Jailed for Freedom

© *Edith Derwent.*

ALICE PAUL

Jailed for Freedom

By

DORIS STEVENS

 BOOKS FOR LIBRARIES PRESS
FREEPORT, NEW YORK

81592

INTERNATIONAL STANDARD BOOK NUMBER:
0-8369-5757-1

LIBRARY OF CONGRESS CATALOG CARD NUMBER:
76-153003

PRINTED IN THE UNITED STATES OF AMERICA

TO

ALICE PAUL

THROUGH WHOSE BRILLIANT
AND DEVOTED LEADERSHIP
THE WOMEN OF AMERICA HAVE
BEEN ABLE TO CONSUMMATE
WITH GLADNESS AND GALLANT
COURAGE THEIR LONG STRUG-
GLE FOR POLITICAL LIBERTY,
THIS BOOK IS AFFECTIONATELY
DEDICATED

PREFACE

This book deals with the intensive campaign of the militant suffragists of America [1913-1919] to win a solitary thing—the passage by Congress of the national suffrage amendment enfranchising women. It is the story of the first organized militant political action in America to this end. The militants differed from the pure propagandists in the woman suffrage movement chiefly in that they had a clear comprehension of the forces which prevail in politics. They appreciated the necessity of the propaganda stage and the beautiful heroism of those who had led in the pioneer agitation, but they knew that this stage belonged to the past; these methods were no longer necessary or effective.

For convenience sake I have called Part II "Political Action," and Part III "Militancy," although it will be perceived that the entire campaign was one of militant political action. The emphasis, however, in Part II is upon political action, although certainly with a militant mood. In Part III dramatic acts of protest, such as are now commonly called militancy, are given emphasis as they acquired a greater importance during the latter part of the campaign. This does not mean that all militant deeds were not committed for a specific political purpose. They were. But militancy is as much a state of mind, an approach to a task, as it is the commission of deeds of protest. It is the state of mind of those who is their fiery idealism do not lose sight of the real springs of human action.

There are two ways in which this story might be told. It might be told as a tragic and harrowing tale of martyrdom. Or it might be told as a ruthless enterprise of compelling a hostile administration to subject women to martyrdom in order to hasten its surrender. The truth is, it has elements of both ruthlessness and martyrdom. And I have tried to make them appear in a true proportion. It is my sincere hope that you will understand and appreciate the martyrdom involved, for it was the conscious voluntary gift of beautiful, strong and young hearts. *But it was never martyrdom for its own sake. It was martyrdom used for a practical purpose.*

The narrative ends with the passage of the amendment by Congress. The campaign for ratification, which extended over fourteen months, is a story in itself. The ratification of the amendment by the 36th and last state legislature proved as difficult to secure from political leaders as the 64th and last vote in the United States Senate.

This book contains my interpretations, which are of course arguable. But it is a true record of events.

DORIS STEVENS.

New York, August, 1920.

CONTENTS

ix

ILLUSTRATIONS

xi

"I do pray, and that most earnestly and constantly, for some terrific shock to startle the women of the nation into a self-respect which will compel them to see the absolute degradation of their present position; which will compel them to break their yoke of bondage and give them faith in themselves; which will make them proclaim their allegiance to women first. . . . The fact is, women are in chains, and their servitude is all the more debasing because they do not realize it. O to compel them to see and feel and to give them the courage and the conscience to speak and act for their own freedom, though they face the scorn and contempt of all the world for doing it!"

Susan B. Anthony, 1872.

PART I
LEADERSHIP

CHAPTER 1

SUSAN B. ANTHONY was the first militant suffragist. She has been so long proclaimed only as the magnificent pioneer that few realize that she was the first woman to defy the law for the political liberty of her sex.

The militant spirit was in her many early protests. Sometimes these protests were supported by one or two followers; more often they were solitary protests. Perhaps it is because of their isolation that they stand out so strong and beautiful in a turbulent time in our history when all those about her were making compromises.

It was this spirit which impelled her to keep alive the cause of the enfranchisement of women during the passionate years of the Civil War. She held to the last possible moment that no national exigency was great enough to warrant abandonment of woman's fight for independence. But one by one her followers deserted her. She was unable to keep even a tiny handful steadfast to this position. She became finally the only figure in the nation appealing for the rights of women when the rights of black men were agitating the public mind. Ardent abolitionist as she was, she could not tolerate without indignant protest the exclusion of women in all discussions of emancipation. The suffrage war policy of Miss Anthony can be compared to that of the militants a half century later when confronted with the problem of this country's entrance into the world war.

The war of the rebellion over and the emancipation of the

3

negro man written into the constitution, women contended they
had a right to vote under the new fourteenth amendment. Miss
Anthony led in this agitation, urging all women to claim the
right to vote under this amendment. In the national election
of 1872 she voted in Rochester, New York, her home city, was
arrested, tried and convicted of the crime of "voting without
having a lawful right to vote."

I cannot resist giving a brief excerpt from the court records
of this extraordinary case, so reminiscent is it of the cases of
the suffrage pickets tried nearly fifty years later in the courts
of the national capital.

After the prosecuting attorney had presented the government's case, Judge Hunt read his opinion, said to have been
written before the case had been heard, and directed the jury
to bring in a verdict of guilty. The jury was dismissed without deliberation and a new trial was refused. On the following
day this scene took place in that New York court room.

JUDGE HUNT (Ordering the defendant to stand up)—Has
the prisoner anything to say why sentence shall not be pronounced?

MISS ANTHONY—Yes, your Honor, I have many things to
say; for in your ordered verdict of guilty, you have trampled
under foot every vital principle of our government. My natural rights, my civil rights, my political rights, my judicial
rights, are all alike ignored. Robbed of the fundamental privilege of citizenship, I am degraded from the status of a citizen
to that of a subject; and not only myself individually, but all
my sex are, by your Honor's verdict doomed to political subjection under this so-called republican form of government.

JUDGE HUNT—The Court cannot listen to a rehearsal of
argument which the prisoner's counsel has already consumed
three hours in presenting.

MISS ANTHONY—May it please your Honor, I am not arguing the question, but simply stating the reasons why sentence

cannot in justice be pronounced against me. Your denial of
my citizen's right to vote, is the denial of my right of consent
as one of the governed, the denial of my right of representation
as one taxed, the denial of my right to a trial by jury of my
peers as an offender against law; therefore, the denial of my
sacred right to life, liberty, property, and——

JUDGE HUNT—The Court cannot allow the prisoner to go
on.

MISS ANTHONY—But, your Honor will not deny me this
one and only poor privilege of protest against this high-
handed outrage upon my citizen's rights. May it please the
Court to remember that since the day of my arrest last November this is the first time that either myself or any person of
my disfranchised class has been allowed a word of defense
before judge or jury——

JUDGE HUNT—The prisoner must sit down, the Court cannot allow it.

MISS ANTHONY—Of all my persecutors from the corner
grocery politician who entered the complaint, to the United
States marshal, commissioner, district attorney, district judge,
your Honor on the bench, not one is my peer, but each and
all are my political sovereigns. . . . Precisely as no disfranchised person is entitled to sit upon the jury and no woman is
entitled to the franchise, so none but a regularly admitted
lawyer is allowed to practice in the courts, and no woman can
gain admission to the bar—hence, jury, judge, counsel, all must
be of superior class.

JUDGE HUNT—The Court must insist—the prisoner has
been tried according to the established forms of law.

MISS ANTHONY—Yes, your Honor, but by forms of law, all
made by men, interpreted by men, administered by men, in
favor of men and against women; and hence your Honor's
ordered verdict of guilty, against a United States citizen for
the exercise of the "citizen's right to vote," simply because that

citizen was a woman and not a man. . . . As then the slaves who got their freedom had to take it over or under or through the unjust forms of the law, precisely so now must women take it to get their right to a voice in this government; and I have taken mine, and mean to take it at every opportunity.

JUDGE HUNT—The Court orders the prisoner to sit down. It will not allow another word.

MISS ANTHONY—When I was brought before your Honor for trial I hoped for a broad interpretation of the constitution and its recent amendments, which should declare all United States citizens under its protecting ægis. . . . But failing to get this justice, failing even to get a trial by a jury—not of my peers—I ask not leniency at your hands but rather the full rigor of the law.

JUDGE HUNT—The Court must insist (here the prisoner sat down). The prisoner will stand up. (Here Miss Anthony rose again.) The sentence of the Court is that you pay a fine of $100.00 and the costs of the prosecution.

MISS ANTHONY—May it please your Honor, I will never pay a dollar of your unjust penalty. . . . And I shall earnestly and persistently continue to urge all women to the practical recognition of the old Revolutionary maxim, "Resistance to tyranny is obedience to God."

JUDGE HUNT—Madam, the Court will not order you stand committed until the fine is paid.

Miss Anthony did not pay her fine and was never imprisoned. I believe the fine stands against her to this day.

On the heels of this sensation came another of those dramatic protests which until the very end she always combined with political agitation. The nation was celebrating its first centenary of the signing of the Declaration of Independence at Independence Square, Philadelphia. After women had been refused by all in authority a humble half moment in which to present to the Centennial the Women's Declaration of Rights,

Miss Anthony insisted on being heard. Immediately after the Declaration of Independence had been read by a patriot, she led a committee of women, who with platform tickets had slipped through the military, straight down the center aisle of the platform to address the chairman, who pale with fright and powerless to stop the demonstration had to accept her document. Instantly the platform, graced as it was by national dignitaries and crowned heads, was astir. The women retired, distributing to the gasping spectators copies of their Declaration. Miss Anthony had reminded the nation of the hollowness of its celebration of an independence that excluded women.

Susan B. Anthony's aim was the national enfranchisement of women. As soon as she became convinced that the constitution would have to be specifically amended to include woman suffrage, she set herself to this gigantic task. For a quarter of a century she appealed to Congress for action and to party conventions for suffrage endorsement. When, however, she saw that Congress was obdurate, as an able and intensely practical leader she temporarily directed the main energy of the suffrage movement to trying to win individual states. With women holding the balance of political power, she argued, the national government will be compelled to act. She knew so well the value of power. She went to the West to get it.

She was a shrewd tactician; with prophetic insight, without compromise. To those women who would yield to party expediency as advised by men, or be diverted into support of other measures, she made answer in a spirited letter to Lucy Stone:

"So long as you and I and all women are political slaves, it ill becomes us to meddle with the weightier discussions of our sovereign masters. It will be quite time enough for us, with self-respect, to declare ourselves for or against any party upon the intrinsic merit of its policy, when men shall recognize us as their political equals. . . .

"If all the suffragists of all the States could see eye to eye on this point, and stand shoulder to shoulder against every party and politician not fully and unequivocally committed to 'Equal Rights for Women,' we should become at once the moral balance of power which could not fail to compel the party of highest intelligence to proclaim woman suffrage the chief plank of its platform. . . . Until that good day comes, I shall continue to invoke the party in power, and each party struggling to get into power, to pledge itself to the emancipation of our enslaved half of the people. . . ."

She did not live to see enough states grant suffrage in the West to form a balance of power with which to carry out this policy. She did not live to turn this power upon an unwilling Congress. But she stood to the last, despite this temporary change of program, the great dramatic protagonist of national freedom for women and its achievement through rebellion and practical strategy.

With the passing of Miss Anthony and her leadership, the movement in America went conscientiously on endeavoring to pile up state after state in the "free column." Gradually her followers lost sight of her aggressive attack and her objective—the enfranchisement of women by Congress. They did not sustain her tactical wisdom. This reform movement, like all others when stretched over a long period of time, found itself confined in a narrow circle of routine propaganda. It lacked the power and initiative to extricate itself. Though it had many eloquent agitators with devoted followings, it lacked generalship.

The movement also lost Miss Anthony's militant spirit, her keen appreciation of the fact that the attention of the nation must be focussed on minority issues by dramatic acts of protest.

Susan B. Anthony's fundamental objective, her political attitude toward attaining it, and her militant spirit were revived in suffrage history in 1913 when Alice Paul, also of Quaker background, entered the national field as leader of the new suffrage forces in America.

CHAPTER 2

MOST people conjure up a menacing picture when a person is called not only a general, but a militant one. In appearance Alice Paul is anything but menacing. Quiet, almost mouselike, this frail young Quakeress sits in silence and baffles you with her contradictions. Large, soft, gray eyes that strike you with a positive impact make you feel the indescribable force and power behind them. A mass of soft brown hair, caught easily at the neck, makes the contour of her head strong and graceful. Tiny, fragile hands that look more like an X-ray picture of hands, rest in her lap in Quakerish pose. Her whole atmosphere when she is not in action is one of strength and quiet determination. In action she is swift, alert, almost panther-like in her movements. Dressed always in simple frocks, preferably soft shades of purple, she conforms to an individual style and taste of her own rather than to the prevailing vogue.

I am going recklessly on to try to tell what I think about Alice Paul. It is difficult, for when I begin to put it down on paper, I realize how little we know about this laconic person, and yet how abundantly we feel her power, her will and her compelling leadership. In an instant and vivid reaction, I am either congealed or inspired; exhilarated or depressed; sometimes even exasperated, but always *moved*. I have seen her very presence in headquarters change in the twinkling of an eye the mood of fifty people. It is not through their affections

10

that she moves them, but through a naked force, a vital force which is indefinable but of which one simply cannot be unaware. Aiming primarily at the intellect of an audience or an individual, she almost never fails to win an emotional allegiance.

I shall never forget my first contact with her. I tell it here as an illustration of what happened to countless women who came in touch with her to remain under her leadership to the end. I had come to Washington to take part in the demonstration on the Senate in July, 1913, en route to a much-needed, as I thought, holiday in the Adirondacks.

"Can't you stay on and help us with a hearing next week?" said Miss Paul.

"I'm sorry," said I, "but I have promised to join a party of friends in the mountains for a summer holiday and . . ."

"Holiday?" said she, looking straight at me. Instantly ashamed at having mentioned such a legitimate excuse, I murmured something about not having had one since before entering college.

"But can't you stay?" she said.

I was lost. I knew I would stay. As a matter of fact, I stayed through the heat of a Washington summer, returned only long enough at the end of the summer to close up my work in state suffrage and came back to join the group at Washington. And it was years before I ever mentioned a holiday again.

Frequently she achieved her end without even a single word of retort. Soon after Miss Paul came to Washington in 1913, she went to call on a suffragist in that city to ask her to donate some funds toward the rent of headquarters in the Capital. The woman sighed. "I thought when Miss Anthony died," she said, "that all my troubles were at an end. She used to come to me for money for a federal amendment and I always told her it was wrong to ask for one, and that besides we would never get it. But she kept right on coming. Then when she died we didn't hear any more about an amendment. And now you come again saying the same things Miss Anthony said."

Miss Paul listened, said she was sorry and departed. Very shortly a check arrived at headquarters to cover a month's rent.

A model listener, Alice Paul has unlimited capacity for letting the other person relieve herself of all her objections without contest. Over and over again I have heard this scene enacted.

"Miss Paul, I have come to tell you that you are all wrong about this federal amendment business. I don't believe in it. Suffrage should come slowly but surely by the states. And although I have been a life-long suffragist, I just want to tell you not to count on me, for feeling as I do, I cannot give you any help."

A silence would follow. Then Miss Paul would say ingenuously, "Have you a half hour to spare?"

"I guess so," would come slowly from the protestant. "Why?"

"Won't you please sit down right here and put the stamps on these letters? We have to get them in the mail by noon."

"But I don't believe . . ."

"Oh, that's all right. These letters are going to women probably a lot of whom feel as you do. But some of them will want to come to the meeting to hear our side."

By this time Miss Paul would have brought a chair, and that ended the argument. The woman would stay and humbly proceed to stick on endless stamps. Usually she would come back, too, and before many days would be an ardent worker for the cause against which she thought herself invincible.

Once the state president of the conservative suffrage forces in Ohio with whom I had worked the previous year wrote me a letter pointing out what madness it was to talk of winning the amendment in Congress "this session," and adding that "nobody but a fool would ever think of it, let alone speak of it publicly." She was wise in politics; we were nice, eager, young girls, but pretty ignorant—that was the gist of her remonstrance. My vanity was aroused. Not wishing to be called "mad" or "foolish" I sat down and answered her in a friendly spirit, with the sole object of proving that we were wiser than she imagined. I had never discussed this point with anybody, as I had been in Washington only a few months and it had never occurred to me that we were not right to talk of getting the amendment in that particular session. But I answered my patronizing friend, in effect, that of course we were not fools, that we knew we would not get the amendment that session, but we saw no reason for not demanding it at once and taking it when we got it.

When Miss Paul saw the carbon of that letter she said quietly, pointing to the part where I had so nobly defended our sagacity, "You must never say that again and never put it on paper." Seeing my embarrassment, she hastened to explain. "You see, we *can* get it this session if enough women care sufficiently to demand it now."

Alice Paul brought back to the fight that note of immediacy which had gone with the passing of Miss Anthony's leadership. She called a halt on further pleading, wheedling, proving, praying. It was as if she had bidden women stand erect, with confidence in themselves and in their own judgments, and compelled them to be self-respecting enough to dare to put their freedom first, and so determine for themselves the day when they should be free. Those who had a taste of begging under the old régime and who abandoned it for demanding, know how fine and strong a thing it is to realize that you must take what is yours and not waste your energy proving that you are or will some day be worthy of a gift of power from your masters. On that glad day of discovery you have first freed yourself to fight for freedom. Alice Paul gave to thousands of women the essence of freedom.

And there was something so cleansing about the way in which she renovated ideas and processes, emotions and instincts. Her attack was so direct, so clear, so simple and unafraid. And her resistance had such a fine quality of strength.

Sometimes it was a roaring politician who was baffled by this non-resistant force. I have heard many an irate one come into her office in the early days to tell her how to run the woman's campaign, and struggle in vain to arouse her to combat. Having begun a tirade, honor would compel him to see it through even without help from a silent adversary. And so he would get more and more noisy until it would seem as if one lone shout from him might be enough to blow away the frail object of his attack. Ultimately he would be forced to retire, perhaps in the face of a serene smile, beaten and angered that he had been able to make so little impression. And many the delicious remark and delightful quip afterward at his expense!

Her gentle humor is of the highest quality. If only her opponents could have seen her amusement at their hysteria. At the very moment they were denouncing some plan of action and calling her "fanatical" and "hysterical" she would fairly beam with delight to see how well her plan had worked. Her intention had been to arouse them to just that state of mind, and how admirably they were living up to the plan. The hysteria was all on their side. She coolly sat back in her chair and watched their antics under pressure.

"But don't you know," would come another thundering one, "that this will make the Democratic leaders so hostile that . . ."

The looked-for note of surprise never came. She had counted ahead on all this and knew almost to the last shade the reaction that would follow from both majority and minority leaders. All this had been thoroughly gone over, first with herself, then with her colleagues. All the "alarms" had been rung. The male politician could not understand why his well-meaning and generously-offered advice caused not a ripple and not a change in plan. Such calm unconcern he could not endure. He was accustomed to emotional panics. He was not accustomed to a leader who had weighed every objection, every attack and counted the cost accurately.

Her ability to marshal arguments for keeping her own followers in line was equally marked. A superficial observer would rush into headquarters with, "Miss Paul, don't you think it was a great tactical mistake to force President Wilson at this time to state his position on the amendment? Will it not hurt our campaign to have it known that he is against us?"

"It is the best thing that could possibly happen to us. If he is against us, women should know it. They will be aroused to greater action if he is not allowed to remain silent upon something in which he does not believe. It will make it easier for us to campaign against him when the time comes."

And another time a friend of the cause would suggest, "Would it not have been better not to have tried for planks in party platforms, since we got such weak ones?"

"Not at all. We can draw the support of women with greater ease from a party which shows a weak hand on suffrage, than from one which hides its opposition behind silence."

She had always to combat the fear of the more timid ones who felt sure with each new wave of disapproval that we would be submerged. "Now, I have been a supporter of yours every step of the way," a "fearful" one would say, "but this is really going a little too far. I was in the Senate gallery to-day when two suffrage senators in speeches denounced the pickets and their suffrage banners. They said that we were setting suffrage back and that something ought to be done about it."

"Exactly so," would come the ready answer from Miss Paul. "And they *will* do something about it only if we continue

to make them uncomfortable enough. Of course even suffrage
senators will object to our pickets and our banners because
they do not want attention called to their failure to compel the
Administration to act. They know that as friends of the
measure their responsibility is greater." And the "fearful"
one was usually convinced and made stronger.

I remember so well when the situation was approaching its
final climax in Washington. Men and women, both, came to
Miss Paul with, "This is terrible! Seven months' sentence is
impossible. You must stop! You cannot keep this up!"

With an unmistakable note of triumph in her voice Miss
Paul would answer, "Yes, it is terrible for us, but not nearly so
terrible as for the government. The Administration has fired
its heaviest gun. From now on we shall win and they will
lose."

Most of the doubters had by this time banished their fears
and had come to believe with something akin to superstition
that she could never be wrong, so swiftly and surely did they
see her policies and her predictions on every point vindicated
before their eyes.

She has been a master at concentration, a master strategist—a great general. With passionate beliefs on all important social questions, she resolutely set herself against being
seduced into other paths. Far from being naturally an ascetic,
she has disciplined herself into denials and deprivations, cultural and recreational, to pursue her objective with the least
possible waste of energy. Not that she did not want above all
else to do this thing. She did. But doing it she had to abandon the easy life of a scholar and the aristocratic environment
of a cultured, prosperous, Quaker family, of Moorestown, New
Jersey, for the rigors of a ceaseless drudgery and frequent imprisonment. A flaming idealist, conducting the fight with the
sternest kind of realism, a mind attracted by facts, not fancies,
she has led fearlessly and with magnificent ruthlessness. Think-

ing, thinking day and night of her objective and never retarding her pace a moment until its accomplishment, I know no modern woman leader with whom to compare her. I think she must possess many of the same qualities that Lenin does, according to authentic portraits of him—cool, practical, rational, sitting quietly at a desk and counting the consequences, planning the next move before the first one is finished. And if she has demanded the ultimate of her followers, she has given it herself. Her ability to get women to work and never to let them stop is second only to her own unprecedented capacity for work.

Alice Paul came to leadership still in her twenties, but with a broad cultural equipment. Degrees from Swarthmore, the University of Pennsylvania, and special study abroad in English universities had given her a scholarly background in history, politics, and sociology. In these studies she had specialized, writing her doctor's thesis on the status of women. She also did factory work in English industries and there acquired first hand knowledge of the industrial position of women. In the midst of this work the English militant movement caught her imagination and she abandoned her studies temporarily to join that movement and go to prison with the English suffragists.

Convinced that the English women were fighting the battle for the women of the world, she returned to America fresh from their struggle, to arouse American women to action. She came bringing her gifts and concentration to this one struggle. She came with that inestimable asset, youth, and, born of youth, indomitable courage to carry her point in spite of scorn and misrepresentation.

Among the thousands of telegrams sent Miss Paul the day the amendment finally passed Congress was this interesting message from Walter Clark, Chief Justice of the Supreme

Court of North Carolina, Southern Democrat, Confederate Veteran and distinguished jurist:

"Will you permit me to congratulate you upon the great triumph in which you have been so important a factor? Your place in history is assured. Some years ago when I first met you I predicted that your name would be written 'on the dusty roll the ages keep.' There were politicians, and a large degree of public sentiment, which could only be won by the methods you adopted. . . . It is certain that, but for you, success would have been delayed for many years to come."

PART II

POLITICAL ACTION

CHAPTER 1

W HERE are the people?" This was Woodrow Wilson's first question as he arrived at the Union Station in Washington the day before his first inauguration to the Presidency in March, 1913.

"On the Avenue watching the suffragists parade," came the answer.

The suffrage issue was brought oftenest to his attention from then on until his final surrender. It lay entirely with him as to how long women would be obliged to remind him of this issue before he willed to take a hand.

"The people" were on the Avenue watching the suffragists parade. The informant was quite right. It seemed to those of us who attempted to march for our idea that day that the whole world was there—packed closely on Pennsylvania Avenue.

The purpose of the procession was to dramatize in numbers and beauty the fact that women wanted to vote—that women were asking the Administration in power in the national government to speed the day. What politicians had not been able to get through their minds we would give them through their eyes—often a powerful substitute. Our first task seemed simple—actually to show that thousands of women wanted immediate action on their long delayed enfranchisement. This we did.

This was the first demonstration under the leadership of Alice Paul, at that time chairman of the Congressional Com-

21

mittee of the National American Woman Suffrage Association. It was also the beginning of Woodrow Wilson's liberal education.

The Administration, without intending it, played into the hands of the women from this moment. The women had been given a permit to march. Inadequate police protection allowed roughs to attack them and all but break up the beautiful pageant. The fact of ten thousand women marching with banners and bands for this idea was startling enough to wake up the government and the country, but not so startling as ten thousand women man-handled by irresponsible crowds because of police indifference.

An investigation was demanded and a perfunctory one held. The police administration was exonerated, but when the storm of protest had subsided the Chief of Police was quietly retired to private life.

It was no longer a secret that women wanted to vote and that they wanted the President and Congress to act.

A few days later the first deputation of suffragists ever to appear before a President to enlist his support for the passage of the national suffrage amendment waited upon President Wilson.[1] Miss Paul led the deputation. With her were Mrs. Genevieve Stone, wife of Congressman Stone of Illinois, Mrs. Harvey W. Wiley, Mrs. Ida Husted Harper, and Miss Mary Bartlett Dixon of Maryland. The President received the deputation in the White House Offices. When the women entered they found five chairs arranged in a row with one chair in front, like a class-room. All confessed to being frightened when the President came in and took his seat at the head of the class. The President said he had no opinion on the subject of woman suffrage; that he had never given it any thought;[2]

---

[1] There had been individual visits to previous presidents.

[2] At Colorado Springs in 1911, when Mr. Wilson was Governor of New Jersey and campaigning for the Presidential nomination, a delegation of Colorado women asked him his position on woman suffrage. He said,

and that above all it was his task to see that Congress concentrated on the currency revision and the tariff reform. It is recorded that the President was somewhat taken aback when Miss Paul addressed him during the course of the interview with this query, "But Mr. President, do you not understand that the Administration has no right to legislate for currency, tariff, and any other reform without first getting the consent of women to these reforms?"

"Get the consent of women?" It was evident that this course had not heretofore occurred to him.

"This subject will receive my most careful consideration," was President Wilson's first suffrage promise.

He was given time to "consider" and a second deputation went to him, and still a third, asking him to include the suffrage amendment in his message to the new Congress assembling in extra session the following month. And still he was obsessed with the paramount considerations of "tariff" and "currency." He flatly said there would be no time to consider suffrage for women. But the "unreasonable" women kept right on insisting that the liberty of half the American people was paramount to tariff and currency.

President Wilson's first session of Congress came together April 7th, 1913. The opening day was marked by the suffragists' second mass demonstration. This time women delegates representing every one of the 435 Congressional Districts in the country bore petitions from the constituencies showing that the people "back home" wanted the amendment passed. The delegates marched on Congress and were received with a warm welcome and their petitions presented to Congress. The same day the amendment which bears the name of Susan B. Anthony, who drafted it in 1875, was reintroduced into both houses of Congress.

"Ladies, this is a very arguable question and my mind is in the midst of the argument."

The month of May saw monster demonstrations in many cities and villages throughout the country, with the direct result that in June the Senate Committee on Suffrage made the first favorable report made by that committee in *twenty-one years*, thereby placing it on the Senate calendar for action.

Not relaxing the pressure for a day we organized the third great demonstration on the last of July when a monster petition signed by hundreds of thousands of citizens was brought to the Senate asking that body to pass the national suffrage amendment. Women from all parts of the country mobilized in the countryside of Maryland where they were met with appropriate ceremonies by the Senate Woman Suffrage Committee. The delegation motored in gaily decorated automobiles to Washington and went direct to the Senate, where the entire day was given over to suffrage discussion.

Twenty-two senators spoke in favor of the amendment in presenting their petitions. Three spoke against it. For the first time in *twenty-six years* suffrage was actually debated in Congress. That day was historic.

Speeches? Yes. Greetings? Yes. Present petitions from their constituencies? Gladly. Report it from the Senate Committee? They had to concede that. But passage of the amendment? That was beyond their contemplation.

More pressure was necessary. We appealed to the women voters, of whom there were then four million, to come into action.

"Four million women voters are watching you," we said to Congress. We might as well have said, "There are in the South Sea Islands four million heathens."

It was clear that these distant women voters had no relation in the senatorial mind to the realism of politics. We decided to bring some of these women voters to Washington. Having failed to get the Senate to act by August, we invited the Council of Women Voters to hold its convention in Washington that Congress might learn this simple lesson: women did vote; there were four million of them; they had a voters' organization; they cared about the enfranchisement of all American women; they wanted the Senate to act; suffrage was no longer a moral problem; it could be made a practical political problem with which men and parties would have to reckon.

Voting women made their first impression on Congress that summer.

Meanwhile the President's "paramount issues"—tariff and currency—had been disposed of. With the December Congress approaching, he was preparing another message. We went to him again. This time it was the women from his own home state, an influential deputation of seventy-three women, including the suffrage leaders from all suffrage organizations in New Jersey. The women urged him to include recommendation of the suffrage resolution in his message to the new Congress. He replied:

"I am pleased, indeed, to greet you and your adherents here, and I will say to you that I was talking only yesterday with several members of Congress in regard to a Suffrage Committee in the House. The subject is one in which I am deeply interested, and you may rest assured that I will give it my earnest attention."

In interesting himself in the formation of a special committee to sit on suffrage in the House, the President was doing the smallest thing, to be sure, that could be done, but he was doing something. This was a distinct advance. It was our task to press on until all the maze of Congressional machinery had been used to exhaustion. Then there would be nothing left to do but to pass the amendment.

A fourth time that year the determination of women to secure the passage of the amendment was demonstrated. In December, the opening week of the new Congress, the annual convention of the National American Woman Suffrage Association was held in Washington. Miss Lucy Burns, vice chairman of its Congressional Committee and also of the Congressional Union, was applauded to the echo by the whole convention when she said:

"The National American Woman Suffrage Association is assembled in Washington to ask the Democratic Party to enfranchise the women of America.

"Rarely in the history of the country has a party been more powerful than the Democratic Party is to-day. It controls the Executive Office, the Senate and more than two-thirds of the members of the House of Representatives. It is in a position to give us effective and immediate help.

"We ask the Democrats to take action now. Those who hold power are responsible to the country for the use of it. They are responsible not only for what they do, but for what they do not do. Inaction establishes just as clear a record as does a policy of open hostility.

"We have in our hands to-day not only the weapon of a just cause; we have the support of ten enfranchised states— states comprising one-fifth of the United States Senate, one-seventh of the House of Representatives, and one-sixth of the electoral vote. More than 3,600,000 women have a vote in Presidential elections. It is unthinkable that a national government which represents women, and which appeals periodically for the suffrages of women, should ignore the issue of the right of all women to political freedom.

"We cannot wait until after the passage of scheduled Administration reforms. . . . Congress is free to take action on our question in the present session. We ask the Administration to support the woman suffrage amendment in Congress with its whole strength."

This represented the attitude of the entire suffrage movement toward the situation in the winter of 1913. At no time did the militant group deviate from this position until the amendment was through Congress.

It was difficult to make the Administration believe that the women meant what they said, and that they meant to use everything in their power and resourcefulness to see it carried out.

Men were used to having women ask them for suffrage. But they were disconcerted at being asked for it now; at being threatened with political chastisement if they did not yield to the demand.

In spite of the repeated requests to President Wilson that he include support of the measure in his message to Congress, he delivered his message December 2nd while the convention was still in session, and failed to make any mention of the suffrage amendment. He recommended self-government for Filipino men instead.

Immediately Miss Paul organized the entire convention into a fifth deputation to protest against this failure and to urge support in a subsequent message. Dr. Anna Howard Shaw led the interview. In reply to her eloquent appeal for his assistance, the President said in part: "I am merely the spokesman of my party. . . . I am not at liberty to urge upon Congress in messages, policies which have not had the organic consideration of those for whom I am spokesman. I am by my own principles shut out, in the language of the street, from 'starting anything.' I have to confine myself to those things which have been embodied as promises to the people at an election."

I shall never forget that day. Shafts of sunlight came in at the window and fell full and square upon the white-haired leader who was in the closing days of her power. Her clear, deep, resonant voice, ringing with the genuine love of liberty, was in sharp contrast to the halting, timid, little and technical answer of the President. He stooped to utter some light pleasantry which he thought would no doubt please the "ladies." It did not provoke even a faint smile. Dr. Shaw had dramatically asked, "Mr. President, if *you* cannot speak for us and your party will not, who then, pray, is there to speak for us?"

"You seem very well able to speak for yourselves, ladies," with a broad smile, followed by a quick embarrassment when no one stirred.

"We mean, Mr. President, who will speak for us with *authority?*" came back the hot retort from Dr. Shaw.

The President made no reply. Instead he expressed a desire to shake the hands of the three hundred delegates. A few felt that manners compelled them to acquiesce; the others filed out without this little political ceremony.

Alice Paul's report to the national convention for her year's work as Chairman of the Congressional Committee of the National American Woman Suffrage Association, and as Chairman also of the Congressional Union for Woman Suffrage, showed that a budget of twenty-seven thousand dollars had been raised and expended under her leadership as against *ten dollars* spent during the previous year on Congressional work. At the beginning of the year there was no interest in work with Congress. It was considered hopeless. At the close of the year 1913 it had become a practical political issue. Suffrage had entered the national field to stay.

At this point the Congressional Union for Woman Suffrage was obliged to become an independent body in order to continue this vigorous policy which the conservative suffrage leaders were unwilling to follow.

Hearings, deputations to the President, petitions to Congress, more persistent lobbying, all these things continued during the following year under Miss Paul's leadership with the result that a vote in the Senate was taken, though at an inopportune moment,—the first vote in the Senate since 1887. The vote stood 36 to 34—thereby failing by 11 votes of the necessary two-thirds majority. This vote, nevertheless, indicated that a new strength in the suffrage battle had forced Congress to take some action.

In the House, the Rules Committee on a vote of 4 to 4

refused to create a suffrage committee. We appealed to the Democratic caucus to see if the party sustained this action. We wished to establish their party responsibility, one way or another, and by securing the necessary signatures to a petition, we compelled the caucus to meet. By a vote of 123 to 57 the caucus declared " . . . that the question of woman suffrage is a state and not a federal question," as a substitute for the milder resolution offered, providing for the creation of a committee on woman suffrage. If this had left any doubt as to how the Democratic Party, as a party, stood, this doubt was conveniently removed by Representative Underwood, the Majority Leader of the House, when he said on the floor of the House the following day: "The Democratic Party last night took the distinctive position that it was not in favor of this legislation because it was in favor of the states controlling the question of suffrage. . . . I not only said I was opposed to it, but I said the Party on this side of the Chamber was opposed to it, and the Party that has control of the legislation in Congress certainly has the right to say that it will not support a measure if it is not in accordance with its principles."

Meanwhile the President had said to a deputation of workingwomen who waited upon him in February, "Until the Party, as such, has considered a matter of this very supreme importance, and taken its position, I am not at liberty to speak for it; and yet I am not at liberty to speak for it as an individual, for I am not an individual."

"But we ask you to speak *to* your party, not *for* it," answered Mrs. Glendower Evans, Chairman of the deputation, amid evident presidential embarrassment.

Those women who had been inclined perhaps to accept the President's words as true to fact, entertained doubts when a few days later he demanded of his party in Congress the repeal of the free tolls provision in the Panama Canal tolls act. In so doing, he not only recommended action not endorsed by his party, but he demanded action which his party had specifically declared against.

It was necessary to appeal again to the nation. We called for demonstrations of public approval of the amendment in every state on May 2. Thousands of resolutions were passed calling for action in Congress. These resolutions were made the center of another great demonstration in Washington, May 9, when thousands of women in procession carried them to the Capitol where beautiful and impressive ceremonies were held on the Capitol steps. The resolutions were formally received by members of Congress and the demonstration ended dramatically with a great chorus of women massed on the steps singing "The March of the Women" to the thousands of spectators packed closely together on the Capitol grounds.

And still the President withheld his support.

Under our auspices five hundred representative club women of the country waited upon him in another appeal for help.[1] To them he explained his "passion for local self-government," which led to his conviction "that this is a matter for settlement by the states [2] and not by the federal government. . . ."

Women had to face the fact that the 63rd Congress had made a distinctly hostile record on suffrage. The President, as leader of his party, had seven times refused all aid; the Democratic Party had recorded its opposition through an adverse vote in the Senate and a caucus vote in the House forbidding even consideration of the measure.

It became clear that some form of political action would have to be adopted which would act as an accelerator to the Administration. This feeling was growing momentarily among many women, but it was conspicuously strong in the mind of Mrs. Oliver H. P. Belmont, recognized as one of the ablest

[1] 7th deputation to the President, June 30, 1914.
[2] This amounted to virtual opposition because of the great difficulties, (some of them almost insuperable) involved in amending many state constitutions.

suffrage leaders in the country. Anticipating the unfriendly record made by the Democrats in the 63rd Congress, Mrs. Belmont had come to Miss Paul and to her vice-chairman, Miss Lucy Burns, to urge the formulation of a plan whereby we could strike at Administration opposition through the women voters of the West. Miss Paul had the same idea and welcomed the support of this plan by so able a leader.

Mrs. Belmont was impatient to do nationally what she had already inaugurated in New York State suffrage work—make suffrage an election issue. She was the first suffragist in America to be "militant" enough to wage a campaign against office-seekers on the issue of woman suffrage. She was roundly denounced by the opposition press, but she held her ground. It is interesting to record that she defeated the first candidate for the New York Assembly ever campaigned against on this issue.

She had associated herself with the Pankhursts in England and was the first suffrage leader here publicly to commend the tactics of the English militants. Through her, Mrs. Pankhurst made her first visits to America, where she found a sympathetic audience. Even among the people who understood and believed in English tactics, the general idea here was that only in the backward country of England was "militancy" necessary. In America, men would give women what women wanted without a struggle.

Mrs. Belmont was the one suffrage leader who foresaw a militant battle here whenever women should determine to ask for their freedom immediately. In a great measure she prepared the way for that battle.

Since the movement had not even advanced to the stage of political action at that time, however, Mrs. Belmont realized that political action would have to be exhausted before attempting more aggressive tactics. Not knowing whether Miss Paul had contemplated inaugurating political action in the national field, she sought out the new leader and urged her to begin at once to organize the women's power for use in the approaching national elections.

Those interested in the woman's movement are fairly familiar with Mrs. Belmont's early state suffrage work and her work with the militants in England, but they do not know as much about her national work. It is not easy for a woman of vast wealth to be credited with much else in America than the fact of generosity in giving money to the cause in which she believes. Wealth dazzles us and we look no further. Mrs. Belmont has given hundreds of thousands of dollars to suffrage, both state and national, but she has given greater gifts in her militant spirit, her political sagacity and a marked tactical sense. She was practically the only leader formerly associated with the conservative forces who had the courage to extricate herself from the old routine propaganda and adventure into new paths. She always approached the struggle for liberty in a wholesome revolutionary mood. She was essentially a leader, and one who believed in action—always action.

Until the movement in America regained its militant spirit, her heart was primarily with the English women, because she thought their fight so magnificent that it would bring suffrage to women in England sooner than our slow-going methods would bring it to us. In 1910, when English militancy was at its height, Mrs. Belmont gave out an interview in London, in which she predicted that English women would have the suffrage before us. She even went so far as to say that we in America would have to create an acute situation here, probably a form of militancy, before we could win. At the same time the President of the International Suffrage Alliance said in London: "The suffrage movement in England resembles a battle. It is cruel and tragic. Ours in America is an evolution—less dramatic, slow but more *sure*." Facts sustained Mrs. Belmont's prophecy. Facts did not sustain the other

MRS. O. H. P. BELMONT

prediction. English women got the vote in 1918. American women were not enfranchised nationally until August, 1920.

The following is the political theory and program approved by Mrs. Belmont and submitted to the Congressional Union, by its chairman, Alice Paul, at a conference of the organization at the home of Mrs. Belmont in Newport in August, 1914:

The dominant party (at that time the Democratic Party) is responsible for all action and therefore for action on suffrage.

This party's action had been hostile to this measure.

The dominant party in the approaching election must be convinced, and through it all other parties, that opposition to suffrage is inexpedient.

All parties will be convinced when they see that their opposition costs them votes.

Our fight is a political one.

We must appeal for support to the constituency which is most friendly to suffrage, that constituency being the voting women.

An attempt must be made, no matter how small, to organize the women's vote.

An appeal must be made to the women voters in the nine suffrage states to withhold their support from the Democrats nationally, until the national Democratic Party ceases to block the suffrage amendment.

This is non-partisanship in the highest degree, as it calls upon women to forego previous allegiance to a party. If they are Democrats in this instance, they must vote against their party. If the Republican Party were in power and pursued a similar course, we would work against that party.

The party which sees votes falling away will change its attitude.

After we have once affected by this means the outcome of a national election, even though slightly, every party will hesitate to trifle with our measure any longer.

All candidates from suffrage states are professing suffragists, and therefore we have nothing to lose by defeating a member of the dominant party in those states. Another suffragist will take his place.

Men will object to being opposed because of their party responsibility in spite of their friendliness individually to suffrage. But women certainly have a right to further through the ballot their wishes on the suffrage question, as well as on other questions like currency, tariff, and what not.

This can only be done by considering the Party record, for as the individual record and individual pledges go, all candidates are practically equal.

We, as a disfranchised class, consider our right to vote, preëminently over any other issue in any party's program.

Political leaders will resent our injecting our issue into their campaign, but the rank and file will be won when they see the loyalty of women to women.

This policy will be called militant and in a sense it is, being strong, positive and energetic.

If it is militant to appeal to women to use their vote to bring suffrage to this country, then it is militant to appeal to men or women to use their vote to any good end.

To the question of "How will we profit if another party comes in?" our answer will be that adequate political chastisement of one party for its bad suffrage record through a demonstration of power by women voters affecting the result of the national election, will make it easier to get action from any party in power.

Amidst tremendous enthusiasm this plan was accepted by the little conference of women at Newport, and $7,000 pledged in a few moments to start it. There was a small group of women, an infinitely small budget with which to wage a campaign in nine states, but here was also enthusiasm and resolute determination.

A tiny handful of women—never more than two, more often only one to a state—journeyed forth from Washington into the nine suffrage states of the West to put before the voting women this political theory, and to ask them to support it.

CHAPTER 2

WOMEN VOTERS ORGANIZE

"I T can't be done." "Women don't care about suffrage."
"Once they've got it, it is a dead issue." "To talk of
arousing the Western women to protest against the Congressional candidates of the National Democratic Party in the
suffrage states, when every one of them is a professing suffragist, is utter folly." So ran the comment of the political wise-
acres in the autumn of 1914.

But the women had faith in their appeal.

It is impossible to give in a few words any adequate picture
of the anger of Democratic leaders at our entrance into the
campaign. Six weeks before election they woke up to find the
issue of national suffrage injected into a campaign which they
had meant should be no more stirring than an orderly and perfunctory endorsement of the President's legislative program.

The campaign became a very hot one during which most of
the militancy seemed to be on the side of the political leaders.
Heavy fists came down on desks. Harsh words were spoken.
Violent threats were made. In Colorado, where I was campaigning, I was invited politely but firmly by the Democratic
leader to leave the state the morning after I had arrived.
"You can do no good here. I would advise you to leave at
once. Besides, your plan is impracticable and the women will
not support it."

"Then why do you object to my being here?" I asked.

"You have no right to ask women to do this. . . ."

Some slight variation of this experience was met by every

woman who took part in this campaign. Of course, the Democratic leaders did not welcome an issue raised unexpectedly, and one which forced them to spend an endless amount of time apologizing for and explaining the Democratic Party's record. Nor did they relish spending more money publishing more literature, in short, adding greatly to the burdens of their campaign. The candidates, a little more suave than the party leaders, proved most eloquently that they had been suffragists "from birth." One candidate even claimed a suffrage inheritance from his great-grandmother.

This first entry of women into a national election on the suffrage amendment was little more than a quick, brilliant dash. With all its sketchiness, however, it had immediate political results, and when the election was over, there came tardily a general public recognition that the Congressional Union had made a real contribution to these results. In the nine suffrage states women voted for 45 members of Congress. For 43 of these seats the Democratic Party ran candidates. We opposed in our campaign all of these candidates. Out of the 43 Democratic candidates running, only 20 were elected. While it was not our primary aim to defeat candidates it was generally conceded that we had contributed to these defeats.

Our aim in this campaign was primarily to call to the attention of the public the bad suffrage record of the Democratic Party. The effect of our campaign was soon evident in Congress. The most backward member realized for the first time that women had voted. Even the President perceived that the movement had gained new strength, though he was not yet politically moved by it. He was still "tied to a conviction" [1] which he had had all his life that suffrage "ought to be brought about state by state."

Enough strength and determination among women had

[1] Statement to Deputation of Democratic women (eighth deputation) at the White House, Jan. 6, 1915.

been demonstrated to the Administration, however, to make them want to do something "just as good" as the thing we asked. The Shafroth-Palmer [1] Resolution was introduced, providing for a constitutional amendment permitting a national initiative and referendum on suffrage in the states, thereby forcing upon women the very course we had sought to circumvent. This red herring drawn across the path had been accepted by the conservative suffragists evidently in a moment of hopelessness, and their strength put behind it, but the politicians who persuaded them to back it knew that it was merely an attempt to evade the issue.

This made necessary a tremendous campaign throughout the country by the Congressional Union, with the result that the compromise measure was eventually abandoned. During its life, however, politicians were happy in the opportunity to divide their support between it and the original amendment, which was still pending. To offset this danger and to show again in dramatic fashion the strength and will of the women voters to act on this issue, we made political work among the western women the principal effort of the year 1915, the year preceding the presidential election. Taking advantage of the Panama-Pacific Exposition in San Francisco, we opened suffrage headquarters in the Palace of Education on the exposition grounds. From there we called the first Woman Voters' Convention ever held in the world for the single purpose of attaching political strength to the movement. Mrs. O. H. P. Belmont was chairman of the committee which signed the convention call.

Women from all the voting states assembled in a mass convention September 14, 15 and 16. There is not time to describe

[1] This resolution was introduced in the Senate by Senator Shafroth of Colorado, Democrat; in the House by Representative A. Mitchell Palmer of Pennsylvania, Democrat, later Attorney General in President Wilson's Cabinet. Both men, although avowed supporters of the original Susan B. Anthony amendment, backed this evil compromise.

the beauty of the pageantry which surrounded that gathering, nor of the emotional quality which was at high pitch throughout the sessions. These women from the deserts of Arizona, from the farms of Oregon, from the valleys of California, from the mountains of Nevada and Utah, were in deadly earnest. They had answered the call and they meant to stay in the fight until it was won. The convention went on record unanimously for further political action on behalf of national suffrage and for the original amendment without compromise, and pledged itself to use all power to this end without regard to the interests of any existing political party.

Two emissaries, Sara Bard Field and Frances Joliffe, both of California, were commissioned by women voters at the final session, when more than ten thousand people were present, to go to the President and Congress bearing these resolutions and hundreds of thousands of signatures upon a petition gathered during the summer. They would speak directly to the President lest he should be inclined to take lightly the women voters' resolutions.

The envoys, symbolic of the new strength that was to come out of the West, made their journey across continent by automobile. They created a sensation all along the way, received as they were by governors, by mayors, by officials high and low, and by the populace. Thousands more added their names to the petition and it was rolled up to gigantic proportions until in December when unrolled it literally stretched over miles as it was borne to the Capitol with honor escorts.

The action of the convention scarcely cold, and the envoys mid-way across the continent, the President hastened to New Jersey to cast his vote for suffrage in a state referendum. He was careful to state that he did so as a private citizen, "not as the leader of my party in the nation." He repeated his position, putting the emphasis upon his opposition to national suffrage, rather than on his belief in suffrage for his state.

"I believe that it (suffrage) should be settled by the states and not by the national government, and that in no circumstances should it be made a party question; and my view has grown stronger at every turn of the agitation." He knew women were asking the powerful aid of the President of the United States, not the aid of Mr. Wilson of Princeton, New Jersey. The state amendment in New Jersey was certain to fail, as President Wilson well knew. Casting a vote for it would help his case with women voters, and still not bring suffrage in the East a step nearer.

The envoys' reception at the Capitol was indeed dramatic. Thousands of women escorted them amid bands and banners to the halls of Congress, where they were received by senators and representatives and addressed with eloquent speeches. The envoys replied by asking that their message be carried by friends of the measure to the floor of the Senate and House, and this was done.

The envoys waited upon the President at the White House. This visit of the representatives of women with power marked rather an advance in the President's position. He listened with an eager attention to the story of the new-found power and what women meant to do with it. For the first time on record, he said he had "an open mind" on the question of national suffrage, and would confer with his party colleagues.

The Republican and Democratic National Committees heard the case of the envoys. They were given a hearing before the Senate Suffrage Committee and before the House Judiciary in one of the most lively and entertaining inquisitions in which women ever participated.

No more questions on mother and home! No swan song on the passing of charm and womanly loveliness! Only agile scrambling by each committee member to ask with eagerness and some heat, "Well, if this amendment has not passed Congress by then, what will you do in the elections of 1916?" It was with difficulty that the women were allowed to tell their story, so eager was the Committee to jump ahead to political consequences. "Sirs, that depends upon what you gentlemen do. We are asking a simple thing——" But they never got any further from the main base of their interest.

"If President Wilson comes out for it and his party does not," from a Republican member, "will you——"

"I object to introducing partisan discussions here," came shamelessly from a Democratic colleague. And so the hearing passed in something of a verbal riot, but with no doubt as to the fact that Congressmen were alarmed by the prospect of women voting as a protest group.

The new year found the Senate promptly reporting the measure favorably again, but the Judiciary Committee foot-balled it to its sub-committee, back to the whole committee, postponed it, marked time, dodged without a blush, and finally defeated it.

The problem of neutrality toward the European war was agitating the minds of political leaders. Nothing like suffrage for women must be allowed to rock the ship even slightly! Oh, no, indeed; it was men's business to keep the nation out of war. Men never had shown marked skill at keeping nations out of war in the history of the world. But never mind! Logic must not be pressed too hard upon the "reasoning" sex. This time, men *would* do it.

The exciting national election contest was approaching. Party conventions were scheduled to meet in June while the amendment languished at the Capitol. It was clear that more highly organized woman-power would have to be called into action before the national government would speed its pace. To the women voters the Eastern women went for decisive assistance. A car known as the "Suffrage Special," carrying distinguished Eastern women and gifted speakers, made an extensive tour of the West and under the banner of the Congressional Union called again upon the women voters to come to Chicago on June 5th to form a new party,—The Woman's Party [1]—to serve as long as should be necessary as the balance of power in national contests, and thus to force action from the old parties.

The instant response which met this appeal surpassed the most optimistic hopes. Thousands of women assembled in Chicago for this convention, which became epoch-making not only in the suffrage fight but in the whole woman movement. *For the first time in history, women came together to organize their political power into a party to free their own sex.* For the first time in history representatives of men's political parties came to plead before these women voters for the support of their respective parties.

The Republican Party sent as its representatives John Hays Hammond and C. S. Osborn, formerly Governor of Michigan. The Democrats sent their most persuasive orator, President Wilson's friend, Dudley Field Malone, Collector of the Port of New York. Allan Benson, candidate for the Presidency on the Socialist ticket, represented the Socialist Party. Edward Polling, Prohibition leader, spoke for the Prohibition Party, and Victor Murdock and Gifford Pinchot for The Progressive Party.

All laid their claims for suffrage support before the women with the result that the convention resolved itself into another political party—The Woman's Party. A new party with but one plank—the immediate passage of the federal suffrage amendment—a party determined to withhold its support from all existing parties until women were politically free, and to punish politically any party in power which did not use its

---

[1] The Woman's Party started with a membership of all Congressional Union members in suffrage states. Anne Martin of Nevada was elected chairman.

power to free women; a party which became a potent factor of protest in the following national election.

This first step towards the solidarity of women quickly brought results. The Republican National Convention, meeting immediately•after the Woman's Party Convention, and the Democratic National Convention the week following, both included suffrage planks in their national platforms for the first time in history. To be sure, they were planks that failed to satisfy us. But the mere hint of organized political action on suffrage had moved the two dominant parties to advance a step. The new Woman's Party had declared suffrage a national political issue. The two major parties acknowledged the issue by writing it into their party platforms.

The Republican platform was vague and indefinite on national suffrage. The Democratic Party made its suffrage plank specific against action by Congress. It precisely said, "We recommend the extension of the franchise to the women of the country *by the states* upon the same terms as men." It was openly stated at the Democratic Convention by leading Administration Democrats that the President himself had written this suffrage plank. If the Republicans could afford to write a vague and indefinite plank, the President and his party could not. They as the party in power had been under fire and were forced to take sides. They did so. The President chose the plank and his subordinates followed his lead. It may be remarked in passing that this declaration so solidified the opposition within the President's party that when the President ultimately sought to repudiate it, he met stubborn resistance.

Protected by the President's plank, the Democratic Congress continued to block national suffrage. It would not permit it even to be reported from the Judiciary Committee. The party platform was written. The President, too, found it easy to hide behind the plank which he had himself written, counting on women to be satisfied. To Mrs. D. E. Hooker of Richmond, Virginia, who as a delegate from the Virginia Federation of Labor, representing 60,000 members, went to him soon after to ask his support of the amendment, the President said, "I am opposed by conviction and political traditions to federal action on this question. Moreover, after the plank which was adopted in the Democratic platform at St. Louis, I could not comply with the request contained in this resolution even if I wished to do so."

President Wilson could not act because the party plank which he had written prevented him from doing so!

Meanwhile the women continued to protest.

Miss Mabel Vernon of Delaware, beloved and gifted crusader, was the first member of the Woman's Party to commit a "militant" act. President Wilson, speaking at the dedication services of the Labor Temple in Washington, was declaring his interest in all classes and all struggles. He was proclaiming his beliefs in the abstractions of liberty and justice, when Miss Vernon, who was seated on the platform from which he was speaking, said in her powerful voice, "Mr. President, if you sincerely desire to forward the interests of all the people, why do you oppose the national enfranchisement of women?" Instant consternation arose, but the idea had penetrated to the farthest corner of the huge assembly that women were protesting to the President against the denial of their liberty.

The President found time to answer, "That is one of the things which we will have to take counsel over later," and resumed his speech. Miss Vernon repeated her question later and was ordered from the meeting by the police.

As the summer wore on, women realized that they would have to enter the national contest in the autumn. Attention was focussed on the two rival presidential candidates, Woodrow Wilson and Charles Evans Hughes, the Republican nominee, upon whom the new Woman's Party worked diligently

for prompt statements of their position on the national
amendment.

The next political result of the new solidarity of women
was Mr. Hughes' declaration on August 1st, 1916: "My view
is that the proposed amendment should be submitted and
ratified and the subject removed from political discussion."

The Democratic Congress adjourned without even reporting the measure to that body for a vote, and went forthwith
to the country to ask reëlection.

We also went to the country. We went to the women voters
to lay before them again the Democratic Party's record—
now complete through one Administration. We asked women
voters again to withhold their support nationally from President Wilson and his party.

The President accepted at once the opportunity to speak
before a convention of suffragists at Atlantic City in an effort
to prove his great belief in suffrage. He said poetically, "The
tide is rising to meet the moon. . . . You can afford to wait."
Whatever we may have thought of his figure of speech, we
disagreed with his conclusion.

The campaign on, Democratic speakers throughout the
West found an unexpected organized force among women, demanding an explanation of the past conduct of the Democratic
Party and insisting on an immediate declaration by the President in favor of the amendment. Democratic orators did their
utmost to meet this opposition. "Give the President time. He
can't do everything at once." "Trust him once more; he will
do it for you next term." "He kept us out of war. He is the
best friend the mothers of the nation ever had." "He stood
by you. Now you women stand by him." "What good will
votes do you if the Germans come over here and take your
country?" And so on. Enticing doctrine to women—the
peace lovers of the human race.

Although we entered this contest with more strength than

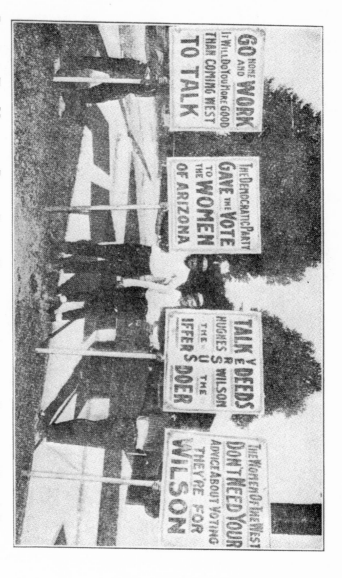

DEMOCRATS HIRE MESSENGER BOYS TO DISPLAY POSTERS IN AN ATTEMPT TO COUNTERACT WOMAN'S PARTY CAMPAIGN

we had had in 1914, with a budget five times as large and with piled-up evidence of Democratic hostility, we could not have entered a more difficult contest. The people were excited to an almost unprecedented pitch over the issue of peace versus war. In spite of the difficulty of competing with this emotional issue which meant the immediate disposal of millions of lives, it was soon evident that the two issues were running almost neck and neck in the Western territory.

No less skilled a campaigner than William Jennings Bryan took the stump in the West against the Woman's Party. At least a third of each speech was devoted to suffrage. He urged. He exorted. He apologized. He explained. He pleaded. He condemned. Often he was heckled. Often he saw huge "VOTE AGAINST WILSON! HE KEPT US OUT OF SUFFRAGE!" banners at the doors of his meetings. One woman in Arizona, who, unable longer to listen in patience to the glory of "a democracy where only were governed those who consented," interrupted him. He coldly answered, "Madam, you cannot pick cherries before they are ripe." By the time he got to California, however, the cherries had ripened considerably, for Mr. Bryan came out publicly for the national amendment.

What was true of Mr. Bryan was true of practically every Democratic campaigner. Against their wills they were forced to talk about suffrage, although they had serenely announced at the opening of the campaign that it was "not an issue in this campaign." Some merely apologized and explained. Others, like Dudley Field Malone, spoke for the federal amendment, and promised to work to put it through the next Congress, "if only you women will stand by Wilson and return him to power."

Space will not permit in this book to give more than a hint of the scope and strength of our campaign. If it were possible to give a glimpse of the speeches made by men in that campaign, you would agree that it was not peace alone that was the dominant issue, but peace and suffrage. It must be made perfectly clear that the Woman's Party did not attempt to elect Mr. Hughes. It did not feel strong enough to back a candidate in its first battle, and did not conduct its fight affirmatively at all. No speeches were made for Mr. Hughes and the Republican Party. The appeal was to vote a vote of protest against Mr. Wilson and his Congressional candidates, because he and his party had had the power to pass the amendment through Congress and had refused to do so. That left the women free to choose from among the Republicans, Socialists and Prohibitionists. It was to be expected that the main strength of the vote taken from Mr. Wilson would go to Mr. Hughes, as few women perhaps threw their votes to the minority parties. But just as the Progressive Party's protest had been effective in securing progressive legislation without winning the election, so the Woman's Party hoped its protest would bring results in Congress without attempting to win the election.

History will never know in round numbers how many women voted against the President and his party at this crisis, for there are no records kept for men and women separately, except in one state, in Illinois. The women there voted two to one against Mr. Wilson and for Mr. Hughes.

Men outnumber women throughout the entire western territory; in some states, two and three to one; in Nevada, still higher. But, whereas, in the election of 1912, President Wilson got 69 electoral votes from the suffrage states, in the 1916 election, when the whole West was aflame for him because of his peace policy, he got only 57. Enthusiasm for Mr. Hughes in the West was not sufficiently marked to account entirely for the loss of these 12 electoral votes. Our claim that Democratic opposition to suffrage had cost many of them was never seriously denied.

The Democratic Judiciary Committee of the House which had refused to report suffrage to the House for a vote, had only one Democratic member from a suffrage state, Mr. Taggart of Kansas, standing for reëlection. This was the only spot where women could strike out against the action of this committee—and Mr. Taggart. They struck with success. He was defeated almost wholly by the women's votes.

With a modest campaign fund of slightly over fifty thousand dollars, raised almost entirely in small sums, the women had forced the campaign committee of the Democratic Party to assume the defensive and to practically double expenditure and work on this issue. As much literature was used on suffrage as on peace in the suffrage states.

Many Democrats although hostile to our campaign said without qualification that the Woman's Party protest was the only factor in the campaign which stemmed the western tide toward Wilson, and which finally made California the pivotal state and left his election in doubt for a week.

Again, with more force, national suffrage had been injected into a campaign where it was not wanted, where the leaders had hoped the single issue of "peace" would hold the center of the stage. Again many women had stood together on this issue and put woman suffrage first. And the actual reëlection of President Wilson had its point of advantage, too, for it enabled us to continue the education of a man in power who had already had four years of lively training on the woman question.

CHAPTER 3

OF the hundreds of women who volunteered for the last Western campaign, perhaps the most effective in their appeal were the disfranchised Eastern women.

The most dramatic figure of them all was Inez Milholland Boissevain, the gallant and beloved crusader who gave her life that the day of women's freedom might be hastened. Her last words to the nation as she fell fainting on the platform in California were, "Mr. President, how long must women wait for liberty?" Her fiery challenge was never heard again. She never recovered from the terrific strain of the campaign which had undermined her young strength. Her death touched the heart of the nation; her sacrifice, made so generously for liberty, lighted anew the fire of rebellion in women, and aroused from inertia thousands never before interested in the liberation of their own sex.

Memorial meetings were held throughout the country at which women not only paid radiant tribute to Inez Milholland, but reconsecrated themselves to the struggle and called again upon the reëlected President and his Congress to act.

The most impressive of these memorials was held on Christmas Day in Washington. In Statuary Hall under the dome of the Capitol—the scene of memorial services for Lincoln and Garfield—filled with statues of outstanding figures in the struggle for political and religious liberty in this country, the first memorial service ever held in the Capitol to honor a woman, was held for this gallant young leader.

Boy choristers singing the magnificent hymn

> "Forward through the darkness
> Leave behind the night,
> Forward out of error,
> Forward into light"

led into the hall the procession of young girl banner-bearers. Garbed in simple surplices, carrying their crusading banners high above their heads, these comrades of Inez Milholland Boissevain seemed more triumphant than sad. They seemed to typify the spirit in which she gave her life.

Still other young girls in white held great golden banners flanking the laurel-covered dais, from which could be read the inscriptions: "Greater love hath no man than this, that he lay down his life for his friend" . . . "Without extinction is liberty; Without retrograde is equality" . . . "As He died to make men holy let us die to make men free" . . .

From behind the heavy velvet curtains came the music of voices and strings, and the great organ sounded its tragic and triumphant tones.

Miss Maud Younger of California was chosen to make the memorial address on this occasion. She said in part:

"We are here to pay tribute to Inez Milholland Boissevain, who was our comrade. We are here in the nation's capital, the seat of our democracy, to pay tribute to one who gave up her life to realize that democracy. . . .

"Inez Milholland walked down the path of life a radiant being. She went into work with a song in her heart. She went into battle with a laugh on her lips. Obstacles inspired her, discouragement urged her on. She loved work and she loved battle. She loved life and laughter and light, and above all else she loved liberty. With a loveliness beyond most, a kindliness, a beauty of mind and soul, she typified always the best and noblest in womanhood. She was the flaming torch that went ahead to light the way—the symbol of light and freedom. . . .

"Symbol of the woman's struggle, it was she who carried to the West the appeal of the unenfranchised, and carrying it, made her last appeal on earth, her last journey in life.

"As she set out upon her last journey, she seems to have had the clearer vision, the spiritual quality of one who has already set out for another world. With infinite understanding and intense faith in her mission, she was as one inspired. Her meetings were described as 'revival meetings,' her audiences as 'wild with enthusiasm.' Thousands acclaimed her, thousands were turned away unable to enter. . . .

"And she made her message very plain.

"She stood for no man, no party. She stood only for woman. And standing thus she urged:

" 'It is women for women now and shall be until the fight is won! Together we shall stand shoulder to shoulder for the greatest principle the world has ever known, the right of self-government.

" 'Whatever the party that has ignored the claims of women we as women must refuse to uphold it. We must refuse to uphold any party until all women are free.

" 'We have nothing but our spirits to rely on and the vitality of our faith, but spirit is invincible.

" 'It is only for a little while. Soon the fight will be over. Victory is in sight.'

"Though she did not live to see that victory, it is sweet to know that she lived to see her faith in women justified. In one of her last letters she wrote:

" 'Not only did we reckon accurately on women's loyalty to women, but we likewise realized that our appeal touched a certain spiritual, idealistic quality in the western woman voter, a quality which is yearning to find expression in political life. At the idealism of the Woman's Party her whole nature flames into enthusiasm and her response is immediate. She gladly transforms a narrow partisan loyalty into loyalty to a principle, the establishment of which carries with it no personal advantage to its advocate, but merely the satisfaction of achieving one more step toward the emancipation of mankind. . . . We are bound to win. There never has been a fight yet where interest was pitted against principle that principle did not triumph!'

" . . . The trip was fraught with hardship. Speaking day and night, she would take a train at two in the morning to arrive at eight; then a train at midnight to arrive at five in the morning. Yet she would not change the program; she would not leave anything out. . . .

"And so . . . her life went out in glory in the shining cause of freedom.

"And as she had lived loving liberty, working for liberty, fighting for liberty, so it was that with this word on her lips she fell. 'How long must women wait for liberty?' she cried and fell—as surely as any soldier upon the field of honor—as truly as any who ever gave up his life for an ideal.

"As in life she had been the symbol of the woman's cause so in death she is the symbol of its sacrifice. The whole daily sacrifice, the pouring out of life and strength that is the toll of woman's prolonged struggle.

"Inez Milholland is one around whom legends will grow up. Generations to come will point out Mount Inez and tell of the beautiful woman who sleeps her last sleep on its slopes.

"They will tell of her in the West, tell of the vision of loveliness as she flashed through on her last burning mission, flashed through to her death—a falling star in the western heavens.

"But neither legend nor vision is liberty, which was her life. Liberty cannot die. No work for liberty can be lost. It lives on in the hearts of the people, in their hopes, their aspirations, their activities. It becomes part of the life of the nation. What Inez Milholland has given to the world lives on forever.

"We are here to-day to pay tribute to Inez Milholland Boissevain, who was our comrade. Let our tribute be not words which pass, nor song which flies, nor flower which fades. Let it be this: that we finish the task she could not finish; that with new strength we take up the struggle in which fighting beside us she fell; that with new faith we here consecrate ourselves to the cause of woman's freedom until that cause is won; that with new devotion we go forth, inspired by her sacrifice, to the end that her sacrifice be not in vain, for dying she shall bring to pass that which living she could not achieve—full freedom for women, full democracy for the nation.

"Let this be our tribute, imperishable, to Inez Milholland Boissevain."

Miss Anne Martin of Nevada, chairman of the Woman's Party, presided over the services. Other speakers were Honorable George Sutherland, United States Senator from Utah, representing the United States Congress; and Honorable Rowland S. Mahany, former member of Congress and lifelong friend of the Milholland family.

Mrs. William Kent of California, wife of Representative Kent, presented two resolutions which the vast audience approved by silently rising. One resolution, a tribute of rare beauty, prepared by Zona Gale, a friend of Inez Milholland, was a compelling appeal to all women to understand and to reverence the ideals of this inspiring leader. The other was an appeal to the Administration for action.

The pageantry of surpliced choristers and the long line of girl standard-bearers retired to the strains of the solemn recessional. The great audience sat still with bowed heads as the voices in the distance dropped in silence. Instantly the strains of the Marseillaise, filling the great dome with its stirring and martial song of hope, were taken up by the organ and the strings, and the audience was lifted to its feet singing as if in anticipation of the triumph of liberty.

The women were in no mood merely to mourn the loss of a comrade-leader. The government must be shown again its share of responsibility. Another appeal must be made to the President who, growing steadily in control over the people and over his Congress, was the one leader powerful enough to direct his party to accept this reform. But he was busy gathering his power to lead them elsewhere. Again we would have to compete with pro-war anti-war sentiment. But it was no time to relax.

Following the holiday season a deputation of over three hundred women carried to the White House the Christmas Day memorial for Inez Milholland and other memorials from similar

services. The President was brought face to face with the
new protest of women against the continued waste of physical
and spiritual energy in their battle. There is no better way
to picture the protest than to give you something verbatim
from the speeches made that memorable day. This was the first
meeting of suffragists with the President since the campaign
against him in the previous autumn. It was only because of the
peculiar character of the appeal that he consented to hear
them.

Miss Younger presented the national memorial to him and
introduced Mrs. John Winters Brannan, who made no plea to
the President but merely gave him the New York memorial
which read as follows:

"This gathering of men and women, assembled on New
Year's day in New York to hold a memorial service in honor
of Inez Milholland Boissevain, appeals to you, the President
of the United States, to end the outpouring of life and effort
that has been made for the enfranchisement of women for more
than seventy years in this country. The death of this lovely
and brave women symbolizes the whole daily sacrifice that vast
numbers of women have made and are making for the sake of
political freedom. It has made vivid the 'constant unnoticed
tragedy of this prolonged effort for a freedom that is acknowledged just, but still denied.'

"It is not given to all to be put to the supreme test and to
accept that test with such gallant gladness as she did. The
struggle, however, has reached the point where it requires such
intensity of effort—relentless and sustained—over the whole
vast country, that the health of thousands of noble women is
being insidiously undermined. If this continues, and it will
continue until victory is won, we know only too surely that
many women whom the nation can ill spare will follow in the
footsteps of Inez Milholland.

"We desire to make known to you, Mr. President, our deep
sense of wrong being inflicted upon women in making them
spend their health and strength and forcing them to abandon
other work that means fuller self-expression, in order to win

freedom under a government that professes to believe in democracy.

"There is only one cause for which it is right to risk health and life. No price is too high to pay for liberty. So long as lives of women are required, these lives will be given.

"But we beg of you, Mr. President, so to act that this ghastly price will not have to be paid. Certainly it is a grim irony that a Republic should exact it. Upon you at this moment rests a solemn responsibility; for with you it rests to decide whether the life of this brilliant, dearly-loved woman whose glorious death we commemorate to-day, shall be the *last* sacrifice of life demanded of American women in their struggle for self-government.

"We ask you with all the fervor and earnestness of our souls to exert your power over Congress in behalf of the national enfranchisement of women in the same way you have so successfully used it on other occasions and for far less important measures.

"We are confident that if the President of the United States decides that this act of justice shall be done in the present session of Congress, it will be done. We know further that if the President does not urge it, it will not be done. . . ."

A fraction of a moment of silence follows, but it is long enough to feel strongly the emotional state of mind of the President. It plainly irritates him to be so plainly spoken to. We are conscious that his distant poise on entering is dwindling to petty confusion. There is something inordinately cool about the fervor of the women. This too irritates him. His irritation only serves to awaken in every woman new strength. It is a wonderful experience to feel strength take possession of your being in a contest of ideas. No amount of trappings, no amount of authority, no number of plainclothes men, nor the glamour of the gold-braided attaches, nor the vastness of the great reception hall, nor the dazzle of the lighted crystal chandeliers, and above all not the mind of your opponent can cut in on your slim, hard strength. You are more than invincible. Your mind leaps ahead to the infinite liberty of which yours is only a small part. You feel his strength in authority, his weakness in vision. He does not follow. He feels sorrow for us. He patronizes us. He must temper his irritation at our undoubted fanaticism and unreason. We, on the other hand, feel so superior to him. Our strength to demand is so much greater than his power to withhold. But he does not perceive this.

In the midst of these currents the serene and appealing voice of Sara Bard Field came as a temporary relief to the President—but only temporary. She brought tears to the eyes of the women as she said in presenting the California memorial resolutions:

"Mr. President, a year ago I had the honor of calling upon you with a similar deputation. At that time we brought from my western country a great petition from the voting women urging your assistance in the passage of the federal amendment for suffrage. At that time you were most gracious to us. You showed yourself to be in line with all the progressive leaders by your statement to us that you could change your mind and would consider doing so in connection with this amendment. We went away that day with hope in our hearts, but neither the hope inspired by your friendly words nor the faith we had in you as an advocate of democracy kept us from working day and night in the interest of our cause.

"Since that day when we came to you, Mr. President, one of our most beautiful and beloved comrades, Inez Milholland, has paid the price of her life for this cause. The untimely death of a young woman like this—a woman for whom the world has such bitter need—has focussed the attention of the men and women of the nation on the fearful waste of women which this fight for the ballot is entailing. The same maternal instinct for the preservation of life—whether it be the physical life of a child or the spiritual life of a cause—is sending women into this battle for liberty with an urge which gives them no rest night or day. Every advance of liberty has demanded its quota of human sacrifice, but if I had time I could show you that we have paid in a measure that is running over. In the light of Inez Milholland's death, as we look over the long backward trail through which we have sought our political liberty, we are asking how long must this struggle go on.

"Mr. President, to the nation more than to women alone is this waste of maternal force significant. In industry such a waste of money and strength would not be permitted. The modern trend is all toward efficiency. Why is such waste permitted in the making of a nation?

"Sometimes I think it must be very hard to be a President, in respect to his contacts with people as well as in the great business he must perform. The exclusiveness necessary to a great dignitary holds him away from that democracy of communion, necessary to a full understanding of what the people are really thinking and desiring. I feel that this deputation to-day fails in its mission if, because of the dignity of your office and the formality of such an occasion, we fail to bring you the throb of woman's desire for freedom and her eagerness to ally herself when once the ballot is in her hand, with all those activities to which you, yourself, have dedicated your life. Those tasks which this nation has set itself to do are her tasks as well as man's. We women who are here to-day are close to this desire of women. We cannot believe that you are our enemy or indifferent to the fundamental righteousness of our demand.

"We have come here to you in your powerful office as our helper. We have come in the name of justice, in the name of democracy, in the name of all women who have fought and died for this cause, and in a peculiar way with our hearts bowed in sorrow, in the name of this gallant girl who died with the word 'liberty' on her lips. We have come asking you this day to speak some favorable word to us that we may know that you will use your good and great office to end this wasteful struggle of women."

The highest point in the interview had been reached. Before the President began his reply, we were aware that the high moment had gone. But we listened.

"Ladies, I had not been apprised that you were coming here to make any representations that would issue an appeal to me.

Inez Milholland Boissevain

I had been told that you were coming to present memorial resolutions with regard to the very remarkable woman whom your cause has lost. I, therefore, am not prepared to say anything further than I have said on previous occasions of this sort.

"I do not need to tell you where my own convictions and my own personal purpose lie, and I need not tell you by what circumscriptions I am bound as leader of a party. As the leader of a party my commands come from that party and not from private personal convictions.

"My personal action as a citizen, of course, comes from no source but my own conviction and, therefore, my position has been so frequently defined, and I hope so candidly defined, and it is so impossible for me until the orders of my party are changed, to do anything other than I am doing as a party leader, that I think nothing more is necessary to be said.

"I do want to say this: I do not see how anybody can fail to observe from the utterances of the last campaign that the Democratic Party is more inclined than the opposition to assist in this great cause, and it has been a matter of surprise to me, and a matter of very great regret that so many of those who were heart and soul for this cause seemed so greatly to misunderstand and misinterpret the attitude of parties. *In this country*, as in every other self-governing country, *it is really through the instrumentality of parties that things can be accomplished. They are not accomplished by the individual voice but by concerted action, and that action must come only so fast as you can concert it.* I have done my best and shall continue to do my best to concert it in the interest of a cause in which I personally believe."

Dead silence. The President stands for a brief instant at the end of his words as if waiting for some faint stir of approval which does not come. He has the baffled air of a disappointed actor who has failed to "get across." Then he turns abruptly on his heel and the great doors swallow him up. Silently the women file through the corridor and into the fresh air.

The women returned to the spacious headquarters across

the park all of one mind. How little the President knew about women! How he underestimated their intelligence and penetration of things political! Was it possible that he really thought these earnest champions of liberty would merely carry resolutions of sorrow and regret to the President?

But this was not the real irony. How lightly he had shifted the responsibility for getting results to his party. With what coldness he had bade us "concert opinion," a thing which he alone could do. That was pretty hard to bear, coming as it did when countless forms of appeal had been exhausted by which women without sufficient power could "concert" anything. The movement was almost at the point of languishing so universal was the belief in the nation that suffrage for women was inevitable. And yet he and his party remained immovable.

The three hundred women of the memorial deputation became on their return to headquarters a spirited protest meeting.

Plans of action in the event the President refused to help had been under consideration by Miss Paul and her executive committee for some time, but they were now presented for the first time for approval. There was never a more dramatic moment at which to ask the women if they were ready for drastic action.

Harriot Stanton Blatch, daughter of Elizabeth Cady Stanton and a powerful leader of women, voiced the feeling of the entire body when she said, in a ringing call for action:

"We have gone to Congress, we have gone to the President during the last four years with great deputations, with small deputations. We have shown the interest all over the country in self-government for women—something that the President as a great Democrat ought to understand and respond to instantly. Yet he tells us to-day that we must win his party. He said it was strange that we did not see before election that his party was more favorable to us than the Republican party. How did it show its favor? How did he show his favor to-day to us? He says we have got to convert his party . . . Why? Never before did the Democratic Party lie more in the hands of one man than it lies to-day in the hands of President Wilson. Never did the Democratic Party have a greater leader, and never was it more susceptible to the wish of that leader, than is the Democratic Party of to-day to President Wilson. He controls his party, and I don't think he is too modest to know it. He can mould it as he wishes and he has moulded it. He moulded it quickly before election in the matter of the eight-hour law. Was that in his party platform? He had to crush and force his party to pass that measure. Yet he is not willing to lay a finger's weight on his party to-day for half the people of the United States. . . . Yet to-day he tells us that we must wait more—and more.

"We can't organize bigger and more influential deputations. We can't organize bigger processions. We can't, women, do anything more in that line. We have got to take a new departure. We have got to keep the question before him all the time. We have got to begin and begin immediately.

"Women, it rests with us. We have got to bring to the President, individually, day by day, week in and week out, the idea that great numbers of women want to be free, *will* be free, and want to know what he is going to do about it.

"Won't you come and join us in standing day after day at the gates of the White House with banners asking, 'What will you do, Mr. President, for one-half the people of this nation?' Stand there as sentinels—sentinels of liberty, sentinels of self-government—silent sentinels. Let us stand beside the gateway where he must pass in and out, so that he can never fail to realize that there is a tremendous earnestness and insistence back of this measure. Will you not show your allegiance to-day to this ideal of liberty? Will you not be a silent sentinel of liberty and self-government?"

Deliberations continued. Details were settled. Three thousand dollars was raised in a few minutes among these women, fresh from the President's rebuff. No one suggested waiting until the next Presidential campaign. No one even mentioned the fact that time was precious, and we could wait no longer. Every one seemed to feel these things without troubling to put them into words. Volunteers signed up for sentinel duty and the fight was on.

SCENE OF MEMORIAL SERVICE—STATUARY HALL, THE CAPITOL

© Harris & Ewing.

PART III

MILITANCY

*"I will write a song for the President, full of menacing signs,
And, back of it all, millions of discontented eyes."*
WALT WHITMAN.

CHAPTER 1

WHEN all suffrage controversy has died away it will be the little army of women with their purple, white and gold banners, going to prison for their political freedom, that will be remembered. They dramatized to victory the long suffrage fight in America. The challenge of the picket line roused the government out of its half-century sleep of indifference. It stirred the country to hot controversy. It made zealous friends and violent enemies. It produced the sharply-drawn contest which forced the surrender of the government in the second Administration of President Wilson.

The day following the memorial deputation to the President, January 10th, 1917, the first line of sentinels, a dozen in number, appeared for duty at the White House gates. In retrospect it must seem to the most inflexible person a reasonably mild and gentle thing to have done. But at the same time it caused a profound stir. Columns of front page space in all the newspapers of the country gave more or less dispassionate accounts of the main facts. Women carrying banners were standing quietly at the White House gates "picketing" the President; women wanted President Wilson to put his power behind the suffrage amendment in Congress. That did not seem so shocking and only a few editors broke out into hot condemnation.

When, however, the women went back on the picket line the next day and the next and the next, it began to dawn upon the excited press that such persistence was "undesirable" . . .

"unwomanly" . . . "dangerous." Gradually the people most hostile to the idea of suffrage in any form marshaled forth the fears which accompany every departure from the prescribed path. Partisan Democrats frowned. Partisan Republicans chuckled. The rest remained in cautious silence to see how "others" would take it. Following the refrain of the press, the protest-chorus grew louder.

"Silly women" . . . "unsexed" . . . "pathological" . . . "They must be crazy" . . . "Don't they know anything about politics?" . . . "What can Wilson do? He does not have to sign the constitutional amendment." . . . So ran the comment from the wise elderly gentlemen sitting buried in their cushioned chairs at the gentlemen's club across the Park, watching eagerly the "shocking," "shameless" women at the gates of the White House. No wonder these gentlemen found the pickets irritating! This absorbing topic of conversation, we are told, shattered many an otherwise quiet afternoon and broke up many a quiet game. Here were American women before their very eyes daring to shock them into having to think about liberty. And what was worse—liberty for women. Ah well, this could not go on,—this insult to the President. They could with impunity condemn him and gossip about his affairs. But that women should stand at his gates asking for liberty,— that was a sin without mitigation.

Disapproval was not confined merely to the gentlemen in their Club. I merely mention them as an example, for they were our neighbors, and the strain on them day by day, as our beautiful banners floated gaily out from our headquarters was, I am told, a heavy one.

Yet, of course, we enjoyed irritating them. Standing on the icy pavement on a damp, wintry day in the penetrating cold of a Washington winter, knowing that within a stone's throw of our agony there was a greater agony than ours— there was a joy in that!

There were faint rumblings also in Congress, but like so many of its feelings they were confined largely to the cloak rooms. Representative Emerson of Ohio did demand from the floor of the House that the "suffrage guard be withdrawn, as it is an insult to the President," but his protest met with no response whatever from the other members. His oratory fell on indifferent ears. And of course there were always those in Congress who got a vicarious thrill watching women do in their fight what they themselves had not the courage to do in their own. Another representative, an anti-suffrage Democrat, inconsiderately called us "Iron-jawed angels," and hoped we would retire. But if by these protests these congressmen hoped to arouse their colleagues, they failed.

We were standing at the gates of the White House because the American Congress had become so supine that it could not or would not act without being compelled to act by the President. They knew that if they howled at us it would only afford an opportunity to retort—"Very well then, if you do not like us at the gates of your leader; if you do not want us to 'insult' the President, end this agitation by taking the matter into your own hands and passing the amendment." Such a suggestion would be almost as severe a shock as our picketing. The thought of actually initiating legislation left a loyal Democratic follower transfixed.

The heavy dignity of the Senate forbade their meddling much in this controversy over tactics. Also they were more interested in the sporting prospect of our going into the world war. There was no appeal to blood-lust in the women's fight. There were no shining rods of steel. There was no martial music. We were not pledging precious lives and vast billions in our crusade for liberty. The beginning of our fight did indeed seem tiny and frail by the side of the big game of war, and so the senators were at first scarcely aware of our presence.

But the intrepid women stood their long vigils, day

by day, at the White House gates, through biting wind and driving rain, through sleet and snow as well as sunshine, waiting for the President to act. Above all the challenges of their banners rang this simple, but insistent one:

MR. PRESIDENT!
HOW LONG MUST WOMEN WAIT FOR LIBERTY?

The royal blaze of purple, white and gold—the Party's tricolored banners—made a gorgeous spot of color against the bare, blacklimbed trees.

There were all kinds of pickets and so there were all kinds of reactions to the experience of picketing. The beautiful lady, who drove up in her limousine to do a twenty minute turn on the line, found it thrilling, no doubt. The winter tourist who had read about the pickets in her home paper thought it would be "so exciting" to hold a banner for a few minutes. But there were no illusions in the hearts of the women who stood at their posts day in and day out. None of them will tell you that they felt exalted, ennobled, exhilarated, possessed of any rare and exotic emotion. They were human beings before they were pickets. Their reactions were those of any human beings called upon to set their teeth doggedly and hang on to an unpleasant job.

"When *will* that woman come to relieve me? I have stood here an hour and a half and my feet are like blocks of ice," was a more frequent comment from picket to picket than "Isn't it glorious to stand here defiantly no matter what the stupid people say about us?"

"I remember the thousand and one engaging things that would come to my mind on the picket line. It seemed that anything but standing at a President's gate would be more diverting. But there we stood.

And what were the reflections of a President as he saw the indomitable little army at his gates? We can only venture to say from events which happened. At first he seemed amused and interested. Perhaps he thought it a trifling incident staged by a minority of the extreme "left" among suffragists and anticipated no popular support for it. When he saw their persistence through a cruel winter his sympathy was touched. He ordered the guards to invite them in for a cup of hot coffee, which they declined. He raised his hat to them as he drove through the line. Sometimes he smiled. As yet he was not irritated. He was fortified in his national power.

With the country's entrance into the war and his immediate elevation to world leadership, the pickets began to be a serious thorn in his flesh. His own statements of faith in democracy and the necessity for establishing it throughout the world left him open to attack. His refusal to pay the just bill owed the women and demanded by them brought irritation.

What would *you* do if you owed a just bill and every day some one stood outside your gates as a quiet reminder to the whole world that you had not paid it?

You would object. You would get terribly irritated. You would call the insistent one all kinds of harsh names. You might even arrest him. But the scandal would be out.

Rightly or wrongly, your sincerity would be touched; faith in you would be shaken a bit. Perhaps even against your will you would yield.

But you *would* yield. And that was the one important fact to the women.

This daily sight, inspiring, gallant and impressive, escaped no visitor to the national capital. Distinguished visitors from the far corners of the earth passed by the pickets on those days which made history. Thousands read the compelling messages on the banners, and literally hundreds of thousands learned the story, when the visitors got "back home."

Real displeasure over the sentinels by those who passed was negligible. There was some mirth and joking, but the vast majority were filled with admiration, either silent or expressed.

"Keep it up." . . . "You are on the right track." . . . "Congratulations." . . . "I certainly admire your pluck—stick to it and you will get it." . . . This last from a military officer. . . . "It is an outrage that you women should have to stand here and beg for your rights. We gave it to our women in Australia long ago." . . . This from a charming gentleman who bowed approvingly.

Often a lifted hat was held in sincere reverence over the heart as some courteous gentleman passed along the picket line. Of course there were some who came to try to argue with the pickets; who attempted to dissuade them from their persistent course. But the serene, good humor and even temper of the women would not allow heated arguments to break in on the military precision of their line. If a question was asked, a picket would answer quietly. An occasional sneer was easy to meet. That required no acknowledgment.

A sweet old veteran of the Civil War said to one of my comrades: "Yous all right; you gotta fight for your rights in this world, and now that we are about to plunge into another war, I want to tell you women there'll be no end to it unless you women get power. We can't save ourselves and we need you. . . . I am 84 years old, and I have watched this fight since I was a young man. Anything I can do to help, I want to do. I am living at the Old Soldiers' Home and I ain't got much money, but here's something for your campaign. It's all I got, and God bless you, you've gotta win." He spoke the last sentence almost with desperation as he shoved a crumpled $2.00 bill into her hand. His spirit made it a precious gift.

Cabinet members passed and repassed. Congressmen by the hundreds came and went. Administration leaders tried to conceal under an artificial indifference their sensitiveness to our strategy.

And domestic battles were going on inside the homes

throughout the country, for women were coming from every state in the Union, to take their place on the line. For the first time good "suffrage-husbands" were made uncomfortable. Had they not always believed in suffrage? Had they not always been uncomplaining when their wife's time was given to suffrage campaigning? Had they not, in short, been good sports about the whole thing? There was only one answer. They had. But it had been proved that all the things that women had done and all the things in which their menfolk had coöperated, were not enough. Women were called upon for more intensive action. "You cannot go to Washington and risk your health standing in front of the White House. I cannot have it."

"But the time has come when we have to take risks of health or anything else."

"Well, then, if you must know, I don't believe in it. Now I am a reasonable man and I have stood by you all the way up to now, but I object to this. It isn't ladylike, and it will do the cause more harm than good. You women lay yourselves open to ridicule."

"That's just it—that's a fine beginning. As soon as men get tired laughing at us, they will do something more about it. They won't find our campaign so amusing before long."

"But I protest. You've no right to go without considering me."

"But if your country called you in a fight for democracy, as it is likely to do at any moment, you'd go, wouldn't you?"

"Why, of course."

"Of course you would. You would go to the front and leave me to struggle on as best I could without you. That is the way you would respond to your country's call, whether it was a righteous cause or not. Well, I am going to the front too. I am going to answer the women's call to fight for democracy. I would be ashamed of myself if I were not willing to join my comrades. I am sorry that you object, but if you will just put yourself in my place you will see that I cannot do otherwise."

It must be recorded that there were exceptional men of sensitive imaginations who urged women against their own hesitancy. They are the handful who gave women a hope that they would not always have to struggle alone for their liberation. And women passed by the daily picket line as spectators, not as participants. Occasionally a woman came forward to remonstrate, but more often women were either too shy to advance or so enthusiastic that nothing could restrain them. The more kind-hearted of them, inspired by the dauntless pickets in the midst of a now freezing temperature, brought mittens, fur pieces, golashes, wool-lined raincoats; hot bricks to stand on, coffee in thermos bottles and what not.

Meanwhile the pickets became a household word in Washington, and very soon were the subject of animated conversation in practically every corner of the nation. The Press cartoonists, by their friendly and satirical comments, helped a great deal in popularizing the campaign. In spite of the bitter editorial comment of most of the press, the humor of the situation had an almost universal appeal.

At the Washington dinner of the Gridiron Club, probably the best known press club in the world,—a dinner at which President Wilson was a guest,—one of the songs sung for his benefit was as follows:

"We're camping to-night on the White House grounds
        Give us a rousing cheer;
Our golden flag we hold aloft, of cops we have no fear.
        Many of the pickets are weary to-night,
Wishing for the war to cease; many are the chilblains and
        frost-bites too;
        It is no life of ease.

Camping to-night, camping to-night,
Camping on the White House grounds."

SCENES ON THE PICKET LINE

Top—"We Shall Fight" Banner *
Silent Sentinel—Joy Young
Middle—Picketing in the Rain
Bottom—Working Women March to White House *
Pickets in June

* © Harris & Ewing.

The White House police on duty at the gates came to treat the picketers as comrades.

"I was kinda worried," confessed one burly officer when the pickets were five minutes late one day. "We thought perhaps you weren't coming and we would have to hold down this place alone."

The bitter-enders among the opponents of suffrage broke into such violent criticism that they won new friends to the amendment.

People who had never before thought of suffrage for women had to think of it, if only to the extent of objecting to the way in which we asked for it. People who had thought a little about suffrage were compelled to think more about it. People who had believed in suffrage all their lives, but had never done a stroke of work for it, began to make speeches about it, if only for the purpose of condemning us.

Some politicians who had voted for it when there were not enough votes to carry the measure loudly threatened to commit political suicide by withdrawing their support. But it was easy to see at a glance that they would not dare to run so great a political risk on an issue growing daily more important.

As soon as the regular picket line began to be accepted as a matter of course, we undertook to touch it up a bit to sustain public interest. State days were inaugurated, beginning with Maryland. The other states took up the idea with enthusiasm. There was a College Day, when women representing 15 American colleges stood on the line; a Teachers' Day, which found the long line represented by almost every state in the Union, and a Patriotic Day, when American flags mingled with the party's banners carried by representatives of the Women's Reserve Corps, Daughters of the Revolution and other patriotic organizations. And there were professional days when women doctors, lawyers and nurses joined the picket appeal.

Lincoln's birthday anniversary saw another new feature.

A long line of women took out banners bearing the slogans:

LINCOLN STOOD FOR WOMAN SUFFRAGE 60 YEARS AGO.
MR. PRESIDENT, WHY DO YOU BLOCK THE NATIONAL
SUFFRAGE AMENDMENT TO-DAY?

WHY ARE YOU BEHIND LINCOLN?

and another:

AFTER THE CIVIL WAR, WOMEN ASKED FOR POLITICAL
FREEDOM. THEY WERE TOLD TO WAIT—THIS WAS THE
NEGRO'S HOUR. IN 1917 AMERICAN WOMEN STILL ASK
FOR FREEDOM.
WILL YOU, MR. PRESIDENT, TELL THEM TO WAIT—
THAT THIS IS THE PORTO RICAN'S HOUR? [1]

A huge labor demonstration on the picket line late in February brought women wage earners from office and factory throughout the Eastern States.

A special Susan B. Anthony Day on the anniversary of the birth of that great pioneer, served to remind the President who said, "You can afford to wait," that the women had been waiting and fighting for this legislation to pass Congress since the year 1878.

More than one person came forward to speak with true religious fervor of the memory of the great Susan B. Anthony. Her name is never mentioned nor her words quoted without finding such a response.

In the face of heavy snow and rain, dozens of young women stood in line, holding special banners made for this occasion. Thousands of men and women streaming home from work in the early evening read words of hers spoken during the Civil

---

[1] President Wilson had just advocated self-government for Porto Rican men.

War, so completely applicable to the policy of the young banner-bearers at the gates.

WE PRESS OUR DEMAND FOR THE BALLOT AT THIS TIME IN NO NARROW, CAPIOUS OR SELFISH SPIRIT, BUT FROM PUREST PATRIOTISM FOR THE HIGHEST GOOD OF EVERY CITIZEN, FOR THE SAFETY OF THE REPUBLIC AND AS A GLORIOUS EXAMPLE TO THE NATIONS OF THE EARTH.

AT THIS TIME OUR GREATEST NEED IS NOT MEN OR MONEY, VALIANT GENERALS OR BRILLIANT VICTORIES, BUT A CONSISTENT NATIONAL POLICY BASED UPON THE PRINCIPLE THAT ALL GOVERNMENTS DERIVE THEIR JUST POWERS FROM THE CONSENT OF THE GOVERNED.

THE RIGHT OF SELF-GOVERNMENT FOR ONE-HALF OF ITS PEOPLE IS OF FAR MORE VITAL CONSEQUENCE TO THE NATION THAN ANY OR ALL OTHER QUESTIONS.

During the reunion week of the Daughters and Veterans of the Confederacy, the picket line was the center of attraction for the sight-seeing veterans and their families. For the first time in history the troops of the Confederacy had crossed the Potomac and taken possession of the capital city. The streets were lined with often tottering but still gallant old men, white-haired and stooped, wearing their faded badges on their gray uniforms, and carrying their tattered flags.

It seemed to the young women on picket duty during those days that not a single veteran had failed to pay his respects to the pickets. They came and came; and some brought back their wives to show them the guard at the gates.

One old soldier with tears in his dim eyes came to say, "I've done sentinel duty in my time. I know what it is. . . .

And now it's your turn. You young folks have the strength and the courage to keep it up. . . . You are going to put it through!"

One sweet old Alabamian came shyly up to one of the pickets and said, "I say, Miss, this *is* the White House, isn't it?"

Before she could answer, he added: "We went three times around the place and I told the boys, the big white house in the center was the White House, but they wasn't believing me and I wasn't sure, but as soon as I saw you girls coming with your flags, to stand here, I said, 'This *must* be the White House. This is sure enough where the President lives; here are the pickets with their banners that we read about down home.'" A note of triumph was in his frail voice.

The picket smiled, and thanked him warmly, as he finished with, "You are brave girls. You are bound to get him"— pointing his shaking finger toward the White House.

President Wilson's second inauguration was rapidly approaching. Also war clouds were gathering with all the increased emotionalism that comes at such a crisis. Some additional demonstration of power and force must be made before the President's inauguration and before the excitement of our entry into the war should plunge our agitation into obscurity. This was the strategic moment to assemble our forces in convention in Washington.

Accordingly, the Congressional Union for Woman Suffrage and the Woman's Party, that section of the Congressional Union in suffrage states made up of women voters, convened in Washington and decided unanimously to unite their strength, money and political power in one organization, and called it the National Woman's Party.

The following officers were unanimously elected to direct the activities of the new organization: Chairman of the National Woman's Party, Miss Alice Paul, New Jersey; vice-chairman, Miss Anne Martin, Nevada; secretary, Miss Mabel Vernon, Nevada; treasurer, Miss Gertrude Crocker, Illinois; executive members, Miss Lucy Burns, Mrs. O. H. P. Belmont, Mrs. John Winters Brannan, New York; Mrs. Gilson Gardner, Illinois; Mrs. Robert Baker, Washington, D. C.; Mrs. William Kent and Miss Maud Younger, California; Mrs. Florence Bayard Hilles, Delaware; Mrs. Donald Hooker, Maryland; Mrs. J. A. H. Hopkins, New Jersey; Mrs. Lawrence Lewis, Pennsylvania, and Miss Doris Stevens, Nebraska.

The convention came to a close on the eve of inauguration, culminating in the dramatic picket line made up of one thousand delegates who sought an interview with the President. The purpose of the interview was to carry to him the resolutions of the convention, and further plead with him to open his second administration with a promise to back the amendment.

In our optimism we hoped that this glorified picket-pageant might form a climax to our three months of picketing. The President admired persistence. He said so. He also said he appreciated the rare tenacity shown by our women. Surely "now" he would be convinced! No more worrying persistence would be needed! The combined political strength of the western women and the financial strength of the eastern women would surely command his respect and entitle us to a hearing.

What actually happened?

It was a day of high wind and stinging, icy rain, that March 4th, 1917, when a thousand women, each bearing a banner, struggled against the gale to keep their banners erect. It is always impressive to see a thousand people march, but the impression was imperishable when these thousand women marched in rain-soaked garments, hands bare, gloves roughly torn by the sticky varnish from the banner poles and the streams of water running down the poles into the palms of their hands. It was a sight to impress even the most hardened spectator who had seen all the various forms of the suffrage agitation in Washington. For more than two hours the women circled the White House—the rain never ceasing for an instant—hoping to the last moment that at least their leaders would be allowed to take in to the President the resolutions which they were carrying.

Long before the appointed hour for the march to start, thousands of spectators sheltered by umbrellas and raincoats lined the streets to watch the procession. Two bands whose men managed to continue their spirited music in spite of the driving rain led the march playing "Forward Be Our Watchword"; "The Battle Hymn of the Republic"; "Onward Christian Soldiers"; "The Pilgrim's Chorus" from Tannhäuser; "The Coronation March" from Le Prophēte, the Russian Hymn and "The Marsellaise."

Miss Vida Milholland led the procession carrying her sister's last words, "Mr. President, how long must women wait for liberty?" She was followed by Miss Beulah Amidon of North Dakota, who carried the banner that the beloved Inez Milholland carried in her first suffrage procession in New York.

The long line of women fell in behind.

Most extraordinary precautions had been taken about the White House. Everything had been done except the important thing. There were almost as many police officers as marchers. The Washington force had been augmented by a Baltimore contingent and squads of plainclothes men. On every fifty feet of curb around the entire White House grounds there was a policeman. About the same distance apart on the inside of the tall picket-fence which surrounds the grounds were as many more.

We proceeded to the main gate. Locked! I was marshalling at the head of the line and so heard first hand what passed between the leaders and the guards. Miss Anne Martin addressed the guard—

"We have come to present some important resolutions to the President of the United States."

"I have orders to keep the gates locked, Ma'am."

"But there must be some mistake. Surely the President does not mean to refuse to see at least . . ."

"Those are my only orders, Ma'am."

The procession continued on to the second gate on Pennsylvania Avenue. Again locked. Before we could address the somewhat nervous policeman who stood at the gates, he hastened to say, "You can't come in here; the gates are locked."

"But it is imperative; we are a thousand women from all States in the Union who have come all the way to Washington to see the President and lay before him . . ."

"No orders, Ma'am."

The line made its way to the third and last gate—the gate leading to the Executive offices. As we came up to this gate a small army of grinning clerks and secretaries manned the windows of the Executive offices, evidently amused at the sight of the women struggling in the wind and rain to keep their banners intact. Miss Martin, Mrs. William Kent of California, Mrs. Florence Bayard Hilles of Delaware, Miss Mary Patterson of Ohio, niece of John C. Patterson of Dayton, Mrs. J. A. H. Hopkins of New Jersey, Miss Eleanor Barker of Indiana, and Mrs. Mary Darrow Weible of North Dakota,—the leaders —stayed at the gate, determined to get results from the guard, while the women continued to circle the White House.

"Will you not carry a message to the President's Secretary asking him to tell the President that we are here waiting to see him?"

"Can't do that, Ma'am."

"Will you then take our cards to the Secretary to the President, merely announcing to him that we are here, so that he may send somebody to carry in our resolutions?"

Still the guard hesitated. Finally he left the gate and

carried the message a distance of a few rods into the Executive offices. He had scarcely got inside when he rushed back to his post. When we sought to ascertain what had happened to the cards—had they been given and what the answer was—he quietly confided to us that he had been reprimanded for even attempting to bring them in and informed us that the cards were still in his pocket.

"I have orders to answer no questions and to carry no messages. If you have anything to leave here you might take it to the entrance below the Executive offices, and when I go off my beat at six o'clock I will leave it as I go by the White House."

We examined this last entrance suggested. It did not strike us as the proper place to leave an important message for the President.

"What is this entrance used for?" I asked the guard.

"It's all right, lady. If you've got something you'd like to leave, leave it with me. It will be safe."

I retorted that we were not seeking safety for our message, but speed in delivery.

The guard continued: "This is the gate where Mrs. Wilson's clothes and other packages are left."

It struck us as scarcely fitting that we should leave our resolutions amongst "Mrs. Wilson's clothes and other packages," so we returned to the last locked gate to ask the guard if he had any message in the meantime for us. He shook his head regretfully.

Meanwhile the women marched and marched, and the rain fell harder and as the afternoon wore on the cold seemed almost unendurable.

The white-haired grandmothers in the procession—there were some as old as 84—were as energetic as the young girls of 20. What was this immediate hardship compared to eternal subjection! Women marched and waited—waited and marched,

MONSTER PICKET FORMING

LOCKED GATES MET THE LEADERS

SECTION OF PICKET CIRCLING WHITE HOUSE IN RAIN

"THEY MARCHED AND WAITED—WAITED AND MARCHED"

© Harris & Ewing.

under the sting of the biting elements and under the worse
sting of the indignities heaped upon them. It was impossible
to believe that in democratic America they could not see the
President to lay before him their grievance.

It was only when they saw the Presidential limousine, in
the late afternoon, roll luxuriously out of the grounds, and
through the gates down Pennsylvania Avenue, that the weary
marchers realized that President Wilson had deliberately
turned them away unheard!

The car for an instant, as it came through the gates,
divided the banner-bearers on march. President and Mrs. Wilson
looked straight ahead as if the long line of purple, white
and gold were invisible.

All the women who took part in that march will tell you
what was burning in their hearts on that dreary day. Even
if reasons had been offered—and they were not—genuine
reasons why the President could not see them, it would not have
cooled the women's heat. Their passionate resentment went
deeper than any reason could possibly have gone.

This one single incident probably did more than any other
to make women sacrifice themselves. Even something as thin as
diplomacy on the part of President Wilson might have saved
him many restless hours to follow, but he did not take the
trouble to exercise even that.

The women returned to headquarters and there wrote a
letter which was dispatched with the resolutions to President
Wilson. In a letter to the National Woman's Party, acknowledging the receipt of them, he concluded by saying: "May I
not once more express my sincere interest in the cause of woman
suffrage?"

Three months of picketing had not been enough. We must
not only continue on duty at his gates but also at the gates
of Congress.

CHAPTER 2

P RESIDENT WILSON called the War Session of the Sixty-fifth Congress on April 2, 1917.

On the opening day of Congress not only were the pickets again on duty at the White House, but another picket line was inaugurated at the Capitol. Returning senators and congressmen were surprised when greeted with great golden banners reading:

RUSSIA AND ENGLAND ARE ENFRANCHISING THEIR WOMEN IN WAR-TIME. HOW LONG MUST AMERICAN WOMEN WAIT FOR THEIR LIBERTY?

The last desperate flurries in the pro-war and anti-war camps were focused on the Capitol grounds that day. There swarmed about the grounds and through the buildings pacifists from all over the country wearing white badges, and advocates of war, wearing the national colors. Our sentinels at the Capitol stood strangely silent, and almost aloof, strong in their dedication to democracy, while the peace and war agitation circled about them.

With lightning speed the President declared that a state of war existed. Within a fortnight following, Congress declared war on Germany and President Wilson voiced his memorable, "We shall fight for the things we have always carried nearest our hearts—for democracy—for the right of those who submit to authority to have a voice in their own government." Inspiring words indeed! The war message concluded with still another defense of the fight for political liberty: "To such a task we can dedicate our lives and our fortunes, everything that we are and everything that we have, with the pride of those who know that the day has come when America is privileged to spend her blood and her might for the principles that gave her birth and happiness and the peace which she has treasured. God helping her, she can do no less."

Now that the United States was actually involved in war, we were face to face with the question, which we had considered at the convention the previous month, when war was rumored, as to what position we, as an organization, should take in this situation.

The atmosphere of that convention had been dramatic in the extreme. Most of the delegates assembled had been approached either before going to Washington or upon arriving, and urged to use their influence to persuade the organization to abandon its work for the freedom of women and turn its activities into war channels. Although war was then only rumored, the hysterical attitude was already prevalent. Women were asked to furl their banners and give up their half century struggle for democracy, to forget the liberty that was most precious to their hearts.

"The President will turn this Imperialistic war into a crusade for democracy." . . . "Lay aside your own fight and help us crush Germany, and you will find yourselves rewarded with a vote out of the nation's gratitude," were some of the appeals made to our women by government officials high and low and by the rank and file of men and women. Never in history did a band of women stand together with more sanity and greater solidarity than did these 1000 delegates representing thousands more throughout the States.

As our official organ, *The Suffragist,* pointed out editorially, in its issue of April 21st, 1917: Our membership was made up of women who had banded together to secure political freedom for women. We were united on no other subject. Some would offer passive resistance to the war; others would become devoted followers of a vigorous military policy. Between these, every shade of opinion was represented. Each was loyal to the ideas which she held for her country. With the character of these various ideals, the National Woman's Party, we maintained, had nothing to do. It was concerned only with the effort to obtain for women the opportunity to give effective expression, through political power, to their ideals, whatever they might be.

The thousand delegates present at the convention, though differing widely on the duty of the individual in war, were unanimous in voting that in the event of war, the National Woman's Party, *as an organization*, should continue to work for political liberty for women and for that alone, believing as the convention stated in its resolutions, that in so doing the organization "serves the highest interest of the country." They were also unanimous in the opinion that all service which *individuals* wished to give to war or peace should be given through groups organized for such purposes, and not through the Woman's Party, a body created, according to its constitution, for one purpose only—"to secure an amendment to the United States Constitution enfranchising women."

We declared officially through our organ that this held "as the policy of the Woman's Party, whatever turn public events may take."

Very few days after we were put upon a national war basis it became clear that never was there greater need of work for internal freedom in the country. Europe, then approaching her third year of war, was increasing democracy in the midst of the terrible conflict. In America at that very moment women were being told that no attempt at electoral reform had any place in the country's program "until the war is over." The Democrats met in caucus and decided that only "war measures" should be included in the legislative program, and announced that no subjects would be considered by them, unless the President urged them as war measures.

Our task was, from that time on, to make national suffrage a war measure.

We at once urged upon the Administration the wisdom of accepting this proposed reform as a war measure, and pointed out the difficulty of waging a war for democracy abroad while democracy was denied at home. But the government was not willing to profit by the experience of its Allies in extending suffrage to women, without first offering a terrible and brutal resistance.

We must confess that the problem of dramatizing our fight for democracy in competition with the drama of a world-war, was most perplexing. Here were we, citizens without power and recognition, with the only weapons to which a powerless class which does not take up arms can resort. We could not and would not fight with men's weapons. Compare the methods women adopted to those men use in the pursuit of democracy,— bayonets, machine guns, poison gas, deadly grenades, liquid fire, bombs, armored tanks, pistols, barbed wire entanglements, submarines, mines—every known scientific device with which to annihilate the enemy!

What did we do?

We continued to fight with our simple, peaceful, almost quaint device—a banner. A little more fiery, perhaps; pertinent to the latest political controversy, but still only a banner inscribed with militant truth!

Just as our political strategy had been to oppose, at elections, the party in power which had failed to use its power to free women, so now our military strategy was based on the military doctrine of concentrating all one's forces on the enemy's weakest point. To women the weakest point in the

Administration's political lines during the war was the inconsistency between a crusade for world democracy and the denial of democracy at home. This was the untenable position of President Wilson and the Democratic Administration, from which we must force them to retreat. We could force such a retreat when we had exposed to the world this weakest point.

Just as the bluff of a democratic crusade must be called, so must the knight-leader of the crusade be exposed to the critical eyes of the world. Here was the President, suddenly elevated to the position of a world leader with the almost pathetic trust of the peoples of the world. Here was the champion of their democratic aspirations. Here was a kind of universal Moses, expected to lead all peoples out of bondage—no matter what the bondage, no matter of how long standing.

The President's elevation to this unique pinnacle of power was at once an advantage and a disadvantage to us. It was an advantage to us in that it made our attack more dramatic. One supposed to be impeccable was more vulnerable. It was a disadvantage to have to overcome this universal trust and world-wide popularity. But this conflict of wits and brains against power only enhanced our ingenuity.

On the day the English mission headed by Mr. Balfour, and the French mission headed by M. Viviani, visited the White House, we took these inscriptions to the picket line:

WE SHALL FIGHT FOR THE THINGS WE HAVE ALWAYS CARRIED
NEAREST OUR HEARTS

DEMOCRACY SHOULD BEGIN AT HOME

WE DEMAND JUSTICE AND SELF-GOVERNMENT IN OUR OWN LAND

Embarrassing to say these things before foreign visitors? We hoped it would be. In our capacity to embarrass Mr. Wilson in his Administration, lay our only hope of success. We had to keep before the country the flagrant inconsistency of

the President's position. We intended to know why, if democracy were so precious as to demand the nation's blood and
treasure for its achievement abroad, its execution at home was
so undesirable.

Meanwhile:—

"I tell you solemnly, ladies and gentlemen, we cannot any
longer postpone justice in these United States"—President
Wilson.

"I don't wish to sit down and let any man take care of me
without my at least having a voice in it, and if he doesn't listen
to my advice, I am going to make it as unpleasant as I can."—
President Wilson,—and other challenges were carried on
banners to the picket line.

Some rumblings of political action began to be heard. The
Democratic majority had appointed a Senate Committee on
Woman Suffrage whose members were overwhelmingly for federal action. The chairman, Senator Andreas Jones of New
Mexico, promised an early report to the Senate. There were
scores of gains in Congress. Representatives and Senators were
tumbling over each other to introduce similar suffrage resolutions. We actually had difficulty in choosing the man whose
name should stamp our measure.

A minority party also was moved to act. Members of the
Progressive Party met in convention in St. Louis on April 12,
13 and 14 and adopted a suffrage plank which demanded "the
nation-wide enfranchiseemnt of women. . . ."

In addition to this plank they adopted a resolution calling
for the establishment of democracy at home "at a time when
the United States is entering into an international war for
democracy" and instructing the chairman of the convention "to
request a committee consisting of representatives of all liberal
groups to go to Washington to present to the President and
the Congress of the United States a demand for immediate sub-

mission of an amendment to the United States constitution enfranchising women."

They appointed a committee from the convention to carry these resolutions to the President. The committee included Mr. J. A. H. Hopkins of the Progressive Party, as chairman; Dr. E. A. Rumley of the Progressive-Republican Party and Vice President of the New York *Evening Mail;* Mr. John Spargo of the Socialist Party; Mr. Virgil Hinshaw, chairman of the Executive Committee of the Prohibition Party; and Miss Mabel Vernon, Secretary of the National Woman's Party. It was the first suffrage conference with the President after the declaration of war, and was the last deputation on suffrage by minority party leaders. The conference was one of the utmost informality and friendliness.

The President was deeply moved, indeed, almost to the point of tears, when Miss Mabel Vernon said, "Mr. President, the feelings of many women in this country are best expressed by your own words in your war message to Congress. . . . To every woman who reads that message must come at once this question: If the right of those who submit to authority to have a voice in their own government is so sacred a cause to foreign people as to constitute the reason for our entering the international war in its defense, will you not, Mr. President, give immediate aid to the measure before Congress demanding self-government for the women of this country?"

The President admitted that suffrage was constantly pressing upon his mind for reconsideration. He added, however, that the program for the session was practically complete and intimated that it did not include the enfranchisement of women.

He informed the Committee that he had written a letter to Mr. Pou, Chairman of the Rules Committee of the House, expressing himself as favoring the creation of a Woman Suffrage Committee in that body. While we had no objection to having the House create a Suffrage Committee, we were not primarily interested in the amplification of Congressional machinery, unless this amplification was to be followed by the passage of the amendment. The President could as easily have written the Senate Committee on Suffrage or the Judiciary Committee of the House, advising an immediate report on the suffrage resolution, as have asked for the creation of another committee to report on the subject.

He made no mention of his state-by-state conviction, however, as he had in previous interviews, and the Committee of Progressives understood him to have at least tacitly accepted federal action.

The House Judiciary Committee continued to refuse to act and the House Rules Committee steadily refused to create a Suffrage Committee.

Hoping to win back to the fold the wandering Progressives who had thus demonstrated their allegiance to suffrage and seeing an opportunity to embarrass the Administration, the Republicans began to interest themselves in action on the amendment. In the midst of Democratic delays, Representative James R. Mann, Republican leader of the House, moved to discharge the Judiciary Committee from further consideration of the suffrage amendment. No matter if the discussion which followed did revolve about the authorization of an expenditure of $10,000 for the erection of a monument to a dead President as a legitimate war measure. It was clear from the partisan attitude of those who took part in the debate that we were advancing to that position where we were as good political material to be contested over by opposing political groups as was a monument to a dead President. And if the Democrats could defend such an issue as a war measure, the Republicans wanted to know why they should ignore suffrage for women as a war measure. And it was encouraging to find ourselves thus suddenly and spontaneously sponsored by the Republican leader.

The Administration was aroused. It did not know how far the Republicans were prepared to go in their drive for action, so on the day of this flurry in the House the snail-like Rules Committee suddenly met in answer to the call of its chairman, Mr. Pou, and by a vote of 6 to 5 decided to report favorably on the resolution providing for a Woman Suffrage Committee in the House "*after all pending war measures have been disposed of.*"

Before the meeting, Mr. Pou made a last appeal to the Woman's Party to remove the pickets. . . . "We can't possibly win as long as pickets guard the White House and Capitol," Mr. Pou had said. The pickets continued their vigil and the motion carried.

Still uncertain as to the purposes of the Republicans, the Democrats were moved to further action.

The Executive Committee of the Democratic National Committee, meeting in Washington a few days later, voted 4 to 2 to "officially urge upon the President that he call the two Houses of Congress together and recommend the immediate submission of the Susan B. Anthony amendment." This action which in effect reversed the plank in the Democratic platform evidently aroused protests from powerful quarters. Also the Republicans quickly subsided when they saw the Democrats making an advance. And so the Democratic Executive Committee began to spread abroad the news that its act was not really official, but merely reflected the "personal conviction" of the members present. It extracted the official flavor, and so of course no action followed in Congress.

And so it went—like a great game of chess. Doubtless the politicians believed they were moved from their own true and noble motives. The fact was that the pickets had moved the Democrats a step. The Republicans had then attempted to take two steps, whereupon the Democrats must continue to move more rapidly than their opponents. Behind this matching of political wits by the two parties stood the faithful pickets compelling them both to act.

Simultaneously with these moves and counter-moves in political circles, the people in all sections of this vast country began to speak their minds. Meetings were springing up everywhere, at which resolutions were passed backing up the picket line and urging the President and Congress to act. Even the South, the Administration's stronghold, sent fiery telegrams demanding action. Alabama, South Carolina, Texas, Maryland, Mississippi, as well as the West, Middle West, New England and the East—the stream was endless.

Every time a new piece of legislation was passed,—the war tax bill, food conservation or what not,—women from unexpected quarters sent to the Government their protest against the passage of measures so vital to women without women's consent, coupled with an appeal for the liberation of women. Club women, college women, federations of labor,—various kinds of organizations sent protests to the Administration leaders. The picket line, approaching its sixth month of duty, had aroused the country to an unprecedented interest in suffrage; it had rallied widespread public support to the amendment as a war measure, and had itself become almost universally accepted if not universally approved. And in the midst of picketing and in spite of all the prophecies and fears that "picketing" would "set back the cause," within one month, Michigan, Nebraska and Rhode Island granted Presidential suffrage to women.

The leaders were busy marshaling their forces behind the President's war program, which included the controversial Conscription and Espionage Bills, then pending, and did not relish having our question so vivid in the public mind. Even when the rank and file of Congress gave consideration to questions not in the war program, they had to face a possible charge of inconsistency, insincerity or bad faith.   The freedom of Ireland, for example, was not in the program.   And when 132 members of the House cabled Lloyd George that nothing would do more for American enthusiasm in the war than a settlement of the Irish question, we took pains to ascertain the extent of the belief in liberty at home of these easy champions of Irish liberty.   When we found that of the 132 men only 57 believed in liberty for American women, we were not delicate in pointing out to the remaining 75 that their belief in liberty for Ireland would appear more sincere if they believed in a democratic reform such as woman suffrage here.

The manifestations of popular approval of suffrage, the constant stream of protests to the Administration against its delay nationally, and the shame of having women begging at its gates, could result in only one of two things.   The Administration had little choice.   It must yield to this pressure from the people or it must suppress the agitation which was causing such interest.   It must pass the amendment or remove the troublesome pickets.

It decided to remove the pickets.

CHAPTER 3

THE FIRST ARRESTS

THE Administration chose suppression. They resorted to force in an attempt to end picketing. It was a policy doomed to failure as certainly as all resorts to force to kill agitation have failed ultimately. This marked the beginning of the adoption by the Administration of tactics from which they could never extricate themselves with honor. Unfortunately for them they were entering upon this policy toward women which savored of czarist practices, at the very moment they were congratulating the Russians upon their liberation from the oppression of a Czar. This fact supplied us with a fresh angle of attack.

President Wilson sent a Mission to Russia to add America's appeal to that of the other Allies to keep that impoverished country in the war. Such was our democratic zeal to persuade Russia to continue the war and to convince her people of its democratic purposes, and of the democratic quality of America, that Elihu Root, one of the President's envoys, stated in Petrograd that he represented a republic where "universal, direct, equal and secret suffrage obtained." We subjected the President to attack through this statement.

Russia also sent a war mission to our country for purposes of coöperation. This occasion offered us the opportunity again to expose the Administration's weakness in claiming complete political democracy while women were still denied their political freedom.

It was a beautiful June day when all Washington was agog

with the visit of the Russian diplomats to the President. As
the car carrying the envoys passed swiftly through the gates
of the White House there stood on the picket line two silent
sentinels, Miss Lucy Burns of New York and Mrs. Lawrence
Lewis of Philadelphia, both members of the National Executive
Committee, with a great lettered banner which read:

TO THE RUSSIAN ENVOYS

PRESIDENT WILSON AND ENVOY ROOT ARE DECEIVING
RUSSIA WHEN THEY SAY "WE ARE A DEMOCRACY, HELP
US WIN THE WORLD WAR SO THAT DEMOCRACY MAY
SURVIVE."

WE THE WOMEN OF AMERICA TELL YOU THAT AMER-
ICA IS NOT A DEMOCRACY. TWENTY-MILLION AMERI-
CAN WOMEN ARE DENIED THE RIGHT TO VOTE. PRESI-
DENT WILSON IS THE CHIEF OPPONENT OF THEIR NA-
TIONAL ENFRANCHISEMENT.

HELP US MAKE THIS NATION REALLY FREE. TELL OUR
GOVERNMENT IT MUST LIBERATE ITS PEOPLE BEFORE
IT CAN CLAIM FREE RUSSIA AS AN ALLY.

Rumors that the suffragists would make a special demonstration before the Russian Mission had brought a great crowd
to the far gate of the White House; a crowd composed almost
entirely of men.

Like all crowds, this crowd had its share of hoodlums and
roughs who tried to interfere with the women's order of the
day. There was a flurry of excitement over this defiant message of truth, but nothing that could not with the utmost ease
have been settled by one policeman.

There was the criticism in the press and on the lips of men
that we were embarrassing our Government before the eyes of
foreign visitors. In answering the criticism, Miss Paul publicly stated our position thus: "The intolerable conditions

against which we protest can be changed in the twinkling of an eye. The responsibility for our protest is, therefore, with the Administration and not with the women of America, if the lack of democracy at home weakens the Administration in its fight for democracy three thousand miles away."

This was too dreadful. A flurry at the gates of the Chief of the nation at such a time would never do. Our allies in the crusade for democracy must not know that we had a day-by-day unrest at home. Something must be done to stop this exposé at once. Had these women no manners? Had they no shame? Was the fundamental weakness in our boast of pure and perfect democracy to be so wantonly displayed with impunity?

Of course it was embarrassing. We meant it to be. The truth must be told at all costs. This was no time for manners.

Hurried conferences behind closed doors! Summoning of the military to discuss declaring a military zone around the White House! Women could not advance on drawn bayonets. And if they did . . . What a picture! Common decency told the more humane leaders that this would never do. I daresay political wisdom crept into the reasoning of others.

Closing the Woman's Party headquarters was discussed. Perhaps a raid! And all for what? Because women were holding banners asking for the precious principle at home that men were supposed to be dying for abroad.

Finally a decision was reached embodying the combined wisdom of all the various conferees. The Chief of Police, Major Pullman, was detailed to "request" us to stop "picketing" and to tell us that if we continued to picket, we would be arrested.

"We have picketed for six months without interference," said Miss Paul. *"Has the law been changed?"*

"No," was the reply, "but you must stop it."

"But, Major Pullman, we have consulted our lawyers and know we have a legal right to picket."

"I warn you, you will be arrested if you attempt to picket again."

The following day Miss Lucy Burns and Miss Katherine Morey of Boston carried to the White House gates "We shall fight for the things we have always held nearest our hearts, for democracy, for the right of those who submit to authority to have a voice in their own government," and were arrested.

News had spread through the city that the pickets were to be arrested. A moderately large crowd had gathered to see the "fun." One has only to come into conflict with prevailing authority, whether rightly or wrongly, to find friendly hosts vanishing with lightning speed. To know that we were no longer wanted at the gates of the White House and that the police were no longer our "friends" was enough for the mob mind.

Some members of the crowd made sport of the women. Others hurled cheap and childish epithets at them. Small boys were allowed to capture souvenirs, shreds of the banners torn from non-resistant women, as trophies of the sport.

Thinking they had been mistaken in believing the pickets were to be arrested, and having grown weary of their strenuous sport, the crowd moved on its way. Two solitary figures remained, standing on the sidewalk, flanked by the vast Pennsylvania Avenue, looking quite abandoned and alone, when suddenly without any warrant in law, they were arrested on a completely deserted avenue.

Miss Burns and Miss Morey upon arriving at the police station, insisted, to the great surprise of all the officials, upon knowing the charge against them. Major Pullman and his entire staff were utterly at a loss to know what to answer. The Administration had looked ahead only as far as threatening arrest. They doubtless thought this was all they would have to do. People could not be arrested for picketing. Picketing is a guaranteed right under the Clayton Act of

Congress. Disorderly conduct? There had been no disorderly conduct. Inciting to riot? Impossible! The women had stood as silent sentinels holding the President's own eloquent words.

Doors opened and closed mysteriously. Officials and sub-officials passed hurriedly to and fro. Whispered conversations were heard. The book on rules and regulations was hopefully thumbed. Hours passed. Finally the two prisoners were pompously told that they had "obstructed the traffic" on Pennsylvania Avenue, were dismissed on their own recognizance, and never brought to trial.

The following day, June 23rd, more arrests were made; two women at the White House, two at the Capitol. All carried banners with the same words of the President. There was no hesitation this time. They were promptly arrested for "obstructing the traffic." They, too, were dismissed and their cases never tried. It seemed clear that the Administration hoped to suppress picketing merely by arrests. When, however, women continued to picket in the face of arrest, the Administration quickened its advance into the venture of suppression. It decided to bring the offenders to trial.

On June 26, six American women were tried, judged guilty on the technical charge of "obstructing the traffic," warned by the court of their "unpatriotic, almost treasonable behavior," and sentenced to pay a fine of twenty-five dollars or serve three days in jail.

"Not a dollar of your fine will we pay," was the answer of the women. "To pay a fine would be an admission of guilt. We are innocent."

The six women who were privileged to serve the first terms of imprisonment for suffrage in this country, were Miss Katherine Morey of Massachusetts, Mrs. Annie Arneil and Miss Mabel Vernon of Delaware, Miss Lavinia Dock of Pennsylvania, Miss Maud Jamison of Virginia, and Miss Virginia Arnold of

North Carolina. "Privileged" in spite of the foul air, the rats, and the mutterings of their strange comrades in jail!

*   *   *   *

Independence Day, July 4, 1917, is the occasion for two demonstrations in the name of liberty. Champ Clark, late Democratic speaker of the House, is declaiming to a cheering crowd behind the White House, "Governments derive their just powers from the consent of the governed." In front of the White House thirteen silent sentinels with banners bearing the same words, are arrested. It would have been exceedingly droll if it had not been so tragic. Champ Clark and his throng were not molested. The women with practically a deserted street were arrested and served jail terms for "obstructing traffic."

The trial of this group was delayed to give the jail authorities time to "vacate and tidy up," as one prisoner confided to Miss Joy Young. It developed that "orders" had been received at the jail immediately after the arrests and before the trial, "to make ready for the suffragettes." What did it matter that their case had not yet been heard? To jail they must go.

Was not the judge who tried and sentenced them a direct appointee of President Wilson? Were not the District Commissioners who gave orders to prepare the cells the direct appointees of President Wilson? And was not the Chief of Police of the District of Columbia a direct appointee of these same commissioners? And was not the jail warden who made life for the women so unbearable in prison also a direct appointee of the commissioners?

It was all a merry little ring and its cavalier attitude toward the law, toward justice, and above all toward women was of no importance. The world was on fire with a grand blaze. This tiny flame would scarcely be visible. No one would notice a few "mad" women thrown into jail. And if the world should find it out, doubtless public opinion would agree that the women ought to stay there. And even if it should not agree,

OFFICER ARRESTS PICKETS
Miss Catherine Flanagan, Mrs. William U. Watson

WOMEN PUT INTO POLICE PATROL

this little matter could all be explained away before another election.

Meanwhile the President could proclaim through official channels his disinterestedness. Observe the document, of which I give the substance, which he caused or allowed to be published at this time, through his Committee on Public Information.

"OFFICIAL BULLETIN"

"Published Daily under order of the President of the United States, by the Committee on Public Information.

GEORGE CREEL, Chairman.

"Furnished without charge to all newspapers, post offices, government officials and agencies of a public character for the dissemination of official news of the United States Government."

* * * *

"Washington, July 3, 1917. No. 46—Vol. i."

There follows a long editorial [1] which laments the public attention which has centered on the militant campaign, appeals to editors and reporters not to "encourage" us in our peculiar conduct by printing defies to the President of the United States even when "flaunted on a pretty little purple and gold banner" and exhorts the public to control its thrills. The official bulletin concludes with:

"It is a fact that there remains in America one man who has known exactly the right attitude to take and maintain toward the pickets. A whimsical smile, slightly puckered at the roots by a sense of the ridiculous, a polite bow—and for the rest a complete ignoring of their existence. He happens to be the man around whom the little whirlwind whirls—the President of the United States." And finally with an admonition that "the rest of the country . . . take example from him in its emotional reaction to the picket question."

[1] From the *Woman Citizen.*

The Administration pinned its faith on jail—that institution of convenience to the oppressor when he is strong in
power and his weapons are effective. When the oppressor
miscalculates the strength of the oppressed, jail loses its
convenience.

SUFFRAGISTS IN PRISON COSTUME*

Left to Right:—†Miss Doris Stevens;   ‡Mrs. J. A. H. Hopkins;
*Mrs. John Winters Brannan

* © *Underwood;* † © *Ira Hill;* ‡ © *Edmonston.*

CHAPTER 4

IT is Bastille Day, July fourteenth. Inspiring scenes and tragic sacrifices for liberty come to our minds. Sixteen women march in single file to take their own "Liberty, Equality, Fraternity" to the White House gates. It is the middle of a hot afternoon. A thin line of curious spectators is seen in the park opposite the suffrage headquarters. The police assemble from obscure spots; some afoot, others on bicycles. They close in on the women and follow them to the gates.

The proud banner is scarcely at the gates when the leader is placed under arrest. Her place is taken by another. She is taken. Another, and still another steps into the breach and is arrested.

Meanwhile the crowd grows, attracted to the spot by the presence of the police and the patrol wagon. Applause is heard. There are cries of "shame" for the police, who, I must say, did not always act as if they relished carrying out what they termed "orders from higher up." An occasional hoot from a small boy served to make the mood of the hostile ones a bit gayer. But for the most part an intense silence fell upon the watchers, as they saw not only younger women, but white-haired grandmothers hoisted before the public gaze into the crowded patrol, their heads erect, their eyes a little moist and their frail hands holding tightly to the banner until wrested from them by superior brute force.

This is the first time most of the women have ever seen a

police station, and they are interested in their surroundings. They are not interested in helping the panting policeman count them over and identify them. Who arrested whom? That becomes the gigantic question.

"Will the ladies please tell which officer arrested them?"

They will not. They do not intend to be a party to this outrage. Finally the officers abandon their attempt at identification. They have the names of the arrestees and will accept bail for their appearance Monday.

"Well girls, I've never seen but one other court in my life and that was the Court of St. James. But I must say they are not very much alike," was the cheery comment of Mrs. Florence Bayard Hilles, [1] as we entered the court room on Monday.

The stuffy court room is packed to overflowing. The fat, one-eyed bailiff is perspiring to no purpose. He cannot make the throng "sit down." In fact every one who has anything to do with the pickets perspires to no purpose. Judge Mullowny takes his seat, looking at once grotesque and menacing on his red throne.

"Silence in the court room," from the sinister-eyed bailiff. And a silence follows so heavy that it can be heard.

Saturday night's disorderlies—both black and white—are tried first. The suffrage prisoners strain their ears to hear the pitiful pleas of these unfortunates, most of whom come to the bar without counsel or friend. Scraps of evidence are heard.

JUDGE: "You say you were not quarreling, Lottie?"

LOTTIE: "I sho' do yo' hono'. We wuz jes singin'—we wuz sho' nuf, sah."

JUDGE: "Singing, Lottie? Why your neighbors here testify to the fact that you were making a great deal of noise—so much that they could not sleep."

---

[1] Mrs. Hilles is the daughter of the late Thomas Bayard, formerly America's ambassador to Great Britain, and Secretary of State in President Cleveland's cabinet.

LOTTIE: "I tells yo' honor' we wuz jes singin' lak we allays do."

JUDGE: "What were you singing?"

LOTTIE: "Why, hymns, sah."

The judge smiles cynically.

A neatly-attired white man with a wizened face again takes the stand against Lottie. Hymns or no hymns he could not sleep. The judge pronounces a sentence of "six months in the workhouse," for Lottie.

And so it goes on.

The suffrage prisoners are the main business of the morning. Sixteen women come inside the railing which separates "tried" from "untried" and take their seats.

"Do the ladies wish the government to provide them with counsel?"

They do not.

"We shall speak in our own behalf. We feel that we can best represent ourselves," we announce. Miss Anne Martin and I act as attorneys for the group.

The same panting policemen who could not identify the people they had arrested give their stereotyped, false and illiterate testimony. The judge helps them over the hard places and so does the government's attorney. They stumble to an embarrassed finish and retire.

An aged government clerk, grown infirm in the service, takes the stand and the government attorney proves through him that there is a White House; that it has a side-walk in front of it, and a pavement, and a hundred other overwhelming facts. The pathetic clerk shakes his dusty frame and slinks off the stand. The prosecuting attorney now elaborately proves that we walked, that we carried banners, that we were arrested by the aforesaid officers while attempting to hold our banners at the White House gates.

Each woman speaks briefly in her own defense. She denounces the government's policy with hot defiance. The blame is placed squarely at the door of the Administration, and in unmistakable terms. Miss Anne Martin opens for the defense:

"This is what we are doing with our banners before the White Hosue, petitioning the most powerful representative of the government, the President of the United States, for a redress of grievances; we are asking him to use his great power to secure the passage of the national suffrage amendment.

"As long as the government and the representatives of the government prefer to send women to jail on petty and technical charges, we will go to jail. Persecution has always advanced the cause of justice. The right of American women to work for democracy must be maintained. . . . We would hinder, not help, the whole cause of freedom for women, if we weakly submitted to persecution now. Our work for the passage of the amendment must go on. It *will* go on."

Mrs. John Rogers, Jr., descendant of Roger Sherman, one of the signers of the Declaration of Independence, speaks: "We are not guilty of any offence, not even of infringing a police regulation. We know full well that we stand here because the President of the United States refuses to give liberty to American women. We believe, your Honor, that the wrong persons are before the bar in this Court. . . ."

"I object, your Honor, to this woman making such a statement here in Court," says the District Attorney.

"We believe the President is the guilty one and that we are innocent."

"Your Honor, I object," shouts the Government's attorney.

The prisoner continues calmly: "There are votes enough and there is time enough to pass the national suffrage amendment through Congress at this session. More than 200 votes in the House and more than 50 in the Senate are pledged to this amendment. The President puts his power behind all measures in which he takes a genuine interest. If he will say one frank word advocating this measure it will pass as a piece of war emergency legislation."

Mrs. Florence Bayard Hilles speaks in her own defense: "For generations the men of my family have given their services to their country. For myself, my training from childhood has been with a father who believed in democracy and who belonged to the Democratic Party. By inheritance and connection I am a Democrat, and to a Democratic President I went with my appeal. . . . What a spectacle it must be to the thinking people of this country to see us urged to go to war for democracy in a foreign land, and to see women thrown into prison who plead for that same cause at home.

"I stand here to affirm my innocence of the charge against me. This court has not proven that I obstructed traffic. My presence at the White House gate was under the constitutional right of petitioning the government for freedom or for any other cause. During the months of January, February, March, April and May picketing was legal. In June it suddenly becomes illegal. . . .

"My services as an American woman are being conscripted by order of the President of the United States to help win the world war for democracy. . . . 'for the right of those who submit to authority to have a voice in their own government.' I shall continue to plead for the political liberty of American women—and especially do I plead to the President, since he is the one person who . . . can end the struggles of American women to take their proper places in a true democracy."

There is continuous objection from the prosecutor, eager advice from the judge, "you had better keep to the charge of obstructing traffic." But round on round of applause comes from the intent audience, whenever a defiant note is struck by the prisoners, and in spite of the sharp rapping of the gavel confusion reigns. And how utterly puny the "charge" is! If it were true that the prisoners actually obstructed the traffic, how grotesque that would be. The importance of their demand, the purity of their reasoning, the nobility and gentle quality of the prisoners at the bar; all conspire to make the charge against them, and the attorney who makes it, and the judge who hears it, petty and ridiculous.

But justice must proceed.

Mrs. Gilson Gardner of Washington, D. C., a member of the Executive Committee of the National Woman's party, and the wife of Gilson Gardner, a well-known Liberal and journalist, speaks:

"It is impossible for me to believe that we were arrested because we were obstructing traffic or blocking the public highway.

"We have been carrying on activities of a distinctly political nature, and these political activities have seemingly disturbed certain powerful influences. Arrests followed. I submit that these arrests are purely political and that the charge of an unlawful assemblage and of obstructing traffic is a political subterfuge. Even should I be sent to jail which, I could not, your Honor, anticipate, I would be in jail, not because I obstructed traffic, but because I have offended politically, because I have demanded of this government freedom for women."

It was my task to sum up for the defense. The judge sat bored through my statement. "We know and I believe the Court knows also," I said, "that President Wilson and his Administration are responsible for our being here to-day. It is a fact that they gave the orders which caused our arrest and appearance before this bar.

"We know and you know, that the District Commissioners are appointed by the President, that the present commissioners were appointed by President Wilson. We know that you, your Honor, were appointed to the bench by President Wilson, and that the district attorney who prosecutes us was appointed by the President. These various officers would not dare bring us here under these false charges without the policy having been decided upon by the responsible leaders.

"What is our real crime? What have these distinguished and liberty-loving women done to bring them before this court of justice? Why, your Honor, their crime is that they peacefully petitioned the President of the United States for liberty. What must be the shame of our nation before the world when it becomes known that here we throw women into jail who love liberty and attempt to peacefully petition the President for it? These women are nearly all descended from revolutionary ancestors or from some of the greatest libertarian statesmen this country has produced. What would these men say now if they could see that passion for liberty which was in their own hearts rewarded in the twentieth century with foul and filthy imprisonment!

"We say to you, this outrageous policy of stupid and brutal punishment will not dampen the ardor of the women. Where sixteen of us face your judgment to-day there will be sixty to-morrow, so great will be the indignation of our colleagues in this fight."

The trial came to an end after a tense two days. The packed court-room sat in a terrible silence awaiting the judge's answer.

There were distinguished men present at the trial—men who also fight for their ideals. There was Frederic C. Howe, then Commissioner of Immigration of the Port of New York, Frank P. Walsh, International labor leader, Dudley Field Malone, then Collector of the Port of New York, Amos Pinchot, liberal leader, John A. H. Hopkins, then liberal-progressive leader in New Jersey who had turned his organization to the support of the President and become a member of the President's Campaign Committee, now chairman of the Committee of Forty-eight and whose beautiful wife was among the prisoners, Allen McCurdy, secretary of the Committee of Forty-eight and many others. One and all came forward to protest to us during the adjournment. "This is monstrous." . . . "Never have I seen evidence so disregarded." . . . "This is a tragic farce." . . . "He will never dare sentence you." . . .

It was reported to us that the judge used the interim to telephone to the District building, where the District Commissioners sit. He returned to pronounce, "Sixty days in the workhouse in default of a twenty-five dollar fine."

The shock was swift and certain to all the spectators. We would not of course pay the unjust fine imposed, for we were not guilty of any offense.

The judge attempted persuasion. "You had better decide to pay your fines," he ventured. And "you will not find jail a pleasant place to be." It was clear that neither he nor his confreres had imagined women would accept with equanimity so drastic a sentence. It was now their time to be shocked. Here were "ladies"—that was perfectly clear—"ladies" of unusual distinction. Surely they would not face the humiliation of a workhouse sentence which involved not only imprisonment but penal servitude! The Administration was wrong again.

"We protest against this unjust sentence and conviction," we said, "but we prefer the workhouse to the payment of a fine imposed for an offense of which we are not guilty." We filed into the "pen," to join the other prisoners, and wait for the "black maria" to carry us to prison.

* * * *

We are all taken to the District Jail, where we are put through the regular catechism: "Were you ever in prison before?—Age—birthplace—father—mother—religion and what not?" We are then locked up,—two to a cell. What will happen next?

The sleek jailer, whose attempt to be cordial provokes a certain distrust, comes to our corridor to "turn us over" to our next keeper—the warden of Occoquan. We learn that the workhouse is not situated in the District of Columbia but in Virginia.

Other locked wagons with tiny windows up near the driver now take us, side by side with drunks and disorderlies, prostitutes and thieves, to the Pennsylvania Station. Here we embark for the unknown terrors of the workhouse, filing through crowds at the station, driven on by our "keeper," who resembles Simon Legree, with his long stick and his pushing and shoving to hurry us along. The crowd is quick to realize that we are prisoners, because of our associates. Friends try to bid us a last farewell and slip us a sweet or fruit, as we are rushed through the iron station gates to the train.

Warden Whittaker is our keeper, thin and old, with a cruel mouth, brutal eyes and a sinister birthmark on his temple. He guards very anxiously his "dangerous criminals" lest they try to leap out of the train to freedom! We chat a little and attempt to relax from the strain that we have endured since Saturday. It is now late in the afternoon of Tuesday.

The dusk is gathering. It is almost totally dark when we alight at a tiny station in what seems to us a wilderness. It is a deserted country. Even the gayest member of the party, I am sure, was struck with a little terror here.

More locked wagons, blacker than the dusk, awaited us. The prison van jolted and bumped along the rocky and hilly road. A cluster of lights twinkled beyond the last hill, and we knew that we were coming to our temporary summer residence. I can still see the long thin line of black poplars against the smouldering afterglow. I did not know then what tragic things they concealed.

* * * *

We entered a well-lighted office. A few guards of ugly demeanor stood about. Warden Whittaker consulted with the hard-faced matron, Mrs. Herndon, who began the prison routine. Names were called, and each prisoner stepped to the desk to get her number, to give up all jewelry, money, hand-bags, letters, eye-glasses, traveling bags containing toilet necessities, in fact everything except the clothes on her body.

From there we were herded into the long bare dining room where we sat dumbly down to a bowl of dirty sour soup. I say dumbly—for now began the rule of silence. Prisoners are punished for speaking to one another at table. They cannot even whisper, much less smile or laugh. They must be conscious always of their "guilt." Every possible thing is done to make the inmates feel that they are and must continue to be anti-social creatures.

We taste our soup and crust of bread. We try so hard to eat it for we are tired and hungry, but no one of us is able to get it down. We leave the table hungry and slightly nauseated.

Another long march in silence through various channels into a large dormitory and through a double line of cots! Then we stand, weary to the point of fainting, waiting the next ordeal. This seemed to be the juncture at which we lost all that is left us of contact with the outside world,—our clothes.

An assistant matron, attended by negress prisoners, relieves us of our clothes. Each prisoner is obliged to strip naked without even the protection of a sheet, and proceed across what seems endless space, to a shower bath. A large tin bucket stands on the floor and in this is a minute piece of dirty soap, which is offered to us and rejected. We dare not risk the soap used by so many prisoners. Naked, we return from the bath to receive our allotment of coarse, hideous prison clothes, the outer gar-ments of which consist of a bulky mother-hubbard wrapper, of bluish gray ticking and a heavy apron of the same dismal stuff. It takes a dominant personality indeed to survive these clothes. The thick unbleached muslin undergarments are of designs never to be forgotten! And the thick stockings and forlorn shoes! What torture to put on shoes that are alike for each foot and made to fit just anybody who may happen along.

Why are we being ordered to dress? It is long past the bed-time hour.

Our suspense is brief. All dressed in cloth of "guilt" we are led into what we later learn is the "recreation" room. Lined up against its wall, we might any other time have bantered about the possibility of being shot, but we are in no mood to jest. The door finally opens and in strides Warden Whittaker with a stranger beside him.

He reviews his latest criminal recruits, engaging the stranger meanwhile in whispered conversation. There are short, uncertain laughs. There are nods of the head and more whispers.

"Well, ladies, I hope you are all comfortable. Now make yourselves at home here. I think you will find it healthy here. You'll weigh more when you go out than when you came in. You will be allowed to write one letter a month—to your family. Of course we open and read all letters coming in and going out. To-morrow you will be assigned your work. I hope you will sleep well. Good night!"

We did not answer. We looked at each other.

News leaked through in the morning that the stranger had been a newspaper reporter. The papers next morning were full of the "comfort" and "luxury" of our surroundings. The "delicious" food sounded most reassuring to the nation. In fact no word of the truth was allowed to appear.

The correspondent could not know that we went back to our cots to try to sleep side by side with negro prostitutes. Not that we shrank from these women on account of their color, but how terrible to know that the institution had gone out of its way to bring these prisoners from their own wing to the white wing in an attempt to humiliate us. There was plenty of room in the negro wing. But prison must be made so unbearable that no more women would face it. That was the policy attempted here.

We tried very hard to sleep and forget our hunger and weariness. But all the night through our dusky comrades padded by to the lavatory, and in the streak of bright light which shot across the center of the room, startled heads could be seen bobbing up in the direction of a demented woman in the end cot. Her weird mutterings made us fearful. There was no sleep in this strange place.

Our thoughts turn to the outside world. Will the women care? Will enough women believe that through such humiliation all may win freedom? Will they believe that through our imprisonment their slavery will be lifted the sooner? Less philosophically, will the government be moved by public protest? Will such protest come?

The next morning brought us a visitor from suffrage headquarters. The institution hoped that the visitor would use her persuasion to make us pay our fines and leave and so she was admitted. We learned the cheering news, that immediately after sentence had been pronounced by the Court, Dudley Field Malone had gone direct to the White House to protest to the President. His protest was delivered with heat. The President said that he was "shocked" at the sixty day sentence, that he did not know it had been done, and made other evasions. Mr. Malone's report of his interview with the President is given in full in a subsequent chapter.

Following Mr. Malone, Mr. J. A. H. Hopkins went to the White House. "How would you like to have your wife sleep in a dirty workhouse next to prostitutes?" was his direct talk to the President. Again the President was "shocked." No wonder! Mr. and Mrs. Hopkins had been the President's dinner guests not very long before, celebrating his return to power. They had supported him politically and financially in New Jersey. Now Mrs. Hopkins had been arrested at his gate and thrown into prison.

In reporting the interview, Mr. Hopkins said:

"The President asked me for suggestions as to what might be done, and I replied that in view of the seriousness of the present situation the only solution lay in immediate passage of the Susan B. Anthony amendment."

Gilson Gardner also went to the White House to leave his hot protest. And there were others.

Telegrams poured in from all over the country. The press printed headlines which could not but arouse the sympathy of thousands. Even people who did not approve of picketing the White House said, "After all, what these women have done is certainly not 'bad' enough to merit such drastic punishment."

And women protested. From coast to coast there poured in at our headquarters copies of telegrams sent to Administration leaders. Of course not all women by any means had approved this method of agitation. But the government's action had done more than we had been able to do for them. It had made them feel sex-conscious. Women were being unjustly treated. Regardless of their feelings about this particular procedure, they stood up and objected.

For the first time, I believe, our form of agitation began to seem a little more respectable than the Administration's handling of it. But the Administration did not know this fact yet.

*　*　*　*

"Everybody in line for the work-room!"

We were thankful to leave our inedible breakfast. We were unable to drink the greasy black coffee. The pain in the tops of our heads was acute.

"What you all down here for?" asked a young negress, barely out of her teens, as she casually fingered her sewing material.

"Why, I held a purple, white and gold banner at the gates of the White House."

"You don' say so! What de odders do?"

"Same thing. We all held banners at the White House gates asking President Wilson to give us the vote."

"An' yo' all got sixty days fo' *dat?*"

"Yes. You see the President thought it would be a good idea to send us to the workhouse for asking for the vote. You know women want to vote and have wanted to for a long time in our country."

"O—Yass'm, I know. I seen yo' parades, an' meetin's, an' everythin'. I know whah yo' all live, right near the White House. You's alright. I hopes yo' git it, fo' women certainly do need protextion against men like Judge Mullowny. He has us allatime picked up an' sen' down here.

"They sen' yo' down here once, an' then yo' come out without a cent, and try to look fo' a job, an' befo' yo' can fin' one a cop walks up an' asks yo' whah yo' live, an' ef yo' haven't got a place yet, becaus' yo' ain' got a cent to ren' one with, he says, 'Come with me, I'll fin' yo' a home,' an' hustles yo' off to the p'lice station an' down heah again, an' you're called a 'vag' (vagrant). What chanct has we niggahs got, I ask ya? I hopes yo' all gits a vote an' fixes up *somethings* for women!"

"You see that young girl over there?" said another prisoner, who in spite of an unfortunate life had kept a remnant of her early beauty. I nodded.

"Well, Judge Mullowny gave her thirty days for her first offense, and when he sentenced her, she cried out desperately, 'Don't send me down there, Judge! If you do, I'll kill myself!' What do you think he said to that?—'I'll give you six months in which to change your mind!'"

I reflected. The judge that broke this pale-faced, silent girl was the appointee of the President. It was the task of such a man to sentence American women to the workhouse for demanding liberty.

Conversing with the "regulars" was forbidden by the

wardress, but we managed, from time to time, to talk to our fellow prisoners with stealthiness.

"We knew somethin' was goin' to happen," said one negro girl, "because Monday the close we had on wer' took off us an' we were giv' these old patched ones. We wuz told they wanted to take 'stock,' but we heard they wuz bein' washed fo' you-all suff'agettes."

The unpleasantness at wearing the formless garments of these unfortunates made us all wince. But the government's calculation aroused our hot indignation. We were not convicted until Tuesday and our prison garments were ready Monday!

"You must not speak against the President," said the servile wardress, when she discovered we were telling our story to the inmates. "You know you will be thrashed if you say anything more about the President; and don't forget you're on Government property and may be arrested for treason if it happens again."

We doubted the seriousness of this threat of thrashing until one of the girls confided to us that such outrages happened often. We afterward obtained proof of these brutalities.[1]

"Old Whittaker beat up that girl over there just last week and put her in the 'booby' house on bread and water for five days."

"What did she do?" I asked.

"Oh, she an' another girl got to scrapping in the blackberry patch and she didn't pick enough berries. . . ."

"All put up your work, girls, and get in line." This from the wardress, who sped up the work in the sewing room. It was lunch time, and though we were all hungry we dreaded going to the silence and the food in that gray dining room with the vile odors. We were counted again as we filed out, carrying our heavy chairs with us as is the workhouse custom.

[1] See affidavit of Mrs. Bovee, page 144.

"Do they do this all the time?" I asked. It seemed as though needless energy was being spent counting and recounting our little group.

"Wouldn't do anybody any good to try to get away from here," said one of the white girls. "Too many bloodhounds!"

"Bloodhounds!" I asked in amazement, for after all these women were not criminals but merely misdemeanants.

"Oh, yes. Just a little while ago three men tried to get away and they turned bloodhounds after them and shot them dead—and they weren't bad men either."

*   *   *   *

When our untasted supper was over that night we were ordered into the square, bare-walled "recreation" room, where we and the other prisoners sat, and sat, and sat, our chairs against the walls, a dreary sight indeed, waiting for the forty-five minutes before bedtime to pass. The sight of two negro girl prisoners combing out each other's lice and dressing their kinky hair in such a way as to discourage permanently a return of the vermin did not produce in us exactly a feeling of "recreation." But we tried to sing. The negroes joined in, too, and soon outsang us, with their plaintive melodies and hymns. Then back to our cells and another attempt to sleep.

*   *   *   *

A new ordeal the next morning! Another of the numberless "pedigrees" is to be taken. One by one we were called to the warden's office.

"Were your father or mother ever insane?"

"Are you a confirmed drunkard, chronic or moderate drinker?"

"Do you smoke or chew or use tobacco in any form?"

"Married or single?"

"Single."

"How many children?"

"None."

FELLOW PRISONERS

SEWING ROOM AT OCCOQUAN WORKHOUSE

"What religion do you profess?"

"Christian."

"What *religion* do you profess?" in a higher pitched voice.

I did not clearly comprehend. "Do you mean 'Am I a Catholic or a Protestant?' I am a Christian."

But it was of no avail. She wrote down, "None."

I protested. "That is not accurate. I insist that I am a Christian, or at least I *try* to be one."

"You must learn to be polite," she retorted almost fiercely, and I returned to the sewing room.

For the hundredth time we asked to be given our toothbrushes, combs, handkerchiefs and our own soap. The third day of imprisonment without any of these essentials found us depressed and worried over our unsanitary condition. We plead also for toilet paper. It was senseless to deny these necessities. It is enough to imprison people. Why seek to degrade them utterly?

* * * *

The third afternoon we were mysteriously summoned into the presence of Superintendent Whittaker. He seemed warm and cordial. We were ordered drawn up in a semi-circle.

"Ladies, there is a rumor that you may be pardoned," he began.

"By whom?" asked one.

"For what?" asked another. "We are innocent women. There is nothing to pardon us for."

"I have come to ask you what you would do if the President pardoned you."

"We would refuse to accept it," came the ready response from several.

"I shall leave you for a while to consider this. Mind! I have not yet received information of a pardon, but I have been asked to ascertain your attitude."

Our consultation was brief. We were of one mind. We

were unanimous in wishing to reject a pardon for a crime which we had never committed. We said so with some spirit when Mr. Whittaker returned for our decision.

"You have no choice. You are obliged to accept a pardon."

That settled it, and we waited. That the protest on the outside had been strong enough to precipitate action from the government was the subject of our conversation. Evidently it had not been strong enough to force action on the suffrage amendment, but it was forcing action, and that was important.

Mr. Whittaker returned triumphant.

"Ladies, you are pardoned by the President. You are free to go as soon as you have taken off your prison clothes and put on your own."

It was sad to leave the other prisoners behind. Especially pathetic were the girls who helped us with our clothes. They whispered such eager appeals in our ears, telling us of their drastic sentences for trifling offenses and of the cruel punishments. It was hard to resist digressing into some effort at prison reform. That way lay our instincts. Our reason told us that we must first change the status of women.

As we were leaving the workhouse to return to Washington we had an unexpected revelation of the attitude of officialdom toward our campaign. Addressing Miss Lucy Burns, who had arrived to assist us in getting on our way, Superintendent Whittaker, in an almost unbelievable rage, said, "Now that you women are going away, I have something to say and I want to say it to *you*. The next lot of women who come here won't be treated with the same consideration that these women were." I will show later on how he made good this terrible threat.

*   *   *   *

Receiving a Presidential pardon through the Attorney General had its amusing aspect. My comrades shared this amusement when I told them the following incident.

On the day after our arrest, I was having tea at the Chevy

Chase Country Club in Washington. Quite casually a gentleman introduced me to Mr. Gregory, the Attorney General.

"I see you were mixed up with the suffragettes yesterday," was the Attorney General's first remark to the gentleman. And before the latter could explain that he had settled accounts quietly but efficiently with a hoodlum who was attempting to trip the women up on their march, the *chief law officer* of the United States contributed this important suggestion: "You know what I'd do if I was those policemen. I'd just take a hose out with me and when the women came out with their banners, why I'd just squirt the hose on 'em. . . ."

"But Mr. Gregory . . ."

"Yes, sir! If you can just make what a woman does look ridiculous, you can sure kill it. . . ."

"But, Mr. Attorney General, what right would the police have to assault these or any other women?" the gentleman managed finally to interpolate.

"Hup—hup——" denoting great surprise, came from the Attorney General, as he looked to me for reassurance.

His expectant look vanished when I said, "Mr. Gregory, did it ever occur to you that it might make the government look ridiculous instead of the women?"

You can imagine how the easy manner of one who is sure of his audience melted from his face.

"This is one of the women arrested yesterday," continued the gentleman, while the Attorney General smothered a "Well, I'll be . . ."

"I am out on bail," I said. "To-morrow we go to jail. It is all prearranged, you understand. The trial is merely a matter of form."

The highest law officer of the land fled gurgling.

* * * *

The day following our release Mrs. J. A. H. Hopkins carried a picket banner to the gates of the White House to test the validity of the pardon. Her banner read, "We do not ask pardon for ourselves but justice for all American women." A curious crowd, as large as had collected on those days when the police arrested women for "obstructing traffic," stood watching the lone picket. The President passed through the gates and saluted. The police did not interfere.

Daily picketing was resumed and no arrests followed for the moment.

It was now August, three months since the Senate Suffrage Committee authorized its chairman, Mr. Jones, to report the measure to the Senate for action. Mr. Jones said, however, that he was too busy to make a report; that he wanted to make a particularly brilliant one, one that would "be a contribution to the cause"; that he did not approve of picketing, but that he would report the measure "in a reasonable time." So much for the situation in the Senate!

From the House we gathered some interesting evidence. We reminded Mr. Webb, Chairman of the Judiciary Committee, that out of a total membership of twenty-one men on his committee, twelve were Democrats, two-thirds of whom were opposed to the measure; we reminded him that the Republicans on the committee were for action. Mr. Webb wrote in answer:

"The Democratic caucus passed a resolution that only war emergency measures would be considered during this extra session, and that the President might designate from time to time special legislation which he regarded as war legislation, and such would be acted on by the House. The President, not having designated woman suffrage and national prohibition so far as war measures, the judiciary committee up to this time has not felt warranted under the caucus rule, in reporting either of these measures. If the President should request either or both of them as war measures, then I think the Committee would attempt to take some action on them promptly. *So you see after all it is important to your cause to make the*

President see that woman suffrage comes within the rules laid down." [1]

Here was a frank admission of the assumption upon which women had gone to jail—that the President was responsible for action on the amendment.

Now that we were again allowed to picket the White House, the Republicans seized the opportunity legitimately to embarrass their opponents by precipitating a bitter debate.

Senator Cummins of Iowa, Republican member of the Suffrage Committee, moved, as had Mr. Mann in the House at an earlier date, to discharge the Suffrage Committee for failing to make the report authorized by the entire Committee. Mr. Cummins said, among other things:

". . . I look upon the resolution as definitely and certainly a war measure. There is nothing that this country could do which would strengthen it more than to give the disfranchised women . . . the opportunity to vote. . . .

"Last week . . . I went to the Chairman of the Committee and told him that . . . we had finished the hearings, reached a conclusion and that it was our bounden duty to make the report to the Senate. . . . I asked him if he would not call a meeting of the Committee. He said that it would be impossible, that he had some other engagements which would prevent a meeting of the Committee."

Senator Cummins explained that he finally got the promise of the Chairman that a meeting of the Committee would be called on a given date. When it was not called he made his motion.

Chairman Jones made some feeble remarks and some evasive excuses which meant nothing, and which only further aroused Republican friends of the measure on the Committee.

Senator Gronna of North Dakota, Republican, interrupted

[1] Italics are mine.

him with the direct question, "I ask the chairman of this committee *why* this joint resolution has not been reported? The Senator, who is chairman of the committee, I suppose, knows as well as I do that the people of the entire country are anxious to have this joint resolution submitted and to be given an opportunity to vote upon it. . . ."

Senator Johnson of California, Republican, proposed that Chairman Jones consent to call the Committee together to consider reporting out the bill, which Senator Jones flatly refused to do.

Senator Jones of Washington, another Republican member of the Committee, added:

"I agree with the Senator from Iowa that this is a war measure and ought to be considered as such at this time. I do not see how we can very consistently talk democracy while disfranchising the better half of our citizenship—*I may not approve of the action of the women picketing the White House, but neither do I approve of what I consider the lawless action toward these women in connection with the picketing.* . . ."

"I do not want to think the chairman does not desire to call the committee together because of some influence outside of Congress as some have suggested. . . ."

At this point Senator Hollis of New Hampshire, Democrat, arose to say:

"There is a small but very active group of women suffragists who have acted in such a way that some who are ardently in favor of woman suffrage believe that their action should not be encouraged by making a favorable report at this time."

Senator Johnson protested at this point, but Senator Hollis continued:

"*To discharge the committee would focus the attention of the country upon the action and would give undue weight to what has been done by the active group of woman suffragists.*"

I think that any student of psychology will acknowledge that our picketing had stimulated action in Congress, and that what was now needed was some still more provocative action from us.

CHAPTER 5

IMPRISONING women had met with considerable public disapproval, and attendant political embarrassment to the Administration. That the presidential pardon would end this embarrassment was doubtless the hope of the Administration. The pickets, however, returned to their posts in steadily increasing numbers. Their presence at the gates was desired by the Administration no more now than it had been before the arrests and imprisonments. But they had found no way to rid themselves of the pickets. And as another month of picketing drew to an end the Administration ventured to try other ways to stop it and with it the consequent embarrassment. Their methods became physically more brutal and politically more stupid. Their conduct became lawless in the extreme.

Meanwhile the President had drafted the young men of America in their millions to die on foreign soil for foreign democracy. He had issued a special appeal to women to give their work, their treasure and their sons to this enterprise. At the same time his now gigantic figure stood obstinately across the path to our main objective. It was our daily task to keep vividly in his mind that objective. It was our responsibility to compel decisive action from him.

Using the return of Envoy Root from his mission to Russia

122

as another dramatic opportunity to speak to the President we took to the picket line these mottoes:

TO ENVOY ROOT

YOU SAY THAT AMERICA MUST THROW ITS MANHOOD TO THE SUPPORT OF LIBERTY.

WHOSE LIBERTY?

THIS NATION IS NOT FREE. TWENTY MILLION WOMEN ARE DENIED BY THE PRESIDENT OF THE UNITED STATES THE RIGHT TO REPRESENTATION IN THEIR OWN GOVERNMENT.

TELL THE PRESIDENT THAT HE CANNOT FIGHT AGAINST LIBERTY AT HOME WHILE HE TELLS US TO FIGHT FOR LIBERTY ABROAD.

TELL HIM TO MAKE AMERICA SAFE FOR DEMOCRACY BEFORE HE ASKS THE MOTHERS OF AMERICA TO THROW THEIR SONS TO THE SUPPORT OF DEMOCRACY IN EUROPE.

ASK HIM HOW HE CAN REFUSE LIBERTY TO AMERICAN CITIZENS WHEN HE IS FORCING MILLIONS OF AMERICAN BOYS OUT OF THEIR COUNTRY TO DIE FOR LIBERTY.

At no time during the entire picketing was the traffic on Pennsylvania Avenue so completely obstructed as it was for the two hours during which this banner made its appearance on the line. Police captains who three weeks before were testifying that the police could not manage the crowds, placidly looked on while these new crowds increased.

We did not regard Mr. Wilson as *our* President. We felt that he had neither political nor moral claim to our allegiance. War had been made without our consent. The war would be finished and very likely a bad peace would be written without our consent. Our fight was becoming increasingly difficult—I might almost say desperate. Here we were, a band of women fighting with banners, in the midst of a world armed to the teeth. And so it was not very difficult to understand how high spirited women grew more resentful, unwilling to be a party to the President's hypocrisy, the hypocrisy so eager to sacrifice life without stint to the vague hope of liberty abroad, while refusing to assist in the peaceful legislative steps which would lead to self-government in our own country. As a matter of fact the President's constant oratory on freedom and democracy moved them to scorn. They were stung into a protest so militant as to shock not only the President but the public. We inscribed on our banner what countless American women had long thought in their hearts.

The truth was not pleasant but it had to be told. We submitted to the world, through the picket line, this question:

KAISER WILSON

HAVE YOU FORGOTTEN HOW YOU SYMPATHIZED WITH THE POOR GERMANS BECAUSE THEY WERE NOT SELF-GOVERNED?

20,000,000 AMERICAN WOMEN ARE NOT SELF-GOVERNED.

TAKE THE BEAM OUT OF YOUR OWN EYE.

We did not expect public sympathy at this point. We knew that not even the members of Congress who had occasionally in debate, but more frequently in their cloak rooms, and often to us privately, called the President "autocrat"—"Kaiser"—"Ruler"—"King"—"Czar"—would approve our telling the truth publicly.

Nor was it to be expected that eager young boys, all agog to fight Germans, would be averse to attacking women in the meantime. They were out to fight and such was the public hysteria that it did not exactly matter whom they fought.

And so those excited boys of the Army and Navy attacked the women and the banner. The banner was destroyed. Another was brought up to take its place. This one met the same fate. Meanwhile a crowd was assembling in front of the White House either to watch or to assist in the attacks. At the very moment when one banner was being snatched away and destroyed, President and Mrs. Wilson passed through the gates on their way to a military review at Fort Myer. *The President saw American women being attacked, while the police refused them protection.*

Not a move was made by the police to control the growing crowd. Such inaction is always a signal for more violence on the part of rowdies. As the throng moved to and fro between the White House and our Headquarters immediately opposite, so many banners were destroyed that finally Miss Lucy Burns, Miss Virginia Arnold and Miss Elizabeth Stuyvesant took those remaining to the second and third floor balconies of our building and hung them out. At this point there was not a picket left on the street. The crowd was clearly obstructing the traffic, but no attempt was made to move them back or to protect the women, some of whom were attacked by sailors on their own doorsteps. The two police officers present watched without interference while three sailors brought a ladder from the Belasco Theater in the same block, leaned it against the side of the Cameron House, the Headquarters, climbed up to the second floor balcony, mounted the iron railing and tore down all banners and the American flag. One sailor administered a severe blow in the face with his clenched fist upon Miss Georgina Sturgis of Washington.

"Why did you do that?" she demanded.

The man halted for a brief instant in obvious amazement and said, "I don't know." And with a violent wrench he tore the banner from her hands and ran down the ladder.

The narrow balcony was the scene of intense excitement.

But for Miss Burns' superb strength she would have been dragged over the railing of the balcony to be plunged to the ground. The mob watched with fascination while she swayed to and fro in her wrestle with two young sailors. And still no attempt by the police to quell the riot!

The climax came when in the late afternoon a bullet was fired through one of the heavy glass windows of the second floor, embedding itself in the ceiling. The bullet grazed past the head of Mrs. Ella Morton Dean of Montana. Captain Flather of the 1st Precinct, with two detectives, later examined the holes and declared they had been made by a 38 caliber revolver, but no attempt was ever made to find the man who had drawn the revolver.

Meanwhile eggs and tomatoes were hurled at our fresh banners flying from the flag poles on the building.

Finally police reserves were summoned and in less than five minutes the crowd was pushed back and the street cleared. Thinking now that they could rely on the protection of the police, the women started with their banners for the White House. But the police looked on while all the banners were destroyed, a few paces from Headquarters. More banners went out,—purple, white and gold ones. They, too, were destroyed before they reached the White House.

This entire spectacle was enacted on August 14, within a stone's throw of the White House.

Miss Paul summed up the situation when she said:

"The situation now existing in Washington exists because President Wilson permits it. Orders were first handed down to the police to arrest suffragists. The clamor over their imprisonments made this position untenable. The police were then ordered to protect suffragists. They were then ordered to attack suffragists. They have now been ordered to encourage irresponsible crowds to attack suffragists. No police head would dare so to besmirch his record without orders from his responsible chief. The responsible chief in the National Capital is the President of the United States."

Shortly after the incident of the "Kaiser banner" I was speaking in Louisville, Kentucky. The auditorium was packed and overflowing with men and women who had come to hear the story of the pickets.

Up to this time we had very few members in Kentucky and had anticipated in this Southern State, part of President Wilson's stronghold, that our Committee would meet with no enthusiasm and possibly with warm hostility.

I had related briefly the incidents leading up to the picketing and the Government's suppressions. I was rather cautiously approaching the subject of the "Kaiser banner," feeling timid and hesitant, wondering how this vast audience of Southerners would take it. Slowly I read the inscription on the famous banner, "Kaiser Wilson, have you forgotten how you sympathized with the poor Germans because they were not self-governed? Twenty million American women are not self-governed. Take the beam out of your own eye."

I hardly reached the last word, still wondering what the intensely silent audience would do, when a terrific outburst of applause mingled with shouts of "Good! Good! He is, he is!" came to my amazed ears. As the applause died down there was almost universal good-natured laughter. Instead of the painstaking and eloquent explanation which I was prepared to offer, I had only to join in their laughter.

A few minutes later a telegram was brought to the platform announcing further arrests. I read:

"Six more women sentenced to-day to 30 days in Occoquan workhouse."

Instant cries of "Shame! Shame! It's an outrage!" Scores of men and two women were on their feet calling for the passage of a resolution denouncing the Administration's policy of persecution. The motion of condemnation was put. It seemed as if the entire audience seconded it. It went through instantly, unanimously, and again with prolonged shouts and applause.

The meeting continued and I shall never forget that audience. It lingered to a late hour, almost to midnight, asking questions, making brief "testimonials" from the floor with almost evangelical fervor. Improvised collection baskets were piled high with bills. Women volunteered for picket duty and certain imprisonment, and the following day a delegation left for Washington.

I cite this experience of mine because it was typical. Every one who went through the country telling the story had similar experiences at this time. Indignation was swift and hot. Our mass meetings everywhere became meetings of protest during the entire campaign.

And resolutions of protest which always went immediately by wire from such meetings to the President, his cabinet and to his leaders in Congress, of course created increasing uneasiness in Democratic circles.

On August 15th the pickets again attempted to take their posts on the line.

On this day one lettered banner and fifty purple, white and gold flags were destroyed by a mob led by sailors in uniform. Alice Paul was knocked down three times by a sailor in uniform and dragged the width of the White House sidewalk in his frenzied attempt to tear off her suffrage sash.

Miss Katharine Morey of Boston was also knocked to the pavement by a sailor, who took her flag and then darted off into the crowd. Miss Elizabeth Stuyvesant was struck by a soldier in uniform and her blouse torn from her body. Miss Maud Jamison of Virginia was knocked down and dragged along the sidewalk. Miss Beulah Amidon of North Dakota was knocked down by a sailor.

In the midst of these riotous scenes, a well-known Washington correspondent was emerging from the White House, after an interview with the President. Dr. Cary Grayson, the President's physician, accompanying him to the door, advised:

"You had better go out the side entrance. Those damned women are in the front."

In spite of this advice the correspondent made his exit through the same gate by which he had entered, and just in time to ward off an attack by a sailor on one of the frailest girls in the group.

The Administration, in its desperation, ordered the police to lawlessness. On August 16th, fifty policemen led the mob in attacking the women. Hands were bruised and arms twisted by police officers and plainclothes men. Two civilians who tried to rescue the women from the attacks of the police were arrested. The police fell upon these young women with more brutality even than the mobs they had before encouraged. Twenty-five lettered banners and 123 Party flags were destroyed by mobs and police on this afternoon.

As the crowd grew more dense, the police temporarily retired from the attack. When their activities had summoned a sufficiently large and infuriated mob, they would rest.

And so the passions of the mob continued unchecked upon these irrepressible women, and from day to day the Administration gave its orders.

Finding that riots and mob attacks had not terrorized the pickets, the Administration decided again to arrest the women in the hope of ending the agitation. Having lost public sympathy through workhouse sentences, having won it back by pardoning the women, the Administration felt it could afford to risk losing it again, or rather felt that it had supplied itself with an appropriate amount of stage-setting.

And so on the third day of the riotous attacks, when it was clear that the pickets would persist, the Chief of Police called at headquarters to announce to Miss Paul that "orders have been changed and henceforth women carrying banners will be arrested."

Meanwhile the pickets heard officers shout to civilian friends as they passed—"Come back at four o'clock."

Members of the daily mob announced at the noon hour in various nearby restaurants that "the suffs will be arrested to-day at 4 o'clock."

Four o'clock is the hour the Government clerks begin to swarm homewards. The choice of this hour by the police to arrest the women would enable them to have a large crowd passing the White House gates to lend color to the fiction that "pickets were blocking the traffic."

Throughout the earlier part of the afternoon the silent sentinels stood unmolested, carrying these mottoes:

ENGLAND AND RUSSIA ARE ENFRANCHISING WOMEN IN
WAR-TIME.

HOW LONG MUST WOMEN WAIT FOR LIBERTY?

THE GOVERNMENT ORDERS OUR BANNERS DESTROYED
BECAUSE THEY TELL THE TRUTH.

At four o'clock the threatened arrests took place. The women arrested were Miss Lavinia Dock of Pennsylvania, Miss Edna Dixon of Washington, D. C., a young public school teacher; Miss Natalie Gray of Colorado, Mrs. Wm. Upton Watson and Miss Lucy Ewing of Chicago, and Miss Catherine Flanagan of Connecticut.

Exactly forty minutes were allowed for the trial of these six women. One police officer testified that they were "obstructing traffic."

None of the facts of the hideous and cruel manhandling by the mobs and police officers was allowed to be brought out. Nothing the women could say mattered. The judge pro-

RIOTOUS SCENES ON PICKET LINE WHEN HOODLUMS WERE PERMITTED TO ATTACK WOMEN

© Harris & Ewing.

nounced: "Thirty days in Occoquan workhouse in lieu of a $10.00 fine."

And so this little handful of women, practically all of them tiny and frail of physique, began the cruel sentence of 30 days in the workhouse, while their cowardly assailants were not even reprimanded, nor were those who destroyed over a thousand dollars' worth of banners apprehended.

The riots had attracted sufficient attention to cause some anxiety in Administration circles. Protests against us and others against the rioters pressed upon them. Congress was provoked into a little activity; activity which reflected some doubt as to the wisdom of arresting women without some warrant in law.

Two attempts were made, neither of which was successful, to give the Administration more power and more law.

Senator Culberson of Texas, Democrat, offered a bill authorizing President Wilson at any time to prohibit any person from approaching or entering any place—in short a blanket authority granting the President or his officials limitless power over the actions of human beings. Realizing that this could be used to prohibit picketing the White House we appeared before a committee hearing on the bill and spoke against it. The committee did not have the boldness to report such a bill.

Senator Myers of Montana, an influential member of the Democratic majority, introduced into the Senate a few days later a resolution making it illegal to picket the White House. The shamelessness of admitting to the world that acts for which women had been repeatedly sentenced to jail, and for which women were at that moment lying in prison, were so legal as to make necessary a special act of Congress against them, was appalling. The Administration policy seemed to be "Let us put women in jail first—let us enact a law to keep them there afterwards."

This tilt between Senator Brandegee, of Connecticut, anti-suffrage Republican, and Senator Myers, suffrage Democrat, took place when Mr. Myers presented his bill:

MR. BRANDEGEE: . . . Was there any defect in the legal proceedings by which these trouble makers were sentenced and put in jail a few weeks ago?

MR. MYERS: None that I know of. I am not in a position to pass upon that. I do not believe any was claimed. . . .

MR. BRANDEGEE: Inasmuch as the law was sufficient to land them in jail . . . I fail to see why additional legislation is necessary on the subject.

MR. MYERS: There seems to be a doubt in the mind of some whether the present law is sufficient and I think it ought to be put beyond doubt. I think . . . the laws are not stringent or severe enough. . . .

MR. BRANDEGEE: They were stringent enough to land the malefactors in jail. . . .

In spite of Senator Myers' impassioned appeal to his colleagues, he was unable to command any support for his bill. I quote this from his speech in the Senate August 18, 1917:

MR. MYERS: Mr. President, I wish to say a few words about the bill I have just introduced. It is intended for the enactment of better and more adequate legislation to prevent the infamous, outrageous, scandalous, and, I think, almost treasonable actions that have been going on around the White House for months past, which have been a gross insult to the President of the United States and to the people of the United States; I mean the so-called picketing of the White House. . . . These disgusting proceedings have been going on for months, and if there is no adequate law to stop them, I think there ought to be.

"I believe the President, in the generosity of his heart, erred when he pardoned some of the women who have been conducting these proceedings, after they had been sentenced to

60 days in the workhouse. I believe they deserved the sentence, and they ought to have been compelled to serve it. . . .

"I for one am not satisfied longer to sit here idly day by day and submit to having the President of the United States insulted with impunity before the people of the country and before all the world. It is a shame and reproach.

"I hope this bill . . . will receive careful consideration and that it may be enacted into law and may be found an adequate preventive and punishment for such conduct."

This bill, which died a well-deserved death, is so amusing as to warrant reproduction. Although lamenting our comparison between the President and the Kaiser, it will be seen that Senator Myers brought forth a thoroughly Prussian document:

A BILL

For the better protection and enforcement of peace and order and the public welfare in the District of Columbia.

Be it enacted by the Senate and House of Representatives of the United States of America in Congress assembled, That when the United States shall be engaged in war it shall be unlawful for any person or persons to carry, hold, wave, exhibit, display, or have in his or her possession in any public road, highway, alley, street, thoroughfare, park, or other public place in the District of Columbia, any banner, flag, streamer, sash, or other device having thereon any words or language with reference to the President or the Vice President of the United States, or any words or language with reference to the Constitution of the United States, or the right of suffrage, or right of citizenship, or any words or language with reference to the duties of any executive official or department of the United States, or with reference to any proposed amendment to the Constitution of the United States, or with reference to any law or proposed law of the United States, calculated to bring the President of the United States or the Government of the United States into contempt, or which may tend to cause confusion, or excitement, or obstruction of the streets or sidewalks thereof, or any passage in any public place.

SEC. 2. That any person committing any foregoing described offense shall, upon conviction thereof, for each offense be fined not less than $100 nor more than $1,000 or imprisoned not less than thirty days nor more than one year, or by both such fine and imprisonment.

Voices were raised in our behalf, also, and among them I note the following letter written to Major Pullman by Gilson Gardner:[1]

Mr. Raymond Pullman,
    Chief of Police,
        Washington, D. C.
My dear Pullman,—

    I am writing as an old friend to urge you to get right in this matter of arresting the suffrage pickets. Of course the only way for you to get right is to resign. It has apparently become impossible for you to stay in office and do your duty. The alternative is obvious.

    You must see, Pullman, that you cannot be right in what you have done in this matter. You have given the pickets adequate protection; but you have arrested them and had them sent to jail and the workhouse; you have permitted the crowd to mob them, and then you have had your officers do much the same thing by forcibly taking their banners from them. In some of the actions you must have been wrong. If it was right to give them protection and let them stand at the White House for five months, both before and after the war, it was not right to do what you did later.

    You say that it was not right when you were "lenient" and gave them protection. You cannot mean that. The rightness or wrongness must be a matter of law, not of personal discretion, and for you to attempt to substitute your discretion is to set up a little autocracy in place of the settled laws of the land. This would justify a charge of "Kaiserism" right here in our capital city.

    The truth is, Pullman, you were right when you gave these women protection. That is what the police are for. When

---

[1] The distinguished journalist who went to Africa to meet Theodore Roosevelt and accompanied him on his return journey to America.

there are riots they are supposed to quell them, not by quelling the "proximate cause," but by quelling the rioters.

I know your police officers now quite well and know that they are most happy when they are permitted to do their duty. They did not like the dirty business of permitting a lot of sailors and street rifraff to rough the girls. All that went against the grain, but when you let them protect the pickets, as you did March third, when a thousand women marched around and around the White House, the officers were as contented as they were efficient.

Washington has a good police force and there has never been a minute when they could not have scattered any group gathered at the White House gates and given perfect protection to the women standing there.

You know why they did not do their duty.

In excusing what you have done, you say that the women carried banners with "offensive" inscriptions on them. You refer to the fact that they have addressed the President as "Kaiser Wilson." As a matter of fact not an arrest you have made—and the arrests now number more than sixty—has been for carrying one of those "offensive" banners. The women were carrying merely the suffrage colors or quotations from President Wilson's writings.

But, suppose the banners were offensive. Who made you censor of banners? The law gives you no such power. Even when you go through the farce of a police court trial the charge is "obstructing traffic"; which shows conclusively that you are not willing to go into court on the real issue.

No. As Chief of Police you have no more right to complain of the sentiments of a banner than you have of the sentiments in an editorial in the Washington *Post*, and you have no more right to arrest the banner-bearer than you have to arrest the owner of the Washington *Post*. . . . Congress refused to pass a press censorship law. There are certain lingering traditions to the effect that a people's liberties are closely bound up with the right to talk things out and those who are enlightened know that the only proper answer to words is words. When force is opposed to words there is ground for the charge of "Kaiserism." . . .

There was just one thing for you to have done, Pullman,

and that was to give full and adequate protection to these women, no matter what banners they carried or what ideas their banners expressed. If there is any law that can be invoked against the wording of the banners it was the business of others in the government to start the legal machinery which would abate them. It was not lawful to abate them by mob violence, or by arrests. And if those in authority over you were not willing that you thus do your duty, it was up to you to resign.

After all it would not be such a terrible thing, Pullman, for you to give up being Chief of Police, particularly *when you are not permitted to be chief of police, but must yield your judgment to the district commissioners who have yielded their judgment to the White House.* Being Chief of Police under such circumstances can hardly be worth while. You are a young man and the world is full of places for young men with courage enough to save their self-respect at the expense of their jobs. You did that once,—back in the Ballinger-Pinchot days. Why not now?

Come out and help make the fight which must be made to recover and protect the liberties which are being filched from us here at home. There is a real fight looming up for real democracy. You will not be alone. There are a lot of fine young men, vigorous and patriotic, in and out of the Administration who are preparing for this fight. Yours will not be the only resignation. But why not be among the first? Don't wait. Let them have your resignation now and let me be the first to welcome and congratulate you.

Sincerely,

(Signed) GILSON GARDNER.

Representative John Baer of North Dakota, having witnessed for himself the riotous scenes, immediately introduced into the House a resolution [1] demanding an investigation of conditions in the Capital which permitted mobs to attack women. This, too, went to certain death. Between the members who did not dare denounce the Administration and the others who did dare denounce the women, we had to stand quite

[1] See Appendix 3 for full text of resolution.

solidly on our own program, and do our best to keep them nervous over the next step in the agitation.

The press throughout the entire country at this time protested against mob violence and the severe sentences pronounced upon the women who had attempted to hold their banners steadfast.

The Washington (D. C.) *Herald*, August 19, printed the following editorial:

There is an echo of the President's phrase about the "firm hand of stern repression" in the arrest, conviction and jailing of the six suffragists; a touch of ruthlessness in their incarceration at Occoquan along with women of the street, pickpockets and other flotsam and jetsam. Still, the suffragists are not looking for sympathy, and it need not be wasted upon them.

The police have arrived at a policy, although no one knows whether it will be sufficiently stable and consistent to last out the week. . . . Washington is grateful that the disgraceful period of rioting and mob violence in front of the White House is at an end, and another crisis in the militant crusade to bring the Susan B. Anthony amendment before Congress has been reached.

What is the next step? No one knows. Picketing doubtless will continue, or an effort will be made to continue it; and militancy, if the police continue to arrest, instead of giving the women protection, will pass into a new phase. The suffragists as well as the public at large are thankful that the police department has finally determined to arrest the pickets, instead of allowing them to be mobbed by hoodlums.

. . . The public eye will be on Occoquan for the next few weeks, to find out how these women bear up under the Spartan treatment that is in store for them. If they have deliberately sought martyrdom, as some critics have been unkind enough to suggest, they have it now. And if their campaign, in the opinion of perhaps the great majority of the public, has been misguided, admiration for their pluck will not be withheld.

The Boston *Journal* of August 20, 1917, said in an editorial written by Herbert N. Pinkham, Jr.:

That higher authorities than the Washington police were responsible for the amazing policy of rough house employed against the suffrage pickets has been suspected from the very beginning. Police power in Washington is sufficient to protect a handful of women against a whole phalanx of excited or inspired government clerks and uniformed hoodlums, if that power were used.

. . . In our nation's capital, women have been knocked down and dragged through the streets by government employees—including sailors in uniform. The police are strangely absent at such moments, as a rule, and arrive only in time to arrest a few women. . . .

Perhaps the inscriptions on the suffrage banners were not tactful. It is sometimes awkward indeed to quote the President's speeches after the speeches have "grown cold." Also a too vigorous use of the word "democracy" is distasteful to some government dignitaries, it seems. But right or wrong, the suffragists at Washington are entitled to police protection, even though in the minds of the Administration they are not entitled to the ballot.

Perhaps, even in America, we must have a law forbidding people to carry banners demanding what they consider their political rights. Such a law would, of course, prohibit political parades of all kinds, public mass meetings and other demonstrations of one set of opinions against another set. Such a law has been proposed by Senator Myers of Montana, the author of the latest censorship and anti-free speech bill. It may be necessary to pass the law, if it is also necessary that the public voice be stilled and the nation become dumb and subservient.

But until there is such a law . . . people must be protected while their actions remain within the law. If their opinions differ from ours, we must refrain from smashing their faces, if a certain number of people believe that they have the right to vote we may either grant their claim or turn them sadly away, but we may not roll them into the gutter; if they see fit to tell us our professions of democracy are empty, we may smile sorrowfully and murmur a prayer for their ignorance but we may not pelt them with rotten eggs and fire a shot through the window of their dwelling; if, denied a properly

dignified hearing, they insist upon walking through the streets
with printed words on a saucy banner, we may be amazed at
their zeal and pitiful of their bad taste, but even for the sake
of keeping their accusations out of sight of our foreign visitors
(whom we have trained to believe us perfect) we may not send
them to jail. . . .

All this suffrage shouting in Washington has as its single
object the attainment of President Wilson's material support
for equal suffrage. . . .

President Wilson's word would carry the question into
Congress. . . .

Would there be any harm in letting Congress vote on a
suffrage resolution? That would end the disturbance and it
would make our shield of national justice somewhat brighter.

It looks like President Wilson's move.

Between these opposing currents of protest and support,
the Administration drifted helplessly. Unwilling to pass the
amendment, it continued to send women to prison.

On the afternoon of September 4th, President Wilson led
his first contingent of drafted "soldiers of freedom" down
Pennsylvania Avenue in gala parade, on the first lap of their
journey to the battlefields of France. On the same afternoon
a slender line of women—also "soldiers of freedom"—attempted
to march in Washington.

As they attempted to take up their posts, two by two, in
front of the Reviewing Stand, opposite the White House, they
were gathered in and swept away by the police like common
street criminals—their golden banners scarcely flung to the
breeze.

MR. PRESIDENT, HOW LONG MUST WOMEN BE DE-
NIED A VOICE IN A GOVERNMENT WHICH IS CON-
SCRIPTING THEIR SONS?

was the offensive question on the first banner carried by Miss
Eleanor Calnan of Massachusetts and Miss Edith Ainge of
New York.

The Avenue was roped off on account of the parade. There was hardly any one passing at the time; all traffic had been temporarily suspended, so there was none to obstruct. But the Administration's policy must go on. A few moments and Miss Lucy Branham of Maryland and Mrs. Pauline Adams of Virginia marched down the Avenue, their gay banners waving joyously in the autumn sun, to fill up the gap of the two comrades who had been arrested. They, too, were shoved into the police automobile, their banners still high and appealing, silhouetted against the sky as they were hurried to the police station.

The third pair of pickets managed to cross the Avenue, but were arrested immediately they reached the curb. Still others advanced. The crowd began to line the ropes and to watch eagerly the line of women indomitably coming, two by two, into the face of certain arrest. A fourth detachment was arrested in the middle of the Avenue on the trolley tracks. But still they came.

A few days later more women were sent to the workhouse for carrying to the picket line this question:

"President Wilson, what did you mean when you said: 'We have seen a good many singular things happen recently. We have been told there is a deep disgrace resting upon the origin of this nation. The nation originated in the sharpest sort of criticism of public policy. We originated, to put it in the vernacular, in a kick, and if it be unpatriotic to kick, why then the grown man is unlike the child. We have forgotten the very principle of our origin if we have forgotten how to object, how to resist, how to agitate, how to pull down and build up, even to the extent of revolutionary practices, if it be necessary to readjust matters. I have forgotten my history if that be not true history.'"

The Administration had not yet abandoned hope of removing the pickets. They persisted in their policy of arrests and longer imprisonments.

CHAPTER 6

D URING all this time the suffrage prisoners were enduring the miserable and petty tyranny of the government
workhouse at Occoquan. They were kept absolutely
incommunicado. They were not allowed to see even their nearest relatives, should any be within reach, until they had been
in the institution two weeks.

Each prisoner was allowed to write one outgoing letter a
month, which, after being read by the warden, could be sent or
withheld at his whim.

All incoming mail and telegrams were also censored by the
Superintendent and practically all of them denied the prisoners. Superintendent Whittaker openly boasted of holding up
the suffragists' mail: "I am boss down here," he said to
visitors who asked to see the prisoners, or to send in a note.
"I consider the letters and telegrams these prisoners get are
treasonable. They cannot have them." He referred to messages commending the women for choosing prison to silence,
and bidding them stand steadfast to their program.

Of course all this was done in the hope of intimidating not
only the prisoners, but also those who came wanting to see
them.

It was the intention of the women to abide as far as possible
by the routine of the institution, disagreeable and unreasonable
as it was. They performed the tasks assigned to them. They
ate the prison food without protest. They wore the coarse
prison clothes. But at the end of the first week of detention

141

they became so weak from the shockingly bad food that they began to wonder if they could endure such a system. The petty tyrannies they could endure. But the inevitable result of a diet of sour bread, half-cooked vegetables, rancid soup with worms in it, was serious.

Finally the true condition of affairs trickled to the outside world through the devious routes of prison messengers.

Senator J. Hamilton Lewis, of Illinois, Democratic whip in the Senate, heard alarming reports of two of his constituents, Miss Lucy Ewing, daughter of Judge Ewing, niece of Adlai Stevenson, Vice-President in Cleveland's Administration, niece of James Ewing, minister to Belgium in the same Administration, and Mrs. William Upton Watson of Chicago. He made a hurried trip to the workhouse to see them. The fastidious Senator was shocked—shocked at the appearance of the prisoners, shocked at the tale they told, shocked that "ladies" should be subjected to such indignities. "In all my years of criminal practice," said the Senator to Gilson Gardner, who had accompanied him to the workhouse, "I have never seen prisoners so badly treated, either before or after conviction." He is a gallant gentleman who would be expected to be uncomfortable when he actually saw ladies suffer. It was more than gallantry in this instance, however, for he spoke in frank condemnation of the whole "shame and outrage" of the thing.

It is possible that he reported to other Administration officials what he had learned during his visit to the workhouse for very soon afterwards it was announced that an investigation of conditions in the workhouse would be held. That was, of course, an admirable manœuvre which the Administration could make. "Is the President not a kind man? He pardoned some women. Now he investigates the conditions under which others are imprisoned. Even though they are lawless women, he wishes them well treated."

It would sound "noble" to thousands.

Immediately the District Commissioners announced this investigation, Miss Lucy Burns, acting on behalf of the National Woman's Party, sent a letter to Commissioner Brownlow. After summing up the food situation Miss Burns wrote:

When our friends were sent to prison, they expected the food would be extremely plain, but they also expected that . . . enough eatable food would be given them to maintain them in their ordinary state of health. This has not been the case.

The testimony of one of the prisoners, Miss Lavinia Dock, a trained nurse, is extremely valuable on the question of food supplied at Occoquan. Miss Dock is Secretary of the American Federation of Nurses. She has had a distinguished career in her profession. She assisted in the work after the Johnstown flood and during the yellow fever epidemic in Florida. During the Spanish war she organized the Red Cross work with Clara Barton. 'I really thought,' said Miss Dock, when I last saw her, 'that I could eat everything, but here I have hard work choking down enough food to keep the life in me.'

I am sure you will agree with me that these conditions should be instantly remedied. When these and other prisoners were sentenced to prison they were sentenced to detention and not to starvation or semi-starvation.

The hygienic conditions have been improved at Occoquan since a group of suffragists were imprisoned there. But they are still bad. The water they drink is kept in an open pail, from which it is ladled into a drinking cup. The prisoners frequently dip the drinking cup directly into the pail.

The same piece of soap is used for every prisoner. As the prisoners in Occoquan are sometimes seriously afflicted with disease, this practice is appallingly negligent.

Concerning the general conditions of the person, I am enclosing with this letter, affidavit of Mrs. Virginia Bovee, an ex-officer of the workhouse. . . . The prisoners for whom I am counsel are aware that cruel practices go on at Occoquan. On one occasion they heard Superintendent Whittaker kicking a woman in the next room. They heard Whittaker's voice, the sound of blows, and the woman's cries.

I lay these facts before you with the knowledge that you will be glad to have the fullest possible information given you concerning the institution for whose administration you as Commissioner of the District of Columbia are responsible.

Very respectfully yours,

(Signed) Lucy Burns.

Mrs. Bovee, a matron, was discharged from the workhouse because she tried to be kind to the suffrage prisoners. She also gave them warnings to guide them past the possible contamination of hideous diseases. As soon as she was discharged from the workhouse she went to the headquarters of the Woman's Party and volunteered to make an affidavit. The affidavit of Mrs. Bovee follows:

I was discharged yesterday as an officer of Occoquan workhouse. For eight months I acted as night officer, with no complaint as to my performance of my duties. Yesterday Superintendent Whittaker told me I was discharged and gave me two hours in which to get out. I demanded the charges from the matron, Mrs. Herndon, and I was told that it was owing to something that Senator Lewis has said.

I am well acquainted with the conditions at Occoquan. I have had charge of all the suffragist prisoners who have been there. I know that their mail has been withheld from them. Mrs. Herndon, the matron, reads the mail, and often discussed it with us at the officers' table. She said of a letter sent to one of the suffragist pickets now in the workhouse, "They told her to keep her eyes open and notice everything. She will never get that letter," said Mrs. Herndon. Then she corrected herself, and added, "Not until she goes away." Ordinarily the mail not given the prisoners is destroyed. The mail for the suffragists is saved for them until they are ready to go away. I have seen three of the women have one letter each, but that is all. The three were Mrs. Watson, Miss Ewing, and I think Miss Flanagan.

The blankets now being used in the prison have been in use since December without being washed or cleaned. Blankets are washed once a year. Officers are warned not to touch any of the bedding. The one officer who handles it is compelled by the regulations to wear rubber gloves while she does so. The sheets for the ordinary prisoners are not changed completely, even when one is gone and another takes her bed. Instead the top sheet is put on the bottom, and one fresh sheet is given them. I was not there when these suffragists arrived, and I do not know how their bedding was arranged. I doubt whether the authorities would have dared to give them one soiled sheet.

The prisoners with disease are not always isolated, by any means. In the colored dormitory there are two women in the advanced stages of consumption. Women suffering from syphilis, who have open sores, are put in the hospital. But those whose sores are temporarily healed are put in the same dormitory with the others. There have been several such in my dormitory.

When the prisoners come they must undress and take a shower bath. For this they take a piece of soap from a bucket in the store room. When they are finished they throw the soap back in the bucket. The suffragists are permitted three showers a week and have only these pieces of soap which are common to all inmates. There is no soap at all in wash rooms.

The beans, hominy, rice, cornmeal (which is exceedingly coarse, like chicken feed) and cereal have all had worms in them. Sometimes the worms float on top of the soup. Often they are found in the cornbread. The first suffragists sent the worms to Whittaker on a spoon. On the farm is a fine herd of Holsteins. The cream is made into butter and sold to the tuberculosis hospital in Washington. At the officers' table we have very good milk. The prisoners do not have any butter or sugar, and no milk except by order of the doctor.

Prisoners are punished by being put on bread or water, or by being beaten. I know of one girl who has been kept seventeen days on only water this month in the "booby house." The same was kept nineteen days on water last year because she beat Superintendent Whittaker when he tried to beat her.

Superintendent Whittaker or his son are the only ones who beat the girls. Officers are not allowed to lay a hand on them in punishment. I know of one girl beaten until the blood had to be scrubbed from her clothing and from the floor of the "booby house." I have never actually seen a girl beaten, but I have seen her afterwards and I have heard the cries and blows. Dorothy Warfield was beaten and the suffragists heard the beating.

(Signed)   MRS. VIRGINIA BOVEE.

Subscribed and sworn to before
me this day of August, 1917.
                JOSEPH H. BATT, *Notary Public.*

While the Administration was planning an investigation of the conditions in the workhouse, which made it difficult for women to sustain health through a thirty day sentence, it was, through its police court, sentencing more women to *sixty day sentences,* under the same conditions. The Administration was giving some thought to its plan of procedure, but not enough to master the simple fact that women would not stop going to prison until something had been done which promised passage of the amendment through Congress.

New forms of intimidation and hardship were offered by Superintendent Whittaker.

Mrs. Frederick Kendall of Buffalo, New York, a frail and highly sensitive woman, was put in a "punishment cell" on bread and water, under a charge of "impudence." Mrs. Kendall says that her impudence consisted of "protesting to the matron that scrubbing floors on my hands and knees was too severe work for me as I had been unable for days to eat the prison food. My impudence further consisted in asking for lighter work."

Mrs. Kendall was refused the clean clothing she should have had the day she was put in solitary confinement and was thus forced to wear the same clothing eleven days. She was refused a nightdress or clean linen for the cot. Her only toilet accommodations was an open pail. For four days she was allowed no water for toilet purposes. Her diet consisted of three thin slices of bread and three cups of water, carried to her in a paper cup which frequently leaked out half the meagre supply before it got to Mrs. Kendall's cell.

Representative and Mrs. Charles Bennet Smith, of Buffalo, friends of Mrs. Kendall, created a considerable disturbance when they learned of this cruel treatment, with the result that Mrs. Kendall was finally given clean clothing and taken from her confinement. When she walked from her cell to greet Mrs. Genevieve Clark Thompson, daughter of Champ Clark, Speaker of the House, and Miss Roberta Bradshaw, other friends, who, through the Speaker's influence, had obtained special permission to see Mrs. Kendall, she fell in a dead faint. It was such shocking facts as these that the Commissioners and their investigating board were vainly trying to keep from the country for the sake of the reputation of the Administration.

For attempting to speak to Mrs. Kendall through her cell door, to inquire as to her health, while in solitary, Miss Lucy Burns was placed on a bread and water diet.

Miss Jeannette Rankin of Montana, the only woman member of Congress, was moved by these and similar revelations to introduce a resolution [1] calling for a Congressional investigation of the workhouse.

There were among the suffrage prisoners women of all shades of social opinion.

The following letter by Miss Gvinter, the young Russian worker, was smuggled out of the workhouse. This appeal to Meyer London was rather pathetic, since not even he, the only Socialist member in Congress, stood up to denounce the treatment of the pickets.

Comrade Meyer London:
I am eight years in this movement, three and a half years a member of the Socialist Party, Branches 2 and 4 of the Bronx, and I have been an active member of the Waist Makers' Union since 1910. I am from New York, but am now in Balti-

[1] For text of Miss Rankin's resolution see Appendix 3.

more, where I got acquainted with the comrades who asked me to picket the White House, and of course I expressed my willingness to help the movement. I am now in the workhouse. I want to get out and help in the work as I am more revolutionary than the Woman's Party, yet conditions here are so bad that I feel I must stay here and help women get their rights. We are enslaved here. I am suffering very much from hunger and nearly blind from bad nourishment. The food is chiefly soup, cereal with worms, bread just baked and very heavy. Even this poor food, we do not get enough. I do not eat meat. When I told the doctor that he said, "You must eat, and if you don't like it here, you go and tell the judge you won't picket any more, and then you can get out of here." But I told him that I could not go against my principles and my belief. He asked, "Do you believe you should break the law?" I replied, "I have picketed whenever I had a chance for eight years and have never broken the law. Picketing is legal."

Please come here as quickly as possible, as we need your help.

Will you give the information in this letter to the newspapers?

Please pardon this scrap of paper as I have nothing else to write on. I would write to other comrades, to Hillquit or Paulsen, but you are in the Congress and can do more.

Yours for the Cause,

(Signed) ANNA GVINTER.

OCCOQUAN WORKHOUSE, Friday, Sept. 21.

Miss Gvinter swore to an affidavit when she came out in which she said in part:

. . . The days that we had to stand on scaffolds and ladders to paint the dormitories, I was so weak from lack of food I was dizzy and in constant danger of falling.

. . . When they told me to *scrub the floors of the lavatories* I refused, because I have to work for my living and I could not afford to get any of the awful diseases that women down there have.

I obeyed all the rules of the institution. The only times I stopped working was because I was too sick to work.

(Signed)   ANNA GVINTER.

Sworn to before me and subscribed in my presence this 13th day of October, 1917.

(Signed)   C. LARIMORE KEELEY,
Notary Public, D. C.

Half a hundred women was the government's toll for one month. Continuous arrests kept the issue hot and kept people who cared in constant protest. It is impossible to give space to the countless beautiful messages which were sent to the women, or the fervent protests which went to government officials. Among the hundreds of thousands of protests was a valuable one by Dr. Harvey Wiley, the celebrated food expert, in a letter to Dr. George M. Kober, member of the Board in control of the jail and workhouse, and a well-known sanitarian. Dr. Wiley wrote:

November 3, 1917.
Dear Dr. Kober:
I am personally acquainted with many of the women who have been confined at Occoquan, and at the District jail, and have heard from their own lips an account of the nutrition and sanitary conditions prevailing at both places.

I, therefore, feel constrained to make known to you the conditions as they have been told to me, and as I believe them actually to exist.

As I understand it, there is no purpose in penal servitude of lowering the vitality of the prisoner, or in inviting disease. Yet both of these conditions prevail both at Occoquan and at the District jail. First of all, the food question. The diet furnished the prisoners at Occoquan especially is of a character to invite all kinds of infections that may prevail, and to lower the vitality so that the resistance to disease is diminished. I have fortunately come into possession of samples of the food actually given to these women. I have kept samples of the milk religiously for over two weeks to see if I could detect the least particle of fat, and have been unable to perceive any. The fat of milk is universally recognized by dieticians as its most important nutritive character. I understand that a dairy is kept on the farm at Occoquan, and yet it is perfectly certain that no whole milk is served or ever has been served to one of the so-called "picketers" in that jail. I have not had enough of the sample to make a chemical analysis, but being somewhat experienced in milk, I can truthfully say that it seems to me to be watered skimmed milk. I also have a sample of the pea soup served. The pea grains are coarsely broken, often more than half of a pea being served in one piece. They never have been cooked, but are in a perfectly raw state, and found to be inedible by the prisoners.

I have also samples of the corn bread which is most unattractive and repellant to the eye and to the taste. All of these witnesses say that the white bread apparently is of good quality, but the diet in every case is the cause of constipation, except in the case of pea soup, which brings on diarrhœa and vomiting. As nutrition is the very foundation of sanitation, I wish to call to your special attention, as a sanitarian, the totally inadequate sustenance given to these prisoners.

The food at the county jail at Washington is much better than the food at Occoquan, but still bad enough. This increased excellence of food is set off by the miserable ventilation of the cells, in which these noble women are kept in solitary confinement. Not only have they had a struggle to get the windows open slightly, but also at the time of their morning meal, the sweeping is done. The air of the cells is filled with dust and they try to cover their coffee and other food with such articles as they can find to keep the dust out of their food. Better conditions for promoting tuberculosis could not be found.

I appeal to you as a well-known sanitarian to get the Board of Charities to make such rules and regulations as would secure to prisoners of all kinds, and especially to political prisoners, as humane an environment as possible.

I also desire to ask that the Board of Charities would authorize me to make inspections of food furnished to prisoners at Occoquan and at the District Jail, and to have physical and chemical analysis made without expense to the Board, in order to determine more fully the nutritive environment in which the prisoners live.

Sincerely,
(Signed)   HARVEY WILEY.

This striking telegram from Richard Bennett, the distinguished actor, must have arrested the attention of the Administration.

September 22, 1917.

Hon. Newton Baker,
Secretary of War,
War Department,
Washington, D. C.

I have been asked to go to France personally, with the film of "Damaged Goods," as head of a lecture corps to the American army. On reliable authority I am told that American women, because they have dared demand their political freedom, are held in vile conditions in the Government workhouse in Washington; are compelled to paint the negro toilets for eight hours a day; are denied decent food and denied communication with counsel. Why should I work for democracy in Europe when our American women are denied democracy at home? If I am to fight for social hygiene in France, why not begin at Occoquan workhouse?

RICHARD BENNETT.

Mr. Bennett never received a reply to this message.

Charming companionships grew up in prison. Ingenuity at lifting the dull monotony of imprisonment brought to light many talents for camaraderie which amused not only the suffrage prisoners but the "regulars." Locked in separate cells, as in the District Jail, the suffragists could still communicate by song. The following lively doggerel to the tune of "Captain Kidd" was sung in chorus to the accompaniment of a hair comb. It became a saga. Each day a new verse was added, relating the day's particular controversy with the prison authorities.

We worried Woody-wood,
As we stood, as we stood,
We worried Woody-wood,
As we stood.
We worried Woody-wood,
And we worried him right good;
We worried him right good as we stood.

We asked him for the vote,
As we stood, as we stood,
We asked him for the vote
As we stood,
We asked him for the vote,
But he'd rather write a note,
He'd rather write a note—so we stood.

We'll not get out on bail,
Go to jail, go to jail—
We'll not get out on bail,
We prefer to go to jail,
We prefer to go to jail—we're not frail.

We asked them for a brush,
For our teeth, for our teeth,
We asked them for a brush
For our teeth.
We asked them for a brush,
They said, "There ain't no rush,"
They said, "There ain't no rush—darn your teeth."

We asked them for some air,
As we choked, as we choked,
We asked them for some air
As we choked.
We asked them for some air
And they threw us in a lair,
They threw us in a lair, so we choked.

We asked them for our nightie,
As we froze, as we froze,
We asked them for our nightie
As we froze.
We asked them for our nightie,
And they looked—hightie-tightie—
They looked hightie-tightie—so we froze.

Now, ladies, take the hint,
As ye stand, as ye stand,
Now, ladies, take the hint,
As ye stand.
Now, ladies, take the hint,
Don't quote the Presidint,
Don't quote the Presidint, as ye stand.

Humor predominated in the poems that came out of prison. There was never any word of tragedy.

Not even an intolerable diet of raw salt pork, which by actual count of Miss Margaret Fotheringham, a teacher of Domestic Science and Dietetics, was served the suffragists *sixteen times in eighteen days*, could break their spirit of gayety. And when a piece of fish of unknown origin was slipped through the tiny opening in the cell door, and a specimen carefully preserved for Dr. Wiley—who, by the way, was unable to classify it—they were more diverted than outraged.

Sometimes it was a "prayer" which enlivened the evening hour before bedtime. Mary Winsor of Haverford, Pennsylvania, was the master prayer-maker. One night it was a Baptist prayer, another a Methodist, and still another a stern Presbyterian prayer. The prayers were most disconcerting to the matron for the "regulars" became almost hysterical with laughter, when they should be slipping into sleep. It was trying also to sit in the corridor and hear your daily cruelties narrated to God and punishment asked. This is what happened to the embarrassed warden and jail attendants if they came to protest.

Sometimes it was the beautiful voice of Vida Milholland which rang through the corridors of the dreary prison, with a stirring Irish ballad, a French love song, or the Woman's Marseillaise.

Again the prisoners would build a song, each calling out from cell to cell, and contributing a line. The following song to the tune of "Charlie Is My Darling" was so written and sung with Miss Lucy Branham leading:

SHOUT THE REVOLUTION OF WOMEN

Shout the revolution
  Of women, of women,
Shout the revolution
  For liberty.
Rise, glorious women of the earth,
  The voiceless and the free
United strength assures the birth
  Of true democracy.

REFRAIN

Invincible our army,
  Forward, forward,
Triumphant daughters pressing
  To victory.

Shout the revolution
  Of women, of women,
Shout the revolution
  For liberty.
Men's revolution born in blood,
  But ours conceived in peace,
We hold a banner for a sword,
  Till all oppression cease.

REFRAIN

Prison, death, defying,
  Onward, onward,
Triumphant daughters pressing
  To victory.

The gayety was interspersed with sadness when the suffragists learned of new cruelties heaped upon the helpless ones, those who were without influence or friends. They learned of that barbarous punishment known as "the greasy pole" used upon girl prisoners. This method of punishment consisted of strapping girls with their hands tied behind them to a greasy pole from which they were partly suspended. Unable to keep themselves in an upright position, because of the grease on the pole, they slipped almost to the floor, with their arms all but severed from the arm sockets, suffering intense pain for long periods of time. This cruel punishment was meted out to prisoners for slight infractions of the prison rules.

The suffrage prisoners learned also of the race hatred which the authorities encouraged. It was not infrequent that the jail officers summoned black girls to attack white women, if the latter disobeyed. This happened in one instance to the suffrage prisoners who were protesting against the warden's forcibly taking a suffragist from the workhouse without telling her or her comrades whither she was being taken. Black girls were called and commanded to physically attack the suffragists. The negresses, reluctant to do so, were goaded to deliver blows upon the women by the warden's threats of punishment.

And as a result of our having been in prison, our headquarters has never ceased being the mecca of many discouraged "inmates," when released. They come for money. They come for work. They come for spiritual encouragement to face life after the wrecking experience of imprisonment. Some regard us as "fellow prisoners." Others regard us as "friends at court."

Occasionally we meet a prison associate in the workaday world. Long after Mrs. Lawrence Lewis' imprisonment, when she was working on ratification of the amendment in Delaware, she was greeted warmly by a charming young woman who came forward at a meeting. "Don't you remember me?" she asked, as

Mrs. Lewis struggled to recollect. "Don't you remember me? I met you in Washington."

"I'm sorry but I seem to have forgotten where I met you," said Mrs. Lewis apologetically.

"In jail," came the answer hesitantly, whereupon Mrs. Lewis listened sympathetically while her fellow prisoner told her that she had been in jail at the time Mrs. Lewis was, that *her* crime was bigamy and that she was one of the traveling circus troupe then in Dover.

"She brought up her husband, also a member of the circus," said Mrs. Lewis in telling of the incident, "and they both joined enthusiastically in a warm invitation to come and see them in the circus."

As each group of suffragists was released an enthusiastic welcome was given to them at headquarters and at these times, in the midst of the warmth of approving and appreciative comrades, some of the most beautiful speeches were delivered. I quote a part of Katharine Fisher's speech at a dinner in honor of released prisoners:

Five of us who are with you to-night have recently come out from the workhouse into the world. A great change? Not so much of a change for women, disfranchised women. In prison or out, American women are not free. Our lot of physical freedom simply gives us and the public a new and vivid sense of what our lack of political freedom really means.

Disfranchisement is the prison of women's power and spirit. Women have long been classed with criminals so far as their voting rights are concerned. And how quick the Government is to live up to its classification the minute women determinedly insist upon these rights. Prison life epitomizes all life under undemocratic rule. At Occoquan, as at the Capitol and the White House, we faced hypocrisy, trickery and treachery on the part of those in power. And the constant appeal to us to "coöperate" with the workhouse authorities sounded wonderfully like the exhortation addressed to all women to "support the Government."

"Is that the law of the District of Columbia?" I asked Superintendent Whittaker concerning a statement he had made to me. "It is the law," he answered, "because it is the rule I make." The answer of Whittaker is the answer Wilson makes to women every time the Government, of which he is the head, enacts a law and at the same time continues to refuse to pass the Susan B. Anthony amendment. . . .

We seem to-day to stand before you free, but I have no sense of freedom because I have left comrades at Occoquan and because other comrades may at any moment join them there. . . .

While comrades are there what is our freedom? It is as empty as the so-called political freedom of women who have won suffrage by a state referendum. Like them we are free only within limits. . . .

We must not let our voice be drowned by war trumpets or cannon. If we do, we shall find ourselves, when the war is over, with a peace that will only prolong our struggle, a democracy that will belie its name by leaving out half the people.

The Administration continued to send women to the workhouse and the District Jail for thirty and sixty day sentences.

CHAPTER 7

D UDLEY FIELD MALONE was known to the country as sharing the intimate confidence and friendship of President Wilson. He had known and supported the President from the beginning of the President's political career. He had campaigned twice through New Jersey with Mr. Wilson as Governor; he had managed Mr. Wilson's campaigns in many states for the nomination before the Baltimore Convention; he had toured the country with Mr. Wilson in 1912; and it was he who led to victory President Wilson's fight for California in 1916.

So when Mr. Malone went to the White House in July, 1917, to protest against the Administration's handling of the suffrage question, he went not only as a confirmed suffragist, but also as a confirmed supporter and member of the Wilson Administration—the one who had been chosen to go to the West in 1916 to win women voters to the Democratic Party.

Mr. Malone has consented to tell for the first time, in this record of the militant campaign, what happened at his memorable interview with President Wilson in July, 1917, an interview which he followed up two months later with his resignation as Collector of the Port of New York. I quote the story in his own words:

Frank P. Walsh, Amos Pinchot, Frederic C. Howe, J. A. H. Hopkins, Allen McCurdy and I were present throughout the trial of the sixteen women in July. Immediately after the police court judge had pronounced his sentence of sixty days in the Occoquan workhouse upon these "first offenders," on the alleged charge of a traffic violation, I went over to Anne Martin, one of the women's counsel, and offered to act as attorney on the appeal of the case. I then went to the court clerk's office and telephoned to President Wilson at the White House, asking him to see me at once. It was three o'clock. I called a taxicab, drove direct to the executive offices and met him.

I began by reminding the President that in the seven years and a half of our personal and political association we had never had a serious difference. He was good enough to say that my loyalty to him had been one of the happiest circumstances of his public career. But I told him I had come to place my resignation in his hands as I could not remain a member of any administration which dared to send American women to prison for demanding national suffrage. I also informed him that I had offered to act as counsel for the suffragists on the appeal of their case. He asked me for full details of my complaint and attitude. I told Mr. Wilson everything I had witnessed from the time we saw the suffragists arrested in front of the White House to their sentence in the police court. I observed that although we might not agree with the "manners" of picketing, citizens had a right to petition the President or any other official of the government for a redress of grievances. He seemed to acquiesce in this view, and reminded me that the women had been unmolested at the White House gates for over five months, adding that he had even ordered the head usher to invite the women on cold days to come into the White House and warm themselves and have coffee.

"If the situation is as you describe it, it is shocking," said the President. "The manhandling of the women by the police was outrageous and the entire trial (before a judge of your own appointment) was a perversion of justice," I said. This seemed to annoy the President and he replied with asperity, "Why do you come to me in this indignant fashion for things which have been done by the police officials of the city of Washington?"

"Mr. President," I said, "the treatment of these women is the result of carefully laid plans made by the District Com-

missioners of the city of Washington, who were appointed to
office by you. Newspaper men of unquestioned information
and integrity have told me that the District Commissioners
have been in consultation with your private secretary, Mr.
Tumulty, and that the Secretary of the Treasury, Mr. Mc-
Adoo, sat in at a conference when the policy of these arrests
was being determined."

The President asserted his ignorance of all this.

"Do you mean to tell me," he said, "that you intend to
resign, to repudiate me and my Administration and sacrifice
me for your views on this suffrage question?"

His attitude then angered me and I said, "Mr. President,
if there is any sacrifice in this unhappy circumstance, it is I
who am making the sacrifice. I was sent twice as your spokesman in the last campaign to the Woman Suffrage States of
the West. You have since been good enough to say publicly
and privately that I did as much as any man to carry California for you. After my first tour I had a long conference
with you here at the White House on the political situation in
those states. I told you that I found your strength with
women voters lay in the fact that you had with great patience
and statesmanship kept this country out of the European war.
But that your great weakness with women voters was that you
had not taken any step throughout your entire Administration
to urge the passage of the Federal Suffrage Amendment, which
Mr. Hughes was advocating and which alone can enfranchise
all the women of the nation. You asked me then how I met
this situation, and I told you that I promised the women
voters of the West that if they showed the political sagacity
to choose you as against Mr. Hughes, I would do everything
in my power to get your Administration to take up and pass
the suffrage amendment. You were pleased and approved of
what I had done. I returned to California and repeated this
promise, and so far as I am concerned, I must keep my part of
that obligation."

I reiterated to the President my earlier appeal that he
assist suffrage as an urgent war measure and a necessary part
of America's program for world democracy, to which the
President replied: "The enfranchisement of women is not at
all necessary to a program of democracy and I see nothing in

the argument that it is a war measure unless you mean that American women will not loyally support the war unless they are given the vote." I firmly denied this conclusion of the President and told him that while American women with or without the vote would support the United States Government against German militarism, yet it seemed to me a great opportunity of his leadership to remove this grievance which women generally felt against him and his administration. "Mr. President," I urged, "if you, as the leader, will persuade the administration to pass the Federal Amendment you will release from the suffrage fight the energies of thousands of women which will be given with redoubled zeal to the support of your program for international justice." But the President absolutely refused to admit the validity of my appeal, though it was as a "war measure" that the President some months later demanded that the Senate pass the suffrage amendment.

The President was visibly moved as I added, "You are the President now, reëlected to office. You ask if I am going to sacrifice you. You sacrifice nothing by my resignation. But I lose much. I quit a political career. I give up a powerful office in my own state. I, who have no money, sacrifice a lucrative salary, and go back to revive my law practice. But most of all I sever a personal association with you of the deepest affection which you know has meant much to me these past seven years. But I cannot and will not remain in office and see women thrown into jail because they demand their political freedom."

The President earnestly urged me not to resign, saying, "What will the people of the country think when they hear that the Collector of the Port of New York has resigned because of an injustice done to a group of suffragists by the police officials of the city of Washington?"

My reply to this was, "With all respect for you, Mr. President, my explanation to the public will not be as difficult as yours, if I am compelled to remind the public that you have appointed to office and can remove all the important officials of the city of Washington."

The President ignored this and insisted that I should not resign, saying, "I do not question your intense conviction about this matter as I know you have always been an ardent suffragist; and since you feel as you do I see no reason why you should not become their counsel and take this case up on appeal without resigning from the Administration."

"But," I said, "Mr. President, that arrangement would be impossible for two reasons; first, these women would not want me as their counsel if I were a member of your Administration, for it would appear to the public then as if your Administration was not responsible for the indignities to which they have been subjected, and your Administration *is* responsible; and, secondly, I cannot accept your suggestion because it may be necessary in the course of the appeal vigorously to criticize and condemn members of your cabinet and others close to you, and I could not adopt this policy while remaining in office under you." The President seemed greatly upset and finally urged me as a personal service to him to go at once and perfect the case on appeal for the suffragists, but not to resign until I had thought it over for a day, and until he had had an opportunity to investigate the facts I had presented to him. I agreed to this, and we closed the interview with the President saying, "If you consider my personal request and do not resign, please do not leave Washington without coming to see me." I left the executive offices and never saw him again.

There was just a day and a half left to perfect the exceptions for the appeal under the rules of procedure. No stenographic record of the trial had been taken, which put me under the greatest legal difficulties. I was in the midst of these preparations for appeal the next day when I learned to my surprise that the President had pardoned the women. He had not even consulted me as their attorney. Moreover, I was amazed that since the President had said he considered the treatment of the women "shocking," he had pardoned them without stating that he did so to correct a grave injustice. I felt certain that the high-spirited women in the workhouse would refuse to accept the pardon as a mere "benevolent" act on the part of the President.

I at once went down to the workhouse in Virginia. My opinion was confirmed. The group refused to accept the President's pardon. I advised them that as a matter of law no one could compel them to accept the pardon, but that as a matter of fact they would have to accept it, for the Attorney

DUDLEY FIELD MALONE

General would have them all put out of the institution bag and baggage. So as a solution of the difficulty and in view of the fact that the President had said to me that their treatment was "shocking" I made public the following statement:

"The President's pardon is an acknowledgment by him of the grave injustice that has been done." This he never denied.

Under this published interpretation of his pardon the women at Occoquan accepted the pardon and returned to Washington. The incident was closed. I returned to New York. During the next two months I carefully watched the situation. Six or eight more groups of women in that time were arrested on the same false charges, tried and imprisoned in the same illegal way. Finally a group of women was arrested in September under the identical circumstances as those in July, was tried in the same lawless fashion and given the same sentence of "sixty days in the workhouse." The President may have been innocent of responsibility for the first arrests, but he was personally and politically responsible for all the arrests that occurred after his pardon of the first group. Under this development it seemed to me that self-respect demanded action, so I sent my resignation to the President, publicly stated my attitude and regretfully left his Administration."

Mr. Malone's resignation in September, 1917, came with a sudden shock, because the entire country and surely the Administration thought him quieted and subdued by the President's personal appeal to him in July.

Mr. Malone was shocked that the policy of arrests should be continued. Mr. Wilson and his Administration were shocked that any one should care enough about the liberty of women to resign a lucrative post in the Government. The nation was shocked into the realization that this was not a street brawl between women and policemen, but a controversy between suffragists and a powerful Administration. We had said so but it would have taken months to convince the public that the President was in any way responsible. Mr. Malone did what we could only have done with the greatest difficulty and after more prolonged sacrifices. He laid the responsibility squarely and dramatically where it belonged. It is impossible to over-emphasize what a tremendous acceleration Mr. Malone's fine, solitary and generous act gave to the speedy break-down of the Administration's resistance. His sacrifice lightened ours.

Women ought to be willing to make sacrifices for their own liberation, but for a man to have the courage and imagination to make such a sacrifice for the liberation of women is unparalleled. Mr. Malone called to the attention of the nation the true cause of the obstruction and suppression. He reproached the President and his colleagues after mature consideration, in the most honorable and vital way,—by refusing longer to associate himself with an Administration which backed such policies.

And Mr. Malone's resignation was not only welcomed by the militant group. The conservative suffrage leaders, although they heartily disapproved of picketing, were as outspoken in their gratitude.

Alice Stone Blackwell, the daughter of Lucy Stone, herself a pioneer suffrage leader and editor, wrote to Mr. Malone:

"May I express my appreciation and gratitude for the excellent and manly letter that you have written to President Wilson on woman suffrage? I am sure that I am only one of many women who feel thankful to you for it.

"The picketing seems to me a very silly business, and I am sure it is doing the cause harm instead of good; but the picketers are being shamefully and illegally treated, and it is a thousand pities, for President Wilson's own sake, that he ever allowed the Washington authorities to enter on this course of persecution. It was high time for some one to make a protest, and you have made one that has been heard far and wide. . . ."

Mrs. Carrie Chapman Catt, the President of the National American Woman Suffrage Association, wrote:

"I was in Maine when your wonderful letter announcing your resignation came out. It was the noblest act that any man ever did on behalf of our cause. The letter itself was a high minded appeal. . . ."

Mrs. Norman de R. Whitehouse, the President of the New York State Woman Suffrage Party, with which Mr. Malone had worked for years, wired:

"Although we disagree with you on the question of picketing every suffragist must be grateful to you for the gallant support you are giving our cause and the great sacrifice you are making."

Mrs. James Lees Laidlaw, Vice Chairman of the New York Suffrage Party, said:

"No words of mine can tell you how our hearts have been lifted and our purposes strengthened in this tremendous struggle in New York State by the reading of your powerful and noble utterances in your letter to President Wilson. There flashed through my mind all the memories of Knights of chivalry and of romance that I have ever read, and they all paled before your championship, and the sacrifice and the high-spirited leadership that it signifies. Where you lead, I believe, thousands of other men will follow, even though at a distance, and most inadequately. . . ."

And from the women voters of California with whom Mr. Malone had kept faith came the message:

"The liberty-loving women of California greet you as one of the few men in history who have been willing to sacrifice material interests for the liberty of a class to which they themselves do not belong. We are thrilled by your inspiring words. We appreciate your sympathetic understanding of the viewpoint of disfranchised women. We are deeply grateful for the incalculable benefit of your active assistance in the struggle of American women for political liberty and for a real Democracy."

I reprint Mr. Malone's letter of resignation which sets forth in detail his position.

The President,   September 7, 1917.
    The White House,
        Washington, D. C.
Dear Mr. President:
    Last autumn, as the representative of your Administration, I went into the woman suffrage states to urge your reëlection. The most difficult argument to meet among the seven million voters was the failure of the Democratic party, throughout four years of power, to pass the federal suffrage amendment looking toward the enfranchisement of all the women of the country. Throughout those states, and particularly in California, which ultimately decided the election by the votes of women, the women voters were urged to support you, even though Judge Hughes had already declared for the federal suffrage amendment, because you and your party, through liberal leadership, were more likely nationally to enfranchise the rest of the women of the country than were your opponents.
    And if the women of the West voted to reëlect you, I promised them that I would spend all my energy, at any sacrifice to myself, to get the present Democratic Administration to pass the federal suffrage amendment.
    But the present policy of the Administration, in permitting splendid American women to be sent to jail in Washington, not for carrying offensive banners, not for picketing, but on the technical charge of obstructing traffic, is a denial even of their constitutional right to petition for, and demand the passage of, the federal suffrage amendment. It, therefore, now becomes my profound obligation actively to keep my promise to the women of the West.
    In more than twenty states it is a practical impossibility to amend the state constitutions; so the women of those States can only be enfranchised by the passage of the federal suffrage amendment. Since England and Russia, in the midst of the great war, have assured the national enfranchisement of their women, should we not be jealous to maintain our democratic leadership in the world by the speedy national enfranchisement of American women?
    To me, Mr. President, as I urged upon you in Washington two months ago, this is not only a measure of justice and democracy, it is also an urgent war measure. The women of

the nation are, and always will be, loyal to the country, and
the passage of the suffrage amendment is only the first step
toward their national emancipation. But unless the government takes at least this first step toward their enfranchisement,
how can the government ask millions of American women, educated in our schools and colleges, and millions of American
women, in our homes, or toiling for economic independence in
every line of industry, to give up by conscription their men
and happiness to a war for democracy in Europe, while these
women citizens are denied the right to vote on the policies of
the Government which demands of them such sacrifice?

For this reason many of your most ardent friends and
supporters feel that the passage of the federal suffrage amendment is a war measure which could appropriately be urged by
you at this session of Congress. It is true that this amendment would have to come from Congress, but the present Congress shows no earnest desire to enact this legislation for the
simple reason that you, as the leader of the party in power,
have not yet suggested it.

For the whole country gladly acknowledges, Mr. President,
that no vital piece of legislation has come through Congress
these five years except by your extraordinary and brilliant
leadership. And what millions of men and women to-day hope
is that you will give the federal suffrage amendment to the
women of the country by the valor of your leadership now.
It will hearten the mothers of the nation, eliminate a just
grievance, and turn the devoted energies of brilliant women to
a more hearty support of the Government in this crisis.

As you well know, in dozens of speeches in many states I
have advocated your policies and the war. I was the first man
of your Administration, nearly five years ago, to publicly
advocate preparedness, and helped to found the first Platts-
burg training camp. And if, with our troops mobilizing in
France, you will give American women this measure for their
political freedom, they will support with greater enthusiasm
your hope and the hope of America for world freedom.

I have not approved all the methods recently adopted by
women in pursuit of their political liberty; yet, Mr. President,
the Committee on Suffrage of the United States Senate was
formed in 1883, when I was one year old; this same federal

suffrage amendment was first introduced in Congress in 1878, brave women like Susan B. Anthony were petitioning Congress for the suffrage before the Civil War, and at the time of the Civil War men like William Lloyd Garrison, Horace Greeley, and Wendell Phillips assured the suffrage leaders that if they abandoned their fight for suffrage, when the war was ended the men of the nation "out of gratitude" would enfranchise the women of the country.

And if the men of this country had been peacefully demanding for over half a century the political right or privilege to vote, and had been continuously ignored or met with evasion by successive Congresses, as have the women, you, Mr. President, as a lover of liberty, would be the first to comprehend and forgive their inevitable impatience and righteous indignation. Will not this Administration, reëlected to power by the hope and faith of the women of the West, handsomely reward that faith by taking action now for the passage of the federal suffrage amendment?

In the Port of New York, during the last four years, billions of dollars in the export and import trade of the country have been handled by the men of the customs service; their treatment of the traveling public has radically changed, their vigilance supplied the evidence of the Lusitania note; the neutrality was rigidly maintained; the great German fleet guarded, captured, and repaired—substantial economies and reforms have been concluded and my ardent industry has been given to this great office of your appointment.

But now I wish to leave these finished tasks, to return to my profession of the law, and to give all my leisure time to fight as hard for the political freedom of women as I have always fought for your liberal leadership.

It seems a long seven years, Mr. President, since I first campaigned with you when you were running for Governor of New Jersey. In every circumstance throughout those years I have served you with the most respectful affection and unshadowed devotion. It is no small sacrifice now for me, as a member of your Administration, to sever our political relationship. But I think it is high time that men in this generation, at some cost to themselves, stood up to battle for the national enfranchisement of American women. So in order effectively to keep my promise made in the West and more freely to go into this larger field of democratic effort, I hereby resign my office as Collector of the Port of New York, to take effect at once, or at your earliest convenience.

Yours respectfully,
(Signed) DUDLEY FIELD MALONE.

The President's answer has never before been published:

THE WHITE HOUSE   U. S. S. MAYFLOWER,
WASHINGTON   12 September, 1917.

My dear Mr. Collector:

Your letter of September 7th reached me just before I left home and I have, I am sorry to say, been unable to reply to it sooner.

I must frankly say that I cannot regard your reasons for resigning your position as Collector of Customs as convincing, but it is so evidently your wish to be relieved from the duties of the office that I do not feel at liberty to withhold my acceptance of your resignation. Indeed, I judge from your letter that any discussion of the reasons would not be acceptable to you and that it is your desire to be free of the restraints of public office. I, therefore, accept your resignation, to take effect as you have wished.

I need not say that our long association in public affairs makes me regret the action you have taken most sincerely.

Very truly yours,
(Signed) WOODROW WILSON.

Hon. Dudley Field Malone,
Collector of Customs,
New York City.

To this Mr. Malone replied:

New York, N. Y.,
The President,   September 15th, 1917.
The White House,
     Washington, D. C.

Dear Mr. President:

Thank you sincerely for your courtesy, for I knew you were on a well-earned holiday and I did not expect an earlier reply to my letter of September 7th, 1917.

After a most careful re-reading of my letter, I am unable to understand how you could judge that any discussion by you of my reasons for resigning would not be acceptable to me since my letter was an appeal to you on specific grounds for action now by the Administration on the Federal Suffrage amendment.

However, I am profoundly grateful to you for your prompt acceptance of my resignation.

Yours respectfully,
(Signed)   DUDLEY FIELD MALONE.

It may have been accidental but it is interesting to note that the first public statement of Mr. Byron Newton, appointed by the Administration to succeed Mr. Malone as Collector of the Port of New York, was a bitter denunciation of all woman suffrage whether by state or national action.

CHAPTER 8

IMMEDIATELY after Mr. Malone's sensational resignation the Administration sought another way to remove the persistent pickets without passing the amendment. It yielded on a point of machinery. It gave us a report in the Senate and a committee in the House and expected us to be grateful.

The press had turned again to more sympathetic accounts of our campaign and exposed the prison régime we were undergoing. We were now for a moment the object of sympathy; the Administration was the butt of considerable hostility. Sensing their predicament and fearing any loss of prestige, they risked a slight advance.

Senator Jones, Chairman of the Suffrage Committee, made a visit to the workhouse. Scarcely had the women recovered from the surprise of his visit when the Senator, on the following day, September 15th, filed the favorable report which had been lying with his Committee since May 15th, exactly six months.

The Report, which he had so long delayed because he wanted [he said] to make it a particularly brilliant and elaborate one, read:

"The Committee on Woman Suffrage, to which was referred the joint resolution proposing an amendment to the Constitution of the United States, conferring upon women the right of suffrage, having the same under consideration, beg leave to report it back to the Senate with the recommendation that the joint resolution do pass."

This report to the Senate was immediately followed by a vote of 181 to 107 in the House of Representatives in favor of creating a Committee on Woman Suffrage in the House. This vote was indicative of the strength of the amendment in the House. The resolution was sponsored by Representative Pou, Chairman of the Rules Committee and Administration leader, himself an anti-suffragist.

It is an interesting study in psychology to consider some of. the statements made in the peculiarly heated debate the day this vote was taken.

Scores of Congressmen, anxious to refute the idea that the indomitable picket had had anything to do with their action, revealed naïvely how surely it had.

Of the 291 men present, not one man stood squarely up for the right of the hundreds of women who petitioned for justice. Some indirectly and many, inadvertently, however, paid eloquent tribute to the suffrage picket.

From the moment Representative Pou in opening the debate spoke of the nation-wide request for the committee, and the President's sanction of the committee, the accusations and counter-accusations concerning the wisdom of appointing it in the face of the pickets were many and animated.

Mr. Meeker of Missouri, Democrat, protested against Congress "yielding to the nagging of a certain group."

Mr. Cantrill of Kentucky, Democrat, believed that "millions of Christian women in the nation should not be denied the right of having a Committee in the House to study the problem of suffrage because of the mistakes of some few of their sisters."

"One had as well say," he went on, "that there should be no police in Washington because the police force of this city permitted daily thousands of people to obstruct the streets and impede traffic and permitted almost the mobbing of the women without arresting the offenders. There was a lawful and peaceful way in which the police of this city could have taken charge of the banners of the pickets without permitting the women carrying them to be the objects of mob violence. To see women roughly handled by rough men on the streets of the capital of the nation is not a pleasing sight to Kentuckians and to red-blooded Americans, and let us hope the like will never again be seen here."

Mr. Walsh, an anti-suffrage Democrat from Massachusetts, deplored taking any action which would seem to yield to the demand of the pickets who carried banners which "if used by a poor workingman in an attempt to get his rights would speedily have put him behind the bars for treason or sedition, and these poor, bewildered, deluded creatures, after their disgusting exhibition can thank their stars that because they wear skirts they are now incarcerated for misdemeanors of a minor character. . . . To supinely yield to a certain class of women picketing the gates of the official residence,—yes, even posing with their short skirts and their short hair within the view of this 'very capitol and our office buildings,' with banners which would seek to lead the people to believe that because we did not take action during this war session upon suffrage, if you please, and grant them the right of the ballot that we were traitors to the American Republic, would be monstrous."

The subject of the creation of a committee on suffrage was almost entirely forgotten. The Congressmen were utterly unable to shake off the ghosts of the pickets. The pickets had not influenced their actions! The very idea was appalling to Representative Stafford of Wisconsin, anti-suffrage Republican, who joined in the Democratic protests. He said:

"If a Suffrage Committee is created the militant class will exclaim, 'Ah, see how we have driven the great House of Representatives to recognize our rights. If we keep up this sort of practices, we will compel the House, when they come to vote on the constitutional amendment, to surrender obediently likewise'."

He spoke the truth, and finished dramatically with:

"Gentlemen, there is only one question before the House to-day and that is, if you look at it from a political aspect, whether you wish to approve of the practices of these women who have been disgracing their cause here in Washington for the past several months."

Representative Volstead, of Minnesota, Republican, came the closest of all to real courage in his protest:—

"In this discussion some very unfair comments have been made upon the women who picketed the White House. While I do not approve of picketing, I disapprove more strongly of the hoodlum methods pursued in suppressing the practice. I gather from the press that this is what took place. Some women did in a peaceable, and perfectly lawful manner, display suffrage banners on the public street near the White House. To stop this the police allowed the women to be mobbed, and then because the mob obstructed the street, the women were arrested and fined, while the mob went scot-free. . . ."

The Suffrage Committee in the House was appointed. The creation of this committee, which had been pending since 1913, was now finally granted in September, 1917. To be sure this was accomplished only after an inordinate amount of time, money and effort had been spent on a sustained and relentless campaign of pressure. But the Administration had yielded.

As a means to remove the pickets, however, this yielding had failed. "We ask no more machinery; we demand the passage of the amendment," said the pickets as they lengthened their line.

CHAPTER 9

POLITICAL PRISONERS

FINDING that a Suffrage Committee in the House and a report in the Senate had not silenced our banners, the Administration cast about for another plan by which to stop the picketing. This time they turned desperately to longer terms of imprisonment. They were indeed hard pressed when they could choose such a cruel and stupid course.

Our answer to this policy was more women on the picket line, on the outside, and a protest on the inside of prison.

We decided, in the face of extended imprisonment, to demand to be treated as political prisoners. We felt that, as a matter of principle, this was the dignified and self-respecting thing to do, since we had offended politically, not criminally. We believed further that a determined, organized effort to make clear to a wider public the political nature of the offense would intensify the Administration's embarrassment and so accelerate their final surrender.

It fell to Lucy Burns, vice chairman of the organization, to be the leader of the new protest. Miss Burns is in appearance the very symbol of woman in revolt. Her abundant and glorious red hair burns and is not consumed—a flaming torch. Her body is strong and vital. It is said that Lucy Stone had the "voice" of the pioneers. Lucy Burns without doubt possessed the "voice" of the modern suffrage movement. Musical, appealing, persuading—she could move the most resistant person. Her talent as an orator is of the kind that makes for instant

intimacy with her audience. Her emotional quality is so powerful that her intellectual capacity, which is quite as great, is not
always at once perceived.

I find myself wanting to talk about her as a human being
rather than as a leader of women. Perhaps it is because she has
such winning, lovable qualities. It was always difficult for her
to give all of her energy and power to a movement. She
yearned to play, to read, to study, to be luxuriously indolent,
to revel in the companionship of her family, to which she is
ardently devoted; to do any one of a hundred things more pleasant than trying to reason with a politician or an unawakened
member of her own sex. But for these latter labors she had a
most gentle and persuasive genius, and she would not shrink
from hours of close argument to convince a person intellec-
tually and emotionally.

Unlike Miss Paul, however, her force is not nonresistant.
Once in the combat she takes delight in it; she is by nature a
rebel. She is an ideal leader for the stormy and courageous
attack—reckless and yet never to the point of unwisdom.

From the time Miss Burns and Miss Paul met for the first
time in Cannon Row Police Station, London, they have been
constant co-workers in suffrage. Both were students abroad at
the time they met. They were among the hundred women arrested for attempting to present petitions for suffrage to Parliament. This was the first time either of them had participated
in a demonstration. But from then on they worked together
in England and Scotland organizing, speaking, heckling members of the government, campaigning at bye-elections; going to
Holloway Prison together, where they joined the Englishwomen
on hunger strike. Miss Burns remained organizing in Scotland
while Miss Paul was obliged to return to America after serious
illness following a thirty day period of imprisonment, during
all of which time she was forcibly fed.

Miss Burns and she did not meet again until 1913—three

years having intervened—when they undertook the national work on Congress. Throughout the entire campaign Miss Burns and Miss Paul counseled with one another on every point of any importance. This combination of the cool strategist and passionate rebel—each sharing some of the attributes of the other—has been a complete and unsurpassed leadership.

You have now been introduced, most inadequately, to Lucy Burns, who was to start the fight inside the prison.

She had no sooner begun to organize her comrades for protest than the officials sensed a "plot," and removed her at once to solitary confinement. But they were too late. Taking the leader only hastened the rebellion. A forlorn piece of paper was discovered, on which was written their initial demand. It was then passed from prisoner to prisoner through holes in the wall surrounding leaden pipes, until a finished document had been perfected and signed by all the prisoners.

This historic document—historic because it represents the first organized group action ever made in America to establish the status of political prisoners—said:

To the Commissioners of the District of Columbia:

As political prisoners, we, the undersigned, refuse to work while in prison. We have taken this stand as a matter of principle after careful consideration, and from it we shall not recede.

This action is a necessary protest against an unjust sentence. In reminding President Wilson of his pre-election promises toward woman suffrage we were exercising the right of peaceful petition, guaranteed by the Constitution of the United States, which declares peaceful picketing is legal in the District of Columbia. That we are unjustly sentenced has been well recognized—when President Wilson pardoned the first group of suffragists who had been given sixty days in the workhouse, and again when Judge Mullowny suspended sentence for the last group of picketers. We wish to point out the inconsistency and injustice of our sentences—some of us have been given sixty days, a later group thirty days, and another group given a suspended sentence for exactly the same action.

Conscious, therefore, of having acted in accordance with the highest standards of citizenship, we ask the Commissioners of the District to grant us the rights due political prisoners. We ask that we no longer be segregated and confined under locks and bars in small groups, but permitted to see each other, and that Miss Lucy Burns, who is in full sympathy with this letter, be released from solitary confinement in another building and given back to us.

We ask exemption from prison work, that our legal right to consult counsel be recognized, to have food sent to us from outside, to supply ourselves with writing material for as much correspondence as we may need, to receive books, letters, newspapers, our relatives and friends.

Our united demand for political treatment has been delayed, because on entering the workhouse we found conditions so very bad that before we could ask that the suffragists be treated as political prisoners, it was necessary to make a stand for the ordinary rights of human beings for all the inmates. Although this has not been accomplished we now wish to bring the important question of the status of political prisoners to the attention of the commissioners, who, we are informed, have full authority to make what regulations they please for the District prison and workhouse.

The Commissioners are requested to send us a written reply so that we may be sure this protest has reached them.

Signed by,

MARY WINSOR, LUCY BRANHAM, ERNESTINE HARA, HILDA BLUMBERG, MAUD MALONE, PAULINE F. ADAMS, ELEANOR A. CALNAN, EDITH AINGE, ANNIE ARNEIL, DOROTHY J. BARTLETT, MARGARET FOTHERINGHAM.

The Commissioners' only answer to this was a hasty transfer of the signers and the leader, Miss Burns, to the District Jail, where they were put in solitary confinement. The women were not only refused the privileges asked but were denied some of the usual privileges allowed to ordinary criminals.

Generous publicity was given to these reasonable demands,

LUCY BURNS

and a surprisingly wide-spread protest followed the official denial of them. Scores of committees went to the District Commissioners. Telegrams backing up the women's demand again poured in upon all responsible administrators, from President Wilson down. Not even foreign diplomats escaped protest or appeal.

Miss Vera Samarodin sent to the Russian Ambassador the following touching letter, concerning her sister, which is translated from the Russian:—

The Russian Ambassador,
    Washington, D. C.
Excellency:

I am appealing to you to help a young Russian girl imprisoned in the workhouse near Washington. Her name is Nina Samarodin. I have just come from one of the two monthly visits I am allowed to make her, as a member of her family.

The severity and cruelty of the treatment she is receiving at Occoquan are so much greater than she would have to suffer in Russia for the simple political offense she is accused of having committed that I hope you will be able to intercede with the officials of this country for her.

Her offense, aside from the fact that she infringed no law nor disturbed the peace, had only a political aim, and was proved to be political by the words of the judge who sentenced her, for he declared that because of the innocent inscription on her banner he would make her sentence light.

Since her imprisonment she has been forced to wear the dress of a criminal, which she would not in Russia; she has had to eat only the coarse and unpalatable food served the criminal inmates, and has not been allowed, as she would in Russia, to have other food brought to her; nor has she, as she would be there been under the daily care of a physician. She is not permitted to write letters, nor to have free access to books and other implements of study. Nina Samarodin has visibly lost in weight and strength since her imprisonment, and she has a constant headache from hunger.

Her motive in holding the banner by the White House, I

feel, cannot but appeal to you, Excellency, for she says it was the knowledge that her family were fighting in Russia in this great war for democracy, and that she was cut off from serving with them that made her desire to do what she could to help the women of this nation achieve the freedom her own people have.

Will you, if it is within your power, attempt to have her recognized as a political prisoner, and relieve the severity of the treatment she is receiving for obeying this impulse born of her love of liberty and the dictates of her conscience?

I have, Excellency, the honor to be,

Respectfully, your countrywoman,

(Signed) VERA SAMARODIN,

Baltimore, Maryland.

Another Russian, Maria Moravsky, author and poet, who had herself been imprisoned in Czarist Russia and who was touring America at the time of this controversy, expressed her surprise that our suffrage prisoners should be treated as common criminals. She wrote:[1] "I have been twice in the Russian prison; life in the solitary cell was not sweet; but I can assure you it was better than that which American women suffragists must bear.

"We were permitted to read and write; we wore our own clothes; we were not forced to mix with the criminals; we did no work. (Only a few women exiled to Siberia for extremely serious political crimes were compelled to work.) And our guardians and even judges respected us; they felt we were victims, because we struggled for liberty."

The Commissioners, who had to bear the responsibility of an answer to these protests and to the demand of the prisoners, contended to all alike that political prisoners did not exist.

"We shall be happy to establish a precedent," said the women.

"But in America," stammered the Commissioners, "there is no need for such a thing as political prisoners."

[1] Reprinted from The Suffragist, Feb. 8, 1919.

"The very fact that we can be sentenced to such long terms for a political offense shows that there does exist, in fact, a group of people who have come into conflict with state power for dissenting from the prevailing political system," our representatives answered.

We cited definitions of political offenses by eminent criminologists, penologists, sociologists, statesmen and historians. We declared that all authorities on political crime sustained our contention and that we clearly came under the category of political, if any crime. We pointed as proof to James Bryce, George Sigerson, Maurice Parmelee and even to Clemenceau, who defined the distinction between political offenses and common law crimes thus: " . . . theoretically a crime committed in the interest of the criminal is a common law crime, while an offense committed in the public interest is a political crime." [1]

We called to their attention the established custom of special treatment of political prisoners in Russia, France, Italy and even Turkey. [2]

We told them that as early as 1872 the International Prison Congress meeting in London recommended a distinction in the treatment of political and common law criminals and the resolution of recommendation was "agreed upon by the representatives of *all the Powers of Europe and America*—with the tacit concurrence of British and Irish officials." [3]

Mr. John Koren, International Prison Commissioner [4] for the United States, was throughout this agitation making a study of this very problem. As chairman of a Special Commit-

---

[1] Speech before the French Chamber of Deputies May 16, 1876, advocating amnesty for those who participated in the Commune of 1871. From the Annales de la Chambre des Députés, 1876, v. 2, pp. 44-48.

[2] Those interested in the question of political prisoners and their treatment abroad may want to read *Concerning Political Prisoners,* Appendix 6.

[3] Siegerson, *Political Prisoners at Home and Abroad,* p. 10.

[4] Appointed and sponsored by the Department of State as delegate to the International Prison Congress.

tee of the American Prison Association, empowered to investigate the problem of political prisoners for America, he made a report at the annual meeting of the American Prison Association in New York, October, 1919, entitled "The Political Offenders and their Status in Prison" [1] in which he says:

"The political offender . . . must be measured by a different rule, and . . . is a creature of extraordinary and temporary conditions. . . .

"There are times in which the tactics used in the pursuit of political recognition may result in a technical violation of the law for which imprisonment ensues, as witness the suffragist cases in Washington. . . . These militants were completely out of place in a workhouse, . . . they could not be made to submit to discipline fashioned to meet the needs of the derelicts of society, and . . . they therefore destroyed it for the entire institution."

There was no doubt in the official mind but that our claim was just. But the Administration would not grant this demand, as such, of political prisoners. It must continue to persuade public opinion that our offense was not of a political nature; that it was nothing more than unpleasant and unfortunate riotous conduct in the capital. The legend of "a few slightly mad women seeking notoriety" must be sustained. Our demand was never granted, but it was kept up until the last imprisonment and was soon reinforced by additional protest tactics. Our suffrage prisoners, however, made an important contribution toward establishing this reform which others will consummate. They were the first in America to organize and sustain this demand over a long period of time. In America we maintain a most backward policy in dealing with political prisoners. We have neither regulation nor precedent for special treatment of them. Nor have we official flexibility.

[1] Mr. Koren discusses the political offender from the penological, not the social, point of view.

This controversy was at its height in the press and in the public mind when President Wilson sent the following message, through a New York State suffrage leader, on behalf of the approaching New York referendum on state woman suffrage:

"May I not express to you my very deep interest in the campaign in New York for the adoption of woman suffrage, and may I not say that I hope no voter will be influenced in his decision with regard to the great matter by anything the so-called pickets may have done here in Washington. However justly they may have laid themselves open to serious criticism, their action represents, I am sure, so small a fraction of the women of the country who are urging the adoption of woman suffrage that it would be most unfair and argue a narrow view to allow their actions to prejudice the cause itself. I am very anxious to see the great state of New York set a great example in this matter."

This statement showed a political appreciation of the growing power of the movement. Also it would be difficult to prove that the "small fraction" had not shown political wisdom in injecting into the campaign the embarrassment of a controversy which was followed by the above statement of the President. In the meantime he continued to imprison in Washington the "so-called pickets" whom he hoped would not influence the decision of the men voters of New York. It will be remembered, in passing, that the New York voters adopted suffrage at this time, although they had rejected it two years earlier. If the voters of New York were influenced at all by the "so-called pickets," could even President Wilson himself satisfactorily prove that it had been an adverse influence?

CHAPTER 10

THE HUNGER STRIKE—A WEAPON

WHEN the Administration refused to grant the demand of the prisoners and of that portion of the public which supported them, for the rights of political prisoners, it was decided to resort to the ultimate protest-weapon inside prison. A hunger strike was undertaken, not only to reinforce the verbal demand for the rights of political prisoners, but also as a final protest against unjust imprisonment and increasingly long sentences. This brought the Administration face to face with a more acute embarrassment. They had to choose between more stubborn resistance and capitulation. They continued for a while longer on the former path.

Little is known in this country about the weapon of the hunger strike. And so at first it aroused tremendous indignation. "Let them starve to death," said the thoughtless one, who did not perceive that that was the very thing a political administration could least afford to do. "Mad fanatics," said a kindlier critic. The general opinion was that the hunger strike was "foolish."

Few people realize that this resort to the refusal of food is almost as old as civilization. It has always represented a passionate desire to achieve an end. There is not time to go into the religious use of it, which would also be pertinent, but I will cite a few instances which have tragic and amusing likenesses to the suffrage hunger strike.

According to the Brehon Law,[1] which was the code of

[1] Joyce, *A Social History of Ancient Ireland,* Vol. I, Chapter VIII.

ancient Ireland by which justice was administered under ancient Irish monarchs (from the earliest record to the 17th century), it became the duty of an injured person, when all else failed, to inflict punishment directly, for wrong done. "The plaintiff 'fasted on' the defendant." He went to the house of the defendant and sat upon his doorstep, remaining there without food to force the payment of a debt, for example. The debtor was compelled by the weight of custom and public opinion not to let the plaintiff die at his door, and yielded. Or if he did not yield, he was practically outlawed by the community, to the point of being driven away. A man who refused to abide by the custom not only incurred personal danger but lost all character.

If resistance to this form of protest was resorted to it had to take the form of a counter-fast. If the victim of such a protest thought himself being unjustly coerced, he might fast in opposition, "to mitigate or avert the evil."

"Fasting on a man" was also a mode of compelling action of another sort. St. Patrick fasted against King Trian to compel him to have compassion on his [Trian's] slaves.[1] He also fasted against a heretical city to compel it to become orthodox.[2] He fasted against the pagan King Loeguire to "constrain him to his will."[3]

This form of hunger strike was further used under the Brehon Law as compulsion to obtain a request. For example, the Leinstermen on one occasion fasted on St. Columkille till they obtained from him the promise that an extern King should never prevail against them.

It is interesting to note that this form of direct action was adopted because there was no legislative machinery to enforce justice. These laws were merely a collection of customs attaining the force of law by long usage, by hereditary habit, and by

[1] *Tripartite Life of St. Patrick,* CLXXVII, p. 218.
[2] *Ibid.* CLXXVII, p. 418.
[3] *Ibid.* CLXXVII, p. 556.

public opinion. Our resort to this weapon grew out of the same situation. The legislative machinery, while empowered to give us redress, failed to function, and so we adopted the fast.

The institution of fasting on a debtor still exists in the East. It is called by the Hindoos "sitting dharna."

The hunger strike was continuously used in Russia by prisoners to obtain more humane practices toward them. Kropotkin [1] cites an instance in which women prisoners hunger struck to get their babies back. If a child was born to a woman during her imprisonment the babe was immediately taken from her and not returned. Mothers struck and got their babies returned to them.

He cites another successful example in Kharkoff prison in 1878 when six prisoners resolved to hunger strike to death if necessary to win two things—to be allowed exercise and to have the sick prisoners taken out of chains.

There are innumerable instances of hunger strikes, even to death, in Russian prison history. But more often the demands of the strikers were won. Breshkovsky [2] tells of a strike by 17 women against outrage, which elicited the desired promises from the warden.

As early as 1877 members of the Land and Liberty Society [3] imprisoned for peaceful and educational propaganda, in the Schlusselburg Fortress for political prisoners, hunger struck against inhuman prison conditions and frightful brutalities and won their points.

During the suffrage campaign in England this weapon was used for the double purpose of forcing the release of imprisoned militant suffragettes, and of compelling the British government to act.

Among the demonstrations was a revival of the ancient Irish

[1] See *In Russian and French Prisons*, P. Kropotkin.
[2] *For Russia's Freedom*, by Ernest Poole,—An Interview with Breshkovsky.
[3] See *The Russian Bastille*, Simon O. Pollock.

custom by Sylvia Pankhurst, who in addition to her hunger strikes within prison, "fasted on" the doorstep of Premier Asquith to compel him to see a deputation of women on the granting of suffrage to English women. She won.

Irish prisoners have revived the hunger strike to compel either release or trial of untried prisoners and have won. As I write, almost a hundred Irish prisoners detained by England for alleged nationalist activities, but not brought to trial, hunger struck to freedom. As a direct result of this specific hunger strike England has promised a renovation of her practices in dealing with Irish rebels.

And so it was that when we came to the adoption of this accelerating tactic, we had behind us more precedents for winning our point than for losing. We were strong in the knowledge that we could "fast on" President Wilson and his powerful Administration, and compel him to act or "fast back."

Among the prisoners who with Alice Paul led the hunger strike was a very picturesque figure, Rose Winslow (Ruza Wenclawska) of New York, whose parents had brought her in infancy from Poland to become a citizen of "free" America. At eleven she was put at a loom in a Pennsylvania mill, where she wove hosiery for fourteen hours a day until tuberculosis claimed her at nineteen. A poet by nature she developed her mind to the full in spite of these disadvantages, and when she was forced to abandon her loom she became an organizer for the Consumers' League, and later a vivid and eloquent power in the suffrage movement.

Her group preceded Miss Paul's by about a week in prison.

These vivid sketches of Rose Winslow's impressions while in the prison hospital were written on tiny scraps of paper and smuggled out to us, and to her husband during her imprisonment. I reprint them in their original form with cuts but no editing.

"If this thing is necessary we will naturally go through with it. Force is so stupid a weapon. I feel so happy doing my bit for decency—for *our* war, which is after all, real and fundamental."

*　　*　　*　　*

"The women are all so magnificent, so beautiful. Alice Paul is as thin as ever, pale and large-eyed. We have been in solitary for five weeks. There is nothing to tell but that the days go by somehow. I have felt quite feeble the last few days—faint, so that I could hardly get my hair brushed, my arms ached so. But to-day I am well again. Alice Paul and I talk back and forth though we are at opposite ends of the building and a hall door also shuts us apart. But occasionally—thrills—we escape from behind our iron-barred doors and visit. Great laughter and rejoicing!"

*　　*　　*　　*

To her husband:—

"My fainting probably means nothing except that I am not strong after these weeks. I know you won't be alarmed.

"I told about a syphilitic colored woman with one leg. The other one was cut off, having rotted so that it was alive with maggots when she came in. The remaining one is now getting as bad. They are so short of nurses that a little colored girl of twelve, who is here waiting to have her tonsils removed, waits on her. This child and two others share a ward with a syphilitic child of three or four years, whose mother refused to have it at home. It makes you absolutely ill to see it. I am going to break all three windows as a protest against their confining Alice Paul with these!

"Dr. Gannon is chief of a hospital. Yet Alice Paul and I found we had been taking baths in one of the tubs here, in which this syphilitic child, an incurable, who has his eyes bandaged all the time, is also bathed. He has been here a year. Into the room where he lives came yesterday two children to be

operated on for tonsillitis. They also bathed in the same tub.
The syphilitic woman has been in that room seven months.
Cheerful mixing, isn't it? The place is alive with roaches,
crawling all over the walls, everywhere. I found one in my bed
the other day. . . ."

*   *   *   *

"There is great excitement about my two syphilitics. Each
nurse is being asked whether she told me. So, as in all institutions where an unsanitary fact is made public, no effort is
made to make the wrong itself right. All hands fall to, to find
the culprit, who made it known, and he is punished."

*   *   *   *

"Alice Paul is in the psychopathic ward. She dreaded
forcible feeding frightfully, and I hate to think how she must
be feeling. I had a nervous time of it, gasping a long time
afterward, and my stomach rejecting during the process. I
spent a bad, restless night, but otherwise I am all right. The
poor soul who fed me got liberally besprinkled during the process. I heard myself making the most hideous sounds. . . .
One feels so forsaken when one lies prone and people shove a
pipe down one's stomach."

*   *   *   *

"This morning but for an astounding tiredness, I am
all right. I am waiting to see what happens when the President
realizes that brutal bullying isn't quite a statesmanlike method
for settling a demand for justice at home. At least, if men are
supine enough to endure, women—to their eternal glory—are
not.

"They took down the boarding from Alice Paul's window
yesterday, I heard. It is so delicious about Alice and me. Over
in the jail a rumor began that I was considered insane and
would be examined. Then came Doctor White, and said he had
come to see 'the thyroid case.' When they left we argued about
the matter, neither of us knowing which was considered 'suspi-

cious.' She insisted it was she, and, as it happened, she was right. Imagine any one thinking Alice Paul needed to be 'under observation!' The thick-headed idiots!''

* * * *

"Yesterday was a bad day for me in feeding. I was vomiting continually during the process. The tube has developed an irritation somewhere that is painful.

"Never was there a sentence [1] like ours for such an offense as ours, even in England. No woman ever got it over there even for tearing down buildings. And during all that agitation *we* were busy saying that never would such things happen in the United States. The men told us they would not endure such frightfulness."

* * * *

"Mary Beard and Helen Todd were allowed to stay only a minute, and I cried like a fool. I am getting over that habit, I think.

"I fainted again last night. I just fell flop over in the bathroom where I was washing my hands and was led to bed when I recovered, by a nurse. I lost consciousness just as I got there again. I felt horribly faint until 12 o'clock, then fell asleep for awhile."

* * * *

"I was getting frantic because you seemed to think Alice was with me in the hospital. She was in the psychopathic ward. The same doctor feeds us both, and told me. Don't let them tell you we take this well. Miss Paul vomits much. I do, too, except when I'm not nervous, as I have been every time against my will. I try to be less feeble-minded. It's the nervous reaction, and I can't control it much. I don't imagine bathing one's food in tears very good for one.

"We think of the coming feeding all day. It is horrible.

---

[1] Sentence of seven months for "obstructing traffic."

The doctor thinks I take it well. I hate the thought of Alice Paul and the others if I take it well."

*   *   *   *

"We still get no mail; we are 'insubordinate.' It's strange, isn't it; if you ask for food fit to eat, as we did, you are 'insubordinate'; and if you refuse food you are 'insubordinate.' Amusing. I am really all right. If this continues very long I perhaps won't be. I am interested to see how long our so-called 'splendid American men' will stand for this form of discipline.

"All news cheers one marvelously because it is hard to feel anything but a bit desolate and forgotten here in this place.

"All the officers here know we are making this hunger strike that women fighting for liberty may be considered political prisoners; we have told them. God knows we don't want other women ever to have to do this over again."

*   *   *   *

There have been sporadic and isolated cases of hunger strikes in this country but to my knowledge ours was the first to be organized and sustained over a long period of time. We shall see in subsequent chapters how effective this weapon was.

CHAPTER 11

THE Administration tried in another way to stop picketing. It sentenced the leader, Alice Paul, to the absurd and desperate sentence of seven months in the Washington jail for "obstructing traffic."

With the "leader" safely behind the bars for so long a time, the agitation would certainly weaken! So thought the Administration! To their great surprise, however, in the face of that reckless and extreme sentence, the longest picket line of the entire campaign formed at the White House in the late afternoon of November 10th. Forty-one women picketed in protest against this wanton persecution of their leader, as well as against the delay in passing the amendment. Face to face with an embarrassing number of prisoners the Administration used its wits and decided to reduce the number to a manageable size before imprisoning this group. Failing of that they tried still another way out. They resorted to imprisonment with terrorism.

In order to show how widely representative of the nation this group of pickets was, I give its personnel complete:

First Group

New York—Mrs. John Winters Brannan, Miss Belle Sheinberg, Mrs. L. H. Hornsby, Mrs. Paula Jakobi, Mrs. Cynthia Cohen, Miss M. Tilden Burritt, Miss Dorothy Day, Mrs. Henry Butterworth, Miss Cora Week, Mrs. P. B. Johns, Miss

Elizabeth Hamilton, Mrs. Ella O. Guilford, New York City; Miss Amy Juengling, Miss Hattie Kruger, Buffalo.

Second Group

Massachusetts—Mrs. Agnes H. Morey, Brookline; Mrs. William Bergen and Miss Camilla Whitcomb, Worcester; Miss Ella Findeisen, Lawrence; Miss L. J. C. Daniels, Boston.

New Jersey—Mrs. George Scott, Montclair.

Pennsylvania—Mrs. Lawrence Lewis, Miss Elizabeth McShane, Miss Katherine Lincoln, Philadelphia.

Third Group

California—Mrs. William Kent, Kentfield.

Oregon—Miss Alice Gram, Miss Betty Gram, Portland.

Utah—Mrs. R. B. Quay, Mrs. T. C. Robertson, Salt Lake City.

Colorado—Mrs. Eva Decker, Colorado Springs, Mrs. Genevieve Williams, Manitou.

Fourth Group

Indiana—Mrs. Charles W. Barnes, Indianapolis.

Oklahoma—Mrs. Kate Stafford, Oklahoma City.

Minnesota—Mrs. J. H. Short, Minneapolis.

Iowa—Mrs. A. N. Beim, Des Moines; Mrs. Catherine Martinette, Eagle Grove.

Fifth Group

New York—Miss Lucy Burns, New York City.

District of Columbia—Mrs. Harvey Wiley.

Louisiana—Mrs. Alice M. Cosu, New Orleans.

Maryland—Miss Mary Bartlett Dixon, Easton; Miss Julia Emory, Baltimore.

Florida—Mrs. Mary I. Nolan, Jacksonville.

There were exceptionally dramatic figures in this group. Mrs. Mary Nolan of Florida, seventy-three years old, frail in

health but militant in spirit, said she had come to take her
place with the women struggling for liberty in the same spirit
that her revolutionary ancestor, Eliza Zane, had carried bullets
to the fighters in the war for independence.

Mrs. Harvey Wiley looked appealing and beautiful as she
said in court, "We took this action with great consecration of
spirit, with willingness to sacrifice personal liberty for all the
women of the country."

Judge Mullowny addressed the prisoners with many high-
sounding words about the seriousness of obstructing the traffic
in the national capital, and inadvertently slipped into a discourse on Russia, and the dangers of revolution. We always
wondered why the government was not clever enough to eliminate political discourses, at least during trials, where the
offenders were charged with breaking a slight regulation. But
their minds were too full of the political aspect of our offense
to conceal it. "The truth of the situation is that the court has
not been given power to meet it," the judge lamented. "It is
very, very puzzling—I find you guilty of the offense charged,
but will take the matter of sentence under advisement."

And so the "guilty" pickets were summarily released.

The Administration did not relish the incarceration of
forty-one women for another reason than limited housing
accommodations. Forty-one women representing sixteen states
in the union might create a considerable political dislocation.
But these same forty-one women were determined to force the
Administration to take its choice. It could allow them to continue their peaceful agitation or it could stand the reaction
which was bound to come from imprisoning them. And so the
forty-one women returned to the White House gates to resume
their picketing. They stood guard several minutes before the
police, taken unawares, could summon sufficient force to arrest
them, and commandeer enough cars to carry them to police
headquarters. As the Philadelphia *North American* pointed

out: "There was no disorder. The crowd waited with interest and in a noticeably friendly spirit to see what would happen. There were frequent references to the pluck of the silent sentinels."

The following morning the women were ordered by Judge Mullowny to "come back on Friday. I am not yet prepared to try the case."

Logic dictated that either we had a right to stand at the gates with our banners or we did not have that right; but the Administration was not interested in logic. It had to stop picketing. Whether this was done legally or illegally, logically or illogically, clumsily or dexterously, was of secondary importance. Picketing must be stopped!

Using their welcome release to continue their protest, the women again marched with their banners to the White House in an attempt to picket. Again they were arrested. No one who saw that line will ever forget the impression it made, not only on friends of the suffragists, but on the general populace of Washington, to see these women force with such magnificent defiance the hand of a wavering Administration. On the following morning they were sentenced to from six days to six months in prison. Miss Burns received six months.

In pronouncing the lightest sentence upon Mrs. Nolan, the judge said that he did so on account of her age. He urged her, however, to pay her fine, hinting that jail might be too severe on her and might bring on death. At this suggestion, tiny Mrs. Nolan pulled herself up on her toes and said with great dignity: "Your Honor, I have a nephew fighting for democracy in France. He is offering his life for his country. I should be ashamed if I did not join these brave women in their fight for democracy in America. I should be proud of the honor to die in prison for the liberty of American women." Even the judge seemed moved by her beautiful and simple spirit.

In spite of the fact that the women were sentenced to serve

their sentences in the District Jail, where they would join Miss Paul and her companions, all save one were immediately sent to Occoquan workhouse.

It had been agreed that the demand to be treated as political prisoners, inaugurated by previous pickets, should be continued, and that failing to secure such rights they would unanimously refuse to eat food or do prison labor.

Any words of mine would be inadequate to tell the story of the prisoners' reception at the Occoquan workhouse. The following is the statement of Mrs. Nolan, dictated upon her release, in the presence of Mr. Dudley Field Malone:

It was about half past seven at night when we got to Occoquan workhouse. A woman [Mrs. Herndon] was standing behind a desk when we were brought into this office, and there were five or six men also in the room. Mrs. Lewis, who spoke for all of us, . . . said she must speak to Whittaker, the superintendent of the place.

"You'll sit here all night, then," said Mrs. Herndon.

I saw men begin to come upon the porch, but I didn't think anything about it. Mrs. Herndon called my name, but I did not answer. . . .

Suddenly the door literally burst open and Whittaker burst in like a tornado; some men followed him. We could see a crowd of them on the porch. They were not in uniform. They looked as much like tramps as anything. They seemed to come in—and in—and in. One had a face that made me think of an ourang-outang. Mrs. Lewis stood up. Some of us had been sitting and lying on the floor, we were so tired. She had hardly begun to speak, saying we demanded to be treated as political prisoners, when Whittaker said:

"You shut up. I have men here to handle you." Then he shouted, "Seize her!" I turned and saw men spring toward her, and then some one screamed, "They have taken Mrs. Lewis."

A man sprang at me and caught me by the shoulder. I am used to remembering a bad foot, which I have had for years, and I remember saying, "I'll come with you; don't drag me;

MISS MATILDA YOUNG—YOUNGEST PICKET
MRS. MARY NOLAN—OLDEST PICKET

I have a lame foot." But I was jerked down the steps and away into the dark. I didn't have my feet on the ground. I guess that saved me. I heard Mrs. Cosu, who was being dragged along with me, call, "Be careful of your foot."

Out of doors it was very dark. The building to which they took us was lighted up as we came to it. I only remember the American flag flying above it because it caught the light from a window in the wing. We were rushed into a large room that we found opened on a large hall with stone cells on each side. They were perfectly dark. Punishment cells is what they call them. Mine was filthy. It had no window save a slip at the top and no furniture but an iron bed covered with a thin straw pad, and an open toilet flushed from outside the cell. . . .

In the hall outside was a man called Captain Reems. He had on a uniform and was brandishing a thick stick and shouting as we were shoved into the corridor, "Damn you, get in here."

I saw Dorothy Day brought in. She is a frail girl. The two men handling her were twisting her arms above her head. Then suddenly they lifted her up and banged her down over the arm of an iron bench—twice. As they ran me past, she was lying there with her arms out, and we heard one of the men yell, "The —— suffrager! My mother ain't no suffrager. I'll put you through ——."

At the end of the corridor they pushed me through a door. Then I lost my balance and fell against the iron bed. Mrs. Cosu struck the wall. Then they threw in two mats and two dirty blankets. There was no light but from the corridor. The door was barred from top to bottom. The walls and floors were brick or stone cemented over. Mrs. Cosu would not let me lie on the floor. She put me on the couch and stretched out on the floor on one of the two pads they threw in. We had only lain there a few minutes, trying to get our breath, when Mrs. Lewis, doubled over and handled like a sack of something, was literally thrown in. Her head struck the iron bed. We thought she was dead. She didn't move. We were crying over her as we lifted her to the pad on my bed, when we heard Miss Burns call:

"Where is Mrs. Nolan?"

I replied, "I am here."

Mrs. Cosu called out, "They have just thrown Mrs. Lewis in here, too."

At this Mr. Whittaker came to the door and told us not to dare to speak, or he would put the brace and bit in our mouths and the straitjacket on our bodies. We were so terrified we kept very still. Mrs. Lewis was not unconscious; she was only stunned. But Mrs. Cosu was desperately ill as the night wore on. She had a bad heart attack and was then vomiting. We called and called. We asked them to send our own doctor, because we thought she was dying. . . . They [the guards] paid no attention. A cold wind blew in on us from the outside, and we three lay there shivering and only half conscious until morning.

"One at a time, come out," we heard some one call at the barred door early in the morning. I went first. I bade them both good-by. I didn't know where I was going or whether I would ever see them again. They took me to Mr. Whittaker's office, where he called my name.

"You're Mrs. Mary Nolan," said Whittaker.

"You're posted," said I.

"Are you willing to put on prison dress and go to the workroom?" said he.

I said, "No."

"Don't you know now that I am Mr. Whittaker, the superintendent?" he asked.

"Is there any age limit to your workhouse?" I said. "Would a woman of seventy-three or a child of two be sent here?"

I think I made him think. He motioned to the guard.

"Get a doctor to examine her," he said.

In the hospital cottage I was met by Mrs. Herndon and taken to a little room with two white beds and a hospital table.

"You can lie down if you want to," she said.

I took off my coat and hat. I just lay down on the bed and fell into a kind of stupor. It was nearly noon and I had had no food offered me since the sandwiches our friends brought us in the courtroom at noon the day before.

The doctor came and examined my heart. Then he examined my lame foot. It had a long blue bruise above the ankle, where they had knocked me as they took me across the night before. He asked me what caused the bruise. I said, "Those fiends when they dragged me to the cell last night." It was paining me. He asked if I wanted liniment and I said only hot water. They brought that, and I noticed they did not lock the door. A negro trusty was there. I fell back again into the same stupor.

The next day they brought me some toast and a plate of food, the first I had been offered in over 36 hours. I just looked at the food and motioned it away. It made me sick. . . . I was released on the sixth day and passed the dispensary as I came out. There were a group of my friends, Mrs. Brannan and Mrs. Morey and many others. They had on coarse striped dresses and big, grotesque, heavy shoes. I burst into tears as they led me away.

(Signed) MARY I. NOLAN.

November 21, 1917.

The day following their commitment to Occoquan Mr. O'Brien, of counsel, was directed to see the women, to ascertain their condition. Friends and relatives were alarmed, as not a line of news had been allowed to penetrate to the world. Mr. O'Brien was denied admission and forced to come back to Washington without any report whatsoever.

The next day Mr. O'Brien again attempted to see his clients, as did also the mother of Miss Matilda Young, the youngest prisoner in Mr. Whittaker's care, and Miss Katherine Morey, who went asking to see her mother. Miss Morey was held under armed guard half a mile from the prison. Admission was denied to all of them.

The terrible anxiety at Headquarters was not relieved the third day by a report brought from the workhouse by one of the marines stationed at Quantico Station, Virginia, who had been summoned to the workhouse on the night the women arrived. He brought news that unknown tortures were going on. Mr. O'Brien immediately forced his way through by a court order, and brought back to Headquarters the astounding news of the campaign of terrorism which had started the moment the prisoners had arrived, and which was being continued at that moment. Miss Lucy Burns, who had asssumed responsibility for the welfare of the women, had managed to secrete small scraps of paper and a tiny pencil, and jot down briefly the day by day events at the workhouse.

This week of brutality, which rivaled old Russia, if it did not outstrip it, was almost the blackest page in the Administration's cruel fight against women.

Here are some of the scraps of Miss Burn's day-by-day log, smuggled out of the workhouse. Miss Burns is so gifted a writer that I feel apologetic for using these scraps in their raw form, but I know she will forgive me.

WEDNESDAY, NOVEMBER 14. Demanded to see Superintendent Whittaker. Request refused. Mrs. Herndon, the matron, said we would have to wait up all night. One of the men guards said he would "put us in sardine box and put mustard on us." Superintendent Whittaker came at 9 p. m. He refused to hear our demand for political rights. Seized by guards from behind, flung off my feet, and shot out of the room. All of us were seized by men guards and dragged to cells in men's part. Dorothy Day was roughly used—back twisted. Mrs. Mary A. Nolan (73-year-old picket from Jacksonville, Florida) flung into cell. Mrs. Lawrence Lewis shot past my cell. I slept with Dorothy Day in a single bed. I was handcuffed all night and manacled to the bars part of the time for asking the others how they were, and was threatened with a straitjacket and a buckle gag.

THURSDAY, NOVEMBER 16. . . . Asked for Whittaker, who came. He seized Julia Emory by the back of her neck and threw her into the room very brutally. She is a little girl. I asked for counsel to learn the status of the case. I was told to "shut up," and was again threatened with a straitjacket and a buckle gag. Later I was taken to put on prison clothes, refused and resisted strenuously. I was then put in a room where delirium tremens patients are kept.

On the seventh day, when Miss Lucy Burns and Mrs. Lawrence Lewis were so weak that Mr. Whittaker feared their death, they were forcibly fed and taken immediately to the jail in Washington. Of the experience Mrs. Lewis wrote:—

I was seized and laid on my back, where five people held me, a young colored woman leaping upon my knees, which seemed to break under the weight. Dr. Gannon then forced the tube through my lips and down my throat, I gasping and suffocating with the agony of it. I didn't know where to breathe from and everything turned black when the fluid began pouring in. I was moaning and making the most awful sounds quite against my will, for I did not wish to disturb my friends in the next room. Finally the tube was withdrawn. I lay motionless. After a while I was dressed and carried in a chair to a waiting automobile, laid on the back seat and driven into Washington to the jail hospital. Previous to the feeding I had been forcibly examined by Dr. Gannon, I struggling and protesting that I wished a woman physician.

Of this experience, Miss Burns wrote on tiny scraps of paper:

WEDNESDAY, 12 m.   Yesterday afternoon at about four or five, Mrs. Lewis and I were asked to go to the operating room. Went there and found our clothes. Told we were to go to Washington. No reason as usual. When we were dressed, Dr. Gannon appeared, and said he wished to examine us. Both refused. Were dragged through halls by force, our clothing partly removed by force, and we were examined, heart tested, blood pressure and pulse taken. Of course such data was of no value after such a struggle. Dr. Gannon told me then I must be fed. Was stretched on bed, two doctors, matron, four colored prisoners present, Whittaker in hall. I was held down by five people at legs, arms, and head. I refused to open mouth. Gannon pushed tube up left nostril. I turned and twisted my head all I could, but he managed to push it up. It hurts nose and throat very much and makes nose bleed freely. Tube drawn out covered with blood. Operation leaves one very sick. Food dumped directly into stomach feels like a ball

of lead. Left nostril, throat and muscles of neck very sore all
night. After this I was brought into the hospital in an ambulance. Mrs. Lewis and I placed in same room. Slept hardly
at all. This morning Dr. Ladd appeared with his tube. Mrs.
Lewis and I said we would not be forcibly fed. Said he would
call in men guards and force us to submit. Went away and
we were not fed at all this morning. We hear them outside
now cracking eggs.

With Miss Burns and Mrs. Lewis, who were regarded as
leaders in the hunger strike protest, removed to the district
jail, Mr. Whittaker and his staff at Occoquan began a systematic attempt to break down the morale of the hunger
strikers. Each one was called to the mat and interrogated.

"Will you work?"—"Will you put on prison clothes?"—
"Will you eat?"—"Will you stop picketing?"—"Will you go
without paying your fine and promise never to picket again?"

How baffled he must have been! The answer was definite
and final. Their resistance was superb.

"One of the few warning incidents during the gray days of
our imprisonment was the unexpected sympathy and understanding of one of the government doctors," wrote Miss Betty
Gram of Portland, Oregon.

" 'This is the most magnificent sacrifice I have ever seen
made for a principle [he said]. I never believed that American
women would care so much about freedom. I have seen women
in Russia undergo extreme suffering for their ideals, but unless
I had seen this with my own eyes I never would have believed it.
My sister hunger struck in Russia, where she was imprisoned for
refusing to reveal the whereabouts of two of her friends indicted
for a government offense. She was fed after three days. You
girls are on your ninth day of hunger strike and your condition
is critical. It is a great pity that such women should be subjected to this treatment. I hope that you will carry your point
and force the hand of the government soon'."

Left to Right

MISS MARION BURRITT   MRS. ALICE COSU
MRS. HARVEY W. WILEY   MRS. R. B. QUAY
MRS. JOHN WINTERS BRANNAN   MRS. A. N. BEIM
MRS. HENRY BUTTERWORTH   MRS. PHOEBE SCOTT
MRS. CYNTHIA COHEN

Left to Right

MRS. CATHERINE MARTINETTE   MISS CORA WEEK
MRS. WILLIAM KENT   MISS AMY JUENGLING
MISS MARY BARTLETT DIXON   MISS HATTIE KRUGER
MRS. C. T. ROBERTSON   MISS BELLE SHEINBERG
MISS JULIA EMORY

FACE JAIL

Left to Right

Mrs. Peggy Johns	Miss Alice Gram
Mrs. Mary Nolan	Mrs. W. Bergen
Miss Betty Gram	Miss Camilla Whitcomb
Miss Ella Findeisen	Mrs. Charles W. Barnes
Mrs. Kate Stafford	Mrs. Ella Guilford

Left to Right

Miss Elizabeth Hamilton	Miss Elizabeth McShane
Miss Catherine Lincoln	Mrs. Lawrence Lewis
Mrs. Eva Decker	Mrs. Paula Jakobi
Mrs. J. H. Short	Miss Dorothy Day
Mrs. Genevieve Williams	Mrs. L. H. Hornsby

The mother of Matilda Young, the youngest picket, anxiously appealed to Mr. Tumulty, Secretary to President Wilson, and a family friend, to be allowed to see the President and ask for a special order to visit her daughter. Failing to secure this, she went daily to Mr. Tumulty's office asking if he himself would not intercede for her. Mr. Tumulty assured her that her daughter was in safe hands, that she need give herself no alarm, the stories of the inhuman treatment at Occoquan were false, and that she must not believe them. Finally Mrs. Young pleaded to be allowed to send additional warm clothing to her daughter, whom she knew to be too lightly clad for the vigorous temperature of November. Mr. Tumulty assured her that the women were properly clothed, and refused to permit the clothing to be sent. The subsequent stories of the women showed what agonies they had endured, because they were inadequately clad, from the dampness of the cells into which they were thrown.

Mrs. John Winters Brannan was among the women who endured the "night of terror." Mrs. Brannan is the daughter of Charles A. Dana, founder of the New York *Sun* and that great American patriot of liberty who was a trusted associate and counselor of Abraham Lincoln. Mrs. Brannan, life-long suffragist, is an aristocrat of intellect and feeling, who has always allied herself with libertarian movements. This was her second term of imprisonment. She wrote a comprehensive affidavit of her experience. After narrating the events which led up to the attack, she continues:

Superintendent Whittaker . . . then shouted out in a loud tone of voice, "Seize these women, take them off, that one, that one,—take her off." The guards rushed forward and an almost indescribable scene of violent confusion ensued. I . . . saw one of the guards seize her [Lucy Burns] by the arms, twist or force them back of her, and one or two other guards seize her by the shoulders, shaking her violently. . . .

I then . . . took up my heavy sealskin coat, which was lying by, and put it on, in order to prepare myself if attacked. . . . I was trembling at the time and was stunned with terror at the situation as it had developed, and said to the superintendent, "I will give my name under protest," and started to walk towards the desk whereon lay the books. The superintendent shouted to me, "Oh, no, you won't; don't talk about protest; I won't have any of that nonsense."

I . . . saw the guards seizing the different women of the party with the utmost violence, the furniture being overturned and the room a scene of the utmost disturbance. I saw Miss Lincoln lying on the floor, with every appearance of having just been thrown down by the two guards who were standing over her in a menacing attitude. Seeing the general disturbance, I gave up all idea of giving my name at the desk, and instinctively joined my companions, to go with them and share whatever was in store for them. The whole group of women were thrown, dragged or herded out of the office on to the porch, down the steps to the ground, and forced to cross the road . . . to the Administration Building.

During all of this time, . . . Superintendent Whittaker was . . . directing the whole attack. . . .

. . . All of us were thrown into different cells in the men's prison, I being put in one with four other women, the cell containing a narrow bed and one chair, which was immediately removed. . . .

During the time that we were being forced into the cells the guards kept up an uproar, shouting, banging the iron doors, clanging bars, making a terrifying noise.

I and one of my companions were lying down on the narrow bed, on which were a blanket and one pillow. The door of the cell was opened and a mattress and a blanket being thrown in, the door was violently banged to. . . . My other . . . companions arranged the mattress on the floor and lay down, covering themselves with the blanket.

. . . I looked across the corridor and saw Miss Lincoln, . . . and asked her whether she was all right, being anxious to know whether she had been hurt by the treatment in the office building. . . . Instantly Superintendent Whittaker rushed forward, shouting at me, "Stop that; not another word from your mouth, or I will handcuff you, gag you and put you in a straitjacket. . . .

I wish to state again that the cells into which we were put were situated in the men's prison. There was no privacy for the women, and if any of us wished to undress we would be subject to the view or observation of the guards who remained in the corridor and who could at any moment look at us. . . . Furthermore, the water closets were in full view of the corridor where Superintendent Whittaker and the guards were moving about. The flushing of these closets could only be done from the corridor, and we were forced to ask the guards to do this for us,—the men who had shortly before attacked us. . . .

None of the matrons or women attendants appeared at any time that night. No water was brought to us for washing, no food was offered to us. . . .

I was exhausted by what I had seen and been through, and spent the night in absolute terror of further attack and of what might still be in store for us. I thought of the young girls who were with us and feared for their safety. The guards . . . acted brutal in the extreme, incited to their brutal conduct towards us, . . . by the superintendent. I thought of the offense with which we had been charged,—merely that of obstructing traffic,—and felt that the treatment that we had received was out of all proportion to the offense with which we were charged, and that the superintendent, the matron and guards would not have dared to act towards us as they had acted unless they relied upon the support of higher authorities. It seemed to me that everything had been done from the time we reached the workhouse to terrorize us, and my fear lest the extreme of outrage would be worked upon the young girls of our party became intense.

It is impossible for me to describe the terror of that night. . . .

The affidavit then continues with the story of how Mrs. Brannan was compelled the following morning to put on prison clothes, was given a cup of skimmed milk and a slice of toast, and then taken to the sewing room, where she was put to work sewing on the underdrawers of the male prisoners.

I was half fainting all of that day and . . . requested permission to lie down, feeling so ill. . . . I could not sleep, having a sense of constant danger. . . . I was almost paralyzed and in wretched physical condition.

On Friday afternoon Mrs. Herndon [matron] . . . led us through some woods nearby, for about three-quarters of a mile, seven of us being in the party. We were so exhausted and weary that we were obliged to stop constantly to rest. On our way back from the walk we heard the baying of hounds very near us in the woods. The matron said, "You must hurry, the bloodhounds are loose." One of the party, Miss Findeisen, asked whether they would attack us, to which the matron replied, "That is just what they would do," and hurried us along. The baying grew louder and nearer at times and then more distant, as the dogs rushed back and forth, and this went on until we reached the sewing room. The effect of this upon our nerves can better be imagined than described. . . .

Every conceivable lie was tried in an effort to force the women to abandon their various form of resistance. They were told that no efforts were being made from the outside to reach them, and that their attorney had been called off the case. Each one was told that she was the only one hunger striking. Each one was told that all the others had put on prison clothes and were working. Although they were separated from one another they suspected the lies and remained strong in their resistance. After Mr. O'Brien's one visit and the subsequent reports in the press he was thereafter refused admission to the workhouse.

The judge had sentenced these women to the jail, but the District Commissioners had ordered them committed to the workhouse. It was evident that the Administration was anxious to keep this group away from Alice Paul and her companions, as they counted on handling the rebellion more easily in two groups than one.

Meanwhile the condition of the prisoners in the workhouse grew steadily worse. It was imperative that we force the Administration to take them out of the custody of Superintendent Whittaker immediately. We decided to take the only course open—to obtain a writ of habeas corpus. A hurried journey by counsel to United States District Judge Waddill of Norfolk, Virginia, brought the writ. It compelled the government to bring the prisoners into court and show cause why they should not be returned to the district jail. This conservative Southern judge said of the petition for the writ, "It is shocking and blood-curdling."

There followed a week more melodramatic than the most stirring moving picture film. Although the writ had been applied for in the greatest secrecy, a detective suddenly appeared to accompany Mr. O'Brien from Washington to Norfolk, during his stay in Norfolk, and back to Washington. Telephone wires at our headquarters were tapped.

It was evident that the Administration was cognizant of every move in this procedure before it was executed. No sooner was our plan decided upon than friends of the Administration besought us to abandon the habeas corpus proceedings. One member of the Administration sent an emissary to our headquarters with the following appeal:

"If you will only drop these proceedings, I can absolutely guarantee you that the prisoners will be removed from the workhouse to the jail in a week."

"In a week? They may be dead by that time," we answered. "We cannot wait."

"But I tell you, you must not proceed."

"Why this mysterious week?" we asked. "Why not to-morrow? Why not instantly?"

"I can only tell you that I have a positive guarantee of the District Commissioners that the women will be removed," he said in conclusion. We refused to grant his request.

There were three reasons why the authorities wished for a week's time. They were afraid to move the women in their

weakened condition and before the end of the week they hoped
to increase their facilities for forcible feeding at the workhouse.
They also wished to conceal the treatment of the women, the
exposure of which would be inevitable in any court proceedings.
And lastly, the Administration was anxious to avoid opening up
the whole question of the legality of the very existence of the
workhouse in Virginia.

Persons convicted in the District for acts committed in
violation of District law were transported to Virginia—alien
territory—to serve their terms. It was a moot point whether
prisoners were so treated with sufficient warrant in law. Eminent jurists held that the District had no right to convict a person under its laws and commit that person to confinement in
another state. They contended that sentence imposed upon a
person for unlawful acts in the District should be executed in
the District.

Hundreds of persons who had been convicted in the District
of Columbia and who had served their sentences in Virginia had
been without money or influence enough to contest this doubtful
procedure in the courts. The Administration was alarmed.

We quickened our pace. A member of the Administration
rushed his attorney as courier to the women in the workhouse
to implore them not to consent to the habeas corpus proceedings. He was easily admitted and tried to extort from one prisoner at a time a promise to reject the plan. The women suspected his solicitude and refused to make any promise whatsoever without first being allowed to see their own attorney.

We began at once to serve the writ. Ordinarily this would
be an easy thing to do. But for us it developed into a very
difficult task. A deputy marshal must serve the writ. Counsel
sought a deputy. For miles around Washington, not one was
to be found at his home or lodgings. None could be reached
by telephone.

Meanwhile Mr. Whittaker had sped from the premises of

PRISONERS RELEASED

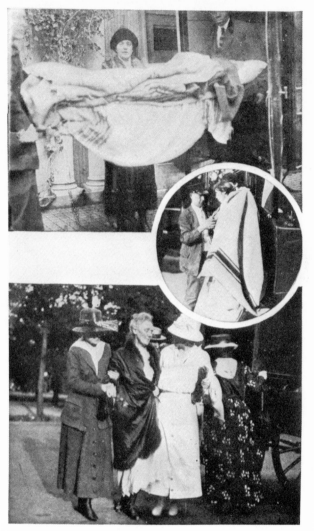

Top—Miss Elizabeth Kalb on Stretcher*
Center—Miss Kate Heffelfinger Brought to Headquarters
by Jail Attendant
Lower—Mrs. Lawrence Lewis Assisted from Ambulance

the workhouse to the District, where he kept himself discreetly hidden for several days. When a deputy was found, six attempts were made to serve the writ. All failed. Finally by a ruse, Mr. Whittaker was caught at his home late at night. He was aroused to a state of violent temper and made futile threats of reprisal when he learned that he must produce the suffrage prisoners at the Court in Alexandria, Virginia, on the day of November twenty-third.

CHAPTER 12

Great passions when they run through a whole population, inevitably find a great spokesman. A people cannot remain dumb which is moved by profound impulses of conviction; and when spokesmen and leaders are found, effective concert of action seems to follow as naturally. Men spring together for common action under a common impulse which has taken hold upon their very natures, and governments presently find that they have those to reckon with who know not only what they want, but also the most effective means of making governments uncomfortable until they get it. Governments find themselves, in short, in the presence of *Agitation,* of systematic movements of opinion, which do not merely flare up in spasmodic flames and then die down again, but burn with an accumulating ardor which can be checked and extinguished only by removing the grievances and abolishing the unacceptable institutions which are its fuel. Casual discontent can be allayed, but agitation fixed upon conviction cannot be. To fight it is merely to augment its force. It burns irrepressibly in every public assembly; quiet it there, and it gathers head at street corners; drive it thence, and it smoulders in private dwellings, in social gatherings, in every covert of talk, only to break forth more violently than ever because denied vent and air. It must be reckoned with. . . .

Governments have been very resourceful in parrying agitation, in diverting it, in seeming to yield to it, and then cheating it of its objects, in tiring it out or evading it. . . . But the end, whether it comes soon or late, is quite certain to be always the same.

—*"Constitutional Government in the United States."*
WOODROW WILSON, PH.D., LL.D.,
President of Princeton University.

THE special session of the 65th Congress, known as the "War Congress," adjourned in October, 1917, having passed every measure recommended as a war measure by the President.

In addition, it found time to protect by law migratory birds, to appropriate forty-seven million dollars for deepening rivers and harbors, and to establish more federal judgeships. No honest person would say that lack of time and pressure of

210

war legislation had prevented its consideration of the suffrage measure. If one-hundredth part of the time consumed by its members in spreading the wings of the overworked eagle, and in uttering to bored ears "home-made" patriotic verse, had been spent in considering the liberty of women, this important legislation could have been dealt with. Week after week Congress met only for three days, and then often merely for prayer and a few hours of purposeless talking.

We had asked for liberty, and had got a suffrage committee appointed in the House to consider the pros and cons of suffrage, and a favorable report in the Senate from the Committee on Woman Suffrage, nothing more.

On the very day and hour of the adjournment of the special session of the War Congress, Alice Paul led eleven women to the White House gates to protest against the Administration's allowing its lawmakers to go home without action on the suffrage amendment.

Two days later Alice Paul and her colleagues were put on trial.

Many times during previous trials I had heard the District Attorney for the government shake his finger at Miss Paul and say, "We'll get you yet. . . . Just wait; and when we do, we'll give you a year!"

It was reported from very authentic sources that Attorney General Gregory had, earlier in the agitation, seriously considered arresting Miss Paul for the Administration, on the charge of conspiracy to break the law. We were told this plan was abandoned because, as one of the Attorney General's staff put it, "No jury would convict her."

However, here she was in their hands, in the courtroom.

Proceedings opened with the customary formality. The eleven prisoners sat silently at the bar, reading their morning papers, or a book, or enjoying a moment of luxurious idleness, oblivious of the comical movements of a perturbed court.

Nothing in the world so baffles the pompous dignity of a court as non-resistant defendants. The judge cleared his throat and the attendants made meaningless gestures.

"Will the prisoners stand up and be sworn?"

They will not.

"Will they question witnesses?"

They will not.

"Will they speak in their own behalf?"

The slender, quiet-voiced Quaker girl arose from her seat. The crowded courtroom pressed forward breathlessly. She said calmly and with unconcern: "We do not wish to make any plea before this court. We do not consider ourselves subject to this court, since as an unenfranchised class we have nothing to do with the making of the laws which have put us in this position."

What a disconcerting attitude to take! Miss Paul sat down as quietly and unexpectedly as she had arisen. The judge moved uneasily in his chair. The gentle way in which it was said was disarming. Would the judge hold them in contempt? He had not time to think. His part of the comedy he had expected to run smoothly, and here was this defiant little woman calmly stating that we were not subject to the court, and that we would therefore have nothing to do with the proceedings. The murmurs had grown to a babel of conversation. A sharp rap of the gavel restored order and permitted Judge Mullowny to say: "Unfortunately, I am here to support the laws that are made by Congress, and, of course, I am bound by those laws; and you are bound by them as long as you live in this country, notwithstanding the fact that you do not recognize the law."

Everybody strained his ears for the sentence. The Administration had threatened to "get" the leader. Would they dare?

Another pause!

"I shall suspend sentence for the time being," came solemnly from the judge.

Was it that they did not dare confine Miss Paul? Were they beginning actually to perceive the real strength of the movement and the protest that would be aroused if she were imprisoned? Again we thought perhaps this marked the end of the jailing of women.

But though the pickets were released on suspended sentences, there was no indication of any purpose on the part of the Administration of acting on the amendment. Two groups, some of those on suspended sentence, others first offenders, again marched to the White House gates. The following motto:

THE TIME HAS COME TO CONQUER OR SUBMIT; FOR US THERE CAN BE BUT ONE CHOICE—WE HAVE MADE IT.

a quotation from the-President's second Liberty Loan appeal, was carried by Miss-Paul.

Dr. Caroline E. Spencer of Colorado carried:

RESISTANCE TO TYRANNY IS OBEDIENCE TO GOD.

All were brought to trial again.

The trial of Miss Paul's group ran as follows:

MR. HART (Prosecuting Attorney for the Government): Sergeant Lee, were you on Pennsylvania Avenue near the White House Saturday afternoon?

SERGEANT LEE: I was.

MR. HART: At what time?

LEE: About 4:35 in the afternoon.

HART: Tell the court what you saw.

LEE: A little after half-past four, when the department clerks were all going home out Pennsylvania Avenue, I saw four suffragettes coming down Madison Place, cross the Avenue and continue on Pennsylvania Avenue to the gate of the White House, where they divided two on the right and two on the left side of the gate.

HART: What did you do?

LEE: I made my way through the crowd that was surrounding them and told the ladies *they were violating the law by standing at the gates,* and wouldn't they please move on?

HART: Did they move on?

LEE: They did not; and they didn't answer either.

HART: What did you do then?

LEE: I placed them under arrest.

HART: What did you do then?

LEE: *I asked the crowd to move on.*

Mr. Hart then arose and summing up said: "Your Honor, these women have said that *they will picket again.* I ask you to impose the maximum sentence."

Such confused legal logic was indeed drôle!

"You ladies seem to feel that we discriminate in making arrests and in sentencing you," said the judge heavily. "The result is that you force me to take the most drastic means in my power to compel you to obey the law."

More legal confusion!

"Six months," said the judge to the first offenders, "and then you will serve one month more," to the others.

Miss Paul's parting remark to the reporters who intercepted her on her way from the courtroom to begin her seven months' sentence was:

"We are being imprisoned, not because we obstructed traffic, but because we pointed out to the President the fact that he was obstructing the cause of democracy at home, while Americans were fighting for it abroad."

I am going to let Alice Paul tell her own story, as she related it to me one day after her release:

It was late afternoon when we arrived at the jail. There we found the suffragists who had preceded us, locked in cells.

The first thing I remember was the distress of the prisoners about the lack of fresh air. Evening was approaching, every window was closed tight. The air in which we would be obliged to sleep was foul. There were about eighty negro and white prisoners crowded together, tier upon tier, frequently two in a cell. I went to a window and tried to open it. Instantly a group of men, prison guards, appeared; picked me up bodily, threw me into a cell and locked the door. Rose Winslow and the others were treated in the same way.

Determined to preserve our health and that of the other prisoners, we began a concerted fight for fresh air. The windows were about twenty feet distant from the cells, and two sets of iron bars intervened between us and the windows, but we instituted an attack upon them as best we could. Our tin drinking cups, the electric light bulbs, every available article of the meagre supply in each cell, including my treasured copy of Browning's poems which I had secretly taken in with me, was thrown through the windows. By this simultaneous attack from every cell, we succeeded in breaking one window before our supply of tiny weapons was exhausted. The fresh October air came in like an exhilarating gale. The broken window remained untouched throughout the entire stay of this group and all later groups of suffragists. Thus was won what the "regulars" in jail called the first breath of air in their time.

The next day we organized ourselves into a little group for the purpose of rebellion. We determined to make it impossible to keep us in jail. We determined, moreover, that as long as we were there we would keep up an unremitting fight for the rights of political prisoners.

One by one little points were conceded to quiet resistance. There was the practice of sweeping the corridors in such a way that the dust filled the cells. The prisoners would be choking to the gasping point, as they sat, helpless, locked in the cells, while a great cloud of dust enveloped them from tiers above and below. As soon as our tin drinking cups, which were sacrificed in our attack upon the windows, were restored to us, we instituted a campaign against the dust. Tin cup after tin cup was filled and its contents thrown out into the corridor from every cell, so that the water began to trickle down from tier to tier. The District Commissioners, the Board of Charities, and other officials were summoned by the prison authorities. Hurried consultations were held. Nameless officials passed by in review and looked upon the dampened floor. Thereafter the corridors were dampened and the sweeping into the cells ceased. And so another reform was won.

There is absolutely no privacy allowed a prisoner in a cell. You are suddenly peered at by curious strangers, who look in at you all hours of the day and night, by officials, by attendants, by interested philanthropic visitors, and by prison reformers, until one's sense of privacy is so outraged that one rises in rebellion. We set out to secure privacy, but we did not succeed, for, to allow privacy in prison, is against all institutional thought and habit. Our only available weapon was our blanket, which was no sooner put in front of our bars than it was forcibly taken down by Warden Zinkhan.

Our meals had consisted of a little almost raw salt pork, some sort of liquid—I am not sure whether it was coffee or soup—bread and occasionally molasses. How we cherished the bread and molasses! We saved it from meal to meal so as to try to distribute the nourishment over a longer period, as almost every one was unable to eat the raw pork. Lucy Branham, who was more valiant than the rest of us, called out from her cell, one day, "Shut your eyes tight, close your mouth over the pork and swallow it without chewing it. Then you can do it." This heroic practice kept Miss Branham in fairly good health, but to the rest it seemed impossible, even with our eyes closed, to crunch our teeth into the raw pork.

However gaily you start out in prison to keep up a rebellious protest, it is nevertheless a terribly difficult thing to do in the face of the constant cold and hunger of undernourishment. Bread and water, and occasional molasses, is not a diet destined to sustain rebellion long. And soon weakness overtook us.

At the end of two weeks of solitary confinement, without any exercise, without going outside of our cells, some of the prisoners were released, having finished their terms, but five of us were left serving seven months' sentences, and two, one month sentences. With our number thus diminished to seven, the authorities felt able to cope with us. The doors were unlocked and we were permitted to take exercise. Rose Winslow fainted as soon as she got into the yard, and was carried back to her cell. I was too weak to move from my bed. Rose and I were taken on stretchers that night to the hospital.

For one brief night we occupied beds in the same ward in the hospital. Here we decided upon the hunger strike, as the ultimate form of protest left us—the strongest weapon left with which to continue within the prison our battle against the Administration.

Miss Paul was held absolutely incommunicado in the prison hospital. No attorney, no member of her family, no friend could see her. With Miss Burns in prison also it became imperative that I consult Miss Paul as to a matter of policy. I was peremptorily refused admission by Warden Zinkhan, so I decided to attempt to communicate with her from below her window. This was before we had established what in prison parlance is known as the "grape-vine route." The grape-vine route consists of smuggling messages oral or written via a friendly guard or prisoner who has access to the outside world.

Just before twilight, I hurried in a taxi to the far-away spot, temporarily abandoned the cab and walked past the dismal cemetery which skirts the prison grounds. I had fortified myself with a diagram of the grounds, and knew which entrance to attempt, in order to get to the hospital wing where Miss Paul lay. We had also ascertained her floor and room. I must first pick the right building, proceed to the proper corner, and finally select the proper window.

The sympathetic chauffeur loaned me a very seedy looking overcoat which I wrapped about me. Having deposited my hat inside the cab, I turned up the collar, drew in my chin and began surreptitiously to circle the devious paths leading to a side entrance of the grounds. My heart was palpitating, for the authorities had threatened arrest if any suffragists were found on the prison grounds, and aside from my personal feelings, I could not at that moment abandon headquarters.

Making a desperate effort to act like an experienced and trusted attendant of the prison, I roamed about and tried not to appear roaming. I successfully passed two guards, and reached the desired spot, which was by good luck temporarily deserted. I succeeded in calling up loudly enough to be heard by Miss Paul, but softly enough not to be heard by the guards.

I shall never forget the shock of her appearance at that window in the gathering dusk. Everything in the world seemed black-gray except her ghost-like face, so startling, so inaccessible. It drove everything else from my mind for an instant. But as usual she was in complete control of herself. She began to hurl questions at me faster than I could answer. "How were the convention plans progressing?" . . . "Had the speakers been secured for the mass meeting?" . . . "How many women had signed up to go out on the next picket line?" And so on.

"Conditions at Occoquan are frightful," said I. "We are planning to . . ."

"Get out of there, and move quickly," shouted the guard, who came abruptly around the corner of the building. I tried to finish my message. "We are planning to habeas corpus the women out of Occoquan and have them transferred up here."

"Get out of there, I tell you. Damn you!" By this time he was upon me. He grabbed me by the arm and began shaking me. "You will be arrested if you do not get off these grounds." He continued to shake me while I shouted back, "Do you approve of this plan?"

I was being forced along so rapidly that I was out of range of her faint voice and could not hear the answer. I plead with the guard to be allowed to go back quietly and speak a few more words with Miss Paul, but he was inflexible. Once out of the grounds I went unnoticed to the cemetery and sat on a tombstone to wait a little while before making another attempt, hoping the guard would not expect me to come back. The lights were beginning to twinkle in the distance and it was now almost total darkness. I consulted my watch and realized that in forty minutes Miss Paul and her comrades would again be going through the torture of forcible feeding. I waited five minutes—ten minutes—fifteen minutes. Then I went back to the grounds again. I started through another entrance, but had proceeded only a few paces when I was forcibly evicted. Again I returned to the cold tombstone. I believe that I never in my life felt more utterly miserable and impotent. There were times, as I have said, when we felt inordinately strong. This was one of the times when I felt that we were frail reeds in the hands of cruel and powerful oppressors. My thoughts were at first with Alice Paul, at that moment being forcibly fed by men jailers and men doctors. I remembered then the man warden who had refused the highly reasonable request to visit her, and my thoughts kept right on up the scale till I got to the man-President—the pinnacle of power against us. I was indeed desolate. I walked back to the hidden taxi, hurried to headquarters, and plunged into my work, trying all night to convince myself that the sting of my wretchedness was being mitigated by activity toward a release from this state of affairs.

Later we established daily communication with Miss Paul through one of the charwomen who scrubbed the hospital floors. She carried paper and pencil carefully concealed upon her. On entering Miss Paul's room she would, with very comical stealth, first elaborately push Miss Paul's bed against the door, then crawl practically under it, and pass from this point of concealment the coveted paper and pencil. Then she would linger over the floor to the last second, imploring Miss Paul to hasten her writing. Faithfully every evening this silent, dusky messenger made her long journey after her day's work, and patiently waited while I wrote an answering note to be delivered to Miss Paul the following morning. Thus it was that while in the hospital Miss Paul directed our campaign, in spite of the Administration's most painstaking plans to the contrary.

Miss Paul's story continues here from the point where I interrupted it.

From the moment we undertook the hunger strike, a policy of unremitting intimidation began. One authority after another, high and low, in and out of prison, came to attempt to force me to break the hunger strike.

"You will be taken to a very unpleasant place if you don't stop this," was a favorite threat of the prison officials, as they would hint vaguely of the psycopathic ward, and St. Elizabeth's, the Government insane asylum. They alternately bullied and hinted. Another threat was "You will be forcibly fed immediately if you don't stop"—this from Dr. Gannon. There was nothing to do in the midst of these continuous threats, with always the "very unpleasant place" hanging over me, and so I lay perfectly silent on my bed.

After about three days of the hunger strike a man entered my room in the hospital and announced himself as Dr. White, the head of St. Elizabeth's. He said that he had been asked by District Commissioner Gardner to make an investigation. I later learned that he was Dr. William A. White, the eminent alienist.

Coming close to my bedside and addressing the attendant, who stood at a few respectful paces from him, Dr. White said: "Does this case talk?"

"Why wouldn't I talk?" I answered quickly.

"Oh, these cases frequently will not talk, you know," he continued in explanation.

"Indeed I'll talk," I said gaily, not having the faintest idea that this was an investigation of my sanity.

"Talking is our business," I continued, "we talk to any one on earth who is willing to listen to our suffrage speeches."

"Please talk," said Dr. White. "Tell me about suffrage;

why you have opposed the President; the whole history of your campaign, why you picket, what you hope to accomplish by it. Just talk freely."

I drew myself together, sat upright in bed, propped myself up for a discourse of some length, and began to talk. The stenographer whom Dr. White brought with him took down in shorthand everything that was said.

I may say it was one of the best speeches I ever made. I recited the long history and struggle of the suffrage movement from its early beginning and narrated the political theory of our activities up to the present moment, outlining the status of the suffrage amendment in Congress at that time. In short, I told him everything. He listened attentively, interrupting only occasionally. to say, "But, has not President Wilson treated you women very badly?" Whereupon, I, still unaware that I was being examined, launched forth into an explanation of Mr. Wilson's political situation and the difficulties he had confronting him. I continued to explain why we felt our relief lay with him; I cited his extraordinary power, his influence over his party, his undisputed leadership in the country, always painstakingly explaining that we opposed President Wilson merely because he happened to be President, not because he was President Wilson. Again came an interruption from Dr. White, "But isn't President Wilson directly responsible for the abuses and indignities which have been heaped upon you? You are suffering now as a result of his brutality, are you not?" Again I explained that it was impossible for us to know whether President Wilson was personally acquainted in any detail with the facts of our present condition, even though we knew that he had concurred in the early decision to arrest our women.

Presently Dr. White took out a small light and held it up to my eyes. Suddenly it dawned upon me that he was examining me personally; that his interest in the suffrage agitation and the jail conditions did not exist, and that he was merely interested in my reactions to the agitation and to jail. Even then I was reluctant to believe that I was the subject of mental investigation and I continued to talk.

But he continued in what I realized with a sudden shock, was an attempt to discover in me symptoms of the persecution mania. How simple he had apparently thought it would be, to prove that I had an obsession on the subject of President Wilson!

The day following he came again, this time bringing with him the District Commissioner, Mr. Gardner, to whom he asked me to repeat everything that had been said the day before. For the second time we went through the history of the suffrage movement, and again his inquiry suggested his persecution mania clue? When the narrative touched upon the President and his responsibility for the obstruction of the suffrage amendment, Dr. White would turn to his associate with the remark: "Note the reaction."

Then came another alienist, Dr. Hickling, attached to the psychopathic ward in the District Jail, with more threats and suggestions, if the hunger strike continued. Finally they departed, and I was left to wonder what would happen next. Doubtless my sense of humor helped me, but I confess I was not without fear of this mysterious place which they continued to threaten.

It appeared clear that it was their intention either to discredit me, as the leader of the agitation, by casting doubt upon my sanity, or else to intimidate us into retreating from the hunger strike.

After the examination by alienists, Commissioner Gardner, with whom I had previously discussed our demand for treatment as political prisoners, made another visit. "All these things you say about the prison conditions may be true," said Mr. Gardner, "I am a new Commissioner, and I do not know. You give an account of a very serious situation in the jail. The jail authorities give exactly the opposite. Now I promise you we will start an investigation at once to see who is right, you or they. If it is found you are right, we shall correct the conditions at once. If you will give up the hunger strike, we will start the investigation at once."

"Will you consent to treat the suffragists as political prisoners, in accordance with the demands laid before you?" I replied.

Commissioner Gardner refused, and I told him that the hunger strike would not be abandoned. But they had by no means exhausted every possible facility for breaking down our resistance. I overheard the Commissioner say to Dr. Gannon on leaving, "Go ahead, take her and feed her."

I was thereupon put upon a stretcher and carried into the psycopathic ward.

* * * *

There were two windows in the room. Dr. Gannon immediately ordered one window nailed from top to bottom. He then ordered the door leading into the hallway taken down and an iron-barred cell door put in its place. He departed with the command to a nurse to "observe her."

Following this direction, all through the day once every hour, the nurse came to "observe" me. All through the night, once every hour she came in, turned on an electric light sharp in my face, and "observed" me. This ordeal was the most terrible torture, as it prevented my sleeping for more than a few minutes at a time. And if I did finally get to sleep it was only to be shocked immediately into wide-awakeness with the pitiless light.

Dr. Hickling, the jail alienist, also came often to "observe" me. Commissioner Gardner and others—doubtless officials— came to peer through my barred door.

One day a young interne came to take a blood test. I protested mildly, saying that it was unnecessary and that I objected. "Oh, well," said the young doctor with a sneer and a supercilious shrug, "you know you're not mentally competent to decide such things." And the test was taken over my protest.

It is scarcely possible to convey to you one's reaction to such an atmosphere. Here I was surrounded by people on their way to the insane asylum. Some were waiting for their commitment papers. Others had just gotten them. And all the while everything possible was done to attempt to make me feel that I too was a "mental patient."

At this time forcible feeding began in the District Jail. Miss Paul and Miss Winslow, the first two suffragists to undertake the hunger strike, went through the operation of forcible feeding this day and three times a day on each succeeding day until their release from prison three weeks later. The hunger strike spread immediately to other suffrage prisoners in the jail and to the workhouse as recorded in the preceding chapter.

One morning [Miss Paul's story continues] the friendly face of a kindly old man standing on top of a ladder suddenly appeared at my window. He began to nail heavy boards across the window from the outside. He smiled and spoke a few kind words and told me to be of good cheer. He confided to me in a sweet and gentle way that he was in prison for drinking, that he had been in many times, but that he believed he had never seen anything so inhuman as boarding up this window and depriving a prisoner of light and air. There was only time for a few hurried moments of conversation, as I lay upon my bed watching the boards go up until his figure was completely hidden and I heard him descending the ladder.

After this window had been boarded up no light came into the room except through the top half of the other window, and almost no air. The authorities seemed determined to deprive me of air and light.

Meanwhile in those gray, long days, the mental patients in the psycopathic ward came and peered through my barred door. At night, in the early morning, all through the day there were cries and shrieks and moans from the patients. It was terrifying. One particularly melancholy moan used to keep up hour after hour, with the regularity of a heart beat. I said to myself, "Now I have to endure this. I have got to live through this somehow. I'll pretend these moans are the noise of an elevated train, beginning faintly in the distance and getting louder as it comes nearer." Such childish devices were helpful to me.

The nurses could not have been more beautiful in their spirit and offered every kindness. But imagine being greeted in the morning by a kindly nurse, a new one who had just come on duty, with, "I know you are not insane." The nurses explained the procedure of sending a person to the insane asylum. Two alienists examine a patient in the psycopathic ward, sign an order committing the patient to St. Elizabeth's Asylum, and there the patient is sent at the end of one week.

No trial, no counsel, no protest from the outside world! This was the customary procedure.

I began to think as the week wore on that this was probably their plan for me. I could not see my family or friends; counsel was denied me; I saw no other prisoners and heard nothing of them; I could see no papers; I was entirely in the hands of alienists, prison officials and hospital staff.

I believe I have never in my life before feared anything or any human being. But I confess I was afraid of Dr. Gannon, the jail physician. I dreaded the hour of his visit.

"I will show you who rules this place. You think you do. But I will show you that you are wrong." Some such friendly greeting as this was frequent from Dr. Gannon on his daily round. "Anything you desire, you shall not have. I will show you who is on top in this institution," was his attitude.

After nearly a week had passed, Dudley Field Malone finally succeeded in forcing an entrance by an appeal to court officials and made a vigorous protest against confining me in the psychopathic ward. He demanded also that the boards covering the window be taken down. This was promptly done and again the friendly face of the old man became visible, as the first board disappeared.

"I thought when I put this up America would not stand for this long," he said, and began to assure me that nothing dreadful would happen. I cherish the memory of that sweet old man.

The day after Mr. Malone's threat of court proceedings, the seventh day of my stay in the psychopathic ward, the attendants suddenly appeared with a stretcher. I did not know whither I was being taken, to the insane asylum, as threatened, or back to the hospital—one never knows in prison where one is being taken, no reason is ever given for anything. It turned out to be the hospital.

*   *   *   *

After another week spent by Miss Paul on hunger strike in the hospital, the Administration was forced to capitulate. The doors of the jail were suddenly opened, and all suffrage prisoners were released.

With extraordinary swiftness the Administration's almost

incredible policy of intimidation had collapsed. Miss Paul had been given the maximum sentence of seven months, and at the end of five weeks the Administration was forced to acknowledge defeat. They were in a most unenviable position. If she and her comrades had offended in such degree as to warrant so cruel a sentence, (with such base stupidity on their part in administering it) she most certainly deserved to be detained for the full sentence. The truth is, every idea of theirs had been subordinated to the one desire of stopping the picketing agitation. To this end they had exhausted all their weapons of force.

From my conversation and correspondence with Dr. White, it is clear that as an alienist he did not make the slightest allegation to warrant removing Miss Paul to the psychopathic ward. On the contrary he wrote, "I felt myself in the presence of an unusually gifted personality" and . . . "she was wonderfully alert and keen . . . possessed of an absolute conviction of her cause . . . with industry and courage sufficient to avail herself of them [all diplomatic possibilities]. He praised the "most admirable, coherent, logical and forceful way" in which she discussed with him the purpose of our campaign.

And yet the *Administration put her in the psychopathic ward and threatened her with the insane asylum.*

An interesting incident occurred during the latter part of Miss Paul's imprisonment. Having been cut off entirely from outside communication, she was greatly surprised one night at a late hour to find a newspaper man admitted for an interview with her. Mr. David Lawrence, then generally accepted as the Administration journalist, and one who wrote for the various newspapers throughout the country defending the policies of the Wilson Administration, was announced. It was equally well known that this correspondent's habit was to ascertain the position of the leaders on important questions, keeping intimately in touch with opinion in White House circles at the same time.

Mr. Lawrence came, as he said, of his own volition, and not as an emissary from the White House. But in view of his close relation to affairs, his interview is significant as possibly reflecting an Administration attitude at that point in the campaign.

The conversation with Miss Paul revolved first about our fight for the right of political prisoners, Miss Paul outlining the wisdom and justice of this demand.

"The Administration could very easily hire a comfortable house in Washington and detain you all there," said Mr. Lawrence, "but don't you see that your demand to be treated as political prisoners is infinitely more difficult to grant than to give you the federal suffrage amendment? If we give you these privileges we shall have to extend them to conscientious objectors and to all prisoners now confined for political opinions. This the Administration cannot do."

The political prisoners protest, then, had actually encouraged the Administration to choose the lesser of two evils— some action on behalf of the amendment.

"Suppose," continued Mr. Lawrence, "the Administration should pass the amendment through one house of Congress next session and go to the country in the 1918 elections on that record and if sustained in it, pass it through the other house a year from now. Would you then agree to abandon picketing?"

"Nothing short of the passage of the amendment through Congress will end our agitation," Miss Paul quietly answered for the thousandth time.

Since Mr. Lawrence disavows any connection with the Administration in this interview, I can only remark that events followed exactly in the order he outlined; that is, the Administration attempted to satisfy the women by putting the amendment through the House and not through the Senate.

It was during Miss Paul's imprisonment that the forty-one women went in protest to the picket line and were sent to the workhouse, as narrated in the previous chapter. The terrorism they endured at Occoquan ran simultaneously with the attempted intimidation of Miss Paul and her group in the jail.

CHAPTER 13

IN August, 1917, when it was clear that the policy of imprisoning suffragists would be continued indefinitely, and under longer sentences, the next three groups of pickets to be arrested asked for a decision from the highest court, the District Court of Appeals. Unlike other police courts in the country, there is no absolute right of appeal from the Police Court of the District of Columbia. Justice Robb, of the District Court of Appeals, after granting two appeals, refused to grant any more, upon the ground that he had discretionary power to grant or withhold an appeal. When further right of appeal was denied us, and when the Administration persisted in arresting us, we were compelled either to stop picketing or go to prison.

The first appealed case was heard by the Court of Appeals on January 8, 1918, and the decision [1] handed down in favor of the defendants on March 4, 1918. This decision was concurred in by all three judges, one of whom was appointed by President Wilson, a second by President Roosevelt and the third by President Taft.

In effect the decision declared that every one of the 218 suffragists arrested up to that time was illegally arrested, illegally convicted, and illegally imprisoned. The whole policy of the Administration in arresting women was by this decision held up to the world as lawless. The women could, if they had chosen, have filed suits for damages for false arrest and imprisonment at once.

[1] See Hunter vs. District of Columbia, 47 App. Cas. (D. C.) p. 406.

The appeal cases of the other pickets were ordered dismissed and stricken from the records. Dudley Field Malone was chief counsel in the appeal.

Another example of ethical, if not legal lawlessness, was shown by the Administration in the following incident. Throughout the summer and early autumn we had continued to press for an investigation of conditions at Occoquan, promised almost four months earlier.

October 2nd was the date finally set for an investigation to be held in the District Building before the District Board of Charities. Armed with 18 affidavits and a score of witnesses as to the actual conditions at Occoquan, Attorney Samuel C. Brent and Judge J. K. N. Norton, both of Alexandria, Virginia, acting as counsel with Mr. Malone, appeared before the Board on the opening day and asked to be allowed to present their evidence. They were told by the Board conducting the investigation that this was merely "an inquiry into the workhouse conditions and therefore would be held in secret without reporters or outsiders present." The attorneys demanded a public hearing, and insisted that the question was of such momentous importance that the public was entitled to hear both sides of it. They were told they might submit in writing any evidence they wished to bring before the Board. They refused to produce testimony for a "star chamber proceeding," and refused to allow their witnesses to be heard unless they could be heard in public.

Unable to get a public hearing, counsel left the following letter with the President of the Board:

Hon. John Joy Edson,
    President Board of Charities,
        Washington, D. C.
    Dear Sir:—We are counsel for a large group of citizens, men and women, who have in the past been associated with Occoquan work house as officials or inmates and who are ready

to testify to unspeakable conditions of mismanagement, graft, sanitary depravity, indignity and brutality at the institution.

We are glad you are to conduct this long-needed inquiry and shall coöperate in every way to get at the truth of conditions in Occoquan through your investigation, provided you make the hearings public, subpœna all available witnesses, including men and women now prisoners at Occoquan, first granting them immunity, and provided you give counsel an opportunity to examine and cross examine all witnesses so called.

We are confident your honorable board will see the justice and wisdom of a public inquiry. If charges so publicly made are untrue the management of Occoquan work house is entitled to public vindication, and if these charges are true, the people of Washington and Virginia should publicly know what kind of a prison they have in their midst, and the people of the country should publicly know the frightful conditions in this institution which is supported by Congress and the government of the United States.

We are ready with our witnesses and affidavits to aid your honorable board in every way, provided you meet the conditions above named. But if you insist on a hearing behind closed doors we cannot submit our witnesses to a star chamber proceeding and shall readily find another forum in which to tell the American public the vivid story of the Occoquan work house.

Respectfully yours,
(Signed) DUDLEY FIELD MALONE,
J. K. N. NORTON,
SAMUEL G. BRENT.

Subsequently the District Board of Charities reported findings on their secret investigation. After a lengthy preamble, in which they attempted to put the entire blame upon the suffrage prisoners, they advised:

That the investigation directed by the Commissioners of the District of Columbia be postponed until the conditions of unrest, excitement, and disquiet at Occoquan have been overcome:

That the order relieving W. H. Whittaker as superintendent, temporarily and without prejudice, be revoked, and Mr. Whittaker be restored to his position as superintendent: [1]

That the members of the National Woman's Party now at Occoquan be informed that unless they obey the rules of the institution and discontinue their acts of insubordination and riot, they will be removed from Occoquan to the city jail and placed in solitary confinement.

In announcing the report to the press the District Commissioners stated that they approved the recommendations of the Board of Charities "after most careful consideration," and that "as a matter of fact, the District workhouse at Occoquan is an institution of which the commissioners are proud, and is a source of pride to every citizen of the nation's Capital."

That the Administration was in possession of the true facts concerning Mr. Whittaker and his conduct in office there can be no doubt. But they supported him until the end of their campaign of suppression.

Another example of the Administration's lawlessness appeared in the habeas corpus proceedings by which we rescued the prisoners at the workhouse from Mr. Whittaker's custody. The trial occurred on November 23rd.

No one present can ever forget the tragi-comic scene enacted in the little Virginia court room that cold, dark November morning. There was Judge Waddill [2]—who had adjourned his sittings in Norfolk to hasten the relief of the prisoners—a mild mannered, sweet-voiced Southern gentleman. There was Superintendent Whittaker in his best Sunday clothes, which mitigated very little the cruel and nervous demeanor which no one who has come under his control will ever forget. His thugs were there, also dressed in their best clothes, which only exaggerated their coarse features and their shifty eyes. Mrs. Herndon, the thin-lipped matron, was there, looking nervous

[1] Pending the investigation Mr. Whittaker was suspended, and his first assistant, Alonzo Tweedale, served in the capacity of superintendent.

[2] Appointed to the bench by President Roosevelt.

and trying to seem concerned about the prisoners in her charge. Warden Zinkhan was there seeming worried at the prospect of the prisoners being taken from the care of Superintendent Whittaker and committed to him—he evidently unwilling to accept the responsibility.

Dudley Field Malone and Mr. O'Brien of counsel, belligerent in every nerve, were ready to try the case. The two dapper government attorneys, with immobile faces, twisted nervously in their chairs. There was the bevy of newspaper reporters struggling for places in the little courtroom, plainly sympathetic, for whatever they may have had to write for the papers they knew that this was a battle for justice against uneven odds. There were as many eager spectators as could be crowded into so small an area. Upon the whole an air of friendliness prevailed in this little court at Alexandria which we had never felt in the Washington courts. And the people there experienced a shock when the slender file of women, haggard, red-eyed, sick, came to the bar. Some were able to walk to their seats; others were so weak that they had to be stretched out on the wooden benches with coats propped under their heads for pillows. Still others bore the marks of the attack of the "night of terror." Many of the prisoners lay back in their chairs hardly conscious of the proceedings which were to free them. Mrs. Brannan collapsed utterly and had to be carried to a couch in an ante-room.

It was discovered just as the trial was to open that Miss Lucy Burns and Mrs. Lawrence Lewis, who it will be remembered had been removed to the jail before the writ had been issued, were absent from among the prisoners.

"They are too ill to be brought into court," Mr. Whittaker replied to the attorneys for the defense.

"We demand that they be brought into court at our risk," answered counsel for the defense.

The government's attorneys sustained Mr. Whittaker in

not producing them. It was clear that the government did not wish to have Miss Burns with the marks still fresh on her wrists from her manacling and handcuffing, and Mrs. Lewis with a fever from the shock of the first night, brought before the judge who was to decide the case.

"If it was necessary to handcuff Miss Burns to the bars of her cell, we consider her well enough to appear," declared Mr. O'Brien. "We consider we ought to know what has happened to all of these petitioners since these events. While I was at Occoquan Sunday endeavoring to see my clients, Mr. Whittaker was trying to induce the ladies, who, he says, are too sick to be brought here, to dismiss this proceeding. Failing in that, he refused to let me see them, though I had an order from Judge Mullowny, and they were taken back to the District of Columbia. From that time to this, though I had your Honor's order which you signed in Norfolk, the superintendent of the Washington jail also refused to allow me to see my clients, saying that your order had no effect in the District of Columbia."

"If there are any petitioners that you claim have not been brought here because they have been carried beyond the jurisdiction of the courts, I think we should know it," ruled the court. "Counsel for these ladies want them here; and they say that they ought to be here and are well enough to be here; that the respondent here has spirited them away and put them beyond the jurisdiction of the court. On that showing, unless there is some reason why they ought not to come, they should be here."

Miss Burns and Mrs. Lewis were accordingly ordered brought to court.

This preliminary skirmish over, the opening discussion revolved about a point of law as to whether the Virginia District Court had authority to act in this case.

After hearing both sides on this point, Judge Waddill said:

"These are not state prisoners; they are prisoners of the District of Columbia. They are held by an order of the court claiming to have jurisdiction in the District of Columbia. But they are imprisoned in the Eastern District of Virginia, in Occoquan workhouse which, very much to our regret, is down here, and is an institution that we alone have jurisdiction over. No court would fail to act when such a state of affairs as is set forth in this petition is brought to its attention.

"Here was a case concerning twenty-five or thirty ladies. The statement as to their treatment was bloodcurdling; it was shocking to man's ideas of humanity if it is true. They are here in court, and yet your answer denies all these facts which they submit. It is a question whether you can do that and yet deny these petitioners the right of testimony."

Proceeding with this argument, the defense contended that the act itself of the District Commissioners in sending prisoners to the Occoquan workhouse was illegal; that no formal transfer from one institution to another had ever been made, the sentencing papers distinctly stating that all prisoners were committed to "the Washington Asylum and Jail."

"We deny that the records of the Commissioners of the District of Columbia can show that there was any order made by the Board for the removal of these women. The liberty of a citizen cannot be so disregarded and trifled with that any police official or jailer may at his own volition, commit and hold him in custody and compel him to work. The liberty of the people depends upon a broader foundation."

Repeated questions brought out from Mr. Zinkhan, Warden of the Jail, the fact that the directions given by the Commissioners to transfer prisoners from the jail to Occoquan rested entirely upon a verbal order given "five or six years ago."

"Do you really mean," interrupted the court, "that the only authority you have on the part of the Commissioners of the District of Columbia to transfer parties down to Occoquan is a verbal order made five or six years ago?"

Questions by the defense brought out the fact also that Mr. Zinkhan could remember in detail the first oral orders he had received for such a transfer, dating back to 1911, although he could not remember important details as to how he had received the orders concerning the suffragists committed to his care! He only knew that "orders were oral and explicit."

Q. [By defense in court] You say the three commissioners were present?

A. Sure.

Q. Who else was present?

A. I am not sure just now who else was present. I remember somebody else was there, but I don't remember just who. . . .

Q. Were the three commissioners present at the time Mr. [Commissioner] Brownlow gave you this order?

A. Yes.

Q. You say it was a verbal order of the Commissioners?

A. Yes.

Q. Was the clerk of the Board present?

A. I think not.

Q. And you cannot remember who was present aside from the three Commissioners?

A. No, I cannot remember just now.

Q. Try to recollect who was present at that meeting when this order was given, aside from the Commissioners. There was somebody else present?

A. It is my impression that there was some one other person present, but I am not sure just now who it was.

Q. It was some official, some one well known, was it not. . . . ?

A. I am not sure. . . .

[This conference was one in which Mr. McAdoo was reported to have participated.]

The gentle judge was distressed when in answer to a question by the government's attorney as to what Mr. Zinkhan did when the prisoners were given into his charge, the warden replied:

A. I heard early in the afternoon of the sentence, and I did not get away from the Commissioners' meeting until nearly 4 o'clock and I jumped in my machine and went down to the jail, and I think at that time six of them had been delivered there and were in the rotunda of the jail, and a few minutes after that a van load came. The remaining number of ten or twelve had not arrived, but inasmuch as the train had to leave at 5 o'clock and there would not be time enough to receive them in the jail and get them there in time for the train, I took the van that was there right over to the east end of the Union Station, and I think I took some of the others in my machine and another machine we had there carried some of the others over, and we telephoned the other van at Police Court to go direct to the east end of the Union Station and to deliver them to me. I had of course the commitments of those that were brought up to the jail—about 20 of them—and received from the officer of the court the other commitments of the last van load, and there I turned all of them except one that I kept back . . . over to the receiving and discharging officer representing the District Workhouse, and they were taken down there that evening.

There followed some questioning of the uneasy warden as to how he used this power to decide which prisoners should remain in jail and which should be sent to Occoquan. Warden Zinkhan stuttered something about sending "all the able bodied prisoners to Occoquan—women able to perform useful work"— and that "humanitarian motives" usually guided him in his selection. It was a difficult task for the warden for he had to conceal just *why* the suffrage prisoners were sent to Occoquan, and in so doing had to invent "motives" of his own.

Q. [By defense.] Mr. Zinkhan, were you or were you not actuated by humanitarian motives when you sent this group of women to the Occoquan Workhouse?

A. Yes.

Q. Were you actuated by humanitarian motives when you sent Mrs. Nolan, a woman of 73 years, to the workhouse? Did you think that she could perform some service at Occoquan that it was necessary to get her out of the District Jail and down there?

Warden Zinkhan gazed at the ceiling, shifted in his chair and hesitated to answer. The question was repeated, and finally the warden admitted uncomfortably that he believed he was inspired by "humanitarian motives."

"Mrs. Nolan, will you please stand up?" called out Mr. Malone.

All eyes turned toward the front row, where Mrs. Nolan slowly got to her feet. The tiny figure of a woman with pale face and snowy hair, standing out dramatically against her black bonnet and plain black dress, was answer enough.

Warden Zinkhan's answers after that came even more haltingly. He seemed inordinately fearful of trapping himself by his own words.

"The testimony has brought out the fact," the judge remarked at this point, "that two of these ladies were old and one of them is a delicate lady. Her appearance would indicate that she is not strong. Under this rule, if one of these ladies had been eighty years old and unable to walk she would have gone along with the herd and nobody would have dared to say 'ought this to be done?' Would the Commissioners in a case of that sort, if they gave consideration to it, think of sending such an individual there? Was not that what the law expected them to do, and not take them off in droves and inspect them at the Union Station and shoot them on down? Yet that is about what was done in this case."

In summing up this phase of the case in an eloquent appeal, Mr. Malone said:

"Can the Commissioners, with caprice and no order and no record except that orally given five or six years ago, and one which this warden now says was given 'oral and explicit,' transfer defendants placed in a particular institution, and under a particular kind of punishment arbitrarily to another institution, and add to their punishment?

"Even if we admit that the Commissioners had power, did Congress ever contemplate that any District Commissioners would dare to exercise power affecting the life and health of defendants in this fashion? Did Congress ever contemplate that, by mere whim, these things could be done? I am sure it did not, and even on the admission of the government that they had the power, they have exercised this power in such a scandalous fashion that it is worthy of the notice of the court and worthy of the remedy which we seek—the removal of the suffrage prisoners from the Occoquan workhouse."

After a brief recess, Judge Waddill rendered this decision: "The locking up of thirty human beings is an unusual sort of thing and judicial officers ought to be required to stop long enough to see whether some prisoners ought to go and some not; whether some might not be killed by going; or whether they should go dead or alive. *This class of prisoners* and this number of prisoners *should have been given special consideration.* There cannot be any controversy about this question . . . . You ought to lawfully lock them up instead of unlawfully locking them up—if they are to be locked up. . . . *The petitioners are, therefore, one and all, in the Workhouse without semblance of authority or legal process of any kind. . . . and they will accordingly be remanded to the custody of the Superintendent of the Washington Asylum and Jail."* . . .

It having been decided that the prisoners were illegally detained in the workhouse, it was not necessary to go into a discussion of the cruelties committed upon the prisoners while there.

The government's attorneys immediately announced that they would appeal from the decision of Judge Waddill. Pending such an appeal the women were at liberty to be paroled in the custody of counsel. But since they had come from the far corners of the continent and since some of them had served out almost half of their sentence, and did not wish in case of an adverse decision on the appeal, to have to return later to undergo the rest of their sentence, they preferred to finish their sentences.

These were the workhouse prisoners thus remanded to the jail who continued the hunger strike undertaken at the workhouse, and made a redoubtable reinforcement to Alice Paul and Rose Winslow and their comrades on strike in the jail when the former arrived.

CHAPTER 14

THE ADMINISTRATION OUTWITTED

WITH thirty determined women on hunger strike, of whom eight were in a state of almost total collapse, the Administration capitulated. It could not afford to feed thirty women forcibly and risk the social and political consequences; nor could it let thirty women starve themselves to death, and likewise take the the consequences. For by this time one thing was clear, and that was that the discipline and endurance of the women could not be broken. And so all the prisoners were unconditionally released on November 27th and November 28th.

On leaving prison Miss Paul said: "The commutation of sentences acknowledges them to be unjust and arbitrary. The attempt to suppress legitimate propaganda has failed.

"We hope that no more demonstrations will be necessary, that the amendment will move steadily on to passage and ratification without further suffering or sacrifice. But what we do depends entirely upon what the Administration does. We have one aim: the immediate passage of the federal amendment."

Running parallel to the protest made inside the prison, a public protest of nation-wide proportions had been made against continuing to imprison women. Deputations of influential women had waited upon all party leaders, cabinet officials, heads of the war boards, in fact every friend of the Administration, pointing out that we had broken no law, that we were unjustly held, and that the Administration would suffer politically for their handling of the suffrage agitation.

A committee of women, after some lively fencing with the Secretary of War, finally drove Mr. Baker to admit that women had been sent to prison for a political principle; that they were *not* petty disturbers but part of a great fundamental struggle. Secretary Baker said, "This [the suffrage struggle] is a revolution. There have been revolutions all through history. Some have been justified and some have not. The burden of responsibility to decide whether your revolution is justified or not is on you. The whole philosophy of your movement seems to be to obey no laws until you have a voice in those laws."

At least one member of the Cabinet thus showed that he had caught something of the purpose and depth of our movement. He never publicly protested, however, against the Administration's policy of suppression.

Mr. McAdoo, then Secretary of the Treasury, gave no such evidence of enlightenment as Mr. Baker. A committee of women endeavored to see him. He was reported "out. But we expect him here soon."

We waited an hour. The nervous private secretary returned to say that he had been mistaken. "The Secretary will not be in until after luncheon."

"We shall wait," said Mrs. William Kent, chairman of the deputation. "We have nothing more important to do to-day than to see Secretary McAdoo. We are willing to wait the whole day, if necessary, only it is imperative that we see him."

The private secretary's spirits sank. He looked as if he would give anything to undo his inadvertence in telling us that the Secretary was expected after luncheon! Poor man! We settled down comfortably to wait, a formidable looking committee of twenty women.

There was the customary gentle embarrassment of attend-

ants whose chief is in a predicament from which they seem
powerless to extricate him, but all were extremely courteous.
The attendant at the door brought us the morning papers to
read.   Gradually groups of men began to arrive and cards
were sent in the direction of the spot where we inferred the
Secretary of the Treasury was safely hidden, hoping and
praying for our early retirement.

Whispered conversations were held.   Men disappeared in
and out of strange doors.   Still we waited.

Finally as the fourth hour of our vigil was dragging on, a
lieutenant appeared to announce that the Secretary was very
sorry but that he would not be able to see us "at all."   We
consulted, and finally sent in a written appeal, asking for "five
minutes of his precious time on a matter of grave importance."
More waiting!   Finally a letter was brought to us directed to
Mrs. William Kent, with the ink of the Secretary of the Treasury's signature still wet.   With no concealment of contempt,
he declared that under no circumstances could he speak with
women who had conducted such an outrageous campaign in
such an "illegal" way.   We smiled as we learned from his pro-
nouncement that "picketing" was "illegal," for we were not
supposed to have been arrested for picketing.   The tone of
his letter, its extreme bitterness, tended to confirm what we had
always been told, that Mr. McAdoo assisted in directing the
policy of arrests and imprisonment.

I have tried to secure this letter for reproduction but unfortunately Mrs. Kent did not save it.   We all remember its
bitter passion, however, and the point it made about our
"illegal picketing."

Congress convened on December 4th.   President Wilson
delivered a message, restating our aims in the war.   He also
recommended a declaration of a state of war against Austria;
the control of certain water power sites; export trade-com-
bination; railway legislation; and the speeding up of all neces-

sary appropriation legislation. But he did not mention the suffrage amendment. Having been forced to release the prisoners, he again rested.

Immediately we called a conference in Washington of the Executive Committee and the National Advisory Council of the Woman's Party. Past activities were briefly reviewed and the political situation discussed. It is interesting to note that the Treasurer's report made at this conference showed that receipts in some months during the picketing had been double what they were the same month the previous year when there was no picketing. In one month of picketing the receipts went as high as six times the normal amount. For example in July of 1917, when the arrests had just begun, receipts for the month totalled $21,623.65 as against $3,690.62 for July of 1916. In November, 1917, when the militant situation was at its highest point, there was received at National Headquarters $31,117.87 as against $15,008.18 received in November, 1916. Still there were those who said we had no friends!

A rumor that the President would act persisted. But we could not rely on rumor. We decided to accelerate him and his Administration by filing damage suits amounting to $800,000 against the District Commissioners, against Warden Zinkhan, against Superintendent Whittaker and Captain Reams, a workhouse guard. [1] They were brought in no spirit of revenge, but merely that the Administration should not be allowed to forget its record of brutality, unless it chose to amend its conduct by passing the amendment. The suits were brought by the women who suffered the greatest abuse during the "night of terror" at the workhouse.

If any one is still in doubt as to the close relation between the Court procedure in our case and the President's actions,

---

[1] We were obliged to bring the suits against individuals, as we could not in the law bring them against the government.

this letter to one of our attorneys in January, 1918, must convince him.

My dear Mr. O'Brien:—

I wish you would advise me as soon as you conveniently can, what will be done with the suffragist cases now pending against Whittaker and Reams in the United States District Court at Alexandria.

I have heard rumors, the truth of which you will understand better than I, that *these cases will be dropped if the President comes out in favor of woman suffrage. This, I understand, he will do and certainly hope so,* as I am personally in favor of it and have been for many years. *But in case of his delay in taking any action, will you agree to continue these cases for the present?*

Very truly yours,
(Signed) F. H. Stevens,
Assistant Corporation Counsel, D. C.

In order to further fortify themselves, the District Commissioners, when the storm had subsided, quietly removed Warden Zinkhan from the jail and Superintendent Whittaker resigned his post at the workhouse, presumably under pressure from the Commissioners.

The Woman's Party conference came to a dramatic close during that first week in December with an enormous mass meeting in the Belasco Theatre in Washington. On that quiet Sunday afternoon, as the President came through his gates for his afternoon drive, a passageway had to be opened for his motor car through the crowd of four thousand people who were blocking Madison Place in an effort to get inside the Belasco Theatre. Inside the building was packed to the rafters. The President saw squads of police reserves, who had been for the past six months arresting pickets for him, battling with a crowd that was literally storming the theatre in their eagerness to do honor to those who had been arrested. Inside there was a fever heat of enthusiasm, bursting cheers, and thundering applause which shook the building. America has never before nor since seen such a suffrage meeting.

Mrs. O. H. P. Belmont, chairman, opened the meeting by saying:

"We are here this afternoon to do honor to a hundred gallant women, who have endured the hardship and humiliation of imprisonment because they love liberty.

"The suffrage pickets stood at the White House gates for ten months and dramatized the women's agitation for political liberty. Self-respecting and patriotic American women will no longer tolerate a government which denies women the right to govern themselves. A flame of rebellion is abroad among women, and the stupidity and brutality of the government in this revolt have only served to increase its heat.

"As President Wilson wrote, 'Governments have been very successful in parrying agitation, diverting it, in seeming to yield to it and then cheating it, tiring it out or evading it. But the end, whether it comes soon or late, is quite certain to be the same.' While the government has endeavored to parry, tire, divert, and cheat us of our goal, the country has risen in protest against this evasive policy of suppression until to-day the indomitable pickets with their historic legends stand triumphant before the nation."

Mrs. William Kent, who had led the last picket line of forty-one women, was chosen to decorate the prisoners.

"In honoring these women, who were willing to go to jail for liberty," said Mrs. Kent, "we are showing our love of country and devotion to democracy." The long line of prisoners filed past her and amidst constant cheers and applause, received a tiny silver replica of a cell door, the same that appears in miniature on the title page of this book.

As proof of this admiration for what the women had done, the great audience in a very few moments pledged $86,326 to continue the campaign. Many pledges were made in honor of

Alice Paul, Inez Milholland, Mrs. Belmont, Dudley Field Malone, and all the prisoners. Imperative resolutions calling upon President Wilson and his Administration to act, were unanimously passed amid an uproar.

CHAPTER 15

IMMEDIATELY following the release of the prisoners and the magnificent demonstration of public support of them, culminating at the mass meeting recorded in the preceding chapter, political events happened thick and fast. Committees in Congress acted on the amendment. President Wilson surrendered and a date for the vote was set.

The Judiciary Committee of the House voted 18 to 2 to report the amendment to that body. The measure, it will be remembered, was reported to the Senate in the closing days of the previous session, and was therefore already before the Senate awaiting action. [1]

To be sure, the Judiciary Committee voted to report the amendment without recommendation. But soon after, the members of the Suffrage Committee, provision for which had also been made during the war session, were appointed. All but four members of this committee were in favor of national suffrage, and immediately after its formation it met to organize and decided to take the suffrage measure out of the hands of the Judiciary Committee and to press for a vote.

A test of strength came on December 18th.

On a trivial motion to refer all suffrage bills to the new suffrage committee, the vote stood 204 to 107. This vote, although unimportant in itself, clearly promised victory for the amendment in the House. In a few days, Representative Mon-

[1] See Chapter 8.

dell of Wyoming, Republican, declared that the Republican side of the House would give more than a two-thirds majority of its members to the amendment.

"It is up to our friends on the Democratic side to see that the amendment is not defeated through hostility or indifference on their side," said Mr. Mondell.

Our daily poll of the House showed constant gains. Pledges from both Democratic and Republican members came thick and fast; cabinet members for the first time publicly declared their belief in the amendment. A final poll, however, showed that we lacked a few votes of the necessary two-thirds majority to pass the measure in the House.

No stone was left unturned in a final effort to get the President to secure additional Democratic votes to insure the passage of the amendment. Finally, on the eve of the vote President Wilson made his first declaration of support of the amendment through a committee of Democratic Congressmen. During the vote the following day Representative Cantrill of Kentucky, Democrat, reported the event to the House. He said in part:

It was my privilege yesterday afternoon to be one of a committee of twelve to ask the President for advice and counsel on this important measure (prolonged laughter and jeers). Mr. Speaker, in answer to the sentiment expressed by part of the House, I desire to say that at no time and upon no occasion am I ever ashamed to confer with Woodrow Wilson upon any important question (laughter, applause, and jeers) and that part of the House that has jeered that statement before it adjourns to-day will follow absolutely the advice which he gave this committee yesterday afternoon. (Laughter and applause.) After conference with the President yesterday afternoon he wrote with his own hands the words which I now read to you, and each member of the committee was authorized by the President to give full publicity to the following:

"The committee found that the President had not felt at liberty to volunteer his advice to Members of Congress in this

important matter, but when we sought his advice (laughter)
he very frankly and earnestly advised us to vote for the amend-
ment as an act of right and justice to the women of the country
and of the world."

. . . To my Democratic brethren who have made these halls
ring with their eloquence in their pleas to stand by the President, I will say that now is your chance to stand by the President and vote for this amendment, "as an act of right and
justice to the women of the country and of the world" . . .

Do you wish to do that which is right and just toward the
women of your own country? If so, follow the President's
advice and vote for this amendment. It will not do to follow
the President in this great crisis in the world's history on those
matters only which are popular in your own districts. The
true test is to stand by him, even though your own vote is un-
popular at home. The acid test for a Member of Congress is
for him to stand for right and justice even if misunderstood
at home at first. In the end, right and justice will prevail
everywhere.

. . . No one thing connected with the war is of more
importance at this time than meeting the reasonable demand
of millions of patriotic and Christian women of the Nation
that the amendment for woman suffrage be submitted to the
States. . . .

The amendment passed the House January 10, 1918, by a
vote of 274 to 136—a two-thirds majority with one vote to
spare—*exactly forty years to a day from the time the suffrage
amendment was first introduced into Congress, and exactly one
year to a day from the time the first picket banner appeared at
the gates of the White House.*

Eighty-three per cent of the Republicans voting on the
measure, voted in favor of it, while only fifty per cent of the
Democrats voting, voted for it. Even after the Republicans
had pledged their utmost strength, more than two-thirds of
their membership, votes were still lacking to make up the Democratic deficiency, and the President's declaration that the measure ought to pass the House, produced them from his own

party. Those who contend that picketing had "set back the clock,"—that it did "no good,"—that President Wilson would "not be moved by it"—have, we believe, the burden of proof on their side of the argument. It is our firm belief that the solid year of picketing, with all its political ramifications, did compel the President to abandon his opposition and declare himself for the measure. I do not mean to say that many things do not coöperate in a movement toward a great event. I do mean to say that picketing was the most vital force amongst the elements which moved President Wilson. That picketing had compelled Congress to see the question in terms of political capital is also true. From the first word uttered in the House debate, until the final roll-call, political expediency was the chief motif.

Mr. Lenroot of Wisconsin, Republican, rose to say:

"May I suggest that there is a distinction between the Democratic members of the Committee on Rules and the Republican members, in this, that all of the Republican members are for this proposition?" This was met with instant applause from the Republican side.

Representative Cantrill prefaced his speech embodying the President's statement, which caused roars and jeers from the opposition, with the announcement that he was not willing to risk another election, with the voting women of the West, and the amendment still unpassed.

Mr. Lenroot further pointed out that: "From a Republican standpoint—from a partisan standpoint, it would be an advantage to Republicans to go before the people in the next election and say that this resolution was defeated by southern Democrats."

An anti-suffragist tried above the din and noise to remind Mr. Lenroot that three years before Mr. Lenroot had voted "No," but a Republican colleague came suddenly to the rescue with "What about Mr. Wilson?" which was followed by, "He kept us out of war," and the jeers on the Republican side became more pronounced.

This interesting political tilt took place when Representatives Dennison and Williams of Illinois, and Representative Kearns of Ohio, Republicans, fenced with Representative Raker of California, Democrat, as he attempted, with an evident note of self-consciousness, to make the President's reversal seem less sudden.

MR. DENNISON: It was known by the committee that went to see the President that the Republicans were going to take this matter up and pass it in caucus, was it not?

MR. RAKER: I want to say to my Republican friends upon this question that I have been in conference with the President for over three years upon this question. . . .

MR. KEARNS: How did the women of California find out and learn where the President stood on this thing just before election last fall? Nobody else seemed to know it.

MR. RAKER: They knew it.

MR. KEARNS: How did they find it out?

MR. RAKER: I will take a minute or two—

MR. KEARNS: I wish the gentleman would.

MR. RAKER: The President went home and registered. The President went home and voted for woman suffrage.

MR. KEARNS: He said he believed in it for the several states. . . .

MR. RAKER: One moment——

MR. KEARNS: That is the only information they had upon the subject, is it?

MR. WILLIAMS: . . . Will the gentleman yield?

MR. RAKER: I cannot yield.

MR. WILLIAMS: Just for a question.

MR. RAKER: I cannot yield. . . .

That the President's political speed left some overcome was clear from a remark of Mr. Clark of Florida when he said:

"I was amused at my friend from Oklahoma, Mr. Ferris, who wants us to stand with the President. God knows I want to stand with him. I am a Democrat, and I want to follow the leader of my party, and I am a pretty good lightning-change artist myself sometimes (laughter); but God knows I cannot keep up with his performance. (Laughter.) Why, the President wrote a book away back yonder" . . . and he quoted generously from President Wilson's many statements in defense of state rights as recorded in his early writings.

Mr. Hersey of Maine, Republican, drew applause when he made a retort to the Democratic slogan, "Stand by the President." He said:

"Mr. Speaker, I am still 'standing with the President,' or, in other words, the President this morning is standing with me."

The resentment at having been forced by the pickets to the point of passing the amendment was in evidence throughout the debate.

Representative Gordon of Ohio, Democrat, said with bitterness: "We are threatened by these militant suffragettes with a direct and lawless invasion by the Congress of the United States of the rights of those States which have refused to confer upon their women the privilege of voting. This attitude on the part of some of the suffrage Members of this House is on an exact equality with the acts of these women militants who have spent the last summer and fall, while they were not in the district jail or workhouse, in coaxing, teasing, and nagging the President of the United States for the purpose of inducing him, by coercion, to club Congress into adopting this joint resolution."

Shouts of "Well, they got him!" and "They got it!" from all sides, followed by prolonged laughter and jeers, interrupted the flow of his oratory.

Mr. Ferris of Oklahoma, Democrat, hoped to minimize the effectiveness of the picket.

"Mr. Speaker," he said, "I do not approve or believe in picketing the White House, the National Capitol, or any other station to bring about votes for women. I do not approve of wild militancy, hunger strikes, and efforts of that sort. I do not approve of the course of those women that . . . become agitators, lay off their womanly qualities in their efforts to secure votes. I do not approve of anything unwomanly any-where, any time, and my course to-day in supporting this suf-frage amendment is not guided by such conduct on the part of a very few women here or elsewhere." (Applause.)

Representative Langley of Kentucky, Republican, was able to see picketing in a fairer light:

"Much has been said pro and con about 'picketing',—that rather dramatic chapter in the history of this great move-ment. It is not my purpose to speak either in criticism or con-demnation of that; but if it be true—I do not say that it is, because I do not know—but if it be true, as has been alleged, that certain promises were made, as a result of which a great campaign was won, and those promises were not kept, I wonder whether in that silent, peaceful protest that was against this broken faith, there can be found sufficient warrant for the in-dignities which the so-called 'pickets' suffered; and when in passing up and down the Avenue I frequently witnessed cul-tured, intellectual women arrested and dragged off to prison because of their method of giving publicity to what they be-lieved to be the truth, I will confess that the question sometimes arose in my mind whether when the impartial history of this great struggle has been written their names may not be placed upon the roll of martyrs to the cause to which they were con-secrating their lives in the manner that they deemed most effective."

Mr. Mays of Utah was one Democrat who placed the re-sponsibility for militancy where it rightly belonged when he said:

"Some say to-day that they are ashamed of the action of the militants in picketing the Capitol. . . . But we should be more ashamed of the unreasonable stubbornness on the part of the men who refused them the justice they have so long and patiently asked."

And so the debate ran on. Occasionally one caught a glimmer of real comprehension amongst these men about to vote upon our political liberty; but more often the discussion stayed on a very inferior level.

And there were gems imperishable!

Even friends of the measure had difficulty not to romanticize about "Woman—God's noblest creature" . . . "man's better counterpart" . . . "humanity's perennial hope" . . . "the world's object most to be admired and loved" . . . and so forth.

Representative Elliott of Indiana, Republican, favored the resolution because—"A little more than four hundred years ago Columbus discovered America. Before that page of American history was written he was compelled to seek the advice and assistance of a woman. From that day until the present day the noble women of America have done their part in times of peace and of war. . . ."

If Queen Isabella was an argument in favor for Mr. Elliott of Indiana, Lady Macbeth played the opposite part for Mr. Parker of New Jersey, Republican. . . . "I will not debate the question as to whether in a time of war women are the best judges of policy. That great student of human nature, William Shakespeare, in the play of Macbeth, makes Lady Macbeth eager for deeds of blood until they are committed and war is begun and then just as eager that it may be stopped." . . .

Said Mr. Gray of New Jersey, Republican: "A nation will endure just so long as its men are virile. History, physiology, and psychology all show that giving woman equal political rights with man makes ultimately for the deterioration of manhood. It is, therefore, not only because I want our country to win this war but because I want our nation to possess the male virility necessary to guarantee its future existence that I am opposed to the pending amendment."

The hope was expressed that President Wilson's conversion would be like that of St. Paul, "and that he will become a master-worker in the vineyards of the Lord for this proposition." (Applause.)

Mr. Gallivan, Democrat, although a representative of Massachusetts, "the cradle of American liberty," called upon a great Persian philosopher to sustain him in his support. " 'Dogs bark, but the caravan moves on.' . . . Democracy cannot live half free and half female."

Mr. Dill of Washington, Democrat, colored his support with the following tribute: " . . . It was woman who first learned to prepare skins of animals for protection from the elements, and tamed and domesticated the dog and horse and cow. She was a servant and a slave. . . . To-day she is the peer of man."

Mr. Little of Kansas, Republican, tried to bring his colleagues back to a moderate course by interpolating:

"It seems to me, gentlemen, that it is time for us to learn that woman is neither a slave nor an angel, but a human being, entitled to be treated with ordinary common sense in the adjustment of human affairs. . . ."

But this calm statement could not allay the terror of Representative Clark of Florida, Democrat, who cried: "In the hearings before the committee it will be found that one of the leaders among the suffragettes declared that they wanted the ballot for 'protection', and when asked against whom she desired 'protection' she promptly and frankly replied, 'men.' My God, has it come to pass in America that the women of the land need to be protected from the men?" The galleries quietly nodded their heads, and Mr. Clark continued to predict either the complete breakdown of family life. . . . or "they [man and wife] must think alike, act alike, have the same ideals of life, and look forward with like vision to the happy consummation 'beyond the vale.' . . .

"God knows that . . . when you get factional politics limited to husband and wife, oh, what a spectacle will be presented, my countrymen. . . . Love will vanish, while hate ascends the throne. . . .

"To-day woman stands the uncrowned queen in the hearts of all right-thinking American men; to her as rightful sovereign we render the homage of protection, respect, love, and may the guiding hand of an all-wise Providence stretch forth in this hour of peril to save her from a change of relation which must bring in its train, discontent, sorrow, and pain," he concluded desperately, with the trend obviously toward "crowning" the queens.

There was the disturbing consideration that women know too much to be trusted. "I happen to have a mother," said Mr. Gray of New Jersey, Republican, "as most of us have, and incidentally I think we all have fathers, although a father does not count for much any more. My mother has forgotten more political history than he ever knew, and she knows more about the American government and American political economy than he has ever shown symptoms of knowing, and for the good of mankind as well as the country she is opposed to women getting into politics."

The perennial lament for the passing of the good old days was raised by Representative Welty of Ohio, Democrat, who said:

"The old ship of state has left her moorings and seems to be sailing on an unknown and uncharted sea. The government founded in the blood of our fathers is fading away. Last fall, a year ago, both parties recognized those principles in their platforms, and each candidate solemnly declared that he would abide by them if elected. But lo, all old things are passing away, and the lady from Montana has filed a bill asking

that separate citizenship be granted to American women mar-
rying foreigners."

Representative Greene of Massachusetts, Republican, all
but shed tears over the inevitable amending of the Constitution:

"I have read it [the Constitution] many times, and there
have been just 17 amendments adopted since the original Constitution was framed by the master minds whom God had inspired in the cabin of the Mayflower to formulate the Constitution of the Plymouth Colony which was made the basis of the
Constitution of Massachusetts and subsequently resulted in the
establishment of the Constitution of the United States under
which we now live. . . ."

Fancy his shock at finding the pickets triumphant.

"Since the second session of the Sixty-fifth Congress
opened," he said, "I have met several women suffragists from
the State of Massachusetts. I have immediately propounded
to them this one question: 'Do you approve or disapprove of
the suffrage banners in front of the White House . . . ?' The
answer in nearly every case to my question was: 'I glory in
that demonstration' . . . the response to my question was very
offensive, and I immediately ordered these suffrage advocates
from my office."

And again the pickets featured in the final remarks of Mr.
Small of North Carolina, Democrat, who deplored the fact
that advocates of the amendment had made it an issue inducing
party rivalry. "This is no party question, and such efforts
will be futile. It almost equals in intelligence the scheme of
that delectable and inane group of women who picketed the
White House on the theory that the President could grant them
the right to vote."

Amid such gems of intellectual delight the House of the
great American Congress passed the national suffrage amendment.

We turned our entire attention then to the Senate.

SOME PUBLIC MEN WHO PROTESTED AGAINST
IMPRISONMENT OF SUFFRAGISTS

© *Underwood*
COL. WILLIAM BOYCE THOMPSON

© *Harris & Ewing*
GILSON GARDNER

J. A. H. HOPKINS

© *Harris & Ewing*
DR. HARVEY W. WILEY

CHAPTER 16

AN INTERLUDE (SEVEN MONTHS)

THE President had finally thrown his power to putting the amendment through the House. We hoped he would follow this up by insisting upon the passage of the amendment in the Senate. We ceased our acts of dramatic protest for the moment and gave our energies to getting public pressure upon him, to persuade him to see that the Senate acted. We also continued to press directly upon recalcitrant senators of the minority party who could be won only through appeals other than from the President.

There are in the Senate 96 members—2 elected from each of the 48 states. To pass a constitutional amendment through the Senate, 64 votes are necessary, a two-thirds majority. At this point in the campaign, 53 senators were pledged to support the measure and 43 were opposed. We therefore had to win 11 more votes. A measure passed through one branch of Congress must be passed through the other branch during the life of that Congress, otherwise it dies automatically and must be born again in a new Congress. We therefore had only the remainder of the first regular session of the 65th Congress and, failing of that, the short second session from December, 1918, to March, 1919, in which to win those votes.

Backfires were started in the states of the senators not yet committed to the amendment. Organized demand for action in the Senate grew to huge proportions.

We turned also to the leading influential members of the respective parties for active help.

Colonel Roosevelt did his most effective suffrage work at this period in a determined attack upon the few unconvinced Republican Senators. The Colonel was one of the few leaders in our national life who was never too busy to confer or to offer and accept suggestions as to procedure. He seemed to have imagination about women. He never took a patronizing attitude nor did he with moral unction dogmatically tell you how the fight should be waged and won. He presupposed ability among women leaders. He was not offended, morally or politically, by our preferring to go to jail rather than to submit in silence. In fact, he was at this time under Administration fire, because of his bold attacks upon some of their policies, and remarked during an interview at Oyster Bay:

"I may soon join you women in jail. One can never tell these days."

His sagacious attitude toward conservative and radical suffrage forces was always delightful and indicative of his appreciation of the political and social value of a movement's having vitality enough to disagree on methods. None of the banal philosophy that "you can never win until all your forces get together" from the Colonel. One day, as I came into his office for an interview, I met a member of the conservative suffragists just leaving, and we spoke. In his office the Colonel remarked, "You know, I contemplated having both you and Mrs. Whitney come to see me at the same time, since it was on a similar mission, but I didn't quite know whether the lion and the lamb would lie down together, and I thought I'd better take no chances. . . . But I see you're on speaking terms," he added. I answered that our relations were extremely amiable, but remarked that the other side might not like to be called "lambs."

"You delight in being the lions—on that point I am safe, am I not?" And he smiled his widest smile as he plunged into a vivid expository attack upon the Senatorial opponents of suffrage in his own party. He wrote letters to them. If this failed, he invited them to Oyster Bay for the week-end. Never did he abandon them until there was literally not a shadow of hope to bank on.

When the Colonel got into action something always happened on the Democratic side. He made a public statement to Senator Gallinger of New Hampshire, Republican leader in the Senate, in which he pointed to the superior support of the Republicans and urged even more liberal party support to ensure the passage of the amendment in the Senate. Action by the Democrats followed fast on the heels of this public statement.

The National Executive Committee of the Democratic party, after a referendum vote of the members of the National Committeemen, passed a resolution calling for favorable action in the Senate. Mr. A. Mitchell Palmer wrote to the Woman's Party saying that this resolution must be regarded as "an official expression of the Democratic Party through the only organization which can speak for it between national conventions."

The Republican National Committee meeting at the same time commended the course taken by Republican Representatives who had voted for the amendment in the House, and declared their position to be "a true interpretation of the thought of the Republican Party."

Republican and Democratic state, county and city committees followed the lead and called for Senate action.

State legislatures in rapid succession called upon the Senate to pass the measure, that they in turn might immediately ratify. North Dakota, New York, Rhode Island, Arizona, Texas and other states acted in this matter.

Intermittent attempts on the Republican side to force action, followed by eloquent speeches from time to time, piquing their opponents, left the Democrats bison-like across the path. The majority of them were content to rest upon the action taken in the House.

I was at this time Chairman of the Political Department of the Woman's Party, and in that capacity interviewed practically every national leader in both majority parties. I can not resist recording a few impressions.

Colonel William Boyce Thompson of New York, now Chairman of Ways and Means of the Republican National Committee, who with Raymond Robins had served in Russia as member of the United States Red Cross Mission, had just returned. The deadlock was brought to his attention. He immediately responded in a most effective way. In a brief but dramatic speech at a great mass meeting of the Woman's Party, at Palm Beach, Florida, he said:

"The story of the brutal imprisonment in Washington of women advocating suffrage is shocking and almost incredible. I became accustomed in Russia to the stories of men and women who served terms of imprisonment under the Czar, because of their love of liberty, but did not know that women in my own country had been subjected to brutal treatment long since abandoned in Russia.

"I wish now to contribute ten thousand dollars to the campaign for the passage of the suffrage amendment through the Senate, one hundred dollars for each of the pickets who went to prison because she stood at the gates of the White House, asking for the passage of the suffrage measure."

This was the largest single contribution received during the national agitation. Colonel Thompson had been a suffragist all his life, but he now became actively identified with the work for the national amendment. Since then he has continued to give generously of his money and to lend his political prestige as often as necessary.

Colonel House was importuned to use his influence to win additional Democratic votes in the Senate, or better still to urge the President to win them. Colonel House is an interesting but not unfamiliar type in politics. Extremely courteous, mild mannered, able, quickly sympathetic, he listens with undistracted attention to your request. His round bright eyes snap as he comes at you with a counter-proposal. It seems so reasonable. And while you know he is putting back upon you the very task you are trying to persuade him to undertake, he does it so graciously that you can scarcely resist liking it. He has the manner of having done what you ask without actually doing more than to make you feel warm at having met him. It is a kind of elegant statecraft which has its point of grace, but which is exasperating when effectiveness is needed. Not that Colonel House was not a supporter of the federal amendment. He was. But his gentle, soft and traditional kind of diplomacy would not employ high-powered pressure. "I shall be going to Washington soon on other matters, and I shall doubtless see the President. Perhaps he may bring up the subject in conversation, and if he does, and the opportunity offers itself, I may be able to do something." Some such gentle threat would come from the Colonel. He was not quite so tender, however, in dealing with Democratic senators, after the President declared for the amendment. He did try to win them.

Ex-President Taft, then joint Chairman of the National War Labor Board, was interviewed at his desk just after rendering an important democratic labor award.

"No, indeed! I'll do nothing for a proposition which adds more voters to our electorate. I thought my position on this question was well known," said Mr. Taft.

"But we thought you doubtless had changed your mind since the beginning of our war for democracy——" I started to answer.

"This is *not* a war for democracy," he said emphatically, looking quizzically at me for my assertion; "if it were, I wouldn't be doing anything for it. . . . The trouble in this country is we've got too many *men* voting as it is. Why, I'd take the vote away from most of the men," he added. I wanted to ask him what men he would leave voting. I wanted also to tell him they were taking the vote away from one class of men in Russia at that moment.

Instead, I said, "Well, I'm not quite sure whom we could trust to sit in judgment"—while he looked smiling and serene, as much as to say, "Oh, that would be a simple matter."

"However," I said, "we have no quarrel with you. You are an avowed aristocrat, and we respect your candor. Our quarrel is with democrats who will not trust their own doctrines." Again he smiled with as much sophistication as such a placid face could achieve, and that was all. I believe Mr. Taft has lately modified his attitude toward women voting. I do not know how he squares that with his distaste of democracy.

There was Samuel Gompers, President of the American Federation of Labor, high in Administration confidence. It was a long wait before Abby Scott Baker and I were allowed into his sanctum.

"Well, ladies, what can I do for you?" was the opening question, and we thought happily here is a man who will not bore us with his life record on behalf of women. He comes to the point with direction.

"Will you speak to the President on behalf of your organization, which has repeatedly endorsed national suffrage, to induce him to put more pressure behind the Senate which is delaying suffrage?" we asked with equal direction. We concealed a heavy sigh as a reminiscent look came into his shrewd, wan eyes, and he began:

"Doubtless you ladies do not know that as long ago as 1888"—I believe that was the date—"my organization sent a petition to the United States Congress praying for the adoption of this very amendment and we have stood for it ever since. . . ."

"Don't you think it is about time that prayer was answered?" we ventured to interrupt. But his reverie could not be disturbed. He looked at us coldly, for he was living in the past, and continued to recount the patient, enduring qualities of his organization.

"I will speak to my secretary and see what the organization can do," he said finally. We murmured again that it was the President we wished him to speak to, but we left feeling reasonably certain that there would be no dynamic pressure from this cautious leader.

Herbert Hoover was the next man we sought. Here we encountered the well-groomed secretary who would not carry our cards into his chief.

"Mr. Hoover has appointments a week ahead," he said. "For example, his chart for to-day includes a very important conference with some grain men from the Northwest," . . . and he continued to recite the items of the chart, ending with "a dinner at the White House to-night."

"If we could see him for just five minutes," we persisted, "he could do what we ask this very night at the White House." But the trained-to-protect secretary was obdurate.

"We shall leave a written request for five minutes at Mr. Hoover's convenience," we said, and prepared the letter.

Time passed without answer. Mrs. Baker and I were compelled to go again to Mr. Hoover's office.

Again we were greeted by the affable secretary, who on this occasion recounted not only his chief's many pressing engagements, but his devoted family life—his Saturday and Sunday habits which were "so dreadfully cut into by his heavy work." We were sympathetic but firm. Would Mr. Hoover not be willing to answer our letter? Would he not be willing to state publicly that he thought the amendment ought to be passed

in the Senate? Would the secretary, in short, please go to
him to ascertain if he would be willing to say a single word in
behalf of the political liberty of women? The secretary disappeared and returned to say, "Mr. Hoover wishes me to tell
you ladies he can give no time whatever to the consideration of
your question until after the war is over. This is final."

The Chief Food Administrator would continue to demand
sacrifices of women throughout the war, but he would not give
so much as a thought to their rights in return. Mr. Hoover
was the only important man in public life who steadfastly
refused to see our representatives. After announcing his
candidacy for nomination to the Presidency he authorized his
secretary to write us a letter saying he had always been for
woman suffrage.

Mr. Bainbridge Colby, then member of the Emergency
Fleet Corporation of the Shipping Board and member of the
Inter-Allied Council which sat on shipping problems, now
Secretary of State in President Wilson's Cabinet, was ap-
proached as a suffragist, known to have access to the President.
Mr. Colby had just returned from abroad when I saw him.
He is a cultivated gentleman, but he knows how to have super-
lative enthusiasm.

"In the light of the world events," he said, "this reform is
insignificant. No time or energy ought to be diverted from
the great program of crushing the Germans."

"But can we not do that," I asked, "without neglecting
internal liberties?"

Mr. Colby is a strong conformist. He became grave.
When I was indiscreet enough to reveal that I was inclined
to pin my faith to the concrete liberty of women, rather than
to a vague and abstract "human freedom," which was supposed to descend upon the world, once the Germans were beaten,
I know he wanted to call me "seditious." But he is a gallant

gentleman and he only frowned with distress. He continued with enthusiasm to plan to build ships.

Bernard Baruch, then member of the Advisory Committee of the Council of National Defense, later economic expert at the Peace Conference, was able to see the war and the women's problem at the same time. He is an able politician and was therefore sensitive to our appeal; he saw the passage of the amendment as a political asset. I do not know how much he believed in the principle. That was of minor importance. What was important was that he agreed to tell the President that he believed it wise to put more pressure on the measure in the Senate. Also I believe Mr. Baruch was one member of the Administration who realized in the midst of the episode that arresting women was bad politics, to say nothing of the doubtful chivalry of it.

George Creel, chairman of the Committee on Public Information, was also asked for help. We went to him many times, because his contact with the President was constant. A suffragist of long standing, he nevertheless hated our militant tactics, for he knew we were winning and the Administration was losing. He is a strange composite. Working at terrific tension and mostly under fire, he was rarely in calm enough mood to sit down and devise ways and means.

"But I talk to the President every day on this matter"—and—"I am doing all I can"—and—"The President is doing all he can"—he would drive at you—without stopping for breath.

"But if you will just ask him to get Senator ———"

"He is working on the Senator now. You people must give him time. He has other things to do," he would say, sweeping aside every suggestion. Familiar advice!

Charles D. Hilles, former Chairman of the Republican National Committee, was a leader who had come slowly to believe in national suffrage. But, once convinced, he was a faithful and dependable colleague who gave practical political assistance.

William Randolph Hearst in powerful editorials called upon the Senators to act. Mr. R. J. Caldwell of New York, life-long suffragist, financier and man of affairs, faithfully and persistently stood by the amendment and by the militants. A more generous contributer and more diligent ally could not be found. A host of public men were interviewed and the great majority of them did help at this critical juncture. It is impossible to give a list that even approaches adequacy, so I shall not attempt it.

Our pressure from below and that of the leaders from above began to have its effect. An attempt was made by Administration leaders to force a vote on May 19, 1918. Friends interceded when it was shown that not enough votes were pledged to secure passage. Again the vote was tentatively set for June 27th and again postponed.

The Republicans, led by Senator Gallinger, provided skirmishes from time to time. The Administration was accused on the floor of blocking action, to which accusation its leaders did not even reply.

Still unwilling to believe that we would be forced to resume our militancy we attempted to talk to the President again. A special deputation of women munition workers was sent to him under our auspices. The women waited for a week, hoping he would consent to see them among his receptions—to the Blue Devils of France, to a Committee of Indians, to a Committee of Irish Patriots, and so forth.

"No time," was the answer. And the munition workers were forced to submit their appeal in writing.

"We are only a few of the thousands of American women," they wrote the President, "who are forming a growing part of the army at home. The work we are doing is hard and dangerous to life and health, making detonators, handling TNT, the highest of all explosives. We want to be recognized by our country, as much her citizens as our soldiers are."

Mr. Tumulty replied for the President:

"The President asks me to say that nothing you or your associates could say could possibly increase his very deep interest in this matter and that he is doing everything that he could with honor and propriety do in behalf of the [suffrage] amendment."

An opportunity was given the President to show again his sympathy for a world-wide endeavor just after having ignored this specific opportunity at home. He hastened to accept the larger field. In response to a memorial transmitted through Mrs. Carrie Chapman Catt, President of the International Woman Suffrage Alliance, the French Union for Woman Suffrage urged the President to use his aid on their behalf "which will be a powerful influence for woman suffrage in the entire world." The memorial was endorsed by the suffrage committee of Great Britain, Italy, Belgium, and Portugal. The President took the occasion to say: "The democratic reconstruction of the world will not have been completely or adequately obtained until women are admitted to the suffrage. As for America it is my earnest hope that the Senate of the United States will give an unmistakable answer by passing the federal amendment before the end of this session."

Meanwhile four more Democratic Senators pledged their support to the amendment. Influenced by the President's declaration of support, and by widespread demands from their constituents, Senators Phelan of California, King of Utah, Gerry of Rhode Island, and Culberson of Texas abandoned the ranks of the opposition.

During this same period the Republican side of the Senate gave five more Republican Senators to the amendment. They were Senators McCumber of North Dakota, Kellogg of Minnesota, Harding of Ohio, Page of Vermont, and Sutherland of

West Virginia. All of these men except Senator McCumber [1] were won through the pressure from Republican Party leaders.

This gain of nine recruits reduced to two the number of votes to be won.

When at the end of seven months from the time the amendment had passed the House, we still lacked these two votes, and the President gave no assurance that he would put forth sufficient effort to secure them, we were compelled to renew our attacks upon the President.

[1] Senator McCumber, though opposed, was compelled to support the measure, by the action of the N. D. legislature commanding him to do so.

"Lafayette, We Are Here."

Wholesale Arrests

CHAPTER 17

THE Senate was about to recess. No assurance was given by the majority that suffrage would be considered either before or after the recess. Alarmed and aroused, we decided upon a national protest in Washington August 6th, the anniversary of the birth of Inez Milholland.

The protest took the form of a meeting at the base of the Lafayette monument in the park, directly opposite the White House. Women from many states in the Union, dressed in white, hatless and coatless in the midsummer heat of Washington, marched to the monument carrying banners of purple, white and gold, led by a standard-bearer carrying the American flag. They made a beautiful mass of color as they grouped themselves around the statue, against the abundant green foliage of the park.

The Administration met this simple reasonable form of protest by further arrests.

Mrs. Lawrence Lewis of Philadelphia, the first speaker, began: "We are here because when our country is at war for liberty and democracy . . ." At that point she was roughly seized by a policeman and placed under arrest. The great audience stood in absolute and amazed silence.

Miss Hazel Hunkins of Montana took her place. "Here at the statue of Lafayette, who fought for the liberty of this country," she began, "and under the American flag, I am asking for . . ." She was immediately arrested.

Miss Vivian Pierce of California began: "President Wilson

271

has said . , ." She was dragged from the plinth to the waiting patrol.

One after another came forward in an attempt to speak, but no one was allowed to continue. Wholesale arrests followed. Just as the women were being taken into custody, according to the New York *Evening World* of August 13th, "the President walked out of the northeast gate of the White House and up Pennsylvania Avenue for a conference with Director General of Railroads McAdoo. The President glanced across the street and smiled."

Before the crowd could really appreciate what had happened, forty-eight women had been hustled to the police station by the wagon load, their gay banners floating from the backs of the somber patrols. They were told that the police had arrested them under the orders of Col. C. S. Ridley, the President's military aide, and assistant to the Chief Engineer attached to the War Department. All were released on bail and ordered to appear in court the following day.

When they appeared they were informed by the Government's attorney that he would have to postpone the trial until the following Tuesday so that he might examine witnesses to see "what offense, if any, the women would be charged with."

"I cannot go on with this case," he said, "*I have had no orders.* There are no precedents for cases like these. . . ."

The women demanded that their cases be dismissed, or else a charge made against them. They were merely told to return on the appointed day. Such was the indignation aroused against the Administration for taking this action that Senator Curtis of Kansas, Republican whip, could say publicly:

"The truth of this statement is made evident by the admission of the court that the forty-eight suffragists are arrested upon absolutely no charges, and that these women, among them munition workers and Red Cross workers, are held in Washington until next Tuesday, under arrest, while the United

States attorney for the District of Columbia decides for what offense, 'if any,' they were arrested.

"The meeting was called to make a justified protest against continued blocking of the suffrage amendment by the Democratic majority in the Senate. It is well known that three-fourths of the Republican membership in the Senate are ready to vote for the amendment, but under the control of the Democratic majority the Senate has recessed for six weeks without making any provision for action on this important amendment.

"In justice to the women who have been working so hard for the amendment it should be passed at the earliest date, and if action is not taken on it soon after the resumption of business in the Senate there is every possibility that it will not be taken during this Congress, and the hard-won victory in the House of Representatives will have been won for nothing."

When they finally came to trial ten days after their arrest, to face the charge of "holding a meeting in public grounds," and for eighteen of the defendants an additional charge of "climbing on a statue," the women answered the roll call but remained silent thereafter. The familiar farce ensued. Some were released for lack of identification. The others were sentenced to the District Jail—for ten days if they had merely assembled to hold a public meeting, for fifteen days if they had also "climbed on a statue."

The Administration evidently hoped by lighter sentences to avoid a hunger strike by the prisoners.

The women were taken immediately to a building, formerly used as a man's workhouse, situated in the swamps of the District prison grounds. This building, which had been declared unfit for human habitation by a committee appointed under President Roosevelt in 1909, and which had been uninhabited ever since, was now reopened, nine years later, to receive twenty-six women who had attempted to hold a meeting in a public park in Washington. The women protested in a body and demanded to be treated as political prisoners. This being refused, all save two very elderly women, too frail to do so, went on hunger strike at once.

This last lodgment was the worst. Hideous aspects which had not been encountered in the workhouse and jail proper were encountered here. The cells, damp and cold, were below the level of the upper door and entirely below the high windows. The doors of the cell were partly of solid steel with only a small section of grating, so that a very tiny amount of light penetrated the cells. The wash basins were small and unsightly; the toilet open, with no pretense of covering. The cots were of iron, without any spring, and with only a thin straw pallet to lie upon. The heating facilities were antiquated and the place was always cold. So frightful were the nauseating odors which permeated the place, and so terrible was the drinking water from the disused pipes, that one prisoner after another became violently ill.

"I can hardly describe that atmosphere," said Mrs. W. D. Ascough, of Connecticut. "It was a deadly sort of smell, insidious and revolting. It oppressed and stifled us. There was no escape."

As a kind of relief from these revolting odors, they took their straw pallets from the cells to the floor outside. They were ordered back to their cells but refused in a body to go. They preferred the stone floors to the vile odors within, which kept them nauseated.

Conditions were so shocking that Senators began to visit their constituents in this terrible hole. Many of them protested to the authorities. Protests came in from the country, too.

At the end of the fifth day the Administration succumbed to the hunger strike and released the prisoners, trembling with weakness, some of them with chills and some of them in a high

ABANDONED JAIL

PRISONERS ON STRAW PALLETS ON JAIL FLOOR

fever, scarcely able even to walk to the ambulance or motor car.

We had won from the Administration, however, a concession to our protest. Prior to the release of the prisoners we had announced that in spite of the previous arrests a second protest meeting would be held on the same spot. A permit to hold this second protest meeting was granted us.

"I have been advised [Col. Ridley wrote to Miss Paul] that you desire to hold a demonstration in Lafayette Square on Thursday, August 22d. By direction of the chief of engineers, U. S. Army, you are hereby *granted permission to hold this demonstration.* You are advised good order must prevail."

"We received yesterday [Miss Paul replied] your permit for a suffrage demonstration in Lafayette Park this afternoon, and are very glad that our meetings are no longer to be interfered with. Because of the illness of so many of our members, due to their treatment in prison this last week, and with the necessity of caring for them at headquarters, we are planning to hold our next meeting a little later. We have not determined on the exact date but we will inform you of the time as soon as it is decided upon."

It was reported on credible authority that this concession was the result of a conference at which the President, Secretary of War Baker and Colonel Ridley were present. It was said that Secretary Baker and Colonel Ridley persuaded the President to withdraw the orders to arrest us and allow our meetings to go on, even though they took the form of attacks upon the President.

Two days after the release of the women, the Republican Party, for the first time in the history of woman suffrage, caucused in the Senate in favor of forcing suffrage to a vote.

The resolution which was passed unanimously by the caucus determined to "insist upon consideration immediately" and "also to insist upon a final vote . . . at the earliest possible moment. . . . *Provided*, That this resolution shall not be construed as in any way binding the action or vote of any Member of the Senate upon the merits of the said woman suffrage amendment."

While not a direct attempt, therefore, to win more Republican Senators, this proved a very great tactical contribution to the cause. The Republicans were proud of their suffrage strength. They knew the Democrats were not. With the Congressional elections approaching the Republicans meant to do their part toward acquainting the country with the Administration's policy of vacillation and delay. This was not only helpful to the Republicans politically; it was also advantageous to the amendment in that it goaded the majority into action.

Nine months had passed since the vote in the House and we were perilously near the end of the session, when on the 16th of September, Senator Overman, Democrat, Chairman of the Rules Committee, stated to our Legislative Chairman that suffrage was "not on the program for this session" and that the Senate would recess in a few days for the election campaigns without considering any more legislation. On the same day Senator Jones, Chairman of the Suffrage Committee, announced to us that he would not even call his Committee together to consider taking a vote.

We had announced a fortnight earlier that another protest meeting would be held at the base of the Lafayette Monument that day, September 16th, at *four* o'clock. No sooner had this protest been announced than the President publicly stated that he would receive a delegation of Southern and Western women partisans on the question of the amendment at *two* o'clock the same day.

To this delegation he said, "I am, as I think you know, heartily in sympathy with you. I have endeavored to assist you in every way in my power, and I shall continue to do so.

SUFFRAGISTS MARCH TO LAFAYETTE MONUMENT TO BURN
PRESIDENT WILSON'S WORDS

© Harris & Ewing.

TORCHBEARER AND ESCORTS AT BASE OF MONUMENT.

I will do all I can to urge the passage of the amendment by an early vote."

Presumably this was expected to disarm us and perhaps silence our demonstration. However, it merely moved us to make another hasty visit to Senator Overman, Chairman of the Rules Committee, and to Senator Jones, Chairman of the Suffrage Committee, between the hours of two and four to see if the President's statement that he would do all he could to secure an early vote had altered their statements made earlier in the day.

These Administration leaders assured us that their statements stood; that no provision had been made for action on the amendment; that the President's statement did not mean that a vote would be taken this session; and that they did not contemplate being so advised by him.

Such a situation was intolerable. The President was uttering more fine words, while his Administration leaders interpreted them to mean nothing, because they were not followed up by action on his part.

We thereupon changed our demonstration at four o'clock to a more drastic form of protest. We took these words of the President to the base of Lafayette Monument and burned them in a flaming torch.

A throng gathered to hear the speakers. Ceremonies were opened with the reading of the following appeal by Mrs. Richard Wainwright, wife of Rear-Admiral Wainwright:

"Lafayette, we are here!

"We, the women of the United States, denied the liberty which you helped to gain, and for which we have asked in vain for sixty years, turn to you to plead for us.

"Speak, Lafayette, dead these hundred years but still living in the hearts of the American people. Speak again to plead for us like the bronze woman at your feet, condemned like us to a silent appeal. She offers you a sword. Will you not use for us the sword of the spirit, mightier far than the sword she holds out to you?

"Will you not ask the great leader of democracy to look upon the failure of our beloved country to be in truth the place where every one is free and equal and entitled to a share in the government? Let that outstretched hand of yours pointing to the White House recall to him his words and promises, his trumpet call for all of us, to see that the world is made safe for democracy.

"As our army now in France spoke to you there, saying here we are to help your country fight for liberty, will you not speak here and now for us, a little band with no army, no power but justice and right, no strength but in our Constitution and in the Declaration of Independence; and win a great victory again in this country by giving us the opportunity we ask,—to be heard through the Susan B. Anthony amendment.

"Lafayette, we are here!"

Before the enthusiastic applause for Mrs. Wainwright's appeal had died away, Miss Lucy Branham of Baltimore stepped forward with a flaming torch, which she applied to the President's latest words on suffrage. The police looked on and smiled, and the crowd cheered as she said:

"The torch which I hold symbolizes the burning indignation of the women who for years have been given words without action. . . .

"For five years women have appealed to this President and his party for political freedom. The President has given words, and words, and words. To-day women receive more words. We announce to the President and the whole world to-day, by this act of ours, our determination that words shall not longer be the only reply given to American women—our determination that this same democracy for whose establishment abroad we are making the utmost sacrifice, shall also prevail at home.

"We have protested to this Administration by banners; we have protested by speeches; we now protest by this symbolic act.

"As in the ancient fights for liberty, the crusaders for freedom symbolized their protest against those responsible for injustice by consigning their hollow phrases to the flames, so we, on behalf of thousands of suffragists, in this same way to-day protest against the action of the President and his party in delaying the liberation of American women."

Mrs. Jessie Hardy Mackaye of Washington, D. C., then came forward to the end of the plinth to speak, and as she appeared, a man in the crowd handed her a twenty-dollar bill for the campaign in the Senate. This was the signal for others. Bills and coins were passed up. Instantly marshals ran hither and thither collecting the money in improvised baskets while the cheers grew louder and louder. Many of the policemen present were among the donors.

Burning President Wilson's words had met with popular approval from a large crowd!

The procession of women was starting back to headquarters, the police were eagerly clearing the way for the line; the crowd was dispersing in order; the great golden banner, "Mr. President, what will you *do* for woman suffrage?" was just swinging past the White House gate, when President Wilson stepped into his car for the afternoon drive.

CHAPTER 18

T HE next day the Administration completely reversed its policy. Almost the first Senate business was an announcement on the floor by Senator Jones, Chairman of the Suffrage Committee, that the suffrage amendment would be considered in the Senate September 26th. And Senator Overman, Chairman of the Rules Committee, rather shyly remarked to our legislative chairman that he had been "mistaken yesterday." It was "now in the legislative program." The Senate still stood 62 votes for and 34 against the amendment—2 votes lacking. The President made an effort among individual Democrats to secure them. But it was too feeble an effort and he failed.

Chairman Jones took charge of the measure on the floor. The debate opened with a long and eloquent speech by Senator Vardaman of Mississippi, Democrat, in support of the amendment. "My estimate of woman," said he, in conclusion, "is well expressed in the words employed by a distinguished author who dedicated his book to a 'Little mountain, a great meadow, and a woman,' 'To the mountain for the sense of time, to the meadow for the sense of space, and to the woman for the sense of everything.' "

Senator McCumber of North Dakota, Republican, followed with a curious speech. His problem was to explain why, although opposed to suffrage, he would vote for the amendment. Beginning with the overworked "cave man" and "beasts of the forests," and down to the present day, "the male had always protected the female." He always would! Forgetting recent events in the Capital, he went so far as to say, " . . . In our courts she ever finds in masculine nature an asylum of protection, even though she may have committed great wrong. While the mind may be convinced beyond any doubt, the masculine heart finds it almost impossible to pronounce the word 'guilty' against a woman." Scarcely had the galleries ceased smiling at this idea when he treated them to a novel application of the biological theory of inheritance. "The political field," he declared, "always has been and probably always will be an arena of more or less bitter contest. The political battles leave scars as ugly and lacerating as the physical battles, and the more sensitive the nature the deeper and more lasting the wound. And as no man can enter this contest or be a party to it and assume its responsibilities without feeling its blows and suffering its wounds, much less can woman with her more emotional and more sensitive nature.

"But . . . you may ask why should she be relieved from the scars and wounds of political contest? Because they do not affect her alone but are *transmitted through her to generations yet to come. . . .*"

The faithful story of the sinking ship was invoked by the Senator from North Dakota. One might almost imagine after listening to Congressional debates for some years that traveling on sinking ships formed a large part of human experience. "Fathers, sons, and brothers," said the Senator in tearful voice, "guarding the lifeboats until every woman from the highest to the lowest has been made safe, waving adieu with a smile of cheer on their lips, while the wounded vessel slowly bears them to a strangling death and a watery tomb, belie the charge . . ." that woman needs her citizenship as a form of protection.

In spite of these opinions, however, the Senator was obliged to vote for the amendment because his state had so ordered.

Senator Hardwick of Georgia, Democrat, felt somewhat betrayed that the suffrage plank in the platform of his party in 1916, recommending state action, should be so carelessly set aside. "There is not a Democratic Senator present," said Mr. Hardwick, "who does not know the history that lies back of the adoption of that plank. There is not a Democratic Senator who does not know that the plank was written here in Washington and sent to the convention and represented the deliberate voice of the administration and of the party on this question, which was to remit this question to the several States for action. . . .

"The President of the United States . . . was reported . . . to have sent this particular plank . . . from Washington, supposedly by the hands of one of his Cabinet officers." The fact that his own party and the Republican party were both advancing on suffrage irritated him into denouncing the alacrity with which "politicians and senators are trying to get on the band wagon first."

Senator McKellar of Tennessee, Democrat, reduced the male superiority argument to simple terms when he said: " . . . Taking them by and large, there are brainy men and brainy women, and that is about all there is to the proposition."

Our armies were sweeping victorious toward Germany. There was round on round of eloquence about the glories of war. Rivers of blood flowed. And always the rôle of woman was depicted as a contented binding of wounds. There were those who thought woman should be rewarded for such service. Others thought she ought to do it without asking anything in return. But all agreed that this was her rôle. There was no woman's voice in that body to protest against the perpetuity of such a rôle.

The remarks of Senator Reed of Missouri, anti-suffrage Democrat, typify this attitude. " . . . Women in my state believe in the old-fashioned doctrine that men should fight the battles on the red line; that men should stand and bare their bosoms to the iron hail; and that back of them, if need be, there shall be women who may bind up the wounds and whose tender hands may rest upon the brow of the valiant soldier who has gone down in the fight.

"But, sir, that is woman's work, and it has been woman's work always. . . . The woman who gave her first born a final kiss and blessed him on his way to battle," had, according to the Senator from Missouri, earned a "crown of glory . . . gemmed with the love of the world."

And with Senator Walsh of Montana, Democrat, "The women of America have already written a glorious page in the history of the greatest of wars that have vexed the world. They, like Cornelia, have given, and freely given their jewels to their country."

Some of us wondered.

Senator McLean of Connecticut, anti-suffrage Republican, flatly stated "that all questions involving declarations of war and terms of peace should be left to that sex which must do the fighting and the dying on the battlefield." And he further said that until boys between 18 and 21 who had just been called to the colors should ask for the vote, "their mothers should be and remain both proud and content" without it. He concluded with an amusing account of the history of the ballot box. "This joint resolution," he said, "goes beyond the seas and above the clouds. It attempts to tamper with the ballot box, over which mother nature always has had and always will have supreme control; and such attempts always have ended and always will end in failure and misfortune."

Senator Phelan of California, Democrat, made a straightforward, intelligent speech.

Senator Beckham of Kentucky, Democrat, deplored the idea that man was superior to woman. He pleaded "guilty to the charge of Romanticism." He said, "But I look upon woman as superior to man." Therefore he could not trust her with a vote. He had the hardihood to say further, with the men of the world at each other's throats, . . . "Woman is the civilizing, refining, elevating influence that holds man from barbarism." We charged him with ignorance as well as romanticism when he said in closing, "It is the duty of man to work and labor for woman; to cut the wood, to carry the coal, to go into the fields in the necessary labor to sustain the home where the woman presides and by her superior nature elevates him to higher and better conceptions of life."

Meanwhile Senator Shafroth of Colorado, Democrat, lifelong advocate of suffrage, was painstakingly asking one senator after another, as he had been for years, "Does not the Senator believe that the just powers of government are derived from the consent of the governed?" and then—"But if you have the general principle acknowledged that the just powers of government are derived from the consent of the governed." . . . and so forth. But the idea of applying the Declaration of Independence to modern politics fairly put them to sleep.

These samples of senatorial profundity may divert, outrage, or bore us, but they do not represent the real battle. It is not that the men who utter these sentiments do not believe them. More is the pity, they do. But they are smoke screens—mere skirmishes of eloquence or foolishness. They do not represent the motives of their political acts.

The real excitement began when Senator Pittman of Nevada, Democrat, attempted to reveal to the senators of his party the actual seriousness of the political crisis in which the Democrats were now involved. He also attempted to shift the blame for threatened defeat of the amendment to the Republican side of the chamber. There was a note of desperation in his voice, too, since he knew that President Wilson had not up to that moment won the two votes lacking. The gist of Senator Pittman's remarks was this: The Woman's Party has charged the Senate Woman Suffrage Committee, which is in control of the Democrats, and the President himself, with the responsibility for obstructing a vote on the measure. "I confess," said he, that this is "having its effect as a campaign argument" in the woman suffrage states.

Senator Wolcott of Delaware, Democrat, interrupted him to ask if this was "the party that has been picketing here in Washington?" Senator Pittman, having just paid this tribute to our campaign in the West, hastened to say that it was, but that there was another association, the National American Woman Suffrage Association, which had always conducted its campaign in a "lady-like—modest—and intelligent way" and which had "never mixed in politics."

Waving a copy of the *Suffragist* in the air, Senator Pittman began his attempt to shift responsibility to the Republican side, for the critical condition of the amendment. He denounced the Republicans for caucusing on the amendment and deciding unanimously to press for a vote, when they [the Republicans] knew there were two votes lacking. He scored us for having given so much publicity to the action of the caucus and declared with vehemence that a "trick" had been executed through Senator Smoot which he would not allow to go unrevealed. Senator Pittman charged that the Republicans had promised enough votes to pass the amendment and that upon that promise the Democrats had brought the measure on the floor; that the Republicans thereupon withdrew enough votes to cause the defeat of the amendment. Whether or not this was true, at any rate, as Senator Smoot pointed out, the Democratic Chairman in charge of the measure could at any moment send the measure back to Committee, safe from immediate defeat. This was true, but not exactly a suggestion to be welcomed by the Democrats.

"Yes," replied Senator Pittman, "and then if we move to refer it back to the committee, the Senator from Utah would say again, 'The Democrats are obstructing the passage of this amendment. . . . We told you all the time they wanted to kill it.' . . . If we refer it back to the committee, then we will be charged, as we have been all the time in the suffrage states, with trying to prevent a vote on it, and still the Woman's Party campaign will go on as it is going on now; and if we vote on it they will say: 'We told you the Democrats would kill it, because the President would not make 32 on his side vote for it'."

That was the crux of the whole situation. The Democrats had been manœuvered into a position where they could neither afford to move to refer the amendment back to the committee, nor could they afford to press it to a losing vote. They were indeed in an exceedingly embarrassing predicament.

Throughout hours of debate, Senator Pittman could not get away from the militants. Again and again, he recited our deeds of protest, our threats of reprisal, our relentless strategy of holding his party responsible for defeat or victory.

"I should like the Senator," interpolated Senator Poindexter of Washington, Republican, "so long as he is discussing the action of the pickets, to explain to the Senate whether or not it is the action of the pickets . . . the militant . . . woman's party, that caused the President to change his attitude on the subject. Was he coerced into supporting this measure —after he had for years opposed it—because he was picketed? When did the President change his attitude? If it was not because he was picketed, will the Senator explain what was the cause of the change in the President's attitude?"

Mr. Pittman did not reply directly to these questions.

Senator Reed of Missouri, anti-Administration Democrat, consumed hours reading into the Congressional Record various press reports of militant activities. He dwelt particularly upon the news headlines, such as,

"Great Washington Crowd Cheers Demonstration at White House by National Woman's Party." . . .

"Suffragists Burn Wilson 'Idle Words' . . ."

"Money Instead of Jeers Greet Marchers and Unique Protest Against Withholding Vote" . . .

"Apply Torch to President's Words . . . Promise to Urge Passage of Amendment Not Definite Enough for Militants."

"Suff's Burn Speech . . . Apply Torch to Wilson's Words During Demonstration—Symbol of 'Indignation'—Throngs Witnessing Doings in Lafayette Square Orderly and Contribute to Fund—President Receives Delegation of American Suffrage Association Women."

Senator McKellar of Tennessee, Democrat, asked Mr. Reed if he did not believe that we had a right peaceably to assemble under the "first amendment to our Constitution which I shall read: Congress shall make no law . . . abridging . . . the right of the people peaceably to assemble, and to petition the Government for a redress of grievances." Mr. Reed made no direct answer.

Lest the idea get abroad from the amount of time they spent in discussing the actions of the "wicked militants," that we *had* had something to do with the situation which had resulted in Democratic despair, Senator Thomas of Colorado, the one Democrat who had never been able to conceal his hostility to us for having reduced his majority in 1914, arose to pay a tribute to the conservative suffrage association of America. Their "escutcheon," he said, "is unstained by mob methods or appeals to violence. It has neither picketed Presidents nor populated prisons. . . . It has carried no banners flaunting insults to the Executive," while the militants on the other hand have indulged in "much tumult and vociferous braying, all for notoriety's sake." . . . The galleries smiled as he counseled the elder suffrage leaders "not to lose courage nor yet be faint-hearted," for this "handicap" would soon be overcome. It would have taken an abler man than Senator Thomas, in the face of the nature of this debate, to make any one believe that we had been a "handicap" in forcing them to their position. He was the only one hardy enough to try. After this debate the Senate adjourned, leaving things from the point of view of party politics, tangled in a hopeless knot. It was to untie this knot that the President returned hastily from New York in answer to urgent summons by long distance telephone, and went to the Capitol to deliver his memorable address.

Mr. Vice President and Gentlemen of the Senate: The un-usual circumstances of a world war in which we stand and are judged in the view not only of our own people and our own consciences but also in view of all nations and all peoples will, I hope, justify in your thought, as it does in mine, the message I have come to bring you. I regard the concurrence of the Senate in the constitutional amendment proposing the extension of the suffrage to women as vitally essential to the successful prosecution of the great war of humanity in which we are engaged. I have come to urge upon you the considerations which have led me to that conclusion. It is not only my privilege, it is also my duty to appraise you of every circumstance and element involved in this momentous struggle which seems to me to affect its very processes and its outcome. It is my duty to win the war and to ask you to remove every obstacle that stands in the way of winning it.

I had assumed that the Senate would concur in the amendment because no disputable principle is involved but only a question of the method by which the suffrage is to be extended to women. There is and can be no party issue involved in it. Both of our great national parties are pledged, explicitly pledged, to equality of suffrage for the women of the country. Neither party, therefore, it seems to me, can justify hesitation as to the method of obtaining it, can rightfully hesitate to substitute federal initiative for state initiative, if the early adoption of the measure is necessary to the successful prosecution of the war and if the method of state action proposed in party platforms of 1916 is impracticable within any reasonable length of time, if practicable at all. And its adoption is, in my judgment, clearly necessary to the successful prosecution of the war and the successful realization of the objects for which the war is being fought.

That judgment, I take the liberty of urging upon you with solemn earnestness for reasons which I shall state very frankly and which I shall hope will seem as conclusive to you as they have seemed to me.

This is a peoples' war, and the peoples' thinking constitutes its atmosphere and morale, not the predilections of the drawing room or the political considerations of the caucus. If we be indeed democrats and wish to lead the world to democracy, we can ask other peoples to accept in proof of our sincerity and our ability to lead them whither they wish to be led nothing less persuasive and convincing than our actions. Our professions will not suffice. Verification must be forthcoming when verification is asked for. And in this case verification is asked for, asked for in this particular matter. You ask by whom? Not through diplomatic channels; not by Foreign Ministers, not by the intimations of parliaments. It is asked for by the anxious, expectant, suffering peoples with whom we are dealing and who are willing to put their destinies in some measure in our hands, if they are sure that we wish the same things that they wish. I do not speak by conjecture. It is not alone the voices of statesmen and of newspapers that reach me, *and the voices of foolish and intemperate agitators do not reach me at all!* Through many, many channels I have been made aware what the plain, struggling, workaday folk are thinking upon whom the chief terror and suffering of this tragic war falls. They are looking to the great, powerful, famous democracy of the West to lead them to the new day for which they have so long waited; and they think, in their logical simplicity, that democracy means that women shall play their part in affairs alongside men and upon an equal footing with them. If we reject measures like this, in ignorance or defiance of what a new age has brought forth, of what they have seen but we have not, they will cease to follow or to trust us. They have seen their own governments accept this interpretation of democracy,—seen old governments like Great Britain, which did not profess to be democratic, promise readily and as of course this justice to women, though they had before refused it, the strange revelations of this war having made many things new and plain to governments as well as to peoples.

Are we alone to refuse to learn the lesson? Are we alone to ask and take the utmost that women can give,—service and sacrifice of every kind,—and still say that we do not see what title that gives them to stand by our sides in the guidance of the affairs of their nation and ours? We have made partners of the women in this war; shall we admit them only to a partnership of sacrifice and suffering and toil and not to a partnership of privilege and of right? This war could not have been fought, either by the other nations engaged or by America, if it had not been for the services of the women,— services rendered in every sphere,—not only in the fields of effort in which we have been accustomed to see them work, but wherever men have worked and upon the very skirts and edges of the battle itself. We shall not only be distrusted but shall deserve to be distrusted if we do not enfranchise them with the fullest possible enfranchisement, as it is now certain that the other great free nations will enfranchise them. We cannot isolate our thought or our action in such a matter from the thought of the rest of the world. We must either conform or deliberately reject what they propose and resign the leadership of liberal minds to others.

The women of America are too noble and too intelligent and too devoted to be slackers whether you give or withhold this thing that is mere justice; but I know the magic it will work in their thoughts and spirits if you give it them. I propose it as I would propose to admit soldiers to the suffrage, the men fighting in the field for our liberties and the liberties of the world, were they excluded. The tasks of the women lie at the very heart of the war, and I know how much stronger that heart will beat if you do this just thing and show our women that you trust them as much as you in fact and of necessity depend upon them.

Have I said that the passage of this amendment is a vitally necessary war measure, and do you need further proof? Do you stand in need of the trust of other peoples and of the trust of our women? Is that trust an asset or is it not? I tell you plainly, as commander-in-chief of our armies and of the gallant men in our fleets, as the present spokesman of this people in our dealings with the men and women throughout the world who are now our partners, as the responsible head of a great government which stands and is questioned day by day as to its purposes, its principles, its hopes, whether they be serviceable to men everywhere or only to itself, and who must himself answer these questionings or be shamed, as the guide and director of forces caught in the grip of war and by the same token in need of every material and spiritual resource this great nation possesses,—I tell you plainly that this measure which I urge upon you is vital to the winning of the war and to the energies alike of preparation and of battle.

And not to the winning of the war only. It is vital to the right solution of the great problems which we must settle, and settle immediately, when the war is over. We shall need then a vision of affairs which is theirs, and, as we have never needed them before, the sympathy and insight and clear moral instinct of the women of the world. The problems of that time will strike to the roots of many things that we have not hitherto questioned, and I for one believe that our safety in those questioning days, as well as our comprehension of matters that touch society to the quick, will depend upon the direct and authoritative participation of women in our counsels. We shall need their moral sense to preserve what is right and fine and worthy in our system of life as well as to discover just what it is that ought to be purified and reformed. Without their counselings we shall be only half wise.

That is my case. This is my appeal. Many may deny its validity, if they choose, but no one can brush aside or answer the arguments upon which it is based. The executive tasks of this war rest upon me. I ask that you lighten them and place in my hands instruments, spiritual instruments, which I do not now possess, which I sorely need, and which I have daily to apologize for not being able to employ. (Applause).

It was a truly beautiful appeal.

When the applause and the excitement attendant upon the occasion of a message from the President had subsided, and the floor of the chamber had emptied itself of its distinguished visitors, the debate was resumed.

"If this resolution fails now," said Senator Jones of Washington, ranking Republican member of the Suffrage Committee, "it fails for lack of Democratic votes."

Senator Cummins of Iowa, Republican, also a member of the Suffrage Committee, reminded opponents of the measure of the retaliatory tactics used by President Wilson when repudiated by senators on other issues. "I sincerely hope," he said tauntingly, "that the President may deal kindly and leniently with those who are refusing to remove this obstacle which stands in his way. It has not been very long since the President retired the junior Senator from Mississippi [Mr. Vardaman] from public life. Why? Because he refused at all times to obey the commands which were issued for his direction. The junior Senator from Georgia [Mr. Hardwick] suffered the same fate. How do you hope to escape? . . . My Democratic friends are either proceeding upon the hypothesis that the President is insincere or that they may be able to secure an immunity from him that these other unfortunate aspirants for office failed to secure."

Senator Cummins chided Senator Reed for denouncing "the so-called militants who sought to bring their influence to bear upon the situation in rather a more forcible and decisive method than was employed by the national association. . . . I did not believe in the campaign they were pursuing (not one senator was brave enough to say outright that he did). . . .

"But that was simply a question for them to determine; and if they thought that in accordance with the established custom the President should bring his influence to bear more effectively than he had, they had a perfect right to burn his message; they had a perfect right to carry banners in Lafayette Park, in front of the White House, or anywhere else; they had a perfect right to bring their banners into the Capitol and display them with all the force and vigor which they could command. I did not agree with them; but they also were making a campaign for an inestimable and a fundamental right.

"What would you have done, men, if you had been deprived of the right to vote? What would you have done if you had been deprived of the right of representation? Have the militants done anything worse than the revolutionary forces who gathered about the tea chests and threw them into the sea? . . .

"I do not believe they [the militants] committed any crime; and while I had no particle of sympathy with the manner in which they were conducting their campaign, I think their arrest and imprisonment and the treatment which they received while in confinement are a disgrace to the civilized world, and much the more a disgrace to the United States, which assumes to lead the civilized world in humane endeavor. They disturbed nobody save that disturbance which is common to the carrying forward of all propaganda by those who are intensely and vitally interested in it. I wish they had not done it, but I am not to be the judge of their methods so long as they confine themselves to those acts and to those words which are fairly directed to the accomplishment of their purposes. I cannot accept the conclusion that because these women burned a message in Lafayette Park or because they carried banners upon the streets in Washington therefore they are criminals."

The time had come to take the vote, but we knew we had not won. The roll was called and the vote stood 62 to 34 [Oct. 1, 1918], counting all pairs. We had lost by 2 votes.

Instantly Chairman Jones, according to his promise to the women, changing his vote from "yea" to "nay," moved for a reconsideration of the measure, and thus automatically kept it on the calendar of the Senate. That was all that could be done.

The President's belief in the power of words had lost the amendment. Nor could he by a speech, eloquent as it was, break down the opposition in the Senate which he had so long protected and condoned.

Our next task was to secure a reversal of the Senate vote. We modified our tactics slightly.

CHAPTER 19

OUR immediate task was to compel the President to secure a reversal of two votes in the Senate. It became necessary to enter again the Congressional elections which were a month away.

By a stroke of good luck there were two senatorial contests—in New Jersey and New Hampshire—for vacancies in the short term. That is, we had an opportunity to elect two friends who would take their seats in time to vote on the amendment before the end of this session. It so happened that the Democratic candidates were pledged to vote for the amendment if elected, and that the Republican candidates were opposed to the amendment. We launched our campaign in this instance for the election of the Democratic candidates. We went immediately to the President to ask his assistance in our endeavor. We urged him personally to appeal to the voters of New Jersey and New Hampshire on behalf of his two candidates. As Party leader he was at the moment paying no attention whatever to the success of these two suffragists. Both of the Democratic candidates themselves appealed to President Wilson for help in their contests, on the basis of their suffrage advocacy. His speech to the Senate scarcely cold, the President refused to lend any assistance in these contests, which with sufficient effort might have produced the last two votes.

At the end of two weeks of such pressure upon the President we were unable to interest him in this practical endeavor. It was clear that he would move again only under attack. We went again, therefore, to the women voters of the West and asked them to withhold their support from the Democratic Senatorial candidates in the suffrage states in order to compel the President to assist in the two Eastern contests. This campaign made it clear to the President that we were still holding him and his party to their responsibility.

And as has been pointed out, our policy was to oppose the Democratic candidates at elections so long as their party was responsible for the passage of the amendment and did not pass it. Since there is no question between individuals in suffrage states—they are all suffragists—this could not increase our numerical strength. It could, however, and did demonstrate the growing and comprehensive power of the women voters.

Shortly before election, when our campaign was in full swing in the West, the President sent a letter appealing to the voters of New Jersey to support Mr. Hennessey, the Democratic candidate for the Senate. He subsequently appealed to the voters of New Hampshire to elect Mr. Jameson, candidate for Democratic Senator in New Hampshire.

We continued our campaign in the West as a safeguard against relaxation by the President after his appeal. There were seven senatorial contests in the western suffrage states. In all but two of thse contests—Montana and Nevada—the Democratic Senatorial candidates were defeated. In these two states the Democratic majority was greatly reduced.

Republicans won in New Jersey and New Hampshire and a Republican Congress was elected to power throughout the country.

The election campaign had had a wholesome effect, however, on both parties and was undoubtedly one of the factors in persuading the President to again appeal to the Senate.

Immediately after the defeat in the Senate, and throughout the election campaign, we attempted to hold banners at the Capitol to assist our campaign and in order to weaken the

PICKETS AT CAPITOL

© *Harris & Ewing.*

SENATE PAGES AND CAPITOL POLICE ATTACK PICKETS

resistance of the senators of the opposition. The mottoes on the banners attacked with impartial mercilessness both Democrats and Republicans. One read:

> SENATOR WADSWORTH'S REGIMENT IS FIGHTING FOR DEMOCRACY ABROAD.
> SENATOR WADSWORTH LEFT HIS REGIMENT AND IS FIGHTING AGAINST DEMOCRACY IN THE SENATE.
> SENATOR WADSWORTH COULD SERVE HIS COUNTRY BETTER BY FIGHTING WITH HIS REGIMENT ABROAD THAN BY FIGHTING WOMEN AT HOME.

Another read:

> SENATOR SHIELDS TOLD THE PEOPLE OF TENNESSEE HE WOULD SUPPORT THE PRESIDENT'S POLICIES.
> THE ONLY TIME THE PRESIDENT WENT TO THE SENATE TO ASK ITS SUPPORT SENATOR SHIELDS VOTED AGAINST HIM.
> DOES TENNESSEE BACK THE PRESIDENT'S WAR PROGRAM OR SENATOR SHIELDS?

And still a third:

> GERMANY HAS ESTABLISHED "EQUAL, UNIVERSAL, SECRET, DIRECT FRANCHISE."
> THE SENATE HAS DENIED EQUAL, UNIVERSAL, SECRET SUFFRAGE TO AMERICA.
> WHICH IS MORE OF A DEMOCRACY, GERMANY OR AMERICA?

As the women approached the Senate, Colonel Higgins, the Sergeant at Arms of the Senate, ordered a squad of Capitol policemen to rush upon them. They wrenched their banners from them, twisting their wrists and manhandling them as they took them up the steps, through the door, and down

into the guardroom,—their banners confiscated and they themselves detained for varying periods of time. When the
women insisted on knowing upon what charges they were held,
they were merely told that "peace and order must be maintained on the Capitol grounds," and further, "It don't make
no difference about the law, Colonel Higgins is boss here, and
he has taken the law in his own hands."

Day after day this performance went on. Small detach-
ments of women attempted to hold banners outside the United
States Senate, as the women of Holland had done outside the
Parliament in the Hague. It was difficult to believe that
American politicians could be so devoid of humor as they
showed themselves. The panic that overwhelms our official
mind in the face of the slightest irregularity is appalling!
Instead of maintaining peace and order, the squads of police
managed to keep the Capitol grounds in a state of confusion.
They were assisted from time to time by Senate pages, small
errand boys who would run out and attack mature women
with impunity. The women would be held under the most rigid
detention each day until the Senate had safely adjourned.
Then on the morrow the whole spectacle would be repeated.

While the United States Senate was standing still under our
protest world events rushed on. German autocracy had collapsed. The Allies had won a military victory. The Kaiser
had that very week fled for his life because of the uprising of
his people.

"We are all free voters of a free republic now," was the
message sent by the women of Germany to the women of the
United States through Miss Jane Addams. We were at that
moment heartily ashamed of our government. German women
voting! American women going to jail and spending long
hours in the Senate guardhouse without arrests or charges.
The war came to an end. Congress adjourned November 21st.

When the 65th Congress reconvened for its short and final

session, December 2nd, 1918 [less than a month after our election campaign], President Wilson, for the first time, included suffrage in his regular message to Congress, the thing that we had asked of him at the opening of every session of Congress since March, 1913.

There were now fewer than a hundred days in which to get action from the Senate and so avoid losing the benefit of our victory in the House.

In his opening address to Congress, the President again appealed to the Senate in these words:

"And what shall we say of the women—of their instant intelligence, quickening every task that they touched; their capacity for organization and coöperation, which gave their action discipline and enhanced the effectiveness of everything they attempted; their aptitude at tasks to which they had never before set their hands; their utter self-sacrifice alike in what they did and in what they gave? Their contribution to the great result is beyond appraisal. They have added a new luster to the annals of American womanhood.

"The least tribute we can pay them is to make them the equals of men in political rights, as they have proved themselves their equals in every field of practical work they have entered, whether for themselves or for their country. These great days of completed achievement would be sadly marred were we to omit that act of justice. Besides the immense practical services they have rendered, the women of the country have been the moving spirits in the systematic economies in which our people have voluntarily assisted to supply the suffering peoples of the world and the armies upon every front with food and everything else we had, that might serve the common cause. The details of such a story can never be fully written but we carry them at our hearts and thank God that we can say that we are the kinsmen of such."

Again we looked for action to follow this appeal. Again

we found that the President had uttered these words but had made no plan to translate them into action.

And so his second appeal to the Senate failed, coming as it did after the hostility of his party to the idea of conferring freedom on women nationally, had been approved and fostered by President Wilson for five solid years. He could not overcome with additional eloquence the opposition which he himself had so long formulated, defended, encouraged and solidified, especially when that eloquence was followed by either no action or only half-hearted efforts.

It would now require a determined assertion of his political power as the leader of his party. We made a final appeal to him as leader of his party and while still at the height of his world power, to make such an assertion and to demand the necessary two votes.

CHAPTER 20

NO sooner had we set ourselves to a brief, hot campaign to compel President Wilson to win the final votes than he sailed away to France to attend the Peace Conference, sailed away to consecrate himself to the program of liberating the oppressed peoples of the whole world. He cannot be condemned for aiming to achieve so gigantic a task. But we reflected that again the President had refused his specific aid in an humble aspiration, for the rosy hope of a more boldly conceived ambition.

It was positively impossible for us, by our own efforts, to win the last 2 votes. We could only win them through the President. That he had left behind him his message urging the Senate to act, is true. That Administration leaders did not consider these words a command, is also true. It must be realized that even after the President had been compelled to publicly declare his support of the measure, it was almost impossible to get his own leaders to take seriously his words on suffrage. And so again the Democratic Chairman of the Rules Committee, in whose keeping the program lay, had no thought of bringing it to a vote. The Democratic Chairman of the Woman Suffrage Committee assumed not the slightest responsibility for its success, nor could he produce any plan whereby the last votes could be won. They knew, as well as did we, that the President only could win those last 2 votes. They made it perfectly clear that until he had done so, they could do nothing.

Less than fifty legislative days remained to us. Something had to be done quickly, something bold and offensive enough to threaten the prestige of the President, as he was riding in sublimity to unknown heights as a champion of world liberty; something which might penetrate his reverie and shock him into concrete action. We had successfully defied the full power of his Administration, the odds heavily against us. We must now defy the popular belief of the world in this apostle of liberty. This was the feeling of the four hundred officers of the National Woman's Party, summoned to a three days' conference in Washington in December, 1918. It was unanimously decided to light a fire in an urn, and, on the day that the President was officially received by France, to burn with fitting public ceremonies all the President's past and present speeches or books concerning "liberty", "freedom" and "democracy."

It was late afternoon when the four hundred women proceeded solemnly in single file from headquarters, past the White House, along the edge of the quiet and beautiful Lafayette Park, to the foot of Lafayette's statue. A slight mist added beauty to the pageant. The purple, white and gold banners, so brilliant in the sunshine, became soft pastel sails. Half the procession carried lighted torches; the other half banners. The crowd gathered silently, somewhat awe-struck by the scene. Massed about that statue, we felt a strange strength and solidarity, we felt again that we were a part of the universal struggle for liberty.

The torch was applied to the pine-wood logs in the Grecian Urn at the edge of the broad base of the statue. As the flames began to mount, Vida Milholland stepped forward and without accompaniment sang again from that spot of beauty, in her own challenging way, the Woman's Marseillaise. Even the small boys in the crowd, always the most difficult to please, cheered and clapped and cried for more.

Mrs. John Rogers, Jr., chairman of the National Advisory Council, said, as president of the ceremony:

"We hold this meeting to protest against the denial of liberty to American women. All over the world to-day we see surging and sweeping irresistibly on, the great tide of democracy, and women would be derelict in their duty if they did not see to it that it brings freedom to the women of this land. . . .

"Our ceremony to-day is planned to call attention to the fact that President Wilson has gone abroad to establish democracy in foreign lands when he has failed to establish democracy at home. We burn his words on liberty to-day, not in malice or anger, but in a spirit of reverence for truth.

"This meeting is a message to President Wilson. We expect an answer. If the answer is more words we will burn them *again*. The only answer the National Woman's Party will accept is the instant passage of the amendment in the Senate."

The few hoots and jeers which followed all ceased, when a tiny and aged woman stepped from her place to the urn in the brilliant torch light. The crowd recognized a veteran. It was the most dramatic moment in the ceremony. Reverend Olympia Brown of Wisconsin, one of the first ordained women ministers in the country, then in her eighty-fourth year, gallant pioneer, friend and colleague of Susan B. Anthony, said, as she threw into the flames the speech made by the President on his arrival in France:

" . . . I have fought for liberty for seventy years, and I protest against the President's leaving our country with this old fight here unwon."

The crowd burst into applause and continued to cheer as she was assisted from the plinth of the statue, too frail to dismount by herself. Then came the other representative women, from Massachusetts to California, from Georgia to Michigan, each one consigning to the flames a special declaration of the

President's on freedom. The flames burned brighter and brighter and leapt higher as the night grew black.

The casual observer said, "They must be crazy. Don't they know the President isn't at home? Why are they appealing to him in the park opposite the White House when he is in France?"

The long line of bright torches shone menacingly as the women marched slowly back to headquarters, and the crowd dispersed in silence. The White House *was* empty. But we knew our message would be heard in France.

CHAPTER 21

DECEMBER came to an end with no plan for action on the amendment assured. This left us January and February only before the session would end. The President had not yet won the necessary 2 votes. We decided therefore to keep a perpetual fire to consume the President's speeches on democracy as fast as he made them in Europe.

And so on New Year's Day, 1919, we light our first watch-fire of freedom in the Urn dedicated to that purpose. We place it on the sidewalk in a direct line with the President's front door. The wood comes from a tree in Independence Square, Philadelphia. It burns gaily. Women with banners stand guard over the watchfire. A bell hung in the balcony at headquarters tolls rhythmically the beginning of the watch. It tolls again as the President's words are tossed to the flames. His speech to the workingmen of Manchester; his toast to the King at Buckingham Palace: "We have used great words, all of us. We have used the words 'right' and 'justice' and now we are to prove whether or not we understand these words;" his speech at Brest; all turn into ignominious brown ashes.

The bell tolls again when the watch is changed. All Washington is reminded hourly that we are at the President's gate, burning his words. From Washington the news goes to all the world.

People gather to see the ceremony. The omnipresent small boys and soldiers jeer, and some tear the banners. A soldier rushes to the scene with a bucket of water which does not extinguish the flames. The fire burns as if by magic. A policeman arrives and uses a fire extinguisher. But the fire burns on! The flames are as indomitable as the women who guard them! Rain comes, but all through the night the watchfire burns. All through the night the women stand guard.

Day and night the fire burns. Boys are permitted by the police to scatter it in the street, to break the urn, and to demolish the banners. But each time the women rekindle the fire. A squad of policemen tries to demolish the fire. While the police are engaged at the White House gates, other women go quietly in the dusk to the huge bronze urn in Lafayette Park and light another watchfire. A beautiful blaze leaps into the air from the great urn. The police hasten hither. The burning contents are overturned. Alice Paul refills the urn and kindles a new fire. She is placed under arrest. Suddenly a third blaze is seen in a remote corner of the park. The policemen scramble to that corner. When the watchfires have been continued for four days and four nights, in spite of the attempts by the police to extinguish them, general orders to arrest are sent to the squad of policemen.

Five women are taken to the police station. The police captain is outraged that the ornamental urn valued at $10,000 should have been used to hold a fire which burned the President's words! His indignation leaves the defendants unimpressed, however, and he becomes conciliatory. Will the "ladies" promise to be good and light no more fires in the park?"

Instead, the "ladies" inquire on what charge they are held. Not even the police captain knows. They wait at the police station to find out, refusing to give bail unless they are told. Meanwhile other women address the crowd lingering about the watchfire. The crowd asks thoughtful questions. Little knots of men can be seen discussing "what the whole thing is about anyway."

Miss Mildred Morris, one of the participants, overheard

THE URN GUARDED BY MISS BERTHE ARNOLD

© *Harris & Ewing.*

THE BELL WHICH TOLLED THE CHANGE OF WATCH

the following discussion in one group composed of an old man, a young sailor and a young soldier.

"But whatever you think of them," the sailor was telling the soldier, "you have to admire their sincerity and courage. They've got to do this thing. They want only what's their right and real men want to give it to them."

"But they've got no business using a sidewalk in front of the White House for a bonfire," declared the soldier. "It's disloyal to the President, I tell you, and if they weren't women I'd slap their faces."

"Listen, sonny," said the old man, patting the soldier's arm, "I'm as loyal to the President as any man alive, but I've got to admit that he ain't doing the right thing towards these women. He's forced everything else he's wanted through Congress, and if he wanted to give these women the vote badly enough he could force the suffrage amendment through. If you and I were in these women's places, sonny, we'd act real vicious. We'd want to come here and clean out the whole White House."

"But if the President doesn't want to push their amendment through, it's his right not to," argued the soldier. "It's nobody's business how he uses his power."

"Good God!" the sailor burst out. "Why don't you go over and get a job shining the Kaiser's boots?"

The women were released without bail, since no one was able to supply a charge. But a thorough research was instituted and out of the dusty archives some one produced an ancient statute that would serve the purpose. It prohibits the building of fires in a public place in the District of Columbia between sunset and sunrise. And so the beautiful Elizabethan custom of lighting watchfires as a form of demonstration was forbidden!

In a few days eleven women were brought to trial. There was a titter in the court room as the prosecuting attorney read with heavy pomposity the charge against the prisoners "to wit: That on Pennsylvania Avenue, Northwest, in the District of Columbia they did aid and abet in setting fire to certain combustibles consisting of logs, paper, oil, etc., *between the setting of the sun in the said District of Columbia on the fifth day of January and the rising of the sun in the said District of Columbia of the sixth day of January*, 1919, *A. D.*"

The court is shocked to hear of this serious deed. The prisoners are unconcerned.

"Call the names of the prisoners," the judge orders.

The clerk calls, "Julia Emory."

No answer!

"Julia Emory," he calls a second time.

Dead silence!

The clerk tries another name, a second, a third, a fourth. Always there is silence!

In a benevolent tone, the judge asks the policeman to identify the prisoners. They identify as many as they can. An attempt is made to have the prisoners rise and be sworn. They sit.

"We will go on with the testimony," says the judge.

The police testify as to the important details of the crime. They were on Pennsylvania Avenue—they looked at their watch—they learned it was about 5:30—they saw the ladies in the park putting wood on fires in urns. "I threw the wood on the pavement; they kept putting it back," says one policeman. "Each time I tried to put out the fire they threw on more wood," says another. "They kept on lighting new fires, and I'd keep putting them out," says a third with an injured air.

The prosecuting attorney asks an important question, "Did you command them to stop?"

Policeman—"I did sir, and I said, 'You ladies don't want to be arrested do you?' They made no answer but went on attending to their fires."

WATCHFIRE "LEGAL."*

WATCHFIRE SCATTERED BY POLICE—DR. CAROLINE SPENCER
REBUILDING IT.

The statute is read for the second time. Another witness is called. This time the district attorney asks the policeman,— "Do you know what time the sun in the District of Columbia set on January 5th and rose on January 6th?"

At this profound question, the policeman hesitates, looks abashed, then says impressively, "The sun in the District of Columbia set at 5 o'clock January 5th, and rose at 7:28 o'clock January 6th."

The prosecutor is triumphant. He looks expectantly at the judge.

"How do you know what time the sun rose and set on those days?" asks the judge.

"From the weather bureau," answers the policeman.

The judge is perplexed.

"I think we should have something more official," he says.

The prosecutor suggests that perhaps an almanac would settle the question. The judge believes it would. The government attorney disappears to find an almanac.

Breathless, the prisoners and spectators wait to hear the important verdict of the almanac. The delay is interminable. The court room is in a state of confusion. The prisoners, especially, are amused at the proceedings. It is clear their fate may hang upon a minute or two of time. An hour goes by, and still the district attorney has not returned. Another half hour! Presently he returns to read in heavy tones from the almanac. The policeman looks embarrassed. His information from the weather bureau differs from that of the almanac. His sun rose two minutes too early and continued to shine twelve minutes too long! However, it doesn't matter. The sun shone long enough to make the defendants guilty.

The judge looks at the prisoners and announces that they are "guilty" and "shall pay a fine of $5.00 or serve five days in jail." The Administration has learned its lesson about hunger strikes and evidently fears having to yield to another strike. And so it seeks safety in lighter sentences. The judge pleads almost piteously with them not to go to jail at all, and says that he will put them on probation if they will promise to be good and not light any more fires in the District of Columbia. The prisoners make no promise. They have been found guilty according to the almanac and they file through the little gate into the prisoners' pen.

Somehow they did not believe that whether the sun rose at 7:26 or 7:28 was the issue which had decided whether they should be convicted or not, and it was not in protest against the almanac that they straightway entered upon a hunger strike.

Meanwhile the watchfires continued in the capital. January thirteenth, the day the great world Peace Conference under the President's leadership, began to deliberate on the task of administering "right" and "justice" to all the oppressed of the earth, twenty-three women were arrested in front of the White House.

Another trial! More silent prisoners! They were to be tried this time in groups. A roar of applause from friends in the courtroom greeted the first four as they came in. The judge said that he could not possibly understand the motive for this outburst, and added, "If it is repeated, I shall consider it contempt of court." He then ordered the bailiff to escort the four prisoners out and bring them in again.—Shades of school days!

"And if there is any applause *this time* . . ."

With this threat still in the air, the prisoners reëntered and the applause was louder than before. Great Confusion! The judge roared at the bailiff. The bailiff roared at the prisoners and their friends.

Finally they rushed to the corners of the courtroom and evicted three young women.

"Lock the doors, and see that they do not return," shouted

the angry judge. Thus the dignity of the court was restored. But the group idea had to be abandoned. The prisoners were now brought in one at a time, and one policeman after another testified that, "she kep' alightin' and alightin' fires."

Five days' imprisonment for each woman who "kep' alightin' " watchfires!

On January 25th, in Paris, President Wilson received a delegation of French working women who urged woman suffrage as one of the points to be settled at the Peace Conference. The President expressed admiration for the women of France, and told them of his deep personal interest in the enfranchisement of women. He was 'honored' and 'touched' by their tribute. It was a great moment for the President. He had won the position in the eyes of the world of a devout champion of the liberty of women, but at the very moment he was speaking to these French women American women were lying in the District of Columbia jail for demanding liberty at his gates.

Mrs. Mary Nolan, the eldest suffrage prisoner, took to the watchfire those vain words of the President to the French women. The flames were just consuming—"All sons of freedom are under oath to see that freedom never suffers," when a whole squadron of police dashed up to arrest her. There was a pause when they saw her age. They drew back for an instant. Then one amongst them, more "dutiful" than the rest, quietly placed her under arrest. As she marched along by his side, cheers for her went up from all parts of the crowd.

"Say what you think about them, but that little old lady has certainly got pluck," they murmured.

At the bar Mrs. Nolan's beautiful speech provoked irrepressible applause. The judge ordered as many offenders as could be recognized brought before him. Thirteen women were hastily produced. The trial was suspended while the judge sentenced these thirteen to "forty-eight hours in jail for contempt of court."

And so, throughout January and the beginning of February, 1919, the story of protest continued relentlessly. Watchfires—arrests—convictions—hunger strikes — release — until again the nation rose in protest against imprisoning the women and against the Senate's delay. Peremptory cables went to the President at the Peace Conference, commanding him to act. News of our demonstrations were well reported in the Paris press. The situation must have again seemed serious to him, for although reluctantly and perhaps unwillingly, he did begin to cable to Senate leaders, who in turn began to act. On February 2d, the Democratic Suffrage Senators called a meeting at the Capitol to "consider ways and means." On February 3d, Senator Jones announced in the Senate that the amendment would be•brought up for discussion February 10th. The following evening, February 4th, a caucus of all Democratic Senators was called together at the Capitol by Senator Martin of Virginia, Democratic floor leader in the Senate. This was the first Democratic caucus held in the Senate since war was declared, which would seem to point to the anxiety of the Democrats to marshal two votes.

Several hours of very passionate debate occurred, during which Senator Pollock of South Carolina announced for the first time his support of the measure.

Senator Pollock had yielded to pressure by cable from the President as well as to the caucus. This gain of one vote had reduced the number of votes lacking to one.

Many Democratic leaders now began to show alarm lest the last vote be not secured. William Jennings Bryan was one leader who, rightly alarmed over such a situation, personally consulted with the Democratic opponents. The argument which he presented to them he subsequently gave to the press.

"Woman suffrage is coming to the country and to the world. It will be submitted to the states by the next Congress, if it is not submitted by the present Congress.

"I hope the Democrats of the South will not handicap the Democrats of the North by compelling them to spend the next twenty-five years explaining to the women of the country why their party prevented the submission of the suffrage amendment to the states.

"This is our last chance to play an important part in bringing about this important reform, and it is of vital political concern that the Democrats of the Northern Mississippi Valley should not be burdened by the charge that our party prevented the passage of the suffrage amendment, especially when it is known that it is coming in spite of, if not with the aid of, the Democratic Party."

As we grew nearer the last vote the President was meeting what was perhaps his most bitter resistance from within. It was a situation which he could have prevented. His own early hostility, his later indifference and negligence, his actual protection given to Democratic opponents of the measure, his own reversal of policy practically at the point of a pistol, the half-hearted efforts made by him on its behalf, were all coming to fruition at the moment when his continued prestige was at stake. His power to get results on this because of belated efforts was greatly weakened. This also undermined his power in other undertakings essential to his continued prestige. Whereas more effort, at an earlier time, would have brought fairer results, now the opponents were solidified in their opposition, were through their votes publicly committed to the nation as opponents, and were unwilling to sacrifice their heavy dignity to a public reversal of their votes. This presented a formidable resistance, indeed.

Therefore the Democratic blockade continued.

And so did the watchfires!

CHAPTER 22

THE suffrage score now stood as follows: One vote lacking in the Senate, 15 days in which to win it, and President Wilson across the sea! The Democrats set February 10 as the date on which the Senate would again vote on the amendment, without any plan as to how the last vote would be won.

We were powerless to secure the last vote. That was still the President's problem. Knowing that he always put forth more effort under fire of protest from us than when not pressed, we decided to make as a climax to our watchfire demonstrations a more drastic form of protest. We wanted to show our contempt for the President's inadequate support which promised so much in words and which did so little in deeds to match the words.

And so on the day preceding the vote we burned in effigy a portrait of President Wilson even as the Revolutionary fathers had burned a portrait of King George. [1]

---

[1] This is the inscription on a tablet at the State House, Dover Green, Dover, in commemoration of Delaware's revolutionary leaders.

Signers of the Declaration of Independence.

Caeser Rodney—Thomas McKain—George Read

At the urgent request of Thomas McKain, Caesar Rodney being then in Delaware, rode post haste on horseback to Philadelphia and reached Independence Hall July 4, 1776.

The following day news of the adoption of the Declaration of Independence reaching Dover a portrait of King George was burned on Dover Green at the order of the Committee of Safety. The following historic words being uttered by the chairman:

"Compelled by strong necessity thus we destroy even the shadow of that king who refused to reign over a free people."

One Hundred Women Hold Public Conflagration

A hundred women marched with banners to the center of the sidewalk opposite the White House. Mingling with the party's tri-colored banners were two lettered ones which read:

ONLY FIFTEEN LEGISLATIVE DAYS ARE LEFT IN THIS CONGRESS.

FOR MORE THAN A YEAR THE PRESIDENT'S PARTY HAS BLOCKED SUFFRAGE IN THE SENATE.

IT IS BLOCKING IT TO-DAY.

THE PRESIDENT IS RESPONSIBLE FOR THE BETRAYAL OF AMERICAN WOMANHOOD.

And—

WHY DOES NOT THE PRESIDENT INSURE THE PASSAGE OF SUFFRAGE IN THE SENATE TO-MORROW?

WHY DOES HE NOT WIN FROM HIS PARTY THE ONE VOTE NEEDED?

HAS HE AGREED TO PERMIT SUFFRAGE AGAIN TO BE PUSHED ASIDE?

PRESIDENT WILSON IS DECEIVING THE WORLD.

HE PREACHES DEMOCRACY ABROAD AND THWARTS DEMOCRACY HERE.

As the marchers massed their banners, and grouped themselves about the urn, a dense crowd of many thousand people closed in about them, a crowd so interested that it stood almost motionless for two hours while the ceremonies continued. The fire being kindled, and the flames leaping into the air, Miss Sue White of Tennessee and Mrs. Gabrielle Harris of South Carolina dropped into the fire in the urn a figure of President Wilson sketched on paper in black and white—a sort of effigy de luxe, we called it, but a symbol of our contempt none the less.

Mrs. Henry O. Havemeyer of New York, life-long suffragist and woman of affairs, said as master of the ceremonies, "Every

Anglo-Saxon government in the world has enfranchised its women. In Russia, in Hungary, in Austria, in Germany itself, the women are completely enfranchised, and thirty-four women are now sitting in the new Reichstag. We women of America are assembled here to-day to voice our deep indignation that . . . American women are still deprived of a voice in their government at home. We mean to show that the President. . . ." She was caught by the arm, placed under arrest, and forced into the waiting patrol wagon.

Thereupon the police fell upon the ceremonies, and indiscriminate arrests followed. Women with banners were taken; women without banners were taken. Women attempting to guard the fire; women standing by doing nothing at all; all were seized upon and rushed to the patrol. While this uproar was going on, others attempted to continue the speaking where Mrs. Havemeyer had left it, but each was apprehended as she made her attempt. Some that had been scheduled to speak, but were too shy to utter a word in the excitement, were also taken. When the "Black Marias" were all filled to capacity, nearby automobiles were commandeered, and more patrols summoned. And still not even half the women were captured.

The police ceased their raids suddenly. Orders to arrest no more had evidently been given. Some one must have suggested that a hundred additions to the already overcrowded jail and workhouse would be too embarrassing. Perhaps the ruse of arresting some, and hoping the others would scamper away at the sight of authority, was still in their minds.

After a brief respite they turned their attention to the fascinated crowd. They succeeded in forcing back these masses of people half way across Pennsylvania Avenue, and stationed an officer every two feet in front of them. But still women came to keep the fire burning. Was there no end of this battalion of women? The police finally declared a "military zone" between the encircling crowd and the remaining women, and no person was allowed to enter the proscribed area. For another hour, then, the women stood on guard at the urn, and as night fell, the ceremonies ended. Sixty of them marched back to headquarters. Thirty-nine had been arrested.

The following morning, February 10th, saw two not unrelated scenes in the capital. Senators were gathering in their seats in the senate chamber to answer to the roll call on the suffrage amendment. A few blocks away in the courthouse, thirty-nine women were being tried for their protest of the previous day.

There was no uncertainty either in the minds of the galleries or of the senators. Every one knew that we still lacked *one* vote. The debate was confined to two speeches, one for and one against.

When the roll was called, there were voting and paired in favor of the amendment, 63 senators; there were voting and paired against the amendment 33 senators. The amendment lost therefore, by one vote. Of the 63 favorable votes 32 were Republicans and 31 Democrats. Of the 33 adverse votes 12 were Republicans and 21 Democrats. This means that of the 44 Republicans in the Senate, 32 or 73 per cent voted for the amendment. Of the 52 Democrats in the Senate 31 or 60 per cent voted for it. And so it was again defeated by the opposition of the Democratic Administration, and by the failure of the President to put behind it enough power to win.

Meanwhile another burlesque of justice dragged wearily on in the dim courtroom. The judge was sentencing thirty-nine women to prison. When the twenty-sixth had been reached, he said wearily, "How many more are out there?"

When told that he had tried only two-thirds of the defendants, he dismissed the remaining thirteen without trial!

They were as guilty as their colleagues. But the judge was tired. Twenty-six women sent to jail is a full judicial day's work, I suppose.

There was some rather obvious shame and unhappiness in the Senate because of the petty thing they had done. The prisoners in the courtroom were proud because they had done their utmost for the principle in which they believed.

Senator Jones of New Mexico, Chairman of the Committee, and his Democratic colleagues refused to reintroduce the Susan B. Anthony amendment in the Senate immediately after this defeat. But on Monday, February 17, Senator Jones of Washington, ranking Republican on the Suffrage Committee, obtained unanimous consent and reintroduced it, thereby placing it once more on its way to early reconsideration.

CHAPTER 23

BOSTON MILITANTS WELCOME THE PRESIDENT

IT was announced that the President would return to America on February 24th. That would leave seven days in which he could act before the session ended on March 3d. We determined to make another dramatic effort to move him further.

Boston was to be the President's landing place. Boston, where ancient liberties are so venerated, and modern ones so abridged! No more admirable place could have been found to welcome the President home in true militant fashion.

Wishing the whole world to know that women were greeting President Wilson, why they were greeting him, and what form of demonstration the greetings would assume, we announced our plans in advance. Upon his arrival a line of pickets would hold banners silently calling to the President's attention the demand for his effective aid. In the afternoon they would hold a meeting in Boston Common and there burn the parts of the President's Boston speech which should pertain to democracy and liberty. These announcements were met with official alarm of almost unbelievable extent. Whereas front pages had been given over heretofore to publishing the elaborate plans for the welcome to be extended to the President, eulogies of the President, and recitals of his great triumph abroad, now the large proportion of this space was devoted to clever plans of the police to outwit the suffragists. The sustained publicity of this demonstration was unprecedented. It actually filled the Boston papers for all of two weeks.

A "deadline," a diagram of which appeared in the press, was to be established beyond which no suffragist, no matter how enterprising, could penetrate to harass the over-worked President with foolish ideas about the importance of liberty for women. Had not this great man the cares of the world on his shoulders? This was no time to talk about liberty for women! The world was rocking and a great peace conference was sitting, and the President was just returning to report on the work done so far. The Boston descendants of the early revolutionists would do their utmost to see that no untoward event should mar the perfection of their plans. They would see to it that the sacred soil of the old Boston Common should not be disgraced.

It was a perfect day. Lines of marines whose trappings shone brilliantly in the clear sunshine were in formation to hold back the crowds from the Reviewing stand where the President should appear after heading the procession in his honor. It seemed as if all Boston were on hand for the welcome. A slender file of twenty-two women marched silently into the sunshine, slipped through the "deadline," and made its way to the base of the Reviewing stand. There it unfurled its beautiful banners and took up its post directly facing the line of marines which was supposed to keep all suffragists at bay. Quite calmly and yet triumphantly, they stood there, a pageant of beauty and defiant appeal, which not even the most hurried passerby could fail to see and comprehend.

There were consultations by the officials in charge of the ceremonies. The women looked harmless enough, but had they not been told that they must not come there? They were causing no riot, in fact they were clearly adding much beauty—people seemed to take them as part of the elaborate ceremony—but officials seldom have sense of humor enough or adaptability enough to change quickly, especially when they have made

PICKETS IN FRONT OF REVIEWING STAND, BOSTON

threats. It would be a taint on their honor, if they did not "pick up" the women for the deed.

One could hear the people reading slowly the large lettered banner:

Mr. President, You said in the Senate on September 20 "We shall not only be distrusted but we shall deserve to be distrusted if we do not enfranchise women." You alone can remove this distrust now by securing the one vote needed to pass the suffrage amendment before March 4.

The American flag carried by Miss Katherine Morey of Brookline held the place of honor at the head of the line and there were the familiar, "Mr. President, how long must women wait for liberty?" and "Mr. President, what will you do for woman suffrage?" The other banners were simply purple, white and gold.

"When we had stood there about three quarters of an hour," said Katherine Morey, "Superintendent Crowley came to me and said, 'We want to be as nice as we can to you suffragette ladies, but you cannot stand here while the President goes by, so you might as well go back now.' I said I was sorry, but as we had come simply to be there at that very time, we would not be able to go back until the President had gone by. He thereupon made a final appeal to Miss Paul, who was at headquarters, but she only repeated our statement. The patrol wagons were hurried to the scene and the arrests were executed in an exceedingly gentlemanly manner. But the effect on the crowd was electric. The sight of 'ladies' being put into patrols, seemed to thrill the Boston masses as nothing the President subsequently said was able to.

"We were taken to the House of Detention and there charged with 'loitering more than seven minutes'."

As Mrs. Agnes H. Morey, Massachusetts Chairman of the Woman's Party, later remarked:

"It is a most extraordinary thing. Thousands loitered from curiosity on the day the President arrived. Twenty-two loitered for liberty, and only those who loitered for liberty were arrested."

Realizing that the event of the morning had diverted public attention to our issue, and undismayed by the arrests, other women entered the lists to sustain public attention upon our demand to the President.

The ceremony on the Common began at three o'clock. Throngs of people packed in closely in an effort to hear the speakers, and to catch a glimpse of the ceremony, presided over by Mrs. Louise Sykes of Cambridge, whose late husband was President of the Connecticut College for Women. From three o'clock until six, women explained the purpose of the protest, the status of the amendment, and urged those present to help. At six o'clock came the order to arrest. Mrs. C. C. Jack, wife of Professor Jack of Harvard University, Mrs. Mortimer Warren of Boston, whose husband was head of a base hospital in France, and Miss Elsie Hill, daughter of the late Congressman Hill, were arrested and were taken to the House of Detention, where they joined their comrades.

"Dirty, filthy hole under the Court House," was the general characterization of the House of Detention. "Jail was a Paradise compared to this depraved place," said Miss Morey. "We slept in our clothes, four women to a cell, on iron shelves two feet wide. In the cell was an open toilet. The place slowly filled up during the night with drunks and disorderlies until pandemonium reigned. In the evening, Superintendent Crowley and Commissioner Curtis came to call on us. I don't believe they had ever been there before, and they were painfully embarrassed. Superintendent Crowley said to me, "If you were

MRS. LOUISE SYKES BURNING PRESIDENT WILSON'S SPEECH ON BOSTON COMMON

drunk we could release you in the morning, but unfortunately since you are not we have got to take you into court."

When the prisoners were told next morning the decision of Chief Justice Bolster to try each prisoner separately and in closed court, they all protested against such proceedings. But guards took the women by force to a private room. "The Matron, who was terrified," said Miss Morey, "shouted to the guards, 'You don't handle the drunks that way. You know you don't.' But they continued to push, shove and shake the women while forcing them to the ante room."

"As an American citizen under arrest, I demand a public trial," was the statement of each on entering the judge's private trial room.

While the trial was proceeding without the women's co-operation,—some were tried under wrong names, some were tried more than once under different names, but most of them under the name of Jane Doe—vigorous protests were being made to all the city officials by individuals among the throngs who had come to the court house to attend the trial. This protest was so strong that the last three women were tried in open court. The judge sentenced everybody impartially to eight days in jail in lieu of fines, with the exception of Miss Wilma Henderson, who was released when it was learned that she was a minor.

The women were taken to the Charles Street Jail to serve their sentences. "The cells were immaculately clean," said Miss Morey, "but there was one feature of this experience which obliterated all its advantages. The cells were without modern toilet facilities. The toilet equipment consisted of a heavy wooden bucket, about two and a half feet high and a foot and a half in diameter, half filled with water. No one of us will ever forget that foul bucket. It had to be carried to the lower floor—we were on the third and fourth floors—every morning. I could hardly lift mine off the floor, to say nothing of getting it down stairs (Miss Morey weighs 98 pounds), so there it stayed. Berry Pottier managed to get hers down, but was so exhausted she was utterly unable to get it back to her cell.

"The other toilet facility provided was a smaller bucket of water to wash in, but it was of such a strangely unpleasant odor that we did not dare use it."

The Boston reporters were admitted freely—and they wrote columns of copy. There was the customary ridicule, but there were friendly light touches such as, "Militant Highlights—To be roommates at Vassar College and then to meet again as cellmates was the experience of Miss Elsie Hill and Mrs. Lois Warren Shaw." . . . "Superintendent Kelleher didn't know when he was in Congress with Elsie Hill's father he would some day have Congressman Hill's daughter in his jail."

And there were friendly serious touches in these pages of sensational news—such as this excerpt from the front page of the Boston *Traveler* of February 25, 1919. "The reporter admired the spirit of the women. Though weary from loss of sleep, the fire of a great purpose burned in their eyes. . . .

"It was a sublime forgetting of self for the goal ahead, and whether the reader is in sympathy with the principle for which these women are ready to suffer or not, he will be forced to admire the spirit which leads them on."

Photographs of the women were printed day by day— giving their occupations, if any, noting their revolutionary ancestors, ascertaining the attitude of husbands and fathers. Mrs. Shaw's husband's telegram was typical of the support the women got. "Don't be quitters," he wired, "I have competent nurses to look after the children." Mr. Shaw is a Harvard graduate and a successful manufacturer in Manchester, New Hampshire.

Telegrams of protest from all over the country poured in upon all the Boston officials who had had any point of contact with the militants. All other work was for the moment suspended. Such is the quality of Mrs. Morey's organizing genius that she did not let a solitary official escape. Telegrams also went from Boston, and especially from the jail, to President Wilson.

Official Boston was in the grip of this militant invasion when suddenly a man of mystery, one E. J. Howe, appeared and paid the women's fines. It was later discovered that the mysterious E. J. Howe alleged to have acted for a "client." Whether the "client" was a part of Official Boston, no one ever knew. There were rumors that the city wished to end its embarrassment.

Sedate Boston had been profoundly shaken. Sedate Boston gave more generously than ever before to militant finances. And when the "Prison Special" arrived a few days later a Boston theatre was filled to overflowing with a crowd eager to hear more about their local heroines, and to cheer them while they were deccrated with the already famous prison pin.

Something happened in Washington, too, after the President's safe journey thither from Boston.

CHAPTER 24

IT would be folly to say that President Wilson was not at this time aware of a very damning situation.

The unanswerable "Prison Special"—a special car of women prisoners—was touring the country from coast to coast to keep the public attention, during the closing days of the session, fixed upon the suffrage situation in the Senate. The prisoners were addressing enormous meetings and arousing thousands, especially in the South, to articulate condemnation of Administration tactics. It is impossible to calculate the number of cables which, as a result of this sensational tour, reached the President during his deliberations at the Peace Table. The messages of protest which did not reach the President at the Peace Conference were waiting for him on his desk at the White House.

Even if some conservative Boston suffragists did present him with a beautiful bouquet of jonquils tied with a yellow ribbon, as their welcome home, will any one venture to say that that token of trust was potent enough to wipe from his consciousness the other welcome which led his welcomers to jail? Will any one contend that President Wilson upon his arrival in Washington, and after changing his clothes, piously remarked:

"By the way, Tumulty, I want to show you some jonquils tied with a yellow ribbon that were presented to me in Boston. I am moved, I think I may say deeply moved by this sincere tribute, to do something this morning for woman suffrage.

Just what is the state of affairs? And does there seem to be any great demand for it?" We do not know what, if anything, he did say to Secretary Tumulty, but we know what he did. He hurried over to the Capitol, and there made his first official business a conference with Senator Jones of New Mexico, Chairman of the Senate Suffrage Committee. After expressing chagrin over the failure of the measure in the Senate, the President discussed ways and means of getting it through.

An immediate result of the conference was the introduction in the Senate, February 28th, by Senator Jones, of another resolution on suffrage. Senator Jones had refused to reintroduce the original suffrage resolution immediately after the Senate defeat, February 10th. Now he came forward with this one, a little differently worded, but to the same purpose as the original amendment. [1]

This resolution was a concession to Senator Gay of Louisiana, Democrat, who had voted against the measure on February 10th, but who immediately pledged his vote in favor of the new resolution. Thus the sixty-fourth and last vote was won. The majority instantly directed its efforts toward getting a vote on the new resolution.

On March 1st Senator Jones attempted to get unanimous consent to consider it. Senator Wadsworth, of New York, Republican anti-suffragist, objected. When consent was again asked, the following day, Senator Weeks of Massachusetts, Republican anti-suffragist, objected. On the last day of the session, Senator Sherman of Illinois, Republican suffragist, objected. And so the Democratic Congress ended without passing the amendment.

On the face of it, these parliamentary objections from Republicans prevented action, when the Democrats had finally

[1] This amendment, although to the same purpose as the original amendment, was not as satisfactory because of possible controversial points in the enforcement article. The original amendment is of course crystal clear in this regard.

secured the necessary votes. As a matter of fact, however, the President and his party were responsible for subjecting the amendment to the tactical obstruction of individual anti-suffrage Senators. They waited until the last three days to make the supreme effort. That the President did finally get the last vote even at a moment when parliamentary difficulties prevented it from being voted upon, proved our contention that he could pass the amendment at any time he set himself resolutely to it. This last ineffective effort also proved how hard the President had been pushed by our tactics.

But it seems to me that President Wilson has a pathetic aptitude for acting a little too late. The fact that the majority of the Southern contingent in his party stood stubbornly against him on woman suffrage, was of course a real obstacle. But we contended that the business of a statesman who declared himself to be a friend of a measure was to remove even real obstacles to the success of that measure. Perhaps our standard was too high. It must be confessed that people in general are distressingly patient, easily content with pronouncements, and shockingly inert about seeing to it that political leaders act as they speak.

We had seen the President overcome far greater obstacles than stood in his way on this issue. We had seen him lead a country which had voted to stay out of the European war into battle almost immediately after they had so voted. We had seen him conscript the men of the same stubborn South, which had been conspicuously opposed to conscription. We had seen him win mothers to his war point of view after they had fought passionately for him and his peace program at election time. He had taken pains to lead men and women— influential and obscure—to his way of thinking. I do not condemn him—I respect him for being able to do this. The point is that he *did* overcome obstacles when his heart and head were set to the task.

Since our problem was neither in his head nor his heart, it was our task to put it there. Having got it there, it was our responsibility to see that it churned and churned there, until he had to act. We did our utmost.

For six full years, through three Congresses under President Wilson's power, the continual Democratic resistance, meandering, delays, deceits had left us still disfranchised. A world war had come and gone during this span of effort. Vast millions had died in pursuit of liberty. A Czar and a Kaiser had been deposed. The Russian people had revolutionized their whole social and economic system. And here in the United States of America we couldn't even wrest from the leader of democracy and his poor miserable associates the first step toward our political liberty—the passage of an amendment through Congress, submitting the question of democracy to the states!

What a magnificent thing it was for those women to rebel! Their solitary steadfastness to their objective stands out in this world of confused ideals and half hearted actions, clear and lonely and superb!

CHAPTER 25

THE Republican Congress elected in November, 1918, would not sit until December, 1919—such is our unfortunate system—unless called together by the President in a special session. We had polled the new Congress by personal interviews and by post, and found a safe two-thirds majority for the amendment in the House. In the new Senate we still lacked a fateful one vote.

Our task was, therefore, to induce the President to call a special session of Congress at the earliest possible moment, and to see that he did not relax his efforts toward the last vote.

"He won't do it!" . . . "President Wilson will never let the Republican Congress come together until the regular time." . . . "Especially with himself in Europe!" The usual points of objection were raised. But we persisted. We felt that the President could win this last vote. And the fear that a Republican Congress might, if he did not, was an accelerating factor.

One feature of the campaign to force a special session was a demonstration in New York, on the eve of President Wilson's return to Europe, at the time he addressed a mass meeting in the Metropolitan Opera House on behalf of his proposed League of Nations. The plan of demonstration was to hold outside of the Opera House banners addressed to President Wilson, and to consign his speech to the flames of a torch at a public meeting nearby.

It was a clear starry night in March when the picket line
of 25 women proceeded with tri-colored banners from New
York headquarters in Forty-first street to the Opera House.
As we neared the corner of the street opposite the Opera House
and before we could cross the street a veritable battalion of
policemen in close formation rushed us with unbelievable
ferocity. Not a word was spoken by a single officer of the
two hundred policemen in the attack to indicate the nature of
our offense. Clubs were raised and lowered and the women
beaten back with such cruelty as none of us had ever witnessed
before.

The women clung to their heavy banner poles, trying to
keep the banners above the maelstrom. But the police seized
them, tore the pennants, broke the poles, some of them over
our backs, trampled them underfoot, pounded us, dragged us,
and in every way behaved like frantic beasts. It would have
been so simple quietly to detain our little handful until after
the President's speech, if that seemed necessary. But to launch
this violent attack under the circumstances was madness. Not
a pedestrian had paid any except friendly attention to the
slender file of women. But the moment this happened an
enormous crowd gathered, made up mostly of soldiers and
sailors, many of whom had just returned from abroad and
were temporarily thronging the streets of New York. They
joined forces with the police in the attack.

Miss Margaretta Schuyler, a beautiful, fragile young girl,
was holding fast a silken American flag which she had carried
at the head of the procession when a uniformed soldier jumped
upon her, twisted her arms until she cried in pain, cursed,
struggled until he had torn her flag from its pole, and then
broke the pole across her head, exulting in his triumph over
his frailer victim.

When I appealed to the policeman, who was at the moment
occupied solely with pounding me on the back, to intercept the

soldier in his cruel attack, his only reply was: "Oh, he's helping me." He thereupon resumed his beating of me and I cried,
"Shame, shame! Aren't you ashamed to beat American women
in this brutal way?" I offered no other resistance. "If we
are breaking any law, arrest us! Don't beat us in this cowardly fashion!"

"We'll rush you like bulls," was his vulgar answer, "we've
only just begun."

Another young woman, an aviatrice, was seized by the
coat collar and thrown to the pavement for trying to keep
hold of her banner. Her fur cap was the only thing that saved
her skull from serious injury. As it was, she was trampled
under foot and her face severely cut before we could rescue her
with the assistance of a sympathetic member of the crowd.
The sympathetic person was promptly attacked by the policeman for helping his victim to her feet. There were many
shouts of disapproval of the police conduct and many cheers
for the women from the dense crowd.

By this time the crowd had massed itself so thickly that
we could hardly move an inch. It was perfectly apparent that
we could neither make our way to the Opera House nor could
we extricate ourselves. But the terrors continued. Women
were knocked down and trampled under foot, some of them
almost unconscious, others bleeding from the hands and face;
arms were bruised and twisted; pocketbooks were snatched
and wrist-watches stolen.

When it looked as if the suffocating mêlée would result in
the death or permanent injury to some of us, I was at last
dragged by a policeman to the edge of the crowd. Although
I offered not the slightest resistance, I was crushed continuously in the arm by the officer who walked me to the police
station, and kept muttering: "You're a bunch of cannibals,—
cannibals,—Bolsheviks."

Upon arriving at the police station I was happily relieved

to find five of my comrades already there. We were all impartially cursed at; told to stand up; told to sit down; forbidden to speak to one another; forbidden even to smile at one another. One by one we were called to the desk to give our name, age, and various other pieces of information. We stood perfectly silent before the station lieutenant as he coaxingly said, "You'd better tell."—"You'd better give us your name." —"You'd better tell us where you live—it will make things easier for you." But we continued our silence.

Disorderly conduct, interfering with the police, assaulting the police (Shades of Heaven! assaulting the police!), were the charges entered against us.

We were all locked in separate cells and told that we would be taken to the Woman's Night Court for immediate trial.

While pondering on what was happening to our comrades and wondering if they, too, would be arrested, or if they would just be beaten up by the police and mob, a large, fat jail matron came up and began to deliver a speech, which ran something like this:

"Now, shure and you ladies must know that this is goin' a bit too far. Now, I'm for suffrage alright, and I believe women ought to vote, but why do you keep botherin' the President? Don't you know he has got enough to think about with the League of Nations, the Peace Conference and fixin' up the whole world on his mind?"

In about half an hour we were taken from our cells and brought before the Lieutenant, who now announced, "Well, you ladies may go now,—I have just received a telephone order to release you."

We accepted the news and jubilantly left the station house, returning at once to our comrades. There the battle was still going on, and as we joined them we were again dragged and cuffed about the streets by the police and their aids, but there were no more arrests. Elsie Hill succeeded in speaking from a balcony above the heads of the crowd:

"Did you men turn back when you saw the Germans coming? What would you have thought of any one who did? Did you expect us to turn back? We never turn back, either—and we won't until democracy is won! Who rolled bandages for you when you were suffering abroad? Who bound your wounds in your fight for democracy? Who spent long hours of the night and the day knitting you warm garments? There are women here to-night attempting to hold banners to remind the President that democracy is not won at home, who have given their sons and husbands for your fight abroad. What would they say if they could see you, their comrades in the fight over there, attacking their mothers, their sisters, their wives over here? Aren't you ashamed that you have not enough sporting blood to allow us to make our fight in our own way? Aren't you ashamed that you accepted the help of women in your fight, and now to-night brutally attack them?"

And they did listen until the police, in formation—looking now like wooden toys—advanced from both sides of the street and succeeded in entirely cutting off the crowd from Miss Hill.

The meeting thus broken up, we abandoned a further attempt that night. As our little, bannerless procession filed slowly back to headquarters, hoodlums followed us. The police of course gave us no protection and just as we were entering the door of our own building a rowdy struck me on the side of the head with a heavy banner pole. The blow knocked me senseless against the stone building; my hat was snatched from my head, and burned in the street. We entered the building to find that soldiers and sailors had been periodically rushing it in our absence, dragging out bundles of our banners, amounting to many hundreds of dollars, and burning them in the street, without any protest from the police.

One does not undergo such an experience without arriving

at some inescapable truths, a discussion of which would interest me deeply but which would be irrelevant in this narrative.

"Two hundred maddened women try to see the President." . . . "Two hundred women attack the police," and similar false headlines, appeared the next morning in the New York papers. It hurt to have the world think that we had attacked the police. That was a slight matter, however, for that morning at breakfast, aboard the *George Washington*, the President also read the New York papers. He saw that we were not submitting in silence to his inaction. It seems reasonable to assume that on sailing down the harbor that morning past the Statue of Liberty the President had some trouble to banish from his mind the report that "two hundred maddened women" had tried to "make the Opera House last night."

CHAPTER 26

T HE "Prison Special," which was nearing the end of its
dramatic tour, was arousing the people to call for a
special session of Congress, as the President sailed
away.

Although a Republican Congress had been elected, President Wilson, as the head of the Administration, was still
responsible for initiating and guiding legislation. We had to
see to it that, with his Congress out of power, he did not relax
his efforts on behalf of the amendment.

There was this situation which we were able to use to our
advantage. Two new Democratic Senators, Senator Harrison
of Mississippi and Senator Harris of Georgia, had been elected
to sit in the incoming Congress through the President's influence. He, therefore, had very specific power over these two
men, who were neither committed against suffrage by previous
votes nor were they yet won to the amendment.

We immediately set ourselves to the task of getting the
President to win one of these men. From the election of these
two men in the autumn to early spring, constant pressure was
put upon the President to this end. When we could see no
activity on the part of the President to secure the support of
one of them, we again threatened publicly to resume dramatic
protests against him. We kept the idea abroad that he was
still responsible, and that we would continue to hold him so,
until the amendment was passed.

Such a situation gave friends of the Administration considerable alarm. They realized that the slightest attack on the President at that moment would jeopardize his many other endeavors. And so these friends of the President undertook to acquaint him with the facts.

Senator Harris was happily in Europe at the time. A most anxious cable, signed by politicians in his own party, was sent to the President in Paris explaining the serious situation and urging him to do his utmost to secure the vote of the Senator at once.

Senator Harris was in Italy when he received an unexpected telegram asking him to come to Paris. He journeyed with all speed to the President, perhaps even thinking that he was about to be dispatched to some foreign post, to learn that the conference was for the purpose of securing his vote on the national suffrage amendment.

Senator Harris there and then gave his vote, the 64th vote.

On that day the passage by Congress of the original Susan B. Anthony amendment was assured.

Instantly a cable was received at the White House carrying news to the suffragists of the final capture of the elusive last vote. Following immediately on the heels of this cable came another cable calling the new Congress into special session May 19th.

In the light of the President's gradual yielding and final surrender to our demand, it will not be out of place to summarize briefly just what happened.

President Wilson began his career as President of the United States an anti-suffragist. He was opposed to suffrage for women both by principle and political expediency. Sometimes I think he regarded suffragists as a kind of sect—good women, no doubt, but tiresome and troublesome. Whether he has yet come to see the suffrage battle as part of a great movement embracing the world is still a question. It is not an important question, for in any case it was not inward conviction but political necessity that made him act.

Believing then that suffragists were a sect, he said many things to them at first with no particular care as to the bearing of these things upon political theory or events. He offered, successively, "consideration," an "open mind," a "closed mind," and "age-long conviction deeply matured," party limitations, party concert of action, and what not. He saw in suffrage the "tide rising to meet the moon," but waited and advised us to wait with him. But we did not want to wait, and we proceeded to try to make it impossible for him to wait, either. We determined to make action upon this issue politically expedient for him.

When the President began to perceive the potential political power of women voters, he first declared, as a "private citizen," that suffrage was all right for the women of his home state, New Jersey, but that it was altogether wrong to ask him as President to assist in bringing it about for all the women of the nation. He also interested himself in writing the suffrage plank in the Democratic Party's national platform, specifically relegating action on suffrage to the states. Then he calmly announced that he could not act nationally, "even if I wanted to," because the platform had spoken otherwise.

The controversy was lengthened. The President's conspicuous ability for sitting still and doing nothing on a controversial issue until both sides have exhausted their ammunition was never better illustrated than in this matter. He allowed the controversy to continue to the point of intellectual sterility. He buttressed his delays with more evasions, until finally the women intensified their demand for action. They picketed his official gates. But the President still recoiled from action. So mightily did he recoil from it that he was willing to imprison women for demanding it.

It is not extraordinary to resent being called upon to act,

for it is only the exceptional person who springs to action, even when action is admitted to be desirable and necessary. And the President is *not* exceptional. He is surprisingly ordinary.

While the women languished in prison, he fell back upon words—beautiful words, too—expressions of friendliness, good wishes, hopes, and may-I-nots. In this, too, he was acting like an ordinary human being, not like the statesman he was reputed to be. He had habituated himself to a belief in the power of words, and every time he uttered them to us he seemed to refortify himself in his belief in their power.

It was the women, not the President, who were exceptional. They refused to accept words. They persisted in demanding acts. Step by step under terrific gunfire the President's resistance crumbled, and he yielded, one by one, every minor facility to the measure, always withholding from us, however, the main objective. Not until he had exhausted all minor facilities, and all possible evasions, did he publicly declare that the amendment should pass the House, and put it through. When he had done that we rested from the attack momentarily, in order to let him consummate with grace, and not under fire, the passage of the amendment in the Senate. He rested altogether. We were therefore compelled to renew the attack. He countered at first with more words. But his reliance upon them was perceptibly shaken when we burned them in public bonfires. He then moved feebly but with a growing concern toward getting additional votes in the Senate. And when, as an inevitable result of his policy—and ours—the political embarrassment became too acute, calling into question his honor and prestige, he covertly began to consult his colleagues. We pushed him the harder. He moved the faster toward concrete endeavor. He actually undertook to win the final votes in the Senate.

There he found, however, that quite an alarming situation

had developed—a situation which he should have anticipated, but for which he was totally unprepared. Opposition in his own party had been growing more and more rigid and cynical. His own opposition to the amendment, his grant of immunity to those leaders in his party who had fought the measure, his isolating himself from those who might have helped—all this was coming to fruition among his subordinates at a time when he could least afford to be beaten on anything. What would have been a fairly easy race to win, if he had begun running at the pistol shot, had now become most difficult.

Perceiving that he had now not only to move himself, but also to overcome the obstacle which he had allowed to develop, we increased the energy of our attack. And finally the President made a supreme assertion of his power, and secured the last and 64th vote in the Senate. He did this too late to get the advantage—if any advantage is to be gained from granting a just thing at the point of a gun—for this last vote arrived only in time for a Republican Congress to use it.

It seems to me that Woodrow Wilson was neither devil nor God in his manner of meeting the demand of the suffragists. There has persisted an astounding myth that he is an extraordinary man. Our experience proved the contrary. He behaved toward us like a very ordinary politician. Unnecessarily cruel or weakly tolerant, according as you view the justice of our fight, but a politician, not a statesman. He did not go out to meet the tide which he himself perceived was "rising to meet the moon." That would have been statesmanship. He let it all but engulf him before he acted. And even as a politician he failed, for his tactics resulted in the passage of the amendment by a Republican Congress.

CHAPTER 27

THE Republican Congress convened in Special Session May 19.

Instantly Republican leaders in control of the 66th Congress caucussed and organized for a prompt passage of the amendment. May 21st the Republican House of Representatives passed the measure by a vote of 304 to 89—the first thing of any importance done by the new House. This was 42 votes above the required two-thirds majority, whereas the vote in the House in January, 1918, under Democratic control had given the measure only one vote more than was required.

Immediately the Democratic National Committee passed a resolution calling on the legislatures of the various states to hold special legislative sessions where necessary, to ratify the amendment as soon as it was through Congress, in order to "enable women to vote in the national elections of 1920."

When the 64th vote was assured two more Republican Senators announced their support, Senator Keyes of New Hampshire and Senator Hale of Maine, and on June 4th the measure passed the Senate by a vote of 66 to 30,—2 votes more than needed.[1] Of the 49 Republicans in the Senate, 40 voted for the amendment, 9 against. Of the 47 Democrats in the Senate, 26 voted for it and 21 against.

And so the assertion that "the right of citizens of the United States to vote shall not be denied or abridged by the

---

[1] These figures include all voting and paired.

United States or by any state on account of sex," introduced into Congress by the efforts of Susan B. Anthony in 1878, was finally submitted to the states for ratification [1] on June 4th, 1919.

I do not need to explain that the amendment was not won from the Republican Congress between May 19th and June 4th, 1919. The Republican Party had been gradually coming to appreciate this opportunity throughout our entire national agitation from 1913 to date. And our attack upon the party in power, which happened to be President Wilson's party, had been the most decisive factor in stimulating the opposition party to espouse our side. It is perhaps fortunate for the Republican Party that it was their political opponents who inherited this lively question in 1913. However, the political advantage is theirs for having promptly and ungrudgingly passed the amendment the moment they came into power. But it will not be surprising to any one who has read this book that I conclude by pointing out that the real triumph belongs to the women.

Our objective was the national enfranchisement of women. A tiny step, you may say. True! But so long as we know that this is but the first step in the long struggle of women for political, economic and social emancipation, we need not be disturbed. If political institutions as we know them to-day in their discredited condition break down, and another kind of organization—perhaps industrial—supplants them, women will battle for their place in the new system with as much determination as they have shown in the struggle just ended.

That women have been aroused never again to be content with their subjection there can be no doubt. That they will ultimately secure for themselves equal power and responsibility

[1] When a constitutional amendment has passed Congress it must be ratified by a majority vote of 36 state legislatures and thereupon proclaimed operative by the Secretary of State of the United States before it becomes the law of the land. For ratification data see Appendix 1.

in whatever system of government is evolved is positive. How revolutionary will be the changes when women get this power and responsibility no one can adequately foretell. One thing is certain. They will not go back. They will never again be good and willing slaves.

It has been a long, wearying struggle. Although drudgery has persisted throughout, there have been compensatory moments of great joy and beauty. The relief that comes after a great achievement is sweet. There is no residue of bitterness. To be sure, women have often resented it deeply that so much human energy had to be expended for so simple a right. But whatever disillusionments they have experienced, they have kept their faith in women. And the winning of political power by women will have enormously elevated their status.

*1. Mrs. Lawrence Lewis; 2. Mrs. George Roewer; 3. Mrs. Jessica Henderson; | 4. Mrs. Naomi Barrett; 5. Miss Elizabeth Huff; 6. Dr. Caroline E. Spencer; *7. Miss Ruth Crocker; 8. Miss Rose Winslow; 9. Miss Berry Pottier; *10. Miss Julia Hurbut; 11. Miss Ernestine Hara; 12. Mrs. Betsey Reyneau.

1. Mrs. Kate Winston; *2. Miss Hazel Hunkins; 3. Miss Mary H. Ingham; *4. Miss Elizabeth Kalb; 5. Miss Maud Jamison; *6. Mrs. Louise Mayo; 7. Mrs. Annie J. McGee; 8. Miss Nell Mercer; *9. Mrs. Bertha C. Moller; *10. Miss Katherine C. Morey; 11. Mrs. Agnes H. Morey; 12. Miss Maud Malone; 13. Mrs. Elsie Vervane; †14. Mrs. John Rogers, Jr.

1. Miss Eleanor Calnan; 2. Mrs. W. D. Ascough; 3. Miss Julia Emory; 4. Mrs. Dorothy Bartlett; 5. Mrs. Abby Scott Baker; 6. Miss Louise Bryant; *7. Miss Mary Gertrude Fendall; *8. Miss Katharine Fisher; 9. Miss Alice Gram; 10. Dr. Sarah H. Lockrey; 11. Mrs. Frederick W. Kendall; 12. Mrs. Elizabeth Walmsley; 13. Miss Sue White; 14. Mrs. Iris Calderhead Walker.

1. Miss Edna Dixon; 2. Miss Gertrude L. Crocker;
*3. Miss Clara Wold; 4. Miss Jennie Bronenberg; 5.
Miss Lucy Branham; 6. Mrs. Mary E. Brown; †7. Mrs.
Kate J. Boeckh; 8. Mrs. Paula Jakobi; *9. Miss Mary
Dubrow; 10. Mrs. Pauline Adams; 11. Mrs. Rebecca
Winsor Evans; ‡12. Miss Virginia Arnold; *13. Mrs. A.
R. Colvin; 14. Miss Edith Ainge.

*© Harris & Ewing; †Clinedinst; ‡Edmonston.

1. Miss Lavinia L. Dock; 2. Miss Rose Fishstein; 3. Mrs. Wm. F. Dowell; 4. Miss Reba Gomborov; 5. Mrs. Lucy Branham; 6. Mrs. Annie Arneil; 7. Miss Cora Crawford; *8. Mrs. Gilson Gardner; *9. Miss Elsie Hill; *10. Miss Natalie Gray; 11. Mrs. J. Irving Gross; 12. Mrs. Lucille Calmes; 13. Mrs. H. E. Russian; 14. Mrs. Ruby E. Koenig.

*© *Harris & Ewing.*

1. Miss Margaret Fotheringham; *2. Miss Anne Martin; 3. Mrs. Martha Reed Shoemaker; *4. Mrs. M. Toscan Bennett; 5. Miss Lucy Ewing; 6. Miss Betty Gram; 7. Miss Gladys Greiner; 8. Mrs. H. O. Havemeyer; *9. Miss Kate Heffelfinger; 10. Mrs. Rosa Fishstein; †11. Mrs. Florence Bayard Hilles; 12. Mrs. Effie M. Main; 13. Mrs. Margaret Oaks; 14. Miss Vida Milholland.

*ⓒ Harris & Ewing; †Edmonston.

*1. Mrs. Harvey W. Wiley; 2. Mrs. Phoebe C. Munnecke;
†3. Miss Nina Samarodin; 4. Miss Mary Winsor; 5. Miss
Rhoda Kellogg; 6. Mrs. Lois Warren Shaw; 7. Miss
Ruth Small; 8. Mrs. Alexander Shields; †9. Mrs.
Helena Hill Weed; *10. Miss Mabel Vernon; 11. Mrs.
Robert H. Walker; 12. Miss Margaret F. Whittemore;
13. Miss Martha W. Moore; 14. Miss Ellen Winsor.

APPENDICES

APPENDIX 1

Text of the National Suffrage Amendment

Proposing an amendment to the Constitution of the United States extending the right of suffrage to women.

Resolved by the Senate and House of Representatives of the United States of America in Congress assembled (two-thirds of each House concurring therein), That the following articles be proposed to the legislatures of the several States as an amendment to the Constitution of the United States, which when ratified by three-fourths of the said legislatures, shall be valid as part of said Constitution, namely:

"ARTICLE—SEC. 1. The right of citizens of the United States to vote shall not be denied or abridged by the United States or by any State on account of sex.

"SEC. 2. Congress shall have power, by appropriate legislation, to enforce the provisions of this article."

RECORD OF ACTION ON NATIONAL SUFFRAGE AMENDMENT

In Congress

Drafted

By Susan B. Anthony in 1875

First Introduced

January 10, 1878, by Hon. A. A. Sargent, in the Senate

Reported from Committee

In the Senate

1878, Adverse majority.
1879, Favorable minority.
1882, Favorable majority,
    adverse minority.
1884, Favorable majority,
    adverse minority.
1886, Favorable majority.
1890, Favorable majority.
1892, Favorable majority,
    adverse minority.
1896, Adverse majority.
1913, Favorable majority.
1914, Favorable majority.
1917, Favorable majority.
1919, Unanimously favorably.

In the House

1883, Favorable majority.
1884, Adverse majority,
    favorable minority.
1886, Favorable minority.
1890, Favorable majority.
1894, Adverse majority.
1914, Without recommendation.
1916, Without recommendation.
1917, Without recommendation.
1918, Favorable majority.
1919, Favorable majority.

Voted Upon

In the Senate

January 25, 1887. Yeas 16, nays 34.
Absent 25 (of whom 4 were announced as for and 2 against).
March 19, 1914. Yeas 35, nays 34, failing by 11 of the necessary two-thirds vote.
October 1, 1918. Yeas 54, nays 30, failing by 2 of the two-thirds vote.
February 10, 1919. Yeas 55, nays 29, failing by 1 of the necessary two-thirds vote.
June 4, 1919. Yeas 56, nays 25, passing by 2 votes over necessary two-thirds majority.

In the House

January 12, 1915. Yeas 174, nays 204, failing by 78 of the necessary two-thirds vote.
January 10, 1918. Yeas 274, nays 136, passing by 1 vote over necessary two-thirds majority.
May 21, 1919. Yeas 304, nays 89, passing by 42 votes over necessary two-thirds majority.

In the States

State	Date of Ratification	Vote Senate	Vote House	Party of Governor	Party Controlling Legislature
1 Wisconsin	June 10, 1919	24-1	54-2	Rep.	Rep.
2 *Michigan	June 10, 1919	Unan.	Unan.	Rep.	Rep.
3 *Kansas	June 16, 1919	Unan.	Unan.	Rep.	Rep.
4 *Ohio	June 16, 1919	27-3	73-6	Dem.	Rep.
5 *New York	June 16, 1919	Unan.	Unan.	Rep.	Rep.
6 Illinois	June 17, 1919	Unan.	133-4	Rep.	Rep.
7 Pennsylvania	June 24, 1919	32-6	153-44	Rep.	Rep.
8 Massachusetts	June 25, 1919	34-5	184-77	Dem.	Dem.
9 *Texas	June 28, 1919	Unan.	96-21	Rep.	Rep.
10 *Iowa	July 2, 1919	Unan.	95-5	Rep.	Rep.
11 *Missouri	July 3, 1919	28-3	125-4	Dem.	Div'd.
12 *Arkansas	July 20, 1919	20-2	76-17	Dem.	Dem.
13 *Montana	July 30, 1919	38-1	Unan.	Dem.	Rep.
14 *Nebraska	Aug. 2, 1919	Unan.	Unan.	Rep.	Rep.
15 *Minnesota	Sept. 8, 1919	60-5	120-6	Rep.	Rep.
16 *New Hampshire	Sept. 10, 1919	14-10	212-143	Rep.	Dem.
17 *Utah	Sept. 30, 1919	Unan.	Unan.	Dem.	Rep.
18 *California	Nov. 1, 1919	Unan.	73-2	Rep.	Rep.
19 *Maine	Nov. 5, 1919	24-5	72-68	Rep.	Rep.
20 *North Dakota	Dec. 1, 1919	38-4	103-6	Rep.	Rep.
21 *South Dakota	Dec. 4, 1919	Unan.	Unan.	Rep.	Rep.
22 *Colorado	Dec. 12, 1919	Unan.	Unan.	Rep.	Rep.
23 Rhode Island	Jan. 6, 1920	37-1	89-3	Rep.	Rep.
24 Kentucky	Jan. 6, 1920	30-8	72-25	Rep.	Div'd.
25 *Oregon	Jan. 12, 1920	43-3	Unan.	Rep.	Rep.
26 *Indiana	Jan. 16, 1920	Unan.	Unan.	Rep.	Rep.
27 *Wyoming	Jan. 27, 1920	Unan.	Unan.	Rep.	Rep.
28 *Nevada	Feb. 7, 1920	Unan.	Unan.	Dem.	Div'd.
29 New Jersey	Feb. 10, 1920	18-2	34-24	Rep.	Rep.
30 *Idaho	Feb. 11, 1920	29-6	Unan.	Rep.	Rep.
31 *Arizona	Feb. 12, 1920	Unan.	Unan.	Dem.	Rep.
32 *New Mexico	Feb. 19, 1920	17-5	36-10	Rep.	Rep.
33 *Oklahoma	Feb. 27, 1920	24-15	84-12	Dem.	Dem.
34 *West Virginia	Mar. 10, 1920	15-14	47-40	Rep.	Rep.
35 *Washington	Mar. 22, 1920	Unan.	Unan.	Rep.	Rep.
36 *Tennessee	Aug. 18, 1920	25-4	49-47	Dem.	Dem.

* States ratifying at Special Session.

APPENDIX 2

Countries in Which Women Vote

Azerbaijain (Moslem) Republic	1919	Iceland	1919
Australia	1902	Ireland	1918
Austria	1918	Isle of Man	1881
¹Belgium	1919	Luxembourg	1919
British East Africa	1919	³Mexico	1917
Canada	1918	New Zealand	1893
Czecho Slovakia	1918	Norway	1907
Denmark	1915	Poland	1918
²England	1918	Rhodesia	1919
Finland	1906	Russia	1917
Germany	1918	Scotland	1918
Holland	1919	⁴Sweden	1919
Hungary	1918	United States	1920
		Wales	1918

[1] *Electoral Reform Bill as passed granted suffrage to widows who have not remarried and mothers of soldiers killed in battle or civilians shot by Germans.*

[2] *Women over age of 30—Bill to reduce age to 21 has passed its second reading.*

[3] *No sex qualification for voting in constitution. Women have so far not availed themselves of their right to vote, but are expected to do so in the coming elections.*

[4] *To be confirmed in 1920.*

APPENDIX 3

Resolutions Demanding Investigations

Resolution (171) to authorize an Investigation of the District of Columbia Workhouse.

Introduced in the House by Miss Jeannette Rankin, Representative from Montana.

October 5, 1917.

Text of Resolution:

Resolved, That a select committee of seven Members of the House of Representatives be appointed by the Speaker to investigate the administration of the District of Columbia Workhouse at Occoquan, Virginia, and to report thereon as early as possible during the second session of the Sixty-fifth Congress. Said committee is authorized to sit during the recess in Washington, District of Columbia and elsewhere, to subpœna witnesses, and to call for records relating to the said workhouse. To defray the necessary expenses of such investigation, including the employment of clerical assistance, the' committee is authorized to expend not to exceed $1,000 from the contingent fund of the House.

———

Resolution (130) to authorize an Investigation of Mob Attacks on Suffragists.

Introduced in the House by John Baer, Representative from North Dakota.

August 17, 1917.

Text of Resolution:

WHEREAS, in the city of Washington, D. C., about 350 feet from the White House premises is a building known as the Cameron House, in which is located headquarters and main offices of a woman's organization at which is continually congregated women of character, courage and intelligence, who come from various sections of the United States, and

WHEREAS, on three successive days, to wit: the 14th, 15th and 16th days of August, 1917, on said days immediately following the closing of the day's work by the clerks and employees of the Executive Departments, hundreds of these clerks and employees, acting with sailors, then and now in the service of the United States Navy and in uniform at the time, and soldiers, then and now in the service of the United States Army, also in their uniforms at the time,—and these clerks, employees, sailors and soldiers, and others, formed themselves into mobs and deliberately, unlawfully and violently damaged the said headquarters and offices of the said woman's organization by pelting rotten eggs through the doors and windows, shooting a bullet from a revolver through a window, and otherwise damaging said Cameron House, and also violently and unlawfully did strike, choke, drag and generally mistreat and injure and abuse the said women when they came defenseless upon the streets adjoining as well as when they were in the said building; and

WHEREAS, the organized police of the City of Washington, District of Columbia, made no attempt to properly safeguard the property and persons of the said defenseless women, but, on the contrary, said police even seemed to encourage the lawless acts of the mob; and

WHEREAS, such lawlessness is in the Capital of the United States and within a few hundred feet of the Executive Mansion and offices of the President of the United States; and

WHEREAS, these attacks upon defenseless women are not only an outrage and crime in themselves, that prove the perpetrators and those lending aid to the same to be cowards, but in addition, create throughout the world contempt for the United States and set a vicious example to the people throughout the United States and the world at large, of lawlessness and violence; and encourage designing cowards and manipulators everywhere to form mobs to molest the innocent and defenseless under any pretext whatever; and

WHEREAS, there seems to be no activity or attempt on the part of any one in authority in the City of Washington, District of Columbia, nor by the government officials to apprehend, arrest or punish those perpetrating the violence, on account of which the same may occur indefinitely unless Congress acts in the premises; and

WHEREAS, the legal status upon the premises stated would excuse the occupants of the Cameron House if they were so disposed in firing upon the mobs aforesaid, and thus create a state of greater violence and unlawry, to further injure the prestige and good name of the United States for maintaining law and order and institutions of democracy; therefore be it

Resolved, that the Speaker appoint a Committee of seven members to investigate into all the facts relating to the violence and unlawful acts aforesaid, and make the earliest possible report upon the conditions, with the purpose in view of purging the army and navy of the United States and other official departments, of all lawless men who bring disgrace upon the American flag by participating in mob violence, and also to inquire regarding the conduct of all government employees and the police of the city of Washington, District of Columbia, with a view to maintaining law and order.

APPENDIX 4

SUFFRAGE PRISONERS

NOTE:—Scores of women were arrested but never brought to trial; many others were convicted and their sentences suspended or appealed. It has been possible to list below only those women who actually served prison sentences although more than five hundred women were arrested during the agitation.

MINNIE D. ABBOTT, Atlantic City, N. J., officer of the N.W.P. [National Woman's Party]. Arrested picketing July 14, 1917, sentenced to 60 days in Occoquan workhouse.

MRS. PAULINE ADAMS, Norfolk, Va., wife of leading physician, prominent clubwoman and Congressional District Chairman of the N.W.P. Arrested picketing Sept. 4, 1917. Sentenced to 60 days in Occoquan workhouse. Arrested watchfire demonstration Feb. 9, 1919, but released on account of lack of evidence.

EDITH AINGE, Jamestown, N. Y., native of England, came to America when a child, and has brought up family of nine brothers and sisters. Worked for state suffrage in N. Y. 1915. Served five jail sentences. Sentenced to 60 days in Occoquan for picketing Sept., 1917, 15 days in Aug., 1918, Lafayette Sq. meeting, and three short terms in District Jail in Jan., 1919, watchfire demonstrations.

HARRIET U. ANDREWS, Kansas City, Mo., came to Washington as war worker. Arrested watchfire demonstration and sentenced to 5 days in District Jail Jan., 1919.

MRS. ANNIE ARNEIL, Wilmington, Del., did picket duty from beginning in 1917. One of first six suffrage prisoners. Served eight jail sentences, 3 days, June, 1917; 60 days in Occoquan, Aug.-Sept., 1917, picketing; 15 days, Aug., 1918, Lafayette Sq. meeting, and five sentences of 5 days each in Jan. and Feb., 1919, watchfire demonstrations.

BERTHE ARNOLD, Colorado Springs, Colo., daughter of prominent physician. Educated at Colo. State Univ. Student of music Phila.; member of D.A.R.; kindergarten teacher. Arrested Jan., 1919, watchfire demonstration, sentenced to 5 days in District Jail.

VIRGINIA ARNOLD, North Carolina, student George Washington and Columbia Univs., school teacher, later organizer and executive secretary N.W.P. in Washington. Served 3 days June, 1917, with first pickets sentenced.

MRS. W. D. ASCOUGH, Detroit, Mich.   Former Conn. State Chairman, N.W.P. Studied for concert stage London and Paris. Abandoned concert stage to devote time to suffrage. Sentenced to 15 days Aug., 1918, Lafayette Sq. meeting, and 5 days Feb., 1919, in watchfire demonstration. Member "Prison Special" which toured country in Feb., 1919.

MRS. ABBY SCOTT BAKER, Washington, D. C., wife of Dr. Robert Baker, and descendant long line of army officers. Three sons in service during World War. Known as the diplomat of the N.W.P., and as such has interviewed practically every man prominent in political life. Member executive committee of N.W.P. and has been political chairman since 1918. Arrested picketing and sentenced to 60 days in Occoquan, Sept., 1917.

MRS. CHARLES W. BARNES, Indianapolis, Ind., officer of Ind. Branch, N.W.P. Arrested picketing Nov., 1917, sentenced to 15 days in jail.

MRS. NAOMI BARRETT, Wilmington, Del., arrested watchfire demonstration Jan. 13, 1919. Sentenced to 5 days in District Jail.

MRS. W. J. BARTLETT, Putnam, Conn., leader Conn. State Grange. Arrested Aug., 1917, picketing, sentenced to 60 days.

MRS. M. TOSCAN BENNETT, Hartford, Conn., wife of lawyer and writer, member D.A.R. and Colonial Dames, has been active in state suffrage work for many years. Member National Advisory Council, N.W.P. and Conn. state treasurer. Arrested Jan., 1919, watchfire demonstration. Sentenced to 5 days in District Jail.

HILDA BLUMBERG, New York City, native of Russia, one of youngest prisoners. Educated and taught school in this country. Arrested picketing, Sept., 1917; sentenced to 30 days in Occoquan; arrested again Nov. 10, sentenced to 15 days.

MRS. KATE BOECKH, Washington, D. C., native of Canada, one of first women aeroplane pilots. Arrested picketing Aug., 1917, case appealed. Arrested applauding in court Jan., 1919, served 3 days.

MRS. CATHERINE BOYLE, Newcastle, Del., munitions worker during World War. Arrested Jan., 1919, watchfire demonstration, sentenced to 5 days in jail.

LUCY G. BRANHAM, Baltimore, Md., organizer N.W.P., graduate Washington College, Md.; M. A., Johns Hopkins; graduate student Univ. of Chicago and Ph.D. Columbia. Won Carnegie hero medal for rescuing man and woman from drowning at St. Petersburg, Fla. Arrested picketing Sept., 1917, sentenced to 60 days in Occoquan and District Jail.

MRS. LUCY G. BRANHAM, Baltimore, Md., mother of Miss Lucy Branham, widow of Dr. John W. Branham who lost his life fighting a yellow fever epidemic in Ga. Arrested watchfire demonstration Jan., 1919; sentenced to 3 days in District Jail.

MRS. JOHN WINTERS BRANNAN, New York City, daughter of the late Charles A. Dana, founder and editor N. Y. *Sun*, trusted counselor of President Lincoln; wife of Dr. Brannan, Pres. Board of Trustees Bellevue Hospital; member executive committee N.W.P., state chairman New York Branch. Did brilliant state suffrage work as officer of Woman's Political Union in N. Y. Arrested picketing July 14, 1917, sentenced to 60 days in Occoquan; pardoned by President after serving 3 days. Again arrested picketing Nov. 10, 1917, sentenced to 45 days.

JENNIE BRONENBERG, Philadelphia, Pa. Student Wharton School, Univ. of Pa. Arrested Feb., 1919, sentenced to 5 days in District Jail.

MRS. MARY E. BROWN, Wilmington, Del., state press chairman, N.W.P. Father member First Del. regiment; mother field nurse, Civil War. Descendant Captain David Porter, of Battleship Essex, War of 1812. Arrested watchfire demonstration Jan. 13, 1919, sentenced to 5 days in District Jail.

LOUISE BRYANT, New York City, formerly of Portland, Ore., author, poet and journalist, wife of John Reed. Correspondent for Phila. Public Ledger in Petrograd for six months during Russian revolution. Arrested watchfire demonstration Feb., 1919, sentenced to 5 days in District Jail.

LUCY BURNS, New York City, graduate Vassar College, student of Yale Univ. and Univ. of Bonn, Germany. High School teacher. Joined English militant suffrage movement 1909, where she met Alice Paul, with whom she joined in establishing first permanent suffrage headquarters in Washington in Jan., 1913; helped organize parade of March 3, 1913; vice chairman and member of executive committee Congressional Union for Woman Suffrage [later the N.W.P.], for a time editor of *The Suffragist*. Leader of most of the picket demonstrations and served more time in jail than any other suffragist in America. Arrested picketing June, 1917, sentenced to 3 days; arrested Sept., 1917, sentenced to 60 days; arrested Nov. 10, 1917, sentenced to six months; in January, 1919, arrested watchfire demonstrations for which she served one 3 day and two 5 day sentences. She also served 4 prison terms in England.

MRS. HENRY BUTTERWORTH, New York City, comes of an old Huguenot family. Active in civic and suffrage work in N. Y. for past 20 years. Charter member National Society of Craftsmen. Arrested picketing Nov., 1917, sentenced to 30 days in Occoquan.

MRS. LUCILLE A. CALMES, Princeton, Ia. Great-granddaughter of George Fowler, founder of New Harmony, Ind. Government worker during World War. Arrested watchfire demonstration Jan. 13, 1919, sentenced to 5 days in District Jail.

ELEANOR CALNAN, Methuen, Mass. Congressional district chairman of Mass. Branch N.W.P. Arrested picketing July 14, 1917, sentenced to 60 days in Occoquan, pardoned by President after 3 days; arrested Sept., 1917, sentenced to 60 days in Occoquan. Arrested in Boston, Feb., 1919, for participation in Boston demonstration at home coming of President; sentenced to 8 days in Charles St. Jail.

MRS. AGNES CHASE, Washington, D. C., formerly of Ill.; engaged in scientific research work for U. S. Dept. of Agriculture. Arrested Lafayette Sq. meeting August, 1918, sentenced to 10 days. Arrested watchfire demonstration Jan., 1919, sentenced to 5 days.

Mrs. Palys L. Chevrier, New York City, arrested watchfire demonstration Jan., 1919, sentenced to 5 days. Member "Prison Special" which toured country in Feb., 1919.

Mrs. Helen Chisaski, Bridgeport, Conn., munition worker and member of Machinists' Union. Arrested watchfire demonstration Jan. 13, 1919; sentenced to 5 days in jail.

Mrs. William Chisholm, Huntington, Pa., now deceased; arrested picketing Sept. 4, 1917, sentenced to 60 days in Occoquan.

Josephine Collins, Framingham, Mass., owns and manages the village store at Framingham Center. She encountered serious opposition from some of her customers on account of her militant activities; one of first members N.W.P.; arrested in Boston Feb., 1919, for taking part in welcome to the President; sentenced to 8 days in Charles St. Jail.

Mrs. Sarah Tarleton Colvin, St. Paul, Minn., member famous Tarleton family of Alabama, wife of Dr. A. R. Colvin, Major in the Army, and Acting Surgical Chief at Fort McHenry during World War; graduate nurse Johns Hopkins training school, Red Cross nurse in this country during war; Minnesota state chairman N.W.P. Member "Prison Special." Arrested watchfire demonstrations Jan., 1919; sentenced to 2 terms of 5 days each.

Betty Connolly, West Newton, Mass., household assistant, arrested in Boston, Feb., 1919, demonstration of welcome to President Wilson; sentenced to 8 days in Charles St. Jail.

Mrs. Alice M. Cosu, New Orleans, La., vice chairman La. state branch N.W.P. Arrested picketing Nov., 1917, and sentenced to 30 days in Occoquan workhouse.

Cora Crawford, Philadelphia, Pa., business woman. Marched in 1913 suffrage parade in Washington. Arrested watchfire demonstration Jan., 1919; sentenced to 5 days in District Jail.

Gertrude Crocker, Washington, D. C., formerly of Ill., educated at Vassar College and Univ. of Chicago. National Treasurer N.W.P. 1916; government worker, 1917. Served 3 jail sentences: 30 days for picketing in 1917, 10 days for assisting Lafayette Sq. meeting 1918, and 5 days for participating watchfire 1919.

Ruth Crocker, Washington, D. C., formerly of Ill., sister of Gertrude Crocker. Came to Washington for suffrage, later government worker. Served 30 days at Occoquan for picketing in 1917 and 3 days in District Jail for watchfire demonstration Jan., 1919.

Miss L. J. C. Daniels, Grafton, Vt., and Boston. Arrested picketing Nov. 10, 1917, sentenced to 15 days. Took part in Capitol picketing Nov., 1918; arrested watchfire demonstration Jan. 9, 1919, sentenced to 5 days in District Jail. Arrested in Boston for participation in welcome demonstration to President, sentenced to 8 days in Charles St. Jail.

Dorothy Day, New York City, member of the "Masses" [now the "Liberator"] staff. Arrested picketing Nov. 10, 1917, sentenced to 30 days in Occoquan workhouse.

EDNA DIXON, Washington, D. C., daughter of physician; teacher in public schools. Arrested picketing Aug., 1917, sentenced to 30 days in Occoquan workhouse.

LAVINIA L. DOCK, Fayetteville, Pa., associated with the founders of American Red Cross nursing service; secretary of American Federation of Nurses and member of International Council of Nurses. Assisted in relief work during Johnstown flood and during Fla. yellow fever epidemic; army nurse during Spanish-American War, author of "The History of Nursing," "The Tuberculosis Nurse," and a number of other text books on nursing. One of early workers of Henry St. Settlement in N. Y., and founder of visiting nurse movement in N. Y. On staff of American Journal of Nursing. One of first six pickets to serve prison sentence of 3 days in June, 1917. Later that summer she served 25 days in Occoquan; and in Nov. 15 days.

MRS. MARY CARROLL DOWELL, Philadelphia, Pa., wife of William F. Dowell, magazine editor and writer with whom she has been associated in business. Active club and suffrage worker in Pa. and N. J., state officer Pa. branch N.W.P. Arrested watchfire demonstration Jan. 20, 1919, and served 5 days in District Jail.

MARY DUBROW, Passaic, N. J.; student Univ. of N. Y.; teacher in N. J. until she joined suffrage ranks as organizer and speaker. Arrested watchfire demonstration Jan. 6, 1919, sentenced to 10 days.

JULIA EMORY, Baltimore, Md.; daughter of late state senator, D. H. Emory. Gave up work for Trade Union League to work for suffrage in 1917. Sentenced to 30 days in Occoquan for picketing Nov., 1917. After her release became organizer N.W.P. Aug., 1918, arrested and sentenced to 10 days Lafayette Sq. meeting. Jan. 7, 1919, sentenced to 10 days, and later in that month to 5 days for watchfire demonstrations. Led Capitol picket Oct. and Nov., 1919, and suffered many injuries at hands of police.

MRS. EDMUND C. EVANS, Ardmore, Pa., one of three Winsor sisters who served prison terms for suffrage. Member of prominent Quaker family. Arrested watchfire demonstration Jan., 1919, and sentenced to 5 days in District Jail.

LUCY EWING, Chicago, Ill., daughter of Judge Adlai Ewing, niece of James Ewing, minister to Belgium under Cleveland; niece also of Adlai Stevenson, Vice-President under Cleveland. Officer Ill. Branch N.W.P. Arrested picketing Aug. 17, 1917, sentenced to 30 days in Occoquan workhouse.

MRS. ESTELLA EYLWARD, New Orleans, La. Business woman. Came to Washington to take part in final watchfire demonstration Feb., 1919; arrested and sentenced to 5 days in District Jail.

MARY GERTRUDE FENDALL, Baltimore, Md., graduate of Bryn Mawr College; campaigned for N.W.P. in West 1916; national treasurer of organization June, 1917, to December, 1919. Arrested and sentenced to 3 days, Jan., 1919, for applauding in court.

ELLA FINDEISEN, Lawrence, Mass. Arrested picketing Nov. 10, 1917, sentenced to 30 days at Occoquan.

KATHARINE FISHER, Washington, D. C., native of Mass. Great-great-granddaughter of Artemas Ward, ranking Major General in Revolutionary War. Teacher, social worker and later employee of U. S. War Risk Bureau. Written prose and verse on suffrage and feminist topics. Arrested picketing Sept. 13, 1917, sentenced to 30 days 'at Occoquan workhouse.

MRS. ROSE GRATZ FISHSTEIN, Philadelphia, Pa., native of Russia. Came to America at 15. Had been imprisoned for revolutionary activities in Russia and fled to this country following release on bail. Operator in shirt factory; later union organizer; factory inspector for N. Y. State Factory Commission. Feb. 9, 1919 arrested watchfire demonstration and sentenced to 5 days in District Jail.

ROSE FISHSTEIN, Philadelphia, Pa., sister-in-law of Mrs. Rose G. Fishstein, born in Russia, educated in N. Y. and Phila. Student of Temple Univ., business woman. Arrested watchfire demonstration, Feb., 1919, sentenced to 5 days in District Jail.

CATHERINE M. FLANAGAN, Hartford, Conn., state and national organizer for N.W.P.; formerly secretary for Conn. Woman Suffrage Association. Father came to this country as Irish exile because of his efforts in movement for Irish freedom. Arrested picketing August, 1917, sentenced to 30 days in Occoquan workhouse.

MARTHA FOLEY, Dorchester, Mass., active worker in Mass. labor movement. Arrested in demonstration at homecoming of President in Boston, Feb., 1919; sentenced to 8 days in Charles St. Jail.

MRS. T. W. FORBES, Baltimore, Md., officer of Just Government League of Md.; arrested watchfire demonstration Feb. 9, 1919, sentenced to 5 days in District Jail.

JANET FOTHERINGHAM, Buffalo, N. Y., teacher of physical culture. Arrested picketing July 14, 1917, sentenced to 60 days in workhouse. but pardoned by President after 3 days.

MARGARET FOTHERINGHAM, Buffalo, N. Y., Red Cross dietician, stationed at military hospital at Waynesville, N. C., during war. Later dietician at Walter Reid Military Hospital, Washington, D. C. Arrested picketing Aug., 1917, sentenced to 60 days.

FRANCIS FOWLER, Brookline, Mass., sentenced to 8 days in Charles St. Jail for participation in demonstration of welcome to President, Boston, Feb., 1919.

MRS. MATILDA HALL GARDNER, Washington, D. C., formerly of Chicago, daughter of late Frederick Hall, for many years editor of Chicago *Tribune,* and wife of Gilson Gardner, Washington representative of Scripps papers. Educated Chicago, Paris and Brussels. Associated with Alice Paul and Lucy Burns when they came to Washington to begin agitation for federal suffrage and member of national executive committee of N.W.P. since 1914. Arrested July 14, 1917, sentenced to 60 days in Occoquan; Jan. 13, 1919, sentenced to 5 days in District Jail.

ANNA GINSBERG, New York City; served 5 days in District jail for watchfire demonstration Feb., 1919.

REBA GOMBOROV, Philadelphia, Pa.; born in Kiev, Russia. Educated in U. S. public schools; social worker; assistant secretary and visitor for Juvenile Aid Society of Phila. President Office Workers' Association; secretary of Penn. Industrial Section for Suffrage; member N.W.P., Trade Union League. Sentenced to 5 days in District Jail Jan., 1919, for watchfire demonstration.

ALICE GRAM, Portland, Ore., graduate Univ. of Ore., came to Washington to take part in picket Nov. 10, 1917. Arrested and sentenced to 30 days in Occoquan workhouse. Following release assistant in press dept. N.W.P.

BETTY GRAM, Portland, Ore., graduate Univ. of Ore. Abandoned stage career to take part in picket demonstration of Nov. 10, 1917. Worker in Juvenile courts of Portland. Sentenced to 30 days in Occoquan workhouse; later arrested in Boston demonstration of Feb., 1919, and sentenced to 8 days in Charles St. Jail. Business manager of *The Suffragist* and national organizer for N.W.P.

NATALIE GRAY, Col. Springs, Col., daughter of treasurer Col. Branch N. W. P. Arrested picketing Aug. 17, 1917, sentenced to 30 days in Occoquan workhouse.

MRS. FRANCIS GREEN, New York City, one of second group of women to serve prison sentences for suffrage in this country. Served 3 days in District Jail following picket demonstration of July 4, 1917.

GLADYS GREINER, Baltimore, Md., daughter of John E. Greiner, engineering expert, member of Stevens Railway Commission to Russia in 1917. Graduate of Forest Glen Seminary, Md.; did settlement work in mountain districts of Ky.; has held tennis and golf championships of Md., and for 3 years devoted all time to suffrage. Arrested picketing July 4, 1917, sentenced to 3 days in District Jail; arrested Oct. 20, 1917, sentenced to 30 days in District Jail; arrested Lafayette Sq. meeting Aug., 1918, sentenced to 15 days in District Jail. Recently taken up work in labor movement.

MRS. J. IRVING GROSS. Boston, Mass., charter member of Mass. Branch N.W.P. Father and husband both fought in Civil War. Arrested 5 times Lafayette Sq. meetings Aug., 1918, and sentenced to 15 days in District Jail. Arrested in Boston demonstration on Common following landing of President and sentenced to 8 days in Charles St. Jail.

ANNA GWINTER, New York City, arrested for picketing Nov. 10, 1917, and sentenced to 30 days in Occoquan workhouse.

ELIZABETH HAMILTON, New York City, arrested for picketing Nov. 10, 1917, and sentenced to 30 days in Occoquan workhouse.

ERNESTINE HARA, New York City, young Roumanian, arrested for picketing Sept., 1917, and sentenced to 30 days in Occoquan workhouse.

REBECCA HARRISON, Joplin, Mo., arrested final watchfire demonstration Feb. 10, 1919; sentenced to 5 days in District Jail.

Mrs. H. O. Havemeyer, New York City; widow of late H. O. Havemeyer; leader of suffrage movement for many years; one of its most eloquent speakers, and generous contributor to its funds; active in Liberty Loan campaigns, in the Land Army movement of N. Y. State, and in working for military rank for nurses. As member of "Prison Special" spoke for suffrage in the large cities. Arrested Feb. 10, 1919, for taking part in final watchfire demonstration; sentenced to 5 days in District Jail.

Kate Heffelfinger, Shamokin, Pa.; art student; sentenced to 6 months in District Jail for picketing Oct. 15, 1917; another month later added for previous offense. Aug., 1918, sentenced to 15 days for participating in Lafayette Sq. meeting; Jan., 1919, sentenced to 5 days for participation in watchfire demonstration.

Mrs. Jessica Henderson, Boston, Mass., wife of prominent Bostonian, one of liberal leaders of Boston; identified with many reform movements. Mother of 6 children, one of whom, Wilma, aged 18, was arrested with her mother, spent night in house of detention, and was released as minor. Sentenced to 8 days in Charles St. Jail Feb., 1919, for participation in Boston demonstration of welcome to President.

Minnie Hennesy, Hartford, Conn.; business woman, having supported herself all her life; arrested for picketing Oct. 6, 1917, and sentence suspended. Rearrested Oct. 8, 1917, and sentenced to 6 months.

Anne Herkimer, Baltimore, Md., Child Labor inspector for U. S. Children's Bureau. Arrested Feb., 1919, and sentenced to 5 days in District Jail for participating watchfire demonstration.

Elsie Hill, Norwalk, Conn.; daughter of late Ebenezer J. Hill, 21 years Congressman from Conn.; graduate Vassar College and student abroad. Taught French in District of Columbia High School. Lately devoted all her time to suffrage. Member of executive committee of Congressional Union 1914-1915; President D.C. Branch College Equal Suffrage League, and later national organizer for N.W.P. Aug., 1918, sentenced to 15 days in District Jail for speaking at Lafayette Sq. meeting. Feb., 1919, sentenced to 8 days in Boston for participation in welcome demonstration to President.

Mrs. George Hill, Boston, Mass.; sentenced to 8 days in Boston, Feb., 1919, for participation in welcome to President.

Mrs. Florence Bayard Hilles, Newcastle, Del.; daughter of late Thomas Bayard, first American ambassador to Great Britain and secretary of state under Cleveland. Munitions worker during World War. After the war engaged in reconstruction work in France. Chairman Del. Branch N.W.P. and member of national executive committee. Arrested picketing July 14, 1917, sentenced to 60 days in Occoquan workhouse; pardoned by President after 3 days.

Mrs. J. A. H. Hopkins (Allison Turnbull), Morristown, N. J., state chairman N.W.P., member executive committee N.W.P. 1917, and president and officer of various women's clubs. Her husband was leader Progressive Party and later supported President Wilson, serving on Democratic National Campaign Committee in 1916. At present Chairman Committee of

48. Mrs. Hopkins arrested July 14, 1917, for picketing, sentenced to 60 days in workhouse; pardoned by President after 3 days.

MRS. L. H. HORNSBY, New York City, formerly of Ill., one of first women aviators in this country. Arrested for picketing Nov. 10, 1917; sentenced to 30 days in District Jail.

ELIZABETH HUFF, Des Moines, Ia.; came to Washington to work for war department during war; later with Red Cross. Sentenced to 5 days in jail, Jan., 1919, for watchfire demonstration.

EUNICE HUFF, Des Moines, Ia.; sister of Elizabeth; also engaged in war work in Washington. Sentenced to 3 days in jail Jan., 1919, for applauding suffrage prisoners in court.

HAZEL HUNKINS, Billings, Mont.; graduate Vassar College; later instructor in Chemistry, Univ. of Mo. Joined suffrage movement as organizer for N.W.P. Later investigator for War Labor Board. Active in all picketing campaigns. Aug. 1918, sentenced to 15 days for participation in Lafayette Sq. meeting.

JULIA HURLBUT, Morristown, N. J., vice chairman N. J. Branch N.W.P. In 1916 assisted in Washington state campaign. Arrested picketing July 14, 1917, sentenced to 60 days in Occoquan workhouse; pardoned by President after 3 days. Engaged in war work in France during war.

MARY INGHAM, Philadelphia, Pa.; graduate Bryn Mawr College; Pa. chairman of N.W.P.; secretary of National Progressive League 1912. Has held offices of vice president of Pa. Women's Trade Union League, director of Bureau of Municipal Research of Phila., member of board of corporators of Woman's Medical College of Pa., where she was former student. For several years manager woman's department of Bonbright and Co., investment brokers. Arrested for picketing July 14, 1917; sentenced to 60 days in Occoquan, pardoned by President after 3 days.

MRS. MARK JACKSON, Baltimore, Md., arrested picketing Aug., 1917, sentenced to 30 days.

PAULA JAKOBI, New York City; playwright, author of "Chinese Lily." Once matron of Framingham reformatory for purpose of studying prison conditions. Arrested picketing Nov. 10, 1917, and sentenced to 30 days in Occoquan workhouse.

MAUD JAMISON, Norfolk, Va.; came to Washington in 1916 as volunteer worker of N.W.P. Later became assistant in treasurer's department. Had been school teacher and business woman before joining N.W.P. Took active part in picketing from the beginning; one of first group arrested, June, 1917; served 3 days in District Jail; later served 30 days in District Jail; Oct., 1917, sentenced to 7 months. Released by Government after 44 days. Jan., 1919, served 5 days in jail for participation in watchfire demonstration.

MRS. PEGGY BAIRD JOHNS, New York City, formerly of St. Louis, newspaper woman and magazine writer. Sentenced to 30 days in Occoquan workhouse Aug., 1917; and 30 days in Nov., 1917, for picketing.

WILLIE GRACE JOHNSON, Shreveport, La., state officer, N.W.P. and prominent in civic work. Successful business woman. Arrested in final watchfire demonstration Feb., 1919. Sentenced to 5 days in District Jail.

AMY JUENGLING, Buffalo, N. Y.; of Swiss and German ancestry. Graduated with honors from Univ. of N. Y. Has lived in Porto Rico and North Carolina, in latter state doing educational work among mountaineers. At present engaged in Americanization work. Nov., 1917, sentenced to 30 days in Occoquan workhouse for picketing.

ELIZABETH GREEN KALB, Houston, Texas; graduate Rice Institute, 1916; student Univ. Chicago, 1916. Won Carnegie Peace Prize in Texas state intercollegiate oratory contest in 1915. In 1918 became active worker for N.W.P., taking part in Capitol picket. Arrested watchfire demonstration Jan., 1919, sentenced to 5 days in District Jail. In charge of literature and library dept. of N.W.P. at national headquarters.

RHODA KELLOGG, Minneapolis, Minn.; graduate Univ. of Minn. and Pres. of Univ. Equal Suffrage Club. Sentenced to 24 hours for applauding suffrage prisoners in Court Jan., 1919, sentenced to 5 days in District Jail for participation in watchfire demonstration same month.

MRS. FREDERICK W. KENDALL, Hamburg, N. Y.; wife of one of editors of Buffalo Express; writer, public speaker and club leader. Arrested for picketing, Aug., 1917, and sentenced to 30 days in Occoquan workhouse.

MARIE ERNST KENNEDY, Philadelphia, Pa.; formerly state chairman N.W.P. Arrested Feb., 1919, in watchfire demonstration, sentenced to 5 days in jail.

MRS. MARGARET WOOD KESSLER, Denver, Col.; vice president Woman's Progressive Club of Col. Sept., 1917, sentenced to 30 days in Occoquan for picketing.

ALICE KIMBALL, New York City. Has been engaged in Y.W.C.A. work, and as librarian in N. Y. Public Library, and later as labor investigator. Sentenced to 15 days in District Jail for taking part in Lafayette Sq. meeting Aug. 10, 1918.

MRS. BEATRICE KINKEAD, Montclair, N. J., active member of N.W.P. in N. J. Joined picket of July 14, 1917. Sentenced to 60 days in Occoquan, but pardoned by President after 3 days.

MRS. RUBY E. KOENIG, Hartford, Conn. Took part in Lafayette Sq. meeting of Aug., 1918, and suffered sprained arm from rough treatment by police. Arrested and sentenced to 15 days in District Jail.

HATTIE KRUGER, Buffalo, N. Y. Trained nurse; ran for Congress on Socialist ticket in 1918. Worker in Lighthouse Settlement, Philadelphia, and for time probation officer of Juvenile Court of Buffalo. Nov. 10, 1917, sentenced to 30 days in Occoquan workhouse for picketing.

DR. ANNA KUHN, Baltimore, Md., physician. Arrested picketing Nov. 10, 1917, sentenced to 30 days.

MRS. LAWRENCE LEWIS, Philadelphia, Pa., maternal ancestor of family which took possession 1660 land grant in Conn. from King, paternal ancestor Michael Hillegas who came Phila. 1727, a founder of Phila. Academy Fine Arts, Assembly, etc. Son of Hillegas was first U. S. treasurer; sister of Dr. Howard A. Kelly, well-known surgeon, formerly professor Johns Hopkins Hospital, author of many medical books; sister of Mrs. R. R. P. Bradford, founder and Pres. of Lighthouse Settlement, Phila.; member executive committee of N.W.P. since 1913; chairman of finance 1918; national treasurer, 1919; chairman ratification committee 1920; active in state suffrage work many years; served 3 days in jail for picketing July, 1917; arrested Nov. 10, 1917, sentenced to 60 days; arrested Lafayette Sq. meeting, Aug., 1918, sentenced to 15 days; arrested watchfire demonstration Jan., 1919, sentenced to 5 days in jail.

KATHARINE LINCOLN, New York City, formerly of Philadelphia. Was working for Traveler's Aid when she came to picket Nov. 10, 1917. Sentenced to 30 days in Occoquan workhouse. Worked for N.W.P. for several months; later campaigned for Anne Martin, candidate for U. S. Senate from Nev.

DR. SARAH H. LOCKREY, Philadelphia, Pa.; graduate Woman's Medical College of Pa. Served as interne Woman's Hospital in Phila., and later head of gynecological clinic of same hospital. Surgeon on West Phila. Hospital for Women and Children. Received degree of Fellow of American College of Surgery 1914. Chairman of her Congressional District for the N.W.P. Aug., 1918, sentenced to 15 days in District Jail for taking part in Lafayette Sq. meeting.

ELIZABETH McSHANE, Philadelphia, Pa., graduate Vassar College; principal of school near Indianapolis, later business woman. Assisted in Pa. health survey, working with the American Medical Association. Aug., 1918, sentenced to 15 days in jail for participation in Lafayette Sq. meeting. Jan., 1919, served 5 days for participating in watchfire demonstration. Member of "Prison Special" 1919.

MRS. ANNIE J. MAGEE, Wilmington, Del., one of first Del. supporters of N.W.P. Took part in many pickets. Arrested watchfire demonstration Jan., 1919, and sentenced to 5 days in District Jail.

MRS. EFFIE B. MAIN, Topeka, Kan., arrested for taking part in Lafayette Sq. meeting Aug. 10, 1918; sentenced to 10 days in District Jail.

MAUD MALONE, New York City, librarian in N. Y. Lifelong suffragist; arrested for picketing, Sept. 4, 1917, and served sentence of 60 days at Occoquan workhouse.

ANNE MARTIN, Reno, Nev.; graduate Leland Stanford Univ.; studied in English Univs. Professor of history in Univ. of Nev. As Pres. of Nev. Woman's Civic League led successful fight for state suffrage in 1914. Served as legislative chairman for Congressional Union, and N.W.P. and member of executive committee. When N.W.P. was formed, in 1916, elected its chairman. When it combined with Congressional Union, she became vice chairman. In 1918 ran on independent ticket for U. S. Senate. July 14, 1917, sentenced to 60 days at Occoquan workhouse for picketing. Pardoned by President after 3 days.

MRS. LOUISE PARKER MAYO, Framingham, Mass., of Quaker descent. Taught school for five years before marriage to William I. Mayo, grandson of Chief Justice Isaac Parker of Mass. Mother of 7 children. Arrested for picketing July 14, 1917; sentenced to 60 days in Occoquan workhouse; pardoned by President after 3 days.

NELL MERCER, Norfolk, Va.; member of Norfolk Branch, N.W.P. Business woman. Feb., 1919, sentenced to 5 days in District Jail for participation in final watchfire demonstration.

VIDA MILHOLLAND, New York City; daughter of Mr. and Mrs. John E. Milholland and sister of Inez Milholland Boissevain. Student at Vassar where won athletic championships and dramatic honors. Studied singing here and abroad, but on death of sister gave up career of promise to devote herself to suffrage work. July 4, 1917, arrested and served 3 days in District Jail for picketing. In 1919 toured the country with "Prison Special," singing at all meetings.

MRS. BERTHA MOLLER, Minneapolis, Minn., campaigned for state suffrage before joining N.W.P. Interested in industrial problems. Of Swedish descent, one of ancestors served on staff of Gustavus-Adolphus, and 2 uncles are now members of Swedish parliament. She served 2 jail sentences, one of 24 hours for applauding suffragists in court, and another of 5 days for participation in watchfire demonstration, Jan., 1919.

MARTHA W. MOORE, Philadelphia, Pa., of Quaker ancestry, student at Swarthmore College; charter member of Congressional Union; has devoted herself to social service work, Children's Aid, Traveler's Aid, etc. Arrested and sentenced to 5 days in District Jail Jan., 1919, for participation in watchfire demonstration.

MRS. AGNES H. MOREY, Brookline, Mass., comes of line of Colonial ancestors who lived in Concord. Following picket of Nov. 10, 1917, sentenced to 30 days at District Jail and Occoquan. Chairman of Mass. Branch N.W.P., of which she was one of founders, and member of National Advisory Council N.W.P. Member of "Suffrage Special" of 1916, and a gifted speaker and organizer.

KATHARINE A. MOREY, Brookline, Mass., daughter of Mrs. A. H. Morey; also officer State Branch N.W.P. Organizer election campaign 1916 in Kansas and has many times assisted at national headquarters. One of first group pickets sentenced, served 3 days, June, 1917; Feb., 1919, arrested in Boston demonstration of welcome to President and sentenced to 8 days in Charles St. Jail.

MILDRED MORRIS, Denver, Col., well-known newspaper woman of Denver. Came to Washington for Bureau of Public Information during war. Later investigator for War Labor Board. Now Washington correspondent International News Service. In Jan., 1919, served 5 day sentence in District Jail for lighting watchfire.

MRS. PHOEBE C. MUNNECKE, Detroit, Mich.; assisted with meetings and demonstrations in Washington winter of 1918-19. Jan., 1919, arrested for lighting watchfire, sentenced to 10 days in jail. Later sentenced to 3 days in jail for applauding suffrage prisoners in court.

GERTRUDE MURPHY, Minneapolis, Minn., superintendent of music in Minn. public schools. Jan., 1919, served 24-hour sentence for applauding suffragists in court. Later served 5 days in District Jail for participation in watchfire demonstration.

MRS. MARY A. NOLAN, Jacksonville, Fla., born in Va.; descended from family of Duffy, Cavan, Ireland. Educated at convent of Mont de Chantal in W. Va. As young woman was teacher and leader in Southern library movement. Suffrage pioneer; prominent in Confederate organizations of South. In 1917 joined N.W.P., came to Washington to picket. Arrested Nov. 10, 1917, sentenced to 6 days in District Jail, but sent to Occoquan workhouse. January, 1919, arrested many times in watchfire demonstrations; sentenced to 24 hours in jail. Oldest suffrage prisoner.

MRS. MARGARET OAKES, Idaho; arrested Lafayette Sq. meeting Aug., 1918, and sentenced to 10 days in District Jail.

ALICE PAUL, Moorestown, N. J. English Quaker ancestor imprisoned for Quaker beliefs died in English prison; born of Quaker parentage and brought up in this small Quaker town. Received her A.B. degree from Swarthmore College, and her M.A. and Ph.D. from Univ. of Pa. Graduate of N. Y. School of Philanthropy, and studied at Universities of London and Birmingham, specializing in economics and sociology. While in England took part in militant campaign under Mrs. Pankhurst. On return to America, she was appointed chairman in 1913 of the Congressional Committee of the National American Woman Suffrage Association. Founded Congressional Union for Woman Suffrage; made chairman. When this became an independent organization reappointed chairman. When it merged with the N.W.P. in 1917, she was chosen chairman of the combined organizations, and has continued in this office to the present date. Has served 6 prison terms for suffrage, 3 in England and 3 in United States. In Oct., 1919, she was sentenced to 7 months for picketing and served 5 weeks before released on account of hunger strike. While in jail suffered the severest treatment inflicted upon any suffrage prisoner. In Aug., 1918, sentenced to 10 days for participation in Lafayette Sq. meeting. In Jan., 1919, sentenced to 5 days for lighting a watchfire.

BERRY POTTIER, Boston, Mass., of French descent; art student; participated in Boston demonstration at home-coming of President, and sentenced to 8 days in Charles St. Jail.

EDNA M. PURTELLE, Hartford, Conn., sentenced to 5 days in District Jail for participation in Lafayette Sq. meeting Aug., 1918.

MRS. R. B. QUAY, Salt Lake City, Utah; arrested in Nov. 10, 1917, picket; sentenced to 30 days in District Jail, but sent to Occoquan workhouse.

MRS. BETSY REYNEAU, Detroit, Mich., wife of Paul Reyneau; portrait painter. Arrested picketing July 14, 1917. Sentenced to 60 days in Occoquan, but pardoned by the President after 3 days.

MRS. C. T. ROBERTSON, Salt Lake City, Utah; active worker for reforms affecting women. Arrested in Nov. 10, 1917, picket; sentenced to 30 days in District Jail, but sent to Occoquan workhouse.

Mrs. George E. Roewer, Belmont, Mass., graduate of Radcliffe, active suffragist since college days; wife of well known attorney of Boston and granddaughter of prominent figures in German Revolution of 1848 who were exiled to the United States. Sentenced to 8 days in Boston Charles St. Jail following participation in welcome demonstration to the President, Feb. 1919.

Mrs. John Rogers, Jr., New York City, wife of Dr. John Rogers, Jr., celebrated thyroid expert, is a descendant of Roger Sherman, signer of the Declaration of Independence. A pioneer worker for state suffrage before taking up national work. Before entering suffrage movement active in improving conditions in New York public schools. Chairman Advisory Council of the N.W.P., and one of the most forceful speakers in the suffrage ranks. In 1916 and 1919 as member of "Suffrage Special" and "Prison Special" toured the country speaking for suffrage. July 14, 1917, sentenced to 60 days in Occoquan workhouse for picketing, but was pardoned by the President after 3 days.

Marguerite Rossette, Baltimore, Md., young artist, and niece of Dr. Joshua Rossette, well known social worker. Took part in N.W.P. demonstrations, served 5 days in District Jail for participation in final watchfire demonstration, Feb., 1919.

Mrs. Elise T. Russian, Detroit, Mich., born in Constantinople of Armenian parentage. Educated in this country. Taught school in Mass. until marriage. State officer N.W.P. Sentenced to 5 days in District Jail for participation in Jan., 1919, watchfire demonstration; and 8 days in Boston in the Charles St. Jail for participation in welcome demonstration to President in Feb., 1919.

Nina Samarodin, born in Kiev, Russia, graduate of Kiev University. In 1914 came to America on visit, but entered industrial fight, becoming, first, worker and then union organizer. Teacher Rand School of Social Science, New York. Sentenced to 30 days in Occoquan for picketing September, 1917.

Mrs. Phoebe Persons Scott, Morristown, New Jersey, graduate of Smith College where she specialized in biology and botany. Did settlement work at New York Henry St. Settlement. Worked for state suffrage before joining N.W.P. and becoming one of its officers. Sentenced to 30 days in District Jail for picketing Nov. 10, 1917, but sent to Occoquan workhouse.

Ruth Scott, Bridgeport, Conn., munitions worker. Sentenced to 5 days in District Jail for participation in watchfire demonstration Jan., 1919.

Belle Sheinberg, New York City; of Russian descent; student of New York Univ., who left her studies to picket in Washington Nov. 10, 1917. Sentenced to 30 days in Occoquan workhouse.

Mrs. Lucille Shields, Amarillo, Texas. Picketed regularly during 1917. July 4, 1917, served 3 days in District Jail for picketing; served 5 days Jan. 13, 1919, for participation in watchfire demonstration. Soon after release sentenced to 3 days for applauding suffrage prisoners in Court.

Mrs. Martha Reed Shoemaker, Philadelphia, Pa., graduate of Vassar College. Served 5 days in District Jail for participation in final watchfire demonstration of Feb. 9, 1919.

Mrs. Mary Short, Minneapolis, Minn., state officer N.W.P. Sentenced to 30 days in Occoquan workhouse for picketing November 10, 1917.

Mrs. Lois Warren Shaw, Manchester, N. H., student of Vassar and Radcliffe, mother of six children. Wife of V. P. and General Manager McElwain Shoe Co., N. H., chairman N.W.P. Sentenced to 8 days in Charles St. Jail after participation in Boston demonstration to welcome President Feb., 1919.

Ruth Small, Boston, Mass., participant in several state suffrage campaigns before taking up national work. In charge of Boston headquarters of N.W.P. for a time. For taking part in Boston demonstration on the return of the President in Feb., 1919, sentenced to 8 days in Charles St. Jail.

Dr. Caroline E. Spencer, Colorado Springs, Col., formerly of Philadelphia. Secretary Col. Branch, N.W.P. Graduate Woman's Medical College of Pa. October 20, 1917, arrested for picketing and sentenced to 7 months' imprisonment. For participating in watchfire demonstration Jan. 13, 1919, sentenced to 5 days in District Jail.

Mrs. Kate Stafford, Oklahoma City, Okla., active worker for reforms affecting women and children in her own state. Mother of six children. Picketed Nov. 10, 1917, and was sentenced to 30 days in District Jail.

Doris Stevens, Omaha, Neb., now resident New York City. Graduate of Oberlin College; social worker and teacher; organized and spoke for state suffrage campaigns in Ohio and Michigan; joined Congressional Union in 1913. Organized first Convention of women voters at Panama Pacific Exposition in 1915; managed 1916 election campaign in Cal. for N.W.P. Has acted successively as executive secretary, organizer, legislative chairman, political chairman, and executive committee member of N.W.P. Arrested for picketing July 14, 1917; sentenced to 60 days in Occoquan workhouse; pardoned by President after 3 days. Arrested N. Y. Mar., 1919, picket demonstration Metropolitan Opera House, but not sentenced.

Elizabeth Stuyvesant, New York City, formerly of Cincinnati; dancer by profession; active in settlement work and in campaign for birth-control. July 4, 1917, arrested for picketing and sentenced to 3 days in District Jail.

Elsie Unterman, Chicago, Ill., social worker who took week's vacation in January, 1919, to come to Washington to picket. She served 3 days in District Jail for applauding suffragists in court.

Mabel Vernon, Wilmington, Del., Secretary N.W.P., graduate Swarthmore College. Fellow student with Alice Paul. Gave up position as high school teacher when Congressional Union was founded to become organizer and speaker. With remarkable gifts as a speaker, has addressed large meetings in every part of the country. As brilliant organizer has had charge of many important organization tasks of N.W.P. Organized the transcontinental trip of voting envoys to the President. Campaigned in Nev. 1914 and 1916. Became national organization chairman N.W.P. Organized the Washington picket line for several months. One of the first six women to serve prison sentence for suffrage in District Jail. For picketing June, 1917, served 3 days.

Mrs. ELSIE VERVANE, Bridgeport, Conn., munitions worker and President of Woman's Machinist Union of Bridgeport. In Jan., 1919, came to Washington with group of union women and took part in watchfire demonstration; arrested and served 5 days in District Jail.

IRIS CALDERHEAD [now wife of John Brisben Walker], Marysville, Kansas, now resident of Denver, Colo., daughter of former-Representative Calderhead of Kansas. Graduate of Univ. of `Kansas and student at Bryn Mawr. Abandoned school teaching to work for suffrage; became organizer and speaker for N.W.P. July 4, 1917, arrested for picketing and served 3 days in District Jail.

Mrs. ROBERT WALKER, Baltimore, Md., officer Md. Branch N.W.P. A Quaker and graduate of Swarthmore College; wife of a captain in the late war and mother of 3 children. Arrested July 14, 1917, for picketing and sentenced to 60 days in Occoquan workhouse. Pardoned by President after 3 days.

BERTHA WALLERSTEIN, New York City, student of Barnard College; served 5 days in District Jail Jan., 1919, for watchfire demonstration.

Mrs. BERTHA WALMSLEY, Kansas City, Mo., holding government position at time arrested for applauding suffragists in court; served 3 days in District Jail.

Mrs. WILLIAM UPTON WATSON, Chicago, Ill., treasurer state branch, N.W.P. Sentenced to 30 days Occoquan workhouse for picketing Aug. 17, 1917. Aug., 1918, sentenced to 5 days for participation in Lafayette Sq. meeting.

Mrs. C. WEAVER, Bridgeport, Conn., worked during war in munitions factory. Came to Washington for watchfire demonstration of Jan. 13, 1919; arrested and sentenced to 5 days in District Jail.

EVA WEAVER, Bridgeport, Conn., daughter of Mrs. C. Weaver, also worked in munitions factory; arrested with mother Jan. 13, 1919, and served 5 days in District Jail.

Mrs. HELENA HILL WEED, Norwalk, Conn., graduate of Vassar and Montana School of Mines. One of few qualified women geologists of country. Daughter of late Congressman Ebenezer Hill. At one time vice-president general of D.A.R. Prominent member of Congressional Union and N.W.P. from early days. One of first pickets arrested, July 4, 1917; served 3 days in District Jail. Aug., 1918, arrested for participation in Lafayette Sq. meeting; sentenced to 15 days. Jan., 1918, sentenced to 24 hours for applauding in court.

CORA A. WEEK, New York City, of Norse descent; parents Wisconsin pioneers; studied art in Boston; became member Art Student's League of New York; helped organize Oliver Merson Atelier in Paris; exhibited Paris Salon. Arrested for picketing Nov. 10, 1917; sentenced to 30 days in District Jail. Member of "Prison Special" 1919.

CAMILLA WHITCOMB, Worcester, Mass., chairman 4th Congressional District Mass. N.W.P. Nov. 10, 1917, sentenced to 30 days in jail for picketing.

SUE WHITE, Jackson, Tenn., state chairman N.W.P.; recently edited *The Suffragist;* organizer and research chairman. Belongs to prominent pioneer families of Tenn. and Ky. and is descendant of Marshall and Jefferson families of Va. Court and convention reporter for ten years; 1918 appointed by Governor, Secretary of Tenn. State Commission for the Blind. Identified with U.D.C. and D.A.R.; the Federation of Women's Clubs and Parent Teachers' Association. Has done much to organize suffrage sentiment in her state. Feb. 9, 1919, arrested and served 5 days in District Jail for participating in final watchfire demonstration.

MARGARET FAY WHITTEMORE, Detroit, Mich. Her grandmother, a Quaker, started suffrage work in Michigan. Daughter of one of leading patent attorneys of country. N.W.P. organizer since 1914. Imprisoned 3 days for picketing July 4, 1917. Jan., 1919, served 24 hours in jail for applauding in court.

MRS. HARVEY W. WILEY, Washington, D. C., daughter of General Kelton, and wife of Dr. Harvey Wiley, food expert and ex-director of the pure food department of U. S. Government. Member of national advisory council of N.W.P. Has done lobbying, political work and picketing for N.W.P. Nov. 10, 1917, sentenced to 15 days in District Jail; appealed her case; later sustained by higher court.

ROSE WINSLOW, New York City, born in Poland and brought to this country when child. Began work at age of 11 in Philadelphia; for many years worked in hosiery factory in Pittsburg; later employed in shop in Philadelphia. Recently has won success as an actress. Has brilliant gifts; 1916 spoke throughout West in suffrage campaign of N.W.P. Oct. 15, 1917, sentenced to 7 months in District Jail for picketing.

MARY WINSOR, Haverford, Pa.; comes of family of pioneer Quaker descent. Educated at Drexel Institute of Philadelphia, at Bryn Mawr and abroad. At request of American Academy of Political and Social Science made survey of English suffrage movement. Founder and Pres. of Pa. Limited Suffrage Society. Sept., 1917, sentenced to 60 days at Occoquan workhouse for picketing. Later sentenced to 10 days for participation in Lafayette Sq. meeting. Has worked and spoken for suffrage in many parts of the country. Member "Prison Special" Feb., 1919.

ELLEN WINSOR, Haverford, Pa., sister of Mary Winsor and of Mrs. Edmund C. Evans, both of whom served prison sentences. Jan., 1919, sentenced to 5 days in District Jail for participation in watchfire demonstration.

MRS. KATE WINSTON, Chevy Chase, Md., wife of Prof. A. P. Winston, formerly Professor of economics at Univ. of Col. and at Univ. of Tokio. Jan., 1919, arrested and sentenced to 5 days in District Jail for participation in watchfire demonstration.

CLARA WOLD, Portland, Ore., newspaper writer. Of Norwegian parentage; her family closely related to Henrik Ibsen. Graduate of Univ. of Ore. Took part in Lafayette Sq. meeting of Aug., 1918; sentenced to 15 days. Jan., 1919, arrested for participation in watchfire demonstration and sentenced to 5 days. For several months acted as editor of *The Suffragist*.

JOY YOUNG, New York City, formerly of Washington, D. C., wife of Merrill Rogers. Former assistant on *The Suffragist* and later organizer for N.W.P. in various parts of the country. Served 3 days in District Jail for picketing July 4, 1917.

MATILDA YOUNG, Washington, D. C., sister of Joy Young; has devoted all her time to suffrage for several years. Youngest picket arrested, being 19 years old when she first served a prison term. For picketing Nov. 10, 1917, sentenced to 15 days in District Jail; served two terms in jail in Jan., 1919; 5 days for watchfire demonstration; 3 days for applauding suffrage prisoners in court.

APPENDIX 5

DIRECTORS OF NATIONAL CAMPAIGN

EXECUTIVE COMMITTEES LISTED BY YEARS

——o——

CONGRESSIONAL COMMITTEE

EXECUTIVE COMMITTEE 1913

Miss Alice Paul, N. J., Chairman
Miss Lucy Burns, N. Y., Vice-chairman
Mrs. Mary R. Beard, N. Y.
Miss Crystal Eastman, N. Y.
Mrs. Lawrence Lewis, Pa.

CONGRESSIONAL UNION FOR WOMAN SUFFRAGE

EXECUTIVE COMMITTEE 1914

Miss Alice Paul, N. J., Chairman
Miss Lucy Burns, N. Y., Vice-chairman
Mrs. Mary R. Beard, N. Y.
Mrs. O. H. P. Belmont, N. Y.
Miss Crystal Eastman, N. Y.
Mrs. Gilson Gardner, D. C.
Miss Elsie Hill, Conn.
Mrs. William Kent, Cal.
Mrs. Lawrence Lewis, Pa.

EXECUTIVE COMMITTEE 1915

Miss Alice Paul, N. J., Chairman
Miss Lucy Burns, N. Y., Vice-chairman
Mrs. Mary R. Beard, N. Y.
Mrs. O. H. P. Belmont, N. Y.
Miss Crystal Eastman, N. Y.
Mrs. Gilson Gardner, D. C.
Miss Elsie Hill, Conn.
Mrs. Donald R. Hooker, Md.
Mrs. William Kent, Cal.
Mrs. Lawrence Lewis, Pa.

EXECUTIVE COMMITTEE 1916

Miss Alice Paul, N. J., Chairman
Miss Lucy Burns, N. Y., Vice-chairman

Mrs. O. H. P. Belmont, N. Y.
Mrs. John Winters Brannan, N. Y.
Mrs. Gilson Gardner, D. C.
Mrs. Donald R. Hooker, Md.
Mrs. William Kent, Cal.
Mrs. Lawrence Lewis, Pa.
Miss Anne Martin, Nevada
Mrs. Harriot Stanton Blatch, N. Y.

WOMAN'S PARTY (*Formed June, 1916*)

EXECUTIVE COMMITTEE

Miss Anne Martin, Nev., Chairman
Mrs. Phoebe Hearst, Cal., 1st Vice-chairman
Judge Mary M. Bartelme, Ill., 2nd Vice-chairman
Miss Mabel Vernon, Nev., Secretary
Miss Alice Paul, N. J., ex-officio

NATIONAL WOMAN'S PARTY

(*After Amalgamation of Congressional Union and Woman's Party*)

EXECUTIVE COMMITTEE 1917

Miss Alice Paul, N. J., Chairman
Miss Anne Martin, Nev., Vice-chairman
Miss Mabel Vernon, Del., Secretary
Miss Gertrude L. Crocker, Ill., Treasurer
Mrs. Abby Scott Baker, D. C.
Mrs. O. H. P. Belmont, N. Y.
Mrs. John Winters Brannan, N. Y.
Miss Lucy Burns, N. Y.
Mrs. Gilson Gardner, D. C.
Mrs. Florence Bayard Hilles, Del.
Mrs. Donald R. Hooker, Md.
Mrs. J. A. H. Hopkins, N. J.
Mrs. William Kent, Cal.
Mrs. Lawrence Lewis, Pa.
Miss Doris Stevens, N. Y.
Miss Maud Younger, Cal.

EXECUTIVE COMMITTEE 1918

Miss Alice Paul, N. J., Chairman
Miss Anne Martin, Nev., Vice-chairman
Miss Mabel Vernon, Del., Secretary
Miss Mary Gertrude Fendall, Md., Treasurer
Mrs. Abby Scott Baker, D. C.
Mrs. O. H. P. Belmont, N. Y.
Mrs. John Winters Brannan, N. Y.
Miss Lucy Burns, N. Y.
Mrs. Gilson Gardner, D. C.
Mrs. Thomas N. Hepburn, Conn.
Mrs. Florence Bayard Hilles, Del.

Mrs. Donald R. Hooker, Md.
Mrs. Lawrence Lewis, Pa.
Miss Doris Stevens, N. Y.
Miss Maud Younger, Cal.

EXECUTIVE COMMITTEE 1919-1920

Miss Alice Paul, N. J., Chairman
Miss Mabel Vernon, Del., Secretary
Miss Mary Gertrude Fendall, Md., Treasurer
Mrs. Abby Scott Baker, D. C.
Mrs. O. H. P. Belmont, N. Y.
Mrs. John Winters Brannan, N. Y.
Miss Lucy Burns, N. Y.
Mrs. Gilson Gardner, D. C.
Mrs. Thomas N. Hepburn, Conn.
Mrs. Florence Bayard Hilles, Del.
Mrs. Donald R. Hooker, Md.
Mrs. Henry G. Leach, N. Y.
Mrs. Lawrence Lewis, Pa.
Miss Doris Stevens. N. Y.
Mrs. Richard Wainwright, D. C.
Miss Maud Younger, Cal.

APPENDIX 6

CONCERNING POLITICAL PRISONERS

DEFINITIONS

James Bryce: [1]

"Perhaps we may say that whenever the moral judgment of the community at large does not brand an offence as sordid and degrading, and does not feel the offence to be one which destroys its respect for the personal character of the prisoner, it may there be held that prison treatment ought to be different from that awarded to ordinary criminals."

George Sigerson: [2]

"Men may differ, in thought and deed, on many questions without moral guilt. Forms of government and measures relating to the welfare and organization of society have been, in all ages and countries, questions on which men have entertained divergent convictions, and asserted their sincerity by conflicting action, often at grave personal sacrifice and the loss of life. On the other hand, all people are agreed in condemning certain acts, stigmatized as crimes, which offend against the well-being of the individual or the community.

"Hence, civilized states distinguish between actions concerning which good men may reasonably differ, and actions

[1] James Bryce made this distinction in 1889 between the two kinds of offenders. Letter Introductory to "Political Prisoners at Home and Abroad," Sigerson.

[2] "Political Prisoners at Home and Abroad."

375

which all good men condemn. The latter, if permitted to prevail, would disintegrate and destroy the social life of mankind; the former, if successful, would simply reorganize it, on a different basis. . . . The objects may, in one generation, be branded as crimes, whilst in the next those who fail to make them triumph and suffered as malefactors are exalted as patriot martyrs, and their principles incorporated amongst the foundation principles of the country's constitution.

"Attempts to effect changes by methods beyond the conventions which have the sanction of the majority of a community, may be rash and blameworthy sometimes, but they are not necessarily dishonorable, and may even occasionally be obligatory on conscience."

As to the incumbency upon a government to differentiate in punishments inflicted upon these two classes of offenders, he further says: "When a Government exercises its punitive power, it should, in awarding sentence, distinguish between the two classes of offenders. To confound in a common degradation those who violate the moral law by acts which all men condemn, and those who offend against the established order of society by acts of which many men approve, and for objects which may sometime be accepted as integral parts of established order, is manifestly wrong in principle. It places a Government morally in the wrong in the eyes of masses of the population, a thing to be sedulously guarded against."

George Clemenceau: [1]

"Theoretically a crime committed in the interest of the criminal is a common law crime, while an offense committed in the public interest is a political crime." He says further, "That an act isolated from the circumstances under which it was committed . . . may have the *appearance* of a common

---

[1] Clemenceau in a speech before the French Chamber of Deputies, May 16th, 1876, advocating amnesty for those who participated in the Commune of 1871. From the Annals de la Chambre des Deputies, 1876, v. 2, pp. 44-48.

law crime . . . while viewed in connection with the circumstances under which it is committed (in connection with a movement) . . . it may take on a political character."

Maurice Parmelee: [1]

"Common crimes are acts contrary to the law committed in the interest of the individual criminal or of those personally related to the criminal. Political crimes are acts contrary to the law committed against an existing government or form of government in the interest of another government or form of government. . . . .

"Furthermore, there are other offenses against the law which are not common crimes, and yet are not political crimes in the usual criminological sense. . . . .

"Among these crimes, which are broader than the ordinary political crimes, are offenses in defense of the right to freedom of thought and belief, in defense of the right to express one's self in words in free speech, . . . and many illegal acts committed by conscientious objectors to the payment of taxes or to military service, the offenses of laborers in strikes and other labor disturbances, the violations of law committed by those who are trying to bring about changes in the relations between the sexes, etc.

"Common crimes are almost invariably anti-social in their nature, while offenses which are directly or indirectly political are usually social in their intent, and are frequently beneficial to society in their ultimate effect. We are, therefore, justified in calling them social crimes, as contrasted with the anti-social common crimes. . . . ."

[1] "Criminology" by Maurice Parmelee, Chap. XXVIII. Author also of "Poverty and Social Progress," "The Science of Human Behavior," "The Principles of Anthropology and Sociology in their relation to Criminal Procedure." During the late war Dr. Parmelee was a Representative of the U. S. War Trade Board stationed at the American Embassy, London; economic advisor to the State Department, and Chairman of the Allied Rationing Committee which administered the German Blockade.

Treatment Accorded Political Prisoners Abroad

It is interesting to note what other countries have done toward handling intelligently the problem of political offenders.

Russia was probably the first country in modern history to recognize political prisoners as a class,[1] although the treatment of different groups and individuals varied widely.

First of all, the political offender was recognized as a "political" not by law, but by custom. When sure of a verdict of guilty, either through damaging evidence or a packed jury, the offender was tried. When it was impossible to commit him to trial because there were no proofs against him, "Administrative Exile" was resorted to. These judgments or Administrative orders to exile were pronounced in secret on political offenders; one member of the family of the defendant was admitted to the trial under the law of 1881. Those exiled by Administrative order were transported in cars, but stopped en route at the *etapes*, political prisoners along with common law convicts. Since 1866 politicals condemned by the courts to hard labor or to exile, journeyed on foot with common law convicts.[1]

There were no hospitals for political exiles; doctors and surgeons among the exiled helped their sick comrades.

Families were permitted to follow the loved ones into exile, if they chose. For example, wives were allowed to stay at Lower Kara, and visit their husbands in the prison in Middle Kara twice a week and to bring them books.

When criminal convicts were freed in Siberia after serving a given sentence at hard labor, they received an allotment of land and agricultural implements for purposes of sustenance, and after two years the government troubled no more about

[1] Siberia received its first exiles [non-conformists] in the 17th Century.

them. They became settlers in some province of Southern Siberia. With political exiles it was quite different. When they had finished a seven, ten, or twelve year sentence, they were not liberated but transferred to the tundras within the Arctic Circle.

Fancy a young girl student exiled to a village numbering a hundred houses, with the government allowance of 8 to 10 shillings a month to live on. Occupations were closed to her, and there was no opportunity to learn a trade. She was forbidden to leave the town even for a few hours. The villagers were for the most part in fear of being suspected if seen to greet politicals in the street.

"Without dress, without shoes, living in the nastiest huts, without any occupation, they [the exiles] were mostly dying from consumption," said the *Golos* of February 2, 1881. They lived in constant fear of starvation. And the Government allowance was withdrawn if it became known that an exile received any monetary assistance from family or friends.

Those politicals condemned to hard labor in Siberia worked mostly in gold mines for three months out of twelve, during which period meat was added to their diet. Otherwise black bread was the main food of the diet.

When held in prisons awaiting trial or convicted and awaiting transfer into exile, politicals did no work whatever. Their only occupation was reading. Common criminals had to work in prison as well as in Siberia.

In the fortress of Sts. Peter and Paul,[1] Kropotkin was lodged in a cell big enough to shelter a big fortress gun (25 feet on the diagonal). The walls and floor were lined with felt to prevent communication with others. "The silence in these felt-covered cells is that of a grave," wrote Kropotkin. . . . "Here I wrote my two volumes on The Glacial Period." Here

[1] In the Trubeskoi bastion, one building in the fortress.

he also prepared maps and drawings. This privilege was only granted to him, however, after a strong movement amongst influential circles compelled it from the Czar.[1] The Geographical Society for whom he was writing his thesis also made many pleas on his behalf. He was allowed to buy tobacco, writing paper and to have books—but no extra food.

Kropotkin says that political prisoners were not subjected to corporal punishment, through official fear of bloodshed. But he must mean by corporal punishment actual beatings, for he says also, "The black holes, the chains, the riveting to barrows are usual punishments." And some politicals were alleged to have been put in *oubliettes* in the Alexis Ravelin[2] which must have been the worst feature of all the tortures. This meant immurement alive in cells, in a remote spot where no contact with others was possible, and where the prisoner would often be chained or riveted for years.

More recently there was some mitigation of the worst features of the prison régime and some additional privileges were extended to politicals.

All this applied to old Russia. There is no documentary proof available yet, as to how Soviet Russia treats its offenders against the present government. The Constitution of the Russian Socialist Federated Soviet Republic[3] does not provide a status for political prisoners, but it does provide for their release. It specifically deals with amnesty which is proof of the importance with which it regards the question of political offenders. It says: "The All-Russian Central Executive Committee deal with questions of state such as . . . the right to declare individual and general amnesty."[4]

France has had perhaps the most enlightened attitude of all the nations toward political offenders. She absolutely

[1] See *Memoirs of a Revolutionist*, Kropotkin.
[2] Another section of Sts. Peter and Paul Fortress.
[3] Adopted by the 5th All-Russian Congress of Soviets, July 10, 1918. Reprinted from *The Nation*, January 4, 1919.
[4] Article 3, Chapter 9 . . . 49 q.

guarantees special treatment, by special regulations, and does not leave it to the discretion of changing governments.

On August 7, 1834, Thiers, in a ministerial circular, laid down the fundamental principles upon which France has acted. The only obligation upon the defendant, according to this circular, was to prove the political nature of the offense,— "that it should be demonstrated and incontestable that they have acted under the influence of their opinions." [1] Theirs advocated superior diet for political prisoners and no work.

His edict was followed by special regulations issued for politicals under the Empire, February 9th, 1867, through M. Pietri, Prefect of the Seine. These regulations, illustrative of the care France exercised at an early date over her politicals, defined the housing conditions, diet, intercourse with comrades inside the prison and with family and friends from the outside. Their privacy was carefully guarded. No curious visitor was allowed to see a political unless the latter so desired.

Kropotkin wrote [2] of his incarceration in Clairvaux prison in 1883, to which he and twenty-two others were transferred from Lyons after being prosecuted for belonging to the International Workingmen's Association: "In France, it is generally understood that for political prisoners the loss of liberty and the forced inactivity are in themselves so hard that there is no need to inflict additional hardships."

In Clairvaux he and his comrades were given quarters in spacious rooms, not in cells. Kropotkin and Emile Gautier, the French anarchist, were given a separate room for literary work and the Academy of Sciences offered them the use of its library.

There was no intercourse with common law prisoners. The politicals were allowed to wear their own clothes, to smoke, to buy food and wine from the prison canteen or have it brought

[1] *Sigerson, Political Prisoners at Home and Abroad,* p. 89.
[2] *Memoirs of a Revolutionist,* Kropotkin.

in; they were free of compulsory work, but might, if they chose, do light work for which they were paid. Kropotkin mentions the extreme cleanliness of the prison and the "excellent quality" of the prison food.

Their windows looked down upon a little garden and also commanded a beautiful view of the surrounding country. They played nine-pins in the yard and made a vegetable and flower garden on the surface of the building's wall. For other forms of recreation, they were allowed to organize themselves into classes. This particular group received from Kropotkin lessons in cosmography, geometry, physics, languages and bookbinding. Kropotkin's wife was allowed to visit him daily and to walk with him in the prison gardens.

Sebastian Faure, the great French teacher and orator, was sentenced to prison after the anarchist terrorism in 1894 and while there was allowed to write his "La Douleur Universelle."

Paul La Fargue, son-in-law of Karl Marx, wrote his famous "The Right to be Lazy" in Sainte Pelagie prison.

France has continued this policy to date. Jean Grave, once a shoemaker and now a celebrated anarchist, was condemned to six months in La Sante prison for an offensive article in his paper, *Les Temps Nouveaux*. Such is the liberty allowed a political that while serving this sentence he was given paper and materials with which to write another objectionable article, called "La Société Mourante et l'Anarchie," for the publication of which he received another six months.

It is interesting to note the comparatively light sentences political offenders get in France. And then there is an established practice of amnesty. They rarely finish out their terms. Agitation for their release extends from the extreme revolutionary left to the members of the Chamber of Deputies, frequently backed by the liberal press.

Italy also distinguishes between political and common law

offenders. The former are entitled to all the privileges of *custodia honesta* [1] which means they are allowed to wear their own clothes, work or not, as they choose; if they do work, one half their earnings is given to them. Their only penal obligation is silence during work, meals, school and prayers. A friend of Sr. Serrati, the ex-editor of the Italian journal *Il Proletario*, tells me that Serrati was a political prisoner during the late war; that he was sentenced to three and a half years, but was released at the end of six months, through pressure from the outside. But while there, he was allowed to write an article a day for *Avanti*, of which paper he was then an editor.

Even before the Franco-Prussian War German principalities recognized political offenders as such. The practice continued after the federation of German states through the Empire and up to the overthrow of Kaiser Wilhelm. Politicals were held in "honorable custody" in fortresses where they were deprived only of their liberty.

For revolutionary activities in Saxony in 1849, Bakunin [2] was arrested, taken to a Cavalry Barracks and later to Koenigstein Fortress, where politicals were held. Here he was allowed to walk twice daily under guard. He was allowed to receive books, he could converse with his fellow prisoners and could write and receive numerous letters. In a letter to a friend [3] he wrote that he was occupied in the study of mathematics and English, and that he was "enjoying Shakespeare." And . . . "they treat me with extraordinary humaneness."

Another letter to the same friend a month later said he was writing a defense of his political views in "a comfortable room," with "cigars and food brought in from a nearby inn."

[1] Sigerson, pp. 154-5.
[2] The Life of Michael Bakunin—Eine Biographie von Dr. Max Nettlau. (Privately printed by the author. Fifty copies reproduced by the autocopyist, Longhaus.)
[3] To Adolph R—— (the last name illegible) October 15, 1849.

The death sentence was pronounced against him in 1850 but commuted to imprisonment for life. The same year he was extradited to Austria where the offense was committed, then to Russia and on to Siberia in 1855, whence he escaped in 1860 in an American ship.

In 1869 Bebel[1] received a sentence of *three weeks* in Leipzig (contrast with Alice Paul's seven months' sentence) "for the propagation of ideas dangerous to the state." Later for high treason based upon Social-Democratic agitation he was sentenced to two years in a fortress. For *lèse majesté* he served nine months in Hubertusburg—a fortress prison (in 1871). Here politicals were allowed to pay for the cleaning of their cells, to receive food from a nearby inn, and were allowed to eat together in the corridors. They were only locked in for part of the time, and the rest of the time were allowed to walk in the garden. They were permitted lights until ten at night; books; and could receive and answer mail every day. Bebel received permission to share cell quarters with the elder Liebknecht (Wilhelm), then serving time for his internationalism. He says that political prisoners were often allowed a six weeks' leave of absence between sentences; when finishing one and beginning a second.

According to Sigerson, politicals in Austria also were absolved from wearing prison clothes, might buy their own food and choose their work. I am told the same régime prevailed in Hungary under Franz Joseph.

The new constitution of the German Republic adopted at Weimar July 31, 1919, provides that [2] "The President of the Republic shall exercise for the government the right of pardon. . . . Government amnesties require a national law."

In the Scandinavian countries there is no provision for special consideration of political prisoners, although a proposed

[1] *My Life,* August Bebel.
[2] Article 49.

change in Sweden's penal laws now pending includes special treatment for them, and in Denmark, although politicals are not recognized apart from other prisoners, the people have just won an amnesty for all prisoners convicted of political offense as I write. Neither Switzerland nor Spain makes separate provision for politicals, although there are many prisoners confined in their prisons for political offenses, especially in Spain, where there are nearly always actually thousands in *Monjuich.* Portugal also subjects political offenders to the same régime as criminals.

Concerning Turkey and Bulgaria, I appealed to George Andreytchine, a Bulgarian revolutionist who as protégé of King Ferdinand was educated at Sofia and Constantinople, knowing his knowledge on this point would be authentic. He writes: "Turkey, which is the most backward of all modern states, recognized the status of political prisoners before 1895, or shortly after the Armenian massacres. Thousands of Bulgarian, Greek, Armenian and Arabian insurgents, caught with arms in their hands, conspiring and actually in open rebellion against the Ottoman Empire, were sentenced to exile or hard labor, but were never confined in the same prisons with ordinary criminals and felons. They were put in more hygienical prisons where they were allowed to read and write and to breathe fresh air. Among some of my friends who were exiled to Turkish Africa for rebellion was a young scholar, Paul Shateff, by name, who while there wrote a remarkable monograph on the ethnology and ethnography of the Arabian Tribes in which he incidentally tells of the special treatment given him and his fellow exiles as political prisoners.

"There is something to be said for the political wisdom of the Sultans. Amnesty is an established practice, usually at the birthday of the Sultan or the coming to power of a new Sultan, or on Ramadan,[1] a national holiday.

"In 1908 when the young Turks assumed control of the government, all political prisoners were released and cared for by the state. My friend Paul Shateff was sent at state expense to Bruxelles to finish his studies.

"Bulgaria, another one of those 'backward countries,' established the political régime even earlier than Turkey. Politicals are allowed to read, to write books or articles for publication, to receive food from outside, and are periodically released on amnesty."

And now we come to England. In general England, too, gives political offenders much lighter sentences than does America, but, except in isolated cases, she treats them no better. She does not recognize them as political prisoners. If they are distinguished prisoners like Dr. Jamison, who was permitted to serve the sentence imposed upon him for leading an armed raid into the Transvaal in 1895, in a luxuriously furnished suite, to provide himself with books, a piano, and such food as he chose, and to receive his friends, special dispensation is allowed; or like William Cobbett, who was imprisoned for writing an alleged treasonable article in his journal, *The Register*, in 1809; or Leigh Hunt for maligning the Prince Regent who, he believed, broke his promise to the Irish cause; Daniel O'Connell and six associates in 1844 for "seditious activity"; John Mitchell, who in 1848 was sent to Bermuda and then to Van Dieman's Land.[2] These British prisoners, while not proclaimed as politicals, did receive special privileges.[3]

More recently Bertrand Russell, the distinguished man of letters who served sixty-one days in lieu of payment of fine for

---

[1] The month (the ninth in the Mohammedan year) in which the first part of the Koran is said to have been received.

[2] English penal colony in Tasmania.

[3] For details of their handsome treatment see Sigerson, pp. 19-20.

writing a pamphlet intended to arouse public indignation against the treatment of a certain conscientious objector, received special privileges. In England the matter of treatment rests largely with the will of the Prime Minister, who dictates the policy to the Home Secretary, who in turn directs the Chairman of the Board of Directors of Prisons. The Home Secretary may, however, of his own accord issue an order for special privileges if he so desires, or if there is a strong demand for such an order. Many government commissions and many distinguished British statesmen have recommended complete recognition and guarantee of the status of political prisoners, but the matter has been left to common law custom and precedent, and the character of the prime minister. In the case of Ireland the policy agreed upon is carried out by the Lord Lieutenant of Ireland.

It is difficult to generalize about England's treatment of Irish political offenders. From the earliest nationalist activities she has treated them practically all as common criminals, or worse, if such a thing is possible. She has either filled English prisons, or, as in the sixties, put them in convict ships and sent them to Bermuda and Australia for life sentences along with common convicts where they performed the hardest labor. Irish prisoners have fought with signal and persistent courage for the rights due political offenders. Lately, after militant demonstrations within the prisons and after deaths resulting from concerted hunger striking protests, some additional privileges have been extended. But these can be and are withheld at will. There is no guarantee of them.

As early as 1835 Canadian nationalists who had taken part in an insurrection in Upper Canada on behalf of self-government and who were sent to Van Dieman's Land in convict ships, entered a vigorous protest to Lord Russell, the Home Secretary, against not receiving the treatment due political prisoners.

England has to her credit, then, some flexibility about extending privileges to politicals. We have none. England has to her credit lighter sentences—Irish cases excepted. No country, not excluding imperial Germany, has ever given such cruelly long sentences to political offenders as did America during the late war.

I have incorporated this discussion in such a book for two reasons: first, because it seemed to me important that you should know what a tremendous contribution the suffrage prisoners made toward this enlightened reform. They were the first in America to make a sustained demand to establish this precedent which others will consummate. They kept up the demand to the end of the prison episode, reënforcing it by the hunger strike protest. The other reason for including this discussion here is that it seems to me imperative that America recognize without further delay the status of political offenders. As early as 1872 the International Prison Congress meeting in London recommended a distinction in the treatment of common law criminals and politicals, and the resolution was agreed upon by the representatives of *all the Powers of Europe and America* with the tacit concurrence of British and Irish officials. And still we are behind Turkey in adopting an enlightened policy. We have neither regulation, statute nor precedent. Nor have we the custom of official flexibility.

Note.—The most conspicuous political prisoner from the point of view of actual power the United States has ever held in custody was Jefferson Davis, the President of the Confederate States, during the rebellion of the South against the Union. He was imprisoned in Fortress Monroe and subjected to the most cruel and humiliating treatment conceivable. For details of his imprisonment see the graphic account given in "Jefferson Davis—A Memoir" by his wife, Vol. II, pp. 653-95.

POETS
AND
POEMS

BLOOM'S LITERARY CRITICISM **20**TH **ANNIVERSARY COLLECTION**

Dramatists and Dramas
The Epic
Essayists and Prophets
Novelists and Novels
Poets and Poems
Short Story Writers and Short Stories

POETS
AND
POEMS

BLOOM'S LITERARY CRITICISM 20TH ANNIVERSARY COLLECTION

Harold Bloom
Sterling Professor of the Humanities
Yale University

CHELSEA HOUSE
PUBLISHERS
A Haights Cross Communications ◀ Company ®
Philadelphia

A Haights Cross Communications ⬧ Company ®

www.chelseahouse.com

Printed and bound in the United States of America.
10 9 8 7 6 5 4 3 2 1

Library of Congress Cataloging-in-Publication Data

Bloom, Harold.
  Poets and poems / Harold Bloom.
    p. cm. — (Bloom's 20th anniversary collection)
  ISBN 0-7910-8225-3 (hc) — ISBN 0-7910-8364-0 (pb) 1. Poetry, Modern—
History and criticism. I. Title.
  PN1161.B56 2005
  809.1'03—dc22
                                        2005008636

Cover designed by Takeshi Takahashi
Cover illustration by David Levine
Layout by EJB Publishing Services

Table of Contents

Preface

Harold Bloom

I BEGAN EDITING ANTHOLOGIES OF LITERARY CRITICISM FOR CHELSEA House in early 1984, but the first volume, *Edgar Allan Poe: Modern Critical Views*, was published in January, 1985, so this is the twentieth anniversary of a somewhat Quixotic venture. If asked how many separate books have been issued in this project, I no longer have a precise answer, since in so long a span many volumes go out of print, and even whole series have been discontinued. A rough guess would be more than a thousand individual anthologies, a perhaps insane panoply to have been collected and introduced by a single critic.

Some of these books have surfaced in unlikely places: hotel rooms in Bologna and Valencia, Coimbra and Oslo; used-book stalls in Frankfurt and Nice; on the shelves of writers wherever I have gone. A batch were sent by me in answer to a request from a university library in Macedonia, and I have donated some of them, also by request, to a number of prisoners serving life sentences in American jails. A thousand books across a score of years can touch many shores and many lives, and at seventy-four I am a little bewildered at the strangeness of the endeavor, particularly now that it has leaped between centuries.

It cannot be said that I have endorsed every critical essay reprinted, as my editor's notes have made clear. Yet the books have to be reasonably reflective of current critical modes and educational fashions, not all of them provoking my own enthusiasm. But then I am a dinosaur, cheerfully naming myself as "Bloom Brontosaurus Bardolator." I accept only three criteria for greatness in imaginative literature: aesthetic splendor, cognitive power, wisdom. What is now called "relevance" will be in the dustbins in less than a generation, as our society (somewhat tardily) reforms prejudices and inequities. The fashionable in literature and criticism always ebbs away into Period Pieces. Old, well-made furniture survives as valuable antiques, which is not the destiny of badly constructed imaginings and ideological exhortings.

Time, which decays and then destroys us, is even more merciless in obliterating weak novels, poems, dramas, and stories, however virtuous these may be. Wander into a library and regard the masterpieces of thirty years ago: a handful of forgotten books have value, but the iniquity of oblivion has rendered most bestsellers instances of time's revenges. The other day a friend and former student told me that the first of the Poets Laureate of twentieth-century America had been Joseph Auslander, concerning whom even my still retentive memory is vacant. These days, Mrs. Felecia Hemans is studied and taught by a number of feminist Romantic scholars. Of the poems of that courageous wisdom, who wrote to support her brood, I remember only the opening line of "Casabianca" but only because Mark Twain added one of his very own to form a couplet:

The boy stood on the burning deck
Eating peanuts by the peck.

Nevertheless, I do not seek to affirm the social inutility of literature, though I admire Oscar Wilde's grand declaration: "All art is perfectly useless." Shakespeare may well stand here for the largest benign effect of the highest literature: properly appreciated, it can heal part of the violence that is built into every society whatsoever. In my own judgment, Walt Whitman is the central writer yet brought forth by the Americas—North, Central, South, Caribbean—whether in English, Spanish, Portuguese, French, Yiddish or other tongues. And Walt Whitman is a healer, a poet-prophet who discovered his pragmatic vocation by serving as a volunteer, unpaid wound-dresser and nurse in the Civil War hospitals of Washington, D.C. To read and properly understand Whitman can be an education in self-reliance and in the cure of your own consciousness.

The function of literary criticism, as I conceive it in my gathering old age, is primarily appreciation, in Walter Pater's sense, which fuses analysis and evaluation. When Pater spoke of "art for art's sake' he included in the undersong of his declaration what D.H. Lawrence meant by "art for life's sake," Lawrence, the most provocative of post-Whitmanian vitalists, has now suffered a total eclipse in the higher education of the English-speaking nations. Feminists have outlawed him with their accusations of misogyny, and they describe him as desiring women to renounce sexual pleasure. On this supposed basis, students lose the experience of reading one of the major authors of the twentieth century, at once an unique novelist, story-teller, poet, critic, and prophet.

An enterprise as vast as Chelsea House Literary Criticism doubtless reflects both the flaws and the virtues of its editor. Comprehensiveness has been a goal throughout, and I have (for the most part) attempted to set aside many of my own literary opinions. I sorrow when the market keeps an important volume out of print, though I am solaced by the example of my idol, Dr. Samuel Johnson, in his *Lives of the Poets*. The booksellers (who were both publishers and retailers) chose the poets, and Johnson was able to say exactly what he thought of each. Who remembers such worthies as Yalden, Sprat, Roscommon, and Stepney? It would be invidious for me to name the contemporary equivalents, but their name is legion.

I have been more fully educated by this quest for comprehensivness, which taught me how to write for a larger audience. Literary criticism is both an individual and communal mode. It has its titans: Johnson, Coleridge, Lessing, Goethe, Hazlitt, Sainte-Beuve, Pater, Curtius, Valèry, Frye, Empson, Kenneth Burke are among them. But most of those I reprint cannot be of that eminence: one makes a heap of all that can be found. Over a lifetime in reading and teaching one learns so much from so many that no one can be certain of her or his intellectual debts. Hundreds of those I have reprinted I never will meet, but they have helped enlighten me, insofar as I have been capable of learning from a host of other minds.

Introduction

Harold Bloom

I FIRST FELL IN LOVE WITH POETRY SEVENTY YEARS AGO, WHEN I WAS four. Though born in the Bronx, I spoke and read only Yiddish at that age, and the poets were the best of those who had come to the United States: Moshe Leib Halpern, Mani Leib, H. Leivick, Jacob Glatstein. Thanks to the Melrose branch of the Bronx Public Library, I soon taught myself to read English by immersing myself in the study of Anglo-American poetry. Only dim memories of such early favorites as Vachel Lindsay still abide in me, but I gradually read my way through vast areas of poetry. By the time somewhere between ten and twelve years old, I had begun to love William Blake and Hart Crane with a particular intensity. Memorizing them, without effort because of incessant rereading, I came to possess them with a kind of implicit understanding, which I certainly could not have externalized until many years later.

Sometimes I am asked, by poets who are close friends, why I never began to write my own poems, but from the beginning the art seemed to me daemonic and magical. To have entered it, except as an appreciative reader, would have involved crossing a sacred threshold. I kept on reading Blake and Crane, and they led me to Shelley, Wallace Stevens, Yeats, Milton, and at last to Shakespeare.

At what age I began to comprehend more fully what I reread, I cannot now mark with any certainty. Self-education has its hazards (my English pronunciation is still eccentric) but it armors against reductiveness: political, religious, philosophical, and mere fashions in criticism. T.S. Eliot fascinated me by his poetry, yet repelled me simultaneously by his dogmatic prose. At fifteen or so I read through *The Sacred Wood* and *After Strange Gods*, disliking the latter, and disheartened by the former. At least, *After*

Strange Gods led me to D.H. Lawrence, attracted to him by Eliot's extraordinarily violent denunciation.

The first critic of poetry I admired was G. Wilson Knight, whom much later I came to know and like personally. As a Cornell freshman barely seventeen, I purchased and read to pieces Northrop Frye's *Fearful Symmetry*, his majestic study of Blake. I was a kind of disciple to Frye for nearly two decades, until in the summer of 1967 I woke up from a nightmare on the morning of my thirty-seventh birthday and began writing a curious prose rhapsody called "The Covering Cherub or Poetic Influence". After many revisions, this was published in January 1973 as *The Anxiety of Influence*, but Frye had condemned it when I sent him a version in September 1967, after which we agreed to disagree forever about the nature of poetry and criticism.

At seventy-four, I continue to possess by memory almost all of the poetry I ever have loved. Perhaps memory (without which reading and thinking are alike impossible) over-determined my critical orientation. If you cannot forget Shakespeare, Milton, Wordsworth, Keats, Tennyson, Walt Whitman, Emily Dickinson, then you are not greatly tempted by resentful pronouncements that certain inadequate poets deserve study because of their gender, sexual orientation, ethnic origin, skin pigmentation and similar criteria.

The astonishing richness of Anglo-American poetic traditions is confined in this volume to mostly lyrical and meditative work, since much of it appears in the volumes on *The Epic* and *Dramatists and Dramas* in this six-book series. I regret the omission of a younger poet like Henri Cole, who will prove to be canonical, and of others who will endure, like John Brooks Wheelwright and Leonie Adams in the generation of Hart Crane.

Wallace Stevens remarked that the function of poetry is to help us lead our lives. I tend to modify that to the specific question that Freud called reality testing, which is learning to endure mortality. At moments of danger and of severe illness I have resorted to the fierce comfort of reciting poems to myself, whether out loud or silently. Not being much of a beach-person, I go there only to chant Walt Whitman, Hart Crane, Stevens, generally in solitude addressing the wind and the waves. Poetry cannot heal the organized violence of society, but it can perform a work of healing for the self. Stevens called poetry a violence from within set against a violence from without. He also reminded us that the mind was the most terrible force in the world, for it only could defend us from itself. Hart Crane beautifully and poignantly hoped that poetry could bring him "an improved infancy". Nothing will give us that, or return the beloved dead to us. Consolation, after the work of mourning is complete, reaches some of us from elegiac poetry. Like William and Henry James, I find a profound measure of enhancement in hearing Whitman's "When Lilacs Last in the Dooryard Bloom'd" chanted aloud, whether by another or by myself. Or I find existence heightened by listening to a tape of John Gielgud reciting Milton's *Lycidas* or Ralph Richardson delivering Coleridge's *The Rime of the Ancient Mariner*. I will finish with this because I want to hear Wallace Stevens himself read out *The Auroras of Autumn* on another tape. In the twilight of existence, such an experience accumulates its own value.

Petrarch

(1304–1374)

Idolatry, however repugnant to an Augustinian moralist, is at the linguistic level the essence of poetic autonomy. Because language and
desire are indistinguishable in a literary text, we may say that by accusing his persona of an idolatrous passion Petrarch was affirming his own
autonomy as a poetic: creator.

—JOHN FRECCERO

THE ANGUISH OF CONTAMINATION (OR ANXIETY OF INFLUENCE) NO LONGER
seems to me a particularly modern (or Romantic) malady. Jeremiah the
prophet shadows the poet of the Book of Job, Jesus Ben Sirach in his
Ecclesiasticus is haunted by Ecclesiastes (Koheleth), and Aristophanes savagely mauls Euripides for his misprisions of Aeschylus. If we add Plato's
agon with Homer, and the Gnostics' sense of belatedness in regard both to
Plato and the Hebrew Bible, then we have a considerable catalog of ancient
literary sorrows.

Petrarch's relation to Dante is enormously complex and difficult to
judge, partly because Petrarch's own influence upon poetry after him was
so great that it veils everything that is problematical in Petrarch's over
whelming originality. Each strong poet strives to make himself seem more
different from his central precursor than he actually is, and Petrarch's
strong misreading of Dante, implicit in Petrarch's own poetry, has affected
us more than we can know, particularly in helping to present some among
us with a Dante wholly given over to the allegory of the theologians, and
so apparently altogether free of idolatrous or Petrarchan passion, at least in
the *Commedia*. Here Robert M. Durling returns us to the deep affinities
between Dante's *rime petrose* and Petrarch's *rime sparse*:

1

To see one's experience in terms of myth is to see in the myth the possibility of the kind of allegorical meaning that was called tropological. Petrarch knew and used freely the traditional allegorical interpretations of the Ovidian myths. But he dissociated them from clear-cut moral judgments, and in this he was closer to the Dante of the *petrose* than of the *Commedia*. To say that falling in love and becoming a love poet is a transformation into a laurel tree involves the sense that the channeling of the vital energy of frustrated love into the sublimated, eternizing mode of poetry has consequences not fully subject to conscious choice or to moral judgment. For Petrarch the perfection of literary form, which exists polished and unchanging on the page in a kind of eternity, is achieved only at the cost of the poet's natural life. His vitality must be metamorphosed into words, and this process is profoundly ambiguous. If on the one hand Petrarch subscribes to—even in a sense almost single-handedly founds—the humanistic cult of literary immortality and glory, on the other hand he has an acute awareness that writing poetry involves a kind of death. This recognition has something very modern about it; it gives a measure of the distance that separates Petrarch from Dante, who gambled recklessly on the authority his poem would have as a total integration. Petrarch is always calling attention to the psychologically relative, even suspect, origin of individual poems and thus of writing itself. His hope is that ultimately the great theme of praise will redeem even the egotism of the celebrant.

It is fascinating to me that one could substitute Rilke's name for Petrarch's here, and still retain coherence, particularly if one also substituted Goethe for Dante. What Freccero calls an idolatrous passion (for Laura, for poetry, for literary immortality and glory), Durling calls a kind of death. Both critics are true to Petrarch, and to Rilke, or Yeats, or Wallace Stevens, all of them in a profound sense still Petrarchans. Or perhaps we could say that all of them, like Petrarch himself, come out of the strongest of Dante's stony lyrics, the great sestina "To the Dim Light and the Large Circle of Shade." I give it here in Dante Gabriel Rossetti's piercing version, the best poem that Rossetti ever wrote:

To the dim light and the large circle of shade
I have clomb, and to the whitening of the hills,

There where we see no colour in the grass.
Natheless my longing loses not its green,
It has so taken root in the hard stone
Which talks and hears as though it were a lady.

Utterly frozen is this youthful lady,
Even as the snow that lies within the shade;
For she is no more moved than is the stone
By the sweet season which makes warm the hills
And alters diem afresh from white to green,
Covering their sides again with flowers and grass.

When on her hair she sets a crown of grass
The thought has no more room for other lady,
Because she weaves the yellow with the green
So well that Love sits down there in the shade,—
Love who has shut me in among low hills
Faster than between walls of granite-stone.

She is more bright than is a precious stone;
The wound she gives may not be healed with grass:
I therefore have fled far o'er plains and hills
For refuge from so dangerous a lady;
But from her sunshine nothing can give shade,—
Not any hill, nor wall, nor summer-green.

A while ago, I saw her dressed in green,—
So fair, she might have wakened in a stone
This love which I do feel even for her shade;
And therefore, as one woos a graceful lady,
I wooed her in a field that was all grass
Girdled about with very lofty hills.

Yet shall the streams turn back and climb the hills
Before Love's flame in this damp wood and green
Burn, as it burns within a youthful lady,
For my sake, who would sleep away in stone
My life, or feed like beasts upon the grass,
Only to see her garments cast a shade.

How dark soe'er the hills throw out their shade,

Under her summer-green the beautiful lady
Covers it, like a stone covered in grass.

The Lady Pietra degli Scrovigni, sublimely hard-hearted, takes her
place with Shakespeare's Dark Lady of the Sonnets as a muse stimulating
one of the two greatest Western poets since Homer and the Bible to
unprecedented depths of imaginative degradation. Dante, already quester
if not yet pilgrim, climbs the high hills, presumably at twilight, or on a
winter day, in search of fulfillment, only to find that he is in love with a
Medusa. Petrarch's Laura, in one of her aspects, is also a Medusa who
transforms her poet into a stone man. Freccero and Durling agree that
Petrarch is properly ambivalent about being the object of such a transformation. The ironies of Dante doubtless transcend those of his son
Petrarch, but all the ironies of Dante's sestina seem directed against the
poet himself, and not against the superbly cruel Pietra, who reduces her
lover to the condition of Nebuchadnezzar, feeding like beasts upon the
grass. Troubadour love, culminating in the poetry of Arnaut Daniel,
emphasized the oxymoronic destructiveness of the obsessive image of the
beloved that the poet carried in his head. This is the disaster of a particular moment, the precise time when the poet falls in love, akin to falling in
battle. A purely secularized moment so intense is bound to become a confrontation with the Medusa. Here is Poem 30 of the *rime sparse*, a sestina
in which Petrarch has the courage to confront Dante's stony sestina:

A youthful lady under a green laurel
I saw, whiter and colder than snow
not touched by the sun many and many years,
and her speech and her lovely face and her locks
pleased me so that I have her before my eyes
and shall always have wherever I am, on slope or shore.

Then my thoughts will have come to shore
when green leaves are not to be found on a laurel;
when I have a quiet heart and dry eyes
we shall see the fire freeze, and burning snow;
I have not so many hairs in these locks
as I would be willing, in order to see that day, to wait years.

But because time flies and the years flee
and one arrives quickly at death
either with dark or with white locks,

I shall follow the shadow of that sweet laurel
in the most ardent sun or through the snow,
until the last day closes these eyes.

There never have been seen such lovely eyes,
either in our age or in the first years;
they melt me as the sun does the snow:
whence there comes forth a river of tears
that Love leads to the foot of the harsh laurel
that has branches of diamond and golden locks.

I fear I shall change my face and my locks
before she with true pity will show me her eyes,
my idol carved in living laurel;
for, if I do not err, today it is seven years
that I go sighing from shore to shore
night and day, in heat and in snow.

Inwardly fire:, though outwardly white snow,
alone with these thoughts, with changed locks,
always weeping I shall go along every shore,
to make pity perhaps come into the eyes
of someone who will be born a thousand years from now—
if a well-tended laurel can live so long.

Gold and topaz in the sun above the snow
are vanquished by the golden locks next to those eyes
that lead my years so quickly to shore.

Durling's translation is prose, and attempts to be literal; Rossetti breaks through his own rhetorical sublimations and repressions in the impassioned verse of his Dante translations. Yet, without prejudice to Petrarch (or to Durling), a contrast of Dante's and Petrarch's Italian texts seems to me productive of results remarkably similar to a juxtaposition of Rossetti and Durling. I cannot conceive of a lyric poet more gifted at what I call "poetic misprision" than Petrarch; his sestina is a beautiful evasion of Dante's, yet an evasion whose gestures depend upon the stony sestina of the great precursor. The unifying element in those gestures is their striking and indeed audaciously deliberate idolatry, cunningly analyzed both by Durling and by Freccero. I wish to add to Durling and Freccero only the speculation that Petrarch's idolatrous gestures, here and elsewhere, are revisionary tropes, figures or ratios intended to widen the distance between Dante and Petrarch. In order to clear a space for his own art, Petrarch overtly takes the spiritual (and aesthetic) risk of substituting idolatry for typology, Laura for Beatrice.

Dante's sestina, if judged by the moral code of the *Commedia*, would condemn its poet to the Inferno, but then that is an overt power of the poem: this is the deep degradation of Dante before his conversion, before his turn (or return) to Beatrice. Still, poetically his degradation is Sublime, and can be said to mark a limit for the erotic Sublime. The obsessive force of his sestina is unmatched and is still productive in our century in poems like the sleepwalker's ballad of Lorca and the laments for barren passion of Yeats. Dante's sestina spares neither the Lady Pietra nor himself. She is stone, not flesh, and utterly frozen, as much a victim of the Medusa as the Medusa herself. You cannot flee from Pietra; her icy sunshine penetrates every covert place, and so allows no shade. She will not take fire for Dante as other ladies do, despite his hyperbolical devotion (or because of it?) and her lovely green is profoundly sinister, because it is the color of Dante's desire, and not nature's green at all. In some dark sense the Lady Pietra is antithetical to Beatrice, so that Dante's passion for her is decidedly idolatrous, anti-Augustinian, and a triumph for the allegory of the poets over the allegory of the theologians.

Petrarch memorializes the seventh anniversary of his falling in love with Laura, which he celebrates as a falling into idolatry, since it is also a falling into poetic strength. Fire indeed will freeze snow, snow burn, before Petrarch gives up poetry, since poetry alone allows him "to make pity perhaps come into the eyes / of someone who will be born a thousand years from now," a prophecy now two-thirds accomplished in time. All that is idolatrous enough, but Petrarch superbly culminates his sestina by giving scandal, by subverting Psalm 119, which in the Vulgate reads, "I have loved Your commandments above gold and topaz," to which Petrarch replies:

> Gold and topaz in the sun above the snow
> are vanquished by the golden locks next to those eyes
> that lead my years so quickly to shore.

The golden locks of Laura have replaced God's commandments, in a remarkable turn upon Dante's Pietra, whose "curling yellow mingles with the green / so beautifully that Love comes to stay in the shade there." Petrarch has won a victory over Dante's trope, but at the high cost of an idolatry beyond nearly all measure. Dante's response to Petrarch's sestina can be heard proleptically throughout the *Commedia*, which teaches us that what we behold must be the truth, since great or small we gaze into that mirror in which, before we think, we behold our thought. What Petrarch beholds is at once poetry, fame, and death; he does not behold a transcendental truth, or for that matter a demonic one. He asserts a limited authority, because after Dante's extraordinary authority no other sort could be persuasive or authentic. Dante, like Milton, casts a shadow of belatedness over those who come after. Petrarch, whose genius had to flourish just one generation later and whose own father had been a friend of Dante's, exiled from Florence with Dante, chose a gorgeous solipsism as his poetic stance. Call that solipsism idolatry or what you will; Petrarch urges you to do so. As a wager with mortality, such a stance invented lyric poetry as we continue to know it today.

William Shakespeare

(1564–1616)

IS THERE AN EQUIVALENT IN SHAKESPEARE'S SONNETS TO HIS MOST ORIGINAL power as a dramatist: to represent changes in his characters as ensuing from their overhearing of what they themselves say, whether to others or to themselves? Does the condensed art of a sonnet allow Shakespeare to become one of his own characters, as it were, caught in the process of changing as a reaction to, or reflection of, his own utterance? I do not mean to ask again how dramatic the Sonnets are or are not. Rather, I wonder if any among the Sonnets fulfill A.D. Nuttall's fine assertion for Shakespearean mimesis, that it makes us see aspects of reality we never could have seen without it.

The aesthetic strength of the Sonnets has little to do with their appearance in a sequence, as more seems to be lost than gained when we read them straight through in order. As a rough series of isolated splendors, the best among them are rightly judged to be the most eminent in the language, superior not only to Spenser, Sidney, and Drayton, but also to Milton, Wordsworth, and Keats. They have a monumental quality difficult to match in any Western language, worthy of the poet of "The Phoenix and the Turtle."

Not many critics have preferred Sonnet 94 to all the other sonnets, but it has intrigued nearly every commentator because of its ambivalences:

> They that have power to hurt, and will do none,
> That do not do the thing they most do show,
> Who moving others, are themselves as stone,
> Unmoved, cold, and to temptation slow,
> They rightly do inherit heaven's graces,
> And husband nature's riches from expense;

They are the lords and owners of their faces,
Others but stewards of their excellence.
The summer's flow'r is to the summer sweet,
Though to itself it only live and die,
But if that flow'r with base infection meet,
The basest weed outbraves his dignity:
> For sweetest things turn sourest by their deeds;
> Lilies that fester smell far worse than weeds.

Stephen Booth sees this as "a stylistic mirror of the speaker's indecision," and observes that "The sentences wander from attribute to attribute in such a way that a reader's response to 'them' who are the subject of lines 1–8 swings repeatedly back and forth between negative and positive." The crucial question then would be: Is the speaker's indecision resolved through the implications of the couplet ending the poem? But that in turn depends upon another question: how undecided truly is the speaker in regard to "them"?

If you choose not to hurt someone else, even as your outward semblance intimates you almost certainly are about to do so, there may be a considerable touch of sadomasochism in you. Or you may be like Hamlet, who most provokes the love of the audience in act 5, where he is beyond the reach of love. An unmoved mover is more a divinity than a magnet, and so rightly inherits heaven's graces. So far at least the poem that I encounter is no mirror of its speaker's supposed indecision.

To "husband nature's riches from expense" may mean to hold one's sexuality in reserve, to abstain from expending it, but I am reluctant, in the context of Sonnet 94, to so restrict the sense of "nature's riches." We think of Hamlet as one of nature's great treasures because we think of him as an adventure of and in the spirit. In act 5, he manifests extraordinary disinterestedness; are we so far from that Hamlet if we speak of him as husbanding nature's riches from expense? In full and final control, the Hamlet of act 5 indeed is the lord and owner of his face, the outward image that he turns to Elsinore and to the audience. That brings us to the puzzling line: "Others but stewards of their excellence," where the emphasis upon "their" clearly gives us not "others" but "lords and owners" as the antecedent. To continue with my *Hamlet* analogue, Horatio is a prime instance of one of those stewards of excellence, who survive to tell the story of the greater figures they admire and love.

On this reading, the hero, Hamlet or another, is "the summer's flower," sweet to Horatio and the audience, but essentially living and dying by and for himself, for ends we can only partly apprehend, let alone accept.

The crisis of meaning turns upon the nature of the base infection that the hero meets. I do not accept a reading that associates the infection with the weed, for the "base" in "base infection" means "debasing" or potentially debasing, whereas "the basest weed" is already debased. Think of poor Othello as summer's flower debased by the infection of jealous madness, and so fallen into the terrible lack of dignity of his madness at its incoherent worst. Hamlet is precisely a being who is not turned sourest by his deeds, not a lily that festers.

I hardly seek to turn the Sonnets (1592 to 1596, or so) into a prophecy of *Hamlet* (1600 to 1601) or rather say of *Othello* (1604), but Sonnet 94 is emblematic of the tragedian who was to come, unless indeed it was written later than most of the other sonnets, which is possible enough. On my reading, it is the negative equivalent of what Wordsworth celebrated when he chanted that feeling comes in aid of feeling, and diversity of strength attends us if but once we have been strong. Strength, in Shakespeare, becomes horror when feeling comes to prey upon feeling, and Othello or Macbeth fall into ruin the more dreadfully because, in their different ways, they were so strong.

I do not find then the ambivalences in Sonnet 94 that so many, including Empson, have found, and so I do not find the speaker changing in the final couplet. I would suppose then that the Sonnets, even at their strongest, are indeed lyric rather than dramatic, marvelously conventional rather than personally expressive. Wordsworth and Keats learn from Shakespeare in their sonnets, but are closer to Milton because they put into their sonnets, as Milton sometimes did, the burden of their prophecy. Shakespeare, who had the power to hurt, nevertheless husbanded nature's riches from expense in his Sonnets and chose rather to live and die not only to himself, in his tragedies.

John Donne and the
17th-Century Metaphysical Poets

(1572-1631)

I

ABRAHAM COWLEY IS A POET REMEMBERED TODAY ONLY BY SCHOLARS, AND I doubt that he has a dozen readers a year among them, whether in America or in Britain. In the later seventeenth century he was regarded as a canonical poet, hugely influential, very much the Ezra Pound of his era. Though faded by Johnson's day, he was still famous enough to lead off the *Lives of the Poets*, where he, rather than Donne, is regarded as the founder and chief ornament (rather dimmed) of the Metaphysical school or line of wit, the bad old way superseded by Dryden and Pope.

Literary history, particularly the history of criticism, has a habit of making ludicrous many of a period's firm judgments. When I was young, Shelley was ignored or deprecated in literary and academic circles, and Donne was considered the paradigm of poetry. In the age of Eliot (or the Pound Era, if you prefer), you were dismissed as barbaric or eccentric if you believed that *Song of Myself* was the central American poem, or that Hart Crane was a permanent poet, and W.H. Auden perhaps something less than that.

Johnson himself thought his *Life of Cowley* the best of the *Lives*, since his discussion of the Metaphysical poets (he took his name for them from Dryden) was a pioneer venture. It may be unfashionable to believe this, but Johnson's discussion of the school of Donne seems to me still the most adequate we possess, despite the perpetual Donne revivals which go on continuously, from Coleridge through Arthur Symons in the nineteenth century, and endlessly in our own.

Johnson, whatever his blindnesses and flaws, remains the most fecund and suggestive literary critic in the language, with only Hazlitt and Ruskin as his near rivals. It could hardly be expected that he should have preferred John Donne to Alexander Pope; I do not, and in any case Johnson's analysis of Metaphysical poetry still seems to me more just than any of the modern defenses, down to the persuasive attempt by Louis Martz to substitute "the meditative poem" for "the metaphysical poem" as a category. Martz gives a very useful account of both terms, and of their complex interaction:

> Meditation points toward poetry, in its use of images, in its technique of arousing the passionate affections of the will ...
>
> For critical and historical purposes we should, I believe, attempt to distinguish between the "metaphysical" and the "meditative" qualities in this poetry ...
>
> ["Metaphysical"] poems tend to begin abruptly, in the midst of an occasion; and the meaning of the occasion is explored and grasped through a peculiar use of metaphor. The old Renaissance "conceit," the ingenious comparison, is developed into a device by which the extremes of abstraction and concreteness, the extremes of unlikeness, may be woven together into a fabric of argument unified by the prevailing force of "wit."

This is responsible and lucid, though a long way from the fierce verve of Johnson on the same matter:

> Wit, like all other things subject by their nature to the choice of man, has its changes and fashions, and at different times takes different forms. About the beginning of the seventeenth century appeared a race of writers that may be termed the metaphysical poets ...
>
> The metaphysical poets were men of learning, and to shew their learning was their whole endeavour ...
>
> If the father of criticism has rightly denominated poetry ... *an imitative art*, these writers will, without great wrong, lose their right to the name of poets; for they cannot be said to have imitated any thing; they neither copied nature nor life; neither painted the forms of matter, nor represented the operations of intellect.
>
> Those however who deny them to be poets, allow them to be wits. Dryden confesses of himself and his contemporaries, that they fall below Donne in wit, but maintains that they surpass him in poetry.

If Wit be well described by Pope, as being "that which has been often thought, but was never before so well expressed," they certainly never attained, nor ever sought it; for they endeavoured to be singular in their thoughts, and were careless of their diction. But Pope's account of wit is undoubtedly erroneous: he depresses it below its natural dignity, and reduces it from strength of thought to happiness of language.

If by a more noble and more adequate conception that be considered as Wit, which is at once natural and new, that which, though not obvious, is, upon its first production, acknowledged to be just; if it be that, which he that never found it, wonders how he missed; to wit of this kind the metaphysical poets have seldom risen. Their thoughts are often new, but seldom natural; they are not obvious, but neither are they just; and the reader, far from wondering that he missed them, wonders more frequently by what perverseness of industry they were ever found.

But Wit, abstracted from its effects upon the hearer, may be more rigorously and philosophically considered as a kind of *discordia concors*; a combination of dissimilar images, or discovery of occult resemblances in things apparently unlike. Of wit, thus defined, they have more than enough. The most heterogeneous ideas are yoked by violence together; nature and art are ransacked for illustrations, comparisons, and allusions; their learning instructs, and their subtilty surprises; but the reader commonly thinks his improvement dearly bought, and though he sometimes admires is seldom pleased.

Wit is, for Johnson, as he says: "strength of thought" and not mere "happiness of language." Though he went on to deny Donne and his followers a share either in "the pathetick" or "the sublime," Johnson gave them what was, for him, a measure of true praise:

Yet great labour, directed by great abilities, is never wholly lost: if they frequently threw away their wit upon false conceits, they likewise sometimes struck out unexpected truth: if their conceits were far-fetched, they were often worth the carriage. To write on their plan, it was at least necessary to read and think. No man cold be born a metaphysical poet, nor assume the dignity of a writer, by descriptions copied from descriptions, by imitations borrowed from imitations, by traditional imagery, and hereditary similies, by readiness of rhyme, and volubility of syllables.

In perusing the works of this race of authours, the mind is exercised either by recollection or inquiry; either something already learned is to be retrieved, or something new is to be examined. If their greatness seldom elevates, their acuteness often surprises; if the imagination is not always gratified, at least the powers of reflection and comparison are employed; and in the mass of materials which ingenious absurdity has thrown together, genuine wit and useful knowledge may be sometimes found, buried perhaps in grossness of expression, but useful to those who know their value; and such as, when they are expanded to perspicuity, and polished to elegance, may give lustre to works which have more propriety, though less copiousness of sentiment.

Reading and thinking are activities Johnson always recommended to poets, particularly at his own moment, yet these paragraphs of praise are qualified by the absence of Johnson's deepest veneration, which is for wisdom and its poetic refinement through elaborate invention. Johnson is careful to deny Cowley (and Donne, his master) invention, the essence of poetry, though his care is uneasily qualified by an implicit realization that is made explicit in *The Rambler* No. 125:

Definitions have been no less difficult or uncertain in criticism than in law. Imagination, a licentious and vagrant faculty, unsusceptible of limitations, and impatient of restraint, has always endeavoured to baffle the logician, to perplex the confines of distinction, and burst the enclosures of regularity. There is therefore scarcely any species of writing, of which we can tell what is its essence, and what are its constituents; every new genius produces some innovation which, when invented and approved, subverts the rules which the practice of foregoing authors had established.

We cannot fault Johnson for not seeing Donne as such a new genius of innovation, and not merely because we would excuse the critic's blindness as a product of the vagaries of taste. Towards Donne, Johnson is both puzzled and respectful. His Donne is "a man of very extensive and various knowledge," "abstruse and profound," "indelicate," whose work, when improper, "is produced by a voluntary deviation from nature in pursuit of something new or strange." But this Donne troubles Johnson, as Cowley does not. What Donne calls into question is Johnson's criteria of the general or the universal, and the natural, and to have provoked the great critic in regard to those criteria is to have manifested indubitable poetic strength.

II

Johnson had a great distrust of devotional verse, which I suspect was a hidden element in his ambivalence towards the Metaphysical poets. Even in the *Life of Cowley*, the distrust is evidenced, when Johnson discusses Cowley's frigid religious epic, the *Davideis*:

> Sacred History has been always read with submissive reverence, and an imagination over-awed and controlled. We have been accustomed to acquiesce in the nakedness and simplicity of the authentick narrative, and to repose on its veracity with such humble confidence, as suppresses curiosity. We go with the historian as he goes, and stop with him when he stops. All amplification is frivolous and vain; all addition to that which is already sufficient for the purposes of religion, seems not only useless, but in some degree profane.
>
> Such events as were produced by the visible interposition of Divine Power are above the power of human genius to dignify. The miracle of Creation, however it may teem with images, is best described with little diffusion of language: *He spake the word, and they were made.*

Two very diverse judgments, moral and aesthetic, uneasily mingle here. "Submissive reverence," with one's imagination "over-awed and controlled," is hardly a proper stance for any critic, let alone the strongest critic in Western literary tradition. This moral position is curiously reinforced by Johnson's keen aesthetic apprehension of the sublime economy of style manifested by the Authorized Version of the Holy Bible, much of it the work of the preternaturally eloquent William Tyndale and of Miles Coverdale. Poor Cowley has little hope of sustaining close comparison to Tyndale, but that is his Johnsonian punishment for daring to provoke a great critic into "submissive reverence." At that, Cowley fared better than the unfortunate Edmund Waller, whose Sacred Poems stimulated Johnson to the most powerful strictures against religious verse ever written:

Contemplative piety, or the intercourse between God and the human soul, cannot be poetical. Man admitted to implore the mercy of his Creator, and plead the merits of his Redeemer, is already in a higher state than poetry can confer.

The essence of poetry is invention; such invention as, by producing something unexpected, surprises and delights. The topicks of devotion are few, and being few are universally known; but few as they are, they can be made no more; they can receive no grace from novelty of sentiment, and very little from novelty of expression.

Poetry pleases by exhibiting an idea more grateful to the mind than things themselves afford. This effect proceeds from the display of those parts of nature which attract, and the concealment of those which repel the imagination: but religion must be shewn as it is; suppression and addition equally corrupt it; and such as it is, it is known already.

From poetry the reader justly expects, and from good poetry always obtains, the enlargement of his comprehension and elevation of his fancy; but this is rarely to be hoped by Christians from metrical devotion. Whatever is great, desireable, or tremendous, is comprised in the name of the Supreme Being. Omnipotence cannot be exalted; Infinity cannot be amplified; Perfection cannot be improved.

The employments of pious meditation are Faith, Thanksgiving, Repentance, and Supplication. Faith, invariably uniform, cannot be invested by fancy with decorations. Thanksgiving, the most joyful of all holy effusions, yet addressed to a Being without passions, is confined to a few modes, and is to be felt rather than expressed. Repentance, trembling in the presence of the Judge, is not at leisure for cadences and epithets. Supplication of man to man may diffuse itself through many topicks of persuasion; but supplication to God can only cry for mercy.

Of sentiments purely religious, it will be found that the most simple expression is the most sublime. Poetry loses its lustre and its power, because it is applied to the decoration of something more excellent than itself. All that verse can do is to help the memory, and delight the ear, and for these purposes it may be very useful; but it supplies nothing to the mind. The ideas of Christian Theology are too simple for eloquence, too sacred for fiction, and too majestick for ornament; to recommend them by tropes and figures, is to magnify by a concave mirror the sidereal hemisphere.

How well do Donne's devotional poems, or Herbert's, or those of Crashaw, Vaughan, Traherne withstand this formidable theoretical assault? Do the meditative poems of the Metaphysical school escape the indictment that their tropes merely "magnify by a concave mirror the sidereal hemisphere"?

Perhaps Johnson could be accused of overstating the aesthetic risk of devotional verse, yet he is refreshingly original and all but unique among critics in addressing himself to this difficult, and for him painful matter. It should be noted that Johnson's exalted praise of Milton, extraordinary in a critic who opposed Milton in politics, religion, and cultural vision, is founded upon the critic's conviction that Milton almost uniquely overcomes the limitations of a religious poetry:

> Pleasure and terrour are indeed the genuine sources of poetry; but poetical pleasure must be such as human imagination can at least conceive, and poetical terrour such as human strength and fortitude may combat. The good and evil of Eternity are too ponderous for the wings of wit; the mind sinks under them in passive helplessness, content with calm belief and humble adoration.
>
> Known truths, however, may take a different appearance, and be conveyed to the mind by a new train of intermediate images. This Milton has undertaken, and performed with pregnancy and vigour of mind peculiar to himself. Whoever considers the few radical positions which the Scriptures afforded him, will wonder by what energetick operation he expanded them to such extent, and ramified them to so much variety, restrained as he was by religious reverence from licentiousness of fiction.

It is by the standard of *Paradise Lost* as a Christian poem that Johnson found the meditative poetry of the school of Donne unpersuasive and uninteresting. As readers of Donne's sublime hymns, or Herbert's *The Temple*, we rightly are convinced that Johnson's sensibility was surprisingly narrow when he read the Metaphysicals. On the basis of his quotations from Donne in the *Life of Cowley*, Johnson seems to have shied away from Donne's divine poems, and he avoids quoting from Herbert. What seems an overwhelming virtue of Metaphysical devotional verse, its detailed imagery and highly individualized figurations, must have offended Johnson's Horatian passion for the universal. Certainly he had little patience for the minute particulars of the Metaphysical trope:

> The fault of Cowley, and perhaps of all the writers of the meta-
> physical race, is that of pursuing his thoughts to their last ram-
> ifications, by which he loses the grandeur of generality; for of
> the greatest things the parts are little; what is little can be but
> pretty, and by claiming dignity becomes ridiculous. Thus all
> the power of description is destroyed by a scrupulous enumer-
> ation; and the force of metaphors is lost, when the mind by the
> mention of particulars is turned more upon the original than
> the secondary sense, more upon that from which the illustra-
> tion is drawn than that to which it is applied.

III

Frank Kermode, a foremost contemporary critic of Donne, accurate-ly remarks: "It remains true that to write of the fortunes of Donne in the past seventy years is, in effect, to write less about him than about the aes-thetic preoccupations of that epoch." I would amplify Kermode's observa-tion, fifteen years later, by suggesting that the years 1915–1955 had very different "aesthetic preoccupations" than the years 1955–1985, or than the years remaining to this century are likely to have. Eliot, as Kermode says, sought to associate his own poetry with the mode of Donne, but Eliot's poetry, as Kermode does not say, in fact derives from Tennyson and Whitman. *The Waste Land* has far more in common with "Maud" and "When Lilacs Last in the Dooryard Bloom'd" than it does with *The Second Anniversarie* or "A Nocturnall upon S. Lucies Day." Kermode associates the restoration of Donne "to his place among the English poets" with the restoration of "wit to its place in poetry." Johnson associated wit with poet-ry and Pope. I myself find more wit in the Shelley of *The Triumph of Life* than in Donne, but then I am of a different critical generation from that of Kermode.

I doubt that future defenses of Donne and of his school will organ-ize themselves as Modernist celebrations of a Metaphysical agility in wit. Donne seems now as archaic as Spenser, and as specialized as Ben Jonson. The Eliotic vogue for him is now over, and with it is gone the New Critical notion that every good short poem must follow the paradigm of a Donne lyric or meditation. Johnson's powerful critique of the Metaphysicals may not be the last word, but it has recovered a good part of its force during the past thirty years. The recent essays reprinted in this volume manifest a serious attempt to appreciate the school of Donne on a basis very different from the one that extends from Eliot to Kermode. Donne and Herbert do not seem to me poets of the eminence of Spenser and Milton, and a critical epoch that preferred them to Spenser and Milton was certain to pass away as an almost grotesque interlude in the history of taste. But they are the principal devotional poets in the language, hardly equalled by Hopkins or by the Eliot of the *Quartets* or the later Auden. Whatever Johnson thought, the sacred Milton was anything but a devotional poet. A sect of one, Milton persuasively redefined Christianity almost as drastically as William Blake did. Curiously enough, it was rather Donne and Herbert, and their fellows, who merited Johnson's praise. For them, the good and evil of Eternity were not "too ponderous for the wings of wit."

Anne Bradstreet

(1612–1672)

It is appropriate that the first considerable American poet should have been a woman, Anne Bradstreet, who addressed her own book with a charming sense of the difference involved in being a woman poet:

> If for thy father asked, say thou hadst none;
> And for thy mother, she alas is poor,
> Which caused her thus to send thee out of door.

A comparison of Bradstreet with Quarles, her indubitable if unexciting precursor, would reveal his greater skill at craft and her far more interesting poetic and human personality. Whether one wishes to believe, with the feminist critic Wendy Martin, that Bradstreet's poetry constitutes a mode of "subversive piety" may depend upon the ideological perspective of the individual reader. But she certainly had more wit, vitality, and humanity, in herself and in her poems, than Quarles possessed.

No American poet, except Walt Whitman, to this day is Emily Dickinson's peer, so that in moving from Bradstreet to Dickinson we enter upon the mystery of what will always remain, beyond all ironies, the American Sublime. Attempts to find women precursors for Dickinson are not likely ever to prove persuasive. Her agon, immense and capable, is with Emerson and with the High Romantic poets, and ultimately with the Bible itself. To undertake such a struggle is beyond the capacity of any American poet except for Dickinson and Whitman, even of Wallace Stevens. Whitman's subtle inventiveness, his uncanny mastery of figuration and nuances of diction, above all his astonishing powers of regenerating multiple selves out of his own abyss of being, more than compensate for his relative lack of cognitive strength. Dickinson is cognitively so endowed, and so original, that her only peers among poets writing in English might be Shakespeare, Milton, and Blake. Like them, she reconceptualizes very nearly every idea she considers, and more in the overt mode of Milton and of Blake than in Shakespeare's extraordinary and deftly misleading manner. Like Milton and the High Romantics, she excels at the difficult art of making herself prior to what genetically precedes her. Consider the remarkable poem 290:

> Of Bronze—and Blaze—
> The North—Tonight—
> So adequate—it forms—
> So preconcerted with itself—
> So distant—to alarms—
> An Unconcern so sovereign
> To Universe, or me—
> Infects my simple spirit
> With Taints of Majesty—
> Till I take vaster attitudes—
> And strut upon my stem—
> Disdaining Men, and Oxygen,
> For Arrogance of them—
>
> My splendors, are Menagerie—
> But their Competeless Show
> Will entertain the Centuries
> When I, am long ago,
> An Island in dishonored Grass—
> Whom none but Beetles—know.

This overtly is "about" the northern lights, but actually is mediated by Emerson's essay, "The Poet" (1843):

> For it is not metres, but a metre-making argument, that makes a poem,—a thought so passionate and alive, that, like the spirit of a plant or an animal, it has an architecture of its own, and adorns nature with a new thing. The thought and the form are equal in order of time, but in the order of genesis the thought is prior to the form. The poet has a new thought: he has a whole new experience to unfold; he will tell us how it was with him, and all men will be the richer in his fortune. For, the experience of each new age requires a new confession, and the

world seems always waiting for its poet. I remember, when I was young, how much I was moved one morning by tidings that genius had appeared in a youth who sat near me at table. He had left his work, and gone rambling none knew whither, and had written hundreds of lines, but could not tell whether that which was in him was therein told: he could tell nothing but that all was changed,—man, beast, heaven, earth, and sea. How gladly we listened! how credulous! Society seemed to be compromised. We sat in the aurora of a sunrise which was to put out all the stars. Boston seemed to be at twice the distance it had the night before, or was much farther than that. Rome, — what was Rome? Plutarch and Shakespeare were in the yellow leaf, and Homer no more should be heard of. It is much to know that poetry has been written this very day, under this very roof, by your side. What! that wonderful spirit has not expired! these stony moments are still sparkling and animated! I had fancied that the oracles were all silent, and nature had spent her fires, and behold! all night, from every pore, these fine auroras have been streaming.

Emerson is frolicking here, and yet his thought is so passionate and alive, his meter-making argument so compelling, that his little fable of the youth has its darker side also. The image of the aurora begins here as dawn, indeed an apocalyptic sunrise that might dim all the stars for good, but by a marvelous crossing is transformed into the aurora borealis proper, streaming from every pore of the night. The northern lights therefore represent, for Emerson, a reversal of belatedness into earliness, executed here with superb irony, since the belatedness belongs to Shakespeare and Homer, and the earliness to "a youth who sat near me at table."

Dickinson, frequently deft at taking hints from Emerson and then swerving away from them (in a process ably studied by Joanne Feit Diehl), seems to have taken the hint with more than usual dialectical agility in "Of Bronze—and Blaze—." I no longer agree with Charles R. Anderson's strong commentary upon this poem, which interprets its teaching as being that "the mortal poet corrupts his true nature if he attempts to be divine" and that "the poet must remain earth-bound." That tends to negate Dickinson's subtler ironies, which dominate the poem. The North, meaning the night sky and the auroras streaming through it, is so adequate as to overwhelm what might seem adequate desire to Dickinson, and infects her "simple spirit" with sublime longings. Her own bronze and blaze becomes the rhetorical stance of her poetry, which rises to the heights ("vaster attitudes")

in order to manifest a sovereign unconcern all her own. Certainly the crucial irony is in "And strut upon my stem," which is a negative or downward
metamorphosis, but only of the natural woman, as it were, and not of the
poet. To say that her Splendors are Menagerie is indeed to admit that she is
a performer, but the ancient Pindaric assertion of canonical renown and
poetic survival follows with enormous authority. To be a "Competelesss
Show," able to entertain the centuries, indeed is to be preconcerted with
oneself, to be distant to alarms, even to the prophecy of one's organic fate.

Why do we apprehend, beyond error, that "Of Bronze—and Blaze"
was written by a woman? In a way more singular and persuasive than any
other woman poet has managed (at least since Sappho), Dickinson in
scores of her strongest poems compels us to confront the part that gender
plays in her poetic identity:

> The Tint I cannot take—is best—
> The Color too remote
> That I could show it in Bazaar—
> A Guinea at a sight—
>
> The fine—impalpable Array—
> That swaggers on the eye
> Like Cleopatra's Company—
> Repeated—in the sky—
>
> The Moments of Dominion
> That happen on the Soul
> And leave it with a Discontent
> Too exquisite—to tell—
>
> The eager look—on Landscapes—
> As if they just repressed
> Some Secret—that was pushing
> Like Chariots—in the Vest—
>
> The Pleading of the Summer—
> That other Prank—of Snow—
> That Cushions Mystery with Tulle,
> For fear the Squirrels—know.
>
> Their Graspless manners—mock us—
> Until the Cheated Eye

Shuts arrogantly—in the Grave
Another way—to see—

"Of Bronze—and Blaze" does not quite name the auroras, which is a typical procedure for Dickinson. "The Tint I cannot take—is best" goes further and avoids naming anything. American male theorists and poets from Emerson and Whitman through Stevens and W.C. Williams are programmatic in urging an unnaming upon us, and Stevens in particular achieves some of his greatest effects in that mode:

This is nothing until in a single man contained,
Nothing until this named thing nameless is
And is destroyed. He opens the door of his house

On flames. The scholar of one candle sees
An Arctic effulgence flaring on the frame
Of everything he is. And he feels afraid.

This is the crisis of "The Auroras of Autumn," where "this named thing" is the aurora borealis, which flames forth to frighten the poet or scholar of one candle and so undoes his attempt to enact the program of unnaming. But Dickinson, shrewdly exploiting her identity as woman poet, chooses another way to see, a way that unnames without defiance or struggle. The best tint is what she cannot take, too remote for showing, impalpable, too exquisite to tell, secret, graspless. Such a tint seems unavailable to the eye of the male poet, even to a Keats or a Shelley, even to Wordsworth's extraordinary mediation between the visual and the visionary. No woman poet since Dickinson has had the power to teach us so urgently and intuitively that women need not see as men see, need not will as men will, need not appropriate for themselves as men perhaps need to do. Freud, when he sadly admitted that women were a mystery, echoed the bafflement of Milton, and might have been echoing Blake. Only three men who wrote in English—Chaucer, Shakespeare, Samuel Richardson— seem able to convey the sense of a difference between women and men in a way comparable to the greatest women writers in the language, Jane Austen, George Eliot, Dickinson. If Austen is comparable to Chaucer as a craftsman in irony and George Eliot comparable to Richardson as a moral psychologist of the Protestant temperament, then Dickinson is quite comparable to some of the subtlest aspects of Shakespearean representation. Without Shakespeare, our sense of reality would be much diminished. Without Dickinson, our sense of reality might not be diminished, but we would know far less than we do about the sufferings and the satisfactions of a really isolated consciousness at its highest powers, particularly if it were the consciousness of a woman.

Andrew Marvell

(1621-1678)

MARVELL IS THE MOST ENIGMATIC, UNCLASSIFIABLE, AND UNAFFILIATED major poet in the language. It is finally unhelpful to call his poetry Metaphysical, Mannerist, Epicurean, Platonist, or Puritan, though all of those terms somehow are applicable. One of the most original poets in Western tradition, Marvell had no strong precursors, though Spenser may be near his hidden root. His poetry has a clear relation to the schools of Donne and Jonson, but is of neither, unlike that of such contemporaries as Randolph, Carew, and Lovelace. The distance from Milton, his greatest contemporary and the subject of one of his most admirable and admiring poems, is remarkable. His authentic affinities were with quite minor French poets who came after the Pléiade, Théophile de Viau (1590–1626) and Antoine–Girard de Saint-Arrant (1594–1661).

Post-Pléiade French pastoralists can be said to have invented Marvell's lyric mode, but there is absolutely nothing Gallic about Marvell's own poetry. Nor are there Marvellian poets after Marvell. T.S. Eliot, though his essay on Marvell has been so influential, is a Tennysonian-Whitmanian elegist of the self, whose actual verse has more in common with that of William Morris than with Marvell.

Eliot's celebrated essay, still being exalted by Frank Kermode and others, is in fact quite bad, being replete with irrelevant assertions as to how much better a poet Marvell is than Shelley, Keats, Wordsworth, Tennyson, Browning, Hardy, and Yeats, all of whom lacked what Eliot "designated tentatively as wit, a tough reasonableness beneath the slight lyric grace." We learn also from Eliot that Marvell surpasses the "L'Allegro" and "Il Penseroso" of Milton, a judgment that might have provoked some amiable skepticism in Marvell himself. Poor William Morris, a poet not very relevant to Marvell's mode, is also dragged in for a drubbing, and Eliot concludes that Browning, whose "A Toccata of Galuppi's" may be the most maturely sophisticated shorter poem in the language, "seems oddly immature, in some way, beside Marvell." Two years after his 1921 essay on Marvell, Eliot changed his mind anyway, in a review of the Nonesuch Press edition of Marvell's *Miscellaneous Poems*, where we learn that Marvell, unlike Chaucer and Pope, is "fantastical," conceit-ridden, and is in any case not as great a poet as Bishop Henry King, author of the "Exequy" but not of much more that engages us now. Though Kermode is Eliot's declared inheritor as a Marvell critic, I find his general emphasis more useful than his precursor's:

> To conclude: Marvell is not a philosophical poet; in his role as poet he engaged his subjects as poetry, bringing to them a mind of great intelligence and intelligently ordered learning. Our knowledge of his religious and political thought helps us only a little more than our knowledge of his personal life (quick temper, preference for solitary drinking) and can be related to the substance of his poetry only very cautiously and generally (the power of a mind engaged but detached, the alertness, leaning on the wind). Negatively, we can learn a lot from other poetry, and from the nature and contemporary use of allegory (habitual intermittency defined by the cult of acuteness or wit, and the resonantly defined detail). Broad categories are misleading; using words such as "puritan; "Platonist," even such as "nature" and "wit," we must constantly discriminate: wit is not seventeenth-century property but an ancient instrument of poetry and of religion, nature an indescribably complex inheritance of assumptions and meanings.

My only dissent here would be to go a bit further; that Marvell was a bad-tempered, hard-drinking lifelong bachelor and controversialist is more helpful knowledge than everything we know of his religion and politics, for the paradoxical reason that such a personality simply does not manifest itself in the poems, except perhaps for the satires. The Mower poems, my subject in this introduction, could have been written by a good-tempered married man who never touched alcohol and had little notion of religious and political quarrels. Yet they are at once absolutely idiosyncratic and personal, and totally universal in scope and emphasis, which is only to say that they are very great, very enigmatic lyric poems rather than philosophical tractates or scholarly investigations.

If Marvell is a poet's poet, then his lyrics and meditations have a particularly refreshing function for us right now, when poetry is studied as everything except poetry, be it politics, societal discontents, gender struggles, historicisms, philosophies, psychologies, semiotics, or what you will. Good critics, when once they still read poems as poems, accurately found in Marvell the culmination of the European pastoral lyric that Theocritus had inaugurated. Thomas G. Rosenmeyer, in his fine book on Theocritus, *The Green Cabinet* (1969), concluded that in the pastoral mode, "the poem as a whole is a trope, rather than any one portion of it." As a principle, this seems truer even of Marvell than of Theocritus and Virgil. Marvell's Mower poems are extended metaphors for a highly individual view of how our fall caused nature's loss of value also, so that the wounding power of sexual love became the wound that sexuality itself ended by being. William Empson interpreted the Mower most grandly:

> In these meadows he feels he has left his mark on a great territory, if not on everything, and as a typical figure he has mown all the meadows of the world; in either case Nature gives him regal and magical honors, and I suppose he is not only the ruler but the executioner of the daffodils—the Clown as Death.

In one aspect the pastoral Mower may be the Clown as Death, but in the enigmatic Mower poems this most original of Marvell's tropes cannot be uncovered once and for all. In "The Mower against Gardens," the Mower ends by insisting that "the gods themselves with us do dwell," presumably because we are not altogether fallen anymore than nature is, since "the sweet fields" still to all dispense / A wild and fragrant innocence." This is very different from the extraordinary triad of "Damon the Mower," "The Mower to the Glowworms," and "The Mower's Song," all of them reliant upon a great text in Isaiah:

> The voice said, Cry. And he said, What shall I cry? All flesh is grass, and all the goodliness thereof is as the flower of the field:
>   The grass withereth, the flower fadeth: because the spirit of the LORD bloweth upon it: surely the people is grass.
>   The grass withereth, the flower fadeth: but the word of our God shall stand for ever.
>
> (Isa. 40:6–8)

In Walt Whitman, the grass becomes flesh, a metamorphosis in which Marvell preceded Whitman. Damon the Mower, stung by Juliana's scorching beams, attains involuntarily a congruence of inner qualities and outer emblems:

> Sharp like his scythe his sorrow was,
> And withered like his hopes the grass.

Marvell's Mower, absurdly enough, is both the ridiculous Polyphemus, the Cyclops of Theocritus, and, I suspect, the Adam Kadmon or unfallen God-Man of Kabbalistic and Hermetic tradition. That is, Damon is Adam, Adam both debased beneath and exalted beyond the Adam of Genesis. Damon is the Clown as Death, if you will, but he is (or was) also the Clown as a more abundant, preexistent life, not so much the Cyclops or Virgil's Corydon as the

Platonic dream of a divine human before the crashing downwards of a catastrophic creation. Marvell's more-than-ironic mode conveys mysteries only through an immensely sophisticated humor, edged by the reality principle of mortality. Ruth Nevo adroitly describes "Damon the Mower" as "a pastoral elegy for the quiet mind disturbed radically by desire unsatisfied," which sensibly leaves undefined whose mind that is, and how cosmological the desire may be. Geoffrey Hartman, sinuously seeking to match the subtle Marvell, finds the theme of the Mower poems in "the labor of hope," with "hope in nature frustrated by love or by the very strength of hope." Hartman's Mower is rather like the afflicted heroine of Wordsworth's "The Ruined Cottage"; what had been cultivated in hope is now destroyed in hope, as the end is hastened. The instrument of that hastening is death's scythe, which dominates the final three exquisite stanzas of this eleven-stanza lyric:

> "How happy might I still have mowed,
> Had not Love here his thistles sowed!
> But now I all the day complain,
> Joining my labour to my pain;
> And with my scythe cut down the grass,
> Yet still my grief is where it was:
> But, when the iron blunter grows,
> Sighing, I whet my scythe and woes."
> While thus he threw his elbow round,
> Depopulating all the ground,
> And, with his whistling scythe, does cut
> Each stroke between the earth and root,
> The edged steel by careless chance

Did into his own ankle glance;
And there among the grass fell down,
By his own scythe, the Mower mown.
"Alas!" said he, "these hurts are slight
To those that die by love's despite.
With shepherd's-purse, and clown's-all-heal,
The blood I staunch, and wound I seal.
Only for him no cure is found,
Whom Juliana's eyes do wound.
'Tis death alone that this must do:
For Death thou art a Mower too."

"The Mower mown" might well have been the poem's title, except for its neglect of Damon in his self-apotheosis:

"I am the Mower Damon, known
Through all the meadows I have mown.
On me the morn her dew distills
Before her darling daffodils.
And, if at noon my toil me heat,
The sun himself licks off my sweat.
While, going home, the evening sweet
In cowslip-water bathes my feet."

That does not seem to me the Clown as Death so much as the Clown as Hermetic Adam, living in a place very much his own, and even more his self, being at home all the time. We see Damon Adam fall again in stanzas 9–11, and so lose his home, possibly forever:

The Mower to the Glowworms

Ye living lamps, by whose dear light
The nightingale does sit so late,
And studying all the summer night,
Her matchless songs does meditate;

Ye country comets, that portend
No war, nor prince's funeral,
Shining unto no higher end
Than to presage the grass's fall;

Ye glowworms, whose officious flame
To wandering mowers shows the way,
That in the night have lost their aim,
And after foolish fires do stray;

Your courteous lights in vain you waste,
Since Juliana here is come,
For she my mind hath so displaced
That I shall never find my home.

This extraordinary lyric, addressed by the fallen Mower to the luminaries of his severely shrunken world, is surely one of the most mysterious
and beautiful poems in the language. I cannot reread it or recite it to
myself without evoking the beautiful quatrains that Blake added to *The
Gates of Paradise* when he reengraved that little Prophetic Book, addressing the quatrains "To the Accuser Who is the God of this World." But
"The Mower to the Glowworms" has no Jobean associations, even if it too
is a lost traveller's dream under the hill. "The grass's fall" is the fall of the
flesh, and the third stanza might almost have been written by William
Blake.

The first stanza of "The Mower's Song" recapitulates the last stanza
here, where the Mower's mind is displaced, but the revision is in a finer tone:

My mind was once the true survey
Of all these meadows fresh and gay,
And in the greenness of the grass
Did see its hopes as in a glass;
When Juliana came, and she
What I do to the grass, does to my thoughts and me.

Juliana is the Charmer as Death, and the remainder of the poem centers itself upon the extraordinary revelations of that last line, Marvell's solitary and unique instance of a refrain:

But these, while I with sorrow pine,
Grew more luxuriant still and fine,
That not one blade of grass you spied,
But had a flower on either side;
When Juliana came, and she
What I do to the grass, does to my thoughts and me.

Unthankful meadows, could you so
A fellowship so true forgo,
And in your gaudy May-games meet,
While I lay trodden under feet?
  When Juliana came, and she
What I do to the grass, does to my thoughts and me.

But what you in compassion ought,
Shall now by my revenge be wrought:
And flow'rs, and grass, and I and all,
Will in one common ruin fall.
  For Juliana comes, and she
What I do to the grass, does to my thoughts and me.

And thus, ye meadows, which have been
Companions of my thoughts more green,
Shall now the heraldry become
With which I will adorn my tomb;
  For Juliana comes, and she
What I do to the grass, does to my thoughts and me.

Damon, resenting the flowers, truly resents a green world that will survive his own now irretrievable fall. But his true resentment is also an apocalyptic paradox, since his "revenge" of "one common ruin" is pragmatically a further riot of what Whitman calls the flag of the poet's disposition, out of hopeful green stuff woven. The heraldry of green will make the entire earth the Mower's tomb, but such a heraldry will bury scythe and scyther alike, give death to Death, and perhaps herald the rebirth of Damon as Adam Kadmon, the Primal Man forever not to be mown down.

William Blake

(1757–1827)

WHAT HAPPENS TO A POEM AFTER IT HAS SUCCEEDED IN CLEARING A SPACE for itself? As the poem itself begins to be misread, both by other poems and by criticism, is it distorted in the same way or differently than it has been distorted by itself, through its own activity in misreading others? Clearly its meanings do change drastically between the time that it first wrestles its way into strength, and the later time that follows its canonization. What kinds of misreading does canonization bring about? Or, to start further back, why call the canonization of texts a necessary misreading of texts?

What is canonization, in a purely secular context, and why ought criticism to talk about it? Criticism in fact hardly has talked about canon-formation, at least for quite a while now, and the process is a troublesome one, and so not easy to discuss. Canon-formation, in the West, began in the creation of Scripture, when the rabbis accepted certain texts and rejected others, so as to arrive at last at the library of thirty-nine books now commonly referred to as the Old Testament. The rabbis were no more unanimous than any other body of literary critics, and some of the disputes about canonization were not settled for several generations. The three main divisions of the Hebrew Bible—the Law, the Prophets, the Writings or Wisdom literature—represent three stages of canon-formation. It is likely that the Law was canonized by about 400 B.C., the Prophets by about 100 B.C., the Writings not until A.D. 90.

"Canon" as a word goes back to a Greek word for a measuring rule, which in Latin acquired the additional meaning of "model." In English we use it to mean a church code, a secular law, a standard or criterion, or a part of the Catholic Mass, or as a musical synonym for a kind of fugue, or in printing for a size of type. But we also use it for authoritative lists of works, sacred or secular, by one author or by many. The Greek word *kanon* was of

Semitic origin, and it is difficult to distinguish between its original meanings of "reed" or "pipe," and "measuring rod." Canon-formation or canonization is a richly suggestive word for a process of classic-formation in poetic tradition, because it associates notions of music and of standards.

But before considering poetic canon-formation, I want to go back to the biblical process of canonization. Samuel Sandmel makes the useful observation that before a text was canonized, it could be copied with inattention, as you or I tend to copy. But, he adds: "Once a writing became canonical, it was copied with such relentless fidelity that even the inherited mistakes and the omissions and the telescoping were retained." The late Edmund Wilson, perhaps not understanding the indirect descent of academic textual scholars from these pious copyists, complained bitterly at its modern continuance, but we can attain a critical realization about how a copying-canonization fosters misreading, of a peculiarly uninteresting, weak, and unproductive kind. A canonical reading, like a canonical copying, attempts to stop the mind by making a text redundantly identical with itself, so as to produce a total presence, an unalterable meaning. So many texts, so many meanings—might be the motto of weak canonization. But there is also strong canonization, and it is more dangerous, whether carried on by the Academy of Ezra, the Church, the universities, or most of all by strong critics from Dr. Samuel Johnson to the present day. Though my own texts-for-reading in this [essay] will be two famous lyrics by Blake, *London* and *The Tyger*, I will try to illustrate the ways in which strong canonization misreads by a religious example, before I turn to Blake. But before I come to my religious example, I want to say something about the transition from religious to secular canon-formation.

Whether in religion or in poetry, or (as I suspect) everywhere else as well, memory is a crucial mode of thought, as Hannah Arendt remarks in the context of political philosophy. We can make a more drastic assertion; in poetry memory is always the most important mode of thought, despite Blake's passionate insistences upon the contrary view. The reason why most strong post-Enlightenment poems end with schemes of transumption or metaleptic reversals, with defensive patterns of projection and/or introjection, with imagery of earliness and/or belatedness, in short with the revisionary ratio I have called the *apophrades* or Return of the Dead, is that, particularly in poems, the past, like the future, is always a force, and indeed, in poems, the future's force is directed to driving the poem back into the past, no matter what the poet is trying to do.

Hannah Arendt tells us that political thought as a tradition goes from Plato to Marx, and ends there. I suppose we could say that moral psychology as a tradition goes from Plato to Freud and ends there. But poetry as a tradition has no Marx or Freud (though Wordsworth came closest to that end-stop position) because you cannot break the tradition without ceasing to write poetry, in the sense that the tradition from Homer to Goethe defines poetry, and Wordsworth's best poetry paradoxically breaks the tradition only to extend it, but at the high cost of narrowing and internalizing the tradition, so that all subsequent attempts to get beyond Wordsworth have failed. Blake was a much less original poet than Wordsworth, as I think we are only beginning to understand. Despite his surface innovations, Blake is closer to Spenser and to Milton than he is to Wordsworth, and far closer than Wordsworth is to Spenser and Milton. Wordsworth imposed himself upon the canon; Blake, though a major intellectual revisionist, was more imposed upon *by* the canon than modern Blake scholarship is willing to accept or admit.

I return to the process of canonic imposition. E.R. Curtius sums it up by saying: "Canon formation in literature must always proceed to a selection of classics." But Curtius, so far as I can tell, hardly distinguishes between religious and secular canon-formation. A secular tradition presumably is open to intruders of genius, rather more readily than a religious tradition, and surely this difference is the crucial one between revisionism and heresy. Revisionism alters *stance*; heresy alters *balance*. A secular canon stands differently, after it subsumes a great revisionist, as British poetry manifested a different relation between the poet and the poem, after Wordsworth. But a religious canon is thrown out of balance by a great heretic, and cannot subsume him unless it is willing to be a different religion, as Lutheranism and Calvinism were very different religions from Catholicism. Joachim of Flora or Eckhart could not become canonical texts, but in the secular canon Blake has been legitimatized. What this has done to Blake is now my concern, a concern I want to illuminate first by one large instance of the reading peculiarities brought about through religious canonization. The book *Koheleth* or Ecclesiastes is, rather astonishingly, a canonical work, part of Scripture. The book Ecclesiasticus, or *The Wisdom of Jesus the Son of Sirach*, was not taken into the canon, and is part of the Old Testament Apocrypha.

As literary works, they both are magnificent; in the King James version, it would be difficult to choose between them for rhetorical power, but Ecclesiastes is far stronger in the original. Their peculiar fascination for my purposes is that they exist in a relation of precursor and ephebe, with Koheleth or Ecclesiastes, written about 250 B.C., being the clearly dominant influence upon Ben Sirach or Ecclesiasticus, written about 200 B.C. By a splendid irony, the canonical Koheleth is a highly problematic text in regard to normative Judaism, while the uncanonical Ben Sirach is explicitly and unquestionably orthodox, a monument to normative Judaism.

Koheleth derives from the Hebrew word *kahal*, meaning "the community" or "the congregation." The Greek "Ecclesiastes," meaning a member of the *ecclesia* or assembly of citizens, is not a very exact equivalent. Neither word, Hebrew or Greek, means "the Preacher," which is a famous mistranslation for Koheleth. Tradition identifies Koheleth with Solomon, a beautiful but false idea. Like his imitator Ben Sirach, Koheleth worked in the literary genre of Wisdom Literature, a vast genre in the ancient Near East. "Instruction" is a synonym for "Wisdom" in this sense, and may be a better modern translation for *Hokmah*, which really meant: "How to live, what to do," but was also used as a synonym for poetry and song, which were not distinguished from Instruction.

Robert Gordis, in the most widely accepted modern study of Koheleth, shows that Koheleth was a teacher in one of the Wisdom academies in third-century B.C. Jerusalem, teaching aristocratic youths, in a quasi-secular way. His ambiance was anything but prophetic, and his highly individual vision of life and religion was much closer to what we would call skeptical humanism than it was to the central traditions of Judaism. God, for Koheleth, is the Being who made us and rules over us, but Koheleth has nothing more to say about Him. God is there at our beginning and at our end; in between what matters is our happiness. How did *this* book become canonized?

Not without a struggle, is part of the answer. The two great interpretative schools of the rabbis Hillel and Shammai fought a long spiritual war over Koheleth, and the Hillelites did not win a final victory until A.D. 90 when the Council of Jamnia (Jabneh) closed out Scripture by affirming that Koheleth was part of the canon. The school of Shammai sensibly asserted that the book was self-contradictory, merely literary, not inspired by God, and was marked plainly by skepticism towards the Torah. The Hillelites insisted that the book was by Solomon (though surely even they knew this was a pious fiction), and pointed to certain passages in the book that were traditionally Torah-oriented. What was the motive of the Hillelites? Theologically, they were liberals, and presumably Koheleth helped them to achieve more daring and open interpretations of the Law. Yet the deeper motive, as with the great Rabbi Akiba's passion for the *Song of Songs*, seems to have been what we call literary or aesthetic esteem. Koheleth was, rhetorically and conceptually, too good a book to lose. Though both a belated and an audacious work, it was taken permanently into Scripture. I myself am a mere amateur at biblical scholarship, yet I want to go further in expressing the misreading of this canonization, for as

I read it, Koheleth is a revisionist poem, a strong misprision of Torah, which suffered the happy irony of being absorbed by the precursor against whom it had rebelled, however ambivalently. Koheleth 3:14 echoes Deuteronomy 4:2 and 13:1 in a revisionist way, so as to change the emphasis from the Law's splendor to human powerlessness. It echoes passages in Kings, Samuel, and Leviticus, so as to undo the moral point from a categorical insistence upon righteousness as a divine commandment to the skeptical view that moral error is inevitable and even necessary, but that righteousness is always more humanly sensible if only you can achieve it. Robert Gordis insightfully remarks that Koheleth refers only to Torah and to Wisdom Scripture, and wholly ignores the canonical prophets, as nothing could be more antithetical to his own vision than Isaiah and Ezekiel.

Let us contrast to Koheleth his eloquent and more traditionally pious ephebe Ben Sirach, who about a half-century later seems to have followed much the same profession, teaching pragmatic Wisdom, of a literary kind, at an upper-class academy in Jerusalem. Ben Sirach can be described as the Lionel Trilling of his day, even as his precursor, Koheleth, seems a figure not wholly unlike Walter Pater or even Matthew Arnold, in Arnold's more skeptical moments, though I hasten to add that Arnold was hardly in Koheleth's class as poet or intellect. Ben Sirach, by a charming but not unexpected antithetical irony, echoes or alludes constantly to Koheleth, but always canonically misreading Koheleth into a Shammai-like high Pharisaic orthodoxy. Wherever Koheleth urges the necessity of pleasure, Ben Sirach invokes the principle of echoing Koheleth while urging restraint, but in the vocabulary of his precursor. Robert Gordis observes that wherever Koheleth is literal in his meaning, Ben Sirach interprets him as being figurative. Any close comparison of the texts of Ecclesiastes and Ecclesiasticus will confirm the analysis that Gordis makes.

Let me sum up this rather intricate excursus upon Koheleth and the book of Jesus Ben Sirach. The revisionist work, through canonization, is misread by being overfigurated by the canonically informed reader. The derivative, orthodox work, left uncanonized because of its belatedness, is misread by being overliteralized by those who come after it, ourselves included.

I turn to two texts of Blake, two famous *Songs of Experience: London* and *The Tyger*. How are we to read these two revisionist lyrics that Blake intended us to canonize, that indeed now are part of the canon of British poetry? What kinds of misreadings are these poems now certain to demand? *London* is a revisionist text with regard to the book of the prophet Ezekiel; *The Tyger* is a revisionist text with regard to the Book of Job, and also in relation to *Paradise Lost*.

Here is the precursor-text for Blake's *London*, chapter 9 of the Book of Ezekiel:

He cried also in mine ears with a loud voice, saying, "Cause them that have charge over the city to draw near, even every man with his destroying weapon in his hand."

And, behold, six men came from the way of the higher gate, which lieth toward the north, and every man a slaughter weapon in his hand; and one man among them was clothed with linen, with a writer's inkhorn by his side: and they went in, and stood beside the brasen altar.

And the glory of the God of Israel was gone up from the cherub, whereupon he was, to the threshold of the house. And he called to the man clothed with linen, which had the writer's inkhorn by his side;

And the Lord said unto him, "Go through the midst of the city, through the midst of Jerusalem, and set a mark upon the foreheads of the men that sigh and that cry for all the abominations that be done in the midst thereof."

And to the others he said in mine hearing, "Go ye after him through the city, and smite: let not your eye spare, neither have ye pity: Slay utterly old and young, both maids, and little children, and women: but come not near any man upon whom is the mark; and begin at my sanctuary." Then they began at the ancient men which were before the house.

And he said unto them, "Defile the house, and fill the courts with the slain: go ye forth." And they went forth, and slew in the city.

And it came to pass, while they were slaying them, and I was left, that I fell upon my face, and cried, and said, "Ah Lord God! wilt thou destroy all the residue of Israel in thy pouring out of thy fury upon Jerusalem?"

Then said he unto me, "The iniquity of the house of Israel and Judah is exceeding great, and the land is full of blood, and the city full of perverseness: for they say, 'The Lord hath forsaken the earth, and the Lord seeth not.'

"And as for me also, mine eye shall not spare, neither will I have pity, but I will recompense their way upon their head."

And, behold, the man clothed with linen, which had the inkhorn by his side, reported the matter, saying, "I have done as thou hast commanded me."

Chapter 8 of Ezekiel ends with God's warning that he will punish the people of Jerusalem for their sins. Chapter 9 is Ezekiel's prophetic vision of the punishment being carried out, despite the prophet's attempt at intercession on behalf of a saving remnant. The crucial verse for Blake's *London* is clearly the fourth one, which gives Blake not only the central image of his poem but even the rhyme of "cry" and "sigh":

> ... And he called to the man clothed with linen, which had the writer's inkhorn by his side;
>   And the Lord said unto him: "Go through the midst of the city, through the midst of Jerusalem, and set a mark upon the foreheads of the men that sigh and that cry for all the abominations that be done in the midst thereof."

This mark is given to the saving remnant of Jerusalem, who alone are to be spared destruction. The Hebrew word for "mark" used here is *taw*, which is the name also of the letter *t*, the last letter of the Hebrew alphabet, even as zed (*z*) is last in ours, or omega is last in the Greek alphabet. Traditional commentary on Ezekiel interpreted this to mean that the taw set upon the forehead of the righteous would be written in ink and signify *tichyeh*, "you shall live," but the *taw* upon the forehead of the wicked would be written in blood and would signify *tamuth*, "you shall die."

The intertextual relationship between Ezekiel and Blake here is quite unmistakable, even though it also has been quite unnoticed, except by myself, in my role as what Blake denounced as a "Satan's Watch-Fiend." How is Blake revising Ezekiel?

Not, so far as I can tell, by his initial equation of London = Jerusalem, which means that from the start all received readings of this poem, including my own, are wholly mistaken in seeing Blake's poem primarily as a protest against repression, whether societal or individual. That is, all received readings have said or intimated that in the poem *London* Blake presents himself as a prophet or prophetic figure, akin to Ezekiel, with the people of London only roughly akin to those of Ezekiel's Jerusalem, in that they are shown as suffering beneath the counterrevolutionary oppression of the regime of William Pitt. On this view the people, however culpable for weakness or lack of will, are the righteous, and only the State and State Church of Pitt are the wicked. From this, a number of other interpretations necessarily follow throughout the poem, down to the famous lines about the harlot and the new-born infant at the poem's close.

I shall demonstrate, with the aid of what I call "antithetical criticism," that all such interpretations are weak, unproductive, canonical misreadings, quite alien to the spirit of Blake's strong misreading or misprision of Ezekiel, and alien in any case to the letter of Blake's text, to the words, images, figurations of the strong poem *London*.

Blake begins: "I wander thro' each charter'd street," and so we begin also, with that wandering and that chartering, in order to define that "L" Is it an Ezekiel-like prophet, or someone whose role and function are altogether different? To "wander" is to have no destination and no purpose. A biblical prophet may wander when he is cast out into the desert, when his voice becomes a voice in the wilderness, but he does not wander when he goes through the midst of the city, through the midst of Jerusalem the City of God. There, his inspired voice always has purpose, and his inspired feet always have destination. Blake knew all this, and knew it with a knowing beyond our knowing. When he begins by saying that he *wanders* in London, his Jerusalem, his City of God, then he begins also by saying "I am not Ezekiel, I am not a prophet, I am too fearful to be the prophet I ought to be, *I am hid*."

"Charter'd" is as crucial as "wander." The word is even richer with multiple significations and rhetorical ironies, in this context, than criticism so far has noticed. Here are the relevant shades-of-meaning: There is certainly a reference to London having been created originally as a city by a charter to that effect. As certainly, there is an ironic allusion to the celebrated political slogan: "the chartered rights of Englishmen." More subtly, as we will see, there is a reference to *writing*, because to be chartered is to be written, since a charter is a written grant from authority, or a document outlining a process of incorporation. In addition, there are the commercial notions of hiring, or leasing, indeed of binding or covenanting, always crucial in a prophetic context. Most important, I think, in this poem that turns upon a mark of salvation or destruction, is the accepted meaning that to be chartered is to be awarded a special privilege or a particular immunity, which is established by a written document. Finally, there is a meaning opposed to "wandering," which is charting or mapping, so as to preclude mere wandering. The streets of London are chartered, Blake says, and so he adds is the Thames, and we can surmise that for Blake, the adjective is primarily negative in its ironies, since his manuscript drafts show that he substituted the word "chartered" for the word "dirty" in both instances.

As is often the case with strong, antithetical poems that are highly condensed in their language, Blake's key-words in *London* are remarkably interrelated, as criticism again has failed to notice. Walter Pater, in his great essay on *Style*, urges that the strong poet, or "literary artist" as he puts it, "will be apt to restore not really obsolete or really worn-out words, but the finer edge of words still in use." Pater meant the restoration of etymological or original meaning, "the finer edge," and in this Pater was again a prophet of modern or belated poetry. But here Blake, who deeply influenced Pater, was already a pioneer. Let us return to "wander" which goes back to the root *wendh*, from which come also "turn," "weave," and "wind." I quote from Blake's *Auguries of Innocence*, notebook jottings clearly related to his *London*:

> The Whore & Gambler by the State
> Licencd build that Nations Fate
> The Harlots cry from Street to Street
> Shall weave Old Englands winding Sheet
> The Winners Shout the Losers Curse
> Dance before dead Englands Hearse
> Every Night & every Morn
> Some to Misery are Born

Contrast this to the final stanza of *London*:

> But most thro' midnight streets I hear
> How the youthful Harlots curse
> Blasts the new-born Infants tear
> And blights with plagues the Marriage hearse.

The harlot's cry or curse, a loser's curse, weaves a winding sheet for England and every marriage in England by blasting the infant's tear and by blighting with plagues. To weave is to wind is to wander is to turn is to blight and blast. Blight and blast what and how? The surprising answer is: voice, which of course is the prophet's one gift. Blake *wendhs* as the harlot *wendhs*, and both to the same result: the loss of human voice. For what is an "infant"? "Infant," "ban," and "prophet" all come from the same root, the Indo-European *Bha*, which is a root meaning "to speak." And "infant" means one incapable of speech; all the infant can do is weep. The Latin *fari* and the Greek *phanai* both mean "to speak," and "prophet" derives from them. A ban is a stated or spoken interdiction, which means that a ban is a curse, while to curse is to put something or someone under a ban. Ban and voice, in Blake's *London*, are natural synonyms and indeed we can say that the poem offers the following equation: every voice = a ban = a curse = weeping or a blasted tear. But the verbal network is even more intricate. The harlot's curse is not, as various interpreters have said, venereal disease, but is indeed what "curse" came to mean in the vernacular after Blake and still means now: menstruation, the natural cycle in the human female. Let us note the complexity of two more key words in the text: "mark" and "forg'd" in "mind-forg'd manacles." A "mark" is a boundary (or, as Blake said, a "Devourer" as opposed to a "Prolific"); it is also a visible trace, a sign in lieu of writing, and a grade of merit or demerit. To "forge" means to "fabricate" in both senses of "fabricate": to make, as a smith or poet makes, but also to counterfeit. The Indo-European root is *dhabh*, meaning "to fit together" and is related to the Hebrew *dabhar* for "word." "Mind-forg'd manacles" is a phrase deliberately evoking the Western metaphysical problem of dualism, since "manacles" for "hand-cuffs" involves *manus* or hand, and hence bodily act, which is at once made and yet feigned or counterfeited by the opposing principle of mind.

I have involved us in all of this verbal interrelation in order to suggest that Blake's *London* centers itself upon an opposition between *voice* and *writing*, by which I don't mean that somehow Jacques Derrida wrote the poem. No—the poem is precisely anti-Nietzschean, anti-Derridaean, and offers us a terrifying nostalgia for a lost prophetic *voice*, the voice of Ezekiel and religious logocentrism, which has been replaced by a demonic *visible trace*, by a mark, by the writing of the apocalyptic letter *taw*. With this as background, I am at last prepared to offer my own, antithetical, strong misreading of Blake's *London*, of which I will assert only that it is more adequate to the text than the weak misreadings now available to us.

I will commence by offering a very plain summary or paraphrase of what I judge to be the difference in meanings when we juxtapose Blake's *London* with its precursor-text in Ezekiel, chapter 9. Then I will proceed to an antithetical account of Blake's *London*, through a charting of its revisionary ratios, tropes, psychic defenses, and images.

In chapter 8 of Ezekiel, the prophet sits in his house of exile in Babylon, surrounded by the elders of Judah. The Spirit of God raises him, and carries him "in the visions of God to Jerusalem," to the outraged Temple, where graven, idolatrous images of Asherah have been placed as substitutes for the Living God. A further and final vision of the *Merkabah*, God's triumphal chariot, is granted Ezekiel, after which four scenes of idolatry *within* the Temple are revealed to him. Chapter 8 concludes with a fierce warning from God:

> Therefore will I also deal in fury; Mine eye shall not spare, neither will I have pity; and though they cry in Mine ears with a loud voice, yet will I not hear them.

Chapter 9, which I have quoted already, mitigates this only for a small remnant. There are six angels of destruction, with only Gabriel (according to the Talmud) armed with the inkhorn that will spare the righteous. Unlike Gabriel, Blake does not necessarily set a mark, since his "mark in every face I meet," primarily is intransitive, meaning "remark" or "observe."

Blake begins *London* with a curious irony, more a scheme than a figure, or if a figure, then more a figure of thought than of speech. For he adopts the outcast role he called Rintrah, the John-the-Baptist or unheeded forerunner, in place of the prophetic vocation, but in the context of Ezekiel's Jerusalem as well as his own London. In the opening dialectic of presence and absence, precisely what is absent is prophetic direction and prophetic purpose; what is present are chartering and marks. So voice is absent, and only demonic writing is present. Blake's defensive reaction-formation to the call he cannot answer is to be a wanderer, and to mark passively rather than mark actively with the *taws* of righteousness and wickedness, life and death. But righteousness and wickedness are alike absent; present only are weakness and woe, neither of which merits a *taw*, whether of ink or of blood. The synecdoche of the universal human face represents Blake's turning against his own self, for he also is weak and woeful, and not the Ezekiel-like prophet he should be.

The litany of "every" becomes a weird metonymic reification, a regression in moving all men back to a state of infancy, but also an isolation, as this is an "every" that separates out rather than unifies people:

> In every cry of every Man,
> In every Infants cry of fear
> In every voice: in every ban
> The mind-forg'd manacles I hear.

"Every Man" includes the Londoner William Blake, whose voice also must betray the clanking sound of "mind-forg'd manacles," where the mind belongs to every man, again including William Blake. An infant's cry of fear is all-too-natural, for the infant is voiceless but for his fear and hunger, which for him is a kind of fear. When the crucial word "voice" enters the poem, it is put into a metonymic, reductive series with "cry of fear" and "ban," with terror and curse, fear and the threat of fear.

When Blake answers this reduction with a Sublime repressive hyperbole, it is governed by the same "I hear," as spoken by a Jonah, a renegade prophet who never does speak in his own poem, but only hears:

> I hear
> How the Chimney-sweepers cry
> Every blackning Church appalls,

And the hapless Soldiers sigh,
Runs in blood down Palace walls.

The chimney-sweepers' cry, as in the two Blakean songs of the sweeps, is "Weep, weep," due to the cockney lisp of the children, as they attempt to advertise their labor with a voiced "sweep, sweep." The cry of weep helps blacken further the perpetually blackening Church, possibly draping it in a pall through the mark of *taw* in a black ink, giving it an edge over the royal palace, which receives the bloody *taw* of destruction. The soldier's hapless sigh prefigures the curse of the harlot, as both are losers, in the term from *Auguries of Innocence*. But what about Blake's synaesthesia? How, even in Sublime representation, can you *hear* a Church being draped in a pall, and how can you *hear* a sigh running in blood down palace walls. The answer, I think, is given by our map of misreading. What Blake is repressing into this hyperbolical hearing-seeing is the visionary power of the *nabi*, the Hebrew prophet, and the running of the repressed voice down the repressive walls represents not only the soldier's hapless sigh, but the more powerful hapless sigh of the prophet who has repressed the voice that is great within us.

We come then to the final stanza, the most weakly misread of all. Here is the characteristic Romantic ending that follows a limiting metaphor by a representing transumption:

But most thro' midnight streets I hear
How the youthful Harlots curse
Blasts the new-born Infants tear
And blights with plagues the Marriage hearse.

I want to reject altogether the customary interpretation that makes "curse" here a variety of venereal infection, and that makes the infant's condition a prenatal blindness. Instead, I want to reaffirm my own earlier interpretation of the Harlot here as Blake's perpetually youthful Harlot, Nature, not the human female, but the natural element in the human, male or female.

The inside/outside perspectivism here gives us Blake as pent-up voice wandering still at midnight *through* the streets, and through that labyrinth he achieves another synaesthetic hearing-seeing, how another curse or ban or natural fact (menstruation) blasts or scatters another natural fact, the tearlessness of the new-born *infant*. For Blake every natural fact equals every other natural fact. The metalepsis that introjects the future here is one that sees enormous plagues riding along in every marriage coach, blighting life into death, as though every marriage carries the *taw* of destruction. Remember again the doggerel of *Auguries of Innocence*:

> The Harlots cry from street to street
> Shall weave Old Englands winding sheet
> The Winners Shout the Losers Curse
> Dance before dead Englands Hearse

If Old England is dead, then all her marriages are funerals. A cry that weaves a shroud is like a mark of *taw* or a ban chartering weakness and woe. Blake's poem is not a protest, not a prophetic outcry, not a vision of judgment. It is a revisionist's self-condemnation, a Jonah's desperation at *knowing* he is not an Ezekiel. We misread Blake's poem when we regard it as prophecy, and see it as primarily sympathy with the wretched of London, because we have canonized the poem, and because we cannot bear to read a canonical poem as being truly so altogether negative and self-destructive a text.

Even as a revisionist strong poem, Blake's *London* is more a deliberate parody of misprision than it is a revisionist text. Blake's tonal complexities are uncanny, *unheimlich*, here and elsewhere, and like Nietzsche Blake is something of a parodist of world history. There is a grotesque element in *London*, and what we take as Sublime hyperbole is actually more the underthrow of litotes, the characteristic rhetorical figure in grotesque representation. This parody is a clearer strain in Blake's *The Tyger*, which I want to introduce more by way of Nietzsche than by way of its origins in Job and Milton.

Like Nietzsche, and like every other revisionist, Blake desired always to keep origin and aim, source and purpose, as far apart as possible. Nietzsche, if I understand him, believed only in comic or preposterous schemes of transumption, in which a future laughter is introjected and a past tragedy is projected. An aphorism in *Beyond Good and Evil* says that we are

> prepared as was no previous age for a Carnival in the grand style, for laughter and a high-spirited revelry, for transcendental flights of Sublime nonsense and an Aristophanes-like mockery of the universe. Perhaps this is where we shall yet discover the realm of our invention, that realm in which we also still can be original, say as parodists of world history and the clowns of God—perhaps, even if nothing else today has a future, our laughter may yet have a future.

We can observe here that a poem, in this view, must be a parody of a parody, just as a man is a parody of God. But Nietzschean repetition is even more bewildering, for any copy is both a parody of its original, yet also a self-parody. In terms of poetic misprision, this means that any poem is both a misreading of a precursor poem and, more crucially, a misreading of itself. Whether Nietzschean parody is universally applicable I do not know, but it illuminates poems of deliberately cyclic repetition like Blake's *The Tyger* or *The Mental Traveller* or *The Crystal Cabinet*.

Blake's Tyger has a pretty exact analogue in a Nietzschean tiger, a grand deconstructive tiger, in the curious text called *Truth and Falsehood in an Extra-Moral Sense*:

> What indeed does man know about himself? Oh! that he could but once see himself complete, placed as it were in an illuminated glass case! Does not nature keep secret from him most things, even about his body ...? Nature threw away the key; and woe to the fateful curiosity which might be able for a moment to look out and down through a crevice in the chamber of consciousness and discover that man, indifferent to his own ignorance, is resting on the pitiless, the greedy, and insatiable, the murderous, and as it were, hanging in dreams on the back of a tiger. Whence, in the wide world, with this state of affairs, arises the impulse to truth?

Nietzsche's tiger is human mortality; our illusive day-to-day existence rests us, in dreams, as we ride the tiger who will be, who is our own death, a metaphorical embodiment of the unbearable truth that the pleasure-principle and the reality-principle are finally one.

Nietzsche's precursors were Goethe, Schopenhauer, Heine, and Wagner; Blake's were Milton and the Bible. Of all the thirty-nine books of the Old Testament, Job obsessed Blake most. The forerunners of Blake's Tyger are the Leviathan and Behemoth of Job, two horrible beasts who represent the God-ordained tyranny of nature over man, two beasts whose final name is human death, for to Blake nature is death.

God taunts Job by asking him if these great beasts will make a covenant with man? Rashi comments on Behemoth by saying: "prepared for the future," and the apocryphal apocalypses, Enoch and IV Ezra and Baruch, all say that Leviathan and Behemoth are parted only to come together one day, in the judgment, when they will be the food of the Righteous. As God says of Leviathan, if none dare face him, then "Who is able to stand before Me?" Milton brings in the Leviathan (evidently a crocodile in Job) as a whale, but Melville's Moby-Dick is closer to the beasts of Job, and to Blake's Tyger.

At this advanced date, I assert an exemption from having to argue against the usual run of merely trivial misreadings of *The Tyger*. I will oppose my antithetical reading to the received misreading of the earlier Bloom, in books like *The Visionary Company* and *Blake's Apocalypse*, or in the notes to *Romantic Poetry and Prose* in the Oxford Anthology. The fundamental principle for reading *The Tyger* is to realize that this is a dramatic lyric in which William Blake is not, cannot be, the speaker. *The Tyger* is a Sublime or hyperbolical monologue, with little movement in its tropes or images. It is dominated by the single trope of repression, by an unconsciously purposeful forgetting, but this is not Blake's repression. The psychic area in which the whole poem centers is hysteria. What does it mean for a major lyric never to deviate from its own hysterical intensity?

The answer is that Blake, more even than Nietzsche, is a master of creative parody, and he is parodying a kind of greatness that he loves and admires, but vehemently does not wish to join. It is the greatness of William Cowper, and the other poets of the Burkean or Miltonic Sublime in the later eighteenth century. The two dominant images of the poem are both fearful-the burning or fire and the symmetry. Fire is the prime perspectivizing trope in all of Romanticism, as we will see again and again. It stands, most often, for discontinuity or for the possibility of, or desire towards discontinuity. Its opposite, the emblem of repetition or continuity, tends to be the inland sound of moving waters. These identifications may seem purely arbitrary now; I will vindicate them in later chapters.

What are we to make of "symmetry"? Symmetry is a one-to-one ratio, whether on opposite sides of a dividing line, or in relation to a center. A one-to-one ratio means that no revisionism has taken place; there has been no *clinamen*, no catastrophe-creation or breaking-of-the-vessels in the making of the Tyger. Like Leviathan and Behemoth, the Tyger is exactly what his creator meant him to be. But who is his creator? Does this poem set itself, for interpretation, in a relatively orthodox Genesis-Milton context, or in the context of some Gnosis? How fearful is the Tyger's maker? Or is it a canonical misreading that we allow this poem to set itself a genetic context for interpretation, at all?

By common consent of interpreters, *The Tyger* is made up of a series of increasingly rhetorical questions. The model for this series certainly is to be found in the Book of Job, where God confronts Job with crushingly rhetorical questions, all of them reducing to the cruelty of: Where were you, anyway, when I made everything? After all, Job's plea had been "Call Thou, and I will answer" (13:22), and God therefore relies upon a continuous irony as figure-of-thought. But the speaker of *The Tyger* is incapable of deliberate irony; every one of his tropes is, as I have noted already, a hyperbole. What is this profound repression defending against? What furnace is coming up, at last, against the will of this daemonizing speaker?

No speaker could be more determined to insist that origin and aim were the same impulse and the same event. We can surmise that the unconsciously purposeful forgetting of this poem's speaker is precisely that he himself, as an aim or purpose, has been separated irreparably from his point of origin. Confronting the Tyger, who represents his own *daemonic* intensity, the form that is his own force, what Blake would have called Vision or his own Imagination, the dramatic speaker is desperately determined to identify completely the Tyger's aim and purpose with the Tyger's supposedly divine origins.

Yet it is not the speaker's text, but Blake's, and the meaning of the text rises parodistically and even with a wild comedy out of the intertextual juxtapositions between the text itself and texts by Cowper, by Milton, and the text cited from Job.

First Cowper, from Book VI of *The Task*:

The Lord of all, himself through all diffused,
Sustains, and is the life of all that lives.
Nature is but a name for an effect
Whose cause is God. He feeds the secret fire
By which the mighty process is maintained,
Who sleeps not, is not weary; in whose sight
Slow circling ages are as transient days,
Whose work is without labour; whose designs
No flaw deforms, no difficulty thwarts;

Here origin and purpose are one, without strain, anxiety, or repression, or so it seems. Next Milton, from Book VII of *Paradise Lost*, part of the most Sublime creation-scene in the language:

The grassy Clods now Calv'd, now half appear'd
The Tawny Lion, pawing to get free
His hinder parts, then springs as broke from Bonds,
And Rampant shakes his Brinded mane; the Ounce,
The Libbard, and the Tiger, as the Mole
Rising, the crumbl'd Earth above them threw
In Hillocks ...

Milton shows rather less creative anxiety than the poet of Job, even allowing himself a transumption of a Lucretian allusion as if to indicate his own corrective confidence that God's origins and Milton's purposes are one and the same. Blake's speaker is not Blake, nor is he Milton, not even Blake's own Milton. He is Cowper or Job, or rather Cowper assimilated to Job, and both assimilated not to the strong poet or revisionist in Blake, but to Blake's own Spectre of Urthona, that is, the time-bound work-a-day ego, and not what Blake liked to call "the Real Man the Imagination."

I approach an antithetical formula. Blake's revisionism in *London* was to measure the ratios by which he fell short of Ezekiel. Blake's revisionism in *The Tyger* is to measure the ratio by which he surpasses Cowper and Job. Cowper's fearful ratio does not frighten Blake, whose entire dialectic depends upon separating origins, natural or natural religion's, from imaginative aims or revisionist purposes. Yet, in *London*, Blake shows himself knowingly incapable of separating prophetic voice as aim or purpose from the cry, curse, ban of natural voice as origin. We have underestimated Blake's complexities, and his own capacity for self-recognition. He is in no danger of falling into the repetition of the Bard confronting the Jobean Tyger. Yet, in the societal context in which a prophet must vindicate himself, Blake falls silent, and falls into the repetition of the wanderer who flees the burden of prophecy. There can no more be a mute prophet than there can be a mute, inglorious Milton. The prophet or *nabi* is precisely a *public orator*, and not a private mutterer or marker. The *nabi* never moans, as Blake did, "I am hid." Blake, who might have been more, by his own account was human—all too human—and gave in to natural fear. His belatedness, in the spiritual more than in the poetic sense, was a shadow that overcame him.

The Blake of *London* has become a canonical writer, unlike the Ben Sirach of Ecclesiasticus, but like Ecclesiasticus Blake gives us in *London* a text he lacks the authority to sustain. The Blake of *The Tyger*, like the Koheleth of Ecclesiastes, gives us a canonical text that tradition necessarily has misread and goes on misreading. Revisionism or belated creations is a hard task, and exacts a very high price, a price that meaning itself must pay for, by being emptied out from a plenitude to a dearth.

I conclude with a final juxtaposition between the skeptical Koheleth and the passionately certain Blake. Both Ecclesiastes and *The Tyger* are texts of conscious belatedness, though *The Tyger* parodies and mocks its own condition of belatedness. For the Tyger itself, as a Sublime representation, is a self-imposed blocking agent, what Blake called a Spectre, and what Ezekiel and Blake called a Covering Cherub. The guilt suffered by the speaker of Blake's *Tyger* is also Cowper's guilt, and the guilt of a very un-Cowperian figure, Milton's Satan. This is the guilt that Nietzsche, in his *Genealogy of Morals*, called the "guilt of indebtedness." I think that Blake meant something like this when he said in *Jerusalem* that it was easier to forgive an enemy than it was to forgive a friend. The speaker of *The Tyger* confronts a burning, fearful symmetry that exists in a one-to-one ratio with its Creator. Like Job confronting Leviathan and Behemoth, the Cowper-like bard confronts an unacceptable surrogate for the divine Precursor, a surrogate who grants him no priority, and who has authority over him insofar as he is natural. Blake, in mocking a canonical kind of poem, nevertheless is subsumed by the canonical traditions of misreading, as any student of *The Tyger*'s interpretative history could testify.

Where Blake's dramatic speaker is trapped in repetition, Koheleth is a theorist of repetition, not far in spirit from the Stoic Marcus Aurelius. "All words toil to weariness," Koheleth says early on in his book, and so he thinks that fundamentally all the books have been written already. Though he praises wisdom, Koheleth is weary of it. He too might have said: "The flesh is sad alas, and I have read all the books." But he adds: "For wisdom is a defense, even as money is a defense," and the Hebrew translated here in the King James version as "defense" is a word literally meaning "shadow." I end on that identification of the defense against influence with the metonymic trope of shade for wisdom or money, and for the forests of the night that frame the menace of the fire that meant a discontinuity from origins.

William Wordsworth

(1770–1850)

There is a human loneliness,
A part of space and solitude,
In which knowledge cannot be denied.
In which nothing of knowledge fails,
The luminous companion, the hand,
The fortifying arm, the profound
Response, the completely answering voice....

—WALLACE STEVENS

THE PRELUDE WAS TO BE ONLY THE ANTECHAPEL TO THE GOTHIC CHURCH
of *The Recluse*, but the poet Wordsworth knew better than the man, and *The Prelude* is a complete and climactic work. The key to *The Prelude* as an internalized epic written in creative competition to Milton is to be found in those lines (754–860) of the *Recluse* fragment that Wordsworth prefaced to *The Excursion* (1814). Wordsworth's invocation, like Blake's to the Daughters of Beulah in his epic *Milton*, is a deliberate address to powers higher than those that inspired *Paradise Lost*:

Urania, I shall need
Thy guidance, or a greater Muse, if such
Descend to earth or dwell in highest heaven!
For I must tread on shadowy ground, must sink
Deep—and, aloft ascending, breathe in worlds
To which the heaven of heavens is but a veil.

The shadowy ground, the depths beneath, and the heights aloft are all in the mind of man, and Milton's heaven is only a veil, separating an allegorical unreality from the human paradise of the happiest and best regions of a poet's mind. Awe of the personal Godhead fades before the poet's reverence for his own imaginative powers:

> All strength—all terror, single or in bands,
> That ever was put forth in personal form—
> Jehovah—with his thunder, and the choir
> Of shouting Angels, and the empyreal thrones—
> I pass them unalarmed.

Blake, more ultimately unorthodox than Wordsworth as he was, had yet too strong a sense of the Bible's power to accept this dismissal of Jehovah. After reading this passage, he remarked sardonically:

> Solomon, when he Married Pharaoh's daughter & became a Convert to the Heathen Mythology, talked exactly in this way of Jehovah as a Very inferior object of Man's Contemplations; he also passed him by unalarm'd & was permitted. Jehovah dropped a tear & follow'd him by his Spirit into the Abstract Void; it is called the Divine Mercy.

To marry Pharaoh's daughter is to marry Nature, the Goddess of the Heathen Mythology, and indeed Wordsworth will go on to speak of a marriage between the Mind of Man and the goodly universe of Nature. Wordsworth is permitted his effrontery, as Solomon the Wise was before him, and, like Solomon, Wordsworth wanders into the Ulro or Abstract Void of general reasoning from Nature, pursued by the ambiguous pity of the Divine Mercy. But this (though powerful) is a dark view to take of Wordsworth's reciprocal dealings with Nature. Courageously but calmly Wordsworth puts himself forward as a renovated spirit, a new Adam upon whom fear and awe fall as he looks into his own Mind, the Mind of Man. As befits a new Adam, a new world with a greater beauty waits upon his steps. The most defiant humanism in Wordsworth salutes the immediate possibility of this earthly paradise naturalizing itself in the here and now:

> Paradise, and groves
> Elysian, Fortunate Fields—like those of old
> Sought in the Atlantic Main—why should they be
> A history only of departed things,
> Or a mere fiction of what never was?
> For the discerning intellect of Man,

> When wedded to this goodly universe
> In love and holy passion, shall find these
> A simple produce of the common day.

No words are more honorific for Wordsworth than "simple" and "common." The marriage metaphor here has the same Hebraic sources as Blake had for his Beulah, or "married land." The true Eden is the child of the common day, when that day dawns upon the great consummation of the reciprocal passion of Man and Nature. What Wordsworth desires to write is "the spousal verse" in celebration of this fulfillment:

> and, by words
> Which speak of nothing more than what we are,
> Would I arouse the sensual from their sleep
> Of Death, and win the vacant and the vain
> To noble raptures.

This parallels Blake's singing in *Jerusalem*:

> Of the sleep of Ulro! and of the passage through
> Eternal Death! and of the awaking to Eternal Life.

But Wordsworth would arouse us by speaking of nothing more than what we already are; a more naturalistic humanism than Blake could endure. Wordsworth celebrates the *given*—what we already possess, and for him it is as for Wallace Stevens

> As if the air, the mid-day air, was swarming
> With the metaphysical changes that occur,
> Merely in living as and where we live.

For Wordsworth, as for Stevens, the earth is enough; for Blake it was less than that all without which man cannot be satisfied. We need to distinguish this argument between the two greatest of the Romantics from the simplistic dissension with which too many readers have confounded it, that between the doctrines of innate goodness and original sin. Wordsworth is not Rousseau, and Blake is not St. Paul; they have more in common with one another than they have with either the natural religionist or the orthodox Christian.

Wordsworth's Imagination is like Wallace Stevens's *Angel Surrounded by Paysans*: not an angel of heaven, but the necessary angel of earth, as, in its sight, we see the earth again, but cleared; and in its hearing we hear the still sad music of humanity, its tragic drone, rise liquidly, not harsh or grating, but like watery words awash, to chasten and subdue us. But the Imagination of Wordsworth and of Stevens is "a figure half seen, or seen for a moment." It rises with the sudden mountain mists, and as suddenly departs. Blake, a literalist of the Imagination, wished for its more habitual sway. To marry Mind and Nature is to enter Beulah; there Wordsworth and Blake are at one. Blake insisted that a man more fully redeemed by Imagination would not need Nature, would regard the external world as hindrance. The split between Wordsworth and Blake is not theological at all, though Blake expresses it in his deliberately displaced Protestant vocabulary by using the metaphor of the Fall where Wordsworth rejects it. For Wordsworth the individual Mind and the external World are exquisitely fitted, each to the other, even as man and wife, and with blended might they accomplish a creation the meaning of which is fully dependent upon the sexual analogy; they give to us a new heaven and a new earth blended into an apocalyptic unity that is simply the matter of common perception and common sexuality raised to the freedom of its natural power. Wordsworthian Man is Freudian Man, but Blake's Human Form Divine is not. "You shall not bring me down to believe such a fitting & fitted" is his reaction to Wordsworth's exquisite adjustings of the Universe and Mind. To accept Nature as man's equal is for Blake the ineradicable error. Blake's doctrine is that either the Imagination totally destroys Nature and puts a thoroughly Human form in its place, or else Nature destroys the Imagination. Wordsworth says of his task that he is forced to hear "Humanity in fields and groves / Pipe solitary anguish" and Blake reacts with ferocity:

> Does not this Fit, & is not Fitting most Exquisitely too, but to
> what?—not to Mind, but to the Vile Body only & to its Laws
> of Good & Evil & its Enmities against Mind.

This is not the comment of an embittered Gnostic. Blake constructs his poetry as a commentary upon Scripture; Wordsworth writes his poetry as a commentary upon Nature. Wordsworth, while not so Bible-haunted as Blake, is himself a poet in the Hebraic prophetic line. The visible body of Nature is more than an outer testimony of the Spirit of God to him; it is our only way to God. For Blake it is the barrier between us and the God within ourselves. Ordinary perception is then a mode of salvation for Wordsworth, provided that we are awake fully to what we see. The common earth is to be hallowed by the human heart's and mind's holy union with it, and by that union the heart and mind in concert are to receive their bride's gift of phenomenal beauty, a glory in the grass, a splendor in the flower. Until at last the Great Consummation will be achieved, and renovated Man will stand in Eden once again. The human glory of Wordsworth, which he bequeathed to Keats, is in this naturalistic celebration of the possibilities inherent in our condition, here and now. That Wordsworth himself, in the second half of his long life, could not sustain this vision is a criticism of neither the vision nor the man, but merely his loss—and ours.

The Old Cumberland Beggar (1797) is Wordsworth's finest vision of the irreducible natural man, the human stripped to the nakedness of primordial condition and exposed as still powerful in dignity, still infinite in value. The Beggar reminds us of the beggars, solitaries, wanderers throughout Wordsworth's poetry, particularly in *The Prelude* and *Resolution and Independence*. He differs from them in that he is not the agency of a revelation; he is not responsible for a sudden release of Wordsworth's imagination. He is not even of visionary utility; he is something finer, beyond use, a vision of reality in himself. I am not suggesting that *The Old Cumberland Beggar* is the best of Wordsworth's poems outside *The Prelude*; it is not in the sublime mode, as are *Tintern Abbey*, the Great Ode, *Resolution and Independence*. But it is the most Wordsworthian of poems, and profoundly moving.

Nothing could be simpler than the poem's opening: "I saw an aged Beggar in my walk." The Old Man (the capitalization is the poet's) has put down his staff, and takes his scraps and fragments out of a flour bag, one by one. He scans them, fixedly and seriously. The plain beginning yields to a music of love, the beauty of the real:

> In the sun,
> Upon the second step of that small pile,
> Surrounded by those wild unpeopled hills,
> He sat, and ate his food in solitude:
> And ever, scattered from his palsied hand,
> That, still attempting to prevent the waste,
> Was baffled still, the crumbs in little showers
> Fell on the ground; and the small mountain birds,
> Not venturing yet to peck their destined meal,
> Approached within the length of half his staff.

It is difficult to describe *how* this is beautiful, but we can make a start by observing that it is beautiful both because it is so matter of fact, and because the fact is itself a transfiguration. The Old Man is in his own state, and he is radically innocent. The "wild unpeopled hills" complement his own solitude; he is a phenomenon of their kind. And he is no more sentimentalized than they are. His lot is not even miserable; he is too absorbed into Nature for that, as absorbed as he can be and still retain human identity.

He is even past further aging. The poet has known him since his childhood, and even then "he was so old, he seems not older now." The Old Man is so helpless in appearance that everyone—sauntering horseman or toll-gate keeper or post boy—makes way for him, taking special care to keep him from harm. For he cannot be diverted, but moves on like a natural process. "He travels on, a solitary Man," Wordsworth says, and then repeats it, making a refrain for that incessant movement whose only meaning is that it remains human though at the edge of our condition:

> He travels on, a solitary Man;
> His age has no companion. On the ground
> His eyes are turned, and, as he moves along,
> *They* move along the ground; and, evermore,
> Instead of common and habitual sight
> Of fields with rural works, of hill and dale,
> And the blue sky, one little span of earth
> Is all his prospect.

He is bent double, like the Leech Gatherer, and his vision of one little span of earth recalls the wandering old man of Chaucer's *Pardoner's Tale*. But Chaucer's solitary longed for death, and on the ground he called his mother's gate he knocked often with his staff, crying, "Dear mother, let me in." Wordsworth's Old Man sees only the ground, but he is tenaciously alive, and is beyond desire, even that of death. He sees, and yet hardly sees. He moves constantly, but is so still in look and motion that he can hardly be seen to move. He is all process, hardly character, and yet almost stasis.

It is so extreme a picture that we can be tempted to ask, "Is this life? Where is its use?" The temptation dehumanizes us, Wordsworth would have it, and the two questions are radically dissimilar, but his answer to the first is vehemently affirmative and to the second an absolute moral passion. There is

> a spirit and pulse of good,
> A life and soul, to every mode of being
> Inseparably linked.

The Old Man performs many functions. The most important is that of a binding agent for the memories of good impulses in all around him. Wherever he goes,

> The mild necessity of use compels
> To acts of love.

These acts of love, added one to another, at last insensibly dispose their performers to virtue and true goodness. We need to be careful in our reaction to this. Wordsworth is not preaching the vicious and mad doctrine that beggary is good because it makes charity possible. That would properly invoke Blake's blistering reply in *The Human Abstract*:

> Pity would be no more
> If we did not make somebody Poor;
> And Mercy no more could be
> If all were as happy as we.

Wordsworth has no reaction to the Old Man which we can categorize. He does not think of him in social or economic terms, but only as a human life, which necessarily has affected other lives, and always for the better. In particular, the Old Man has given occasions for kindness to the very poorest, who give to him from their scant store, and are the kinder for it. Again, you must read this in its own context. Wordsworth's best poetry has nothing directly to do with social justice, as Blake's or Shelley's frequently does. The old beggar is a free man, at home in the heart of the solitudes he wanders, and he does not intend the humanizing good he passively causes. Nor is his social aspect at the poem's vital center; only his freedom is:

> —Then let him pass, a blessing on his head!
> And, long as he can wander, let him breathe
> The freshness of the valleys; let his blood
> Struggle with frosty air and winter snows;
> And let the chartered wind that sweeps the heath
> Beat his grey locks against his withered face.

Pity for him is inappropriate; he is pathetic only if shut up. He is a "figure of capable imagination," in Stevens's phrase, a Man perfectly complete in Nature, reciprocating its gifts by being himself, a being at one with it:

Let him be free of mountain solitudes;
And have around him, whether heard or not,
The pleasant melody of woodland birds.

Mountain solitudes and sudden winds are what suit him, whether he reacts to them or not. The failure of his senses does not cut him off from Nature; it does not matter whether he can hear the birds, but it is fitting that he have them around him. He has become utterly passive toward Nature. Let it be free, then, to come in upon him:

> if his eyes have now
> Been doomed so long to settle upon earth
> That not without some effort they behold
> The countenance of the horizontal sun,
> Rising or setting, let the light at least
> Find a free entrance to their languid orbs.

The Old Man is approaching that identity with Nature that the infant at first knows, when an organic continuity seems to exist between Nature and consciousness. Being so naturalized, he must die in the eye of Nature, that he may be absorbed again:

> And let him, *where* and *when* he will, sit down
> Beneath the trees, or on a grassy bank
> Of highway side, and with the little birds
> Share his chance-gathered meal; and, finally,
> As in the eye of Nature he has lived,
> So in the eye of Nature let him die!

The poem abounds in a temper of spirit that Wordsworth shares with Tolstoy, a reverence for the simplicities of *caritas*, the Christian love that is so allied to and yet is not pity. But Tolstoy might have shown the Old Cumberland Beggar as a sufferer; in Wordsworth he bears the mark of "animal tranquillity and decay," the title given by Wordsworth to a fragment closely connected to the longer poem. In the fragment the Old Man travels on and moves not with pain, but with thought:

> He is insensibly subdued
> To settled quiet ...
> He is by nature led

To peace so perfect that the young behold
With envy, what the Old Man hardly feels.

We know today, better than his contemporaries could, what led Wordsworth to the subject of human decay, to depictions of idiocy, desertion, beggars, homeless wanderers. He sought images of alienated life, as we might judge them, which he could see and present as images of natural communion. The natural man, free of consciousness in any of our senses, yet demonstrates a mode of consciousness which both intends Nature for its object and at length blends into that object. The hiding places of man's power are in his past, in childhood. Only memory can take him there, but even memory fades, and at length fades away. The poet of naturalism, separated by organic growth from his own past, looks around him and sees the moving emblems of a childlike consciousness in the mad, the outcast, and the dreadfully old. From them he takes his most desperate consolation, intimations of a mortality that almost ceases to afflict.

Samuel Taylor Coleridge

(1772-1834)

COLERIDGE, THE YOUNGEST OF FOURTEEN CHILDREN OF A COUNTRY clergyman, was a precocious and lonely child, a kind of changeling in his own family. Early a dreamer and (as he said) a "character," he suffered the loss of his father (who had loved him best of all the children) when he was only nine. At Christ's Hospital in London, soon after his father's death, he found an excellent school that gave him the intellectual nurture he needed, as well as a lifelong friend in the future essayist Charles Lamb. Early a poet, he fell deeply in love with Mary Evans, a schoolfellow's sister, but sorrowfully nothing came of it.

At Jesus College, Cambridge, Coleridge started well, but temperamentally he was not suited to academic discipline and failed of distinction. Fleeing Cambridge, and much in debt, he enlisted in the cavalry under the immortal name of Silas Tomkyn Comberback but kept falling off his horse. Though he proved useful to his fellow dragoons at writing love letters, he was good for little else but stable-cleaning, and the cavalry allowed his brothers to buy him out. He returned to Cambridge, but his characteristic guilt impeded academic labor and when he abandoned Cambridge in 1794 he had no degree.

A penniless young poet, radical in politics, original in religion, he fell in with the then equally radical bard Robert Southey, remembered today as the Conservative Laureate constantly savaged in Byron's satirical verse. Like our contemporary communards, the two poetical youths projected what they named a "pantisocracy." With the right young ladies and, hopefully, other choice spirits, they would found a communistic agrarian-literary settlement on the banks of the Susquehanna in exotic Pennsylvania. At Southey's urging, Coleridge made a pantisocratic engagement to the not very brilliant Miss Sara Fricker, whose sister Southey was to marry.

Pantisocracy died aborning, and Coleridge in time woke up miserably to find himself unsuitably married, the greatest misfortune of his life.

He turned to Wordsworth, whom he had met early in 1795. His poetry influenced Wordsworth's and helped the latter attain his characteristic mode. It is not too much to say that Coleridge's poetry disappeared into Wordsworth's. We remember *Lyrical Ballads* (1798) as Wordsworth's book, yet about a third of it (in length) was Coleridge's, and "Tintern Abbey," the crown of the volume except for "The Rime of the Ancient Mariner," is immensely indebted to Coleridge's "Frost at Midnight." Nor is there much evidence of Wordsworth admiring or encouraging his friend's poetry; toward "The Ancient Mariner" he was always very grudging, and he was discomfited (but inevitably so) by both "Dejection: An Ode" and "To William Wordsworth." Selfless where Wordsworth's poetry was concerned, Coleridge had to suffer his closest friend's neglect of his own poetic ambitions.

This is not an easy matter to be fair about, since literature necessarily is as much a matter of personality as it is of character. Coleridge, like Keats (and to certain readers, Shelley), is lovable. Byron is at least always fascinating, and Blake in his lonely magnificence is a hero of the imagination. But Wordsworth's personality, like Milton's or Dante's, does not stimulate affection for the poet in the common reader. Coleridge has, as Walter Pater observed, a "peculiar charm"; he seems to lend himself to myths of failure, which is astonishing when the totality of his work is contemplated.

Yet it is his life, and his self-abandonment of his poetic ambitions, that continue to convince us that we ought to find in him parables of the failure of genius. His best poetry was all written in the year and half in which he saw Wordsworth daily (1797–8), yet even his best poetry, with the single exception of "The Ancient Mariner," is fragmentary. The pattern of his life is fragmentary also. When he received an annuity from the Wedgwoods, he left Wordsworth and Dorothy to study language and philosophy in Germany (1798–9). Soon after returning, his miserable middle years began, though he was only twenty-seven. He moved near the Wordsworths again and fell in love, permanently and unhappily, with Sara Hutchinson, whose sister Mary was to become Wordsworth's wife in 1802. His own marriage was hopeless, and his health rapidly deteriorated, perhaps for psychological reasons. To help endure the pain he began to drink laudanum, liquid opium, and thus contracted an addiction he never entirely cast off. In 1804, seeking better health, he went to Malta but returned two years later in the worst condition of his life. Separating from Mrs. Coleridge, he moved to London and began another career as lecturer, general man-of-letters, and periodical editor, while his miseries augmented.

The inevitable quarrel with Wordsworth in 1810 was ostensibly reconciled in 1812, but real friendship was not reestablished until 1828.

From 1816 on, Coleridge lived in the household of a physician, James Gillman, so as to be able to keep working and thus avoid total breakdown. Prematurely aged, his poetry period over, Coleridge entered into a major last phase as critic and philosopher, upon which his historical importance depends; but this, like his earlier prose achievements, is beyond the scope of an introduction to his poetry. It remains to ask, What was his achievement as a poet, and extraordinary as that was, why did his poetry effectively cease after about 1807? Wordsworth went on with poetry after 1807 but mostly very badly. The few poems Coleridge wrote, from the age of thirty-five on, are powerful but occasional. Did the poetic will not fail in him, since his imaginative powers did not?

Coleridge's large poetic ambitions included the writing of a philosophic epic on the origin of evil and a sequence of hymns to the sun, moon, and elements. These high plans died, slowly but definitively, and were replaced by the dream of a philosophic *Opus Maximum*, a huge work of synthesis that would reconcile German idealist philosophy with the orthodox truths of Christianity. Though only fragments of this work were ever written, much was done in its place—speculations on theology, political theory, and criticism that were to influence profoundly conservative British thought in the Victorian period and, in quite another way, the American transcendentalism led by Emerson and Theodore Parker.

Coleridge's actual achievement as poet divides into two remarkably diverse groupings—remarkable because they are almost simultaneous. The daemonic group, necessarily more famous, is the triad of "The Ancient Mariner," "Christabel," and "Kubla Khan." The "conversational" group includes the conversation poem proper, of which "The Eolian Harp" and "Frost at Midnight" are the most important, as well as the irregular ode, such as "Dejection" and "To William Wordsworth." The late fragments, "Limbo" and "Ne Plus Ultra," are a kind of return to the daemonic mode. For a poet of Coleridge's gifts to have written only nine poems that really matter is a sorrow, but the uniqueness of the two groups partly compensates for the slenderness of the canon.

The daemonic poems break through the orthodox censor set up by Coleridge's moral fears of his own imaginative impulses. Unifying the group is a magical quest-pattern which intends as its goal a reconciliation between the poet's self-consciousness and a higher order of being, associated with Divine forgiveness; but this reconciliation fortunately lies beyond the border of all these poems. The Mariner attains a state of purgation but cannot get beyond that process. Christabel is violated by

Geraldine, but this too is a purgation rather than a damnation, as her utter innocence is her only flaw. Coleridge himself, in the most piercing moment in his poetry, is tempted to assume the state of an Apollo-rebirth—the youth with flashing eyes and floating hair—but he withdraws from his vision of a poet's paradise, judging it to be only another purgatory.

The conversational group, though so immensely different in mode, speaks more directly of an allied theme: the desire to go home, not to the past but to what Hart Crane beautifully called "an improved infancy." Each of these poems, like the daemonic group, verges upon a kind of vicarious and purgatorial atonement in which Coleridge must fail or suffer so that someone he loves may succeed or experience joy. There is a subdued implication that somehow the poet will yet be accepted into a true home this side of the grave if he can achieve an atonement.

Where Wordsworth, in his primordial power, masters the subjective world and aids his readers in the difficult art of feeling, Coleridge deliberately courts defeat by subjectivity and is content to be confessional. But though he cannot help us to feel, as Wordsworth does, he gives us to understand how deeply felt his own sense of reality is. Though in a way his poetry is a testament of defeat, a yielding to the anxiety of influence and to the fear of self-glorification, it is one of the most enduringly poignant of such testaments that literature affords us.

II

"Psychologically," Coleridge observed, "consciousness is the problem"; and he added somberly: "Almost all is yet to be achieved." How much he achieved Kathleen Coburn and others are showing us. My concern here is the sadder one of speculating yet again about why he did not achieve more as a poet. Walter Jackson Bate has meditated, persuasively and recently, upon Coleridge's human and literary anxieties, particularly in regard to the burden of the past and its inhibiting poetic splendors. I swerve away from Bate to center the critical meditation upon what might be called the poetics of anxiety, the process of misprision by which any latecomer strong poet attempts to clear an imaginative space for himself.

Coleridge could have been a strong poet, as strong as Blake or Wordsworth. He could have been another mighty antagonist for the Great Spectre Milton to engage and, yes, to overcome, but not without contests as titanic as those provided by Blake's *The Four Zoas* and Wordsworth's *The Excursion*, and parental victories as equivocal as those achieved with Blake's *Jerusalem* and Wordsworth's *The Prelude*. But we have no such poems by

Coleridge. When my path winds home at the end of this Introduction, I will speculate as to what these poems should have been. As critical fathers for my quest I invoke first Oscar Wilde, with his glorious principle that the highest criticism sees the object as in itself it really is not, and second, Wilde's critical father, Walter Pater, whose essay of 1866 on "Coleridge's Writings" seems to me still the best short treatment of Coleridge, and this after a century of commentary. Pater, who knew his debt to Coleridge, knew also the anxiety Coleridge caused him, and Pater therefore came to a further and subtler knowing. In the Organic analogue, against which the entire soul of the great Epicurean critic rebelled, Pater recognized the product of Coleridge's profound anxieties as a creator. I begin therefore with Pater on Coleridge, and then will move immediately deep into the Coleridgean interior, to look upon Coleridge's fierce refusal to take on the ferocity of the strong poet.

This ferocity, as both Coleridge and Pater well knew, expresses itself as a near-solipsism, and Egotistical Sublime, or Miltonic godlike stance. From 1795 on, Coleridge knew, loved, envied, was both cheered and darkened by the largest instance of that Sublime since Milton himself. He studied constantly, almost involuntarily, the glories of the truly modern strong poet, Wordsworth. Whether he gave Wordsworth rather more than he received, we cannot be certain; we know only that he wanted more from Wordsworth than he received, but then it was his endearing though exasperating weakness that he always needed more love than he could get, no matter how much he got: "To be beloved is all I need, / And whom I love, I love indeed."

Pater understood what he called Coleridge's "peculiar charm," but he resisted it in the "sacred name of what he called the "relative" spirit against Coleridge's archaizing "absolute" spirit. In gracious but equivocal tribute to Coleridge he observed:

> The literary life of Coleridge was a disinterested struggle against the application of the relative spirit to moral and religious questions. Everywhere he is restlessly scheming to apprehend the absolute; to affirm it effectively; to get it acknowledged. Coleridge failed in that attempt, happily even for him, for it was a struggle against the increasing life of the mind itself.... How did his choice of a controversial interest, his determination to affirm the absolute, weaken or modify his poetic gift.

To affirm the absolute, Pater says—or, as we might say, to reject all dualisms except those sanctioned by orthodox Christian thought—is not *materia poetica* for the start of the nineteenth century, and if we think of a poem like the "Hymn before Sun-Rise, in the Vale of Chamouni," we are likely to agree with Pater. We will agree also when he contrasts Wordsworth favorably with Coleridge, and even with Goethe, commending Wordsworth for "that flawless temperament ... which keeps his conviction of a latent intelligence in nature within the limits of sentiment or instinct, and confines it to those delicate and subdued shades of expression which perfect art allows." Pater goes on to say that Coleridge's version of Wordsworth's instinct is a philosophical idea, which means that Coleridge's poetry had to be "more dramatic, more self-conscious" than Wordsworth's. But this in turn, Pater insists, means that for aesthetic success ideas must be held loosely, in the relative spirit. One idea that Coleridge did not hold loosely was the Organic analogue, and it becomes clearer as we proceed in Pater's essay that the aesthetic critic is building toward a passionate assault upon the Organic principle. He quotes Coleridge's description of Shakespeare as "a nature humanized, a genial understanding, directing self-consciously a power and an implicit wisdom deeper even than our consciousness." "There," Pater comments, with bitter eloquence, "'the absolute' has been affirmed in the sphere of art; and thought begins to congeal." With great dignity Pater adds that Coleridge has "obscured the true interest of art." By likening the work of art to a living organism, Coleridge does justice to the impression the work may give us, but he "does not express the process by which that work was produced."

M.H. Abrams, in his *The Mirror and the Lamp*, defends Coleridge against Pater by insisting that Coleridge knew his central problem "was to use analogy with organic growth to account for the spontaneous, the inspired, and the self-evolving in the psychology of invention, yet not to commit himself as far to the elected figure as to minimize the supervention of the antithetic qualities of foresight and choice." Though Abrams calls Pater "short-sighted," I am afraid the critical palms remain with the relative spirit, for Pater's point was not that Coleridge had no awareness of the dangers of using the Organic analogue but rather that awareness, here as elsewhere, was no salvation for Coleridge. The issue is whether Coleridge, not Shakespeare, was able to direct "self-consciously a power and an implicit wisdom deeper than consciousness." Pater's complaint is valid because Coleridge, in describing Shakespeare, Dante, Milton, keeps repeating his absolute formula that poems grow from within themselves, that their "wholeness is not in vision or conception, but in an inner feeling of totality and absolute being." As Pater says, "that exaggerated inwardness is barren" because it "withdraws us too far from what we can see, hear, and feel," because it cheats the senses and emotions of their triumph. I urge Pater's wisdom here not only against Coleridge, though I share Pacer's love for Coleridge, but against the formalist criticism that continued in Coleridge's absolute spirit.

What is the imaginative source of Coleridge's disabling hunger for the Absolute? On August 9, 1831, about three years before he died, he wrote in his Notebook: "From my earliest recollection I have had a consciousness of Power without Strength—a perception, an experience, of more than ordinary power with an inward sense of Weakness.... More than ever do I feel this now, when all my fancies still in their integrity are, as it were, drawn *inward* and by their suppression and compression rendered a mock substitute for Strength—" Here again is Pater's barren and exaggerated inwardness, but in a darker context than the Organic principle provided.

This context is Milton's "universe of death," where Coleridge apprehended death-in-life as being "the wretchedness of *division*." If we stand in that universe, then "we think of ourselves as separated beings, and place nature in antithesis to the mind, as object to subject, thing to thought, death to life." To be so separated is to become, Coleridge says, "a soul-less fixed star, receiving no rays nor influences into my Being, *a Solitude which I so tremble at, that I cannot attribute it even to the Divine Nature.* "This, we can say, is Coleridge's Counter-Sublime, his answer to the anxiety of influence, in strong poets. The fear of solipsism is greater in him than the fear of not individuating his own imagination.

As with every other major Romantic, the prime precursor poet for Coleridge was Milton. There is a proviso to be entered here; for all these poets—Blake, Wordsworth, Shelley, Coleridge (only Keats is an exception)—there is a greater Sublime poetry behind Milton, but as its author is a people and not a single poet, and as it is far removed in time, its greatness does not inhibit a new imagination—not unless it is taken as the work of the Prime Precursor Himself, to whom all creation belongs. Only Coleridge, among these poets, acquired a double Sublime anxiety of influence. Beyond the beauty that has terror in it of Milton, was beauty more terrible. In a letter to Thelwall, December 17, 1796, Coleridge wrote: "Is not Milton a *sublimer* poet than Homer or Virgil? Are not his Personages more sublimely cloathed? And do you not know, that there is not perhaps *one* page in Milton's *Paradise Lost*, in which he has not borrowed his imagery from the Scriptures?—I allow, and rejoice that *Christ* appealed only to the understanding & the affections; but I affirm that, after reading Isaiah, or St. Paul's Epistle to the Hebrews, Homer & Virgil are disgustingly *tame* to me, & Milton himself barely tolerable." Yet these statements are rare in Coleridge. Frequently, Milton seems to blend with the ultimate influence, which I think is a normal enough procedure. In 1796, Coleridge also says, in his review of Burke's *Letter to a Noble Lord*: "It is lucky for poetry, that Milton did not live in our days...." Here Coleridge moves toward the center of his concern, and we should remember his formula: "Shakespeare was all men, potentially, except Milton." This leads to a more ambiguous formula, reported to us of a lecture that Coleridge gave on November 28, 1811: "Shakespeare became all things well into which he infused himself, while all forms, all things became Milton—the poet ever present to our minds and more than gratifying us for the loss of the distinct individuality of what he represents." Though Coleridge truly professes himself more than gratified, he admits loss. Milton's greatness is purchased at the cost of something dear to Coleridge, a principle of difference he knows may be flooded out by his monistic yearnings. For Milton, to Coleridge, is a mythic monad in himself. Commenting upon the apostrophe to light at the commencement of the third book of *Paradise Lost*, Coleridge notes: "In all modern poetry in Christendom there is an under consciousness of a sinful nature, a fleeting away of external things, the mind or subject greater than the object, the reflective character predominant. In the *Paradise Lost* the sublimest parts are the revelations of Milton's own mind, producing itself and evolving its own greatness; and this is truly so, that when that which is merely entertaining for its objective beauty is introduced, it at first seems a discord." This might be summarized as: where Milton is not, nature is barren, and its significance is that Milton is permitted just such a solitude as Coleridge trembles to imagine for the Divine Being.

Humphry House observed that "Coleridge was quite unbelievably modest about his own poems; and the modesty was of a curious kind, sometimes rather humble and over-elaborate." As House adds, Coleridge "dreaded publication" of his poetry, and until 1828, when he was fifty-six, there was nothing like an adequate gathering of his verse. Wordsworth's attitude was no help, of course, and the Hutchinson girls and Dorothy no doubt followed Wordsworth in his judgments. There was Wordsworth, and before him there had been Milton. Coleridge presumably knew what "Tintern Abbey" owed to "Frost at Midnight," but this knowledge nowhere found expression. Must we resort to psychological speculation in order to see what inhibited Coleridge, or are there more reliable aids available?

In the *Biographia Literaria* Coleridge is not very kind to his pre-Wordsworthian poetry, particularly to the "Religious Musings." Yet this is where we must seek what went wrong with Coleridge's ambitions—here, and if there were space, in "The Destiny of Nations" fragments (not its arbitrarily yoked-together form of 1817), and in the "Ode to the Departing Year," and in the "Monody on the Death of Chatterton" in its earlier versions. After Wordsworth had descended upon Coleridge, supposedly as a "know-thyself" admonition from heaven but really rather more like a new form of the Miltonic blight, then Coleridge's poetic ambitions sustained another kind of inhibition. The Miltonic shadow on early Coleridge needs to be studied first, before a view can be obtained of his maturer struggles with influence.

With characteristic self-destructiveness; Coleridge gave "Religious Musings" the definitive subtitle: "A Desultory Poem, Written on the Christmas Eve of 1794." The root-meaning of "desultory" is "vaulting," and though Coleridge consciously meant that his poem skipped about and wavered, his imagination meant "vaulting," for "Religious Musings" is a wildly ambitious poem. "This is the time ..." it begins, in direct recall of Milton's "Nativity" Hymn, yet it follows not the Hymn but the most sublime moments of *Paradise Lost*, particularly the invocation to Book III. As with the 1802 "Hymn before Sun-Rise," its great fault as a poem is that it never stops whooping; in its final version I count well over one hundred exclamation points in just over four hundred lines. Whether one finds this habit in Coleridge distressing or endearing hardly matters; he just never could stop doing it. He whoops because he vaults; he is a high jumper of the Sublime, and psychologically he could not avoid this. I quote the poem's final passage with relish and with puzzlement, for I am uncertain as to how good it may be, though it seems awful. Yet its awfulness is at least Sublime; it is not the drab, flat awfulness of Wordsworth at *his* common worst in *The Excursion* or even (heresy to admit this!) in so many passages of *The Prelude*—passages that we hastily skip by, feeling zeal and relief in getting at the great moments. Having just shouted out his odd version of Berkeley—that "life is a vision shadowy of truth"—Coleridge sees "the veiling clouds retire" and God appears in a blaze upon His Throne. Raised to a pitch of delirium by this vision, Coleridge soars aloft to join it:

> Contemplant Spirits! ye that hover o'er
> With untired gaze the immeasurable fount
> Ebullient with Creative Deity!
> And ye of plastic power, that interfused
> Roll through the grosser and material mass
> In organizing surge! Holies of God!
> (And what if Monads of the infinite mind?)
> I haply journeying my immortal course

Shall sometime join your mystic choir! Till then
I discipline my young and novice thought
In ministeries of heart-stirring song,
And aye on Meditation's heaven-ward wing
Soaring aloft I breathe the empyreal air
Of Love, omnific, omnipresent Love,
Whose day-spring rises glorious in my soul
As the great Sun, when he his influence
Sheds on the frost-bound waters—The glad stream
Flows to the ray and warbles as it flows.

Scholars agree that this not terribly pellucid passage somehow combines an early Unitarianism with a later orthodox overlay, as well as quantities of Berkeley, Hartley, Newton, Neoplatonism, and possibly more esoteric matter. A mere reader will primarily be reminded of Milton and will be in the right, for Milton counts here and the rest do not. The Spirits Coleridge invokes are Miltonic angels, though their functions seem to be more complicated. Coleridge confidently assures himself and us that his course is immortal, that he may end up as a Miltonic angel and so perhaps also as a monad of the infinite mind. In the meantime, he will study Milton's "heart-stirring song." Otherwise, all he needs is love, which is literally the air he breathes, the sunrise radiating out of his soul in a stream of song, and the natural sun toward which he flows, a sun that is not distinct from God. If we reflect on how palpably sincere this is, how wholehearted, and consider what was to be Coleridge's actual poetic course, we will be moved. Moved to what? Well, perhaps to remember a remark of Coleridge's: "There are many men, especially at the outset of life, who, in their too eager desire for the end, overlook the difficulties in the way; there is another class, who see nothing else. The first class may sometimes fail; the latter rarely succeed." Whatever the truth of this for other men, no poet becomes a strong poet unless he starts out with a certain obliviousness of the difficulties in the way. He will soon enough meet those difficulties, however, and one of them will be that his precursor and inspirer threatens to subsume him, as Coleridge is subsumed by Milton in "Religious Musings" and in his other pre-Wordsworthian poems. And here I shall digress massively before returning to Coleridge's poetry, for my discourse enters now upon the enchanted and baleful ground of poetic influence, through which I am learning to find my way by a singular light—one that will bear a little explanation.

I do not believe that poetic influence is simply something that happens, that it is just the process by which ideas and images are transmitted from earlier to later poets. In that view, whether or not influence causes anxiety in the later poet is a matter of temperament and circumstance. Poetic influence thus reduces to source-study, of the kind performed upon Coleridge by Lowes and later scholars. Coleridge was properly scornful of such study, and I think most critics learn how barren an enterprise it turns out to be. I myself have no use for it as such, and what I mean by the study of poetic influence turns source-study inside out. The first principle of the proper study of poetic influence, as I conceive it, is that no strong poem has sources and no strong poem merely alludes to another poem. The meaning of a strong poem is another strong poem, a precursor's poem which is being misinterpreted, revised, corrected, evaded, twisted askew, made to suffer an inclination or bias which is the property of the later and not the earlier poet. Poetic influence, in this sense, is actually misprision, a poet's taking or doing amiss of a parent-poem that keeps *finding* him, to use a Coleridgean turn of phrase. Yet even this misprision is only the first step that a new poet takes when he advances from the early phase where his precursor floods him to a more Promethean phase where he quests for his own fire—which must nevertheless be stolen from his precursor.

I count some half-dozen steps in the life cycle of the strong poet as he attempts to convert his inheritance into what will aid him without inhibiting him by the anxiety of a failure in priority, a failure to have begotten himself. These steps are revisionary ratios, and for the convenience of a shorthand, I find myself giving them arbitrary names that are proving useful to me and perhaps can be of use to others. I list them herewith, with descriptions but not examples, as this can only be a brief sketch; I must get back to Coleridge's poetry, with this list helpfully in hand, to find my examples in Coleridge.

1. *Clinamen*, which is poetic misprision proper. I take the word from Lucretius, where it means a "swerve" of the atoms so as to make change possible in the universe. The later poet swerves away from the precursor by so reading the parent-poem as to execute a *clinamen* in relation to it. This appears as the corrective movement of his own poem, which implies that the precursor poem went accurately up to a certain point but then should have swerved, precisely in the direction that the new poem moves.

2. *Tessera*, which is completion and antithesis. I take the word not from mosaic-making, where it is still used, but from the ancient Mystery cults, where it meant a token of recognition—the fragment, say, of a small pot which with

the other fragments would reconstitute the vessel. The later poet antithetically "completes" the precursor by so reading the parent-poem as to retain its teens but to mean them in an opposite sense, as though the precursor had failed to go far enough.

3. *Kenosis*, which is a breaking device similar to the defense mechanisms our psyches employ against repetition-compulsions; *kenosis* then is a movement toward discontinuity with the precursor. I take the word from St. Paul, where it means the humbling or emptying out of Jesus by himself when he accepts reduction from Divine to human status. The later poet, apparently emptying himself of his own afflatus, his imaginative godhood, seems to humble himself as though he ceased to be a poet, but this ebbing is so performed in relation to a precursor's poem-of-ebbing that the precursor is emptied out also, and so the later poem of deflation is not as absolute as it seems.

4. *Daemonization*, or a movement toward a personalized Counter-Sublime in reaction to the precursor's Sublime. I take the term from general Neoplatonic usage, where an intermediary being, neither Divine nor human, enters into the adept to aid him. The later poet opens himself to what he believes to be a power in the parent-poem that does not belong to the parent proper but to a range of being just beyond that precursor. He does this, in his poem, by so stationing its relation to the parent-poem as to generalize away the uniqueness of the earlier work.

5. *Askesis*, or a movement of self-purgation which intends the attainment of a state of solitude. I take the term, general as it is, particularly from the practice of pre-Socratic shamans like Empedocles. The later poet does not, as in *kenosis*, undergo a revisionary movement of emptying but of curtailing: he yields up part of his own human and imaginative endowment so as to separate himself from others, including the precursor, and he does this in his poem by so stationing it in regard to the parent-poem as to make that poem undergo an *askesis* also; the precursor's endowment is also truncated.

6. *Apophrades*, or the return of the dead. I take the word from the Athenian dismal or unlucky days upon which the dead returned to reinhabit the houses in which they

had lived. The later poet, in his own final phase, already burdened by an imaginative solitude that is almost a solipsism, holds his own poem so open again to the precursor's work that at first we might believe the wheel has come full circle and we are back in the later poet's flooded apprenticeship, before his strength began to assert itself in the revisionary ratios of *clinamen* and the others. But the poem is now held open to the precursor, where once it was open, and the uncanny effect is that the new poem's achievement makes it seem to us not as though the precursor were writing it, but as though the later poet himself had written the precursor's characteristic work.

These then are six revisionary ratios, and I think they can be observed, usually in cyclic appearance, in the life's work of every post-Enlightenment strong poet—which in English means, for practical purposes, every post-Miltonic strong poet. Coleridge, to return now to where I began, had the potential of the strong poet but—unlike Blake, Wordsworth, and the major poets after them down to Yeats and Stevens in our time—declined the full process of developing into one. Yet his work, even in its fragmentary state, demonstrates this revisionary cycle in spite of himself. My ulterior purpose in this discussion is to use Coleridge as an instance because he is apparently so poor an example of the cycle I have sketched. But that makes him a sterner test for my theory of influence than any other poet I could have chosen.

I return to Coleridge's first mature poetry and to its *clinamen* away from Milton, the Cowperizing turn that gave Coleridge the Conversation Poems, particularly "Frost at Midnight." Hazlitt quotes Coleridge as having said to him in the spring of 1798 that Cowper was the best modern poet, meaning the best since Milton, which was also Blake's judgment. Humphry House demonstrated the relation between "Frost at Midnight" and *The Task*—a happy one, causing no anxieties, where a stronger poet appropriates from a weaker one. Coleridge used Cowper as he used Bowles, Akenside, and Collins, finding in all of them hints that could help him escape the Miltonic influx that had drowned out "Religious Musings." "Frost at Midnight," like *The Task*, swerves away from Milton by softening him, by domesticating his style in a context that excludes all Sublime terrors. When Coleridge rises to his blessing of his infant son at the poem's conclusion he is in some sense poetically "misinterpreting" the beautiful declaration of Adam to Eve: "With thee conversing I forget all time," gentling the darker overtones of the infatuated Adam's declaration of love. Or, more simply, like Cowper he is not so much humanizing Milton—that will take the strenuous, head-on struggles of Blake, Wordsworth, Shelley, Keats—as he is making Milton more childlike, or perhaps better, reading Milton as though Milton loved in a more childlike way.

The revisionary step beyond this, an antithetical completion or *tessera*, is ventured by Coleridge only in a few pantheistic passages that sneaked past his orthodox censor, like the later additions to "The Eolian Harp" or the veiled vision at the end of the second verse paragraph of "This Lime-Tree Bower My Prison." With his horror of division, his endless quest for unity, Coleridge could not sustain any revisionary impulse which involved his reversing Milton or daring to complete that sacred father.

But the next revisionary ratio, the *kenosis* or self-emptying, seems to me almost obsessive in Coleridge's poetry, for what is the total situation of the Ancient Mariner but a repetition-compulsion, which his poet breaks for himself only by the writing of the poem and then only momentarily? Coleridge had contemplated an Epic on the Origin of Evil, but we may ask, Where would Coleridge, if pressed, have located the origin of evil in himself? His Mariner is neither depraved in will nor even disobedient, but merely ignorant, and the spiritual machinery his crime sets into motion is so ambiguously presented as to be finally beyond analysis. I would ask the question, What was Coleridge trying (not necessarily consciously) to do for himself by writing the poem? And by this question I do not mean Kenneth Burke's notion of trying to do something for oneself as a person. Rather, what was Coleridge the poet trying to do for himself as poet? To which I would answer: trying to free himself from the inhibitions of Miltonic influence by humbling his poetic self and so humbling the Miltonic in the process. The Mariner does not empty himself out; he starts empty and acquires a Primary Imagination through his suffering. But for Coleridge the poem is a *kenosis*, and what is being humbled is the Miltonic Sublime's account of the origin of evil. There is a reduction from disobedience to ignorance, from the self-aggrandizing consciousness of Eve to the painful awakening of a minimal consciousness in the Mariner.

The next revisionary step in clearing an imaginative space for a maturing strong poet is the Counter-Sublime, the attaining of which I have termed *daemonization*, and this I take to be the relation of "Kubla Khan" and "Christabel" to *Paradise Lost*. Far more than "The Rime of the Ancient Mariner," these poems demonstrate a tracking by Coleridge with powers that are *daemonic*, even though the "Rime" explicitly invokes Neoplatonic daemons in its marginal glosses. Opium was the avenging *daemon* or *alastor* of Coleridge's life, his Dark or Fallen Angel, his experiential acquaintance with Milton's Satan. Opium was for him what wandering and moral tale-telling became for the Mariner—the personal shape of repetition-compulsion. The lust for paradise in "Kubla Khan," Geraldine's lust for Christabel—these are manifestations of Coleridge's revisionary daemonization of Milton, these are Coleridge's Counter-Sublime. Poetic Genius, the genial spirit itself, Coleridge must see as daemonic when it is his own rather than when it is Milton's.

It is at this point in the revisionary cycle that Coleridge begins to back away decisively from the ferocity necessary for the strong poet. He does not sustain his *daemonization*; he closes his eyes in holy dread, stands outside the circumference of the *daemonic* agent, and is startled by his own sexual daring out of finishing "Christabel." He moved on to the revisionary ratio I have called *askesis*, or the purgation into solitude, the curtailing of some imaginative powers in the name of others. In doing so, he prophesied the pattern for Keats in "The Fall of Hyperion," since in his *askesis* he struggles against the influence of a composite poetic father, Milton-Wordsworth. The great poems of this *askesis* are "Dejection: An Ode" and "To William Wordsworth," where criticism has demonstrated to us how acute the revision of Wordsworth's stance is, and how much of himself Coleridge purges away to make this revision justified. I would add only that both poems misread Milton as sensitively and desperately as they do Wordsworth; the meaning of "Dejection" is in its relation to "Lycidas" as much as in its relation to the "Intimations" ode, even as the poem "To William Wordsworth" assimilates *The Prelude* to *Paradise Lost*. Trapped in his own involuntary dualisms, longing for a monistic wholeness such as he believes is found in Milton and Wordsworth, Coleridge in his *askesis* declines to see how much of his composite parent-poet he has purged away also.

After that, sadly enough, we have only a very few occasional poems of any quality by Coleridge, and they are mostly not the poems of a strong poet—that is, of a man vaulting into the Sublime. Having refused the full exercise of a strong poet's misprisions, Coleridge ceased to have poetic ambitions. But there are significant exceptions—the late manuscript fragment "Limbo" and the evidently still-later fragment "Ne Plus Ultra." Here, and I think here only, Coleridge experiences the particular reward of the strong poet in his last phase—what I have called the *apophrades* or return of the dead: not a Counter-Sublime but a negative Sublime, like the *Last Poems* of Yeats or *The Rock* of Stevens. Indeed negative sublimity is the mode of these Coleridgean fragments and indicates to us what Coleridge might have become had he permitted himself enough of the perverse zeal that the great poet must exhibit in malforming his great precursor.

"Limbo" and "Ne Plus Ultra" show that Coleridge could have become, at last, the poet of the Miltonic abyss, the bard of Demogorgon. Even as they stand, these fragments make us read Book II of *Paradise Lost* a little differently; they enable Coleridge to claim a corner of Milton's Chaos as his own.

Pater thought that Coleridge had succumbed to the Organic analogue because he hungered too intensively for eternity, as Lamb had said of his old school-friend. Pater also quoted De Quincey's summary of Coleridge: "He wanted better bread than can be made with wheat." I would add that Coleridge hungered also for an eternity of generosity between poets, as between people—a generosity that is not allowed in a world where each poet must struggle to individuate his own breath and this at the expense of his forebears as much as of his contemporaries. Perhaps also, to modify De Quincey, Coleridge wanted better poems than can be made without misprision.

I suggest then that the Organic analogue, with all its pragmatic neglect of the processes by which poems have to be produced, appealed so overwhelmingly to Coleridge because it seemed to preclude the anxiety of influence and to obviate the poet's necessity not just to unfold like a natural growth but to develop at the expense of others. Whatever the values of the Organic analogue for literary criticism—and I believe, with Pater, that it does more harm than good—it provided Coleridge with a rationale for a dangerous evasion of the inner steps he had to take for his own poetic development. As Blake might have said, Coleridge's imagination insisted upon slaying itself on the stems of generation—or, to invoke another Blakean image, Coleridge lay down to sleep upon the Organic analogue as though it were a Beulah-couch of soft, moony repose.

What was our loss in this? What poems might a stronger Coleridge have composed? The *Notebooks* list *The Origin of Evil, an Epic Poem*; *Hymns to the Sun, the Moon, and the Elements—six hymns*; and, more fascinating even than these, a scheme for an epic on "the destruction of Jerusalem" by the Romans. Still more compelling is a March 1802 entry in the *Notebooks*: "Milton, a Monody in the metres of Samson's Choruses—only with more rhymes/—poetical influences—political-moral-Dr. Johnson/." Consider the date of this entry—only a month before the first draft of "Dejection"— and some sense of what *Milton, a Monody* might have been begins to be generated. In March 1802, William Blake, in the midst of his sojourn at Hayley's Felpham, was deep in the composition of *Milton: a Poem in 2 Books, To Justify the Ways of God to Men*. In the brief, enigmatic notes for *Milton, a Monody* Coleridge sets down "—poetical influences—political-moral-Dr. Johnson," the last being, we can assume, a refutation of

Johnson's vision of Milton in *The Lives of the Poets*, a refutation that Cowper and Blake would have endorsed. "Poetical influences," Coleridge says, and we may recall that this is one of the themes of Blake's *Milton*, where the Shadow of the Poet Milton is one with the Covering Cherub, the great blocking agent who inhibits fresh human creativity by embodying in himself all the sinister beauty of tradition. Blake's *Milton* is a kind of monody in places, not as a mourning for Milton, but as Milton's own, solitary utterance as he goes down from a premature Eternity (where he is unhappy) to struggle again in fallen time and space. I take it though that *Milton, a Monody* would have been modeled upon Coleridge's early "Monody on the Death of Chatterton" and so would have been Coleridge's lamentation for his Great Original. Whether, as Blake was doing at precisely the same time, Coleridge would have dared to identify Milton as the Covering Cherub, as the angel or *daemon* blocking Coleridge himself out from the poet's paradise, I cannot surmise. I wish deeply that Coleridge had written the poem.

It is ungrateful, I suppose, as the best of Coleridge's recent scholars keep telling us, to feel that Coleridge did not give us the poems he had it in him to write. Yet we have, all apology aside, only a double handful of marvelous poems by him. I close therefore by attempting a description of the kind of poem I believe Coleridge's genius owed us and which we badly need, and always will need. I would maintain that the finest achievement of the High Romantic poets of England was their humanization of the Miltonic Sublime. But when we attend deeply to the works where this humanization is most strenuously accomplished—Blake's *Milton* and *Jerusalem*, Wordsworth's *Prelude*, Shelley's *Prometheus Unbound*, Keats's two *Hyperions*, even in a way Byron's *Don Juan*—we sense at last a quality lacking, a quality in which Milton abounds for all his severity. This quality, though not in itself a tenderness, made Milton's Eve possible, and we miss such a figure in all her Romanic descendants. More than the other five great Romantic poets, Coleridge was able, by temperament and by subtly shaded intellect, to have given us a High Romantic Eve, a total humanization of the tenderest and most appealing element in the Miltonic Sublime. Many anxieties blocked Coleridge from that rare accomplishment, and of these the anxiety of influence was not the least.

Lord Byron

(1788–1824)

> but man's life it thought,
> And he, despite his terror, cannot cease
> Ravening through century after century,
> Ravening, raging, and uprooting that he may come
> Into the desolation of reality.

—W.B. YEATS

PROMETHEAN MAN

Childe Harold's Pilgrimage

BYRON'S PILGRIMAGE AS POET WILL BE INTRODUCED HERE BY A STUDY OF this series of poems, as we might regard them. Cantos I and II (1812) are merely a descriptive medley, mixing travel and history. Canto III (1816) is a poem in the confessional mode of Rousseau and Wordsworth, and marks Byron's first imaginative maturity. Canto IV (1818) attempts a synthesis of the two previous poems. In it, Byron and Italy are alternatively obsessive themes, and fail to balance, so that Canto III remains probably the best poem of the sequence.

The entire series Byron called *A Romaunt*, and both the title and the verse form (the Spenserian stanza) derive from the romance tradition. The quest-theme of romance previously internalized by Blake and Wordsworth appears again in Shelley's *Alastor* and Keats's *Endymion* under Wordsworth's influence. Canto III of *Childe Harold* manifests a more superficial Wordsworthian influence, probably owing both to Byron's relationship with Shelley in 1816 and to his own reading of *The Excursion*. The theme of a quest away from alienation and toward an unknown good is recurrent in the Romantics, and Byron would have come to it without Wordsworth and Shelley, though perhaps then only in the less interesting way of Cantos I and II.

The alienation of Harold in Canto I is hardly profound, though peculiarly relevant both to Byron's time and to ours:

> Worse than adversity the Childe befell;
> He felt the fulness of satiety.

He has run through Sin's long labyrinth, is sick at heart, and more than a little weary. So are we as we read Cantos I and II, though this is more the fault of his imitators than it is of Byron. Too many Byronic heroes have moved across too many screens, and Byron's rhetoric in Cantos I and II is not yet supple enough to keep us from making the association between the master and his disciples:

> Yet oft-times in his maddest mirthful mood
> Strange pangs would flash along Childe Harold's brow,
> As if the memory of some deadly feud
> Or disappointed passion lurk'd below:
> But this none knew, nor haply cared to know;
> For his was not that open, artless soul
> That feels relief by bidding sorrow flow,
> Nor sought he friend to counsel or condole,
> Whate'er this grief more be, which he could not control.

Most of what follows, in these first two cantos, has been described, quite aptly, as "the rhymed diary of two years' travel." What counts in these cantos is the first emergence of Byron's Romantic hero, Promethean Man, who will reach his culmination as Manfred and Cain, and then be replaced by Don Juan. Manfred and Cain are ravaged humanists, though they acquire some diabolical coloring. Childe Harold is scarcely even a vitalist until Canto III, and ends his quest in Canto IV by implying that the posture of pilgrimage is itself a value worth the affirming. We can agree, provided this pilgrimage has an imaginative element, an energy of vision and creation powerful enough to convert its spiritual emptiness into a deliberate theme. This is in fact Byron's great achievement in the third and fourth cantos; his faltering Prometheanism becomes the vehicle for myth. The myth concerns the condition of European man in the Age of Metternich, and is presented in and by the person of the Pilgrim, a complex wanderer who shares only a name with the Childe Harold of the Romantic guidebook that is Cantos I and II.

Canto III opens with Byron's departure into voluntary exile, as he regrets the loss of his child, left behind with the estranged Lady Byron. The poet gives himself to the ocean's guidance, and is content to go "wher'er the surge may sweep." As he is borne on by wind and water, he states the nature of his alienation. No wonder awaits him; his deeds have pierced the depth of life. His heart has grown hard, having endured too much love, sorrow, fame, ambition, strife. Most important, his thought is now turned away from ordinary reality and towards the refuge of "lone caves, yet rife with airy images," and the visionary shapes of "the soul's haunted cell." Fleeing England, he escapes into his poem, and affirms a therapeutic aesthetic idealism:

> 'Tis to create, and in creating live
> A being more intense, that we endow
> With form our fancy, gaining as we give
> The life we image, even as I do now.
> What am I? Nothing: but not so art thou,
> Soul of my thought! with whom I traverse earth,
> Invisible but gazing, as I glow
> Mix'd with thy spirit, blended with thy birth,
> And feeling still with thee in my crush'd feeling's dearth.

Thought seeks refuge in the creation of poetry, for by it we gain more life, even as Byron gains in the life he images. His own limitations are transcended as he blends himself with the birth of what he creates. Rousseau, in Shelley's *Triumph of Life*, returns from this transcendental illusion to the reality of natural limitation. Byron is so wavering in his own aspiration that he turns from it in his very next stanza:

> Yet must I think less wildly:—I *have* thought
> Too long and darkly, till my brain became,
> In its own eddy boiling and o'erwrought,
> A whirling gulf of phantasy and flame.

Yet to cease in this wild thinking is to submit one's thoughts to others, and Byron says of his Childe Harold *persona*:

> He would not yield dominion of his mind
> To spirits against whom his own rebell'd.

This might be Manfred speaking. And again like Manfred, Harold turns to the mountains for companionship, for "they spake a mutual language." But between the Pilgrim and the Alps lies "an Empire's dust," the legacy of the fallen Titan, Napoleon. The poem pauses to brood on the fate of Prometheanism, and to read in Napoleon the same spirit, "antithetically mixt," that reigns in the Pilgrim. Napoleon is either "more or less than man," yet falls through an aspiration beyond man's hope:

> But quiet to quick bosoms is a hell,
> And *there* hath been thy bane; there is a fire
> And motion of the soul which will not dwell
> In its own narrow being, but aspire
> Beyond the fitting medium of desire;
> And, but once kindled, quenchless evermore,
> Preys upon high adventure, nor can tire
> Of aught but rest; a fever at the core,
> Fatal to him who bears, to all who ever bore.

Blake or Shelley would not have acknowledged that desire had a fitting medium, though Shelley frequently emphasizes its fatality to him who bears it. Byron is already caught between admiration and disapproval of those whose "breath is agitation," of "all that expands the spirit, yet appals." Unlike Wordsworth but like Shelley, he seeks the summits of nature not for their own sake but because they show "how Earth may pierce to Heaven, yet leave vain man below." Nor does Byronic solitude much resemble the Wordsworthian kind. Wordsworth goes apart the better to hear humanity's still sad music emanate from nature. Byron desires to be alone that he may "love Earth only for its earthly sake." If he lives not in himself, it is only to become a portion of the nature around him, and so to evade the burden of being a man, "a link reluctant in a fleshly chain."

Rather unfairly, Byron attributes the same desire to Rousseau, a greater Promethean than Napoleon or Byron:

> His love was passion's essence:—as a tree
> On fire by lightning, with ethereal flame
> Kindled he was, and blasted; for to be
> Thus, and enamour'd, were in him the same.

The fire stolen from Heaven both kindles and blasts, and in Rousseau, human love is one with the stolen flame and in turn becomes existence itself. Byron praises Rousseau as inspired, but dismisses him as "phrensied by disease or woe," an anticipation of modern Babbitry toward

Rousseau's genius. Byron's ambivalence is a necessary consequence of the extraordinary view of the natural world that *Childe Harold's Pilgrimage* develops. Every element given to man is simultaneously a way to moral greatness and divine blessing, and also a quicker way to self-deception and damnation. Every human act that widens consciousness increases both exaltation and despair. No other poet has insisted on maintaining both views with equal vigor, and one can wonder if Byron ever justifies his deliberate moral confusion by fully converting its aesthetic consequences into personal myth.

In Canto IV Byron reaches Rome, the goal of his Pilgrimage, and is moved by its aesthetic greatness to intensify his statement of negations. The mind is diseased by its own beauty, and this auto-intoxication fevers into false creation. So much for the Romantic Imagination. Disease, death, bondage become an obsessive litany:

> Our life is a false nature—'tis not in
> The harmony of things,—this hard decree,
> This uneradicable taint of sin,
> This boundless upas, this all-blasting tree
> Whose root is earth, whose leaves and branches be
> The skies which rain their plagues on men like dew—
> Disease, death, bondage—all the woes we see,
> And worse, the woes we see not—which throb through
> The immedicable soul, with heart-aches ever new.

As Mr. Flosky says in Peacock's *Nightmare Abbey*, after hearing Mr. Cypress (Byron) paraphrase this stanza, we have here "a most delightful speech, Mr. Cypress. A most amiable and instructive philosophy. You have only to impress its truth on the minds of all living men, and life will then, indeed, be the desert and the solitude." But this is to miss, however wittily, the direction of Byron's rhetoric, which does not seek to persuade, but to expose. Mr. Cypress is a marvelous creation, and we are sad to see him depart "to rake seas and rivers, lakes and canals, for the moon of ideal beauty," but he is a better satire upon Childe Harold than he is on Byron the Pilgrim. Mr. Cypress sings a song that ends as Childe Harold might be pleased to end, knowing that "the soul is its own monument." Byron as the Pilgrim of Eternity refuses to yield the human value of his life to his own vision of all-consuming sin:

> But I have lived, and have not lived in vain:
> My mind may lose its force, my blood its fire,

And my frame perish even in conquering pain;
But there is that within me which shall tire
Torture and Time, and breathe when I expire;
Something unearthly, which they deem not of,
Like the remember d tone of a mute lyre,
Shall on their soften'd spirits sink, and move
In hearts all rocky now the late remorse of love.

What survives, as in Shelley, is "like the remember'd tone of a mute lyre." In this case, that means the continued reverberation of this stanza, which accurately predicts its own survival. Seeking an image for such aesthetic immortality, Byron turns to the plastic art around him in Rome. Gazing at the Apollo Belvedere, he sees the statue with the approving eye of neoclassic aesthetics, a doctrine of stoic and firm control, of the selected moment or incident that shall be both representative and exemplary:

Or view the Lord of the unerring bow,
The God of life, and poesy, and light
The Sun in human limbs array'd, and brow
All radiant from his triumph in the fight;
The shaft hath just been shot—the arrow bright
With an immortal's vengeance; in his eye
And nostril beautiful disdain, and might
And majesty, flash their full lightnings by,
Developing in that one glance the Deity.

In the next stanza this statue's informing conception is called "a ray of immortality." Just as Byron, in this poem, makes no attempt to reconcile his conviction of the value of human aspiration with his conviction of sin, so he does not try to bring into harmony this neoclassic aesthetic and Rousseau's vision of art as expressive therapy or Wordsworth's more active theory of a poet's creation. A subsequent stanza demonstrates Byron's awareness of the conflict within his own views:

And if it be Prometheus stole from Heaven
The fire which we endure, it was repaid
By him to whom the energy was given
Which this poetic marble hath array'd
With an eternal glory—which, if made
By human hands, is not of human thought;
And Time himself hath hallow'd it, nor laid

One ringlet in the dust—nor hath it caught
A tinge of years, but breathes the flame with which 'twas
wrought.

The Promethean fire we "endure" rather than enjoy, for its origin is illicit; it was stolen. We repay the Titan for the gift of creative energy by a work like this statue, but though the work is of human hands, it is not of human thought. Byron is enough of a Romantic to credit the artist with Promethean energy, but is also too uneasy about the autonomy of Imagination to credit timelessness to a merely human conception. The statue breathes the stolen flame that wrought it, but the aid of more than human inspiration vivifies it.

The timelessness of art ends the wanderings of Byron's Pilgrim, for he comes to rest before the beauty of Rome, his search accomplished. Byron concludes the poem by offering his Pilgrim to the reader as a means of aesthetic grace of the kind the statue of Apollo has supplied to the Pilgrim himself:

Ye! who have traced the Pilgrim to the scene
Which is his last, if in your memories dwell
A thought which once was his, if on ye swell
A single recollection, not in vain
He wore his sandal-shoon and scallop-shell;
Farewell! with *him* alone may rest the pain,
If such there were—with *you*, the moral of his strain.

The Pilgrim has been a catharsis for his creator, who has sought by his creation to transvalue exile and wandering into an essential good appropriate for a generation whose Titanic force is spent. In an age of reaction and repression the heroic spirit must roam, must indulge the residue of a Promethean endowment, but without yielding to it utterly. Somewhere in the endurance of human art an ultimate value must lie, but Byron cannot give a final assent to any view of human nature or art available to him. In this powerful skepticism that refuses to be a skepticism, but throws itself intensely at rival modes of feeling and thought, the peculiar moral and aesthetic value of Byron's poetry comes into initial being. *Childe Harold's Pilgrimage* has passion and conflict without balance. We turn elsewhere in Byron to find both a clearer exaltation of the Promethean and a firmer control of the critical attitude that seeks to chasten and correct this immense energy.

"Prometheus"

In July 1816, in Switzerland, Byron wrote a short ode in three stro-phes, "Prometheus." Composed at the same time as the third canto of *Childe Harold's Pilgrimage*, this ode gathers together the diffused Titanism of the romance, and emphasizes the heroic rather than the sinful aspect of Prometheus' achievement and fate. Yet even here there is a troubled undersong, and a refusal to neglect the darker implications of the fire stolen from Heaven. The overt celebration of human aspiration is proper-ly dominant, but is all the more impressive for the juxtaposition of Byron's darker intimations. The gift of fire is the basis of Byron's art and theme, but the gift is unsanctioned by the withdrawn but responsible Power that has lawful possession of energy. Byron's entire poetic career at its most serious—here, in *Manfred, Cain, Don Juan, The Vision of Judgment*—can be understood as an attempt to justify the theft of fire by creating with its aid, while never forgetting that precisely such creation intensifies the original Promethean "Godlike crime." Byron, in this, writes in the line of Milton's prophetic fears, as do Blake in *The Marriage of Heaven and Hell* and Shelley in *Prometheus Unbound*. The fallen Angels in *Paradise Lost* compose poetic laments and celebrations for their Fall and of their deeds respectively, while Satan journeys through Chaos. Milton rises with immense relief from the abyss he so powerfully creates, and the temptations of Prometheanism constitute the dangers he has escaped. The invocations in *Paradise Lost* exist to establish Milton's hope that his inspiration is Divine, and not Promethean and hence Satanic. Byron has no such hope; his inspi-ration is both glorious and sinful, and his creation glorifies human aspira-tion (and his own) and increases human culpability.

The ode "Prometheus" defies the sufferings consequent upon such guilt, though it recognizes their reality:

> Titan! to whose immortal eyes
>   The sufferings of mortality,
>   Seen in their sad reality,
> Were not as things that gods despise;
> What was thy pity's recompense?
> A silent suffering, and intense;
> The rock, the vulture, and the chain,
> All that the proud can feel of pain,
> The agony they do not show,
> The suffocating sense of woe,
>   Which speaks but in its loneliness,

And then is jealous lest the sky
Should have a listener, nor will sigh
      Until its voice is echoless.

This begins as the Prometheus of Aeschylus, but the emphasis on the pride of silent suffering starts to blend the Titan into the figure of Byron the Pilgrim of Eternity, who does not show his agony, but whose sense of radical sin is suffocating, and who speaks to the mountains in the glory of mutual solitude. This first strophe commends Prometheus as an accurate as well as compassionate observer of human reality, the function Byron tries to fulfill in his poetry. The start of the second strophe dares to attribute directly to the Titan the Byronic conflict of negations:

Titan! to thee the strife was given
      Between the suffering and the will,
      Which torture where they cannot kill.

Prometheus suffers most, like Byron, in the conflict between his sympathy for and participation in human suffering, and the impious drive of his will in gloriously but sinfully bringing relief to humanity. Byron's will cannot bring fire to us, but can create an art that returns the Titanic gift with the human offering of a poem, itself a mark of creative grace but also an agency of further suffering, as it increases our guilt. This rather vicious circularity, a distinctive feature of Byron's view of existence, is very evident in *Childe Harold's Pilgrimage* and enters into the final strophe of "Prometheus." Byron rises to his theme's power with a firmness of diction and mastery of rhythm that his lyrical verse does not often manifest:

Thy Godlike crime was to be kind,
      To render with thy precepts less
      The sum of human wretchedness,
And strengthen Man with his own mind;
But baffled as thou Overt from high,
Still in thy patient energy,
In the endurance, and repulse
      Of thine impenetrable Spirit,
Which Earth and Heaven could not convulse,
      A mighty lesson we inherit.

The Titan's kindness was "Godlike," yet remains a crime. The Promethean gift would have strengthened Man by making the human mind immortal, but the gift's full efficacy was baffled by God. The stolen fire, thus imperfectly received, is itself a torture to us. What survives unmixed in our Titanic inheritance is the emblem of "patient energy," the endurance that will make Manfred's Spirit impenetrable. Prometheus and Man alike fall short of perfection, and so share one tragic fate, but they share also in a triumphant force:

> Thou art a symbol and a sign
>> To mortals of their fate and force;
> Like thee, Man is in part divine,
>> A troubled stream from a pure source;
> And Man in portions can foresee
> His own funereal destiny;
> His wretchedness, and his resistance,
> And his sad unallied existence:
> To which his Spirit may oppose
> Itself—and equal to all woes,
>> And a firm will, and a deep sense,
> Which even in torture can descry
>> Its own concenter'd recompense,
>> Triumphant where it dares defy,
>> And making Death a Victory.

What is confused, here and throughout Byron, is the attitude toward divinity. The "inexorable Heaven" of the second strophe, which creates for its own pleasure "the things it may annihilate," is nevertheless to be identified with the "pure source" from which Prometheus and Man are only troubled streams. Byron insists upon having it both ways, and he cannot overcome the imaginative difficulties created by his spiritual shuffling. Man's destiny is "funereal," for his "sad unallied existence" is detached from God; such are the consequences of Man's Promethean fall. Byron is like Blake's Rintrah, a voice presaging a new revelation but too passionate and confused to speak its own clear truth. The concentrated requital for Man's tortured striving is merely the glory of a defiant defeat. It is only by making Heaven altogether remote that Byron goes further in *Manfred*, where a defiant Titanism at last attains to its imaginative limits.

Manfred

Manfred, Byron thought, was "of a very wild, metaphysical, and inexplicable kind." The kind is that of Goethe's *Faust* and Shelley's *Prometheus*, the

Romantic drama of alienation and renewal, of the self purged by the self. *Faust* strives for the universal, and *Prometheus* is apocalyptic; *Manfred* is overtly personal, and is meant as a despairing triumph of self, and a denial of the efficacy of even a Titanic purgation. The crime of Manfred is that of Byron, incest deliberately and knowingly undertaken. Oedipus gropes in the dark, the light bursts upon him, and outwardly he allows the light to pass judgment upon him. Manfred, like Byron, claims the right of judging himself.

The Manfred we first encounter in the drama has elements in him of Faust and of Hamlet. The setting is in the Higher Alps, where he has his castle. The opening scene is as it must be: Manfred alone, in a Gothic gallery, and midnight the time. By his deep art he summons a condemned star, his own, and attendant spirits. He asks forgetfulness of self; they offer him only power, and suggest he seek his oblivion in death, but refuse to vouchsafe he will find it there. They serve him only with scorn for his mortality; he replies with Promethean pride. His star manifests itself as Astarte, his sister and mistress, but she vanishes when he attempts to embrace her, and he falls senseless. A spirit song is sung over him, which marks him of the brotherhood of Cain.

The second scene is the next morning out on the cliffs. Manfred, alone, soliloquizes like Milton's Satan on Mount Niphates. But Byron's reference here is a deliberate and critical parody. Satan on Nephates has his crisis of conscience and realizes the depth of his predicament, but refuses to believe that he can escape the self he has chosen, and so is driven at last to the frightening inversion "Evil, be thou my good." Manfred, like Satan, sees the beauty of the universe, but avers that he cannot feel it and declines therefore to love it. But he then proceeds to declare its felt beauty. Like Hamlet, and curiously like Satan, he proclaims his weariness of the human condition:

> Half dust, half deity, alike unfit
> To sink or soar.

He desires to sink to destruction, or soar to a still greater destruction, but either way to cease being human. His attempted suicide is frustrated by a kindly peasant, but the wine offered to revive him has blood upon the brim, and his incestuous act is made directly equivalent to murder:

> I say 'tis blood—my blood! the pure warm stream
> Which ran in the veins of my fathers, and in ours
> When we were in our youth, and had one heart,
> And loved each other as we should not love,

And this was shed: but still it rises up,
Colouring the clouds, that shut me out from heaven.

With his crime established, Manfred descends to a lower valley in the Alps, where he confronts a cataract that he identifies with the steed of Death in the Apocalypse. In a marvelous invention, he calls up the Witch of the Alps, a Shelleyan spirit of amoral natural beauty. To her he speaks an idealized history of the outcast Romantic poet, the figure of the youth as natural quester for what nature has not to give, akin to the idealized portraits of self in Shelley's *Alastor* and Keats's *Endymion*. But the incest motif transforms the quester myth into the main theme of *Manfred*, the denial of immortality if it means yielding up the human glory of our condition, yet accompanied by a longing to transcend that condition. The Witch stands for everything in *Manfred* that is at once magical and preternatural. She scorns the Mage for not accepting immortality, and offers him oblivion if he will serve her. With the fine contempt that he displays throughout for all spirits that are not human, Manfred dismisses her. At no time in the play is Manfred anything but grave and courteous to his servants, the poor hunter, and the meddling Abbot who comes to save his soul. To the machinery of the poem, which he himself continually evokes, he is hostile always. This is most striking when he glides arrogantly into the Hall of Arimanes, the chief of dark spirits, and a veil for the Christian devil.

Arimanes is a Gnostic Satan; like Blake's Satan, he is the god of the natural world, worshiped by the three Fates and by Nemesis, who is a very rough version of the dialectical entity Shelley was to call Demogorgon. Manfred refuses to worship Arimanes, but the dark god nevertheless yields to the poet's request and the Phantom of Astarte appears. Manfred asks her to forgive or condemn him, but she declines, and cannot be compelled by Arimanes, as she belongs "to the other powers," the infinitely remote hidden god of light. But at an appeal from Manfred which is both very human in its pathos and essentially Calvinistic in its temper, she yields just enough to speak her brother's name, to tell him "tomorrow ends thy earthly ills," and to give a last farewell. She leaves a momentarily convulsed Manfred, who is first scorned and then grimly valued in a fine dialogue of demonic spirits:

> *A Spirit*. He is convulsed—This is to be a mortal
> And seek the things beyond mortality.
> *Another Spirit*. Yet, see, he mastereth himself, and makes
> His torture tributary to his will.

Had he been one of us, he would have made
An awful spirit.

The final act rejects Christian comfort with an intensity that comes
from a ferocious quasi-Calvinism. The Abbot seeks to reconcile Manfred
"with the true church, and through the church to Heaven," but Manfred
has no use for mediators. The last scene is in the mountains again, within
a lonely tower where Manfred awaits his end. The Spirits of Arimanes
come to claim him, as the Abbot utters ineffectual exorcisms. In two
remarkable speeches, Manfred's Prometheanism manifests its glory. By
power of will he thrusts the demons back, in repudiation of the Faust legend, and dies his own human death, yielding only to himself:

> The mind which is immortal makes itself
> Requital for its good or evil thoughts,—
> Is its own origin of ill and end—
> And its own place and time: its innate sense,
> When stripp'd of this mortality, derives
> No colour from the fleeting things without,
> But is absorb'd in sufferance or in joy,
> Born from the knowledge of its own desert.

The ultimate model here is again Milton's Satan, who hails his infernal world and urges it to receive its new possessor:

> One who brings
> A mind not to be chang'd by Place or Time.
> The mind is its own place, and in itself
> Can make a Heav'n of Hell, a Hell of Heav'n.

Marlowe's Mephistopheles tells his Faustus that "where we are is
hell." The Devil is an inverted Stoic; we have an idea of ill, and from it we
taste an ill savor. Iago with his blend of the Stoic and the Calvinist is closer to Manfred; both beings, like Webster's Lodovico, could say of their
work that they had limned their night pieces and took pride in the result.
Manfred is a Gothic poet who has written his own tragedy with himself as
protagonist. The Machiavellian villain plots the destruction of others,
whether he himself be man like Iago or demon like Mephistopheles. But,
as Northrop Frye remarks in his theory of myths, "the sense of awfulness
belonging to an agent of catastrophe can also make him something more
like the high priest of a sacrifice." Frye points to Webster's Bosola in *The*

Duchess of Malfi as an example. In the Romantic period this figure becomes a high priest who sacrifices himself, like Manfred or Prometheus. The analogue to Christ hovers in the Romantic background. But to what god does Manfred give himself?

Manfred's last words are a proud, naturalistic farewell to the Abbot:

Old man! 'tis not so difficult to die.

Yet even the defiance here is gracious, for the dying Manfred has previously said to the Abbot, "Give me thy hand." Byron insisted that Manfred's last words contained "the whole effect and moral of the poem." The death of Manfred is clearly a release, not a damnation, for his burden of consciousness has long been his punishment. He drives off the demons, who are not so much seeking to drag him down to an inferno of punishment as trying to compel a human will to abandon itself as being inadequate. Manfred has no assurance of oblivion as he dies, but he has the Promethean satisfaction of having asserted the supremacy of the human will over everything natural or preternatural that would oppose it. The supernatural or spiritual world does not enter into the poem; Manfred's relations, if any, with heavenly grace are necessarily a mystery. His rejection of the Abbot is merely to deny a mediator's relevance.

Cain

Byron went further, into mystery itself, in his dramatic piece *Cain* (1821). Manfred's crime of incest is paralleled by Cain's crime of murder, for Manfred's complete knowing of his sister destroyed her, and Cain's destruction of his brother completes an act of knowledge. Byron's radical conception makes Cain the direct ancestor of a tradition that has not yet exhausted itself, that of the artist not just as passive outcast but as deliberate criminal seeking the conditions for his art by violating the moral sanctions of his society.

For Byron, Cain is the first Romantic. Hazlitt best typifies the Romantic in his portrait of Rousseau: "He had the most intense consciousness of his own existence. No object that had once made an impression on him was ever effaced. Every feeling in his mind became a passion." This is true of Byron also, and of Cain. The tragedy of Cain is that he cannot accomplish his spiritual awakening without developing an intensity of consciousness which he is ill-prepared to sustain. His imaginativeness flowers into murderousness, as it will later in the terrible protagonists of Dostoevsky. The dialectic that entraps Byron's Cain is simplistic and inexorable. Cain suspects that Jehovah is malicious, and identifies his own exclusion from Paradise with the ultimate punishment of death, which he does not feel he deserves. Lucifer presents him with evidence that an age of innocence existed even before Adam. Cain fears death, but Lucifer hints that death leads to the highest knowledge. As Northrop Frye points out, this "links itself at once with Cain's own feeling that the understanding of death is his own ultimate victory—in other words, with the converse principle that the highest knowledge leads to death." Cain is mistaken because he does not go far enough imaginatively; he moves to a mere negation of the moral law, a simple inversion of Jehovah's repressive ethic. And yet Byron gives him a capacity to have accomplished more than this. At the climactic moment, when Abel has offered up a lamb in sacrifice to Jehovah, and urges his brother to emulate him, Cain offers instead the first fruits of the earth. Abel prays, abasing himself. Cain speaks his defiance directly to Jehovah:

> If a shrine without victim,
> And altar without gore, may win thy favour,
> Look on it! and for him who dresseth it,
> He is—such as thou mad'st him; and seeks nothing
> Which must be won by kneeling: if he's evil,
> Strike him! thou art omnipotent, and may'st—
> For what can he oppose? If he be good,
> Strike him, or spare him, as thou wilt! since all
> Rests upon thee; and good and evil seem
> To have no power themselves, save in thy will;
> And whether that be good or ill I know not,
> Not being omnipotent, nor fit to judge
> Omnipotence, but merely to endure
> Its mandate; which thus far I have endured.

This powerfully ironic speech acquires, in context, the further irony of the demonic, for it precedes the sacrifice of Abel to his brother's inadequately awakened consciousness of man's freedom. God accepts Abel's lamb, and rejects the fruits of the earth. Cain overthrows his brother's altar, in the name of the creation. When Abel interposes himself and cries that he loves God far more than life, he provokes his brother to murder in the name of life and the earth. The act done, the terrible irony of having brought death into the world by his very quest for life destroys Cain's spirit:

> Oh, earth!
> For all the fruits thou hast render'd to me, I
> Give thee back this.

This is the self-imposed culmination of Byron's Prometheanism. We can leave Blake to make the apt answer, before we pass to the satiric poems in which Byron found a less arbitrary balance for his divided universe. Blake replied to *Cain* with the dramatic scene he called *The Ghost of Abel* (1822), addressed "to Lord Byron in the wilderness." Byron is in the state that precedes prophecy, an Elijah or John the Baptist prefiguring a coming of the truth, and his *Cain* prepares Blake's way before him for *The Ghost of Abel*. Byron's error, in Blake's judgment, is to have insisted that the Imagination necessarily participates in the diabolical, so that the poet must be exile, outcast, and finally criminal. This is the pattern of Byron's obsession with incest, an element present in *Cain* in the beautiful relationship between Adah and Cain, who are both sister and brother, and husband and wife. The murder of Abel, in Byron, is a crime of Imagination; not of passion or society. In Blake, as Frye says, "murder cannot be part of genius but is always part of morality," for genius breaks not only with conventional virtue but with conventional vice as well. Byron could not free himself from societal conventions, and so his Promethean poems do not show us the real man, the Imagination, fully at work within him. The digressive, satirical poems and the handful of late lyrics of personal reappraisal come closer to a full expressiveness. The values of the sequence from *Childe Harold* to *Cain* still exist, but Byron's achievement in them is dwarfed by the great Romantic poems of Titanic aspiration, the Ninth Night of *The Four Zoas* and *Prometheus Unbound*.

THE DIGRESSIVE BALANCE

Beppo

Writing to his publisher, John Murray, in October 1817, Byron expressed his admiration for a poem by John Hookham Frere published earlier in the same year. This work, under the pseudonym "Whistlecraft," is an imitation of the Italian "medley-poem," written in *ottava rima*, and inaugurated by the fifteenth-century poet Pulci in his *Morgante Maggiore*. The form is mock-heroic or satirical romance, and the style digressive, colloquial, realistic. Byron, in imitating Frere, had at first no notion that he had stumbled on what was to be his true mode of writing:

I have written a story in eighty-nine stanzas in imitation of him, called *Beppo* (the short name for Giuseppe, that is, the *Joe* of the Italian Joseph), which I shall throw you into the balance of the fourth canto to help you round to your money; but you had perhaps better publish it anonymously.

Beppo, thus offered to Murray as a throw-in with the last canto of *Childe Harold*, is a permanent and delightful poem, and hardly one to need anonymous publication, which it received in 1818. Byron's caution and respect for convention were characteristic, but he had embarked nevertheless on the great venture of his career, for out of *Beppo* came the greater poems, *Don Juan* and *The Vision of Judgment*, in which the poet at last found aesthetic balance and an individual ethos.

The story of *Beppo*, based on an anecdote of Venetian life told to Byron by the husband of one of his Venetian mistresses, is so slight as to need only a few stanzas of narration. The final version of the poem contains ninety-nine stanzas, and could as effectively go on for ninety-nine more, for the poem's point is in its charming digressiveness. The Venice of Byron's prose (and life) suddenly flowers in his verse, and the man himself is before us, all but unconcealed.

Venice and the Carnival before Lent set the place and time:

> This feast is named the Carnival, which being
>   Interpreted, implies "farewell to flesh."

As the Venetians "bid farewell to carnal dishes," to "guitars and every other sort of strumming," and to "other things which may be had for asking," Byron moves among them with an eye of kindly irony. *Beppo*, like the Carnival, is an escape into freedom. For a little while, as he thinks, Byron puts aside the world of *Childe Harold*, and the Pilgrim becomes a man who can live in the present. After the introduction, *Beppo* digresses on the happy and parallel themes of Venetian women and gondolas, until Byron introduces his heroine, Laura, whose husband, Beppo, has sailed east on business and failed to return. After a long wait, and a little weeping, she takes a Count as protector:

> He was a lover of the good old school,
> Who still become more constant as they cool.

This leads to a digression on the amiable institution of the "Cavalier Servente," and so to Byron in Italy, who was to play that role for the Countess Teresa Guiccioli, the great love of the poet's life after his half-sister Augusta.

Praises of the Italian climate, landscape, and way of life are followed by Byron's appreciation for Italy's chief adornments, the language and the women:

> I love the language, that soft bastard Latin,
>   Which melts like kisses from a female mouth.

This provides a contrast for a backward glance at England, with its "harsh northern whistling, grunting guttural," its "cloudy climate" and "chilly women." Remembering the circumstances of his exile, Byron shrugs himself off as "a broken Dandy lately on my travels" and takes Laura and the Count, after a six-year relationship, off to a Carnival ball, where Laura encounters a Turk who is the returned Beppo. A digression on Moslem sexual ways flows into another upon authors, which includes an oblique glance at Byron's central theme of lost innocence. The ball ends; Beppo as Turk follows Laura and the Count to the stairs of their palace, and reveals the inconvenient truth. The three go within, drink coffee, and accept a return to the earlier arrangement, Beppo and the Count becoming friends. Byron's pen reaches the bottom of a page:

> Which being finish'd, here the story ends;
>   'Tis to be wish'd it had been sooner done,
> But stories somehow lengthen when begun.

Don Juan

On the back of his manuscript of Canto I of *Don Juan*, Byron scribbled an exemplary stanza:

> I would to heaven that I were so much clay,
>   As I am blood, bone, marrow, passion, feeling—
> Because at least the past were pass'd away—
>   And for the future—(but I write this reeling,
> Having got drunk exceedingly to-day,
>   So that I seem to stand upon the ceiling)
> I say—the future is a serious matter—
>   And so—for God's sake—hock and soda-water!

The empirical world of *Don Juan* is typified in this stanza. The poem is identifiable with Byron's mature life, and excludes nothing vital in that life, and so could not be finished until Byron was. *Don Juan's* extraordinary range of tone is unique in poetry, but Byron's was a unique individuality, pre-eminent even in an age of ferocious selfhood.

Don Juan began (September 1818) as what Byron called simply "a poem in the style and manner of *Beppo*, encouraged by the success of the same." But as it developed, the poem became something more ambitious, a satire of European Man and Society which attempts epic dimensions. In the end the poem became Byron's equivalent to Wordsworth's projected *Recluse*, Blake's *Milton*, Shelley's *Prometheus*, and Keats's *Hyperion*. As each of these attempts to surpass and, in Blake's and Shelley's poems, correct Milton, so Byron also creates his vision of the loss of Paradise and the tribulations of a fallen world of experience. There is no exact precedent for an epic satire of this kind. Byron's poetic idol was Pope, who kept his finest satiric strain for *The Dunciad* and wrote his theodicy, without overt satire, in the *Essay on Man*. Had Pope tried to combine the two works in the form of an Italianate medley or mock-heroic romance, something like *Don Juan* might have resulted. Byron's major work is his *Essay on Man*, *Dunciad*, *Rape of the Lock*, and a good deal more besides. Where Byron falls below his Augustan Master in aesthetic genius, he compensates by the range of his worldly knowledge, and the added complexity of bearing the burden of a Romantic Imagination he could neither trust nor eradicate. Much as he wished to emulate Pope, his epic moves in the poetic world of Wordsworth and Shelley, very nearly as much as *Childe Harold* did.

Yet he wills otherwise. The poem's most acute critic, George Ridenour, emphasizes that Byron has chosen "to introduce his longest and most ambitious work with an elaborately traditional satire in the Augustan manner." The seventeen-stanza "Dedication" savages Southey, Wordsworth, and Coleridge, and suggests that Byron is a very different kind of poet and man, whose faults "are at least those of passion and indiscretion, not of calculation, venality, self-conceit, or an impotence which manifests itself in tyranny," to quote Ridenour again. Byron is establishing his *persona* or dramatized self, the satirical mask in which he will present himself as narrator of *Don Juan*. Southey, Wordsworth, and Coleridge are renegades, revolutionary zealots who have become Tories. Southey indeed is an "Epic Renegade," both more venal than his friends (he is poet laureate) and an offender against the epic form, which he so frequently and poorly attempts. As laureate, he is "representative of all the race" of poets, and his dubious moral status is therefore an emblem of the low estate to which Byron believes poetry has fallen:

> And Coleridge, too, has lately taken wing,
>   But like a hawk encumber'd with his hood,—

Explaining metaphysics to the nation—
I wish he would explain his Explanation.

Coleridge's flight is genuine but blind. Southey's poetic soarings end in a "tumble downward like the flying fish gasping on deck." As for Wordsworth, his "rather long *Excursion*" gives a "new system to perplex the sages." Byron does not make the mistake of mounting so high, not will he fall so low:

For me, who, wandering with pedestrian Muses,
    Contend not with you on the winged steed,
I wish your fate may yield ye, when she chooses,
    The fame you envy, and the skill you need.

He will not attempt the sublime, and thus he need not fall into the bathetic. From Southey he passes to the Master Tory, "the intellectual eunuch Castlereagh," a pillar of the Age of Reaction that followed Napoleon, and the master of Southey's hired song:

Europe has slaves, allies, kings, armies still
And Southey lives to sing them very ill.

The mock dedication concluded, the epic begins by announcing its hero:

I want a hero: an uncommon want,
    When every year and month sends forth a new one,
Till, after cloying the gazettes with cant,
    The age discovers he is not the true one:
Of such as these I should not care to vaunt,
    I'll therefore take our ancient friend Don Juan—
We all have seen him, in the pantomime,
    Sent to the devil somewhat ere his time.

This last may be a reference to Mozart's *Don Giovanni*. Byron's Don Juan shares only a name with the hero of the legend or of Mozart. At the root of the poem's irony is the extraordinary passivity and innocence of its protagonist. This fits the age, Byron insists, because its overt heroes are all military butchers. The gentle Juan, acted upon and pursued, sets off the aggressiveness of society.

The plot of *Don Juan* is too extensive for summary, and the poem's digressive technique would defeat such an attempt in any case. The poem organizes itself by interlocking themes and cyclic patterns, rather than by clear narrative structure. "A deliberate rambling digressiveness," Northrop Frye observes, "is endemic in the narrative technique of satire, and so is a calculated bathos or art of sinking in its suspense." *Don Juan* parodies epic form and even its own digressiveness. Its organization centers, as Ridenour shows, on two thematic metaphors: the Fall of Man, in terms of art, nature, and the passions; and the narrator's style of presentation, in terms of his rhetoric and his *persona*. Juan's experiences tend toward a cyclic repetition of the Fall, and Byron's style as poet and man undergoes the same pattern of aspiration and descent.

Canto I deals with Juan's initial fall from sexual innocence. The tone of this canto is urbanely resigned to the necessity of such a fall, and the description of young love and of Donna Julia's beauty clearly ascribes positive qualities to them. Yet Julia is rather unpleasantly changed by her illicit love affair, and her parting letter to Juan betrays a dubious sophistication when we contrast it to her behavior earlier in the canto. As Byron says, speaking mockingly of his own digressiveness:

> The regularity of my design
> Forbids all wandering as the worst of sinning.

His quite conventional moral design condemns Julia, without assigning more than a merely technical lapse to the seduced sixteen-year-old, Juan. The self-baffled Prometheanism of *Childe Harold* manifests itself again here in *Don Juan*, but now the emphasis is rather more firmly set against it. "Perfection is insipid in this naughty world of ours," and Byron is not prepared to be even momentarily insipid, but the price of passion, with its attendant imperfections, may be damnation. And so Byron writes of "first and passionate love":

>   —it stands alone,
> Like Adam's recollection of his fall;
>   The tree of knowledge has been pluck'd
>   —all's known—
> And life yields nothing further to recall
>   Worthy of this ambrosial sin, so shown,
> No doubt in fable, as the unforgiven
> Fire which Prometheus filch'd for us from heaven.

Imaginatively this is an unfortunate passage, as it reduces both Man's crime and the Promethean theft from the level of disobedience, which is

voluntaristic, to that of sexuality itself, a natural endowment. Byron's paradoxes concerning sexual love are shallow, and finally irksome. It is not
enlightening to be told that "pleasure's a sin, and sometimes sin's a pleasure."

Byron does better when he finds Prometheanism dubiously at work
in human inventiveness:

> One makes new noses, one a guillotine,
> > One breaks your bones, one sets them in their sockets.

In an age full of new inventions, "for killing bodies, and for saving
souls," both alike made with great good will, the satirist finds a true function in exploring the ambiguities of human aspiration. When Byron merely condemns all aspiration as sinful, he repels us. Fortunately, he does not
play Urizen for very long at a time. What is most moving in Canto I is the
final personal focus. After extensive ridicule of Coleridge and
Wordsworth, Byron nevertheless comes closest to his own deep preoccupations in two stanzas that are no more than a weaker version of the
"Intimations" and "Dejection" odes:

> No more—no more—Oh! never more on me
> > The freshness of the heart can fall like dew,
> Which out of all the lovely things we see
> > Extracts emotions beautiful and new;
> Hived in our bosoms like the bag o' the bee.
> > Think'st thou the honey with those objects grew?
> Alas! 'twas not in them, but in thy power
> To double even the sweetness of a flower.

This is a very naive version of the "Dejection" ode. What we receive
is what we ourselves give. Byron's scorn of "metaphysics" and "system" in
Coleridge and Wordsworth, which is actually a rather silly scorn of deep
thought in poetry, betrays him into a very weak though moving performance in the mode of Romantic nostalgia for the innocent vision both of
external and of human nature:

> No more—no more—Oh! never more, my heart,
> > Canst thou be my sole world, my universe!
> Once all in all, but now a thing apart,
> > Thou canst not be my blessing or my curse:
> The illusion's gone for ever, and thou art

Insensible, I trust, but none the worse,
And in thy stead I've got a deal of judgment,
Though heaven knows how it ever found a lodgment.

The last couplet helps the stanza, as an ironic equivalent to Wordsworth's "sober coloring" of mature vision, but the preceding lines are weak in that they recall *Peele Castle*, and fall far short of it. Not that Byron is thinking of either Coleridge or Wordsworth in these two stanzas; it is more to the point to note that he might have done better to think of them, and so avoid the bathos of unconsciously, and awkwardly, suggesting their major poetic concerns.

In Canto II Juan is sent on his travels, and suffers seasickness, shipwreck, and the second and greatest of his loves. The shipwreck affords Byron a gruesome opportunity to demonstrate fallen nature at its helpless worst, as the survivors turn to a cannibalism that is rather nastily portrayed. From the flood of judgment only Juan is saved, for only he refrains from tasting human flesh. He reaches shore, a new Adam, freshly baptized from the waves, to find before him a new Eve, Haidée, daughter of an absent pirate. She seems innocence personified, but for Byron no person is innocent. Though it is an "enlargement of existence" for Haidée "to partake Nature" with Juan, the enlargement carries with it the burden of man's fall. Byron himself keenly feels the lack of human justice in this association. First love, "nature's oracle," is all "which Eve has left her daughters since her fall." Yet these moments will be paid for "in an endless shower of hell-fire":

Oh, Love! thou art the very god of evil,
For, after all, we cannot call thee devil.

Canto III is mostly a celebration of ideal love, but its very first stanza pictures Juan as being

loved by a young heart, too deeply blest
To feel the poison through her spirit creeping,
   Or know who rested there, a foe to rest,
Had soil'd the current of her sinless years,
And turn'd her pure heart's purest blood to tears!

This seems an equivocal deep blessing for Haidée, "Nature's bride" as she is. Yet, Byron goes on to say, they were happy, "happy in the illicit indulgence of their innocent desires." This phrasing takes away with one hand what it gives with the other. When, in the fourth canto, all is over, with Juan wounded and sold into slavery, and Haidée dead of a romantically broken heart, Byron gives us his most deliberate stanza of moral confusion. Haidée has just died, and her unborn child with her:

> She died, but not alone; she held within
>   A second principle of life, which might
> Have dawn'd a fair and sinless child of sin;
>   But closed its little being without light,
> And went down to the grave unborn, wherein
>   Blossom and bough lie wither'd with one blight;
> In vain the dews of Heaven descend above
> The bleeding flower and blasted fruit of love.

This is a pathetic kind of sentimental neo-Calvinism until its concluding couplet, when it becomes a statement of the inefficacy of heavenly grace in the affairs of human passion. At the start of the fourth canto Byron has modulated his tone so as to fit his style to the saddest section of his epic. If a fall is to be portrayed, then the verse too must descend:

> Nothing so difficult as a beginning
>   In poesy, unless perhaps the end;
> For oftentimes when Pegasus seems winning
>   The race, he sprains a wing, and down we tend,
> Like Lucifer when hurl'd from heaven for sinning;
>   Our sin the same, and hard as his to mend,
> Being pride, which leads the mind to soar too far,
> Till our own weakness shows us what we are.

Few stanzas in *Don Juan* or elsewhere are as calmly masterful as that. The poet attempting the high style is likely to suffer the fate of Lucifer. Pride goes before the fall of intellect, and the sudden plunge into bathos restores us to the reality we are. The movement from *Childe Harold* into *Don Juan* is caught with fine self-knowledge:

>   Imagination droops her pinion,
> And the sad truth which hovers o'er my desk
> Turns what was once romantic to burlesque.

Self-recognition leads to a gentler statement of mature awareness than Byron usually makes:

And if I laugh at any mortal thing,
    'Tis that I may not weep; and if I weep,
'Tis that our nature cannot always bring
    Itself to apathy, for we must steep
Our hearts first in the depths of Lethe's spring
    Ere what we least wish to behold will sleep:
Thetis baptized her mortal son in Styx;
A mortal mother would on Lethe fix.

This is noble and restrained, and reveals the fundamental despera-tion that pervades the world of the poem, which is our world. After the death of Haidée most of the tenderness of Byron passes out of the poem, to be replaced by fiercer ironies and a reckless gaiety that can swerve into controlled hysteria. It becomes clearer that Byron's universe is neither Christian not Romantic, nor yet the eighteenth-century cosmos he would have liked to repossess. Neither grace nor the displaced grace of the Secondary Imagination can move with freedom in this universe, and a standard of reasonableness is merely a nostalgia to be studied. What haunts Byron is the specter of meaninglessness, of pointless absurdity. He is an unwilling prophet of our sensibility. The apocalyptic desires of Blake and Shelley, the natural sacramentalism of Coleridge and Wordsworth, the humanistic naturalism of Keats, all find some parallels in Byron, but what is central in him stands apart from the other great Romantics. He lacks their confidence, as he lacks also the persuasiveness of their individual rhetorics. Too traditional to be one of them, too restless and driven to be traditional, impatient of personal myth if only because he incarnates his own too fully, he creates a poem without faith in Nature, Art, Society, or the very Imagination he so capably employs. Yet his obsessions betray his uncertainties of rejection. *Don Juan* cannot let Wordsworth alone, and cannot bring itself to mention Shelley, Byron's companion during much of the poem's composition. Until Shelley's death, Byron could not decide what to make of either the man or the poet, both of whom impressed him more than he cared to acknowledge. After Shelley's death, Byron seems to have preferred to forget him, except for one stanza of *Don Juan* where the puzzle of Shelley continues as a troubling presence:

And that's enough, for love is vanity,
    Selfish in its beginning as its end,
Except where 'tis a mere insanity,
    A maddening spirit which would strive to blend
Itself with beauty's frail inanity,

On which the passion's self seems to depend;
And hence some heathenish philosophers
Make love the main-spring of the universe.

The italics are mine, and indicate the probable Shelley reference. The stanza's first two lines express the mature judgment of Byron on love, a vanity that begins and ends in selfishness, except in the case of the rare spirits who madden themselves and others by questing as though the world could contain the object of their fierce desire. The tone here is uneasy, as it is in Byron's continuous digressions on Wordsworth's *Excursion*. *The Excursion* contains just enough of Wordsworth's greatness both to influence and to repel Byron, and its emphasis on the correction of a misanthropic Solitary may have offended him directly. We cannot know, but a surmise is possible. There are moments in *Don Juan* when Byron longs to make nature his altar, and moments when he is drawn toward a desperate religion of love. His rejection of Wordsworth and evasion of Shelley have deep and mysterious roots within *Don Juan*'s underlying assumptions concerning reality.

After the love-death of Haidée, Byron moves Juan into the world of two rapacious empresses, Gulbeyaz of Turkey and the historical Catherine the Great of Russia. Between these tigresses the poem progresses by an account of a battle between Turks and Russians. After Catherine's court, *Don Juan* starts its last, most interesting and unfinished movement, a view of the English society that Byron had known before his exile. A fierce love, a faithless war, another fierce love, and a social satire of what was closest to Byron's heart form a suggestive sequence. Seduced by a young matron, shipwrecked into an idyll of natural and ideal love, wounded and sold into bondage—the passive Juan has encountered all these adventures without developing under their impact. As he falls further into experience, he does not gain in wisdom, but he does maintain a stubborn Spanish aristocratic pride and a basic disinterestedness. Turkish passion and the horror of battle do not seem to affect him directly, but the embraces of Catherine finally convert his disinterestedness into the sickness of uninterestedness. Probably, like Childe Harold and Byron, the Don begins to feel the "fulness of satiety." His diplomatic rest trip to England is a quest for a renewal of interest, and the quest's goal, Lady Adeline, becomes Byron's last vision of a possible and therefore ultimately dangerous woman. In thus patterning the course of the poem, I have moved ahead of my commentary, and return now to Juan in slavery.

The memorable elements in that episode are the digressions. With Juan pausing, involuntarily, between women, Byron is free to meditate upon the impermanence of all worldly vanities, including poetry. He is back in the mood of *Childe Harold*, from which only the therapy of his own epic can rescue him:

> Yet there will still be bards: though fame is smoke,
>   Its fumes are frankincense to human thought;
> And the unquiet feelings, which first woke
>   Song in the world, will seek what then they sought:
> As on the beach the waves at last are broke,
>   Thus to their extreme verge the passions brought
> Dash into poetry, which is but passion,
> Or at least was so ere it grew a fashion.

Poetry here is expression and catharsis, and nothing more. At most it can help keep the poet (and his readers) sane. Elsewhere in *Don Juan* Byron rates poetry as simultaneously higher and lower, when he sees it as a dangerous mode of evading the consequences of Man's Fall, an evasion that must resolve at last in the consciousness of delusion. The impermanence of poetry is related to human mortality and what lies beyond its limits. Before introducing Juan into a Turkish harem, Byron perplexes himself with the mystery of death, drawing upon "a fact, and no poetic fable." His acquaintance, the local military commandant, has been slain in the street "for some reason, surely bad." As Byron stares at the corpse, he cannot believe that this is death:

> I gazed (as oft I have gazed the same)
> To try if I could wrench aught out of death
> Which should confirm, or shake, or make a faith;
> But it was all a mystery. Here we are,
>   And there we go:—but *where*? five bits of lead,
> Or three, or two, or one, send very far!
>   And is this blood, then, form'd but to be shed?
> Can every element our element mar?
>   And air—earth—water—fire live—and we dead?
> *We*, whose minds comprehend all things. No more;
> But let us to the story as before.

What is effective here is the human attitude conveyed, but Byron's own turbulence weakens the expression. Few great poets have written quite so badly about death. The Muse of Byron was too lively to accommodate the grosser of his private apprehensions. The paradox of an all-comprehensive mind inhabiting a form vulnerable to every element is the basis of Byron's dualism, his own saddened version of "the ghost in the machine." The inevitable corruption of the body obsesses Byron, and this obsession determines his dismissal of passionate love as a value. Julia was self-corrupted, and Haidée the most natural and innocent of sinners, too harshly judged by her father, himself a great cutthroat but perfectly conventional in questions of his own family's morality. Gulbeyaz is further down in the scale of female culpability. Her features have "all the sweetness of the devil" when he played the cherub. She has the charm of her passion's intensity, but her love is a form of imperial, or imperious, bondage, her embrace a chain thrown about her lover's neck. Her love is a variation of war and preludes Byron's ferocious and very funny satire on the siege, capture, and sack of the Turkish town Ismail by the ostensibly Christian imperial Russian army of Catherine the Great, Juan's next and most consuming mistress. Byron introduces Canto VII and its slaughter by parodying Spenser, whose *Faerie Queene* sang of "fierce warres and faithful loves." For Byron, it is altogether too late in the day to sing so innocently, especially when "the fact's about the same," so his themes are "fierce loves and faithless wars":

> "Let there be light!" said God, "and there was light!"
>   "Let there be blood!" says man, and there's a sea!
> The fiat of this spoil'd child of the Night
>   (For Day ne'er saw his merits) could decree
> More evil in an hour, than thirty bright
>   Summers could renovate, though they should be
> Lovely as those which ripen'd Eden's fruit;
> For war cuts up not only branch, but root.

War completes the Fall of Man, costing us our surviving root in Eden and nullifying the renovating power of nature. This does not prevent Byron from an immense and sadistic joy in recording the butchery and rapine, but his persona as Promethean poet, whose every stanza heightens aspiration and deepens guilt, justifies the seeming inconsistency.

Juan has butchered freely, but refrained from ravishing, and next appears as hero at the court of Catherine the Great, where he falls, not into love, but into "that no less imperious passion," self-love. Flattered by Catherine's preference, Juan grows "a little dissipated" and becomes very much a royal favorite. As this is morally something of a further fall, Byron is inspired to reflect again upon his favorite theme:

Man fell with apples, and with apples rose,
    If this be true; for we must deem the mode
In which Sir Isaac Newton could disclose
    Through the then unpaved stars the turnpike road,
A thing to counterbalance human woes:
    For ever since immortal man hath glow'd
With all kinds of mechanics, and full soon
Steam-engines will conduct him to the moon.

The triumphs of reason are now also identified as sinfully and gloriously Promethean, and Sir Isaac observing the apple's fall is responsible for the paradox that Man's initial fall with apples was a fortunate one. The glowing of human intellect is "a thing to counterbalance human woes," and soon enough will take us to the moon. Byron quickly goes on to qualify his counterbalance as "a glorious glow," due only to his internal spirit suddenly cutting a caper. Cheerfulness thus keeps breaking in, but does not alter the fundamental vision of our world as "a waste and icy clime." That clime surrounds us, and we are "chill, and chain'd to cold earth," as our hero Prometheus was upon his icy rock. But we look up, and see the meteors of love and glory, lovely lights that flash and then die away, leaving us "on our freezing way." *Don Juan* is not only, its poet tells us, "a nondescript and ever-varying rhyme," but it is also "a versified Aurora Borealis," a northern light flashing over us.

Love and glory have flashed too often for Juan, and he begins to waste into a clime of decay just as his creator laments that Dante's "obscure wood," the mid-point of life, draws close. In "royalty's vast arms," Juan sighs for beauty, and sickens for travel. The now motherly Catherine sends her wasting lover on his last quest, a mission to England, and Byron returns in spirit to the Age of Elegance of his triumphant youth, the London of the Regency.

This, *Don Juan*'s last and unfinished movement, is its most nostalgic and chastened. Byron, once "the grand Napoleon of the realms of rhyme," revisits in vision his lost kingdom, the Babylon that sent him into exile and pilgrimage. "But I will fall at least as fell my hero," Byron cries, completing his lifelong comparison to the other Titan of the age. The poem of Juan, Byron says, is his Moscow, and he seeks in its final cantos his Waterloo. Juan has met his Moscow in Catherine, and evidently would have found a Waterloo in the Lady Adeline Amundeville, cold heroine of the final cantos and "the fair most fatal Juan ever met."

The English cantos are a litany for an eighteenth-century world, forever lost, and by Byron forever lamented. The age of reason and love is over, the poet insists, and the age of Cash has begun. The poem has seen sex displaced into war, and now sees both as displaced into money. Money and coldness dominate England, hypocritically masked as the morality that exiled Byron and now condemns his epic. There are other and deeper wounds to be revenged. The Greek and Italian women of the poet's life have given fully of their passion and spirits, and Byron has returned what he could. But England stands behind him as a sexual battlefield where he conquered all yet won nothing, and where at last he defeated himself and fled. Incest, separation, mutual betrayal of spirit are his English sexual legacy. In his sunset of poetry he returns to brood upon English womankind, products of "the English winter—ending in July, to recommence in August." Beneath the Lady Adeline's snowy surface is the proverbial *et cetera*, as Byron says, but he refuses to hunt down the tired metaphor. He throws out another figure: a bottle of champagne "frozen into a very vinous ice."

> Yet in the very centre, past all price,
>   About a liquid glassful will remain;
> And this is stronger than the strongest grape
> Could e'er express in its expanded shape.

Severity and courtliness fuse here into definitive judgment, and bring the spirit of this female archetype to a quintessence:

> And thus the chilliest aspects may concentre
> A hidden nectar under a cold presence.

Adeline is mostly a cold potential in this unfinished poem; her fatality is only barely felt when Byron breaks off, in his preparation for his final and genuinely heroic pilgrimage, to battle for the Greeks. She is Byron's "Dian of the Ephesians," but there is more flesh and activity to "her frolic Grace," the amorous Duchess of Fitz-Fulke. No personage, but an atmosphere, dominates these English cantos, with their diffused autumnal tone and their perfectly bred but desperately bored aristocrats, with whose breeding and boredom alike Byron is more than half in sympathy.

Don Juan, begun as satiric epic, ends as a remembrance of things past, with Byron's last glance at home, and the poet's last tone one of weary but loving irony. The last word in a discussion of *Don Juan* ought not to be "irony," but "mobility," one of Byron's favorite terms. Oliver Elton called Byron's two central traits his mobility and self-consciousness, and the former is emphasized in *Don Juan*. Adeline is so graceful a social performer that Juan begins to feel some doubt as to how much of her is *real*:

> So well she acted all and every part
>   By turns—with that vivacious versatility,
> Which many people take for want of heart.
>   They err—'tis merely what is call'd mobility,
> A thing of temperament and not of art,
>   Though seeming so, from its supposed facility;
> And false—though true; for surely they're sincerest
> Who are strongly acted on by what is nearest.

This is Byron's own defense against our charge that he postures, our feeling doubts as to how much of *him* is real. An abyss lies beneath mobility, but Adeline and Byron alike are too nimble to fall into it, and their deftness is more than rhetorical. The world of *Don Juan*, Byron's world, demands mobility; there is indeed no other way to meet it. Byron defines mobility in a note that has a wry quality, too sophisticated to acknowledge the tragic dimension being suggested: "It may be defined as an excessive susceptibility of immediate impressions—at the same time without *losing* the past: and is, though sometimes apparently useful to the possessor, a most painful and unhappy attribute."

This is Byron's social version of the Romantic term "Imagination," for mobility also reveals itself "in the balance or reconciliation of opposite or discordant qualities: of sameness, with difference; the individual, with the representative; the sense of novelty and freshness, with old and familiar objects." The great Romantic contraries—emotion and order, judgment and enthusiasm, steady self-possession and profound or vehement feeling—all find their social balance in the quality of mobility. Viewed thus, Byron's achievement in *Don Juan* is to have suggested the pragmatic social realization of Romantic idealism in a mode of reasonableness that no other Romantic aspired to attain.

Byron lived in the world as no other Romantic attempted to live, except Shelley, and Shelley at the last despaired more fully. *Don Juan* is, to my taste, not a poem of the eminence of *Milton* and *Jerusalem*, of *The Prelude* or *Prometheus Unbound* or the two *Hyperions*. But it is not a poem of their kind, nor ought it to be judged against them. Shelley said of *Don Juan* that "every word of it is pregnant with immortality," and again: "Nothing has ever been written like it in English, nor, if I may venture to prophesy, will there be; without carrying upon it the mark of a secondary and borrowed light." Byron despaired of apocalypse, and yet could not be content with Man or nature as given. He wrote therefore with the strategy of meeting this life with awareness, humor, and an intensity of creative aspiration, flawed necessarily at its origins. Mobility is a curious and sophisticated ideal; it attempts to meet experience with experience's own ironies of apprehension. It may be that, as Byron's best critic says, *Don Juan* offers us "a sophistication which (in a highly debased form, to be sure) we have already too much of." We have, however, so little besides that a higher kind of sophistication can only improve us. Whatever its utility, *Don Juan* is exuberant enough to be beautiful in a Blakean sense, little as Blake himself would have cared for Byron's hard-won digressive balance.

THE BYRONIC ETHOS

The Vision of Judgment

The parody poem *The Vision of Judgment* contains Byron's best work outside of *Don Juan*. It is, as Byron said, "in the Pulci style," like *Beppo* and *Juan*, but its high good nature reveals a firmer balance than Byron maintains else where in his Italian mock-heroic vein. Southey, the battered poet laureate, is the scapegoat again, as he was in the "Dedication" to *Don Juan*. Byron's treatment of his victim is both more humane and more effective in the *Vision*, once the reader gets past the angry prose preface.

George III died in 1820, and poor Southey performed the laureate's task of eulogizing his late monarch in *A Vision of Judgment* (1821), a poem no better than it needed to be, and not much worse than most of Southey. The laureate's misfortune was to write a preface in which he denounced lascivious literature and attacked the "Satanic school" (Byron and Shelley) for producing it: "for though their productions breathe the spirit of Belial in their lascivious parts, and the spirit of Moloch in those loathsome images of atrocities and horrors which they delight to represent, they are more especially characterized by a satanic spirit of pride and audacious impiety, which still betrays the wretched feeling of hopelessness wherewith it is allied."

Byron was not the man to pass this by. His *Vision of Judgment* takes its occasion from Southey's and permanently fixates the laureate as a dunce. But it does something rather more vital besides. *Don Juan* has its Miltonic side, as we have seen, yet the *Vision* as it develops is even closer to *Paradise Lost* in material, though hardly in spirit or tone. Milton's anthropomorphic Heaven is sublime and also sometimes wearisome, too much like an earthly court in its servile aspects. Byron's burlesque Heaven is sublimely funny. St. Peter sits by the celestial gate and can happily drowse, for very little goes in. The Angels are singing out of tune and are by now hoarse, having little else to do. Down below, George III dies, which does not disturb the yawning Peter, who has not heard of him. But the mad old blind king arrives in the angelic caravan, and with him comes a very great being, the patron of the "Satanic school":

> But bringing up the rear of this bright host
>   A Spirit of a different aspect waved
> His wings, like thunder-clouds above some coast
>   Whose barren beach with frequent wrecks is paved;
> His brow was like the deep when tempest-toss'd;
>   Fierce and unfathomable thoughts engraved
> Eternal wrath on his immortal face,
> And *where* he gazed a gloom pervaded space.

Those "fierce and unfathomable thoughts" remind us of Manfred, but this is great Lucifer himself, come to claim George as his own. The gate of heaven opens, and the archangel Michael comes forth to meet his former friend and future foe. There is "a high immortal, proud regret" in the eyes of each immortal being, as if destiny rather than will governs their enmity:

> Yet still between his Darkness and his Brightness
> There pass'd a mutual glance of great politeness.

Michael is a gentleman, but the Prince of Darkness has the superior hauteur of "an old Castilian poor noble." He is not particularly proud of owning our earth, but he does own it, in this quietly Gnostic poem. But, as befits a poor noble with hauteur, he thinks few earthlings worth damnation save their kings, and these he takes merely as a kind of quitrent, to assert his right as lord. Indeed, he shares Byron's theory of the Fall as being perpetually renewed by Man:

> they are grown so bad,
> That hell has nothing better left to do
>   Than leave them to themselves: so much more mad
> And evil by their own internal curse,
>   Heaven cannot make them better, nor I worse.

Lucifer's charges against George and his calling of witnesses are nimbly handled. Life comes exuberantly into the poem with the intrusion of Southey upon the heavenly scene. The devil Asmodeus stumbles in, under the heavy load of the laureate, and the poor devil is moved to lament that he has sprained his left wing in the carry. Southey has been writing his *Vision of Judgment*, thus daring to anticipate the eternal decision upon George. The laureate, glad to get an audience, begins to recite, throwing everyone into a horror and even rousing the deceased King from his stupor in the horrible thought that his former laureate, the abominable Pye, has come again to plague him. After a general tumult, St. Peter

> upraised his keys,
> And at the fifth line knock'd the poet down;
> Who felt like Phaeton.

Phaeton (or Phaethon) attempted to drive the chariot of the sun across the sky, but could not control the horses, who bolted, and so Phaethon fell to his death. Southey attempts to ride in the chariot of Apollo, god of poetry, and suffers a fall into the depths, a bathetic plunge. The same imagery of falling is associated with Southey in the "Dedication" to *Don Juan*, but there it is more direct:

> He first sank to the bottom—like his works,
> But soon rose to the surface—like himself.

In the confusion, King George slips into heaven, and as Byron ends his *Vision*, the late monarch is practicing the hundredth psalm, which is only fitting, as it adjures the Lord's people to "enter into his gates with thanksgiving." The ethos of *The Vision of Judgment* is remarkably refreshing. Byron is so delighted by his fable that his good will extends even to Southey, who does not drown like Phaethon but lurks in his own den, still composing. George is in heaven, and the very dignified and high-minded Lucifer back in hell. In this one poem at least, Byron writes as a whole man, whose inner conflicts have been mastered. If the earth is the Devil's, the Devil is yet disinterested, and damnation a subject for urbane bantering. Peculiar as Byron's variety of Prometheanism was, *The Vision of Judgment* makes it clear that we err in calling the poet any genuine sort of a Calvinist:

> for not one am I
> Of those who think damnation better still:
> I hardly know too if not quite alone am I
> In this small hope of bettering future ill
> By circumscribing, with some slight restriction,
> The eternity of hell's hot jurisdiction.

If there is any mockery in the poem which is not altogether good-humored, it is in Byron's conscious "blasphemy":

> I know one may be damn'd
> For hoping no one else may e'er be so;
>   I know my catechism; I know we're cramm'd
> With the best doctrines till we quite o'erflow;
>   I know that all save England's church have shamm'd,
> And that the other twice two hundred churches
> And synagogues.have made a *damn'd* bad purchase.

Religious cant was no more acceptable to Byron than the social or political varieties, however darkly and deeply his own orthodox currents ran. *The Vision of Judgment* is perhaps only a good parody of aspects of *Paradise Lost*, but few of us would prefer Milton's heaven to Byron's as a place in which to live.

"Stanzas to the Po"

Byron's lyrics are an index to his poetic development, though only a few of them are altogether adequate in the expression of his complex sensibility. The best of them include the "Stanzas to the Po" (1819), the undated "Ode to a Lady," which applies the poet's negative Prometheanism to the theme of lost human passion, and the last poems written under the shadow of death at Missolonghi. Byron's personal ethos, the dignity of disillusioned intensity and disinterested heroism, despairing of love and its human limitations but still longing for them, continued to shine out of this handful of lyrics.

The last poems have the poignancy of their occasion, but the "Stanzas to the Po" constitute Byron's finest short poem, and one perfectly revelatory of his mature spirit.

In April 1819 Byron, aged thirty-one, fell in love with the Countess Teresa Guiccioli, aged nineteen, who had been married only a little over a year to the fifty-eight-year-old Count. Byron had already lamented in *Don Juan* the cooling of his heart, now that he was past thirty, but he proved no prophet in this matter. Momentarily separated from Teresa, he wrote the first draft of his "Stanzas to the Po." The firm diction of this beautiful poem shows an Italian influence, probably that of Dante's *Canzioniere*:

> River, that rollest by the ancient walls,
>   Where dwells the Lady of my love, when she

> Walks by thy brink, and there perchance recalls
>   A faint and fleeting memory of me;
>
> What if thy deep and ample stream should be
>   A mirror of my heart, where she may read
> The thousand thoughts I now betray to thee,
>   Wild as thy wave, and headlong as thy speed!

The movement of this is large and stately, but there is a curious and deliberate reluctance in the rhythm, as if the poet wished to resist the river's swift propulsion of his thoughts toward his absent mistress. As he stares at the river he sees suddenly that it is more than a mirror of his heart. He finds not similitude but identity between the Po and his heart:

> Thou tendest wildly onwards to the main.
>   And I—to loving *one* I should not love.

He should not love only because he had said his farewell to love, and is reluctant to welcome it again. But it has come; he longs desperately for his beloved, yet he still resists the longing:

> The wave that bears my tears returns no more:
>   Will she return by whom that wave shall sweep?—
> Both tread thy banks, both wander on thy shore,
>   I by thy source, she by the dark-blue deep.

As the Po is one with the passion of Byron's heart, a love that Teresa reciprocates, the geographical position of the lovers symbolizes the extent to which they have given themselves to their love. Teresa is "by the dark-blue deep," but Byron still lingers by the source, struggling with the past:

> But that which keepeth us apart is not
>   Distance, nor depth of wave, nor space of earth,
> But the distraction of a various lot,
>   As various as the climates of our birth.
>
> A stranger loves the Lady of the land,
>   Born far beyond the mountains, but his blood
> Is all meridian, as if never fann'd
>   By the black wind that chills the polar flood.

His hesitation keeps them apart, and he traces it to the division with-in his own nature. But his blood triumphs, though in his own despite:

> My blood is all meridian; were it not;
>> I had not left my clime, nor should I be,
> In spite of tortures, ne'er to be forgot,
>> A slave again of love,—at least of thee.
>
> 'Tis vain to struggle—let me perish young—
>> Live as I lived, and love as I have loved;
> To dust if I return, from dust I sprung,
>> And then, at least, my heart can ne'er be moved.

Complex in attitude as these two final stanzas of the poem are, they did not satisfy Byron. As he gives himself again to love, he senses that he also gives himself to self-destruction and welcomes this as a consummation to be wished. By loving again, he is true to both his own past and his own nature, but to a past he had rejected and a nature he had sought to negate. His heart is moved again, and to have its torpor stirred is pain, but this is the pain of life.

Less than two months later, as he made his final decision and moved to join Teresa, he redrafted his poem. Characteristically, the poem is now more indecisive than the man, for he alters the final lines to a lament:

> My heart is all meridian, were it not
>> I had not suffered now, nor should I be
> Despite old tortures ne'er to be forgot
>> The slave again—Oh! Love! at least of thee!
>
> 'Tis vain to struggle, I have struggled long
>> To love again no more as once I loved,
> Oh! Time! why leave this worst of earliest
>>> Passions strong?
>> To tear a heart which pants to be unmoved?

Byron was too courtly to leave the penultimate line as above, and modified it to "why leave this earliest Passion strong?" With either read-ing, this makes for a weaker and less controlled climax to the poem than the first version, as it denies the strength of the poet's own will. The first set of "Stanzas to the Po" makes a permanent imaginative gesture, and deserves to be read repeatedly as the universal human legacy it comes so close to being. The heart divided against itself has found few more eloquent emblems.

Last Poems

On the morning of his thirty-sixth birthday, at Missolonghi, where he was to die three months later, Byron finished the poem that is his epitaph:

> 'Tis time this heart should be unmoved,
>   Since others it hath ceased to move:
> Yet, though I cannot be beloved,
>   Still let me love!

He begins with an echo of the final line of the "Stanzas to the Po," but the emphasis is different. He now fears not that he will love again but that he cannot:

> My days are in the yellow leaf;
>   The flowers and fruits of love are gone;
> The worm, the canker, and the grief
>   Are mine alone!

The Macbeth comparison is perhaps rather too melodramatic, but the next stanza modulates to the more appropriate Promethean image of fire:

> The fire that on my bosom preys
>   Is lone as some volcanic isle;
> No torch is kindled at its blaze—
>   A funeral pile.

The fire is not yet out, the volcano not extinct, but the volcano is isolated and the fire will be consumed with the poet. He wears the chain of love (for the abandoned Teresa?) but he cannot share in its pain and power. In a recovery of great rhetorical power he turns upon his grief and delivers himself up to his destiny:

> Tread those reviving passions down,
>   Unworthy manhood!—unto thee
> Indifferent should the smile or frown
>   Of beauty be.

If thou regrett'st thy youth, *why live?*
   The land of honourable death
Is here:—up to the field, and give
   Away thy breath!

Seek out—less often sought than found—
   A soldier's grave, for thee the best;
Then look around, and choose thy ground,
   And take thy rest.

Byron seems to have intended this as his last poem, but his Muses had it otherwise, and ended him with an intense love poem for his page-boy Loukas. The suffering conveyed by this poem clearly has its sexual element, so that the complex puzzle of Byron is not exactly simplified for us, but this is a problem for his biographers, who have reached no agreement upon it. Certainly Byron had homosexual as well as incestuous experience; his questing and experimental psyche, and his conviction of necessary damnation, could have led him to no less. In his final lines he liberates himself from his last verbal inhibition and writes a very powerful homosexual love poem:

I watched thee when the foe was at our side,
   Ready to strike at him—or thee and me.
Were safety hopeless—rather than divide
   Aught with one loved save love and liberty.

I watched thee on the breakers, when the rock
   Received our prow and all was storm and fear,
And bade thee cling to me through every shock;
   This arm would be thy bark, or breast thy bier.

Love and death come dangerously close together in these tense stanzas, so much so that one can understand why Loukas was wary enough to cause Byron to lament:

And when convulsive throes denied my breath
   The faintest utterance to my fading thought,
To thee—to thee—e'en in the gasp of death
   My spirit turned, oh! oftener than it ought.

Thus much and more; and yet thou lov'st me not,
   And never wilt! Love dwells not in our will.

Nor can I blame thee, though it be my lot
　　To strongly, wrongly, vainly love thee still.

It is very moving that this agonized hymn to hopeless love should be
Byron's last poem. Had he been more of a Promethean he would still not
have achieved a better either sexual or rhetorical balance, when one
remembers the English and European society through which he had to
take his way. But he might have had more faith in his own imaginings,
more confidence in his own inventive power, and so have given us something larger and more relevant than *Manfred* in the Romantic mode, good
as *Manfred* is. We have *Don Juan*, and the record, still incomplete, of
Byron's life. Byron did not seem to regret his not having given us more,
and was himself realistic enough to believe that there was no more to give.

Percy Bysshe Shelley

(1792-1822)

Mesdames, one might believe that Shelley lies
Less in the stars than in their earthy wake,
Since the radiant disclosures that you make
Are of an eternal vista, manqué and gold
And brown, an Italy of the mind, a place
Of fear before the disorder of the strange,
A time in which the poet's politics
Will rule in a poets' world.

—WALLACE STEVENS

PERCY BYSSHE SHELLEY, ONE OF THE GREATEST LYRICAL POETS IN WESTERN tradition, has been dead for more than a hundred and forty years, and critics have abounded, from his own day to ours, to insist that his poetry died with him. Until recently, it was fashionable to apologize for Shelley's poetry, if one liked it at all. Each reader of poetry, however vain, can speak only for himself, and there will be only description and praise in this introduction, for after many years of reading Shelley's poems, I find nothing in them that needs apology. Shelley is a unique poet, one of the most original in the language, and he is in many ways *the* poet proper, as much so as any in the language. His poetry is autonomous, finely wrought, in the highest degree imaginative, and has the spiritual form of vision stripped of all veils and ideological coverings, the vision many readers justly seek in poetry, despite the admonitions of a multitude of churchwardenly critics.

The essential Shelley is so fine a poet that one can feel absurd in urging his claims upon a reader:

> I am the eye with which the Universe
>   Beholds itself and knows itself divine;
> All harmony of instrument or verse,
>   All prophecy, all medicine is mine,
>   All light of art or nature—to my song
>   Victory and praise in its own right belong.

That is Apollo singing, in the "Hymn" that Shelley had the sublime audacity to write for him, with the realization that, like Keats, he was a rebirth of Apollo. When, in *The Triumph of Life*, Rousseau serves as Virgil to Shelley's Dante, he is made to speak lines as brilliantly and bitterly condensed as poetry in English affords:

> And if the spark with which Heaven lit my spirit
> Had been with purer nutriment supplied,
>
> Corruption would not now thus much inherit
> Of what was once Rousseau—nor this disguise
> Stain that which ought to have disdained to wear it.

The urbane lyricism of the "Hymn of Apollo," and the harshly self-conscious, internalized dramatic quality of *The Triumph of Life* are both central to Shelley. Most central is the prophetic intensity; as much a result of displaced Protestantism as it is in Blake or in Wordsworth, but seeming more an Orphic than Hebraic phenomenon when it appears in Shelley. Religious poet as he primarily was, what Shelley prophesied was one restored Man who transcended men, gods, the natural world, and even the poetic faculty. Shelley chants the apotheosis, not of the poet, but of desire itself.

> Man, oh, not men! a chain of linked thought,
> Of love and might to be divided not,
> Compelling the elements with adamantine stress;
>   As the sun rules, even with a tyrant's gaze,
>   The unquiet republic of the maze
> Of planets, struggling fierce towards heaven's free wilderness.
>
>   Man, one harmonious soul of many a soul,
>   Whose nature is its own divine control,
> Where all things flow to all, as rivers to the sea ...

The rhapsodic intensity, the cumulative drive and yet firm control of those last three lines in particular, as the high song of humanistic celebration approaches its goal—that seems to me what is crucial in Shelley, and its presence throughout much of his work constitutes his special excellence as a poet.

Lyrical poetry at its most intense frequently moves toward direct address between one human consciousness and another, in which the "I" of the poet directly invokes the personal "Thou" of the reader. Shelley is an intense lyricist as Alexander Pope is an intense satirist; even as Pope assimilates every literary form he touches to satire, so Shelley converts forms as diverse as drama, prose essay, romance, satire, epyllion, into lyric. To an extent he himself scarcely realized, Shelley's genius desired a transformation of all experience, natural and literary, into the condition of lyric. More than all other poets, Shelley's compulsion is to present life as a direct confrontation of equal realities. This compulsion seeks absolute intensity, and courts straining and breaking in consequence. When expressed as love, it must manifest itself as mutual destruction:

> In one another's substance finding food,
> Like flames too pure and light and unimbued
> To nourish their bright lives with baser prey,
> Which point to Heaven and cannot pass away:
> One Heaven, one Hell, one immortality,
> And one annihilation.

Shelley is the poet of these flames, and he is equally the poet of a particular shadow, which falls perpetually between all such flames, a shadow of ruin that tracks every imaginative flight of fire:

> O, Thou, who plumed with strong desire
>   Wouldst float above the earth, beware!
> A Shadow tracks thy flight of fire—
>   Night is coming!

By the time Shelley had reached his final phase, of which the great monuments are *Adonais* and *The Triumph of Life*, he had become altogether the poet of this shadow of ruin, and had ceased to celebrate the possibilities of imaginative relationship. In giving himself, at last, over to the dark side of his own vision, he resolved (or perhaps merely evaded, judgment being so difficult here) a conflict within his self and poetry that had been present from the start. Though it has become a commonplace of recent criticism and scholarship to affirm otherwise, I do not think that Shelley changed very much, as a poet, during the last (and most important) six years of his life, from the summer of 1816 until the summer of 1822. The two poems of self-discovery, of mature poetic incarnation, written in 1816, "Mont Blanc" and the "Hymn to Intellectual Beauty," reveal the two contrary aspects of Shelley's vision that his entire sequence of major poems reveals. The head and the heart, each totally honest in encountering reality, yield rival reports as to the name and nature of reality. The head, in "Mont Blanc," learns, like Blake, that there is no natural religion. There is a Power, a secret strength of things, but it hides its true shape or its shapelessness behind or beneath a dread mountain, and it shows itself only as an indifference, or even pragmatically a malevolence, towards the well-being of men. But the Power speaks forth, through a poet's act of confrontation with it which is the very act of writing his poem, and the Power, rightly interpreted, can be used to repeal the large code of fraud, institutional and historical Christianity, and the equally massive code of woe, the laws of the nation-states of Europe in the age of Castlereagh and Metternich. In the "Hymn to Intellectual Beauty" a very different Power is invoked, but with a deliberate and even austere tenuousness. A shadow, itself invisible, of an unseen Power, sweeps through our dull dense world, momentarily awakening both nature and man to a sense of love and beauty, a sense just beyond the normal range of apprehension. But the shadow departs, for all its benevolence, and despite the poet's prayers for its more habitual sway. The heart's responses have not failed, but the shadow that is antithetically a radiance will not come to stay. The mind, searching for what would suffice, encountered an icy remoteness, but dared to affirm the triumph of its imaginings over the solitude and vacancy of an inadvertent nature. The emotions, visited by delight, felt the desolation of powerlessness, but dared to hope for a fuller visitation. Both odes suffer from the evident straining of their creator to reach a finality, but both survive in their creator's tough honesty and gathering sense of form.

"Mont Blanc" is a poem of the age of Shelley's father-in-law, William Godwin, while the "Hymn to Intellectual Beauty" belongs to the age of Wordsworth, Shelley's lost leader in the realms of emotion. Godwin became a kind of lost leader for Shelley also, but less on the intellectual than on the personal level. The scholarly criticism of Shelley is full of sand traps, and one of the deepest is the prevalent notion that Shelley underwent an intellectual metamorphosis from being the disciple of Godwin and the French philosophical materialists to being a Platonist or Neoplatonist, an all but mystical idealist. The man Shelley may have undergone such a transformation, though the evidence for it is equivocal; the poet Shelley did not. He started as a split being, and ended as one, but his awareness of the division in his consciousness grew deeper, and produced finally the infernal vision of *The Triumph of Life*.

II

> But even supposing that a man should raise a dead body to life before our eyes, and on this fact rest his claim to being considered the son of God; the Humane Society restores drowned persons, and because it makes no mystery of the method it employs, its members are not mistaken for the sons of God. All that we have a right to infer from our ignorance of the cause of any event is that we do not know it ...
>
> (Shelley, *Notes On Queen Mab*)

The deepest characteristic of Shelley's poetic mind is its skepticism. Shelley's intellectual agnosticism was more fundamental than either his troubled materialism or his desperate idealism. Had the poet turned his doubt against all entities but his own poetry, while sparing that, he would have anticipated certain later developments in the history of literature, but his own work would have lost one of its most precious qualities, a unique sensitivity to its own limitations. This sensitivity can be traced from the very beginnings of Shelley's mature style, and may indeed have made possible the achievement of that style.

Shelley was anything but a born poet, as even a brief glance at his apprentice work will demonstrate. Blake at fourteen was a great lyric poet; Shelley at twenty-two was still a bad one. He found himself, as a stylist, in the autumn of 1815, when he composed the astonishing *Alastor*, a blank verse rhapsodic narrative of a destructive and subjective quest. *Alastor*, though it has been out of fashion for a long time, is nevertheless a great and appalling work, at once a dead end and a prophecy that Shelley finally could not evade.

Shelley's starting point as a serious poet was Wordsworth, and *Alastor* is a stepchild of *The Excursion*, a poem frigid in itself, but profoundly influential, if only antithetically, on Shelley, Byron, Keats, and many later poets. The figure of the Solitary, in *The Excursion*, is the central instance of the most fundamental of Romantic archetypes, the man alienated from others and himself by excessive self-consciousness. Whatever its poetic lapses, *The Excursion* is our most extensive statement of the Romantic mythology of the Self, and the young Shelley quarried in it for imaginatively inescapable reasons, as Byron and Keats did also. Though the poet-hero of *Alastor* is not precisely an innocent sufferer, he shares the torment of Wordsworth's Solitary, and like him:

> sees
> Too clearly; feels too vividly; and longs
> To realize the vision, with intense
> And over-constant yearning—there—there lies
> The excess, by which the balance is destroyed.

Alastor, whatever Shelley's intentions, is primarily a poem about the destructive power of the imagination. For Shelley, every increase in imagination ought to have been an increase in hope, but generally the strength of imagination in Shelley fosters an answering strength of despair. In the spring of 1815 Shelley, on mistaken medical advice, confidently expected a rapid death of consumption. By autumn this expectation was put by, but the recent imagining of his own death lingers on in *Alastor*, which on one level is the poet's elegy for himself.

Most critical accounts of *Alastor* concern themselves with the apparent problem of disparities between the poem's eloquent Preface and the poem itself, but I cannot see that such disparities exist. The poem is an extremely subtle internalization of the quest-theme of romance, and the price demanded for the internalization is first, the death-in-life of what Yeats called "enforced self-realization," and at last, death itself. The *Alastor* or avenging daemon of the title is the dark double of the poet-hero, the spirit of solitude that shadows him even as he quests after his emanative portion, the soul out of his soul that Shelley later called the epipsyche. Shelley's poet longs to realize a vision, and this intense and overconstant yearning destroys natural existence, for nature cannot contain the infinite energy demanded by the vision. Wordsworthian nature, and not the poet-hero, is the equivocal element in *Alastor*, the problem the reader needs to, but cannot, resolve. For this nature is a mirror-world, like that in Blake's "The Crystal Cabinet," or in much of Keats's *Endymion*. Its pyramids and domes are sepulchers for the imagination, and all its appearances are illusive, phantasmagoric, and serve only to thwart the poet's vision, and drive him on more fearfully upon his doomed and self-destructive quest. *Alastor* prophesies *The Triumph of Life*, and in the mocking light of the later poem the earlier work appears also to have been a dance of death.

The summer of 1816, with its wonderful products, "Mont Blanc" and the "Hymn to Intellectual Beauty," was for Shelley, as I have indicated, a rediscovery of the poetic self, a way out of the impasse of *Alastor*. The revolutionary epic, first called *Laon and Cyntha*, and then *The Revolt of Islam*, was Shelley's first major attempt to give his newly directed energies adequate scope, but the attempt proved abortive, and the poem's main distinction is that it is Shelley's longest. Shelley's gifts were neither for narrative nor for straightforward allegory, and the *terza rima* fragment, *Prince Athanase*, written late in 1817, a few months after *The Revolt of Islam* was finished, shows the poet back upon his true way, the study of the isolated imagination. Whatever the dangers of the subjective mode of *Alastor*, it remained always Shelley's genuine center, and his finest poems were to emerge from it. *Prince Athanase* is only a fragment, or fragments, but its first part at least retains something of the power for us that it held for the young Browning and the young Yeats. Athanase, from a Peacockian perspective, is quite like the delightfully absurd Scythrop of *Nightmare Abbey*, but if we will grant him his mask's validity we do find in him one of the archetypes of the imagination, the introspective, prematurely old poet, turning his vision outward to the world from his lonely tower of meditation:

> His soul had wedded Wisdom, and her dower
> Is love and justice, clothed in which he sate
> Apart from men, as in a lonely tower,
>
> Pitying the tumult of their dark estate.

There is a touch of Byron's Manfred, and of Byron himself, in Athanase, and Byron is the dominant element in Shelley's next enduring poem, the conversational *Julian and Maddalo*, composed in Italy in the autumn of 1818, after the poets had been reunited. The middle portion of *Julian and Maddalo*, probably based upon legends of Tasso's madness, is an excrescence, but the earlier part of the poem, and its closing lines, introduce another Shelley, a master of the urbane, middle style, the poet of the "Letter to Maria Gisborne," the "Hymn to Mercury," of parts of *The Witch of Atlas* and *The Sensitive Plant*, and of such beautifully controlled love lyrics as "To Jane: The Invitation" and "Lines Written in the Bay of Lerici." Donald Davie, who as a critic is essentially an anti-Shelleyan of the school of Dr. Leavis, and is himself a poet in a mode antithetical to Shelley's, has written an impressive tribute to Shelley's achievement as a master of the urbane style. What I find most remarkable in this mastery is that Shelley carried it over into his major achievement, the great lyrical drama, *Prometheus Unbound*, a work written almost entirely in the high style, on the precarious level of the sublime, where urbanity traditionally has no place. The astonishingly original tone of *Prometheus Unbound* is not always successfully maintained, but for the most part it is, and one aspect of its triumph is that critics should find it so difficult a tone to characterize. The urbane conversationalist, the relentlessly direct and emotionally uninhibited lyricist, and the elevated prophet of a great age to come join together in the poet of *Prometheus Unbound*, a climactic work which is at once celebratory and ironic, profoundly idealistic and as profoundly skeptical, passionately knowing its truths and as passionately agnostic towards all truth. More than any other of Shelley's poems, *Prometheus Unbound* has been viewed as self-contradictory or at least as containing unresolved mental conflicts, so that a consideration of Shelley's ideology may be appropriate prior to a discussion of the poem.

The clue to the apparent contradictions in Shelley's thought is his profound skepticism, which has been ably expounded by C.E. Pulos in his study, *The Deep Truth*. There the poet's eclecticism is seen as centering on the point "where his empiricism terminates and his idealism begins." This point is the skeptic's position, and is where Shelley judged Montaigne, Hume, and his own older contemporary, the metaphysician Sir William Drummond, to have stood. From this position, Shelley was able to reject both the French materialistic philosophy he had embraced in his youth and the Christianity that he had never ceased to call a despotism. Yet the skeptic's position, though it powerfully organized Shelley's revolutionary polemicism, gave no personal comfort, but took the poet to what he himself called "the verge where words abandon us, and what wonder if we grow dizzy to look down the dark abyss of how little we know." That abyss is Demogorgon's, in *Prometheus Unbound*, and its secrets are not revealed by him, for "a voice is wanting, the deep truth is imageless," and Demogorgon is a shapeless darkness. Yeats, sensing the imminence of his apocalypse, sees a vast image, a beast advancing before the gathering darkness. Shelley senses the great change that the Revolution has heralded, but confronts as apocalyptic harbinger only a fabulous and formless darkness, the only honest vision available to even the most apocalyptic of skeptics. Shelley is the most Humean poet in the language, oddly as his temperament accords with Hume's, and it is Hume, not Berkeley or Plato, whose view of reality informs *Prometheus Unbound* and the poems that came after it. Even Necessity, the dread and supposedly Godwinian governing demon of Shelley's early *Queen Mab*, is more of a Humean than a Holbachian notion, for Shelley's Necessity is "conditional, tentative and philosophically ironical," as Pulos points out. It is also a Necessity highly advantageous to a poet, for a power both sightless and unseen is a power removed from dogma and from philosophy, a power that only the poet's imagination can find the means to approach. Shelley is the unacknowledged ancestor of

Wallace Stevens' conception of poetry as the Supreme Fiction, and *Prometheus Unbound* is the most capable imagining, outside of Blake and Wordsworth, that the Romantic quest for a Supreme Fiction has achieved.

The fatal aesthetic error, in reading *Prometheus Unbound* or any other substantial work by Shelley, is to start with the assumption that one is about to read Platonic poetry. I mean this in either sense, that is, either poetry deeply influenced by or expressing Platonic doctrine, or in John Crowe Ransom's special sense, a poetry discoursing in things that are at any point legitimately to be translated into ideas. Shelley's skeptical and provisional idealism is *not* Plato's, and Shelley's major poems are mythopoeic, and not translatable into any terms but their own highly original ones. Shelley has been much victimized in our time by two rival and equally pernicious critical fashions, one that seeks to "rescue" visionary poetry by reading it as versified Plotinus and Porphyry, and another that condemns visionary poetry from Spenser through Hart Crane as being a will-driven allegorization of an idealistic scientism vainly seeking to rival the whole of experimental science from Bacon to the present day. The first kind of criticism, from which Blake and Yeats have suffered as much as Shelley, simply misreads the entire argument against nature that visionary poetry complexly conducts. The second kind, as pervasively American as the first is British, merely underestimates the considerable powers of mind that Shelley and other poets of his tradition possessed.

Shelley admired Plato as a poet, a view he derived from Montaigne, as Pulos surmises, and he appears also to have followed Montaigne in considering Plato to be a kind of skeptic. Nothing is further from Shelley's mind and art than the Platonic view of knowledge, and nothing is further from Shelley's tentative myths than the dogmatic myths of Plato. It is one of the genuine oddities of critical history that a tough-minded Humean poet, though plagued also by an idealistic and psuedo-Platonic heart, should have acquired the reputation of having sought beauty or truth in any Platonic way or sense whatsoever. No Platonist would have doubted immortality as darkly as Shelley did, or indeed would have so recurrently doubted the very existence of anything transcendent.

The most obvious and absolute difference between Plato and Shelley is in their rival attitudes toward aesthetic experience. Shelley resembles Wordsworth or Ruskin in valuing so highly certain ecstatic moments of aesthetic contemplation precisely because the moments are fleeting, because they occupy, as Blake said, the pulsation of an artery. For Shelley these are not moments to be put aside when the enduring light of the Ideas is found; Shelley never encounters such a light, not even in *Adonais*, where Keats appears to have found a kindred light in death. There is no ladder to climb in Shelley's poetry, any more than there is in Blake's. There are more imaginative states-of-being and less imaginative ones, but no hierarchy to bridge the abyss between them.

III

> It is no longer sufficient to say, like all poets, that minors resemble the water. Neither is it sufficient to consider that hypothesis as absolute and to suppose ... that mirrors exhale a fresh wind or that thirsty birds drink them, leaving empty frames. We must go beyond such things. That capricious desire of a mind which becomes compulsory reality must be manifested—an individual must be shown who inserts himself into the glass and remains in its illusory land (where there are figurations and colors but these are impaired by immobile silence) and feels the shame of being nothing more than an image obliterated by nights and permitted existence by glimmers of light.
>
> (Jorge Luis Borges)

It has been my experience, as a teacher of Shelley, that few recent students enjoy *Prometheus Unbound* at a first reading, and few fail to admire it greatly at a second or later reading. *Prometheus Unbound* is a remarkably subtle and difficult poem. That a work of such length needs to be read with all the care and concentration a trained reader brings to a difficult and condensed lyric is perhaps unfortunate, yet Shelley himself affirmed that his major poem had been written only for highly adept readers, and that he hoped for only a few of these. *Prometheus Unbound* is not as obviously difficult as Blake's *The Four Zoas*, but it presents problems comparable to that work. Blake has the advantage of having made a commonplace understanding of his major poems impossible, while Shelley retains familiar (and largely misleading) mythological names like Prometheus and Jupiter. The problems of interpretation in Shelley's lyrical drama are as formidable as English poetry affords, and are perhaps finally quite unresolvable.

It seems clear that Shelley intended his poem to be a millennial rather than an apocalyptic work. The vision in Act III is of a redeemed nature, but not of an ultimate reality, whereas the vision in the great afterthought of Act IV does concern an uncovered universe. In Act IV the imagination of Shelley breaks away from the poet's apparent intention, and visualizes a world in which the veil of phenomenal reality has been rent, a world like that of the Revelation of St. John, or Night the Ninth of *The Four Zoas*. The audacity of Shelley gives us a vision of the last things without the sanction of religious or mythological tradition. Blake does the same, but Blake is systematic where Shelley risks everything on one sustained imagining.

I think that a fresh reader of *Prometheus Unbound* is best prepared if he starts with Milton in mind. This holds true also for *The Prelude*, for Blake's epics, for Keats's *Hyperion* fragments, and even for Byron's *Don Juan*, since Milton is both the Romantic starting point and the Romantic adversary. Shelley is as conscious of this as Blake or any of the others; the Preface to *Prometheus Unbound* refers to that demigod, "the sacred Milton," and commends him for having been "a bold inquirer into morals and religion." Searching out an archetype for his Prometheus, Shelley finds him in Milton's Satan, "the Hero of Paradise Lost," but a flawed, an imperfect hero, of whom Prometheus will be a more nearly perfect descendant. Shelley's poem is almost an echo chamber for *Paradise Lost*, but all the echoes are deliberate, and all of them are so stationed as to "correct" the imaginative errors of *Paradise Lost*. Almost as much as Blake's "brief epic," *Milton*, Shelley's *Prometheus Unbound* is a courageous attempt to save Milton from himself, and for the later poet. Most modern scholarly critics of Milton sneer at the Blakean or Shelleyan temerity, but no modern critic of Milton is as illuminating as Blake and Shelley are, and none knows better than they did how omnipotent an opponent they lovingly faced, or how ultimately hopeless the contest was.

Paraphrase is an ignoble mode of criticism, but it can be a surprisingly revealing one (of the critic as well as the work of course) and it is particularly appropriate to *Prometheus Unbound*, since the pattern of action in the lyrical drama is a puzzling one. A rapid survey of character and plot is hardly possible, since the poem in a strict (and maddening) sense has neither, but a few points can be risked as introduction. Shelley's source is Aeschylus, insofar as he has a source, but his genuine analogues are in his older contemporary Blake, whom he had never read, and of whom indeed he never seems to have heard. Prometheus has a resemblance both to Blake's Orc and to his Los; Jupiter is almost a double for Urizen, Asia approximates Blake's Jerusalem, while Demogorgon has nothing in common with any of Blake's "Giant Forms." But, despite this last, the shape of Shelley's myth is very like Blake's. A unitary Man fell, and split into torturing and tortured components, and into separated male and female forms as well. The torturer is not in himself a representative of comprehensive evil, because he is quite limited; indeed, he has been invented by his victim, and falls soon after his victim ceases to hate his own invention. Shelley's Jupiter, like Urizen in one of his aspects, is pretty clearly the Jehovah of institutional and historical Christianity. George Bernard Shaw, one of the most enthusiastic of Shelleyans, had some illuminating remarks on *Prometheus Unbound* in *The Perfect Wagnerite*. Jupiter, he said, "is the almighty fiend into whom the Englishman's God had degenerated during two centuries of ignorant Bible worship and shameless commercialism." Shaw rather understated the matter, since it seems indubitable that the Jupiter of Shelley's lyrical drama is one with the cheerfully abominable Jehovah of *Queen Mab*, and so had been degenerating for rather more than two centuries.

Prometheus in Shelley is both the archetypal imagination (Blake's Los) and the primordial energies of man (Blake's Orc). Jupiter, like Urizen again, is a limiter of imagination and of energy. He may masquerade as reason, but he is nothing of the kind, being a mere circumscriber and binder, like the God of *Paradise Lost*, Book III (as opposed to the very different, creative God of Milton's Book VII). Asia is certainly not the Universal Love that Shaw and most subsequent Shelleyans have taken her to be. Though she partly transcends nature she is still subject to it, and she is essentially a passive being, even though the apparently central dramatic action of the poem is assigned to her. Like the emanations in Blake, she may be taken as the total spiritual form or achieved aesthetic form quested after by her lover, Prometheus. She is less than the absolute vainly sought by the poet-hero of *Alastor*, though she is more presumably than the mortal Emilia of *Epipsychidion* can hope to represent. Her function is to hold the suffering natural world open to the transcendent love or Intellectual Beauty that hovers beyond it, but except in the brief and magnificent moment-of-moments of her transfiguration (end of Act II) she is certainly not one with the Intellectual Beauty.

That leaves us Demogorgon, the poem's finest and most frustrating invention, who has been disliked by the poem's greatest admirers, Shaw and Yeats. Had Shaw written the poem, Demogorgon would have been Creative Evolution, and had Yeats been the author, Demogorgon would have been the Thirteenth Cone of *A Vision*. But Shelley was a subtler dialectician than Shaw or Yeats; as a skeptic, he had to be. Shaw testily observed that "flatly, there is no such person as Demogorgon, and if Prometheus does not pull down Jupiter himself, no one else will." Demogorgon, Yeats insisted, was a ruinous invention for Shelley: "Demogorgon made his plot incoherent, its interpretation impossible; it was thrust there by that something which again and again forced him to balance the object of desire conceived as miraculous and superhuman, with nightmare."

Yet Demogorgon, in all his darkness, is a vital necessity in Shelley's mythopoeic quest for a humanized or displaced theodicy. The Demogorgon of Spenser and of Milton was the evil god of chaos, dread father of all the gentile divinities. Shelley's Demogorgon, like the unknown Power of *Mont Blanc*, is morally unallied; he is the god of skepticism, and thus the preceptor of our appalling freedom to imagine well or badly. His only clear attributes are dialectical; he is the god of all those at the turning, at the reversing of the cycles. Like the dialectic of the Marxists, Demogorgon is a necessitarian and materialistic entity, part of the nature of things as they are. But he resembles also the shadowy descent of the Holy Spirit in most Christian dialectics of history, though it would be more accurate to call him a demonic parody of the Spirit, just as the whole of *Prometheus Unbound* is a dark parody of Christian salvation myth. Back of Demogorgon is Shelley's difficult sense of divinity, an apocalyptic humanism like that of Blake's, and it is not possible therefore to characterize *Prometheus Unbound* as being either humanistic or theistic in its ultimate vision. Martin Price, writing of Blake's religion, observes that "Blake can hardly be identified as theist or humanist; the distinction becomes meaningless for him. God can only exist within man, but man must be raised to a perception of the infinite. Blake rejects both transcendental deity and natural man." The statement is equally true for the Shelley of *Prometheus Unbound*, if one modifies rejection of transcendental deity to a skeptical opening toward the possibility of such a Power. Though Demogorgon knows little more than does the Asia who questions him, that little concerns his relationship to a further Power, and the relationship is part of the imagelessness of ultimates, where poetry reaches its limit.

The events of *Prometheus Unbound* take place in the realm of mind, and despite his skepticism Shelley at this point in his career clung to a faith in the capacity of the human mind to renovate first itself, and then the outward world as well. The story of the lyrical drama is therefore an unfolding of renovation after renovation, until natural cycle itself is canceled in the rhapsodies of Act IV. Of actions in the traditional sense, I find only one, the act of pity that Prometheus extends toward Jupiter at line 53 of Act I. Frederick A. Pottle, in the most advanced essay yet written on the poem, insists that there is a second and as crucial action, the descent of Asia, with her subsequent struggle to attain to a theology of love: "Asia's action is to give up her demand for an ultimate Personal Evil, to combine an unshakable faith that the universe is sound at the core with a realization that, as regards man, Time is radically and incurably evil." Behind Pottle's reading is a drastic but powerful allegorizing of the poem, in which Prometheus and Asia occupy respectively the positions of head and heart: "The head must sincerely forgive, must willingly eschew hatred on purely experimental grounds ..." while the heart "must exorcize the demons of infancy." One can benefit from this provisional allegorizing even if one finds *Prometheus Unbound* to be less theistic in its implications than Pottle appears to do.

Further commentary on the complexities of the poem can be sought in works listed in the bibliography of this volume, but the aesthetic achievement needs to be considered here. Dr. Samuel Johnson still knew that invention was the essence of poetry, but this truth is mostly neglected in our contemporary criticism. It may be justly observed that Shelley had conquered the myth of Prometheus even as he had transformed it, and the conquest is the greatest glory of Shelley's poem. One power alone, Blake asserted, made a poet: the divine vision or imagination, by which he meant primarily the inventive faculty, the gift of making a myth or of so re-making a myth as to return it to the fully human truths of our original existence as unfallen men. If Johnson and Blake were right, then *Prometheus Unbound* is one of the greatest poems in the language, a judgment that will seem eccentric only to a kind of critic whose standards are centered in areas not in themselves imaginative.

IV

> Nature has appointed us men to be no base or ignoble animals, but when she ushers us into the vast universe ... she implants in our souls the unconquerable love of whatever is elevated and more divine than we. Wherefore not even the entire universe suffices for the thought and contemplation within the reach of the human mind.
>
> (Longinus, *On the Sublime*)

Published with *Prometheus Unbound* in 1820 were a group of Shelley's major odes, including "Ode to the West Wind," "To a Skylark," and "Ode to Liberty." These poems show Shelley as a lyricist deliberately seeking to extend the sublime mode, and are among his finest achievements.

Wallace Stevens, in one of the marvelous lyrics of his old age, hears the cry of the leaves and knows "it is the cry of leaves that do not transcend themselves," knows that the cry means no more than can be found "in the final finding of the ear, in the thing / Itself." From this it follows, with massive but terrible dignity, that "at last, the cry concerns no one at all." This is Stevens' modern reality of *decreation*, and this is the fate that Shelley's magnificent "Ode to the West Wind" seeks to avert. Shelley hears a cry of leaves that do transcend themselves, and he deliberately seeks a further transcendence that will metamorphosize "the thing itself" into human form, so that at last the cry will concern all men. But in Shelley's "Ode," as in Stevens, "there is a conflict, there is a resistance involved; / And being part is an exertion that declines." Shelley too feels the frightening strength of the *given*, "the life of that which gives life as it is," but here as elsewhere Shelley does not accept the merely "as it is." The function of his "Ode" is apocalyptic, and the controlled fury of his spirit is felt throughout this perfectly modulated "trumpet of a prophecy."

What is most crucial to an understanding of the "Ode" is the realization that its fourth and fifth stanzas bear a wholly antithetical relation to one another. The triple invocation to the elements of earth, air, and water occupies the first three stanzas of the poem, and the poet himself does not enter those stanzas; in them he is only a voice imploring the elements to hear. In the fourth stanza, the poet's ego enters the poem, but in the guise only of a battered job, seeking to lose his own humanity. From this nadir, the extraordinary and poignantly "broken" music of the last stanza rises up, into the poet's own element of fire, to affirm again the human dignity of the prophet's vocation, and to suggest a mode of imaginative renovation that goes beyond the cyclic limitations of nature. Rarely in the history of poetry have seventy lines done so much so well.

Shelley's other major odes are out of critical favor in our time, but this is due as much to actual misinterpretations as to any qualities inherent in these poems. "To a Skylark" strikes readers as silly when they visualize the poet staring at the bird and hailing it as nonexistent, but these readers have begun with such gross inaccuracy that their experience of what they take to be the poem may simply be dismissed. The ode's whole point turns on the lark's being out of sight from the start; the poet *hears* an evanescent song, but can see nothing, even as Keats in the "Ode to a Nightingale" never actually sees the bird. Flying too high almost to be heard, the lark is crucially compared by Shelley to his central symbol, the morning star fading into the dawn of an unwelcome day. What can barely be heard, and not seen at all, is still discovered to be a basis upon which to rejoice, and indeed becomes an inescapable motive for metaphor, a dark justification for celebrating the light of uncommon day. In the great revolutionary "Ode to Liberty," Shelley successfully adapts the English Pindaric to an abstract political theme, mostly by means of making the poem radically its own subject, as he does on a larger scale in *The Witch of Atlas* and *Epipsychidion*.

In the last two years of his life, Shelley subtly modified his lyrical art, making the best of his shorter poems the means by which his experimental intellectual temper and his more traditional social urbanity could be reconciled. The best of these lyrics would include "Hymn of Apollo," "The Two Spirits: An Allegory," "To Night," "Lines ... on ... the Death of Napoleon," and the final group addressed to Jane Williams, or resulting from the poet's love for her, including "When the lamp is shattered," "To

Jane: The Invitation," "The Recollection," "With a Guitar, to Jane," and the last completed lyric, the immensely moving "Lines written in the Bay of Lerici." Here are nine lyrics as varied and masterful as the language affords. Take these together with Shelley's achievements in the sublime ode, with the best of his earlier lyrics, and with the double handful of magnificent interspersed lyrics contained in *Prometheus Unbound* and *Hellas*, and it will not seem as if Swinburne was excessive in claiming for Shelley a rank as one of the two or three major lyrical poets in English tradition down to Swinburne's own time.

The best admonition to address to a reader of Shelley's lyrics, as of his longer poems, is to slow down and read very closely, so as to learn what Wordsworth could have meant when he reluctantly conceded that "Shelley is one of the best artists of us all: I mean in workmanship of style":

> There is no dew on the dry grass tonight,
>   Nor damp within the shadow of the trees;
> The wind is intermitting, dry and light;
>   And in the inconstant motion of the breeze
> The dust and straws are driven up and down,
> And whirled about the pavement of the town.
> ("Evening: Ponte Al Mare, Pisa")

This altogether characteristic example of Shelley's workmanship is taken from a minor and indeed unfinished lyric of 1821. I have undergone many unhappy conversations with university wits, poets, and critics, who have assured me that "Shelley had a tin ear," the assurance being given on one occasion by no less distinguished a prosodist than W.H. Auden, and I am always left wondering if my ears have heard correctly. The fashion of insisting that Shelley was a poor craftsman seems to have started with T.S. Eliot, spread from him to Dr. Leavis and the Fugitive group of Southern poets and critics, and then for a time became universal. It was a charming paradox that formalist and rhetorical critics should have become so affectively disposed against a poet as to be incapable of reading any of his verbal figures with even minimal accuracy, but the charm has worn off, and one hopes that the critical argument about Shelley can now move on into other (and more disputable) areas.

V

> Cruelty has a Human Heart,
> And Jealousy a Human Face;

Terror the Human Form Divine,
And Secrecy the Human Dress.
The Human Dress is forged Iron,
The Human Form a fiery Forge,
The Human Face a Furnace seal'd,
The Human Heart its hungry Gorge.
                    (Blake, "A Divine Image")

The Cenci occupies a curious place in Shelley's canon, one that is overtly apart from the sequence of his major works that goes from *Prometheus Unbound* to *The Triumph of Life*. Unlike the psuedo-Elizabethan tragedies of Shelley's disciple Beddoes, *The Cenci* is in no obvious way a visionary poem. Yet it is a tragedy only in a very peculiar sense, and has little in common with the stage-plays it ostensibly seeks to emulate. Its true companions, and descendants, are Browning's giant progression of dramatic monologues, *The Ring and the Book*, and certain works of Hardy that share its oddly effective quality of what might be termed dramatic solipsism, to have recourse to a desperate oxymoron. Giant incongruities clash in *Prometheus Unbound* as they do in Blake's major poems, but the clashes are resolved by both poets in the realms of a self-generated mythology. When parallel incongruities meet violently in *The Cenci*, in a context that excludes myth, the reader is asked to accept as human characters beings whose states of mind are too radically and intensely pure to be altogether human. Blake courts a similar problem whenever he is only at the borderline of his own mythical world, as in *Visions of the Daughters of Albion* and *The French Revolution*. Shelley's Beatrice and Blake's Oothoon are either too human or not human enough; the reader is uncomfortable in not knowing whether he encounters a Titaness or one of his own kind.

Yet this discomfort need not wreck the experience of reading *The Cenci*, which is clearly a work that excels in character rather than in plot, and more in the potential of character than in its realization. At the heart of *The Cenci* is Shelley's very original conception of tragedy. Tragedy is not a congenial form for apocalyptic writers, who tend to have a severe grudge against it, as Blake and D.H. Lawrence did. Shelley's morality was an apocalyptic one, and the implicit standard for *The Cenci* is set in *The Mask of Anarchy*, which advocates a nonviolent resistance to evil. Beatrice is tragic because she does *not* meet this high standard, though she is clearly superior to every other person in her world. Life triumphs over Beatrice because she does take violent revenge upon an intolerable oppressor. The tragedy Shelley develops is one of a heroic character "violently thwarted from her nature" by circumstances she ought to have defied. This allies Beatrice with a large group of Romantic heroes, ranging from the Cain of Byron's drama to the pathetic daemon of Mary Shelley's *Frankenstein* and, on the cosmic level, embracing Shelley's own Prometheus and the erring Zoas or demigods of Blake's myth.

To find tragedy in any of these, you must persuasively redefine tragedy, as Shelley implicitly did. Tragedy becomes the fall of the imagination, or rather the falling away from imaginative conduct on the part of a heroically imaginative individual.

Count Cenci is, as many critics have noted, a demonic parody of Jehovah, and has a certain resemblance therefore to Shelley's Jupiter and Blake's Tiriel and Urizen. The count is obsessively given to hatred, and is vengeful, anal-erotic in his hoarding tendencies, incestuous, tyrannical, and compelled throughout by a jealous possessiveness even toward those he abhors. He is also given to bursts of Tiriel-like cursing, and like Tiriel or Jupiter he has his dying-god aspect, for his death, symbolizes the necessity of revolution, the breaking up of an old and hopeless order. Like all heavenly tyrants in his tradition, Cenci's quest for dominion is marked by a passion for uniformity, and it is inevitable that he seek to seduce the angelic Beatrice to his own perverse level. His success is an ironic one, since he does harden her into the only agent sufficiently strong and remorseless to cause his own destruction.

The aesthetic power of *The Cenci* lies in the perfection with which it both sets forth Beatrice's intolerable dilemma and presents the reader with a parallel dilemma. The natural man in the reader exults at Beatrice's metamorphosis into a relentless avenger, and approves even her untruthful denial of responsibility for her father's murder. The imaginative man in the reader is appalled at the degeneration of an all-but-angelic intelligence into a skilled intriguer and murderess. This fundamental dichotomy *in the reader* is the theater where the true anguish of *The Cenci* is enacted. The overt theme becomes the universal triumph of life over integrity, which is to say of death-in-life over life.

The Cenci is necessarily a work conceived in the Shakespearean shadow, and it is obvious that Shelley did not succeed in forming a dramatic language for himself in his play. Dr. Leavis has seized upon this failure with an inquisitor's joy, saying that "it takes no great discernment to see that *The Cenci* is very bad and that its badness is characteristic." It takes a very little discernment to see that *The Cenci* survives its palpable flaws and that it gives us what Wordsworth's *The Borderers*, Byron's *Cain*, and Coleridge's *Remorse* give us also in their very different ways, a distinguished example of Romantic, experimental tragedy, in which a crime against nature both emancipates consciousness and painfully turns consciousness in upon itself, with an attendant loss of a higher and more innocent state of being. The Beatrice of Shelley's last scene has learned her full autonomy, her absolute alienation from nature and society, but at a frightful, and to Shelley a tragic, cost.

VI

> But were it not, that *Time* their troubler is,
>   All that in this delightful Gardin growes,
>   Should happie be, and have immortall blis
> (Spenser)

In the spring of 1820, at Pisa, Shelley wrote *The Sensitive Plant*, a remarkably original poem, and a permanently valuable one, though it is little admired in recent years. As a parable of imaginative failure, the poem is another of the many Romantic versions of the Miltonic Eden's transformation into a wasteland, but the limitations it explores are not the Miltonic ones of human irresolution and disobedience. Like all of Shelley's major poems, *The Sensitive Plant* is a skeptical work, the skepticism here manifesting itself as a precariously poised suspension of judgment on the human capacity to perceive whether or not natural *or* imaginative values survive the cyclic necessities of change and decay.

The tone of *The Sensitive Plant* is a deliberate exquisitiveness, of a more-than-Spenserian kind. Close analogues to this tone can be found in major passages of Keats's *Endymion* and in Blake's *The Book of Thel*. The ancestor poet for all these visionary poems, including Shelley's *The Witch of Atlas* and the vision of Beulah in Blake's *Milton*, is of course Spenser, whose mythic version of the lower or earthly paradise is presented as the Garden of Adonis in *The Faerie Queene*, Book III, Canto VI, which is probably the most influential passage of poetry in English, if by "influential" we mean what influences other poets.

The dark melancholy of *The Sensitive Plant* is not Spenserian, but everything else in the poem to some extent is. Like many poems in this tradition, the lament is for mutability itself, for change seen as loss. What is lost is innocence, natural harmony, the mutual interpenetrations of a merely given condition that is nevertheless whole and beyond the need of justification. The new state, experiential life as seen in Part III of the poem, is the world without imagination, a tract of weeds. When Shelley, in the noblest quatrains he ever wrote, broods on this conclusion he offers no consolation beyond the most urbane of his skepticisms. The light that puts out our eyes is a darkness to us, yet remains light, and death may be a mockery of our inadequate imaginations. The myth of the poem—its garden, lady, and plant may have prevailed, while we, the poem's readers, may be too decayed in our perceptions to know this. Implicit in Shelley's poem is a passionate refutation of time, but the passion is a desperation unless the mind's imaginings can cleanse perception of its obscurities. Nothing in the poem proper testifies to the mind's mastery of outward sense. The "Conclusion" hints at what Shelley beautifully calls "a modest creed," but the poet is too urbane and skeptical to urge it upon either us or himself. The creed appears again in *The Witch of Atlas*, but with a playful and amiable disinterestedness that removes it almost entirely from the anguish of human desire.

The Witch of Atlas is Shelley's most inventive poem, and is by any just standards a triumph. In kind, it goes back to the English Renaissance epyllion, the Ovidian erotic-mythological brief epic, but in tone and procedure it is a new departure, except that for Shelley it had been prophesied by his own rendition of the Homeric "Hymn to Mercury." Both poems are in *ottava rima*, both have a Byronic touch, and both have been characterized accurately as possessing a tone of visionary cynicism. Hermes and the Witch of Atlas qualify the divine grandeurs among which they move, and remind us that the imagination unconfined respects no orders of being, however traditional or natural.

G. Wilson Knight first pointed to the clear resemblance between the tone of *The Witch of Atlas* and Yeats's later style, and there is considerable evidence of the permanent effect of the poem's fantastic plot and proper ties upon Yeats. Shelley's *Witch* is Yeats's "Byzantium" writ large; both poems deal with Phase 15 of Yeats's *A Vision*, with the phase of poetic incarnation, and so with the state of the soul in which art is created. In a comparison of the two poems, the immediate contrast will be found in the extraordinary relaxation that Shelley allows himself. The nervous intensity that the theme demands is present in the *Witch*, but has been transmuted into an almost casual acceptance of intolerable realities that art cannot mitigate.

The Witch of Atlas, as Shelley says in the poem's highly ironic dedicatory stanzas to his wife, tells no story, false or true, but is "a visionary rhyme." If the Witch is to be translated at all into terms not her own, then she can only be the mythopoeic impulse or inventive faculty itself, one of whose manifestations is the Hermaphrodite, which we can translate as a poem, or any work of art. The Witch's boat is the emblem of her creative desire, and like the Hermaphrodite it works against nature. The Hermaphrodite is both a convenience for the Witch, helping her to go beyond natural limitations, and a companion of sorts, but a highly inadequate one, being little more than a robot. The limitations of art are involved here, for the Witch has rejected the love of every mortal being, and has chosen instead an automaton of her own creation. In the poignant stanzas in which she rejects the suit of the nymphs, Shelley attains one of the immense triumphs of his art, but the implications of the triumph, and of the entire poem, are as deliberately chilling as the Byzantine vision of the aging Yeats.

Though the Witch turns her playful and antinomian spirit to the labor of upsetting church and state, in the poem's final stanzas, and subverts even the tired conventions of mortality as well as of morality, the ultimate impression she makes upon us is one of remoteness. The fierce aspirations of *Prometheus Unbound*, were highly qualified by a consciously manipulated prophetic irony, yet they retained their force, and aesthetic immediacy, as the substance of what Shelley passionately desired. The ruin that shadows love in *Prometheus Unbound*, the *amphisbaena* or two-headed serpent that could move downward and outward to destruction again, the warning made explicit in the closing stanzas spoken by Demogorgon; it is these antithetical hints that survived in Shelley longer than the vehement hope of his lyrical drama. *The Sensitive Plant* and *The Witch of Atlas* manifest a subtle movement away from that hope. *Epipsychidion*, the most exalted of Shelley's poems, seeks desperately to renovate that hope by placing it in the context of heterosexual love, and with the deliberate and thematic self-combustion of the close of *Epipsychidion* Shelley appears to have put all hope aside, and to have prepared himself for his magnificent but despairing last phase, of which the enduring monuments are *Adonais* and *The Triumph of Life*.

VII

> What man most passionately wants is his living wholeness and his living unison, not his own isolate salvation of his "soul." Man wants his physical fulfillment first and foremost, since now, once and once only, he is in the flesh and potent. For man, as for flower and beast and bird, the supreme triumph is to be most vividly, most perfectly alive. Whatever the unborn and the dead may know, they cannot know the beauty, the marvel of being alive in the flesh. The dead may look after the afterwards. But the magnificent here and now of life in the flesh is ours, and ours alone, and ours only for a time.
>
> (D.H. Lawrence, *Apocalypse*)

Except for Blake's *Visions of the Daughters of Albion*, which it in some respects resembles, *Epipsychidion* is the most outspoken and eloquent appeal for free love in the language. Though this appeal is at the heart of the poem, and dominates its most famous passage (lines 147–54), it is only one aspect of a bewilderingly problematical work. *Epipsychidion* was intended by Shelley to be his *Vita Nuova*, celebrating the discovery of his Beatrice in Emilia Viviani. It proved however to be a climactic and not an initiatory poem, for in it Shelley culminates the quest begun in *Alastor*, only to find after culmination that the quest remains unfulfilled and unfulfillable. The desire of Shelley remains infinite, and the only emblem adequate to that desire is the morning and evening star, Venus, at whose sphere the shadow cast by earth into the heavens reaches its limits. After *Epipsychidion*, in *Adonais* and *The Triumph of Life*, only the star of Venus abides as an image of the good. It is not Emilia Viviani but her image that proves inadequate in *Epipsychidion*, a poem whose most turbulent and valuable element is its struggle to record the process of image-making. Of all Shelley's major poems, *Epipsychidion* most directly concerns itself with the mind in creation. "Mont Blanc" has the same position among Shelley's shorter poems, and has the advantage of its relative discursiveness, as the poet meditates upon the awesome spectacle before him. *Epipsychidion* is continuous rhapsody, and sustains its lyrical intensity of a lovers' confrontation for six hundred lines. The mind in creation, here and in *A Defense of Poetry*, is as a fading coal, and much of Shelley's art in the poem is devoted to the fading phenomenon, as image after image recedes and the poet-lover feels more fearfully the double burden of his love's inexpressibility and its necessary refusal to accept even natural, let alone societal, limitations.

There is, in Shelley's development as a poet, a continuous effort to subvert the poetic image, so as to arrive at a more radical kind of verbal figure, which Shelley never altogether achieved. Tenor and vehicle are imported into one another, and the choice of natural images increasingly favors those already on the point of vanishing, just within the ken of eye and ear. The world is skeptically taken up into the mind, and there are suggestions and overtones that all of reality is a phantasmagoria. Shelley becomes an idealist totally skeptical of the metaphysical foundations of idealism, while he continues to entertain a skeptical materialism, or rather he becomes a fantasist pragmatically given to some materialist hypotheses that his imagination regards as absurd. This is not necessarily a self-contradiction, but it is a kind of psychic split, and it is exposed very powerfully in *Epipsychidion*. Who wins a triumph in the poem, the gambler with the limits of poetry and of human relationship, or the inexorable limits? Space, time, loneliness, mortality, wrong—all these are put aside by vision, yet vision darkens perpetually in the poem. "The world, unfortunately, is real; I, unfortunately, am Borges," is the ironic reflection of a great contemporary seer of phantasmagorias, as he brings his refutation of time to an unrefuting close. Shelley too is swept along by what destroys him and is inescapable, the reality that will not yield to the most relentless of imaginings. In that knowledge, he turns to elegy and away from celebration.

Adonais, Shelley's formal elegy for Keats, is a great monument in the history of the English elegy, and yet hardly an elegy at all. Nearly five hundred lines long, it exceeds in scope and imaginative ambition its major English ancestors, the *Astrophel* of Spenser and the *Lycidas* of Milton, as well as such major descendants as Arnold's Thyrsis and Swinburne's *Ave Atque Vale*. Only Tennyson's *In Memoriam* rivals it as an attempt to make the elegy a vehicle for not less than everything a particular poet has to say on the ultimates of human existence. Yet Tennyson, for all his ambition, stays within the bounds of elegy. *Adonais*, in the astonishing sequence of its last eighteen stanzas, is no more an elegy proper than Yeats's "Byzantium" poems are. Like the "Byzantium" poems (which bear a close relation to it), *Adonais* is a high song of poetic self-recognition in the presence of foreshadowing death, and also a description of poetic existence, even of a poem's state of being.

Whether Shelley holds together the elegiac and visionary aspects of his poem is disputable; it is difficult to see the full continuity that takes the poet from his hopeless opening to his more than triumphant close, from:

> I weep for Adonais—he is dead!
> O, weep for Adonais! though our tears
> Thaw not the frost which binds so dear a head!

to:

> I am borne darkly, fearfully, afar;
> Whilst, burning through the inmost veil of Heaven,
> The soul of Adonais, like a star,
> Beacons from the abode where the Eternal are.

From frost to fire as a mode of renewal for the self: that is an archetypal Romantic pattern, familiar to us from *The Ancient Mariner* and the *Intimations* Ode (see the contrast between the last line of stanza VIII and the first of stanza IX in that poem). But *Adonais* breaks this pattern, for the soul of Shelley's Keats burns through the final barrier to revelation only by means of an energy that is set against nature, and the frost that no poetic tears can thaw yields only to "the fire for which all thirst," but which no natural man can drink, for no living man can drink of the whole wine of the burning fountain. As much as Yeats's "All Souls' Night," *Adonais* reaches out to a reality of ghostly intensities, yet Shelley as well as Yeats is reluctant to leave behind the living man who blindly drinks his drop, and *Adonais* is finally a "Dialogue of Self and Soul," in which the Soul wins a costly victory, as costly as the Self's triumph in Yeats's "Dialogue." The Shelley who cries out, in rapture and dismay, "The massy earth and sphered skies are riven!", is a poet who has given himself freely to the tempest of creative destruction, to a reality beyond the natural, yet who movingly looks back upon the shore and upon the throng he has forsaken. The close of *Adonais* is a triumph of character over personality, to use a Yeatsian dialectic, but the personality of the lyric poet is nevertheless the dominant aesthetic element in the poem's dark and fearful apotheosis.

"Apotheosis is not the origin of the major man," if we are to credit Stevens, but the qualified assertions of Shelley do proclaim such an imaginative humanism in the central poems that preceded *Adonais*. In *Adonais* the imagination forsakes humanism, even as it does in the "Byzantium" poems.

Though *Adonais* has been extensively Platonized and Neoplatonized by a troop of interpreters, it is in a clear sense a materialist's poem, written out of a materialist's despair at his own deepest convictions, and finally a poem soaring above those convictions into a mystery that leaves a pragmatic materialism quite undisturbed. Whatever supernal apprehension it is that Shelley attains in the final third of *Adonais*, it is not in any ordinary sense a religious faith, for the only attitude toward natural existence it fosters in the poet is one of unqualified rejection, and indeed its pragmatic postulate is simply suicide. Nothing could be more different in spirit from Demogorgon's closing lines in *Prometheus Unbound* than the final stanzas of *Adonais*, and the ruthlessly skeptical Shelley must have known this.

He knew also though that we do not judge poems by pragmatic tests, and the splendor of the resolution to *Adonais* is not impaired by its implications of human defeat. Whether Keats lives again is unknown to Shelley; poets are among "the enduring dead," and Keats "wakes or sleeps" with them. The endurance is not then necessarily a mode of survival, and what flows back to the burning fountain is not necessarily the human soul, though it is "pure spirit." Or if it is the soul of Keats as well as "the soul of Adonais," then the accidents of individual personality have abandoned it, making this cold comfort indeed. Still, Shelley is not offering us (or himself) comfort; his elegy has no parallel to Milton's consolation in *Lycidas*:

> There entertain him all the Saints above,
> In solemn troops, and sweet Societies

That sing, and singing in their glory move,
And wipe the tears forever from his eyes.

To Milton, as a Christian poet, death is somehow unnatural. To Shelley, for all his religious temperament, death is wholly natural, and if death is dead, then nature must be dead also. The final third of *Adonais* is desperately apocalyptic in a way that *Prometheus Unbound*, Act IV, was not. For *Prometheus Unbound* ends in a Saturnalia, though there are darker implications also, but *Adonais* soars beyond the shadow that the earth casts into the heavens. Shelley was ready for a purgatorial vision of earth, and no longer could sustain even an ironic hope.

VIII

Mal dare, e mal tener lo mondo pulcro
    ha tolto loro, e posti a questa zuffa;
    qual ella sia, parole non ci appulcro.
                    (*Inferno* 7:58–60)

That ill they gave,
And ill they kept, hath of the beauteous world
Deprived, and set them at this strife, which needs
No labour'd phrase of mine to set it off.
                    (Cary, *The Vision of Dante*)

There are elements in *The Triumph of Life*, Shelley's last poem, that mark it as an advance over all the poetry he had written previously. The bitter eloquence and dramatic condensation of the style are new; so is a ruthless pruning of invention. The mythic figures are few, being confined to the "Shape all light," the charioteer, and Life itself, while the two principal figures, Shelley and Rousseau, appear in their proper persons, though in the perspective of eternity, as befits a vision of judgment. The tone of Shelley's last poem is derived from Dante's *Purgatorio*, even as much in *Epipsychidion* comes from Dante's *Vita Nuova*, but the events and atmosphere of *The Triumph of Life* have more in common with the *Inferno*. Still, the poem is a purgatorial work, for all the unrelieved horror of its vision, and perhaps Shelley might have found some gradations in his last vision, so as to climb out of the poem's impasse, if he had lived to finish it, though I incline to doubt this. As it stands, the poem is in hell, and Shelley is there, one of the apparently condemned, as all men are, he says, save for "the sacred few" of Athens and Jerusalem, martyrs to vision like Socrates, Jesus, and a chosen handful, with whom on the basis of *Adonais* we can place Keats, as he too had touched the world with his living flame, and then fled back up to his native noon.

The highest act of Shelley's imagination in the poem, perhaps in all of his poetry, is in the magnificent appropriateness of Rousseau's presence, from his first entrance to his last speech before the fragment breaks off. Rousseau is Virgil to Shelley's Dante, in the sense of being his imaginative ancestor, his guide in creation, and also in prophesying the dilemma the disciple would face at the point of crisis in his life. Shelley, sadly enough, was hardly in the middle of the journey, but at twenty-nine he had only days to live, and the imagination in him felt compelled to face the last things. Without Rousseau, Shelley would not have written the "Hymn to Intellectual Beauty," and perhaps not "Mont Blanc" either. Rousseau, more even than Wordsworth, was the prophet of natural man, and the celebrator of the state of nature. Even in 1816, writing his hymns and starting the process that would lead to the conception of *Prometheus Unbound*, Shelley fights against the natural man and natural religion, but he fights partly against his own desires, and the vision of Rousseau haunts him still in the "Ode to the West Wind" and in the greatest chant of the apocalyptic fourth act of the lyrical drama, the song of the Earth beginning "It interpenetrates my granite mass." Shelley knew that the spirit of Rousseau was what had moved him most in the spirit of the age, and temperamentally (which counts for most in a poet) it makes more sense to name Shelley the disciple and heir of Rousseau than of Godwin, or Wordsworth, or any of the later French theorists of Revolution. Rousseau and Hume make an odd formula of heart and head in Shelley, but they are the closest parallels to be found to him on the emotional and intellectual sides respectively.

Chastened and knowing, almost beyond knowledge, Rousseau enters the poem, speaking not to save his disciple, but to show him that he cannot be saved, and to teach him a style fit for his despair. The imaginative lesson of *The Triumph of Life* is wholly present in the poem's title: life always triumphs, for life, our life, is after all what the preface to *Alastor* called it, a "lasting misery and loneliness." One Power only, the Imagination, is capable of redeeming life, "but that Power which strikes the luminaries of the world with sudden darkness and extinction, by awakening them to too exquisite a perception of its influences, dooms to a slow and poisonous decay those meaner spirits that dare to abjure its dominion." In *The Triumph of Life*, the world's luminaries are still the poets, stars of evening and morning, "heaven's living eyes," but they fade into a double light, the light of nature or the sun, and the harsher and more blinding light of Life, the destructive chariot of the poem's vision. The chariot of

Life, like the apocalyptic chariots of Act IV, *Prometheus Unbound*, goes back
to the visions of Ezekiel and Revelation for its sources, as the chariots of
Dante and Milton did, but now Shelley gives a demonic parody of his
sources, possibly following the example of Spenser's chariot of Lucifera.
Rousseau is betrayed to the light of life because he began by yielding his
imagination's light to the lesser but seductive light of nature, represented
in the poem by the "Shape all light" who offers him the waters of natural
experience to drink. He drinks, he begins to forget everything in the
mind's desire that had transcended nature, and so he falls victim to Life's
destruction, and fails to become one of "the sacred few." There is small
reason to doubt that Shelley, at the end, saw himself as having shared in
Rousseau's fate. The poem, fragment as it is, survives its own despair, and
stands with Keats's *The Fall of Hyperion* as a marvelously eloquent imaginative testament, fit relic of an achievement broken off too soon to rival
Blake's or Wordsworth%, but superior to everything else in its own age.

IX

> The great instrument of moral good is the imagination.
>
> (A Defence of Poetry)

Anti-Shelleyans have come in all intellectual shapes and sizes, and
have included distinguished men of letters from Charles Lamb and De
Quincey down to T.S. Eliot, Allen Tate, and their school in our day. To distinguish between the kinds of anti-Shelleyans is instructive, though the following categories are by no means mutually exclusive. One can count six
major varieties of anti-Shelleyans, whether one considers them historically or in contemporary terms:

1. The school of "common sense"
2. The Christian orthodox
3. The school of "wit"
4. Moralists, of most varieties
5. The school of "classic" form
6. Precisionists, or concretists.

It is evident that examples of (1), (2), and (4) need not be confuted,
as they are merely irrelevant. We may deal with (3), (5), and (6) in their
own terms, rather than in Shelley's, and still find Shelley triumphant.

The "wit" of Shelley's poetry has little to do with that of seventeenth-
century verse, but has much in common with the dialectical vivacity of

Shaw, and something of the prophetic irony of Blake. If irony is an awareness of the terrible gap between aspiration and fulfillment, then the skeptical Shelley is among the most ironical of poets. If it is something else, as it frequently is in the school of Donne, one can observe that there are many wings in the house of wit, and one ought not to live in all of them simultaneously.

Form is another matter, and too complex to be argued fully here. The late C.S. Lewis justly maintained against the school of Eliot that Shelley was more classical in his sense of form, his balance of harmony and design, than Dryden. One can go further: Shelley is almost always a poet of the highest decorum, a stylist who adjusts his form and tone to his subject, whether it be the hammer-beat low style of *The Mask of Anarchy*, the urbane middle style of the *Letter to Maria Gisborne*, or the sublime inventiveness of the high style as it is renovated in *Prometheus Unbound*. Shelley was sometimes a hasty or careless artist, but he was always an artist, a poet who neither could nor would stop being a poet. Dr. Samuel Johnson would have disliked Shelley's poetry, indeed would have considered Shelley to be dangerously mad, but he would have granted that it was poetry of a high, if to him outmoded, order. Critics less classical than Johnson will not grant as much, because their notions of classical form are not as deeply founded.

The precisionist or concretist is probably Shelley's most effective enemy, since everything vital in Shelley's poetry deliberately strains away from the minute particulars of experience. But this is oddly true of Wordsworth as well, though Wordsworth usually insisted upon the opposite. The poetry of renovation in the United States, in our time, had its chief exemplars in William Carlos Williams and in Wallace Stevens, and it is Stevens who is in the line of both Wordsworth and of Shelley. Williams's famous adage, "no ideas but in things," is the self-justified motto of one valid kind of poetic procedure, but it will not allow for the always relevant grandeurs of the sublime tradition, with its "great moments" of ecstasy and recognition. Wordsworth on the mountainside looks out and finds only a sea of mist, an emblem of the highest imaginative vision, in which the edges of things have blurred and faded out. Stevens, opening the door of his house upon the flames of the Northern Lights, confronts an Arctic effulgence flaring upon the frame of everything he is, but does not describe the flashing auroras. Shelley, at his greatest, precisely chants an energetic becoming that cannot be described in the concrete because its entire purpose is to modify the concrete, to compel a greater reality to appear:

> ... the one Spirit's plastic stress
> Sweeps through the dull dense world, compelling there,

All new successions to the forms they wear;
Torturing th' unwilling dross that checks its flight
To its own likeness, as each mass may bear;
And bursting in its beauty and its might
From trees and beasts and men into the Heaven's light.

Had Shelley been able to accept any known faith, he would have given us the name and nature of that "one Spirit." Unlike Keats, he would not have agreed with Stevens that the great poems of heaven and hell had been written, and that only the great poem of earth remained to be composed. His own spirit was apocalyptic, and the still unwritten poems of heaven and hell waited mute upon the answering swiftness of his own imaginings, when he went on to his early finalities:

As if that frail and wasted human form,
Had been an elemental god.

John Keats

(1795-1821)

ONE OF THE CENTRAL THEMES IN W. J. BATE'S DEFINITIVE *JOHN KEATS* IS the "large, often paralyzing embarrassment ... that the rich accumulation of past poetry, as the eighteenth century had seen so realistically, can curse as well as bless." As Mr. Bate remarks, this embarrassment haunted Romantic and haunts post-Romantic poetry, and was felt by Keats with a particular intensity. Somewhere in the heart of each new poet there is hidden the dark wish that the libraries be burned in some new Alexandrian conflagration, that the imagination might be liberated from the greatness and oppressive power of its own dead champions.

Something of this must be involved in the Romantics' loving struggle with their ghostly father, Milton. The role of wrestling Jacob is taken on by Blake in his "brief epic" *Milton*, by Wordsworth in *The Recluse* fragment, and in more concealed form by Shelley in *Prometheus Unbound* and Keats in the first *Hyperion*. The strength of poetical life in Milton seems always to have appalled as much as it delighted; in the fearful vigor of his unmatched exuberance the English master of the sublime has threatened not only poets, but the values once held to transcend poetry:

> ... the Argument
> Held me a while misdoubting his Intent,
> That he would ruin (for I saw him strong)
> The sacred Truths to Fable and old Song
> (So Sampson grop'd the Temple's Posts in spite)
> The World O'erwhelming to revenge his sight.

The older Romantics at least thought that the struggle with Milton had bestowed a blessing without a crippling; to the younger ones a consciousness of gain and loss came together. Blake's audacity gave him a Milton altogether fitted to his great need, a visionary prototype who could be dramatized as rising up, "unhappy tho' in heav'n," taking off the robe of the promise, and ungirding himself from the oath of God, and then descending into Blake's world to save the later poet and every man "from his Chain of Jealousy." Wordsworth's equal audacity allowed him, after praising Milton's invocatory power, to call on a greater Muse than Urania, to assist him in exploring regions more awful than Milton ever visited. The prophetic Spirit called down in *The Recluse* is itself a child of Milton's Spirit that preferred, before all temples, the upright and pure heart of the Protestant poet. But the child is greater than the father, and inspires, in a fine Shakespearean reminiscence:

> The human Soul of universal earth,
> Dreaming on things to come.

Out of that capable dreaming came the poetic aspirations of Shelley and of Keats, who inherited the embarrassment of Wordsworth's greatness to add to the burden of Milton's. Yielding to few in my admiration for Shelley's blank verse in *Prometheus*, I am still made uneasy by Milton's ghost hovering in it. At times Shelley's power of irony rescues him from Milton's presence by the argument's dissonance with the steady Miltonic music of the lyrical drama, but the ironies pass and the Miltonic sublime remains, testifying to the unyielding strength of an order Shelley hoped to overturn. In the lyrics of *Prometheus* Shelley is free, and they rather than the speeches foretold his own poetic future, the sequence of *The Witch of Atlas*, *Epipsychidion* and *Adonais*. Perhaps the turn to Dante, hinted in *Epipsychidion* and emergent in *The Triumph of Life*, was in part caused by the necessity of finding a sublime antithesis to Milton.

With Keats, we need not surmise. The poet himself claimed to have abandoned the first *Hyperion* because it was too Miltonic, and his critics have agreed in not wanting him to have made a poem "that might have been written by John Milton, but one that was unmistakably by no other than John Keats." In the Great Odes and *The Fall of Hyperion* Keats was to write poems unmistakably his own, as *Endymion* in another way had been his own. Individuality of style, and still more of conception, no critic would now deny to the odes, Keats's supreme poems, or to *The Fall of Hyperion*, which was his testament, and is the work future poets may use as Tennyson, Arnold and Yeats used the odes in the past.

That Keats, in his handful of great poems, surpassed the Milton-haunted poets of the second half of the eighteenth century is obvious to a critical age like our own, which tends to prefer Keats, in those poems, to even the best work of Blake, Wordsworth and Shelley, and indeed to most if not all poetry in the language since the mid-seventeenth century. Perhaps the basis for that preference can be explored afresh through a consideration of precisely how Keats's freedom of the negative weight of poetic tradition is manifested in some of his central poems. Keats lost and gained, as each of the major Romantics did, in the struggle with the greatness of Milton. Keats was perhaps too generous and perceptive a critic, too wonderfully balanced a humanist, not to have lost some values of a cultural legacy that both stimulated and inhibited the nurture of fresh values.

Mr. Bate finely says, commenting on Keats's dedication sonnet to Leigh Hunt, that "when the imagination looks to any past, of course, including one's own individual past, it blends memories and images into a denser, more massive unit than ever existed in actuality." Keats's confrontation with this idealized past is most direct from the *Ode to Psyche* on, as Mr. Bate emphasizes. Without repeating him on that ode, or what I myself have written elsewhere, I want to examine it again in the specific context of Keats's fight against the too-satisfying enrichments with which tradition threatens the poet who seeks his own self-recognition and expressive fulfillment.

Most readers recalling the *Ode to Psyche* think of the last stanza, which is the poem's glory, and indeed its sole but sufficient claim to stand near the poet's four principal odes. The stanza expresses a wary confidence that the true poet's imagination cannot be impoverished. More wonderfully, the poet ends the stanza by opening the hard-won consciousness of his own creative powers to a visitation of love. The paradise within is barely formed, but the poet does not hesitate to make it vulnerable, though he may be condemned in consequence to the fate of the famished knight of his own faery ballad. There is triumph in the closing tone of *To Psyche*, but a consciousness also I think of the danger that is being courted. The poet has given Psyche the enclosed bower nature no longer affords her, but he does not pause to be content in that poet's paradise. It is not Byzantium which Keats has built in the heretofore untrodden regions of his mind but rather a realm that is precisely not far above all breathing human passion. He has not assumed the responsibility of an expanded consciousness for the rewards of self-communing and solitary musing, in the manner of the poet-hero of *Alastor*, and of Prince Athanase in his lonely tower. He seeks "love" rather than "wisdom," distrusting a reality that must be approached apart from men. And he has written his poem, in however light a spirit, as an act of self-dedication and of freedom from the wealth of the past. He will be Psyche's priest and rhapsode in the proud conviction that she has had no others before him, or none at least so naked of external pieties.

The wealth of tradition is great not only in its fused massiveness, but in its own subtleties of internalization. One does poor service by sandbagging this profoundly moving poem, yet even the heroic innovators but tread the shadowy ground their ancestors found before them. Wordsworth had stood on that ground, as Keats well knew, and perhaps had chosen a different opening from it, neither toward love nor toward wisdom, but toward a plain recognition of natural reality and a more sublime recognition-by-starts of a final reality that seemed to contain nature. Wordsworth never quite named that finality as imagination, though Blake had done so and the young Coleridge felt (and resisted) the demonic temptation to do so. Behind all these were the fine collapses of the Age of Sensibility, the raptures of *Jubilate Agno* and the *Ode on the Poetical Character*, and the more forced but highly impressive tumults of *The Bard* and *The Progress of Poesy*. Farther back was the ancestor of all such moments of poetic incarnation, the Milton of the great invocations, whose spirit I think haunts the *Ode to Psyche* and the *Ode to a Nightingale*, and does not vanish until *The Fall of Hyperion* and *To Autumn*.

Hazlitt, with his usual penetration, praises Milton for his power to absorb vast poetic traditions with no embarrassment whatsoever: "In reading his works, we feel ourselves under the influence of a mighty intellect, that the nearer it approaches to others, becomes more distinct from them." This observation, which comes in a lecture Keats heard, is soon joined by the excellent remark that "Milton's learning has the effect of intuition." The same lecture, in its treatment of Shakespeare, influenced Keats's conception of the Poetical Character, as Mr. Bate notes. Whether Keats speculated sadly on the inimitable power of Milton's positive capability for converting the splendor of the past into a private expressiveness we do not know. But the literary archetype of Psyche's rosy sanctuary is the poet's paradise, strikingly developed by Spenser and Drayton, and brought to a perfection by Milton. I am not suggesting Milton as a "source" for Keats's *Ode to Psyche*. Poets influence poets in ways more profound than verbal echoings. The paradise of poets is a recurrent element in English mythopoeic poetry, and it is perhaps part of the critic's burden never to allow himself to yield to embarrassment when the riches of poetic tradition come crowding in upon him. Poets need to be selective; critics need the humility of a bad conscience when they exclude any part of the poetic past from "tradition," though humility is never much in critical fashion. Rimbaud put these matters right in one outburst: "On n'a jamais bien jugé le romantisme. Qui l'aurait jugé? Les Critiques!!"

Milton, "escap't the *Stygian* pool," hails the light he cannot see, and reaffirms his ceaseless wanderings "where the Muses haunt / clear Spring, or shady Grove," and his nightly visits to "*Sion* and the flow'ry Brooks beneath." Like Keats's nightingale, he "sings darkling," but invokes a light that can "shine inward, and the mind through all her powers / Irradiate." The light shone inward, the mind's powers were triumphant, and all the sanctities of heaven yielded to Milton's vision. For the sanctuary of Milton's psyche is his vast heterocosm, the worlds he makes and ruins. His shrine is built, not to the human soul in love, but to the human soul glorious in its solitude, sufficient, with God's aid, to seek and find its own salvation. If Keats had closed the casement, and turned inward, seeking the principle that could sustain his own soul in the darkness, perhaps he could have gone on with the first *Hyperion*, and become a very different kind of poet. He would then have courted the fate of Collins, and pursued the guiding steps of Milton only to discover the quest was:

> In vain—such bliss to one alone
> Of all the sons of soul was known,
> And Heav'n and Fancy, kindred pow'rs,
> Have now o'erturned th'inspiring bow'rs,
> Or curtain'd close such scene from ev'ry future view.

Yeats, in the eloquent simplicities of *Per Amica Silentia Lunae*, saw Keats as having "been born with that thirst for luxury common to many at the outsetting of the Romantic Movement," and thought therefore that the poet of *To Autumn* "but gave us his dream of luxury." Yeats's poets were Blake and Shelley; Keats and Wordsworth he refused to understand, for their way was not his own. His art, from *The Wanderings of Oisin* through the *Last Poems and Plays*, is founded on a rage against growing old, and a rejection of nature. The poet, he thought, could find his art only by giving way to an anti-self, which "comes but to those who are no longer deceived, whose passion is reality." Yeats was repelled by Milton, and found no place for him in *A Vision*, and certainly no poet cared so little as Milton to express himself through an anti-self. In Blake's strife of spectre and emanation, in Shelley's sense of being shadowed by the *alastor* while seeking the epipsyche, Yeats found precedent for his own quest towards Unity of Being, the poet as daimonic man taking his mask from. a phase opposite to that of his own will. Like Blake and Shelley, Yeats sought certainty, but being of Shelley's phase rather than Blake's, he did not find it. The way of Negative Capability, as an answer to Milton, Yeats did not take into account; he did not conceive of a poet "certain of nothing but of the holiness of the Heart's affections and the truth of Imagination." (There is, of course, no irritable reaching after mere fact and reason in Yeats: he reached instead for everything the occult sub-imagination had knocked together in place of fact and reason. But his motive was his incapability "of being in uncertainties, mysteries, doubts," and the results are more mixed than most recent criticism will admit.)

Keats followed Wordsworth by internalizing the quest toward finding a world that answered the poet's desires, and he hoped to follow Shakespeare by making that world more than a sublime projection of his own ego. Shakespeare's greatness was not an embarrassment to Keats, but the hard victories of poetry had to be won against the more menacing values of poetic tradition. The advance beyond the *Ode to Psyche* was taken in the *Ode to a Nightingale*, where the high world within the bird's song is an expansion of the rosy sanctuary of Psyche. In this world our sense of actuality is heightened simultaneously with the widening of what Mr. Bate terms "the realm of possibility." The fear of losing actuality does not encourage the dull soil of mundane experience to quarrel with the proud forests it has fed, the nightingale's high requiem. But to be the breathing garden in which Fancy breeds his flowers is a delightful fate; to become a sod is to suffer what Belial dreaded in that moving speech Milton himself and the late C.S. Lewis have taught too many to despise.

Milton, invoking the light, made himself at one with the nightingale; Keats is deliberate in knowing constantly his own separation from the bird. What is fresh in this ode is not I think a sense of the poet's dialogue with himself; it is surprising how often the English lyric has provided such an undersong, from Spenser's *Prothalamion* to Wordsworth's *Resolution and Independence*. Keats wins freedom from tradition here by claiming so very little for the imagination in its intoxicating but harsh encounter with the reality of natural song. The poet does not accept what is as good, and he does not exile desire for what is not. Yet, for him, what is possible replaces what is not. There is no earthly paradise for poets, but there is a time of all-but-final satisfaction, the fullness of lines 35 to 58 of this ode.

I do not think that there is, before Keats, so individual a setting-forth of such a time, anywhere in poetic tradition since the Bible. The elevation of Wordsworth in *Tintern Abbey* still trembles at the border of a theophany, and so derives from a universe centered upon religious experience. The vatic gift of Shelley's self to the elements, from *Alastor* on, has its remote but genuine ancestors in the sibylline frenzies of traditions as ancient as Orphism. Blake's moments of delight come as hard-won intervals of rest from an intellectual warfare that differs little if at all from the struggles towards a revelatory awareness in Ezekiel or Isaiah, and there is no contentment in them. What Keats so greatly gives to the Romantic tradition in the *Nightingale* ode is what no poet before him had the capability of giving—the sense of the human making choice of a human self, aware of its deathly nature, and yet having the will to celebrate the imaginative richness of mortality. The *Ode to a Nightingale* is the first poem to know and declare, wholeheartedly, that death is the mother of beauty. The *Ode to Psyche* still glanced, with high good humor, at the haunted rituals of the already-written poems of heaven; the *Ode to a Nightingale* turns, almost casually, to the unwritten great poem of earth. There is nothing casual about the poem's tone, but there is a wonderful lack of self-consciousness at the poem's freedom from the past, in the poem's knowing that death, our death, is absolute and without memorial.

The same freedom from the massive beliefs and poetic stances of the past is manifested in the *Ode on a Grecian Urn*, where the consolations of the spirit are afforded merely by an artifice of eternity, and not by evidences of an order of reality wholly other than our own. Part of this poem's strength is in the deliberate vulnerability of its speaker, who contemplates a world of values he cannot appropriate for his own, although nothing in that world is antithetical to his own nature as an aspiring poet. Mr. Bate states the poem's awareness of this vulnerability: "In attempting to approach the urn in its own terms, the imagination has been led at the same time to separate itself—or the situation of man generally—still further from the urn." One is not certain that the imagination is not also separating itself from the essential poverty of man's situation in the poem's closing lines. Mr. Bate thinks we underestimate Keats's humor in the Great Odes, and he is probably right, but the humor that apparently ends the *Grecian Urn* is a grim one. The truth of art may be all of the truth our condition can apprehend, but it is not a saving truth. If this is all we need to know, it may be that no knowledge can help us. Shelley was very much a child of Miltonic tradition in affirming the moral instrumentality of the imagination; Keats is grimly free of tradition in his subtle implication of a truth that most of us learn. Poetry is not a means of good; it is, as Wallace Stevens implied, like the honey of earth that comes and goes at once, while we wait vainly for the honey of heaven.

Blake, Wordsworth, and Shelley knew in their different ways that human splendors had no sources but in the human imagination, but each of these great innovators had a religious temperament, however heterodox, and Keats had not. Keats had a clarity in his knowledge of the uniqueness and finality of human life and death that caused him a particular anguish on his own death-bed, but gave him, before that, the imagination's gift of an absolute originality. The power of Keats's imagination could never be identified by him with an apocalyptic energy that might hope to transform nature. It is not that he lacked the confidence of Blake and of Shelley, or of the momentary Wordsworth of *The Recluse*. He felt the imagination's desire for a revelation that would redeem the inadequacies of our condition, but he felt also a humorous skepticism toward such desire. He would have read the prose testament of Wallace Stevens, *Two Or Three Ideas*, with the wry approval so splendid a lecture deserves. The gods are dispelled in mid-air, and leave "no texts either of the soil or of the soul." The poet does not cry out for their return, since it remains his work to resolve life in his own terms, for in the poet is "the increasingly human self."

Part of Keats's achievement is due then to his being perhaps the only genuine forerunner of the representative post-Romantic sensibility. Another part is centered in the *Ode on Melancholy* and *The Fall of Hyperion*, for in these poems consciousness becomes its own purgatory, and the poet learns the cost of living in an excitement of which he affirms "that it is the only state for the best sort of Poetry—that is all I care for, all I live for." From this declaration it is a direct way to the generally misunderstood rigor of Pater, when he insists that "a counted number of pulses only is given to us of a variegated, dramatic life," and asks: "How may we see in them all that is to be seen in them by the finest senses?" Moneta, Keats's veiled Melancholy, counted those pulses, while the poet waited, rapt in an apprehension attainable only by the finest senses, nearly betrayed by those senses to an even more premature doom than his destined one. What links together *The Fall of Hyperion* and its modern descendants like Stevens's *Notes toward a Supreme Fiction* is the movement of impressions set forth by Pater, when analysis of the self yields to the poet's recognition of how dangerously fine the sells existence has become. "It is with this movement, with the passage and dissolution of impressions, images, sensations, that analysis leaves off—that continual vanishing away, that strange, perpetual weaving and unweaving of ourselves."

Though there is a proud laughter implicit in the *Ode on Melancholy*, the poem courts tragedy, and again makes death the mother of beauty. Modern criticism has confounded Pater with his weaker disciples, and has failed to realize how truly Yeats and Stevens are in his tradition. The *Ode on Melancholy* is ancestor to what is strongest in Pater, and to what came after in his tradition of aesthetic humanism. Pater's "Conclusion" to *The Renaissance* lives in the world of the *Ode on Melancholy*:

> Great passions may give us this quickened sense of life, ecstasy and sorrow of love, the various forms of enthusiastic activity, disinterested or otherwise, which come naturally to many of us. Only be sure it is passion—that it does yield you this fruit of a quickened, multiplied consciousness.

The wakeful anguish of the soul comes to the courter of grief in the very shrine of pleasure, and the renovating powers of art yield the tragedy of their might only to a strenuous and joyful seeker. Keats's problem in *The Fall of Hyperion* was to find again the confidence of Milton as to the oneness of his self and theme, but with nothing of the Miltonic conviction that God had worked to fit that self and theme together. The shrines of pleasure and of melancholy become one shrine in the second *Hyperion*, and in that ruin the poet must meet the imaginative values of tradition without their attendant credences, for Moneta guards the temple of all the dead faiths.

Moneta humanizes her sayings to our ears, but not until a poet's courteous dialectic has driven her to question her own categories for mankind. When she softens, and parts the veils for Keats, she reveals his freedom from the greatness of poetic tradition, for the vision granted has the quality of a new universe, and a tragedy different in kind from the tragedy of the past:

> Then saw I a wan face,
> Not pined by human sorrows, but bright-blanch'd
> By an immortal sickness which kills not;
> It works a constant change, which happy death
> Can put no end to; deathwards progressing
> To no death was that visage; it had pass'd
> The lily and the snow; and beyond these
> I must not think now, though I saw that face.
> But for her eyes I should have fled away.
> They held me back with a benignant light,
> Soft mitigated by divinest lids
> Half closed, and visionless entire they seem'd
> Of all external things—

Frank Kermode finds this passage a prime instance of his "Romantic Image," and believes Moneta's face to be "alive only in a chill and inhuman way," yet Keats is held back from such a judgment by the eyes of his Titaness, for they give forth "a benignant light," as close to the saving light Milton invokes as Keats can ever get. Moneta has little to do with the Yeatsian concept of the poetic vision, for she does not address herself to the alienation of the poet. M.H. Abrams, criticizing Mr. Kermode, points to her emphasis on the poet as humanist, made restless by the miseries of mankind. Shelley's Witch of Atlas, for all her playfulness, has more to do with Yeats's formulation of the coldness of the Muse.

Moneta is the Muse of mythopoeia, like Shelley's Witch, but she contains the poetic and religious past, as Shelley's capricious Witch does not. Taking her in a limited sense (since she incarnates so much more than this), Moneta does represent the embarrassments of poetic tradition, a greatness it is death to approach. Moneta's perspective is close to that of the Rilkean Angel, and for Keats to share that perspective he would have to cease to depend on the visible. Moneta's is a perfect consciousness; Keats is committed still to the oxymoronic intensities of experience, and cannot unperplex joy from pain. Moneta's is a world beyond tragedy; Keats needs to be a tragic poet. Rilke dedicated himself to the task of describing a world regarded no longer from a human point of view, but as it is within the angel. Moneta, like this angel, does not regard external things, and again like Rilke's angel she both comforts and terrifies. Keats, like Stevens, fears the angelic imposition of any order upon reality, and hopes to discover a possible order in the human and the natural, even if that order be only the cyclic rhythm of tragedy. Stevens's definitive discovery is in the final sections of *Notes toward a Supreme Fiction*; Keats's similar fulfillment is in his perfect poem, *To Autumn*.

The achievement of definitive vision in *To Autumn* is more remarkable for the faint presence of the shadows of the poet's hell that the poem tries to exclude. Mr. Bate calls the *Lines to Fanny* (written, like *To Autumn*, in October 1819) "somewhat jumbled as well as tired and flat," but its nightmare projection of the imagination's inferno has a singular intensity, and I think considerable importance:

> Where shall I learn to get my peace again?
> To banish thoughts of that most hateful land,
> Dungeoner of my friends, that wicked strand
> Where they were wrecked and live a wrecked life;
> That monstrous region, whose dull rivers pour,
> Ever from their sordid urns unto the shore,
> Unown'd of any weedy-haired gods;
> Whose winds, all zephyrless, hold scourging rods,
> Iced in the great lakes, to afflict mankind;
> Whose rank-grown forests, frosted, black, and blind,
> Would fright a Dryad; whose harsh herbag'd meads
> Make lean and lank the starv'd ox while he feeds;
> There flowers have no scent, birds no sweet song,
> And great unerring Nature once seems wrong.

This may have begun as a fanciful depiction of an unknown America, where Keats's brother and sister-in-law were suffering, yet it develops into a vision akin to Blake's of the world of experience, with its lakes of menace and its forests of error. The moss-lain Dryads lulled to sleep in the forests of the poet's mind in his *Ode to Psyche*, can find no home in this natural world. This is Keats's version of the winter vision, the more powerful for being so unexpected, and clearly a torment to its seer, who imputes error to Nature even as he pays it his sincere and accustomed homage.

It is this waste land that the auroras of Keats's *To Autumn* transform into a landscape of perfection process. Does another lyric in the language meditate more humanly "the full of fortune and the full of fate"? The question is the attentive reader's necessary and generous tribute; the critical answer may be allowed to rest with Mr. Bate, who is moved to make the finest of claims for the poem: "Here at last is something of a genuine paradise." The paradise of poets bequeathed to Keats by tradition is gone; a tragic paradise of naturalistic completion and mortal acceptance has taken its place.

There are other Romantic freedoms won from the embarrassments of poetic tradition, usually through the creation of new myth, as in Blake and Shelley, or in the thematic struggle not to create a myth, as in the earlier work of Wordsworth and Coleridge. Keats found his dangerous freedom by pursuing the naturalistic implications of the poet's relation to his own poem, and nothing is more refreshing in an art so haunted by aspirations to surpass or negate nature. Shelley, still joined to Keats in the popular though not the critical consciousness, remains the best poet to read in counterpoint to the Great Odes and *The Fall of Hyperion*. There is no acceptance in Shelley, no tolerance for the limits of reality, but only the outrageous desire never to cease desiring, the unflagging intensity that goes on until it is stopped, and never is stopped. Keats did what Milton might have done but was not concerned to do; he perfected an image in which stasis and process are reconciled, and made of autumn the most human of seasons in consequence. Shelley's ode to autumn is his paean to the West Wind, where a self-destroying swiftness is invoked for the sake of dissolving all stasis permanently, and for hastening process past merely natural fulfillment into apocalyptic renewal. Whether the great winter of the world can be relieved by any ode Keats tended to doubt, and we are right to doubt with him, but there is a hope wholly natural in us that no doubt dispels, and it is of this hope that Shelley is the unique and indispensable poet.

Alexandr Pushkin

(1799-1837)

PUSHKIN IS SOMETHING OF AN AMIABLE PUZZLE TO AN AMERICAN CRITIC who has no Russian, if only because the poet, who all Russian critics insist is the foremost in their language, and essentially untranslatable, nevertheless seems to survive translation so extraordinarily well. I have just read *Eugene Onegin* in the very different versions of Charles Johnston and Vladimir Nabokov, and found the verse novel a fascination twice over, though so Nabokovian in that rendering as to make me believe, at moments, that I was reading *Pale Fire*. Byron's *Don Juan* and Jane Austen's novels seem to blend in *Onegin*, though John Bayley usefully cautions that Pushkin had never heard of Austen. Bayley also warns that "Onegin is not Don Juan, or anything like him. Most emphatically he is not on easy terms with the consciousness of his creator." Pushkin made the most useful of critical remarks upon his own verse-novel when he charmingly observed, "Do you know my Tatyana has rejected Onegin. I never expected it of her." These are hardly the accents of George Gordon, Lord Byron, gossiping about his own characters.

The example of Sterne's *Tristram Shandy* does seem to be nearly as decisive for *Onegin* as Byron was. Nabokov, himself a Shandean writer, notes that Pushkin knew Sterne only in French versions, even as he knew Byron in French paraphrases. Whether I can know Pushkin any better than he knew Byron and Sterne is open to doubt, since translation is a puzzling art. Just as nearly every generation of poets declares against "poetical diction" and insists that it (at last!) is bringing poetry closer to the common language, so nearly every fresh wave of translators proclaims triumph over all the malefactors who have gone before. Since most poets, and all translators, of every era, write a period style, a gracious skepticism ought to be maintained as to what it is that we actually are reading, at any time.

Here is the conclusion of *Eugene Onegin*, first as Johnston renders it, and then in Nabokov's diction:

XLVIII

She went—and Eugene, all emotion,
stood thunder-struck. In what wild round
of tempests, in what raging ocean
his heart was plunged! A sudden sound,
the clink of rowels, met his hearing;
Tatyana's husband, now appearing ...
But from the hero of my tale,
just at this crisis of his gale,
reader, we must be separating,
for long ... for evermore. We've chased
him far enough through wild and waste.
Hurrah! let's start congratulating
ourselves on our landfall. It's true,
our vessel's long been overdue.

XLIX

Reader, I wish that, as we parted—
whoever you may be, a friend,
a foe—our mood should be warm-hearted.
Goodbye, for now we make an end.
Whatever in this rough confection
you sought—tumultuous recollection,
a rest from toil and all its aches,
or just grammatical mistakes,
a vivid brush, a witty rattle
God grant that from this little book
for heart's delight, or fun, you took,
for dreams, or journalistic battle,
God grant you took at least a grain.
On this we'll part; goodbye again!

L

And my companion, so mysterious,
goodbye to you, my true ideal,
my task, so vivid and so serious
and yet so light. All that is real
and enviable for a poet,

in your pursuit I've come to know it:
oblivion of life's stormy ways,
sweet talk with friends. How many days
since, through the mist that dreams arise on,
young Tanya first appeared to me,
Onegin too—and there to see,
a free romance's far horizon,
still dim, through crystal's magic glass,
before my gaze began to pass.

LI

Of those who heard my opening pages
in friendly gatherings where I read,
as Sadi sang in earlier ages,
'some are far distant, some are dead'.
They've missed Eugene's completed etching
But she who modelled for the sketching
of Tanya's image ... Ah, how great
the toll of those borne off by fate!
Blest he who's left the hurly-burly
of life's repast betimes, nor sought
to drain its beaker down, nor thought
of finishing its book, but early
has wished it an abrupt goodbye—
and, with my Eugene, so have I.

XLVIII

She has gone. Eugene stands
as if by thunder struck.
In what a tempest of sensations
his heart is now immersed!
But a sudden clink of spurs has sounded,
and Tatiana's husband has appeared,
and here my hero,
at an unkind minute for him,
reader, we now shall leave
for long ... forever.... After him
sufficiently we on one path
roamed o'er the world. Let us congratulate
each other on attaining land. Hurrah!
It long (is it not true?) was time.

XLIX

Whoever you be, O my reader—
friend, foe—I wish with you
to part at present as a pal.
Farewell. Whatever you in my wake
sought in these careless strophes—
tumultuous recollections,
relief from labors,
live pictures or bons mots,
or faults of grammar—
God grant that you, in this book,
for recreation, for the daydream,
for the heart, for jousts in journals,
may find at least a crumb.
Upon which, let us part, farewell!

L

You, too, farewell, my strange traveling companion,
and you, my true ideal,
and you, my live and constant,
though small, work. I have known with you
all that a poet covets:
obliviousness of life in the world's tempests,
the sweet converse of friends.
Many, many days have rushed by
since young Tatiana,
and with her Onegin, in a blurry dream
appeared to me for the first time—
and the far stretch of a free novel
I through a magic crystal
still did not make out clearly.

LI

But those to whom at friendly meetings
the first strophes I read—
"Some are no more, others are distant,"
As erstwhiles Sadi said.
Finished without them is Onegin's portrait.
And she from whom is fashioned
the dear ideal of "Tatyana" ...
Ah, fate has much, much snatched away!

> Blest who life's banquet early
> left, having not drained to the bottom
> the goblet full of wine;
> who did not read life's novel to the end
> and all at once could part with it
> as I with my Onegin.

Johnston writes in the mode of W.H. Auden and Louis MacNeice. We might be in Auden's *Letter to Lord Byron* when we read, "Hurrah! Let's start congratulating / ourselves on our landfall," but not when Nabokov writes, "Let us congratulate / each other on attaining land. Hurrah!" But then, we hear Nabokov pure in "to part at present as a pal," "live pictures or bon mots," "jousts in journals," and "did not read life's novel to the end." Johnston's Audenesque style is appropriate for a Winchester and Balliol man who entered the diplomatic service in 1936, while Nabokov's style is of course his peculiar strength, far surpassing any dubious grasp of psychological realities he ever possessed. Where Pushkin is in either of these versions, I cannot know, but reading them side by side a common gusto emerges which does not seem to be secondhand Auden, or Nabokovian preciosity, and I would suppose that this gusto, this fine verve, somehow belongs to Pushkin.

Perhaps that is why I cannot find in Onegin the "superfluous man," archetype of all those Russian novelistic heroes who waste their lives in mock elegance, or in Tatyana the model for all those superb heroines who represent, for the major Russian novelists, the sincerely passionate virtues of Russian womanhood. Doubtless, to Russian readers these identifications are inevitable, but to an American reader in 1986, particularly to one who despises historicisms, old and new, Pushkin's center is neither in societal observation nor in national archetypes. The novel in verse I have just enjoyed in two rather different versions tells me a story of lovers who are out of phase with one another. That sad irony of experience, that we fall in love in varying rhythms even when with one another, is beautifully exemplified in *Eugene Onegin*. Tatyana first falls in love with Eugene, but he falls in love with her belatedly and only when their appropriate time is past. Call him the belated man rather than the superfluous man and you apprehend his ironic condition, and your own.

Of the prose tales of Pushkin, the most powerful (in translation) is clearly the novella *The Queen of Spades*, though the fuller length of *The Captain's Daughter* does reveal some of Pushkin's more varied narrative resources. Paul Debreczeny has culminated a Russian critical tradition of reading *The Queen of Spades* as a Kabbalistic parable, and to Debreczeny's intricate unpacking of the story's dense symbolism I desire to add nothing. But as a critical Kabbalist myself, I know that a Kabbalistic parable, whether in Pushkin or Kafka, shows us that rhetoric, cosmology, and psychology are not three subjects but three in one, and so I turn to the psychology of *The Queen of Spades*.

What is the secret misfortune that the Countess, Queen of Spades, signifies? Does Hermann frighten her to death, or does she pass on to him the curse of St. Germain and so only then is able to die? What we know most surely about the Countess is that she was, is, and will be rancid, a fit mistress for St. Germain (if that is what she was). What we know most surely about Hermann is that he is just as rancid, but unlike the Countess he is trapped in irony every time he speaks. His most extraordinary entrapments come in the first and last sentences we hear him speak: "The game fascinates me, but I am not in the position to sacrifice the essentials of life in the hope of acquiring the luxuries," and the insane, repetitious mutter, "Three, seven, ace! Three, seven, queen!" He of course does sacrifice the true essentials of life, and the identification of the Countess with the Queen of Spades or death-in-life ironically substitutes for the ace of occult success the Kabbalistic crown that is at once a pinnacle and the abyss of nothingness.

Psychologically Hermann and the Countess are very similar, each being compounded of worldly ambition and the diabolic, but the Countess refuses to accept Hermann as her initiate until after she is dead. While alive, all that she will say to Hermann is "It was a joke." It is again a diabolic irony that Hermann answers, "There's no joking about it," since her final joke will render him insane, the joke being the Kabbalistic substitution of the Queen of Spades for the ace. Yet the Countess's apparition speaks in terms that cannot be reconciled with much in the story's overdetermined symbolism:

> "I have come to you against my will," she said in a firm voice, "but I have been ordered to fulfill your request. Three, seven, ace, played in that order, will win for you, but only on condition that you play not more than one card in twenty-four hours, and that you never play again for the rest of your life. I'll forgive you my death if you marry my ward, Lisaveta Ivanovna."

Is it St. Germain or the Devil himself, each presumably on the other side of life, who compels her to come? Whose is the lie, as to the last card, hers or a power beyond her? Why would she wish the horrible Hermann upon poor Lisaveta Ivanovna? Is it because she now cares for her ward, or is it malice towards all concerned? Why three days for the card game rather than one? I do not think that there are aesthetic answers to these questions. What matters, aesthetically, is that we are compelled to try to answer them, that we also are swept into this Kabbalistic narrative of compulsions, deceptions, betrayals, Napoleonic drives. Pushkin has created an overdetermined cosmos and placed us firmly within it, subject to the same frightening forces that his protagonists have to endure.

The trope that governs the cosmos of *The Queen of Spades* is Dantesque, purgatorial exile: "You shall learn the salt taste of another's bread, and the hard path up and down his stairs." That is Dante at Ravenna and Lisaveta Ivanovna in the house of the Countess, but those purgatorial stairs are ascended also by Hermann and the Countess, both to ill effect. The power of *The Queen of Spades* is both purgatorial and infernal, and the reader, who is exposed to both realms, herself or himself chooses the path of the parable, a narrow, winding stair up, or the madness of Hermann's descent, outwards and downwards into wintry night.

Elizabeth Barrett Browning

(1806-1861)

> Like the bright hair uplifted from the head
> Of some fierce Maenad ...
> —Shelley

IN THE UNIVERSITIES, COLLEGES AND SCHOOLS OF THE ENGLISH-SPEAKING world, the canon wars in one sense are pragmatically over, since the academies, joined by the media, have replaced virtually all aesthetic and cognitive standards by considerations of gender, race, ethnicity, sexual orientation, social class, and other irreducible resentments. There is however no necessary finality in this replacement. A considerable resistance still exists, even in the ruined academies, and an aesthetic underground has formed in many of those who staff the media. Much more important, as I have discovered throughout the last decade, there are hundreds of thousands of common readers, outside of the academies and the media, who are not contaminated by what has become fashionable "cultural criticism." I have given up all guest lecturing at academic institutions, and speak only on book tours, which are not intended as aesthetic revival meetings, but which hearten me nevertheless. One particularly mindless English Marxist cheerleader, waving his pom-poms, nastily compared me to Jimmy Swaggart, but as an aesthetic evangelist I happily acknowledge the influence of the divine Oscar Wilde, who would be rather startled to discover that Elizabeth Barrett Browning has eclipsed her husband, the creator of the strongest dramatic monologues in the English language.

I who have limped off too many canonical battlefields, acknowledge defeat in the academies, and am content to carry on the war elsewhere, and not in this essay. The partisans of Barrett Browning have much to say in her behalf, and many of those reprinted here say it eloquently. I have always loved Barrett Browning's "A Musical Instrument" best among her poems, so I will confine myself to an appreciation of its beauty, and a comparison of it to Shelley's "Hymn of Pan," a lyric at least equal in splendor.

II

Homer and Plato say that Pan, god of the woodlands, was the son of Hermes the messenger. As "panic" intimates, Pan has the effect of a sudden fear, like the night-terror he caused at Marathon, inducing the Persians to flee, and yet he was named "Pan" because, at his birth, he delighted all hearts, but particularly that of Dionysus, who recognized in the babe a kindred spirit of ecstasy. Attended by nymphs, Pan roams the wild places, and yet the other likely origin of his name means the "feeder" or herdsman, presumably of goats in Arcadia. Though sexually human, Pan has goats' ears and horns, and carries remarkably little mythology with him. His love affairs with Syrinx, Echo, and Pitys (nymph of the fir-tree) express his notorious amorousness, as does the music of his reed-pipe. Though Pan acquired no transcendental overtones, in the *Phaedrus* he is among the gods to whom Socrates appeals for an inward beauty.

Here is Barrett Browning's "A Musical Instrument," one of the best and most vitalizing lyrical poems in the language:

> What was he doing, the great god Pan,
>   Down in the reeds by the river?
> Spreading ruin and scattering ban,
> Splashing and paddling with hoofs of a goat,
> And breaking the golden lilies afloat
>   With the dragon-fly on the river.
>
> He tore out a reed, the great god Pan,
>   From the deep cool bed of the river;
> The limpid water turbidly ran,
> And the broken lilies a dying-lay,
> And the dragon-fly had fled away,
>   Ere he brought it out of the river.
>
> High on the shore sat the great god Pan
>   While turbidly flowed the river;
> And hacked and hewed as a great god can,
> With his hard bleak steel at the patient reed,

Till there was not a sign of the leaf indeed
    To prove it fresh from the river.

He cut it short, did the great god Pan
    (How tall it stood in the river!)
Then drew the pith, like the heart of a man.
Steadily from the outside ring,
And notched the poor dry empty thing
    In holes, as he sat by the river.

'This is the way,' laughed the great god Pan
    (Laughed while he sat by the river),
'The only way, since gods began
To make a sweet music, they could succeed.'
Then, dropping his mouth to a hole in the reed,
    He blew in power by the river.

Sweet, sweet, sweet, O Pan!
    Piercing sweet by the river!
Blinding sweet, O great god Pan!
The sun on the hill forgot to die,
And the lilies revived, and the dragon-fly
    Came back to dream on the river.

Yet half a beast is the great god Pan
    To laugh as he sits by the river,
Making a poet out of a man;
The true gods sigh for the cost and pain
For the reed which grows nevermore again
    As a reed with the reeds in the river.

Had she written often thus, she would be beyond praise, and I am puzzled that she did not cultivate her lyric powers. "A Musical Instrument" was published in 1860, a year before her death in Florence, and in it Barrett Browning rejoins the High Romantic vitalism of Shelley, Keats, the young Tennyson, and the young Browning. She knew Shelley's "Hymn of Pan," and I suspect she deftly writes an affectionate critique of it in her darker hymn of Pan:

I.
From the forests and highlands
    We come, we come;

From the river-girt islands,
    Where loud waves are dumb
        Listening to my sweet pipings.
The wind in the reeds and the rushes,
    The bees on the bells of thyme,
The birds on the myrtle bushes,
    The cicale above in the lime,
And the lizards below in the grass,
Were as silent as ever old Tmolus was,
    Listening to my sweet pipings.

II.

Liquid Peneus was flowing,
    And all dark Tempe lay
In Pelion's shadow, outgrowing
    The light of the dying day,
        Speeded by my sweet pipings.
The Sileni, and Sylvans, and Fauns,
    And the Nymphs of the woods and the waves,
To the edge of the moist river-lawns,
    And the brink of the dewy caves,
And all that did then attend and follow,
Were silent with love, as you now, Apollo,
    With envy of my sweet pipings.

III.

I sang of the dancing stars,
I sang of the daedal Earth,
And of Heaven—and the giant wars,
    And Love, and Death, and Birth—
        And then I change my pipings—
Singing how down the vale of Maenalus
    I pursued a maiden and clasped a reed.
Gods and men, we are all deluded thus!
    It breaks in our bosom and then we bleed:
All wept, as I think both ye now would,
If envy or age had not frozen your blood,
    At the sorrow of my sweet pipings.

I love both hymns, and appreciate their differences and originalities.
Shelley's Pan chants in the first person, but sings also for the nymphs who

accompany him, and addresses two auditors, Apollo and the reader. Pan's tone is sublimely exuberant and self-confident, content as he is to have subdued (aesthetically) all nature with his sweet pipings, which are the envy of Apollo, god of Poetry. A music of earth challenges and overgoes the Olympian art. There is both a high Shelleyan irony and a universal male lament in the exquisite:

> I pursued a maiden and clasped a reed.
> Gods and men, we are all deluded thus!

This omits the perspective of the maiden Syrinx, whose metamorphosis saved her from Pan's lust, and thus provided him with a reed he transformed into his musical instrument. Barrett Browning, with her own superb irony, shows us Pan turning a male into a reed-pipe, and at the close reveals that her exquisite lyric is a parable of the incarnation of the poetic character itself:

> Yet half a beast is the great god Pan
>   To laugh as he sits by the river,
> Making a poet out of a man;
> The true gods sigh for the cost and pain
> For the reed which grows nevermore again
>   As a reed with the reeds by the river.

I read this as a profound fable of the denaturalization of the male poet, as opposed to the female, with the "true" or Olympian gods showing a very uncharacteristic sorrow, as if they too had been feminized. That Barrett Browning had the gifts that would have made her into a great lyric poet, I do not doubt. What diverted them, into narrative and sonnet sequence, is a complex matter, not to be discussed in this brief context, but she does seem to me most herself in ballads and dramatic lyrics. Yet the matter of her canonical eminence, or lack of it, remains to be resolved, perhaps when our age of ideology passes into another time.

Robert Browning

(1812–1889)

ONE OF THE PRINCIPLES OF INTERPRETATION THAT WILL ARISE OUT OF THE future study of the intricacies of poetic revisionism, and of the kinds of misreading that canon-formation engenders, is the realization that later poets and their critical followers tend to misread strong precursors by a fairly consistent mistaking of literal for figurative, and of figurative for literal. Browning misread the High Romantics, and particularly his prime precursor, Shelley, in this pattern, and through time's revenges most modern poets and critics have done and are doing the same to Browning. I am going to explore Browning, in this essay, as the master of misprision he was, by attempting to show our tendency to read his epiphanies or "good moments" as ruinations or vastations of quest, and our parallel tendency to read his darkest visions-of-failure as if they were celebrations.

I will concentrate on a small group of Browning's poems including *Cleon*, *Master Hugues of Saxe-Gotha*, *A Toccata of Galuppi's*, *Abt Vogler*, and *Andrea del Sarto*, but I cannot evade for long my own obsession with *Childe Roland to the Dark Tower Came*, and so it and its contrary chant, *Thamuris Marching*, will enter late into this discourse. Indeed, I want to end with a kind of critical self-analysis, and ask myself the question: why am I obsessed by the *Childe Roland* poem, or rather, what does it *mean* to be obsessed by that poem? How is it that I cannot conceive of an antithetical practical criticism of poetry without constantly being compelled to use *Childe Roland* as a test case, as though it were the modern poem proper, more even than say, *Tintern Abbey* or *Byzantium* or *The Idea of Order at Key West*? is there a way to make these questions center upon critical analysis rather than upon psychic self-analysis?

In Browning's prose *Essay on Shelley*, there is an eloquent passage that idealizes poetic influence:

There is a time when the general eye has, so to speak, absorbed its fill of the phenomena around it, whether spiritual or material, and desires rather to learn the exacter significance of what it possesses, than to receive any augmentation of what is possessed. Then is the opportunity for the poet of loftier vision, to lift his fellows.... The influence of such an achievement will not soon die out. A tribe of successors (Homerides) working more or less in the same spirit, dwell on his discoveries and reinforce his doctrine; till, at unawares, the world is found to be subsisting wholly on the shadow of a reality, on sentiments diluted from passions, on the tradition of a fact, the convention of a moral, the straw of last year's harvest.

Browning goes on to posit a mighty ladder of authentic poets, in an objective and subjective alternation, who will replace one another almost endlessly in succession, concerning which, "the world dares no longer doubt that its gradations ascend." Translated, this means: "Wordsworth to Shelley to Browning," in which Browning represents a triumph of what he calls the objective principle. Against Browning's prose idealization, I will set his attack upon the disciples of Keats in his poem *Popularity*:

> And there's the extract, flasked and fine,
>> And priced and saleable at last!
> And Hobbs, Nobbs, Stokes and Nokes combine
>> To paint the future from the past,
> Put blue into their line.

For "Hobbs, Nobbs, Stokes and Nokes" we might read Tennyson, Arnold, Rossetti, and whatever other contemporary Keatsian, whether voluntary or involuntary, that Browning wished to scorn. But the next stanza, the poem's last, would surely have cut against Browning himself if for "John Keats" we substituted "Percy Shelley":

> Hobbs hints blue,—straight he turtle eats:
>> Nobbs prints blue,—claret crowns his cup:
> Nokes outdares Stokes in azure feats,—
>> Both gorge. Who fished the murex up?
> What porridge had John Keats?

The vegetarian Shelley, according to his friend Byron, tended to dine on air and water, not fit fare for the strenuously hearty Browning, who in his later years was to become London's leading diner-out. But though Browning seems not to have had the slightest *personal* consciousness of an anxiety of influence, he wrote the most powerful poem ever to be explicitly concerned with the problem. This is the dramatic monologue *Cleon*, in which the imaginary jack-of-all-arts, Cleon, is in my judgment a kind of version of Matthew Arnold, whose *Empedocles on Etna* Browning had been reading. Arnold's Empedocles keeps lamenting his own and the world's belatedness, a lament that becomes a curious kind of inauthentic overconfidence in Cleon's self-defense:

> I have not chanted verse like Homer, no—
> Nor swept string like Terpander, no—nor carved
> And painted men like Phidias and his friend:
> I am not great as they are, point by point.
> But I have entered into sympathy
> With these four, running these into one soul,
> Who, separate, ignored each other's art.
> Say, is it nothing that I know them all?

Browning could enjoy the belatedness, of Arnold or Rossetti, because no poet ever felt less belated than this exuberant daemon. We remember the malicious epithet applied to him by Hopkins: "Bouncing Browning." I think we can surmise that poetic belatedness as an affliction, whether conscious or unconscious, always rises in close alliance with ambivalence towards the prime precursor. Browning felt no ambivalence towards Shelley, such as Yeats had towards Shelley, or Shelley towards Wordsworth, or Wordsworth towards Milton. Browning loved Shelley unbrokenly and almost unreservedly from the age of fourteen, when he first read him, until his own death at the age of seventy-seven. But ambivalence is not the only matrix from which the anxiety of influence rises. There is perhaps a darker source in the guilt or shame of identifying the precursor with the ego-ideal, and then living on in the sense of having betrayed that identification by one's own failure to have become oneself, by a realization that the ephebe has betrayed his own integrity, and betrayed also the covenant that first bound him to the precursor. That guilt unmistakably was Browning's, as Betty Miller and others have shown, and so the burden of belatedness was replaced in Browning by a burden of dissimulation, a lying-against-the-self, rather than a lying-against-time.

But is not that kind of shame only another mask for the guilt-of-indebtedness, the only guilt that ever troubles a poet-as-poet? Certainly, Shelley for Browning was precisely the "numinous shadow" or ancestor god whose baleful influence is stressed by Nietzsche. Rather than demonstrate this too obviously, whether by recourse to Browning's poem Pauline or by an examination of the unhappy episode in which the young Browning yielded to his stern mother's Evangelical will, I think it more interesting to seek out what is most difficult in Browning, which is the total contrast between his optimism, a quality both temperamental and theoretical, and the self-destructive peculiarities of his men and women. I want to start by puzzling over the grotesque and unique poem, *Master Hugues of Saxe-Gotha*, with its curious and central contrast between the charming organist who speaks the monologue and the heavy pseudo-Bachian composer, also invented by Browning, whose name is the poem's title. The relationship between performer and composer is the poem. This relationship is *not* a displaced form of the ambivalence between ephebe and precursor, because the performer's reading/misreading of the composer is very different from the later poet's interpretation of an earlier one, or anyone's reading/misreading of any poet. It is true that a performance is an interpretation, but a performance lacks the vital element of revisionism that makes for fresh creation. The charm of the poem *Master Hugues of Saxe-Gotha*, like the chill of the somewhat similar but greater poem, *A Toccata of Galuppi's*, is precisely that we are free of the burden of misprision and that the performer in each poem is more like a reciter of a text than he is like a critic of a text. Yet it remains true that you cannot recite any poem without giving some interpretation of it, though I would hazard the speculation that even the strongest recital, acting, or performance is at best a weak reading/misreading, in the technical antithetical senses of "weak" and "strong," for again there is no strength, poetic or critical, without the dialectics of revisionism coming into play.

The organist earnestly wants to understand Hugues without revising him, but evidently the world is right and the poor organist wrong, in that less is meant than meets the ear in Hugues' mountainous fugues. Hugues is a kind of involuntary musical nihilist, who in effect would rather have the void as purpose than be void of purpose. The organist is not only old-fashioned in his devotion to Hugues but, as we might say now, old-fashioned in his devotion to meaning. Yet skepticism, a suspicion concerning both meaning-in-Hugues and meaning-in-life, has begun to gain strength in the organist, despite himself. His quasi-desperate test-performance of Hugues, thematically racing the sacristan's putting-out of the light, moves from one sadly negative conclusion to a larger negation, from "But where's music, the dickens?" to:

Is it your moral of Life?
    Such a web, simple and subtle,
Weave we on earth here in impotent strife,
    Backward and forward each throwing his shuttle,
Death ending all with a knife?

The very reluctance of the organist's interpretation convinces us of its relevance to Hugues. Hugues will not "say the word," despite the organist's plea, and the organist lacks the strength to break out on his revisionary own and do what he wants to do, which is "unstop the full-organ, / Blare out the *mode Palestrina*," akin to the gentle simplicity of his own nature. Yet we must not take the organist too literally; after all, there is nothing whatsoever to prevent him from playing Palestrina to his own satisfaction in the moments of light that remain to him. But it is the problematical, cumbersome, absurdly intricate Hugues who obsesses him, whose secret or lack of a secret he is driven to solve. Despite himself, the organist is on an antithetical quest, like absolutely every other monologist in Browning. The luminous last line of the poem is to be answered, emphatically: "Yes!"

While in the roof, if I'm right there,
    ... Lo you, the wick in the socket!
Hallo, you sacristan, show us a fight there!
    Down it dips, gone like a rocket.
What, you want, do you, to come unawares,
Sweeping the church up for first morning-prayers,
And find a poor devil has ended his cares
At the foot of your rotten-runged rat-riddled stairs?
    Do I carry the moon in my pocket?

If the organist is right, then the gold in the gilt roof is a better emblem of a final reality than the spider web woven by Hugues. But fortunately the darkening of the light breaks in upon an uneasy affirmation, and leaves us instead with the realization that the organist is subject as well as object of his own quest for meaning. Hugues goes on weaving his intricate vacuities; the organist carries the moon in his pocket. Has the poem ended, however humorously, as a ruined quest or as a good moment? Does Browning make it possible for us to know the difference between the two? Or is it the particular achievement of his art that the difference cannot be known? Does the organist end by knowing he has been deceived, or does he end in the beautiful earliness of carrying imagination in his own pocket, in a transumptive allusion to the Second Spirit in one of Browning's favorite poems, Shelley's *The Two Spirits: An Allegory*? There the Second Spirit, overtly allegorizing desire, affirms that the "lamp of love," carried within, gives him the perpetual power to "make night day." Browning is more dialectical, and the final representation in his poem is deeply ambiguous. But that is a depth of repression that I want to stay with, and worry, for a space, if only because it bothers me that *Master Hugues of Saxe-Gotha*, like so many of Browning's poems, ends in an *aporia*, in the reader's uncertainty as to whether he is to read literally or figuratively. Browning personally, unlike Shelley, was anything but an intellectual skeptic, and that he should create figures that abide in our uncertainty is at once his most salient and his most challenging characteristic.

A *Toccata of Galuppi's* can be read as a reversal of this poem, since it appears to end in the performer's conscious admission of belatedness and defeat. But Browning was quite as multi-form a maker as poetic tradition affords, and the *Toccata* is as subtle a poem as ever he wrote. It invokes for us a grand Nietzschean question, from the Third Essay of *On the Genealogy of Morals*: "What does it mean when an artist leaps over into his opposite?" Nietzsche was thinking of Wagner, but Browning in the *Toccata* may be another instance. Nietzsche's ultimate answer to his own question prophesied late Freud, if we take the answer to be: "All great things bring about their own destruction through an act of self-overcoming." I think we can say rather safely that no one was less interested in *Selbstaufhebung* than Robert Browning; he was perfectly delighted to be at once subject and object of his own quest. Like Emerson, whom he resembles only in this single respect, he rejoiced always that there were so many of him, so many separate selves happily picnicking together in a single psyche. From a Nietzschean point of view, he must seem only an epitome of some of the most outrageous qualities of the British empirical and Evangelical minds, but he is actually more sublimely outrageous even than that. There are no dialectics that can subsume him, because he is not so much evasive as he is preternatural, wholly daemonic, with an astonishing alliance perpetual in him between an impish cunning and endless linguistic energy. I think we can surmise why he was so fascinated by poets like Christopher Smart and Thomas Lovell Beddoes, poets who represented the tradition of Dissenting Enthusiasm carried over into actual madness. With energies like Browning's, and self-confidence like Browning's, it took a mind as powerful as Browning's to avoid being carried by Enthusiasm into alienation, but perhaps the oddest of all Browning's endless oddities is that he was incurably sane, even as he imagined his gallery of pathological enthusiasts, monomaniacs, and marvelous charlatans.

There are at least four voices coldly leaping along in *A Toccata of Galuppi's*, and only one of them is more or less Browning's, and we cannot be certain even of that. Let us break in for the poem's conclusion, as the monologist first addresses the composer whose "touch-piece" he is playing, and next the composer answers back, *but only through the monologist's performance*, and finally the speaker-performer acknowledges his defeat by the heartlessly brilliant Galuppi:

> XI
>
> But when I sit down to reason, think to take my stand nor
>   swerve,
> While I triumph o'er a secret wrung from nature's close
>   reserve,
> In you come with your cold music till I creep through every
>   nerve.
>
> XII
>
> Yes, you, like a ghostly cricket, creaking where a house was
>   burned:
> 'Dust and ashes, dead and done with, Venice spent what Venice
>   earned.
> The soul, doubtless, is immortal—where a soul can be
>   discerned.
>
> XIII
>
> 'Yours, for instance: you know physics, something of geology,
> Mathematics are your pastime; souls shall rise in their degree;
> Butterflies may dread extinction,—you'll not die, it cannot be!
>
> XIV
>
> 'As for Venice and her people, merely born to bloom and drop,
> Here on earth they bore their fruitage, mirth and folly were the
>   crop:
> What of soul was left, I wonder, when,the kissing had to stop?
>
> XV
>
> 'Dust and ashes!' So you creak it, and I want the heart to scold.
> Dear dead women, with such hair, too—what's become of all
>   the gold
> Used to hang and brush their bosoms? I feel chilly and grown old.

The, "swerve" is the Lucretian *clinamen*, and we might say that Galuppi, like Lucretius, assaults the monologist-performer with the full strength of the Epicurean argument. One possible interpretation is that Browning, as a fierce Transcendentalist of his own sect, a sect of one, is hammering at the Victorian spiritual compromise, which his cultivated speaker exemplifies. That interpretation would confirm the poem's serio-comic opening:

> Oh Galuppi, Baldassaro, this is very sad to find!
> I can hardly misconceive you; it would prove me deaf and blind;
> But although I take your meaning, 'tis with such a heavy mind!

Galuppi's triumph, on this reading, would be the dramatic one of shaking up this cultivated monologist, who first half-scoffs at Galuppi's nihilism, but who ends genuinely frightened by the lesson Galuppi has taught which is a lesson of mortality and consequent meaninglessness. But I think that is to underestimate the monologist, who is a more consider-able temperament even than the organist who plays Hugues and can bear neither to give Hugues up nor accept Hugues' emptiness. Galuppi is no Hugues, but a powerfully sophisticated artist who gives what was wanted of him, but with a Dance-of-Death aspect playing against his audience's desires. And the speaker, who knows physics, some geology, a little math-ematics, and will not quite abandon his Christian immortality, is at least as enigmatic as the organist, and for a parallel reason. Why cannot he let Galuppi alone? What does he quest for in seeing how well he can perform that spirited and elegant art? Far more even than Galuppi, or Galuppi's audience, or than Browning, the speaker is obsessed with mortality:

> Then they left you for their pleasure: till in due time, one by one,
> Some with lives that came to nothing, some with deeds as well undone,
> Death stepped tacitly and took them where they never see the sun.

One of the most moving elements in the poem is its erotic nostalgia, undoubtedly the single sphere of identity between the monologist and Browning himself. Eros crowds the poem, with an intensity and poignance almost Shakespearean in its strength. Nothing in the poem is at once so moving and so shocking as the monologist's final "Dear dead women, with such hair, too—," for this spiritual trimmer is very much a sensual man, like his robust creator. It is the cold Galuppi who is more the dualist, more the artist fulfilling the Nietzschean insight that the ascetic ideal is a defen-sive evasion by which art preserves itself against the truth. But where, as readers, does that leave us, since this time Browning elegantly has cleared himself away? His overt intention is pretty clear, and I think pretty irrelevant also. He wants us—unlike the monologist, unlike Galuppi, unlike Galuppi's hard-living men and women—to resort to his ferocious version of an antithetical Protestantism, which is I think ultimately his misprision of Shelley's antithetical humanism. Yet Browning's art has freed us of Browning, though paradoxically not of Shelley, or at least of the strong Lucretian element in Shelley. Has the monologist quested after Galuppi's truth, only to end up in a vastation of his own comforting evasions of the truth? That would be the canonical reading, but it would overliteralize a metaleptic figuration that knowingly has chosen not to attempt a reversal of time. When the speaker ends by feeling "chilly and grown old," then he has introjected Galuppi's world and Galuppi's music, and projected his own compromise formulations. But this is an *illusio*, a metaleptic figuration that is on the verge of becoming an opening irony or reaction-formation again, that is, rejoining the tone of jocular evasion that began the poem. Nothing has happened because nothing has changed, and the final grimness of Browning's eerie poem is that its speaker is caught in a repetition. He will pause awhile, and then play a toccata of Galuppi's again.

Let us try a third music-poem or improvisation, the still more formidable Abt Vogler, where the daemonic performer is also the momentary composer, inventing fitfully upon an instrument of his own invention, grandly solitary because there is nothing for him to interpret except his own interpretation of his own creation. The canonical readings available here are too weak to be interesting, since they actually represent the poem as being pious. The historical Vogler was regarded by some as a pious fraud, but Browning's Vogler is too complex to be regarded either as an impostor or as sincerely devout. What matters most is that he is primarily an extemporizer, rather than necessarily an artist, whether as performer or composer. The poem leaves open (whatever Browning's intentions) the problem of whether Vogler is a skilled illusionist, or something more than that. At the least, Vogler is self-deceived, but even the self-deception is most complex. It is worth knowing what I must assume that Browning knew: Vogler's self-invented instruments sounded splendid only when played by Vogler. Though the great temptation in reading this poem is to interpret it as a good moment precariously attained, and then lost, I think the stronger or antithetical reading here will show that this is very nearly as much a poem of ruined quest, as *Childe Roland* or *Andrea del Sarto* is.

Abt Vogler is one of those poems that explain Yeats's remark to the effect that he feared Browning as a potentially dangerous influence upon him. If we could read *Abt Vogler* without interpretative suspicion (and I believe we cannot), then the poem would seem to be a way-station between the closing third of *Adonais* and Yeats's Byzantium poems. It establishes itself in a state of being that seems either to be beyond the antithesis of life and death, or else that seems to be the state of art itself. Yet, in the poem *Abt Vogler*, I think we have neither, but something more puzzling, a willed phantasmagoria that is partly Browning's and partly an oddity, a purely visionary dramatic monologue.

Vogler, we ought to realize immediately, does not seek the purposes of art, which after all is hard work. Vogler is daydreaming, and is seeking a magical power over nature or supernature, as in the debased Kabbalist myth of Solomon's seal. Vogler is not so much playing his organ as enslaving it to his magical purposes, purposes that do not distinguish between angel and demon, heaven and hell. Vogler is no Blakean visionary; he seeks not to marry heaven and hell, but merely to achieve every power that he can. And yet he has a moving purpose, akin to Shelley's in *Prometheus Unbound*, which is to aid earth's mounting into heaven. But, is his vision proper something we can grant the prestige of vision, or is there not a dubious element in it?

Being made perfect, when the subject is someone like Vogler, is a somewhat chancy phenomenon. Unlike the sublimely crazy Johannes Agricola, in one of Browning's earliest and most frightening dramatic monologues, Vogler is not a genuine Enthusiast, certain of his own Election. Stanza VI has a touch of *Cleon* about it, and stanza VII is clearly *unheimlich*, despite the miraculous line: "That out of three sounds he frame, not a fourth sound, but a star." But with stanzas VIII and IX, which are this poem's *askesis* or sublimation, it is not so easy to distinguish Vogler from Browning, or one of the beings always bouncing around in Browning, anyway:

VIII

Well, it is gone at last, the palace of music I reared;
 Gone! and the good tears start, the praises that come too slow;
For one is assured at first, one scarce can say that he feared,
 That he even gave it a thought, the gone thing was to go.
Never to be again! But many more of the kind
 As good, nay, better perchance: is this your comfort to me?
To me, who must be saved because I cling with my mind
 To the same, same self, same love, same God: ay, what was, shall be.

IX

Therefore to whom turn I but to thee, the ineffable Name?

> Builder and maker, thou, of houses not made with hands!
>   What, have fear of change from thee who art ever the same?
>   Doubt that thy power can fill the heart that thy power expands?
> There shall never be one lost good! What was, shall live as before;
>   The evil is null, is nought, is silence implying sound;
> What was good shall be good, with, for evil, so much good more;
>   On the earth the broken arcs; in the heaven, a perfect round.

The poem, from here to the end, in the three final stanzas, is suddenly as much Browning's Magnificat as the *Song to David*, which is deliberately echoed in the penultimate line, is Smart's. But what does that mean, whether in this poem, or whether about Browning himself? Surely he would not acknowledge, openly, that his is the art of the extemporizer, the illusionist improvising? Probably not, but the poem may be acknowledging an anxiety that he possesses, to much that effect. Whether this is so or not, to any degree, how are we to read the final stanza?

> Well, it is earth with me; silence resumes her reign:
>   I will be patient and proud, and soberly acquiesce.
> Give me the keys. I feel for the common chord again,
>   Sliding by semitones, till I sink to the minor,—yes,
> And I blunt it into a ninth, and I stand on alien ground,
>   Surveying awhile the heights I rolled from into the deep;
> Which, hark, I have dared and done, for my resting-place is found,
>   The C Major of this life: so now I will try to sleep.

This descent to C Major separates Vogler totally from Browning again, since of the many keys in which the genuinely musical Browning composes, his resting place is hardly a key without sharps or flats. Browning has his direct imitation of Smart's *Song to David* in his own overtly religious poem, *Saul*, and so we can be reasonably certain that Vogler does not speak for Browning when the improviser belatedly stands on alien ground, surveying the Sublime he had attained, and echoes Smart's final lines:

> Thou at stupendous truth believ'd;—
> And now the matchless deed's achiev'd,
>   DETERMINED, DARED, and DONE.

What Vogler has dared and done is no more than to have dreamed a belated dream; where Browning is, in regard to that Promethean or

Shelleyan a dream, is an enigma, at least in this poem. What *Abt Vogler*, as a text, appears to proclaim is the impossibility of our reading it, insofar as reading means being able to govern the interplay of literal and figurative meanings in a text. Canonically, in terms of all received readings, this poem is almost an apocalyptic version of a Browningesque "Good Moment," a time of privilege or an epiphany, a sudden manifestation of highest vision. Yet the patterns of revisionary misprision are clearly marked upon the poem, and they tend to indicate that the poem demands to be read figuratively against its own letter, as another parable of ruined quest, or confession or imaginative failure, or the shame of knowing such failure.

I turn to *Andrea del Sarto*, which with *Childe Roland to the Dark Tower Came*, and the meditation entitled *The Pope* in *The Ring and the Book*, seems to me to represent Browning at his greatest. Here there would appear to be no question about the main issue of interpretation, for the canonical readings seem fairly close to the poem in its proclamation that this artist's quest is ruined, that Andrea stands self-condemned by his own monologue. Betty Miller has juxtaposed the poem, brilliantly, with this troubled and troublesome passage in Browning's *Essay on Shelley*:

> Although of such depths of failure there can be no question here we must in every case betake ourselves to the review of a poet's life ere we determine some of the nicer questions concerning his poetry,—more especially if the performance we seek to estimate aright, has been obstructed and cut short of completion by circumstances,—a disastrous youth or a premature death. We may learn from the biography whether his spirit invariably saw and spoke from the last height to which it had attained. An absolute vision is not for this world, but we are permitted a continual approximation to it, every degree of which in the individual, provided it exceed the attainment of the masses, must procure him a clear advantage. Did the poet ever attain to a higher platform than where he rested and exhibited a result? Did he know more than he spoke of?

On this juxtaposition, Andrea and Browning alike rested on a level lower than the more absolute vision they could have attained. Certainly Andrea tells us, perhaps even shows us, that he knows more than he paints. But Browning? If he was no Shelley, he was also no Andrea, which in part is the burden of the poem. But only in part, and whether there is some level of *apologia* in this monologue, in its patterning, rather than its overt content, is presumably a question that a more antithetical practical criticism ought to be capable of exploring.

Does Andrea overrate his own potential? If he does, then there is no poem, for unless his dubious gain-in-life has paid for a genuine loss-in-art, then he is too self-deceived to be interesting, even to himself. Browning has complicated this matter, as he complicates everything. The poem's subtitle reminds us that Andrea was called "The Faultless Painter," and Vasari, Browning's source, credits Andrea with everything in execution but then faults him for lacking ambition, for not attempting the Sublime. Andrea, in the poem, persuades us of a wasted greatness not so much by his boasting ("At any rate 'tis easy, all of it! / No sketches first, no studies, that's long past: / I do what many dream of, all their lives ..."), but by his frightening skill in sketching his own twilight-piece, by his showing us how "A common greyness silvers everything—." Clearly, this speaker knows loss, and clearly he is the antithesis of his uncanny creator, whose poetry never suffers from a lack of ambition, who is always Sublime where he is most Grotesque, and always Grotesque when he storms the Sublime. Andrea does not represent anything in Browning directly, not even the betrayed relationship of the heroic precursor, yet he does represent one of Browning's anxieties, an anxiety related to but not identical with the anxiety of influence. It is an anxiety of representation, or a fear of forbidden meanings, or in Freudian language precisely a fear of the return-of-the-repressed, even though such a return would cancel out a poem-as-poem, or is it because such a return would end poetry as such?

Recall that Freud's notion of repression speaks of an unconsciously *purposeful* forgetting, and remind yourself also that what Browning could never bear was a sense of *purposelessness*. It is purposelessness that haunts Childe Roland, and we remember again what may be Nietzsche's most powerful insight, which closes the great Third Essay of *On the Genealogy of Morals*. The ascetic ideal, Nietzsche said, by which he meant also the aesthetic ideal, was the only meaning yet found for human suffering, and mankind would rather have the void for purpose than be void of purpose. Browning's great fear, purposelessness, was related to the single quality that had moved and impressed him most in Shelley: the remorseless purposefulness of the Poet in *Alastor*, of Prometheus, and of Shelley himself questing for death in *Adonais*. Andrea, as an artist, is the absolute antithesis of the absolute idealist Shelley, and so Andrea is a representation of profound Browningesque anxiety.

But how is this an anxiety of representation? We enter again the dubious area of *belatedness*, which Browning is reluctant to represent, but is too strong and authentic a poet to avoid. Though Andrea uses another vocabulary, a defensively evasive one, to express his relationship to Michelangelo, Raphael, and Leonardo, he suffers the burden of the late-comer. His Lucrezia is the emblem of his belatedness, his planned excuse for his failure in strength, which he accurately diagnoses as a failure in will. And he ends in deliberate belatedness, and in his perverse need to be cuck-olded:

> What would one have?
> In heaven, perhaps, new chances, one more chance—
> Four great walls in the New Jerusalem,
> Meted on each side by the angel's reed,
> For Leonard, Rafael, Agnolo and me
> To cover—the three first without a wife,
> While I have mine! So—still they overcome
> Because there's still Lucrezia,—as I choose.
>
> Again the Cousin's whistle! Go, my Love.

Can we say that Andrea represents what Shelley dreaded to become, the extinguished hearth, an ash without embers? We know that Shelley need not have feared, yet the obsessive, hidden fear remains impressive. Browning at seventy-seven was as little burned out as Hardy at eighty-eight, Yeats at seventy-four, or Stevens at seventy-five, and his *Asolando*, his last book, fiercely prefigures Hardy's *Winter Words*, Yeats's *Last Poems*, and Stevens's *The Rock*, four astonishing last bursts of vitalism in four of the strongest modern poets. What allies the four volumes (*The Rock* is actual-ly the last section of Stevens's *Collected Poems*, but he had planned it as a separate volume under the title *Autumn Umber*) is their overcoming of each poet's abiding anxiety of representation. "Representation," in poetry, ultimately means self-advocacy; as Hartman says: "You justify either the self or that which stands greatly against it: perhaps both at once." We could cite Nietzsche here on the poet's Will-to-Power, but the more orthodox Coleridge suffices, by reminding us that there can be no origination with-out discontinuity, and that only the Will can interrupt the repetition-com-pulsion that is nature. In the final phases of Browning, Hardy, Yeats, and Stevens, the poet's Will raises itself against Nature, and this antithetical spirit breaks through a final anxiety and dares to represent itself as what Coleridge called self-determining spirit. Whether Freud would have com-pounded this self-realizing instinct with his "detours towards death" I do not know, but I think it is probable. In this final phase, Browning and his followers (Hardy and Yeats were overtly influenced by Browning, and I would suggest a link between the extemporizing, improvising aspect of Stevens, and Browning) are substituting a transumptive representation for the still-abiding presence of Shelley, their common ancestor.

I want to illustrate this difficult point by reference to Browning's last book, particularly to its *Prologue*, and to the sequence called *Bad Dreams*. My model, ultimately, is again the Lurianic Kabbalah, with its notion of *gilgul*, of lifting up a precursor's spark, provided that he is truly one's pre-cursor, truly of one's own root. *Gilgul* is the ultimate *tikkun*, as far as an act of representation can go. What Browning does is fascinatingly like the pat-tern of *gilgul*, for at the end he takes up precisely Shelley's dispute with Shelley's prime precursor, Wordsworth. By doing for Shelley what Shelley could not do for himself, overcome Wordsworth, Browning lifts up or redeems Shelley's spark or ember, and renews the power celebrated in the *Ode to the West Wind* and Act IV of *Prometheus Unbound*. I will try to illus-trate this complex pattern, after these glances at *Asolando*, by returning for a last time (I hope) to my personal obsession with *Childe Roland to the Dark Tower Came*, and then concluding this discourse by considering Browning's late reversal of *Childe Roland* in the highly Shelleyan celebration, *Thamuris Marching*.

The *Prologue* to *Asolando* is another in that long series of revisions of the *Intimations* Ode that form so large a part of the history of nineteenth- and twentieth-century British and American poetry. But Browning con-sciously gives a revision of a revision, compounding *Alastor* and the *Hymn to Intellectual Beauty* with the parent poem. What counts in Browning's poem is not the Wordsworthian gleam, called here, in the first stanza, an "alien glow," but the far more vivid Shelleyan fire, that Browning recalls seeing for the first time, some fifty years before:

> How many a year, my Asolo,
>   Since—one step just from sea to land—
> I found you, loved yet feared you so—
>   For natural objects seemed to stand
> Palpably fire-clothed! No—
> No mastery of mine o'er these!
>   Terror with beauty, like the Bush
> Burning but unconsumed. Bend knees,
>   Drop eyes to earthward! Language? Tush!
> Silence 'tis awe decrees.
>
> And now? The lambent flame is—where?
>   Lost from the naked world: earth, sky,

Hill, vale, tree, flower,—Italia's rare
    O'er-running beauty crowds the eye—
But flame? The Bush is bare.

When Shelley abandoned the fire, then it was for the transumptive trumpet of a prophecy, or in *Adonais* for the same wind rising ("The breath whose might I have invoked in song / Descends on me") to carry him beyond voice as beyond sight. Browning, as an Evangelical Protestant, fuses the Shelleyan heritage with the Protestant God in a powerfully incongruous transumption:

Hill, vale, tree, flower—they stand distinct,
    Nature to know and name. What then?
A Voice spoke thence which straight unlinked
    Fancy from fact: see, all's in ken:
Has once my eyelid winked?
No, for the purged ear apprehends
    Earth's import, not the eye late dazed:
The voice said 'Call my works thy friends!
    At Nature dost thou shrink amazed?
God is it who transcends.'

This is an absolute logocentrism, and is almost more than any poem can bear, particularly at a time as late as 1889. Browning gets away with it partly by way of a purged ear, partly because his Protestantism condenses what High Romanticism normally displaces, the double-bind situation of the Protestant believer whose God simultaneously says "Be Like Me in My stance towards Nature" and "Do not presume to resemble Me in My stance towards nature." The sheer energy of the Browningesque demonic Sublime carries the poet past what ought to render him imaginatively schizoid.

But not for long, of course, as a glance at *Bad Dreams* will indicate, a glance that then will take us back to the greatest of Browning's nightmares, the demonic romance of *Childe Roland*. *Bad Dreams III* is a poem in which the opposition between Nature and Art has been turned into a double-bind, with its contradictory injunctions:

This was my dream! I saw a Forest
    Old as the earth, no track nor trace
Of unmade man. Thou, Soul, explorest—
    Though in a trembling rapture—space

Immeasurable! Shrubs, turned trees,
Trees that touch heaven, support its frieze
Studded with sun and moon and star:
While—oh, the enormous growths that bar
Mine eye from penetrating past
    Their tangled twine where lurks—nay, lives
Royally lone, some brute-type cast
    In the rough, time cancels, man forgives.

On, Soul! I saw a lucid City
    Of architectural device
Every way perfect. Pause for pity,
    Lightning! Nor leave a cicatrice
On those bright marbles, dome and spire,
Structures palatial,—streets which mire
Dares not defile, paved all too fine
For human footstep's smirch, not thine—
Proud solitary traverser,
    My Soul, of silent lengths of way—
With what ecstatic dread, aver,
    Lest life start sanctioned by thy stay!

Ah, but the last sight was the hideous!
    A city, yes,—a Forest, true,—
But each devouring each. Perfidious
    Snake-plants had strangled what I knew
Was a pavilion once: each oak
Held on his horns some spoil he broke
By surreptitiously beneath
Upthrusting: pavements, as with teeth,
Griped huge weed widening crack and split
    In squares and circles stone-work erst.
Oh, Nature—good! Oh, Art—no whit
    Less worthy! Both in one—accurst!

In the sequence of *Bad Dreams*, Browning himself, as interpreter of his own text, identifies Nature with the husband, Art with the wife, and the marriage of Art and Nature, man and woman—why, with Hell, and a sado-masochistic sexual Hell, at that. But the text can sustain very diverse interpretations, as the defensive intensity of repression here is enormously strong. The City is of Art, but like Yeats's Byzantium, which it prophesies, it is also a City of Death-in-Life, and the previous vision of the forest is one of a Nature that might be called Life-in-Death. Neither realm can bear the other, in both senses of "bear"—"bring forth" or "tolerate." Neither is the other's precursor, and each devours the other, if they are brought together. This is hardly the vision of the *Prologue* to *Asolando*, as there seems no room for either Browning or God in the world of the final stanza. Granted that this is nightmare, or severe repression partly making a return, it carries us back to Browning at his most problematic and Sublime, to his inverted vision of the Center, *Childe Roland to the Dark Tower Came*.

As the author of two full-scale commentaries on this poem (in *The Ringers in the Tower*, 1971, and in *A Map of Misreading*, 1975) I reapproach the text with considerable wariness, fairly determined not only that I will not repeat myself, but also hopefully aiming not merely to uncover my own obsessional fixation upon so grandly grotesque a quest-romance. But I recur to the question I asked at the start of this discourse; is there an attainable critical knowledge to be gathered from this critical obsession?

Roland, though a Childe or ephebe on the road to a demonic version of the Scene of Instruction, is so consciously belated a quester that he seems at least as much an obsessive interpreter as anything else purposive that he might desire to become. He out-Nietzsches Nietzsche's Zarathustra in his compulsive will-to-power over the interpretation of his own text. It is difficult to conceive of a more belated hero, and I know of no more extreme literary instance of a quest emptying itself out. Borges accurately located in Browning one of the precursors of Kafka, and perhaps only Kafka's *The Castle* rivals *Childe Roland* as a Gnostic version of what was once romance. Nearly every figuration in the poem reduces to ruin, yet the poem, as all of us obscurely sense, appears to end in something like triumph, in a Good Moment carried through to a supreme representation:

> There they stood, ranged along the hill-sides, met
>> To view the last of me, a living frame
>> For one more picture! in a sheet of flame
> I saw them and I knew them all. And yet
> Dauntless the slug-horn to my lips I set,
>> And blew, '*Childe Roland to the Dark Tower came.*'

Surely it is outrageous to call this a Supreme or even a Good Moment? The stanza just before ends with the sound of loss: "one moment knelled the woe of years." Wordsworth and Coleridge had viewed the Imagination as compensatory, as trading off experiential loss for poetic gain, a formula that we can begin to believe was an unmitigated calamity.

It is the peculiar fascination of *Childe Roland*, as a poem, that it undoes every High Romantic formula, that it exposes the Romantic imagination as being merely an accumulative principle of repression. But such negation is itself simplistic, and evades what is deepest and most abiding in this poem, which is the representation of *power*. For here, I think, is the kernel of our critical quest, that Kabbalistic point which is at once *ayin*, or nothingness, and *ehyeh*, or the representation of Absolute Being, the rhetorical irony or *illusio* that always permits a belated poem to begin again in its quest for renewed strength. Signification has wandered away, and Roland is questing for lost and forgotten *meaning*, questing for *representation*, for a seconding or re-advocacy of his own self. Does he not succeed, far better than Tennyson's Ulysses and Percivale, and far better even than the Solitaries of the High Romantics, in this quest for representation? Let us grant him, and ourselves, that this is a substitute for his truly impossible original objective, for that was the *antithetical*, Shelleyan dream of rebegetting oneself, of breaking through the web of nature and so becoming one's own imaginative father. Substitution, as Roland shows, needs not be a sublimation, but can move from repression *through* sublimation to climax in a more complex act of defense.

Psychoanalysis has no single name for this act, unless we were willing (as we are not) to accept the pejorative one of paranoia for what is, from any point of view that transcends the analytic, a superbly valuable act of the will. Roland teaches us that what psychoanalysis calls "introjection" and "projection" are figurations for the spiritual processes of identification and apocalyptic rejection that exist at the outer borders of poetry. Roland learns, and we learn with him, that the representation of power *is* itself a power, and that this latter power or strength is the only purposiveness that we shall know. Roland, at the close, is re-inventing the self, but at the considerable expense of joining that self to a visionary company of loss, and loss means loss of *meaning* here. The endless fascination of his poem, for any critical reader nurtured upon Romantic tradition, is that the poem, more clearly than any other, nevertheless does precisely what any strong Romantic poem does, at once de-idealizes itself far more thoroughly than we can de-idealize it, yet points also beyond this self-deconstruction or limitation or reduction to the First Idea, on to a re-imagining, to a power-making that no other discursive mode affords. For Roland, as persuasively as any fictive being, warns us against the poisonous ravishments of truth itself. He and his reader have moved only through discourse together, and he and his reader are less certain about what they know than they were as the poem began, but both he and his reader have endured unto a representation of more strength than they had at the start, and such a representation indeed turns out to be a kind of restitution, a *tikkun* for repairing a fresh breaking-of-the-vessels. Meaning has been more curtailed than restored, but strength is revealed as antithetical to meaning.

I conclude with a great poem by Browning that is his conscious revision of *Childe Roland*: the marvelous late chant, *Thamuris Marching*, which is one of the finest unknown, unread poems by a major poet in the language. Twenty-two years after composing *Childe Roland*, Browning, not at the problematic age of thirty-nine, but now sixty-one, knows well that no spring has followed or flowered past meridian. But *Childe Roland* is a belated poem, except in its transumptive close, while all of *Thamuris Marching* accomplishes a metaleptic reversal, for how could a poem be more overwhelmingly early than this? And yet the situation of the quester is objectively terrible from the start of this poem, for Thamuris *knows* he is marching to an unequal contest, a poetic struggle of one heroic ephebe against the greatest of precursors, the Muses themselves. "Thamuris marching," the strong phrase repeated three times in the chant, expresses the *exuberance of purpose*, the Shelleyan remorseless joy in pure, self-destructive poetic quest, that Browning finally is able to grant himself.

Here is Browning's source, Iliad II, 594 ff:

... and Dorion, where the Muses
encountering Thamyris the Thracian stopped him from
singing, as he came from Oichalia and Oichalian Eurytos;
for he boasted that he would surpass, if the very Muses,
daughters of Zeus who holds the aegis, were singing against
him.
and these in their anger struck him maimed, and the voice of
wonder
they took away, and made him a singer without memory;
(Lattimore version)

Homer does not say that Thamyris lost the contest, but rather that the infuriated Muses lost their divine temper, and unvoiced him by maiming his memory, without which no one can be a poet. Other sources, presumably known to Browning, mention a contest decided in the Muses' favor by Apollo, after which those ungracious ladies blinded Thamyris, and removed his memory, so as to punish him for his presumption. Milton, in the invocation to light that opens Book III of *Paradise Lost*, exalted Thamyris by coupling him with Homer, and then associated his own ambitions with both poets:

Nightly I visit: nor sometimes forget
Those other two equall'd with me in Fate,
So were I equall'd with them in renown,
Blind Thamyris and blind Maemonides.

Milton presumably had read in Plutarch that Thamyris was credited
with an epic about the war waged by the Titans against the Gods, the
theme that Browning would associate with Shelley and with Keats.
Browning's Thamuris marches to a Shelleyan terza rima, and marches
through a visionary universe distinctly like Shelley's, and overtly proclaimed as being early: "From triumph on to triumph, mid a ray / Of early
morn—." Laughing as he goes, yet knowing fully his own doom, Thamuris
marches through a landscape of joy that is the deliberate point-by-point
reversal of Childe Roland's self-made phantasmagoria of ordeal-by-land-
scape:

Thamuris, marching, laughed 'Each flake of foam'
(As sparklingly the ripple raced him by)
'Mocks slower clouds adrift in the blue dome!'

For Autumn was the season; red the sky
Held morn's conclusive signet of the sun
To break the mists up, bid them blaze and die.

Morn had the mastery as, one by one
All pomps produced themselves along the tract
From earth's far ending to near Heaven begun.

Was there a ravaged tree? it laughed compact
With gold, a leaf-ball crisp, high-brandished now,
Tempting to onset frost which late attacked.

Was there a wizened shrub, a starveling bough,
A fleecy thistle filched from by the wind,
A weed, Pan's trampling hoof would disallow?

Each, with a glory and a rapture twined
About it, joined the rush of air and light
And force: the world was of one joyous mind.
(19–36)

From Roland's reductive interpretations we have passed to the imagination's heightened expansions. And though this quest is necessarily for the fearful opposite of poetic divination, we confront, not ruin, but the Good Moment exalted and transfigured, as though for once Browning utterly could fuse literal and figurative:

> Say not the birds flew! they forebore their right—
> Swam, reveling onward in the roll of things.
> Say not the beasts' mirth bounded! that was flight—
>
> How could the creatures leap, no lift of wings?
> Such earth's community of purpose, such
> The ease of earth's fulfilled imaginings—
>
> So did the near and far appear to touch
> In the moment's transport—that an interchange
> Of function, far with near, seemed scarce too much;
> (37–45)

Roland's band of failures has become the glorious band of precursors among whom Thamuris predominates. The Shelleyan west wind of imagination rises, Destroyer and Creater, as Thamuris, eternally early, stands as the true ephebe, "Earth's poet," against the Heavenly Muse:

> Therefore the morn-ray that enriched his face,
> If it gave lambent chill, took flame again
> From flush of pride; he saw, he knew the place.
>
> What wind arrived with all the rhythms from plain,
> Hill, dale, and that rough wildwood interspersed?
> Compounding these to one consummate strain,
>
> It reached him, music; but his own outburst
> Of victory concluded the account,
> And that grew song which was mere music erst.
>
> 'Be my Parnassos, thou Pangaian mount!
> And turn thee, river, nameless hitherto!
> Famed shalt thou vie with famed Pieria's fount!
>
> 'Here I await the end of this ado:

Which wins—Earth's poet or the Heavenly Muse.'

There is the true triumph of Browning's art, for the ever-early Thamuris is Browning as he wished to have been, locked in a solitary struggle against the precursor-principle, but struggling in the visionary world of the precursor. Roland rode through a Gnostic universe in which the hidden God, Shelley, was repressed, a repression that gave Browning a negative triumph of the Sublime made Grotesque. In *Thamuris Marching*, the joyous struggle is joined overtly, and the repressed partly returns, to be repressed again into the true Sublime, as Browning lifts up the sparks of his own root, to invoke that great mixed metaphor of the Lurianic Kabbalah. There is a breaking-of-the-vessels, but the sparks are scattered again, and become Shelley's *and* Browning's words, mixed together, among mankind.

Charles Baudelaire

(1821–1867)

SARTRE ENDED HIS BOOK ON BAUDELAIRE BY INSISTING THAT THIS POET, like Emerson's ideal being, made his own circumstances:

> But we should look in vain for a single circumstance for which he was not fully and consciously responsible. Every event was a reflection of that indecomposable totality which he was from the first to the last day of his life. He refused experience. Nothing came from outside to change him and he learned nothing.

Could there have been such a person? Can any poet refuse the experience of reading his precursors? Was Victor Hugo a circumstance for which Baudelaire was fully and consciously responsible? Valéry, who was (unlike Sartre) a theorist of poetic influence, thought otherwise:

> Thus Baudelaire regarded Victor Hugo, and it is not impossible to conjecture what he thought of him. Hugo reigned; he had acquired over Lamartine the advantage of infinitely more powerful and more precise working materials. The vast range of his diction, the diversity of his rhythms, the superabundance of his images, crushed all rival poetry. But his work sometimes made concessions to the vulgar, lost itself in prophetic eloquence and infinite apostrophes. He flirted with the crowd, he indulged in dialogues with God. The simplicity of his philosophy, the disproportion and incoherence of the developments, the frequent contrasts between the marvels of detail and the fragility of the subject, the inconsistency of the whole—everything, in a word,

which could shock and thus instruct and orientate a pitiless young observer toward his future personal art—all these things Baudelaire was to note in himself and separate from the admiration forced upon him by the magic gifts of Hugo, the impurities, the imprudences, the vulnerable points in his work—that is to say, the possibilities of life and the opportunities for fame which so great an artist left to be gleaned.

With some malice and a little more ingenuity than is called for, it would be only too tempting to compare Victor Hugo's poetry with Baudelaire's, with the object of showing how exactly *complementary* the latter is to the former. I shall say no more. It is evident that Baudelaire sought to do what Victor Hugo had not done; that he refrained from all the effects in which Victor Hugo was invincible; that he returned to a prosody less free and scrupulously removed from prose; that he pursued and almost always captured the production of *unbroken charm*, the inappreciable and quasi-transcendent quality of certain poems—but a quality seldom encountered, and rarely in its pure state, in the immense work of Victor Hugo....

Hugo never ceased to learn by practice; Baudelaire, the span of whose life scarcely exceeded the *half* of Hugo's, developed in quite another manner. One would say he had to compensate for the probable brevity and foreshadowed insufficiency of the short space of time he had to live, by the employment of that critical intelligence of which I spoke above. A score of years were vouchsafed him to attain the peak of his own perfection, to discover his personal field and to define a specific form and attitude which would carry and preserve his name. Time was lacking to realize his literary ambitions by numerous experiments and an extensive output of works. He had to choose the shortest road, to limit himself in his gropings, to be sparing of repetitions and divergences. He had therefore to seek by means of analysis what he was, what he could do, and what he wished to do; and to unite, in himself, with the spontaneous virtues of a poet, the sagacity, the skepticism, the attention and reasoning faculty of a critic.

One can transpose this simply enough into very nearly any of the major instances of poetic influence in English. Attempt Wallace Stevens, a true peer of Valéry, but with a more repressed or disguised relation to Whitman than Baudelaire manifested towards Hugo:

It is evident that Wallace Stevens sought to do what Walt Whitman had not done; that he refrained from all the effects in which Walt Whitman was invincible; that he returned to a prosody less free and scrupulously removed from prose; that he pursued and almost always captured the production of *unbroken charm*, the inappreciable and quasi-transcendent quality of certain poems—but a quality seldom encountered, and rarely in its pure state, in the immense work of Walt Whitman.

Valéry, unlike both Formalist and Post-Structuralist critics, understood that Hugo was to French poetry what Whitman was to American poetry, and Wordsworth was to all British poetry after him: the inescapable precursor. Baudelaire's Hugo problem was enhanced because the already legendary poetic father was scarcely twenty years older than the gatherer of *Les Fleurs du Mal*. All French literary movements are curiously belated in relation to Anglo-American literature. Current French sensibility of the school of Derrida is merely a revival of the Anglo-American literary Modernism of which Hugh Kenner remains the antiquarian celebrant. "Post-Structuralist Joyce" is simply Joyce as we read and discussed him when I was a graduate student, thirty-five years ago. In the same manner, the French Romanticism of Hugo in 1830 repeated (somewhat unknowingly) the movement of British sensibility that produced Wordsworth and Coleridge, Byron and Shelley and Keats, of whom the first two were poetically dead, and the younger three long deceased, well before Hugo made his revolution.

Baudelaire started with the declaration that the Romanticism of 1830 could not be the Romanticism (or anything else) of 1845. T.S. Eliot, as was inevitable, cleansed Baudelaire of Romanticism, baptized the poet into an Original Sinner and a Neo-Classicist, and even went so far as to declare the bard of Lesbos a second Goethe. A rugged and powerful literary thinker, Baudelaire doubtless would have accepted these amiable distortions as compliments, but they do not help much in reading him now.

His attitude towards Hugo, always tinged with ambivalence, became at times savage, but a student of poetic influence learns to regard such a pattern as one of the major modes of misprision, of that strong misreading of strong poets that permits other strong poets to be born. *The Salon of 1845* blames the painter Boulanger on poor Hugo:

> Here we have the last ruins of the old romanticism—this is what it means to come at a time when it is the accepted belief that inspiration is enough and takes the place of everything

else; this is the abyss to which the unbridled course of Mazeppa has led. It is M. Victor Hugo that has destroyed M. Boulanger—after having destroyed so many others; it is the poet that has tumbled the painter into the ditch. And yet M. Boulanger can paint decently enough—look at his portraits. But where on earth did he win his diploma as history-painter and inspired artist? Can it have been in the prefaces and odes of his illustrious friend?

That Baudelaire was determined not to be destroyed by Hugo was clear enough, a determination confirmed by the rather invidious comparison of Delacroix to Hugo in *The Salon of 1846*:

Up to the present, Eugène Delacroix has met with injustice. Criticism, for him, has been bitter and ignorant; with one or two noble exceptions, even the praises of his admirers must often have seemed offensive to him. Generally speaking, and for most people, to mention Eugène Delacroix is to throw into their minds goodness knows what vague ideas of ill-directed fire, of turbulence, of hazardous inspiration, of confusion, even; and for those gentlemen who form the majority of the public, pure chance, that loyal and obliging servant of genius, plays an important part in his happiest compositions. In that unhappy period of revolution of which I was speaking a moment ago and whose numerous errors I have recorded, people used often to compare Eugène Delacroix to Victor Hugo. They had their romantic poet; they needed their painter. This necessity of going to any length to find counterparts and analogues in the different arts often results in strange blunders; and this one proves once again how little people knew what they were about. Without any doubt the comparison must have seemed a painful one to Eugène Delacroix, if not to both of them; for if my definition of romanticism (intimacy, spirituality and the rest) places Delacroix at its head, it naturally excludes M. Victor Hugo. The parallel has endured in the banal realm of accepted ideas, and these two preconceptions still encumber many feeble brains. Let us be done with these rhetorical ineptitudes once and for all. I beg all those who have felt the need to create some kind of aesthetic for their own use and to deduce causes from their results to make a careful comparison between the productions of these two artists.

M. Victor Hugo, whose nobility and majesty I certainly have no wish to belittle, *is* a workman far more adroit than inventive, a labourer much more correct than *creative*. Delacroix is sometimes clumsy, but he is essentially creative. In all his pictures, both lyric and dramatic, M. Victor Hugo lets one see a system of uniform alignment and contrasts. With him even eccentricity takes symmetrical forms. He is in complete possession of, and coldly employs, all the modulations of rhyme, all the resources of antithesis and all the tricks of apposition. He is a composer of the decadence or transition, who handles his tools with a truly admirable and curious dexterity. M. Hugo was by nature an academician even before he was born, and if we were still living in the time of fabulous marvels, I would be prepared to believe that often, as he passed before their wrathful sanctuary, the green lions of the *Institut* would murmur to him in prophetic tones, "Thou shalt enter these portals."

For Delacroix justice is more sluggish. His works, on the contrary, are poems—and great poems, *naïvely* conceived and executed with the usual insolence of genius. In the works of the former there is nothing left to guess at, for he takes so much pleasure in exhibiting his skill that he omits not one blade of grass nor even the reflection of a street-lamp. The latter in his works throws open immense vistas to the most adventurous imaginations. The first enjoys a certain calmness, let us rather say a certain detached egoism, which causes an unusual coldness and moderation to hover above his poetry—qualities which the dogged and melancholy passion of the second, at grips with the obstinacies of his craft, does not always permit him to retain. One starts with detail, the other with an intimate understanding of his subject; from which it follows that one only captures the skin, while the other tears out the entrails. Too earthbound, too attentive to the superficies of nature, M. Victor Hugo has become a painter in poetry; Delacroix, always respectful of his ideal, is often, without knowing it, a poet in painting.

This is grand polemical criticism, deliciously unfair to the greatest French poet ever. Hugo is now adroit, but not inventive; a correct laborer, but not creative. Few critical remarks are as effectively destructive as: "with him even eccentricity takes symmetrical forms." Hugo is somehow a mere, earthbound painter of nature, and an academic impostor, doomed from birth to be an institutional pillar. Baudelaire's stance towards Hugo over the next decade became yet more negative, so that it is at first something of a surprise to read his letters to the exiled Hugo in 1859. Yet the complex rhetoric of the letters is again wholly human, all too human, in the agon of poetic influence:

> So now I owe you some explanations. I know your works by heart and your prefaces show me that I've overstepped the theory you generally put forward on the alliance of morality and poetry. But at a time when society turns away from art with such disgust, when men allow themselves to be debased by purely utilitarian concerns, I think there's no great harm in exaggerating a little in the other direction. It's possible that I've protested too much. But that was in order to obtain what was needed. Finally, even if there were a little Asiatic fatalism mixed up in my reflections I think that would be pardonable. The terrible world in which we live gives one a taste for isolation and fatality.
>
> What I wanted to do above all was to bring the reader's thoughts back to that wonderful little age whose true king you were, and which lives on in my mind like a delicious memory of childhood....
>
> The lines I enclose with this letter have been knocking around in my brain for a long time. The second piece was written with the *aim of imitating you* (laugh at my absurdity, it makes me laugh myself) after I'd reread some poems in your collections, in which such magnificent charity blends with such touching familiarity. In art galleries I've sometimes seen wretched art students copying the works of the masters. Well done or botched, these imitations sometimes contained, unbeknownst to the students, something of their own character, be it great or common. Perhaps (perhaps!) that will excuse my boldness. When *The Flowers of Evil* reappears, swollen with three times as much material as the Court suppressed, I'll have the pleasure of inscribing at the head of these poems the name of the poet whose works have taught me so much and brought such pleasure to my youth.

"That wonderful little age" doubtless referred to the Romanticism of the Revolution of 1830, that enchanted moment when Victor Hugo was king. But the true reference is to the nine-year-old Baudelaire, who found in his precursor "a delicious memory of childhood," and no mere likeness. When Baudelaire goes on to speak of imitation he cannot forbear the qualification: "something of their own character, great or common." A few months later, sending his poem, "The Swan," to Hugo, he asked that the poem be judged "with your paternal eyes." But, a year later, Baudelaire again condemned Hugo for: "his concern with contemporary events ... the belief in progress, the salvation of mankind by the use of balloons, etc."

The whip of ambivalence lashed back and forth in Baudelaire. Though a believer in salvation through balloons, the bardic Hugo was also, in his bad son's estimate, a force of nature: "No other artist is so universal in scope, more adept at coming into contact with the forces of the universe, more disposed to immerse himself in nature." That might seem definitive, but later Baudelaire allowed himself this diatribe, which hardly dents the divine precursor:

> Hugo thinks a great deal about Prometheus. He has placed an imaginary vulture on a breast that is never lacerated by anything more than the flea-bites of his own vanity ...
>
> Hugo-the-Almighty always has his head bowed in thought; no wonder he never sees anything except his own navel.

It is painful to read this; more painful still to read the references to Hugo in Baudelaire's letters of 1865–66. One moment, in its flash of a healthier humor, renders a grand, partly involuntary tribute to the normative visionary who both inspired and distressed Baudelaire:

> It appears that he and the Ocean have quarreled! Either he has not the strength to bear the Ocean longer, or the Ocean has grown weary of his presence.

To confront, thus again, the rock-like ego of that force of nature, your poetic father, is to admit implicitly that he returns in his own colors, and not in your own.

II

Proust, in a letter to Jacques Rivière, compared Baudelaire to Hugo and clearly gave the preference to Baudelaire. What Wallace Stevens, following Baudelaire, called the profound poetry of the poor and of the dead, seemed to Proust wholly Baudelaire's, and not Hugo's. But as love poets, Hugo and Baudelaire seemed more equal, even perhaps with Hugo the superior. Proust said he preferred Hugo to Baudelaire in a great common trope:

Elle me regarda de ce regard suprême
Qui reste à la beauté quand nous en triômphons.

She gazed at me with that supreme look
Which endures in beauty even while it is vanquished.
(Hugo)

Et cette gratitude infinie et sublime
Qui sort de la paupière ainsi qu'un long soupir

And that sublime and infinite gratitude
which glistens under the eyelids like a sigh.
(Baudelaire)

Both tropes are superb; I too prefer Hugo's, but why did Proust have that preference, or pretend to have it? Both beauties have been vanquished, but Hugo's by the potent Victor himself, while Baudelaire's Hippolyta reflects the triumph of Delphine, who stares at her victim with the shining eyes of a lioness. Proust, perhaps rather slyly, says he prefers the heterosexual trope to the Lesbian one, but does not say why. Yet, superb critic that he was, he helps us to expand Valéry's insight. Resolving to do precisely what Hugo had not done, Baudelaire became the modern poet of Lesbos, achieving so complex a vision of that alternative convention of Eros as to usurp forever anyone else's representation of it:

Comme un bétail pensif sur le sable couchées,
Elles tournent leurs yeux vers l'horizon des mers,
Et leurs pieds se cherchant et leurs mains rapprochées
Ont de douces langueurs et des frissons amers.

Les unes, coeurs épris de longues confidences,
Dans le fond des bosquets où jasent les ruisseaux,
Vont épelant l'amour des craintives enfances
Et creusent le bois vert des jeunes arbrisseaux;

D'autres, comme des soeurs, marchent lentes et graves
A travers les rochers pleins d'apparitions,
Où saint Antoine a vu surgir comme des laves
Les seins nus et pourprés de ses tentations;

Il en est, aux lueurs des resines croulantes,

Qui dans le creux muet des vieux antres païens
T'appellent au secours de leurs fièvres hurlantes,
O Bacchus, endormeur des remords anciens!

Et d'autres, dont la gorge aime les scapulaires,
Qui, recélant un fouet sous leurs longs vêtements,
Mêlent, dans le bois sombre et les nuits solitaires,
L'écume du plaisir aux larmes des tourments.

O vierges, ô démons, ô monstres, ô martyres,
De la réalité grands esprits contempteurs,
Chercheuses d'infini, dévotes et satyres,
Tantôt pleines de cris, tantôt pleines de pleurs,

Vous que dans votre enfer mon âme a poursuivies,
Pauvres soeurs, je vous aime autant que je vous plains,
Pour vos mornes douleurs, vos soifs inassouvies,
Et les urnes d'amour dont vos grands coeurs sont pleins!

Pensive as cattle resting on the beach,
they are staring out to sea; their hands and feet
creep toward each other imperceptibly
and touch at last, hesitant then fierce.

How eagerly some, beguiled by secrets shared,
follow a talkative stream among the trees,
spelling out their timid childhood's love
and carving initials in the tender wood;

others pace as slow and grave as nuns
among the rocks where Anthony beheld
the purple breasts of his temptations rise
like lava from the visionary earth;

some by torchlight in the silent caves
consecrated once to pagan rites
invoke—to quench their fever's holocaust—
Bacchus, healer of the old regrets;

others still, beneath their scapulars,
conceal a whip that in the solitude

and darkness of the forest reconciles
tears of pleasure with the tears of pain.

Virgins, demons, monsters, martyrs, all
great spirits scornful of reality,
saints and satyrs in search of the infinite,
racked with sobs or loud in ecstasy,

you whom my soul has followed to your hell,
Sisters! I love you as I pity you
for your bleak sorrows, for your unslaked thirsts,
and for the love that gorges your great hearts!

Richard Howard's superb translation greatly assists my inner ear, inadequate for the nuances of Baudelaire's French, in the labor of apprehending what Erich Auerbach memorably spoke of as Baudelaire's aesthetic dignity, that all-but-unique fusion of Romantic pathos and classical irony, so clearly dominant in these immense quatrains. Yet I would place the emphasis elsewhere, upon that psychological acuity in which Baudelaire surpasses nearly all poets, Shakespeare excepted. Freud, speculating upon female homosexuality, uttered the grand and plaintive cry: "we find masculinity vanishing into activity and femininity into passivity, and that does not tell us enough." Baudelaire does tell us enough, almost more than enough, even as Melanie Klein came, after Freud and Karl Abraham, to tell us much more than enough. The "damned women," really little children, play at being masculine and feminine, for Baudelaire's great insight is that Lesbianism transforms the erotic into the aesthetic, transforms compulsion into a vain play that remains compulsive. "Scornful of reality," and so of the reality principle that is our consciousness of mortality, Baudelaire's great spirits search out the infinite, and discover that the only infinity is the hell of repetition. One thinks back to Delphine and Hippolyta; Baudelaire sees and shows that Delphine is the daughter revenging herself upon the mother, even as Hippolyta revenges herself upon the mother in quite another way. When Hippolyta cries out: "Let me annihilate myself upon / your breast and find the solace of a grave!" then we feel that Baudelaire has made Melanie Klein redundant, perhaps superfluous. The revenge upon the mother is doubtless Baudelaire's revenge upon his own mother, but more profoundly it is the aesthetic revenge upon nature. In Baudelaire's own case, was it not also the revenge upon that force of nature, too conversant with ocean, that victorious poetic father, the so-often reviled but never forgotten Victor Hugo?

Matthew Arnold

(1822–1888)

ARNOLD IS A ROMANTIC POET WHO DID NOT WISH TO BE ONE, AN IMPOSSIBLE conflict which caused him finally to abandon poetry for literary criticism and prose prophecy. From the middle 1850s on, Arnold was primarily a prose writer, and his influence has been largely as a literary critic.

Arnold was born on December 24, 1822, the eldest son of the formidable Dr. Thomas Arnold, who from 1828 on was to be Headmaster of Rugby School. Dr. Arnold, a historian of some limited distinction, was a Protestant moralist of the rationalizing kind. His son did well at Rugby but alarmed Dr. Arnold with a defensive posture of continuous gaiety, which became a mock-dandyism at Balliol College, Oxford, where his closest friend was the poet Arthur Hugh Clough. After a fellowship at Oriel College, Oxford, Arnold went to London in 1847, as private secretary to a high official. In 1849 his early poems were published as *The Strayed Reveller, and Other Poems*. The "Marguerite" of those poems is now known to have been inspired by a youthful infatuation with Mary Claude, a summertime neighbor in the Lake district. In 1850, he fell in love with a judge's daughter, whom he married in 1851, after being appointed an Inspector of Schools.

In 1852 Arnold published his principal poem, the ambitious and uneasy *Empedocles on Etna*. When he brought together his *Poems* in 1853, he excluded *Empedocles*, explaining in the volume's famous anti-Romantic Preface that passive suffering was not a fit theme for poetry. When in 1857 he was elected Professor of Poetry at Oxford, almost all his best poetry had been written. Thus, his next poem, *Merope, A Tragedy*, published in 1858, is rather frigid, and the outstanding poems of his last volume, *New Poems* (1867), were composed many years before.

Whatever his achievement as a critic of literature, society, or religion, his work as a poet may not merit the reputation it has continued to hold in the twentieth century. Arnold is, at his best, a very good but highly derivative poet, unlike Tennyson, Browning, Hopkins, Swinburne, and Rossetti, all of whom individualized their voices. As with Tennyson, Hopkins, and Rossetti, Arnold's dominant precursor was Keats, but this is an unhappy puzzle, since Arnold (unlike the others) professed not to admire Keats greatly, while writing his own elegiac poems in a diction, meter, imagistic procedure, that are embarrassingly close to Keats (any reader who believes that this judgment is too harsh ought to experiment immediately by reading side-by-side the odes of Keats and Arnold's "The Scholar-Gipsy" or "Thyrsis"). Tennyson, Hopkins, and D.G. Rossetti retain distinctive Keatsian elements in their mature styles, but these elements are subdued to larger effects. But Arnold in "The Scholar-Gipsy," his best poem of some length, uses the language and movement of Keats even though the effect is irrelevant to his poem's theme.

Still, it is not a mean distinction to have written lyrics as strong as the famous "To Marguerite—Continued" and "Dover Beach" or a meditative poem as profound as "The Buried Life." Arnold got into his poetry what Tennyson and Browning scarcely needed (but absorbed anyway), the main march of mind in his time. His frequently dry tone and flatness of statement may not have been, as he happily believed, evidences of Classicism, but of a lack of poetic exuberance, a failure in the vitality of his language. But much abides in his work, and he is usefully prophetic also of the anti-Romantic "Modernism" of our time, so much of which, like Arnold, has turned out to be Romantic in spite of itself.

Emily Dickinson

(1830–1886)

IT IS NOT A RARE QUALITY FOR GREAT POETS TO POSSESS SUCH COGNITIVE strength that we are confronted by authentic intellectual difficulties when we read them. "Poems are made by fools like me," yes, and by Dante, Milton, Blake and Shelley, but only God can make a tree, to reappropriate a rejoinder I remember making to W.H. Auden many years ago, when he deprecated the possibilities of poetry as compared with the awful truths of Christian theology. But there are certainly very grand poets who are scarcely thinkers in the discursive modes. Tennyson and Whitman are instances of overwhelming elegiac artists who make us fitful when they argue, and the subtle rhetorical evasions of Wallace Stevens do not redeem his unfortunate essay, "A Collect of Philosophy."

Of all poets writing in English in the nineteenth and twentieth centuries, I judge Emily Dickinson to present us with the most authentic cognitive difficulties. Vast and subtle intellect cannot in itself make a poet; the essential qualities are inventiveness, mastery of trope and craft, and that weird flair for intuiting significance through rhythm to which we can give no proper name. Dickinson has all these, as well as a mind so original and powerful that we scarcely have begun, even now, to catch up with her.

Originality at its strongest—in the Yahwists, Plato, Shakespeare and Freud—usurps immense spaces of consciousness and language, and imposes contingencies upon all who come after. These contingencies work so as to conceal authentic difficulty through a misleading familiarity. Dickinson's strangeness, partly masked, still causes us to wonder at her, as we ought to wonder at Shakespeare or Freud. Like them, she has no single, overwhelming precursor whose existence can lessen her wildness for us. Her agon was waged with the whole of tradition, but particularly with the Bible and with romanticism. As an agonist, she takes care to differ from any male model, and places us upon warning:

> I cannot dance upon my Toes—
> No Man instructed me—
> But oftentimes, among my mind,
> A Glee possesseth me,
>
> . . . .
> Nor any know I know the Art
> I mention—easy—Here—
> Nor any Placard boast me—
> It's full as Opera—
> [326]

The mode is hardly Whitmanian in this lyric of 1862, but the vaunting is, and both gleeful arts respond to the Emersonian prophecy of American Self-Reliance. Each responds with a difference, but it is a perpetual trial to be a heretic whose only orthodoxy is Emersonianism, or the exaltation of whim:

> If nature will not tell the tale
> Jehovah told to her
> Can human nature not survive
> Without a listener?
> [1748]

Emerson should have called his little first book, *Nature*, by its true title of Man, but Dickinson in any case would have altered that title also. Alas, that Emerson was not given the chance to read the other Titan that he fostered. We would cherish his charmed reaction to:

> A Bomb upon the Ceiling
> Is an improving thing—
> It keeps the nerves progressive
> Conjecture flourishing—
> [1128]

Dickinson, after all, could have sent her poems to Emerson rather than to the nobly obtuse Higginson. We cannot envision Whitman addressing a copy of the first *Leaves of Grass* to a Higginson. There is little reason to suppose that mere diffidence prevented Miss Dickinson of

Amherst from presenting her work to Mr. Emerson of Concord. In 1862, Emerson was still Emerson; his long decline dates from after the conclusion of the War. A private unfolding remained necessary for Dickinson, according to laws of the spirit and of poetic reason that we perpetually quest to surmise. Whereas Whitman masked his delicate, subtle and hermetic art by developing the outward self of the rough Walt, Dickinson set herself free to invest her imaginative exuberance elsewhere. The heraldic drama of her reclusiveness became the cost of her confirmation as a poet more original even than Whitman, indeed more original than any poet of her century after (and except) Wordsworth. Like Wordsworth, she began anew upon a *tabula rasa* of poetry, to appropriate Hazlitt's remark about Wordsworth. Whitman rethought the relation of the poet's self to his own vision, whereas Dickinson rethought the entire content of poetic vision. Wordsworth had done both, and done both more implicitly than these Americans could manage, but then Wordsworth had Coleridge as stimulus, while Whitman and Dickinson had the yet more startling and far wilder Emerson, who was and is the American difference personified. I cannot believe that even Dickinson would have written with so absolutely astonishing an audacity had Emerson not insisted that poets were as liberating gods:

> Because that you are going
> And never coming back
> And I, however absolute,
> May overlook your Track—

> Because that Death is final,
> However first it be,
> This instant be suspended
> Above Mortality—

> Significance that each has lived
> The other to detect
> Discovery not God himself
> Could now annihilate

> Eternity, Presumption
> The instant I perceive
> That you, who were Existence
> Yourself forgot to live—

These are the opening quatrains of poem 1260, dated by Thomas Johnson as about 1873, but it must be later, if indeed the reference is to the dying either of Samuel Bowles (1878) or of Judge Otis Lord (1884), the two men Richard Sewall, Dickinson's principal biographer, considers to have been her authentic loves, if not in any conventional way her lovers. The poem closes with a conditional vision of God refunding to us finally our "confiscated Gods." Reversing the traditional pattern, Dickinson required and achieved male Muses, and her "confiscated Gods" plays darkly against Emerson's "liberating gods." Of Emerson, whose crucial work (*Essays*, *The Conduct of Life*, *Society and Solitude*, the *Poems*) she had mastered, Dickinson spoke with the ambiguity we might expect. When Emerson lectured in Amherst in December 1857, and stayed next door with Dickinson's brother and sister-in-law, he was characterized by the poet: "as if he had come from where dreams are born." Presumably the Transcendental Emerson might have merited this, but it is curious when applied to the exalter of "Fate" and "Power" in *The Conduct of Life*, or to the dialectical pragmatist of "Experience" and "Circles," two essays that I think Dickinson had internalized. Later, writing to Higginson, she observed: "With the Kingdom of Heaven on his knee, could Mr. Emerson hesitate?" The question, whether open or rhetorical, is dangerous and wonderful, and provokes considerable rumination.

Yet her subtle ways with other male precursors are scarcely less provocative. Since Shelley had addressed *Epipsychidion* to Emilia Viviani, under the name of "Emily," Dickinson felt authorized to answer a poet who, like herself, favored the image of volcanoes. Only ten days or so before judge Lord died, she composed a remarkable quatrain in his honor (and her own):

> Circumference thou Bride of Awe
> Possessing thou shalt be
> Possessed by every hallowed Knight
> That dares to covet thee
> [1620]

Sewall notes the interplay with some lines in *Epipsychidion*:

> Possessing and possessed by all that is
> Within that calm circumference of bliss,
> And by each other, till to love and live
> Be one:—
> [549–52]

Shelley's passage goes on to a kind of lovers' apocalypse:

> One hope within two wills, one will beneath
> Two overshadowing minds, one life, one death,
> One heaven, one Hell, one immortality,
> And one annihilation...
> [584–87]

In his essay, "Circles," Emerson had insisted: "There is no outside, no inclosing wall, no circumference to us." The same essay declares: "The only sin is limitation." If that is so, then there remains the cost of confirmation, worked out by Dickinson in an extraordinary short poem that may be her critique of Emerson's denial of an outside:

> I saw no Way—The Heavens were stitched
> I felt the Columns close—
> The Earth reversed her Hemispheres—
> I touched the Universe—
>
> And back it slid—and I alone
> A Speck upon a Ball—
> Went out upon Circumference—
> Beyond the Dip of Bell—
> [378]

"My Business is Circumference—" she famously wrote to Higginson, to whom, not less famously, she described herself as "the only Kangaroo among the Beauty." When she wrote, to another correspondent, that "The Bible dealt with the Centre, not with the Circumference—," she would have been aware that the terms were Emerson's, and that Emerson also dealt only with the Central, in the hope of the Central Man who would come. Clearly, "Circumference" is her trope for the Sublime, as consciousness and as achievement or performance. For Shelley, Circumference was a Spenserian cynosure, a Gardens of Adonis vision, while for Emerson it was no part of us, or only another challenge to be overcome by the Central, by the Self-Reliant Man.

If the Bible's concern is Centre, not Circumference, it cannot be because the Bible does not quest for the Sublime. If Circumference or Dickinson is the bride of Awe or of the authority of Judge Lord, then Awe too somehow had to be detached from the Centre:

No man saw awe, nor to his house
Admitted he a man
Though by his awful residence
Has human nature been.

Not deeming of his dread abode
Till laboring to flee
A grasp on comprehension laid
Detained vitality.

Returning is a different route
The Spirit could not show
For breathing is the only work
To be enacted now.

"Am not consumed," old Moses wrote,
"Yet saw him face to face"—
That very physiognomy
I am convinced was this.
[1733]

This might be called an assimilation of Awe to Circumference, where "laboring to flee" and returning via "a different route" cease to be antithetical to one another. "Vitality" here is another trope for Circumference or the Dickinsonian Sublime. If, as I surmise, this undated poem is a kind of proleptic elegy for Judge Lord, then Dickinson identifies herself with "old Moses," and not for the first time in her work. Moses, denied entrance into Canaan, "wasn't fairly used—," she wrote, as though the exclusion were her fate also. In some sense, she chose this fate, and not just by extending her circumference to Bowles and to Lord, unlikely pragmatic choices. The spiritual choice was not to be post-Christian, as with Whitman or Emerson, but to become a sect of one, like Milton or Blake. Perhaps her crucial choice was to refuse the auction of her mind through publication. Character being fate, the Canaan she would not cross to was poetic recognition while she lived.

Of Dickinson's 1,775 poems and fragments, several hundred are authentic, strong works, with scores achieving an absolute aesthetic dignity. To choose one above all the others must reveal more about the critic than he or she could hope to know. But I do not hesitate in my choice, poem 627, written probably in her very productive year, 1862. What precedents are there for such a poem, a work of un-naming, a profound and shockingly original cognitive act of negation?

> The Tint I cannot take—is best—
> The Color too remote
> That I could show it in Bazaar—
> A Guinea at a sight—
>
> The fine—impalpable Array—
> That swaggers on the eye
> Like Cleopatra's Company—
> Repeated—in the sky—
>
> The Moments of Dominion
> That happen on the Soul
> And leave it with a Discontent
> Too exquisite—to tell—
>
> The eager look—on Landscapes—
> As if they just repressed
> Some Secret—that was pushing
> Like Chariots—in the West—
>
> The Pleading of the Summer—
> That other Prank—of Snow—
> That Cushions Mystery with Tulle,
> For fear the Squirrels—know.
>
> Their Graspless manners—mock us—
> Until the Cheated Eye
> Shuts arrogantly—in the Grave—
> Another way—to see—

It is, rugged and complete, a poetics, and a manifesto of Self-Reliance. "The poet did not stop at the color or the form, but read their meaning; neither may he rest in this meaning, but he makes the same objects exponents of his new thought." This Orphic metamorphosis is Emerson's, but is not accomplished in his own poetry, nor is his radical program of un-naming. Dickinson begins by throwing away the lights and the definitions, and by asserting that her jocular procreations are too sub-tle for the Bazaar of publication. The repetition of colors (an old word, after all, for tropes) remains impalpable and provokes her into her own Sublime, that state of Circumference at once a divine discontent and a series of absolute moments that take dominion everywhere. Better perhaps than any other poet, she knows and indicates that what is worth representing is beyond depiction, what is worth saying cannot be said. What she reads, on landscapes and in seasons, is propulsive force, the recurrence of perspectives that themselves are powers and instrumentalities of the only knowledge ever available.

The final stanza does not attempt to break out of this siege of perspectives, but it hints again that her eye and will are receptive, not plundering, so that her power to un-name is not Emersonian finally, but something different, another way to see. To see feelingly, yes, but beyond the arrogance of the self in its war against process and its stand against other selves. Her interplay of perspectives touches apotheosis not in a Nietzschean or Emersonian exaltation of the will to power, however receptive and reactive, but in suggestions of an alternative mode, less an interpretation than a questioning, or an othering of natural process. The poem, like so much of Dickinson at her strongest, compels us to begin again in rethinking our relation to poems, and to the equally troubling and dynamic relation of poems to our world of appearances.

Christina Rossetti

(1830-1894)

CHRISTINA ROSSETTI (1830–94) IS ONE OF A HANDFUL OF MAJOR ENGLISH devotional poets, together with John Donne, George Herbert, Richard Crashaw, Henry Vaughn, and her contemporary, the Jesuit Gerard Manley Hopkins. One might expect the beloved sister of Dante Gabriel Rossetti to manifest a marked difference from other poets of religious sensibility. Like the Pre-Raphaelites, her style and procedures stem from Keats and Tennyson, rather than Donne and Herbert, but then Hopkins also is Keatsian in mode.

Goblin Market doubtless is Christina Rossetti's masterpiece, and rightly has become a favorite text for feminist literary criticism. It fascinates and disturbs me, and though I have included it complete in two anthologies, I never have commented upon the poem, for reasons I can only surmise. In a sense it is poetry for children, though indeed they have to be extremely intelligent children of all ages. Thus they could resist the current academic interpretations: Marxist, feminist, lesbian-incestuous, or imagistic self-gratification, at once erotic, mercantile, and even vampiric.

There certainly is a struggle going on in *Goblin Market*, but it seems to me an agon for poetic incarnation, for the establishment of a strong poetic self. I don't suppose that Christina Rossetti would have accepted John Keats's Scene of Instruction less ambivalently if he had been a woman, since strong poets are not particularly given to communal quilt-making. What troubles *Goblin Market* is not only Keats's magnificent oxymoronic rhetoric but also his naturalistic humanism. Keatsian eroticism is totally free of the melancholy sound of church bells. Christina Rossetti's intense faith was intricately fused with an erotic temperament as exuberant as her brother Dante Gabriel Rossetti's, and her lifelong renunciation (so far as we know) of sexual experience testifies to a rather frightening strength of will, or of faith if you would have it so. The Tempter in *Goblin Market* is in any case John Keats and not John Keble, or Romanticism rather than the Oxford Movement of Anglican Revivalism.

I hasten to insist that I find it grotesque to identify the Goblins as male precursor poets: Milton, Keats, Tennyson, and D.G. Rossetti and his friends. The nursery rhyme stylistics of *Goblin Market* are wonderfully effective swerves away from Keatsian celebrations of natural abundance, but they defend against glories of language, and not against gendered dangers.

That *Goblin Market* is an open-ended allegory is its finest attribute. Such irony invests deeply in the fantastic, challenging us to behold our own idiosyncratic phantasmagorias. Perhaps Friedrich Schlegel's definition of irony as the "permanent parabasis of meaning" could not be better exemplified than by Christina Rossetti's most ambitious poem.

Gerard Manley Hopkins

(1844–1889)

OF ALL VICTORIAN POETS, HOPKINS HAS BEEN THE MOST MISREPRESENTED by modern critics. He has been discussed as though his closest affinities were with Donne on one side, and T.S. Eliot on the other. Yet his poetry stems directly from Keats and the Pre-Raphaelites, and the dominant influences upon his literary thought came from Ruskin and Pater. A disciple of Newman, he is as High Romantic as his master, and his best poetry, with all its peculiarities of diction and metric, is perhaps less of a departure from the Victorian norm than Browning's, or Swinburne's, or even Patmore's. His case is analogous to Emily Dickinson's. Published out of their own century, they became for a time pseudocontemporaries of twentieth-century poets, but perspectives later became corrected, and we learned to read both poets as very much involved in the literature and thought of their own generations. Hopkins was, in many of his attitudes, a representative Victorian gentleman; indeed he was as much a nationalistic jingo as Tennyson or Kipling, and his religious anguish is clearly related to a characteristic sorrow of his age. His more properly poetic anguish is wholly Romantic, like Arnold's, for it derives from an incurably Romantic sensibility desperately striving not to be Romantic, but to make a return to a lost tradition. Hopkins quested for ideas of order that were not available to his poetic mind, and as a poet he ended in bitterness, convinced that he had failed his genius.

Hopkins was born on July 28, 1844, at Stratford in Essex, the eldest of nine children, into a very religious High Anglican family, of comfortable means. He did not enjoy his early school years, but flowered at Balliol College, Oxford, where he studied Classics from 1863 to 1867, and became a student of Walter Pater, who corrected his essays. In the atmosphere of the continuing Oxford Movement, Hopkins underwent a crisis, which came in March 1865 and partly resulted from meeting an enthusiastic, young, religious poet, Digby Dolben, who was to drown in June 1867 at the age of nineteen.

In 1866, under Newman's sponsorship, Hopkins was received into the Roman Catholic Church. Two years later, he began his Jesuit novitiate, and continued faithful to the Order until he died. Ordained a priest in 1877, he preached in Liverpool, taught at Stonyhurst, a Jesuit seminary, and from 1884 until his death in 1889 served as Professor of Greek at the University College in Dublin. Though perfectly free to write poems and paint pictures, so far as his superiors in the Society of Jesus were concerned, Hopkins was a congenital self-torturer, and so much a Romantic that he found the professions of priest and poet to be mutually exclusive.

Austin Warren, one of Hopkins's best and most sympathetic critics, justly remarked that in Hopkins's most ambitious poems there is "a discrepancy between texture and structure: the copious, violent detail is matched by no corresponding intellectual or mythic vigor." Following Keats's advice to Shelley, that an artist must serve Mammon by loading every rift of his poem with ore, Hopkins sometimes went too far, and even a sympathetic reader can decide that the poems are overloaded.

What then is Hopkins's achievement as poet? It remains considerable, for the original, almost incredible, accomplishment of Hopkins is to have made Keatsian poetry into a devotional mode, however strained. In the "Subtle Doctor," the Scottish Franciscan philosopher Duns Scotus (1265–1308), also an Oxonian, Hopkins found doctrine to reconcile a concern for individual form, for the "thisness" of people and natural things, with the universal truths of the church. Following his own understanding of Scotus, Hopkins coined the word "inscape" for every natural pattern he apprehended. "Instress," another coinage, meant for him the effect of each pattern upon his own imagination. Taken together, the terms are an attempt at scholasticizing Keats's fundamental approach to perception: detachment, the poet's recourse to nonidentity, Negative Capability.

Hopkins remained unpublished until his friend, the poet Robert Bridges, brought out a first edition of the poems in 1918, nearly thirty years after Hopkins's death. By chance, this first publication almost coincided with the start of the aggressive literary modernism that dominated British and American poetry until the 1950s, and Hopkins was acclaimed by poets and critics as the true continuator of English poetry in the otherwise benighted nineteenth century, and as a precursor who could help justify modern experiments in diction, metrics, and imagistic procedure.

Hopkins's diction adds to its Keatsian and Pre-Raphaelite base a large stock of language derived from his study of Welsh and Old English, and from an amorphous group of Victorian philologists who sought a "pure English," less contaminated by the Latin and French elements that are incurably part of the language. Hopkins's metric was based, as he said, upon nursery rhymes, the choruses of Milton's *Samson Agonistes*, and Welsh poetry. Against what he called the "running" or "common" rhythm of nineteenth-century poetry, Hopkins espoused "sprung rhythm," which he insisted was inherent in the English language, the older, purely accentual meter of Anglo-Saxon verse. Evidently, Hopkins read Keats's odes as having this rhythm, despite Keats's Spenserian smoothness.

Though Hopkins came to the study of Old English late, his essential metrical achievement was to revive the schemes of Old English poetry. But the main traditions of English poetic rhythm go from Chaucer to Spenser and Milton and on to the major Romantics, and Hopkins's archaizing return to Cynewulf and Langland, though influential for a time, now seems an honorable eccentricity. Nevertheless, its expressive effectiveness is undeniable. The metrical basis of many of Hopkins's poems is a fixed number of primary-stressed syllables, surrounded by a variable number of unstressed ones, or "outrides" as he called them. The alliterations of early Germanic poetry also work powerfully to recast the poetic line into a chain of rhythmic bursts. Thus, in "The Windhover," the first two lines each have five of Hopkins's beats (as opposed to five regularized, alternating, accentual-syllabic ones):

> I caúght this mórning, mórning's minión, kíng-
> dom of dáylight's daúphin, dapple-dáwn-drawn Fálcon, in his
> ríding ...

But the first line has ten syllables, and might be mistaken for an iambic pentameter, while the second has sixteen; and we realize as we read through the poems that what is common to them, their *meter* rather than their individual rhythms, is the sequence of five major stresses. Moreover, the phrase "dapple-*dawn*-drawn" is so accented as to preserve the meaning "drawn by dappled dawn" through its interior rhyme and alliterative clusters. Hopkins's own invented metrical terminology is, like his other philosophical vocabulary, highly figurative: "hangers" or "outrides," "sprung rhythm," "counterpointing" (or superposition of rhythmic schemes), even the blended emotive-linguistic meanings of "stress" itself, all invoke the imagery of his poems, and are as subjective as are his metaphysical concepts, but like those concepts constitute an extraordinary approach to a Catholic poetic transcendentalism.

Alfred, Lord Tennyson

(1850-1892)

When I began to write I avowed for my principles those of Arthur Hallam in his essay upon Tennyson. Tennyson, who had written but his early poems when Hallam wrote, was an example of the school of Keats and Shelley, and Keats and Shelley, unlike Wordsworth, intermixed into their poetry no elements from the general thought, but wrote out of the impression made by the world upon their delicate senses.

—W.B. YEATS, *Art and Ideas*

So vivid was the delight attending the simple exertions of eye and ear, that it became mingled more and more with trains of active thought, and tended to absorb their whole being into the energy of sense.

—HALLAM on Shelley and Keats,
in his review of Tennyson's
Poems, Chiefly Lyrical (1830)

THE *LAUREATE OF DESPAIR* AND *THE ANCIENT SAGE* IS OF COURSE ONE OF the memorable disasters of poetic tradition, surpassing the Wordsworth of the *Ecclesiastical Sonnets* and even the Arnold of *Merope*. The whole being of Tennyson was at no single time absorbed into the energy of sense, and for this failure of experience the price was paid, alas even overpaid:

And more—think well! Do-well will follow thought,
And in the fatal sequence of this world
An evil thought may soil thy children's blood;
But curb the beast would cast thee in the mire,
And leave the hot swamp of voluptuousness
A cloud between the Nameless and thyself,

217

And lay thine uphill shoulder to the wheel,
And climb the Mount of Blessing, whence, if thou
Look higher, then—perchance—thou mayest—beyond
A hundred ever-rising mountain lines,
And past the range of Night and Shadow-see
The high-heaven dawn of more than mortal day
Strike on the Mount of Vision!

So, farewell.

There are still Tennyson scholars who can read this, or say they can, but the indefensible badness of it all is plain enough. Sixty years or so before this, as a boy of fourteen, Tennyson possessed the verbal exuberance of an absolute poetic genius, and manifested it in the splendid speeches of the Devil in *The Devil and the Lady*, and in the remarkable movement of an exercise like the *Ode: O Bosky Brook*. The extremes of a poet's values, if they are manifested merely as a chronological continuum, do not much matter. Vision darkens, life triumphs, the poet becomes the man whose pharynx is bad. So went Wordsworth, the founder of modern poetry, and where a Moses was lost, other losses must follow. Yeats and Wallace Stevens appear today to be the first and only poets in the Romantic tradition who flowered anew both in middle and in old age, and yet it can be questioned if either will rival Tennyson and Browning after the fogs of fashion have been dispelled.

At the center of Tennyson the problem is not whether or why he hardened and kept hardening in poetic character, or just how his vision darkened perpetually into the abysses of much of the later verse, but why and how the sensibility of a major Romantic poet was subverted even in his earlier years. What the most sympathetic reader can still find wanting in the best of Tennyson is a power of imagination shown forth uncompromisingly in *The Fall of Hyperion* and *The Triumph of Life*, in *Resolution and Independence* and *The Mental Traveller*, and on the largest scale in *The Prelude* and *Jerusalem*. Romance, lyric, epic were raised to greatness again in the two generations just before Tennyson. In a lyrical monologue like *Andrea del Sarto*, a romance like "Childe Roland to the Dark Tower Came," and in the curious epic of *The Ring and the Book* a poet of Tennyson's own generation comes close to approximating the Romantic achievement. Tennyson was as legitimately the heir of Keats as Browning was of Shelley, and as much a betrayal of Keats's imaginative honesty and autonomy as Browning was of Shelley's. To make such a point is to reveal in oneself an unreconstructed Romantic bias, like that of Swinburne, or Yeats, or Shaw or Hardy, to bring in four Shelleyans who were contemporaries of the older Browning and Tennyson. There are achievements in Tennyson that are not Romantic, but they are small enough. The Tennyson who counts for most, seen in the longest and clearest perspective we now can begin to recover, is certainly a Romantic poet, and not a Victorian anti-Romantic resembling the Arnold of *Merope* or the straining Hopkins of *The Wreck of the Deutschland*. He is a major Romantic poet, but not perhaps one of the greatest, though there is an antithetical storm-cloud drifting through the center of his work that sometimes shows us what his proper greatness should have been. His affinities in his own time were to no other poet but to Ruskin, a great ruin of a Romantic critic, and his value to us now is rather like Ruskin's, since he shows forth as a most crucial instance of the dilemma of post-Romantic art.

Hallam, who remains Tennyson's best critic, found "five distinctive excellences" in his friend's poetic manner: (1) the control of a luxuriant imagination; (2) accuracy of adjustment in "moods of character," so that narration and feeling naturally corresponded with each other; (3) skill in emotionally fusing a vivid, "picturesque" portrayal of objects ("picturesque" being opposed here to Wordsworthian descriptiveness); (4) modulation of verbal harmony; (5) "mellow soberness of tone," addressed to the understanding heart rather than the mere understanding. Yeats, in his old age, spoke of "the scientific and moral discursiveness of *In Memoriam*," but I cannot recognize the poem from that description. What lives in the elegies for Hallam are precisely the excellences that Hallam picked out in his friend's earlier manner, and the various tracts of discursiveness one learns to step over quickly. Discursiveness became a Tennysonian vice, but it did not in itself inhibit the development of Tennyson's poetry. Tennyson, like Browning, but to a still worse extent, never achieved even a pragmatic faith in the autonomy of his own imagination. Such a faith was a ruling passion in Blake, Shelley, and Keats, and such a faith, though held with earnest misgivings, for a while allowed Wordsworth and Coleridge to yield themselves to their greatest achievements. Though the overt Victorian Romantics of the Pre-Raphaelite group struggled back to a version of this faith, it was not held again with similar intensity in Tennyson's age except by Pater, who fostered Yeats even as he gave the more disjunctive and ironical Stevens a fresh point of departure in America. To trace the conflict in Tennyson's earlier poetry between a Romantic imagination and an emergent societal censor is hardly to conduct a fresh investigation, and I will not attempt it here. Such conflicts, whether found in a Spenser or even in a D.H. Lawrence, seem recurrent in the history of poetry, and belong more to the study of consciousness than to the study of poetic tradition. The more rewarding problem for pondering is the young Tennyson's profounder distrust of his own creative powers. A god spoke in him, or a demon, and a revulsion accompanied the maturing of this voice. No really magical poem by Tennyson ever became quite the work he intended it to be, and this gap between his intention and his actual achievement saved him as a poet, though it could not save him altogether. Most considerable poems by Tennyson do not mean what they meant to mean, and while this is true of all poets whatsoever to some degree, Tennyson is the most extreme instance I know of the imagination going one way and the will going quite another. Blake thought that the Milton of *Paradise Lost* had to be rescued from himself, an opinion that most recent Miltonists find dubious, perhaps without fully understanding it. But Tennyson's best poems are a much more radical version of Blake's paradox; they address themselves simultaneously and overtly to both a conventional and a "diabolic" reading.

Partly this is due to the prevalence in Tennyson's poetic mind of the "damned vacillating state" of the early *Supposed Confessions*. No lyric by Tennyson is more central to his sensibility than *Mariana*, entirely a poem of the autonomous imagination running down into isolated and self-destructive expectation. Wordsworth, in his sublime Tale of Margaret, wrote the contrary to Tennyson's poem, for Margaret is destroyed by an imaginative hope that will not take account of the mundane. The hope is all too willing to be fed, and the prevalence of the imagination could hardly be more dangerous. Wordsworth does, here and in *Michael*, what Tennyson could only approximate in *Dora*; the poet creates a consciousness narrower and purer than his own, and measures his own malady of self-concern by its distance from that pure intensity. Mariana, unlike Margaret, is a poetess, and she sings a Dejection ode that Tennyson scarcely ventured to write in his own person. Her disease is Romantic self-consciousness, and no bridegroom can come to heal her. "She could not look on the sweet heaven," for much the same cause as the singer of Blake's *Mad Song* turns his back to the east and rejects the comforts of the sun. Wilful and unwilling, she is poised between two states of being, one in which the world has been taken up into the mind (the mind of a Picturesque rather than Descriptive poet) and the other in which the solipsistic mind rejects the world as an unreal intruder; hence the landscape of her poem, which as a poetic achievement could not be overpraised. The poplar, seen as a phallic symbol by some recent Tennyson critics, is rather an indication of the border realm between the two states in which Mariana lives. She can neither absorb its presence nor utterly reject it, and it serves therefore to show how precarious her mode of existence is. The poem's strongest impulse is to see the world as phantasmagoria, in which case Mariana's lament would be transvalued and appear as an ironic cry of triumph for the autonomy of her vision. But there are other impulses in the poem, and "He cometh not" remains a lament.

The Shelleyan origins of Tennyson's female solitary, in *Mariana* and other poems, has been demonstrated ably by Lionel Stevenson, who unfortunately reduces this emblematic figure in both Shelley and Tennyson to Jung's archetype of the *anima*. The reduction is unnecessary in any case, since *Epipsychidion* demonstrates how consciously and deliberately Shelley used his epipsyche figure. Tennyson's use of his cynosure-female is presumably not as conscious or as deliberate, though no theory of the two Tennysons, and no prosaic psychoanalytic reduction, need be ventured in consequence. Tennyson's poetry is too many-sided for anyone to suggest plausibly that it was written by uneasy collaboration between a Shelley-Keats and a Victorian Christian humanist, and I intend no such notion in this essay. There is a profound sense of the limitations of poetry in both Keats and Shelley, but each learned how to convert this sense into an overt poetic strength. Tennyson wrote in an age of reform, both voluntary and involuntary, while the younger Romantics faced a time of apparent stasis, an exhaustion following an apocalyptic fervor. The temper of poetic imagination is peculiarly and favorably responsive to the thwarting of political hope, and Shelley and Keats and Byron gained immensely by their good fortune of having the era of Metternich and Castlereagh to contend against, little as they would appreciate so cynical a judgment. Like Beddoes and Darley, a half-generation before him, Tennyson found himself with a fiercely autonomous imagination confronting a time that neither challenged nor repelled such an imagination, yet also gave it no proper arena in which to function. Keats was of course not a political poet, indeed was far less one than Tennyson, but there still existed provocations for Keats's humanism and his naturalism to become combative. Browning found provocation enough in the Evangelicism of his parents, particularly his mother, but *Pauline* records too clearly how his Shelleyan sensibility failed guiltily before such a stimulus. Tennyson had no combative use to which an assertion of the imagination could be put, and no antidote therefore against any aesthetic corrosion that his moral doubts of imagination might bring about. The pride of imagination, and the distrust of it, had nowhere to go but within.

Sexual virginity for any poet, even a Jesuit, as Hopkins shows, is a kind of sickness unto action, a time of fear before the potential disorder of the strange. That Tennyson's Muse was (and always remained) Hallam has given Robert Graves occasion for innocent merriment, but need disturb no one any longer. The death of a beautiful young man strikes our social sense as a less appropriate theme for poetry than Poe's pervasive theme, but is of course much more traditional than Poe's preference in corpses. The sexual longings of a poet *qua* poet appear to have little relation to mere experience anyway, as for instance in the contrast between the sexually highly active Shelley, with his crucial antithetical theme of the inadequacy of nature to the imagination from *Alastor* on, and the probably virginal Keats of *Endymion*, with his profoundly primary sense of satisfaction in natural experience. Still, there is a line of poetry that goes from the complexly sensual aspirations of Spenser through the bitter sexual frustrations of Milton and Blake (particularly relevant to his Notebook poems and *Visions of the Daughters of Albion*), then to the curious argument between Shelley and Keats in *Alastor* and *Endymion*, and on to the astonishingly delayed entries into sexual experience of Tennyson and of Yeats. The analytical sophistication in aesthetic realms that would allow a responsible sexual history of English poetry to be written is not available to us, and yet such a history must and should come. The hidden fulfillment of Wordsworth is the aesthetic puzzle of *The Prelude*, since the 1805 version is marred by the inclusion of the Julia and Vaudracour episode, and the 1850 version suffers from its exclusion. The *malaise* of Tennyson's early poetry is very like that of *The Wanderings of Oisin*, and the existence of Shelley and Keats as ancestor-poets-in-common is insufficient to explain the likeness. The tragedy of sexual intercourse, according to the older Yeats, was the perpetual virginity of the soul. The comedy of sexual intercourse is presumably the initial virginity of the body, but in poetry poised before experience the comedy tends to be negated, or rather displaced into the phantasmagoria of a Mariana, whose poem would be destroyed by the slightest touch of a comic spirit.

I am not, I would hope, alone in my puzzlement as to why Tennyson has not had the prestige of the hieratic in our time, while the more limited but precisely similar Mallarmé has. Tennyson's poems of the *Mariana* kind, centered on a self-embowered consciousness, are not less artful or persuasive than Mallarmé's, and are rather more universal in their implications. The English Decadence has, as its true monument, not Swinburne, admirable poet as he certainly was, but the more masterful Tennyson, whose "metaphysics of night" go beyond Mallarmé's in their elaborately indeliberate subtleties. Hallam's is necessarily a theory of pure poetry (as H.M. McLuhan shows) and while Tennyson could not allow himself to share the theory overtly, he inspired it by his early practice, and fell back on it implicitly to save his poetry time and time again. In a way that *In Memoriam* does not apprehend, the dead Hallam remained Tennyson's guardian angel.

Mariana is too pure a poem to test any argument by, so that an overview of its neighbors in early Tennyson seems likely to be helpful. *Recollections of the Arabian Nights* is a clearly Shelleyan poem, more confident indeed in its Shelleyan faith of imagination than anything else of Tennyson's. It echoes *Kubla Khan* also, but not the third part of that poem in which Coleridge to some degree withdraws from the full implications of his own vision. Like the Poet-hero of *Alastor*, Tennyson voyages through nature in search of a center transcending nature, and he finds it in a pleasure-dome like that of *Kubla Khan* or *The Palace of Art* or *The Revolt of Islam*:

> The fourscore windows' all alight
> As with the quintessence of flame,
> A million tapers flaring bright
> From twisted silvers look'd to shame
> The hollow-vaulted dark, and stream'd
> Upon the mooned domes aloof
> In inmost Bagdat, till there seem'd
> Hundreds of crescents on the roof
>   Of night new-risen ...

This is the young Tennyson's Byzantium, and perhaps it lingered in the mind of the old Yeats, though more likely both poets were recalling, however involuntarily, visions seen by Coleridge and by Shelley. Reasonable sophisticates will smile at my connecting Tennyson's playful *Recollections* to Yeats's supreme lyric, but there is a great deal legitimately to claim (or reclaim) for *Recollections of the Arabian Nights*. It was Hallam's favorite among the 1830 *Poems*, and his choice was a justified one, for the lyric is a complete and perfected miniature of Tennyson's poetic mind, and is even an *In Memoriam* in little. A very great, a consummate poet is at work in the full strength of his sensibility, and can be felt with especial power from the fifth line of this stanza on:

> Far off, and where the lemon grove
> In closest coverture upsprung,
> The living airs of middle night
> Died round the bulbul as he sung;
> Not he: but something which possess'd
> The darkness of the world, delight,
> Life, anguish, death, immortal love,
> Ceasing not, mingled, unrepress'd,

> Apart from place, withholding time,
> But flattering the golden prime
> Of good Haroun Alraschid.

This stanza is at the poem's center of vision, and properly recalls the song of Keats's nightingale, also sung to a poet in darkness, and like this chant an overcoming of the limitations of space and time. The companion poem to *Recollections* is the impressive *Ode to Memory*, and it is palpable that both lyrics are love poems addressed to Hallam. Palpable to us and not presumably to Tennyson and Hallam, I suppose I ought to add, but then the *Ode to Memory* ends:

> My friend, with you to live alone,
> Were how much better than to own
> A crown, a sceptre, and a throne!
>
> O strengthen me, enlighten me!
> I faint in this obscurity,
> Thou dewy dawn of memory.

The *Recollections* opens with an inspiriting breeze that takes the poet back to what Hart Crane in *Passage* beautifully called "an improved infancy." In that unitary joy, Tennyson emulates the Poet-hero of *Alastor* and sets forth on his quest for the good Haroun Alraschid, who is already the supernatural Hallam of *In Memoriam*, a poet-king dwelling at the center of vision, a type of god-man still to come. To reach this absolute being, the poet-voyager sails, with "a majesty of slow motion in every cadence," as Hallam observed, until he enters "another night in night," an "imbower'd" world of "imprisoning sweets." The voyage suggests not only the quest of *Alastor*, but also the journey to the Bower of Bliss in Book II of *The Faerie Queene*. Tennyson, as many critics by now have noted, is the most discreetly powerful erotic poet in the language, and this early lyric is a masterpiece of subdued erotic suggestiveness. The penultimate stanza, with its confectioner's delight of a Persian girl, is merely an erotic evasion, but the final stanza, directly celebrating Hallam, is sustained by a lyric rapture remarkable even in the younger Tennyson.

In section CIII of *In Memoriam*, Tennyson finds an after-morn of content because of another voyage-vision in which Hallam is again at the center, the Muse presiding over a realized quest. But the playfulness of *Recollections of the Arabian Nights* is now gone, that poem's greatest admirer being dead. Perhaps remembering how much Hallam had loved the poem, *Tennyson* returns to its design at one of the climaxes in his book of elegies, in which his grief is assuaged by the compensatory imagination, and Hallam is resurrected as a Titan capable of reviving Tennyson's lesser Muses. In itself, section CIII has rightly been judged to be one of Tennyson's great lyrics, but one can wonder how many of the poet's readers have seen how very little the poem has to do with the supposed faith of *In Memoriam*. Bradley, the definitive commentator on the elegies for Hallam, interpreted the dream of section CHI with his usual good sense, but declined to see its clearly Promethean pattern of *consolation*. In Numbers 13:32–33, the spies of Moses report on the Anakim, "which come of the giants," and the report appals the murmuring Israelites. Like the Titans, the Anakim testify to a time when there were giants in the earth, when men walked with gods as equals. In the titanic section CIII Tennyson dreams "a vision of the sea" during his last sleep in the house of his childhood, and in the vision he leaves behind him not only childhood, but all that precedes a rising Prometheanism as well. The poet's lesser Muses, his Daughters of Beulah as Blake patronizingly would have named them, sing "of what is wise and good / And graceful" to a veiled statue of Hallam, the unknown god who must lead them to a greater music. A dove summons Tennyson to an apocalyptic sea, an outward-flowing tide on which he will be reunited with "him I loved, and love / For ever." The weeping Muses sail with the poet:

> And still as vaster grew the shore
>   And rolled the floods in grander space,
>   The maidens gather'd strength and grace
> And presence, lordlier than before;
> And I myself, who set apart
>   And watch'd them, wax'd in every limb;
>   I felt the thews of Anakim,
> The pulses of a Titan's heart.

Watching the ministering spirits of his own creativity, Tennyson suddenly shares their participation in a daemonic possession, an influx of power as the poet rises in the body to be one again with the giants in the earth. With this transformation his Muses sing not of what is, but ought to be: the death of war, the great race that is to come, and a new cosmos—the shaping of a star. The New Man, the first of the crowning race, Tennyson's Albion "appearing ere the times were ripe," and so dying an early and unnatural death, is necessarily Hallam, whose epiphany "thrice as large as man" is the saving culmination of section CIII, and indeed of all the elegies. The ship of the reunited lovers, both now Titans and accompanied by the nervous Muses, fearful lest their function be gone, sails at last toward a land of crimson cloud, a realm where vapor, sea, and earth come together, a world out of space and time and free of all merely human moralities.

One never ceases to be puzzled that *In Memoriam*, an outrageously personal poem of Romantic apotheosis, a poem indeed of vastly eccentric mythmaking, should have been accepted as a work of consolation and moral resolution in the tradition of Christian humanism. *In Memoriam*, viewed as one poem, is rather a welter of confusions, but its main movement is clear enough, and establishes the work as having considerably less relation to a Christian elegy than even *Adonais* has. Whatever Tennyson thought he was doing, the daemon of imaginative autonomy got hold of the poem's continuity, and made the poem an argument for a personal love about as restrained and societal as Heathcliff's passion, or Blake's in *Visions of the Daughters of Albion* or Shelley's in *Epipsychidion*. The vision of Hallam in sections CXXVI to CXXX for instance is a more extreme version of the transfiguration of Keats in the final stanzas of Adonais, and is a victory for everything in Tennyson that could accept neither God nor nature as adequate to the imaginative demands of a permanently bereaved lover who was also a professional poet.

No poet in English seems to me as extreme and fortuitous as Tennyson in his sudden moments of recognition of his own powers, bursts of radiance against a commonplace conceptual background that cannot accommodate such radiance. The deeply imaginative reader learns instinctively to listen to the song and not the singer, for Lawrence's adage is perfectly relevant to Tennyson. More relevant still was the prophetic warning of Hallam, in one sentence of his review that one wishes Tennyson had brooded upon daily, and so perhaps saved for poetry more fully than he did one of the major Romantic sensibilities:

> That delicate sense of fitness which grows with the growth of artist feelings, and strengthens with their strength, until it acquires a celerity and weight of decision hardly inferior to the correspondent judgments of conscience, is weakened by every indulgence of heterogeneous aspirations, however pure they may be, however lofty, however suitable to human nature.

Had Tennyson heeded this, he might have ended like the sinful soul of his own *The Palace of Art*, howling aloud "I am on fire within." One cannot be sure it would not have been the fitting end his imagination required.

Arthur Rimbaud

(1854-1891)

RIMBAUD, HEIR OF BOTH HUGO AND BAUDELAIRE, WAS POTENTIALLY A stronger poet than either, just as Hart Crane, influenced by Eliot and Stevens, possessed poetic gifts that could have transcended the work of both precursors. Crane's identification with Rimbaud takes on a particular poignancy in this context, reminding us of imaginative losses as great as those involved in the early deaths of Shelley and of Keats. The scandal of Rimbaud, which would have been considerable in any nation's poetic tradition, was magnified because of the relative decorum in terms of form and rhetoric of French Romantic poetry, let alone of the entire course of French poetic tradition. A crisis in French poetry would seem a ripple in the Anglo-American tradition, which is endlessly varied and heterodox.

Except for Rimbaud, and a few more recent figures, French poetry does not have titanic eccentrics who establish entirely new norms. Rimbaud was a great innovator within French poetry, but he would have seemed less so had he written in the language of William Blake and William Wordsworth, of Robert Browning and Walt Whitman. *A Season in Hell* comes more than eighty years after *The Marriage of Heaven and Hell*, and the *Illuminations* do not deconstruct the poetic self any more radically than do the Browning monologues and *Song of Myself*. One must be absolutely modern, yes, and a century after Rimbaud it is clear that no one ever is going to be more absolutely modern that the poet of *The Prelude* and the crisis lyrics of 1802. I once believed that the true difference between English and French poetry was the absence of French equivalents of Chaucer and Spenser, Shakespeare and Milton. A larger difference, I now believe, is Wordsworth, whose astonishing originality ended a continuous tradition that had gone unbroken between Homer and Goethe.

Rimbaud had strong precursors in the later Hugo and in Baudelaire, but so great was Rimbaud's potential that he would have benefited by an even fiercer agon, like the one Wordsworth conducted with Milton, and to a lesser extent with Shakespeare. The strongest French poets, down to Valéry, finally seem to confront a composite precursor, Boileau-Descartes, part classical critic, part philosopher. That develops very different urgencies from those ensuing when you must wrest your literary space from Milton or Wordsworth. The difference, even in the outcast Rimbaud, sets certain limits both to rhetoric and to vision.

Those limits, critics agree, come closest to being transcended, in very different ways, in *Une Saison en enfer* and *Les Illuminations*. Leo Bersani, impressively arguing for the "simplicity" of the *Illuminations*, affirms that Rimbaud's greatness is in his negations. Making poetry mean as little as possible is thus seen as Rimbaud's true ambition. If Rimbaud's "The I is another" is the central formula, then the *Illuminations* becomes the crucial work. But since poetry, like belief, takes place between truth and meaning, the Rimbaldian-Bersanian dream of literary negation may be only a dream. What would a poem be if it were, as Bersani hopes, "nonreferential, non-relational, and devoid of attitudes, feelings and tones"? Bersani is the first to admit that the *Saison* is anything but that; it overwhelmingly reveals a coherent self, though hardly one of durable subjectivity. The trope and topos we call "voice" is so strong in *Saison* that we must judge it to be a High Romantic prose poem, whatever we take the *Illuminations* to be.

Saison, far more than Blake's *Marriage*, is always in danger of falling back into the normative Christianity that Rimbaud wants to deny, and that he evidently ceased to deny only upon his death bed. Kristin Ross, in a brilliant exegesis, reads *Saison* as opening out onto a sociohistorical field of which presumably Marcuse, in the name of Freud, was a prophet. I hear *Eros and Civilization* in Ross's eloquent summation of Rimbaud's stance as: "I *will* be a worker—but only at the moment when work, as we know it, has come to an end." If Bersani beautifully idealizes Rimbaud's aesthetic ambition, then Ross nobly idealizes his supposed socialization, though in a post-apocalyptic beyond. I am condemned to read Rimbaud from the perspective of Romanticism, as does John Porter Houston, and the poet I read has all the disorders of Romantic vision, but much of the meanings as well, and they hardly seem to me social meanings.

So much the worse for the wood that finds it is a violin, or the brass that finds it is a bugle, or the French boy of yeoman stock who at sixteen could write "Le Bateau ivre," transuming Baudelaire's "Le Voyage." Rimbaud's violent originality, from "Le Bateau ivre" on, drives not against meaning but against anyone whatsoever, even Baudelaire, bequeathing Rimbaud any meaning that is not already his own. More even than the later Victor Hugo, to whom he grudgingly granted the poetic faculty of Vision, Rimbaud could tolerate no literary authority. Perhaps, if you could combine the visionary Hugo and Baudelaire into a single poet, Rimbaud would have had a precursor who might have induced in him some useful anxiety, but the Anglo-American poetic habit of creating for oneself an imaginary, composite poetic forerunner was not available to Rimbaud.

Barely two years after "Le Bateau ivre," Rimbaud had finished *Une Saison en enfer*. Blake is supposed to have written "How Sweet I Roam'd from Field to Field" before he was fourteen, but except for Blake there is no great poet as precocious as Rimbaud in all of Western literary history. Like Blake, a poet of extraordinary power at fourteen, Rimbaud quite un-like Blake abandoned poetry at nineteen. A trader and gunrunner in Africa, dead at thirty-seven, having written no poetry in the second half of his life, Rimbaud necessarily became and remains the mythical instance of the modern poet as the image of alienation. The myth obscures the deeper tra-ditionalism of *Saison* in particular. Despite the difference implicit in the belated Romanticism of France, Rimbaud is as High Romantic as Blake or Shelley, or as Victor Hugo.

II

Une Saison en enfer has been called either a prose poem or a *récit*; it could also be named a miniature "anatomy" in Northrop Frye's sense of that genre. Perhaps it ought to be regarded as a belated Gnostic Gospel, like its hidden model, the canonical Gospel of John, a work which I sus-pect was revised away from its original form, one where the Word became, not flesh, but *pneuma*, and dwelt among us. Of all Rimbaud's writings, the *Saison* is most like a Hermetic Scripture. Rimbaud had never heard of Blake, who had promised the world his Bible of Hell, but *Saison* in its form always reminds me of *The Marriage of Heaven and Hell*, though it is very different in spirit from that curiously genial instance of apocalyptic satire.

In no way is it condescending to call *Saison* also the Gospel of Adolescence, particularly when we remember that Rousseau had invented that interesting transition, since literature affords no traces of it before him. To think of Rousseau reading *Saison* is grotesque, but in a clear sense Rimbaud indeed is one of Rousseau's direct descendants. Rimbaud doubt-less attempted to negate every inheritance, but how could Rimbaud negate Romanticism? His negation of Catholicism is nothing but Romantic, par-ticularly in its ambivalences.

The pattern unfolded in the nine sections of *Saison* would have been familiar to any Alexandrian Gnostic of the second century A.D. Rimbaud begins with a Fall that is also a catastrophic Creation, abandoning behind him the feast of life, and yet remembering "la clef du festin ancien," the key of charity. The feast must therefore be a communion table, the *pleroma* or Fullness from which Rimbaud has fallen away into the Gnostic *kenoma*, or emptiness of Hell that is simple, everyday bodily existence. Satan, in *Saison*, is the Gnostic Demiurge rather than the Catholic Devil, but then it is soon clear enough that Rimbaud himself, insofar as there is "himself," is a Demiurge also, a peasant or serf Demiurge, as it were. Perhaps Rimbaud's largest irony is his: "Je ne puis comprendre la révolte," since the serfs rose up only to plunder. The medieval yearnings of the "Mauvais sang" section all resemble the rapaciousness of wolves against an animal they have not killed, and so the wolf Rimbaud, his pagan blood returning, is now passed by:

> Le sang païen revient! L'Esprit est proche, pourquoi Christ ne m'aide-t-il pas, en donnant à mon âme noblesse et liberté. Hélas! l'Évangile a passe! l'Évangile! l'Évangile.
>
> J'attends Dieu avec gourmandise. Je suis de race inférieure de toute éternité.

The Holy Ghost is near, but the gluttonous waiting-for-God only guarantees Christ's withholding of charity. Nobility and freedom do not come to the serf lusting for a preternatural salvation. A riot of barbarism is therefore preferable to a supposed civilization in a world bereft of revelation. This is the dialectic of libertine Gnosticism, and reminds me that the American work closest to Rimbaud in spirit is Nathanael West's *Miss Lonelyhearts*, with its superbly squalid version of the ancient Gnostic doctrine that Gershom Scholem grimly called: "Redemption through Sin." Rimbaud peals throughout the rest of his "Bad Blood" section the iron music of atavism, in a full-scale justification of his own systematic derangement of the senses, only to collapse afterwards into the night of a real hell. Rimbaud's Hell is shot through with glimpses of divinity, and seems to be married to Heaven in a literal way, very different from Blake's ironic dialectic. God and Satan appear to be different names for one and the same spirit of lassitude, and Rimbaud thus prepares himself for his deepest descent, into delirium and its memories of his life of intimacy with Verlaine.

When I think of *Saison* I remember first the sick brilliance of Verlaine, the Foolish Virgin, addressing Rimbaud, the Infernal Bridegroom. If *Saison* has any common readers, in the Johnsonian sense, what else would they remember? Rimbaud, had he wished to, could have been the most consistently savage humorist in the French language. Poor

Verlaine is permanently impaled as that masochistic trimmer, the Foolish Virgin, unworthy either of salvation or damnation. The authority of this impaling is augmented by the portrait of the Infernal Bridegroom's forays into poetic alchemy, which are surely to be read as being just as ridiculous as the Foolish Virgin's posturings. So strong is the Rimbaud myth that his own repudiations of divinity and magic do not altogether persuade us. Thinking back to *Saison*, we all grimace wryly at Verlaine as Foolish Virgin, while remembering with aesthetic respect those verbal experiments that Rimbaud renounces so robustly.

To climb out of Hell, Rimbaud discovers that he must cast off his own Gnostic dualism, which means his not wholly un-Johannine Gnostic Christianity. Much of the sections, "L'Impossible" and "L'Éclair," are given to the quest away from Christianity, or rather the only Christianity that seems available. But since the quest involves those two great beasts of Nineteenth Century Europe, Transcendental Idealism and the Religion of Science, Rimbaud discovers that neither God nor Rimbaud is safely mocked. "Matin," following these dismissed absurdities, first restores Rimbaud's Gnosticism, his sense that what is best and oldest in him goes back to before the Creation-Fall. Hailing the birth of the new labor, the new wisdom, Rimbaud moves into his remarkable "Adieu," with its notorious motto: "Il faut être absolument moderne," the epigraph to the life's work of Rimbaud's Gnostic heir, Hart Crane. No longer a magus or an angel, Rimbaud is given back to the earth, a peasant again, like his ancestors. To think of the earth hardly seems a Gnostic formulation, and the famous closing passage of *Saison* abandons Gnosticism once and for all in an extraordinary breakthrough into visionary monism:

> —j'ai vu l'enfer des femmes là-bas;—et il me sera loisible de *posséder la vérité dans une âme et un corps*.

I take it that Rimbaud saw *down there*—in his relation with Verlaine— "the hell of women," precisely the Oedipal romance that he sought to flee. Possessing the truth in a single mind and a single body—one's own—is a narcissistic revelation akin to that of Walt Whitman's at the close of *Song of Myself*. Christianity *and* Gnosticism alike are rejected, and so are both heterosexuality and homosexuality. *Saison* ends with an inward turning closer to Whitman than to Hugo or to Baudelaire:

> Cependant c'est la veille. Recevons tous les influx de vigueur et
> de tendresse réelle. Et à l'aurore, armés d'une ardente patience,
> nous entrerons aux splendides villes.

It is a passage worthy of the poet whom the late James Wright called: "our father, Walt Whitman." We can hardly murmur: "our father, Arthur Rimbaud," but we can remember Hart Crane's equal devotion to Whitman and to Rimbaud, and we can be grateful again to Crane for teaching us something about our ancestry.

A.E. Housman

(1859-1936)

EDMUND WILSON WAS A REMARKABLE CRITIC, BUT NOT NECESSARILY OF modern poetry. In the decline of his former lover, the Byronic Edna Millay, Wilson found the debacle of modern verse. Against A.E. Housman, Wilson got off the grim shot: "Housman has managed to grow old without in a sense knowing maturity." Cyril Connolly was a touch nastier: "He will live as long as the B.B.C." Tom Stoppard, in his *The Birth of Love*, has juxtaposed Housman with Oscar Wilde, much to Wilde's favor.

As a reader of Housman's poetry since childhood, I tend to be surprised by critical dislike of his work. Housman palpably is not a poet of the eminence of Thomas Hardy and D.H. Lawrence, of Edward Thomas and Wilfred Owen, of T.S. Eliot and Geoffrey Hill, and W.B. Yeats is a mountain range of excellence away. But I greatly prefer Housman to many poets who support critical industries (Pound, Auden, et al.), and I am puzzled how any lover of poetry could fail to respond to this:

> Into my heart an air that kills
>   From yon far country blows:
> What are those blue remembered hills,
>   What spires, what farms are those?
>
> That is the land of lost content,
>   I see it shining plain,
> The happy highways where I went
>   And cannot come again.

The first line: "Into my heart an air that kills" is almost a poem in itself, and is a superb irony. It seems strange that Housman should be so undervalued as an ironist. As a classicist, he tends to favor the irony that says one thing while meaning another, but he is also a Romantic ironist, with a keen sense that meaning breaks under the strain of the irony of irony. "The Land of Lost Content" is precisely what cannot be seen, but Housman risks the Blakean line: "I see it shining plain."

Housman, though he can have a superficial resemblance to the earlier Blake, is anything but a visionary poet. Tom Stoppard, in his brilliant *The Invention of Love*, tells us that Housman's life was a failure, in contrast to Oscar Wilde's. Housman probably would have agreed with Stoppard, but recovering from an open heart operation makes me very wary of terming anyone's life a failure.

Do failures write uncanny poems? I have been upset with one of Housman's poems for longer than I can remember:

> Her strong enchantments failing,
>   Her towers of fear in wreck,
> Her limbecks dried of poisons,
>   And the knife at her neck,
>
> The Queen of air and darkness
>   Begins to shrill and cry,
> 'O young man, O my slayer,
>   To-morrow you shall die.'
>
> O Queen of air and darkness,
>   I think 'tis truth you say,
> And I shall die to-morrow;
>   But you will die to-day.

The Queen of air and darkness is no ordinary witch, and her young slayer is grimmer than any irony. What is the poem for? What did Housman do for himself, whether as person or as poet, by composing this poem? He was not susceptible to female enchantments, however strong, and this morbid little masterpiece of a lyric appears to have no sexual element, as it would if we found it in Kipling or in William Morris, or in the sadomasochistic Swinburne: One feels that Housman is exorcising something, something he cannot quite confront.

If I had to choose only one poem by Housman, it would be the superbly savage "Epitaph upon an Army of Mercenaries." But his subtlest and most beautiful poem probably is this:

Tell me not here, it needs not saying,
　　What tune the enchantress plays
In aftermaths of soft September
　　Or under blanching mays,
For she and I were long acquainted
　　And I knew all her ways.

On russet floors, by waters idle,
　　The pine lets fall its cone;
The cuckoo shouts all day at nothing
　　In leafy dells alone;
And traveller's joy beguiles in autumn
　　Hearts that have lost their own.

On acres of the seeded grasses
　　The changing burnish heaves;
Or marshalled under moons of harvest
　　Stands still all night the sheaves;
Or beeches strip in storms for winter
　　And stain the wind with leaves.

Possess, as I possessed a season,
　　The countries I resign,
Where over elmy plains the highway
　　Would mount the hills and shine,
And full of shade the pillared forest
　　Would murmer and be mine.

For nature, heartless, witless nature,
　　Will neither care nor know
What stranger's feet may find the meadow
　　And trespass there and go,
Nor ask amid the dews of morning
　　If they are mine or no.

Had Ben Jonson lived to read this, he might have said: "Had the poet intended an actual mistress, it would have been something." The poem's language is certainly the most heteroerotic in all of Housman, who nevertheless follows Wordsworthian convention by personifying nature as a beloved woman. Yet Housman's enchantress is "heartless, witless," and this is a poem of loss, of intimations of mortality. But there is magnificence in the loss, and an erotic music of the unlived life.

Edwin Arlington Robinson

(1869–1935)

Emerson himself was a product of New England and a man of strong
moral habits.... He gave to American romanticism, in spite of its irresponsible doctrine, a religious tone which it has not yet lost and which
has often proved disastrous.... there is a good deal of this intellectual
laziness in Robinson; and as a result of the laziness, there is a certain
admixture of Emersonian doctrine, which runs counter to the principles governing most of his work and the best of it.

—YVOR WINTERS

THE TORRENT AND THE NIGHT BEFORE (PUBLISHED LATE IN 1896 BY
Robinson himself) remains one of the best first volumes in our poetry.
Three of its shorter poems—"George Crabbe," "Luke Havergal," "The
Clerks"—Robinson hardly surpassed, and three more—"Credo," "Walt
Whitman" (which Robinson unfortunately abandoned), and "The
Children of the Night" (reprinted as title-poem in his next volume)—are
memorable works, all in the earlier Emersonian mode that culminates in
"Bacchus." The stronger "Luke Havergal" stems from the darker
Emersonianism of "Experience" and "Fate," and has a relation to the sin-
gular principles of *Merlin*. It prophesies Robinson's finest later lyrics, such
as "Eros Turannos" and "For a Dead Lady," and suggests the affinity
between Robinson and Frost that is due to their common Emersonian tradition.

In *Captain Craig* (1902) Robinson published "The Sage," a direct
hymn of homage to Emerson, whose *The Conduct of Life* had moved him
profoundly at a first reading in August 1899. Robinson had read the earlier Emerson well before, but it is fascinating that he came to essays like
"Fate" and "Power" only after writing "Luke Havergal" and some similar

poems, for his deeper nature then discovered itself anew. He called "Luke Havergal" "a piece of deliberate degeneration," which I take to mean what an early letter calls "sympathy for failure where fate has been abused and self demor,alized." Browning, the other great influence upon Robinson, is obsessed with "deliberate degeneration" in this sense; Childe Roland's and Andrea del Sarto's failures are wilful abuses of fate and demoralizations of self. "The Sage" praises Emerson's "fierce wisdom," emphasizes Asia's influence upon him, and hardly touches his dialectical optimism. This Emerson is "previsioned of the madness and the mean," fit seer for "the fiery night" of "Luke Havergal":

> But there, where western glooms are gathering,
> The dark will end the dark, if anything:
> God slays Himself with every leaf that flies,
> And hell is more than half of paradise.

These are the laws of Compensation, "or that nothing is got for nothing," as Emerson says in "Power." At the depth of Robinson is this Emersonian fatalism, as it is in Frost, and even in Henry James. "The world is mathematical," Emerson says, "and has no casualty in all its vast and flowing curve." Robinson, brooding on the end of "Power," confessed: "He really gets after one," and spoke of Emerson as walloping one "with a big New England shingle," the cudgel of Fate. But Robinson was walloped too well, by which I do not mean what Winters means, since I cannot locate any "intellectual laziness" in Emerson. Unlike Browning and Hardy, Robinson yielded too much to Necessity.... Circumstances and temperament share in Robinson's obsession with Nemesis, but poetic misprision is part of the story also, for Robinson's *tessera* in regard to Emerson relies on completing the sage's fatalism. From Emerson's categories of power and circumstance, Robinson fashions a more complete single category, in a personal idealism that is a "philosophy of desperation," as he feared it might be called. The persuasive desperation of "Luke Havergal" and "Eros Turannos" is his best expression of this nameless idealism that is also a fatalism, but "The Children of the Night," for all its obtrusive echoes of Tennyson and even Longfellow, shows more clearly what Robinson found to be a possible stance:

> It is the crimson, not the gray,
>   That charms the twilight of all time;
> It is the promise of the day
>   That makes the starry sky sublime;

It is the faith within the fear
   That holds us to the life we curse;
So let us in ourselves revere
   The Self which is the Universe!

The bitter charm of this is that it qualifies so severely its too-hope-ful and borrowed music. Even so early, Robinson has "completed" Emersonian Self-Reliance and made it his own by emphasizing its Stoic as against its Transcendental or Bacchic aspect. When, in "Credo," Robinson feels "the coming glory of the Light!" the light nevertheless emanates from unaware angels who wove "dead leaves to garlands where no roses are." It is not that Robinson believed, with Melville, that the invisible spheres were formed in fright, but he shrewdly suspected that the ultimate world, though existent, was nearly as destitute as this one. He is an Emersonian incapable of transport, an ascetic of the Transcendental spirit, contrary to an inspired saint like Jones Very or to the Emerson of "The Poet," but a contrary, not a negation, to use Blake's distinction. Not less gifted than Frost, he achieves so much less because he gave himself away to Necessity so soon in his poetic life. Frost's Job quotes "Uriel" to suggest that confu-sion is "the form of forms," the way all things return upon themselves, like rays:

Though I hold rays deteriorate to nothing,
First white, then red, then ultra red, then out.

This is cunning and deep in Frost, the conviction that "all things come round," even the mental confusions of God as He morally blunders. What we miss in Robinson is this quality of savagery, the strength that can end "Directive" by saying:

Here are your waters and your watering place.
Drink and be whole again beyond confusion.

To be beyond confusion is to be beyond the form of forms that is Fate's, and to be whole beyond Fate suggests an end to circlings, a resolu-tion to all the Emersonian turnings that see unity, and yet behold divisions. Frost will play at [yielding to Necessity], many times, but his wariness saved him from Robinson's self-exhaustions.

   There is a fine passage in "Captain Craig" where the talkative cap-tain asks: "Is it better to be blinded by the lights, / Or by the shadows?" This supposes grandly that we are to be blinded in any case, but Robinson was not blinded by his shadows. Yet he was ill-served by American Romanticism, though not for the reasons Winters offers. It demands the exuberance of a Whitman in his fury of poetic incarnation, lest the temptation to join Ananke come too soon and too urgently to be resisted. Robinson was nearly a great poet, and would have prospered more if he had been chosen by a less drastic tradition.

Paul Valéry

(1871–1945)

IN THE PREFACE TO HIS *LEONARDO POE MALLARMÉ*, VALÉRY CALLS THESE precursors "three masters of the art of abstraction." "Man fabricates by abstraction" is a famous Valéryan formula, reminding us that this sense of abstraction is Latin: "withdrawn, taken out from, removed." *It Must Be Abstract*, the first part of Stevens's *Notes toward a Supreme Fiction*, moves in the atmosphere of an American version of Valéry's insight, but the American is Walt Whitman and not Edgar Poe:

> The weather and the giant of the weather,
> Say the weather, the mere weather, the mere air:
> An abstraction blooded, as a man by thought.

Valéry fabricates by withdrawing from a stale reality, which he refuses to associate with the imaginings of his masters. These "enchanted, dominated me, and—as was only fitting—tormented me as well; the beautiful is that which fills us with despair." Had Valéry spoken of pain, rather than despair, he would have been more Nietzschean. The genealogy of imagination is not truly Valéry's subject. Despair is not a staleness in reality, or an absence of it; it is the overwhelming presence of reality, of the reality-principle, or the necessity of death-in-life, or simply of dying. Valéry's beautiful "Palme" concludes with a metaphor that seems central to all of his poetry:

> Pareille à celui qui pense
> Et dont l'âme se dépense
> A s'accroître de ses dons!

The palm is the image of a mind so rich in thinking that the gifts of its own soul augment it constantly. That may be one of the origins of Stevens's death-poem, "Of Mere Being," but Valéry's palm is less pure and less flickering than Stevens's final emblem. The two poets and poetic thinkers do not much resemble one another, despite Stevens's yearning regard for Valéry. Perhaps the largest difference is in the attitudes towards precursors. Valéry is lucid and candid, and he confronts Mallarmé. Stevens insists that he does not read Whitman, condemns Whitman for his tramp *persona*, and yet he cannot cease revising Whitman's poems in his own poems. But then that is how Whitman came to discuss his relation to Ralph Waldo Emerson—clearly they order these matters differently in America.

In a meditation of 1919 on "The Intellectual Crisis," Valéry memorably depicted the European Hamlet staring at millions of ghosts:

> But he is an intellectual Hamlet. He meditates on the life and death of truths. For phantoms he has all the subjects of our controversies; for regrets he has all our titles to glory; he bows under the weight of discoveries and learning, unable to renounce and unable to resume this limitless activity. He reflects on the boredom of recommencing the past, on the folly of always striving to be original. He wavers between one abyss and the other, for two dangers still threaten the world: order and disorder.

This retains its force nearly seventy years later, just as it would baffle us if its subject were the American Hamlet. Valéry's fear was that Europe might "become *what she is in reality*: that is, a little cape of the Asiatic continent." The fear was prophetic, though the prophecy fortunately is not yet wholly fulfilled. When Valéry writes in this mode, he is principally of interest to editorial writers and newspaper columnists of the weightier variety. Yet his concern for European culture, perhaps a touch too custodial, is a crucial element in all his prose writing. Meditating upon Descartes, the archetypal French intellect, Valéry states the law of his own nature: "Descartes is above all, a man of intentional action." Consciousness was for Valéry an intentional adventure, and this sense of deliberate quest in the cultivation of consciousness is partly what makes Valéry a central figure of the Western literary intellect.

Valéry deprecated originality, but his critical insights are among the most original of our century. His *Analects* are crowded with the darker truths concerning literary originality:

The value of men's works is not in the works themselves but in their later development by others, in other circumstances.

Nothing is more "original," nothing more "oneself" than to feed on others. But one has to digest them. A lion is made of assimilated sheep.

The hallmark of the greatest art is that imitations of it are legitimate, worthwhile, tolerable; that it is not demolished or devoured by them, or they by it.

Any production of the mind is important when its existence resolves, summons up, or cancels other works, whether previous to it or not.

An artist wants to inspire jealousy till the end of time.

Valéry's central text on originality is his "Letter about Mallarmé" of 1927 where his relation to his authentic precursor inspired dialectical ironies of great beauty;

> We say that an author is *original* when we cannot trace the hidden transformations that others underwent in his mind; we mean to say that the dependence of *what he does* on *what others have done* is excessively complex and irregular. There are works in the likeness of others, and works that are the reverse of others, but there are also works of which the relation with earlier productions is so intricate that we become confused and attribute them to the direct intervention of the gods.
>
> (To go deeper into the subject, we should also have to discuss the influence of a mind on itself and of a work on its author. But this is not the place.)

Everywhere else in Valéry, in prose and verse, is the place, because that was Valéry's true topos, the influence of Paul Valéry's mind upon itself. Is that not the true subject of Descartes and of Montaigne, and of all French men and women of sensibility and intellect? What never ceases to engage Valéry is the effect of his thought and writings upon himself. Creative misunderstandings induced in others were not without interest, but Valéry's creative misunderstandings of Valéry ravished his heart away. Texts of this ravishment abound, but I choose one of the subtlest and most evasive, the dialogue *Dance and the Soul*. Socrates is made by Valéry to speak of "that poison of poisons, that venom which is opposed to all nature," the reduction of life to things as they are that Stevens called the First Idea:

PHAEDRUS

What venom?

SOCRATES

Which is called: the tedium of living? I mean, understand me, not the passing ennui, the tedium that comes of fatigue, or the tedium of which we can see the germ or of which we know the limits; but that perfect tedium, that pure tedium that is not caused by misfortune or infirmity, that is compatible with apparently the happiest of all conditions—that tedium, in short, the stuff of which is nothing else than life itself, and which has no other second cause than the clearsightedness of the living man. This absolute tedium is essentially nothing but life in its nakedness when it sees itself with unclouded eyes.

ERYXIMACHUS

It is very true that if our soul purges itself of all falseness, strips itself of every fraudulent addition to *what is*, our existence is endangered on the spot by the cold, exact, reasonable and moderate view of human life *as it is*.

PHAEDRUS

Life blackens at the contact of truth, as a suspicious mushroom blackens, when it is crushed, at the contact of the air.

SOCRATES

Eryximachus, I asked you if there were any cure?

ERYXIMACHUS

Why cure so reasonable a complaint? There is nothing, no doubt, nothing more essentially morbid, nothing more inimical to nature than to *see things as they are*. A cold and perfect light is a poison it is impossible to combat. Reality, unadulterated, instantly puts a stop to the heart. One drop of that icy lymph suffices to slacken all the springs of the soul, all the throbbing of desire, to exterminate all hopes and bring to ruin all the gods that inhabited our blood. The Virtues and the noblest colors are turned pale by it in a gradual and devouring consumption. The past is reduced to a handful of ashes, the future to a tiny icicle. The soul appears to itself as an empty and measurable form. Here then are things as they are—a rigorous and deadly chain, where each link joins and limits the next.... O Socrates, the universe cannot endure for a single instant to be only what it is. It is strange to think that that which is the Whole cannot suffice itself! ... Its terror of being what it is has induced it to create and paint for itself thousands of masks; there is no other reason for the existence of mortals. What are mortals for?—Their business is *to know*. Know? And what is *to know?—It is assuredly not to be what one is.*—So here are human beings raving and thinking, introducing into nature the principle of unlimited errors and all these myriads of marvels!

The mistakes, the appearances, the play of the mind's dioptric give depth and animation to the world's miserable mass. The idea introduces into what is, the leaven of what is not.... But truth sometimes shows itself, and sounds a discord in the harmonious system of phantasmagorias and errors.... Everything straightway is threatened with perdition, and Socrates in person comes to beg of me a cure for this desperate case of clearsightedness and ennui!...

We are close again to Stevens's appropriations from Valéry in *Notes toward a Supreme Fiction*. The "clearsightedness of the living man" does not belong to Stevens or to us; it is the particular gift of the reductively lucid Valéry, who is capable of seeing "life in its nakedness." If Socrates here is Valéry the writer, then Eryximachus is Valéry the reader of—Valéry! "A cold and perfect light" is what Valéry has taught himself to see—in Valéry. Reality here is not so much the reality principle of Freud, as it is the next step after the nothingness of the abyss or final void in French Poe and in Mallarmé. A pragmatic Gnosticism, implicit in Poe and developed by Mallarmé, triumphs in Valéry's ironic sermon about "what is to *know*." The universe's terror of its own nothingness causes it to proliferate mortals, as if each one of us were only another desperate figuration. Our errors, our marvels, introduce "into what is, the leaven of what is not."

We encounter here again the vision of "Palme," since we hear the influence upon Valéry himself of

Parfois si l'on désespère,
Si l'adorable rigueur
Malgré tes larmes n'opère
Que sous ombre de langueur.

"There is a strict law in literature that we must never go to the bottom of anything." Valéry almost did not take his own counsel in his endless quest to explain the preternatural prevalence of his intentional self-awareness. He seems now the last person-of-letters in the French tradition to have been capable of reconciling acute consciousness of one's own consciousness with the grand fabrications made possible only by abstraction, by a withdrawal from heightened rhetoricity. Compared to him, Sartre and Blanchot, let alone Derrida, come to creation only in the accents of a severe belatedness.

Paul Laurence Dunbar

(1872-1906)

PAUL LAURENCE DUNBAR WAS THE FIRST MAJOR AFRICAN AMERICAN POET, and in my judgment remains one of the truly authentic poets of his American generation, which included Edwin Arlington Robinson, Trumbull Stickney, Edgar Lee Masters, James Weldon Johnson, and the earlier work of Robert Frost. Dead at thirty-five (tuberculosis augmented by alcoholism), Dunbar essentially wrote in the skeptical strain of Shelley, except in dialect poems. He inherited from Shelley an agonistic spirit, expressed strongly in "The Mystery," one of his undervalued poems, where he deliberately echoes "To a Skylark": "I fain would look before / and after, but can neither do." Caught in an unhappy present for a black poet, Dunbar concludes "The Mystery" with memorable eloquence:

> I question of th'eternal bending skies
> That seem to neighbor with the novice earth;
> But they roll on and daily shut their eyes
> On me, as I one day shall do on them,
> And tell me not the secret that I ask.

The secret is the mystery of being an eternal novice, a kind of Promethean complaint, which leads to what may be Dunbar's best poem, "'Ere Sleep Comes Down to Soothe the Weary Eyes." The fifth of the six stanzas is an epitome of how intensely Dunbar can transcend his situation and its limitations:

> Ere sleep comes down to soothe the weary eyes,
>   How questioneth the soul that other soul,—
> The inner sense which neither cheats nor lies,

247

But self exposes unto self, a scroll
Full writ with all life's acts unwise or wise,
  In characters indelible and known;
So, trembling with the shock of sad surprise,
  The soul doth view its awful self alone,
Ere sleep comes down to soothe the weary eyes.

"That other soul" or "awful self" is what the early African American Baptists called "the little me inside the big me," a spark or breath that is no part of nature or history. After eleven repetitions of: "Ere sleep comes down to soothe the weary eyes," we are startled by the poem's closing line, where "seal" replaces "soothe." In his perpetual struggle between bitterness and the Shelleyan wisdom of casting out personal remorse, Dunbar most frequently yields to a bitterness that transcends his personal sorrows.

One of the lucid voicings of that bitterness is Dunbar's memorial sonnet to Robert Gould Shaw, the Harvard College colonel who commanded the black 54th Massachusetts Regiment in its suicidal attack upon Fort Wagner (near Charleston) in July 1863. The sonnet's sestet laments the sacrifice of Shaw and his African American recruits, in a skepticism still relevant in 2001:

Far better the slow blaze of Learning's light,
  The cool and quiet of her dearer fane,
Than this hot terror of a hopeless fight,
  This cold endurance of the final pain,—
Since thou and those who with thee died for right
  Have died, the Present teaches, but in vain!

Dunbar's emblematic poem remains "Sympathy," popularized by Maya Angelou's autobiographical appropriation of "I know why the caged bird sings!" Though Dunbar's High Romantic lyricism has long been unfashionable, his achievement in it remains considerable.

Robert Frost

(1874–1963)

FROST—AT HIS FREQUENT BEST—RIVALS WALLACE STEVENS AS THE GREAT American poet of this century. He does not much resemble Stevens, ultimately for reasons that have little to do with the "essential gaudiness" of much early Stevens, or even with the austere clairvoyance of the later Stevens, poet of "The Auroras of Autumn" and "The Rock." Both of those aspects of Stevens rise from a powerful, barely repressed influence-relationship to Whitman, a poet who scarcely affected Frost. Indeed, Frost's uniqueness among modern American poets of real eminence partly stems from his independence of Whitman. Eliot, Stevens, Pound, Hart Crane, W.C. Williams, Roethke—all have complex links to Whitman, covert in Eliot and in Stevens. Frost (in this like Whitman himself) is the son of Emerson, of the harsher Emerson that we begin only now to recover. Any deep reader of Frost understands why the poet of "Two Tramps in Mud Time" and "Directive" seriously judged Emerson's "Uriel" to be "the greatest Western poem yet." "Uriel's voice of cherub scorn," once referred to by Frost as "Emersonian scorn," is the essential mode of irony favored throughout Frost's poetry.

"Uriel" is Emerson's own irreverent allegory of the controversy set off by his "Divinity School Address." There are certainly passages in the poem that seem to have been written by Frost and not by Emerson:

> The young deities discussed
> Laws of form, and metre just,
> Orb, quintessence, and sunbeams,
> What subsisteth, and what seems.
> One, with low tones that decide,
> And doubt and reverend use defied,

> With a look that solved the sphere,
> And stirred the devils everywhere,
> Gave his sentiment divine
> Against the being of a line.
> "Line in nature is not found;
> Unit and universe are round;
> In vain produced, all rays return;
> Evil will bless, and ice will burn."

At the center of this is Emerson's law of Compensation: "Nothing is got for nothing," as Emerson phrased it later, in the remorseless essay "Power," in his *The Conduct of Life*. The darker Emersonian essays—"Experience," "Power," "Circles," "Fate," "Illusions"—read like manifestos for Frost's poetry. Richard Poirier has demonstrated this in some detail, and I follow him here in emphasizing how pervasive and crucial the affinity between Emerson and Freud tends to be. If there is a particular motto that states the dialectic of Frost's best poems, then it is to be found in a formulation of Emerson's "Self-Reliance."

> Life only avails, not the having lived. Power ceases in the instant
> of repose; it resides in the moment of transition from a past to a
> new state, in the shooting of the gulf, in the darting to an aim.

One thinks of the extraordinary early poem "The Wood-Pile" (1914), where the poet, "out walking in the frozen swamp one gray day," comes upon "a cord of maple, cut and split / and piled" and then abandoned:

> I thought that only
> Someone who lived in turning to fresh tasks
> Could so forget his handiwork on which
> He spent himself, the labor of his ax,
> And leave it there far from a useful fireplace
> To warm the frozen swamp as best it could
> With the slow smokeless burning of decay.

That "slow smokeless burning" is the metaphor for Emerson's "instant of repose," where power ceases. Frost's restless turnings are his most Emersonian moments, American and agonistic. His Job, in *A Masque of Reason*, puzzling over God's Reason, deliberately relates Jehovah's dialectic to that of Emerson's "Uriel":

Yet I suppose what seems to us confusion
Is not confusion, but the form of forms,
The serpent's tail stuck down the serpent's throat,
Which is the symbol of eternity
And also of the way all things come round,
Or of how rays return upon themselves,
To quote the greatest Western poem yet.
Though I hold rays deteriorate to nothing:
First white, then red, then ultrared, then out.

Job's last two lines here mark Frost's characteristic swerve away from Emerson, except that Emerson is the most difficult of fathers to evade, having been always so subtly evasive himself. Frost's authentic nihilism is considerable, but is surpassed by "Fate" in *The Conduct of Life*, and by a grand more-than-Frostian late entry in Emerson's journals, set down in the autumn of 1866, when the sage felt burned to the socket by the intensities he had experienced during the Civil War:

There may be two or three or four steps, according to the genius of each, but for every seeing soul there are two absorbing facts, *I and the Abyss.*

Frost's religion, as a poet, was the American religion that Emerson founded. A latecomer exegete of that religion, I once offered its credo as *Everything that can be broken should be broken*, a Gnostic motto that eminently suits Frost's poetry, where God, whether in *A Masque of Reason, A Masque of Mercy*, or in "Once by the Pacific," is clearly animated neither by reason nor mercy but only by the blind necessities of being the Demiurge:

It looked as if a night of dark intent
Was coming, and not only a night, an age.
Someone had better be prepared for rage.
There would be more than ocean-water broken
Before God's last *Put out the Light* was spoken.

A God who echoes Othello at his most murderous is himself also crazed by jealousy. Frost's celebrated negativity is a secularized negative theology, almost wholly derived from Emerson, insofar as it was not purely temperamental. Slyly aware of it, Frost used it as the occasion for lovely jokes, as in the marvelous "Two Tramps in Mud Time":

> The water for which we may have to look
> In summertime with a witching wand,
> In every wheelrut's now a brook,
> In every print of a hoof a pond.
> Be glad of water, but don't forget
> The lurking frost in the earth beneath
> That will steal forth after the sun is set
> And show on the water its crystal teeth.

"Two Tramps in Mud Time" hymns the Emersonian negativity of refusing to identify yourself with any work, in order instead to achieve the Gnostic identity of the knower with what is known, when the sparks of the Alien God or true Workman stream through you. A shrewd Gnostic, Frost refuses to lament confusion, though he also will not follow Whitman in celebrating it. In Emerson's "Uriel," confusion precedes the dimming of that Miltonic archangel of the sun, who withers from a sad self-knowledge. Uriel-Emerson (for which read Frost) is himself not responsible for engendering the confusion, which results from the failure of nerve suffered by the heavenly powers when they hear Uriel proclaim that "all rays return; Evil will bless, and ice will burn":

> As Uriel spoke with piercing eye,
> A shudder ran around the sky;
> The stern old war-gods shook their heads,
> The seraphs frowned from myrtle-beds;
> Seemed to the holy festival
> The rash word boded ill to all;
> The balance-beam of Fate was bent;
> The bounds of good and ill were rent;
> Strong Hades could not keep his own,
> But all slid to confusion.

"Confusion" is a mixing or pouring together of entities that would be better off if kept apart. Whether instinctively or overtly, both Emerson and Frost seem to have known that the Indo-European root of "confusion" originally meant "to pour a libation," as if to the gods. Frost's "form of forms," or confusion which is not confusion, identified by him with the Emersonian rays returning upon themselves, is a kind of libation poured out to the Alien God, as in the trope that concludes his great poem "Directive":

Here are your waters and your watering place.
Drink and be whole again beyond confusion.

II

"Directive" is Frost's poem of poems or form of forms, a meditation
whose rays perpetually return upon themselves. "All things come round,"
even our mental confusion as we blunder morally, since the Demiurge is
nothing but a moral blunderer. Frost shares the fine Emersonian wildness
or freedom, the savage strength of the essay "Power" that suggests a way
of being whole beyond Fate, of arriving at an end to circlings, at a resolution to all the Emersonian turnings that see unity, and yet behold divisions:
"The world is mathematical, and has no casualty, in all its vast and flowing
curve." "Directive" appears to be the poem in which Frost measures the
lot, and forgives himself the lot, and perhaps even casts out remorse. In
some sense, it was the poem he always wrote and rewrote, in a revisionary
process present already in *A Boy's Will* (1913) but not fully worked out until
Steeple Bush (1947), where "Directive" was published, when Frost was seventy-three. "The Demiurge's Laugh" in *A Boy's Will* features a mocking
demonic derision at the self-realization that "what I hunted was no true
god."

North of Boston (1914) has its most memorable poem in the famous
"After Apple-Picking," a gracious hymn to the necessity of yielding up the
quest, of clambering down from one's "long two-pointed [ladder] sticking
through a tree / Toward heaven still." Frost's subtlest of perspectivizings is
the true center of the poem:

> I cannot rub the strangeness from my sight
> I got from looking through a pane of glass
> I skimmed this morning from the drinking trough
> And held against the world of hoary grass.
> It melted, and I let it fall and break.

The sheet of ice is a lens upon irreality, but so are Frost's own eyes,
or anyone's, in his cosmos. This supposed nature poet represents his harsh
landscapes as a full version of the Gnostic *kenoma*, the cosmological emptiness into which we have been thrown by the mocking Demiurge. This is
the world of *Mountain Interval* (1916), where "the broken moon" is preferred to the dimmed sun, where the oven bird sings of "that other fall we
name the fall," and where the birches:

> shed crystal shells
> Shattering and avalanching on the snow crust
> Such heaps of broken glass to sweep away
> You'd think the inner dome of heaven had fallen.

Mountain Interval abounds in images of the shattering of human ties, and of humans, as in the horrifying "Out, Out—." But it would be redundant to conduct an overview of all Frost's volumes in pursuit of an experiential darkness that never is dispelled. A measurer of stone walls, as Frost names himself in the remarkable "A Star in a Stoneboat," is never going to be surprised that life is a sensible emptiness. The demiurgic pattern of "Design," with its "assorted characters of death and blight," is the rule in Frost. There are a few exceptions, but they give Frost parodies, rather than poems.

Frost wrote the concluding and conclusive Emersonian irony for all his work in the allegorical "A Cabin in the Clearing," the set-piece of *In the Clearing* (1962), published for his eighty-eighth birthday, less than a year before his death. Mist and Smoke, guardian wraiths and counterparts, eavesdrop on the unrest of a human couple, murmuring in their sleep. These guardians haunt us because we are their kindred spirits, for we do not know where we are, since who we are "is too much to believe." We are "too sudden to be credible," and so the accurate image for us is "an inner haze," full kindred to mist and smoke. For all the genial tone, the spirit of "A Cabin in the Clearing" is negative even for Frost. His final letter, dictated just before his death, states an unanswerable question as though it were not a question: "How can we be just in a world that needs mercy and merciful in a world that needs justice." The Demiurge's laugh lurks behind the sentence, though Frost was then in no frame of spirit to indulge a demiurgic imagination.

Frost would have been well content to give his mentor Emerson the last word, though "content" is necessarily an inadequate word in this dark context. Each time I reread the magnificent essay, "Illusions," which concludes and crowns *The Conduct of Life*, I am reminded of the poetry of Robert Frost. The reminder is strongest in two paragraphs near the end that seem to be "Directive" writ large, as though Emerson had been brooding upon his descendant:

> We cannot write the order of the variable winds. How can we penetrate the law of our shifting moods and susceptibility? Yet they differ as all and nothing. Instead of the firmament of yesterday, which our eyes require, it is to-day an eggshell which

coops us in; we cannot even see what or where our stars of destiny are. From day to day, the capital facts of human life are hidden from our eyes. Suddenly the mist rolls up, and reveals them, and we think how much good time is gone, that might have been saved, had any hint of these things been shown. A sudden rise in the road shows us the system of mountains, and all the summits, which have been just as near us all the year, but quite out of mind. But these alternations are not without their order, and we are parties to our various fortune. If life seem a succession of dreams, yet poetic justice is done in dreams also. The visions of good men are good; it is the undisciplined will that is whipped with bad thoughts and bad fortunes. When we break the laws, we lose our hold on the central reality. Like sick men in hospitals, we change only from bed to bed, from one folly to another; and it cannot signify much what becomes of such castaways,—wailing, stupid, comatose creatures,—lifted from bed to bed, from the nothing of life to the nothing of death.

In this kingdom of illusions we grope eagerly for stays and foundations. There is none but a strict and faithful dealing at home, and a severe barring out of all duplicity or illusion there. Whatever games are played with us, we must play no games with ourselves, but deal in our privacy with the last honesty and truth. I look upon the simple and childish virtues of veracity and honesty as the root of all that is sublime in character. Speak as you think, be what you are, pay your debts of all kinds. I prefer to be owned as sound and solvent, and my word as good as my bond, and to be what cannot be skipped, or dissipated, or undermined, to all the *éclat* in the universe. This reality is the foundation of friendship, religion, poetry, and art. At the top or at the bottom of all illusions, I set the cheat which still leads us to work and live for appearances, in spite of our conviction, in all sane hours, that it is what we really are that avails with friends, with strangers, and with fate or fortune.

Wallace Stevens

(1879-1955)

POETS INFLUENCE US BECAUSE WE FALL IN LOVE WITH THEIR POEMS. ALL love unfortunately changes, if indeed it does not end, and since nothing is got for nothing, we also get hurt when we abandon, or are abandoned by, poems. Criticism is as much a series of metaphors for the acts of loving what we have read as for the acts of reading themselves. Walter Pater liked to use the word "appreciations" for his critical essays, and I present this particular series of metaphors as an appreciation of Wallace Stevens. Precisely, I mean to appreciate his success in writing the poems of our climate more definitively than any American since Whitman and Dickinson. What justifies an estimate that sets him higher than Frost, Pound, Eliot and Williams? If he is, as so many readers now believe, a great poet, at least the equal of such contemporaries as Hardy, Yeats, Rilke and Valéry, what are the qualities that make for greatness in him? How and why does he move us, enlighten us, enlarge our existences, and help us to live our lives?

Though the admirers of Stevens are a mighty band these days, they have not convinced all skeptics or detractors. We have had some difficulty in exporting him to the British, who with a few noble exceptions continue to regard him as a rather luxurious and Frenchified exquisite, a kind of upper-middle-class mock-Platonist who represents at best an American Aestheticism, replete with tropical fruits and aroma-laden invitations to the voyage. Their Stevens is the celebrator of Florida and of pre-Castro Havana, a vulgarian-in-spite-of-himself. Some American apostles of the Pound-Eliot-Williams-Olson axis are holdouts also; thus we find Hugh Kenner growling, in his recent *The Pound Era*, that all Stevens comes to is the ultimate realization of the poetics of Edward Lear. We can find also, apart from different adherents of the Gorgeous Nonsense school, those critics who complain that Stevens increasingly became desiccated and mock-philosophical; here one can remember Jarrell's crack about G.E. Moore at the spinet. Finally, sometimes we can hear the complaint of those who insist they are weary of poems about poetry, and so are rendered weariest by the recorder of *Notes Toward a Supreme Fiction*. Probably new fault-findings, more soundly based upon Stevens' actual limitations, will arrive as the decades pass. Someone will rise to ask the hard question: How many qualifications can you get into a single poem and still have a poem? Do we not get more than enough of these interjections that Stevens himself describes as "a few words, an and yet, and yet, and yet—"?

But an appreciation does not address itself to answering negative critics, or to proposing fresh negations. The reader who loves Stevens learns a passion for Yes, and learns also that such a passion, like the imagination, needs to be indulged. "It must give pleasure," Stevens says, following a supreme tradition, and his poems do give pleasure. This pleasure, though naturalistic, essentially helps to satisfy the never-satisfied mind, and to the pursuit of the meaning of that satisfaction I now turn. Courageously waving before me the gaudy banners of the Affective Fallacy, I ask myself what it is that reading Stevens does for me, and what is it that I then attempt to do for other readers of Stevens? Is it an effectual though reduced Romantic Humanism that is rekindled for us? Is it a last splendid if willfully grotesque triumph of the American Sublime? Is it, O glorious if this be so, an achieved survival of the Genteel Tradition, another final hedge against the barbarians who are, as we all know, not only within the gates but also indistinguishable, alas, except upon certain moonlit nights, from our very selves? Is the prudential Seer of Hartford only the most eloquent elaborator of our way of life, the Grand Defender of our sanctified evasions, our privileged status as the secular clergy of a society we cannot serve, let alone save? Have we committed the further and grievous sin of making a Stevens in our own image, a poet of professors as Auden and Eliot and Arnold used to be? Having employed Stevens as a weapon in the mimic wars of criticism against the anti-Romantic legions of the Eliotics and Arnoldians, are we now confronted by his poems as so many statues in the formal parks of our university culture? Are his poems still Spirit to us, or are they only what Emerson, most prudential of New England seers, shrewdly called Commodity? Have we made him too into Literature? Do we need now to defend him against ourselves?

Several critics have regarded Stevens as essentially a comic poet. I think this characterization is not adequate to even his more sardonic aspect, but at least it reminds us of how humorous he could be. One of my favorite poems in *Harmonium*, which I rarely persuade anyone else to like, is called "Two Figures in Dense Violet Light." I take it as being a superbly

American kind of defeated eroticism, the complaint of a would-be lover who is ruefully content to be discontent, because he rather doubts that high romance can be domesticated anyway in a world still so ruggedly New. One might think of this poem's speaker as being a decadent Huckleberry Finn dressed up to play the part of Romeo:

> I had as lief be embraced by the porter at the hotel
> As to get no more from the moonlight
> Than your moist hand.
>
> Be the voice of night and Florida in my ear.
> Use dusky words and dusky images.
> Darken your speech.
>
> Speak, even, as if I did not hear you speaking,
> But spoke for you perfectly in my thoughts,
> Conceiving words,
>
> As the night conceives the sea-sounds in silence,
> And out of their droning sibilants makes
> A serenade.
>
> Say, puerile, that the buzzards crouch on the ridge-pole
> And sleep with one eye watching the stars fall
> Below Key West.
>
> Say that the palms are clear in a total blue,
> Are clear and are obscure; that it is night;
> That the moon shines.

Though more than usually mocking and self-mocking, this is surely another of Stevens' hymns to the Interior Paramour, another invocation of his Muse, his version of Whitman's Fancy. But Whitman's Fancy, though she rarely emanated very far out from him, did have a touch or two of an exterior existence. Stevens' Paramour, poor girl, is the most firmly Interior being in Romantic tradition. Compared to her, the epipsyches of Nerval, Poe, Shelley and the young Yeats are buxom, open-air, Renoir-like ladies. Stevens knows this, and the violet light of his poem is so dense that the two figures might as well be one. "What a love affair!" we cannot help exclaiming, as the Grand Solipsist murmurs to his Paramour: "Speak, even, as if I did not hear you speaking, / But spoke for you perfectly in my thoughts."

This is a delicious Dialogue of One, all right, and we find its true father in some of Emerson's slyly bland observations on the Self-Reliance of Spheral Man. Recalling one Boscovich, an Italian Newtonian who had formulated a more-than-usually crazy version of the molecular theory of matter, Emerson mused: "Was it Boscovich who found that our bodies never come in contact? Well, souls never touch their objects. An innavigable sea washes with silent waves between us and the things we aim at and converse with."

In Stevens, this "innavigable sea" is called "the dumbfoundering abyss / Between us and the object," and no poet has been more honestly ruthless about the actual dualism of our everyday perceptions and imperceptions. Except for a peculiar roster of fabulistic caricatures, there aren't any *people* in Stevens' poems, and this exclusion is comprehensive enough to include Stevens himself as whole man or as person. But the "whole man" or "person" in a poem is generally only another formalizing device or dramatizing convention anyway, a means of self-presentation that Stevens did not care to employ. In the difficult poem, "The Creations of Sound," written against Eliot, who appears in it as X, Stevens declares himself as:

> ... a separate author, a different poet,
> An accretion from ourselves, intelligent
> Beyond intelligence, an artificial man
>
> At a distance, a secondary expositor,
> A being of sound, whom one does not approach
> Through any exaggeration.

For all his antimythological bias, the old Stevens turned to Ulysses, "symbol of the seeker," to present his own final quest for a transcendental self. Unlike the Ulysses of Tennyson, at once somewhat Homeric, Dantesque, Shakespearean and Miltonic, the Ulysses of Stevens is not seeking to meet anything even partly external to himself. What other Ulysses would start out by saying: "As I know, I am and have / The right to be"? For Stevens, "the right to know / And the right to be are one," but his Ulysses must go on questing because:

> Yet always there is another life,
> A life beyond this present knowing,
> A life lighter than this present splendor,
> Brighter, perfected and distant away,
> Not to be reached but to be known,

> Not an attainment of the will
> But something illogically received,
> A divination, a letting down
> From loftiness, misgivings dazzlingly
> Resolved in dazzling discovery.

There is, despite so many of his critics, no doubt concerning the precursor of this ultimate Stevens. For that "something illogically received," we can recall the divinations of the inescapable father of the American Sublime, who uttered the grand formula: "All I know is reception; I am and I have: but I do not get, and when I have fancied I had gotten anything, I found I did not." In the same essay, the superb "Experience," Emerson mused: "I am very content with knowing, if only I could know." Both Emerson and Stevens hold hard to what both call "poverty," imaginative need, and they believe that holding hard long enough will compel the self to attain its due sphericity. Between the skeptically transcendental grandfather and the transcendentally skeptical grandson came the heroic father, spheral man himself, unqualified in his divinations, who tells us what we miss in Emerson and Stevens alike, and what we cannot resist in him:

> Encompass worlds, but never try to encompass me,
> I crowd your sleekest and best by simply looking toward you.
>
> Writing and talk do not prove me,
> I carry the plenum of proof and every thing else in my face,
> With the hush of my lips I wholly confound the skeptic.

For the absolutely transcendental self, the man-god, we read Whitman only, but I am astonished always how much of it abides in Stevens, despite nearly all his critics, and despite the Idiot Questioner in Stevens himself. His evasive glory is hardly distinguishable from his imperfect solipsism, or from ours. And there I verge upon what I take as the clue to his greatness; in the curiously esoteric but centrally American tradition of Emerson, Whitman, Thoreau and Dickinson, Stevens is uniquely the twentieth century poet of that solitary and inward glory we can none of us share with others. His value is that he describes and even celebrates (occasionally) our selfhood-communings as no one else can or does. He knows that "the sublime comes down / To the spirit and space," and though he keeps acknowledging the spirit's emptiness and space's vacancy, he keeps demonstrating a violent abundance of spirit and a florabundance of the consolations of space. He is the poet we always needed, who would speak for the solitude at our center, who would do for us what his own "Large Red Man Reading" did for those ghosts that returned to earth to hear his phrases, "and spoke the feeling for them, which was what they had lacked." Or, to state this function positively, Stevens, more even than Wordsworth, is the essential poet who can recognize that:

> There is a human loneliness,
> A part of space and solitude,
> In which knowledge cannot be denied,
> In which nothing of knowledge fails,
> The luminous companion, the hand,
> The fortifying arm, the profound
> Response, the completely answering voice,
> That which is more than anything else
> The right within us and about us,
> Joined, the triumphant vigor, felt,
> The inner direction on which we depend,
> That which keeps us the little that we are,
> The aid of greatness to be and the force.

There is nothing communal here. Stevens celebrates an apprehension that has no social aspect whatsoever and that indeed appears resistant to any psychological reductions we might apply. As no one is going to be tempted to call Stevens a mystical poet, or in any way religious, we rightly *confront* a considerable problem in description whenever Stevens is most himself. His True Subject appears to be his own sense of glory, and his true value for his readers appears to be that he reminds us of our own moments of solipsistic bliss, or at least of our aspirations for such moments.

The Stevens I begin to sketch has little in common with the poet of "decreation" most of his better critics have described for us. There is indeed a Stevens as seen by Hillis Miller, a poet of the almost-Paterian flux of *sensations*, of a cyclic near-nihilism returning always upon itself. There is also truly a Stevens as seen by Helen Vendler: Stevens the venerable ironist, apostle of "the total leaflessness." I do not assert that these are merely peripheral aspects of the poet, but they seem to me aspects only, darker saliences that surround the central man, shadows flickering beyond that crucial light cast by the single candle of Stevens' self-joying imagination, his version of "A Quiet Normal Life":

His place, as he sat and as he thought, was not
In anything that he constructed, so frail,
So barely lit, so shadowed over and naught,

As, for example, a world in which, like snow,
He became an inhabitant, obedient
To gallant notions on the part of cold.

It was here. This was the setting and the time
Of year. Here in his house and in his room,
In his chair, the most tranquil thought grew peaked

And the oldest and the warmest heart was cut
By gallant notions on the part of night—
Both late and alone, above the crickets' chords,

Babbling, each one, the uniqueness of its sound.
There was no fury in transcendent forms.
But his actual candle blazed with artifice.

Stevens' customary anxiety about transcendent forms is evident, yet
it is also evident that his actual candle is precisely a transcendent form.
Wordsworth was sanely English in refusing to go too far into his True
Subject, which was his own sense of actual sublimity. Emerson, deliberately and wildly American, made possible for all his descendants the outrageous True Subject of the American Sublime. Mocking as always where he
is most vulnerable and most involved, here is Stevens' "The American
Sublime":

How does one stand
To behold the sublime,
To confront the mockers,
The mickey mockers
And plated pairs?

When General Jackson
Posed for his statue
He knew how one feels.
Shall a man go barefoot
Blinking and blank?

But how does one feel?
One grows used to the weather,
The landscape and that;
And the sublime comes down
To the spirit itself,

The spirit and space,
The empty spirit
In vacant space.
What wine does one drink?
What bread does one eat?

Juxtapose this to one of the pure versions of the American Sublime:

> In the highest moments, we are a vision. There is nothing that can be called gratitude nor properly joy. The soul is raised over passion. It seeth nothing so much as Identity. It is a Perceiving that Truth and Right ARE. Hence it becomes a perfect Peace out of the knowing that all things will go well. Vast spaces of nature, the Atlantic Ocean, the South Sea; vast intervals of time, years, centuries, are annihilated to it; this which I think and feel underlay that former state of life and circumstances, as it does underlie my present, and will always all circumstance, and what is called life and what is called death.

This excerpt from Emerson's 1838 Journal was modified into one of the most famous passages in the essay, "Self-Reliance." Nervous as Stevens is at confronting possible mockers, his American Sublime is no appreciable distance from Emerson's. One doesn't see Stevens posing for his statue, but he still admits that the Sublime comes down to what one feels and what one sees, and his emptiness of spirit and vacancy of space were part of the weather, inner and outer, and not permanent metaphysical reductions. That which he was, that only could he see, and he never wearied of affirming his version of Self-Reliance:

... What
One believes is what matters. Ecstatic identities
Between one's self and the weather and the things
Of the weather are the belief in one's element,
The casual reunions, the long-pondered
Surrenders, the repeated sayings that

There is nothing more and that it is enough
To believe in the weather and in the things and men
Of the weather and in one's self, as part of that
And nothing more.

How can a solipsism present itself in the accents of glory, we may be uneasy enough to ask, and again, can a solipsism be a possible humanism? I begin an answer with the dark Wittgensteinian aphorism: What the solipsist *means* is right. For, though solipsism is refutable by its status as tautology, this is what Wittgenstein means when he speaks of a *deep* tautology, which leads to a true realism. Stevens too knows, as Emerson knew, that what he *says* is wrong, but that his meaning is right. The European Sublime had a communal aspect, however solitary its stimulus, but we are of an even more displaced Protestant national sensibility, and, accordingly, we come to reality only through knowing first the scandalous reality of our own selves. Or, as Stevens said:

The lean cats of the arches of the churches,
That's the old world. In the new, all men are priests.

Stevens is a priest, not of the invisible, but of that visible he labors to make a little hard to see. He serves that visible, not for its own sake, but because he wants to make his own sublimity more visible to himself. Endlessly qualifying his sense of his own greatness, he still endlessly returns to rest upon such a sense. Yet he knows that he needs us, his possible readers, to do for him "what he cannot do for himself, that is to say, receive his poetry." As he proudly tells us, he addresses us as an elite, being in this one respect, at least, more honest than a far more esoteric and difficult poet, Whitman. In *The Noble Rider and the Sound of Words*, Stevens says:

> ... all poets address themselves to someone and it is of the essence of that instinct, and it seems to amount to an instinct, that it should be to an elite, not to a drab but to a woman with the hair of pythoness, not to a chamber of commerce but to a gallery of one's own, if there are enough of one's own to fill a gallery. And that elite, if it responds, not out of complaisance, but because the poet has quickened it, because he has educed from it that for which it was searching in itself and in the life around it and which it had not yet quite found, will thereafter do for the poet what he cannot do for himself, that is to say, receive his poetry.

There are two questions to be asked of this passage: What is it in this poet that gives him the instinct to address himself not to a drab but to a woman with the hair of a pythoness, and what is it that we keep searching for in ourselves that Stevens would quicken in us, that he would educe from us? The answer to both questions must be the same answer: a quality that Stevens calls "nobility." As he knew, it is hardly a word that now moves us, and I suspect he chose the word defiantly and therefore wrongly. Stevens says, in the same essay, that "It is one of the peculiarities of the imagination that it is always at the end of an era." Certainly Stevens now seems peculiarly to have been at the end of an era, where he himself could still be visualized as a *noble* rider moving to the sound of words. I myself have come to think that the principal peculiarity of the imagination is that it does not exist, or to state my thought another way, that people talking about the arts do better when they begin to talk as though the imagination did not exist. Let us reduce to the rocky level, and say, as Hobbes did, that "decaying sense" most certainly does exist. Stevens had then a decaying sense of nobility, which he called an imagination of nobility. "Noble," in its root, means to be knowing or seeing, and Stevens had therefore a decaying sense of a certain seeing that was also a knowing. I turn again to Stevens' central precursor for the inevitable vision of this nobility in its American variety:

> ... This insight, which expresses itself by what is called Imagination, is a very high sort of seeing, which does not come by study, but by the intellect being where and what it sees; by sharing the path or circuit of things through forms, and so making them translucid to others.

"Leave the many and hold the few," Emerson also advises in his late poem, "Terminus," thus sanctioning the democratic poet, like Whitman, in the pragmatic address to an actual elite. Stevens needed little sanctioning as to audience, but he was rather anxious about his own constant emphasis upon the self as solitary "scholar," and his recourse was to plead "poverty." He cannot have been unaware that both "scholar" and "poverty" in his rather precise senses were Emersonian usages. A great coverer of traces, Stevens may be judged nevertheless to have turned more to a tradition than to a man. American Romanticism found its last giant in Stevens, who defines the tradition quite as strongly as it informs him. "The prologues are over.... It is time to choose," and the Stevens I think we must choose writes the poems not of an empty spirit in vacant space, but of a spirit so full of itself that there is room for nothing else. This description hardly appears to flatter Stevens, yet I render it in his praise. Another of his still neglected poems, for which my own love is intense, is entitled simply, "Poem With Rhythms":

> The hand between the candle and the wall
> Grows large on the wall.
>
> The mind between this light or that and space,
> (This man in a room with an image of the world,
> That woman waiting for the man she loves,)
> Grows large against space:
>
> *There the man sees the image clearly at last.*
> *There the woman receives her lover into her heart*
> *And weeps on his breast, though he never comes.*
>
> It must be that the hand
> Has a will to grow larger on the wall,
> To grow larger and heavier and stronger than
> The wall; and that the mind
> Turns to its own figurations and declares,
> *"This image, this love, I compose myself*
> *Of these. In these, I come forth outwardly.*
> *In these, I wear a vital cleanliness,*
> *Not as in air, bright-blue-resembling air,*
> *But as in the powerful mirror of my wish and will."*

The principal difference between Stevens and Whitman appears to be that Stevens admits his mind is alone with its own figurations, while Whitman keeps inaccurately but movingly insisting he wants "contact" with other selves. His "contact" is an Emersonian term, and we know, as Whitman's readers, that he actually cannot bear "contact," any more than Emerson, Dickinson, Frost or Stevens can tolerate it. "Poem With Rhythms," like so much of Stevens, has a hidden origin in Whitman's "The Sleepers," particularly in a great passage apparently describing a woman's disappointment in love:

> I am she who adorn'd herself and folded her hair expectantly,
> My truant lover has come, and it is dark.
> Double yourself and receive me darkness,
> Receive me and my lover too, he will not let me go without him.

I roll myself upon you as upon a bed, I resign myself to the
    dusk.

He whom I call answers me and takes the place of my lover,
He rises with me silently from the bed.

Darkness, you are gentler than my lover, his flesh was sweaty
    and panting,
I feel the hot moisture yet that he left me.

My hands are spread forth, I pass them in all directions.
I would sound up the shadowy shore to which you are journeying.

Be careful, darkness! already, what was it touch'd me?
I thought my lover had gone, else darkness and he are one,
I hear the heart-beat, I follow, I fade away.

This juxtaposition of major Whitman to relatively minor Stevens is
not altogether fair, but then I don't think I hurt Stevens by granting that
Whitman, upon his heights, is likely to make his descendant seem only a
dwarf of disintegration. Whitman-as-Woman invokes the darkness of
birth, and blends himself into the mingled Sublimity of death and the
Native Strain. Stevens-as-Interior-Paramour invokes only his mind's own
figurations, but he sees himself cleansed in the vitalizing mirror of will as
he could never hope to see himself in the mere outwardness of air.
Whitman oddly but beautifully persuades us of a dramatic poignance that
his actual solipsism does not earn, while Stevens rather less beautifully
knows only the nondramatic truth of his own fine desperation.

What then is Stevens giving us? What do we celebrate with and in
him when he leads us to celebrate? His vigorous affirmation, "The Well
Dressed Man With a Beard," centers on "a speech / Of the self that must
sustain itself on speech." Is eloquence enough? I turn again to the fountain
of our will, Emerson, who had the courage to insist that eloquence was
enough, because he identified eloquence with "something unlimited and
boundless," in the manner of Cicero. Here is Stevens mounting through
eloquence to his individual sense of "something unlimited and boundless,"
a "something" not beyond our apprehension:

Last night at the end of night his starry head,
Like the head of fate, looked out in darkness, part
Thereof and part desire and part the sense

Of what men are. The collective being knew
There were others like him safely under roof.

The captain squalid on his pillow, the great
Cardinal, saying the prayers of earliest day;
The stone, the categorical effigy;
And the mother, the music, the name; the scholar,
Whose green mind bulges with complicated hues:

True transfigurers fetched out of the human mountain,
True genii for the diminished, spheres,
Gigantic embryos of populations,
Blue friends in shadows, rich conspirators,
Confiders and comforters and lofty kin.

To say more than human things with human voice,
That cannot be; to say human things with more
Than human voice, that, also, cannot be;
To speak humanly from the height or from the depth
Of human things, that is acutest speech.

A critic who has learned, ruefully, to accept the reductive view that the imagination is only decaying sense, must ask himself. Why is he so moved by this transfiguration of language into acutest speech? He may remember, in this connection, the prose statement by Stevens that moves him most:

> Why should a poem not change in sense when there is a fluc-
> tuation of the whole of appearance? Or why should it not
> change when we realize that the indifferent experience of life is
> the unique experience, the item of ecstasy which we have been
> isolating and reserving for another time and place, loftier and
> more secluded....

The doctrinal voice of Walter Pater, another unacknowledged ancestor, is heard in this passage, as perhaps it must be heard in any modern Epicureanism. Stevens, I suggest, is the Lucretius of our modern poetry, and like Lucretius seeks his truth in mere appearances, seeks his spirit in things of the weather. Both poets are beyond illusions, yet both invest their knowing of the way things are with a certain grim ecstasy. But an American Lucretius, coming after the double alienation of European Romanticism and domestic Transcendentalism, will have lost all sense of the communal in his ecstasy. Stevens fulfilled the unique enterprise of a specifically American poetry by exposing the essential solipsism of our Native Strain. No American feels free when he is not alone, and every American's passion for Yes affirms a hidden belief that his soul's substance is no part of the creation. We are mortal gods, the central strain in our poetry keeps saying, and our aboriginal selves are forbidden to find companionship in one another. Our ecstasy comes only from self-recognition, yet cannot be complete if we reduce wholly to "the evilly compounded, vital I ... made ... fresh in a world of white." We need "The Poems of Our Climate" because we are, happily, imperfect solipsists, unhappy in a happily imperfect and still external world—which is to say, we need Stevens:

> There would still remain the never-resting mind,
> So that one would want to escape, come back
> To what had been so long composed.
> The imperfect is our paradise.
> Note that, in this bitterness, delight,
> Since the imperfect is so hot in us,
> Lies in flawed words and stubborn sounds.

William Carlos Williams

(1883-1963)

IN HIS CRITICAL BIOGRAPHY *WILLIAM CARLOS WILLIAMS: A NEW WORLD Naked*, Paul Mariani wisely asserts the lasting influence of John Keats's poetry upon even the late phases of Williams:

> The voice he was listening to, and the voice that struck paydirt for him, was a matter of a complex crossing with Keats, especially the Keats of the *Hyperion* fragments and the odes. Why this should have been so is difficult to say with any exactness, for Williams himself probably did not understand why. What *he* thought he was "capturing" was the voice of the classics—the stately rhythms and sharp straightforward idiom of the Greeks as he thought they must sound should they be discovered walking the streets of his Paterson. But there was something more, a kinship Williams had felt with Keats for over half a century, the plight of the romantic poet who would have spoken as the gods speak if only he had had the power to render their speech in the accents of his own debased language. *Hyperion* is in part the portrait of the dying of the ephebe into the life of the major poet, and Keats had aborted it at the very moment that his poet was undergoing that transformation.
>
> And so with Williams, opting for the step-down line as his "classic" signature as he surfaced from the realization of his mortality, the new rhythm providing a stately, slow saraband to echo Keats's Miltonic and Dantesque phase with a difference. The crossing with Keats is there too in the nature of Williams's late iconography, in the stasis of his late images, frozen for eternity in the realized artifact, as in Williams's translation from

Theocritus's first idyll, with its images limned on a "two-eared bowl / of ivy-wood," a girl and two young men, an ancient fisherman, and a small boy preoccupied with "plaiting a pretty / cage of locust stalks and asphodel." The images of *Asphodel* too belong to the same strain: sharply realized but without Williams's earlier breathlessness and jagged line cuttings.

Poetic influence, an intensely problematical process, normally brings together a strong poet's earliest and final phases. Williams's true precursor, necessarily composite and in some sense imaginary, was a figure that fused Keats with Walt Whitman. Such a figure has in it the potential for a serious splitting of the poetic ego in its defense against the poetic past. The "negative capability" of Keats sorts oddly with Whitman's rather positive capability for conveying the powerful press of himself. "Memory is a kind / of accomplishment," Williams wrote in "The Descent," a crucial poem in his *The Desert Music* (1954). The descent to dying beckons to a return of the dead precursors in one's own colors, even as Keats and Whitman beckoned Williams to ascend into his own poetry. But the poem "The Descent" Williams shrewdly quarried from Book 2 of his own major long poem, *Paterson*, a quarrying that suggests his pride in his own continuities.

Those continuities are massive throughout Williams's best work, which can be cataloged (against the numerous Williams idolators) as a limited yet still remarkably diverse canon: *Paterson* (Book I), *Kora in Hell*, *Spring and All*, "The Widow's Lament in Springtime," "To Waken an Old Lady," "The Trees," "The Yachts," "A Coronal," "These," "The Poor," "A Marriage Ritual," "Raleigh Was Right," "Burning the Christmas Greens," "A Unison," and the grand return of Keats-as-Williams in *Asphodel, That Greeny Flower*. Every critic I have chosen for this volume would select more, much more, but I am of the school of Wallace Stevens, rather than of Williams, and the Williams I honor is the author of about a dozen shorter poems, and four remarkable long poems and prose or verse sequences. I write this introduction not to dissent, but as an experiment. If you believe—as I do—that Williams is not of the eminence of Stevens and Robert Frost, of Hart Crane and even of T.S. Eliot, then what is the irreducible achievement that survives even an extreme skepticism as to Williams's poetic greatness?

Of the volumes that collect Williams, I return most often to *Imaginations*, edited by Webster Schott (1979), which gathers together four weird American originals—*Kora in Hell*, *Spring and All*, *The Great American Novel*, *The Descent of Winter*—as well as some miscellaneous prose. *Kora in Hell* was subtitled *Improvisations* by Williams, who had a particular fondness for it. He analogized its astonishing "Prologue" to *On the Sublime* by the pseudo-Longinus, a comparison not so farfetched as he himself asserted it to be. Essentially it, and all of *Kora*, is a collection of what Emerson (following Plutarch and Cudworth) called "lustres" (Ezra Pound's *lustra*), aphoristic impressions drawn either from others or from the self. Its center is in Williams's characteristic polemic against Pound and Eliot, with an ironizing boost from Stevens:

> E.P. is the best enemy United States verse has. He is interested, passionately interested—even if he doesn't know what he is talking about. But of course he does know what he is talking about. He does not, however, know everything, not by more than half. The accordances of which Americans have the parts and the colors but not the completions before them pass beyond the attempts of his thought. It is a middle-aging blight of the imagination.
>
> I praise those who have the wit and courage, and the conventionality, to go direct toward their vision of perfection in an objective world where the signposts are clearly marked, viz., to London. But confine them in hell for their paretic assumption that there is no alternative but their own groove.
>
> Dear fat Stevens, thawing out so beautifully at forty! I was one day irately damning those who run to London when Stevens caught me up with his mild: "But where in the world will you have them run to?"

The shrewd link to *On the Sublime* is that Williams (admirably and accurately) shares the conviction of Longinus that the Sublime or strong poetry either is agonistic or it is nothing. Williams too seeks to persuade the reader to forsake easier pleasures (Eliot and Pound) for more difficult pleasures (*Kora in Hell*). And his quest is frankly Emersonian, an overt instance of American cultural nationalism. Unfortunately, *Kora*'s considerable verve and vivacity is shadowed by the immense power of James Joyce's *Ulysses*, still incomplete then, but appearing in magazine installments even as Williams wrote and read. Williams's use of mythology is essentially Joyce's, and to fight Joyce on any ground, let alone his prepared killing field, was beyond Williams's talents:

> Giants in the dirt. The gods, the Greek gods, smothered in filth and ignorance. The race is scattered over the world. Where is its home? Find it if you've the genius. Here Hebe

with a sick jaw and a cruel husband,—her mother left no place for a brain to grow. Herakles rowing boats on Berry's Creek! Zeus is a country doctor without a taste for coin jingling. Supper is of a bastard nectar on rare nights for they will come—the rare nights! The ground lifts and out sally the heroes of Sophokles, of Æschylus. They go seeping down into our hearts, they rain upon us and in the bog they sink again down through the white roots, down—to a saloon back of the railroad switch where they have that girl, you know, the one that should have been Venus by the lust that's in her. They've got her down there among the railroad men. A crusade couldn't rescue her. Up to jail—or call it down to Limbo—the Chief of Police our Pluto. It's all of the gods, there's nothing else worth writing of. They are the same men they always were—but fallen. Do they dance now, they that danced beside Helicon? They dance much as they did then, only, few have an eye for it, through the dirt and fumes.

The question becomes: who shall describe the dance of the gods as it is danced now in America? The answer is: Dr. Williams, who brings American babies into the world, and who sees exquisitely what we cannot see without him, which is how differently the gods come to dance here in America:

This is a slight stiff dance to a waking baby whose arms have been lying curled back above his head upon the pillow, making a flower—the eyes closed. Dead to the world! Waking is a little hand brushing away dreams. Eyes open. Here's a new world.

This dance figures again in the concluding improvisation of *Kora in Hell*, as an American seasonal rhythm akin to the natural year of Stevens's "Credences of Summer" and Emerson's "Experience":

Seeing the leaves dropping from the high and low branches the thought rises: this day of all others is the one chosen, all other days fall away from it on either side and only itself remains in perfect fullness. It is its own summer, of its leaves as they scrape on the smooth ground it must build its perfection. The gross summer of the year is only a halting counterpart of those fiery days of secret triumph which in reality themselves paint the year as if upon a parchment, giving each season a mockery of the warmth or frozenness which is within ourselves. The

true seasons blossom or wilt not in fixed order but so that many of them
may pass in a few weeks or hours whereas sometimes a whole life pass-
es and the season remains of a piece from one end to the other.

The world is largest in the American summer, for Williams and
Stevens, even as it was for their forefather, Emerson. *Spring and All* celebrates not this world, but the more difficult American skepticism of a hard
spring, imperishably rendered in its magnificent opening lyric, "By the
road to the contagious hospital," with its harsh splendor of inception, at
once of vegetation, infants, and of Whitmanian or American poems:

> Lifeless in appearance, sluggish
> dazed spring approaches—
>
> They enter the new world naked,
> cold, uncertain of all
> save that they enter. All about them
> the cold, familiar wind—
>
> Now the grass, tomorrow
> the stiff curl of wildcarrot leaf
> one by one objects are defined—
> It quickens: clarity, outline of leaf
>
> But now the stark dignity of
> entrance—Still, the profound change
> has come upon them: rooted, they
> grip down and begin to awaken

The ancient fiction of the leaves, a continuous tradition from Homer
and Virgil, through Dante and on to Spenser and Milton, Shelley and
Whitman, receives one culmination in Stevens, and a very different apotheosis here in Williams. In the prose of *Spring and All*, Williams protests too
emphatically that: "THE WORLD IS NEW," a protest that has been
taken too much at its own self-mystifying evaluation by the most distinguished of the deconstructive critics of Williams, J. Hillis Miller and
Joseph Riddel. But when the best poems in *Spring and All* unfold themselves, the reader can be persuaded that Williams has invented freshly the
accurate metaphors for our American sense of imaginative belatedness:
"There is / an approach with difficulty from / the dead—," and: "The rose
is obsolete / but each petal ends in / an edge." Except for "By the road to

the contagious hospital," the best poems in *Spring and All* are the justly famous ones: "The pure products of America / go crazy—," and "so much depends / upon / a red wheel / barrow."

More problematical are *The Great American Novel* and *The Descent of Winter*, pugnacious assaults upon Williams's own formal limits, yet assaults masked as ironies directed against the literary conventionalities of others. I prefer *The Descent of Winter*, where the authentic anxiety of belatedness, the only legitimate point of origin for any American literature, is expressed in relation to that most impossible of all influences, Shakespeare:

> By writing he escaped from the world into the natural world of his mind. The unemployable world of his fine head was unnaturally useless in the gross exterior of his day—or any day. By writing he made this active. He melted himself into that grossness, and colored it with his powers. The proof that he was right and they passing, being that he continues always and naturally while their artificiality destroyed them. A man unable to employ himself in his world.
>
> Therefore his seriousness and his accuracies, because it was not his play but the drama of his life. It is his anonymity that is baffling to nitwits and so they want to find an involved explanation—to defeat the plainness of the evidence.
>
> When he speaks of fools he is one; when of kings he is one, doubly so in misfortune.
>
> He is a woman, a pimp, a prince Hal—
>
> Such a man is a prime borrower and standardizer— No inventor. He lives because he sinks back, does not go forward, sinks back into the mass—
>
> He is Hamlet plainer than a theory—and in everything.
>
> You can't buy a life again after it's gone, that's the way I mean.
>
> He drinks awful bad and he beat me up every single month while I was carrying this baby, pretty nearly every week.

As an overview of Shakespeare, this is unquestionably the weakest commentary available since Tolstoy; but as a representation of Williams's dilemmas, it has a curious force, including the weird parody of Hemingway's agonistic stance in the last sentence I have just quoted. Despite his army of hyperbolic exegetes, Williams's nakedness in relation to the literary past is not so much that of "a new world naked" as it is that of a no longer so very new world awkwardly wrapped round by too many fine rags.

II

The best lyrics and Book I of *Paterson* are of a higher order, though they also betray darker anxieties of influence than even Williams's defiances dared to confront. They display also another kind of agon, the anxiety as to contemporary rivals, not so much Pound and Eliot as Wallace Stevens and Hart Crane, heirs to Keats and to Whitman, even as Williams was. No two readers are likely to agree upon just which shorter poems by Williams are his strongest, but the one that impresses and moves me most is "A Unison," where the title seems to comprehend most of the dictionary meanings of "unison": an identity of pitch in music; the same words spoken simultaneously by two or more speakers; musical parts combined in octaves; a concord, agreement, harmony. Thomas R. Whitaker, one of Williams's best and most sympathetic critics but no idolator, gives the best introduction to "A Unison":

> It is like an improvisation from *Kora in Hell*—but one with the quiet maturity of vision and movement that some three decades have brought.... As the implicit analogies and contrasts accumulate, we discover (long before the speaker tells us) that we are attending a "unison and a dance." This "death's festival"— *memento mori* and celebration of the "*Undying*"—evades neither the mystery of transience nor that of organic continuance, though neither can be "parsed" by the analytical mind.... In this composed testament of acceptance, Williams's saxifrage ("through metaphor to reconcile / the people and the stones") quietly does its work.... Not since Wordsworth has this natural piety been rendered so freshly and poignantly.

I would not wish to quarrel with Whitaker's judgment, yet there is very little Wordsworth and (inevitably) much Whitman and considerable Keats in "A Unison." Indeed, the poem opens with what must be called an echo from Whitman, in what I assume was a controlled allusion:

> The grass is very green, my friend,
> And tousled, like the head of—
> your grandson, yes?

We hear one or the uncanniest passages in Whitman, from *Song of Myself* 6:

This grass is very dark to be from the white heads of old mothers,
Darker than the colorless beards of old men,
Dark to come from under the faint red roofs of mouths.

Whitman's great fantasia answers a child's question: *"What is the grass?"* As an Epicurean materialist, Whitman believed that the *what* was unknowable, but his remarkable troping on the grass takes a grand turn after his Homeric line: "And now it seems to me the beautiful uncut hair of graves." Williams simply borrows the trope, and even his "very green" merely follows Whitman's hint that a "very green" becomes a "very dark" color, in the shadow of mortality. "A Unison" insists upon:

—what cannot be escaped: the
mountain riding the afternoon as
it does, the grass matted green,
green underfoot and the air—
rotten wood. *Hear! Hear them!*
the Undying. The hill slopes away,
then rises in the middleground,
you remember, with a grove of gnarled
maples centering the bare pasture,
sacred, surely—for what reason?

Williams does not know whether he can or cannot say the reason, but the allusion is to Keats's characteristic, Saturnian shrine in *Hyperion*. For Williams it is "a shrine cinctured there by / the trees," the girdling effect suggested by the natural sculpture of Keats's shrine. Where Keats as the quester in *The Fall of Hyperion* pledges "all the mortals of the world, / And all the dead whose names are in our lips," and where Whitman insists, "The smallest sprout shows there is really no death," Williams neither salutes the living and the dead, nor folds the two into a single figuration. Rather, he *hears* and urges us to: "*Hear the unison of their voices....*" How are we to interpret such an imaginative gesture? Are we hearing more, or enough more, than the unison of the voices of John Keats and Walt Whitman? Devoted Williamsites doubtless would reject the question, but it always retains its force, nevertheless. It is not less true of *The Waste Land* than it is of Williams. Eliot revises Whitman's "When Lilacs Last in the Dooryard Bloom'd" by fusing it with Tennyson (among others, but prime among those others). Image of voice or the trope of poetic identity then becomes a central problem.

Whitman once contrasted himself to Keats by rejecting "negative capability" and insisting instead that the great poet gave us the "powerful press of himself." Admirable as *Paterson* is (particularly its first book), does even it resolve the antithesis in Williams between his "objectivism" or negative capability, and his own, agonistic, powerful press of himself? Mariani ends his vast, idealizing biography by asserting that Williams established "an American poetic based on a new measure and a primary regard for the living, protean shape of the language as it was actually used." Hillis Miller, even more generously, tells us that Williams gave us a concept of poetry transcending both Homer and Wordsworth, both Aristotle and Coleridge:

> The word is given reality by the fact it names, but the independence of the fact from the word frees the word to be a fact in its own right and at the same time "dynamizes" it with meaning. The word can then carry the facts named in a new form into the realm of imagination.

Mariani and Miller are quite sober compared to more apocalyptic Williamsites. Not even Whitman gave us "a new measure," and not Shakespeare himself freed a single word "to be a fact in its own right." William Carlos Williams was, at his best, a strong American poet, far better than his hordes of imitators. Like Ezra Pound's, Williams's remains a fairly problematical achievement in the traditions of American poetry. Some generations hence, it will become clear whether his critics have canonized him permanently, or subverted him by taking him too much at his own intentions. For now he abides, a live influence, and perhaps with even more fame to come.

H.D. (Hilda Doolittle)

(1886-1961)

LIKE EZRA POUND, HER CLOSE FRIEND AND POETIC COLLEAGUE, H.D. seems to me essentially an American pre-Raphaelite poet, a naming that I intend as a compliment since I deeply love the poetry of the Rossettis, Morris, Meredith, and Swinburne. Even as Pound assimilates Dante Gabriel Rossetti to Walt Whitman, so H.D. compounds Christina Rossetti with Emily Dickinson, and both together with the male sequence of Dante Gabriel Rossetti, William Morris, Pound, and D.H. Lawrence.

Louis L. Martz, in his "Introduction" to H.D.'s *The Collected Poems 1912–1944*, sensitively sketches the relation between the psychosexual and the poetic crises that kept her from publishing any volumes of poetry between 1931 and 1944. Her brief analysis with Freud himself (about three months in 1933, and some five weeks in 1934) issued not only in her *Tribute to Freud* but in a number of fairly strong if problematic poems, three in particular, which Martz reports she grouped in the order of "The Dancer," "The Master," and "The Poet." "The Dancer" is the most problematic of these and perhaps would not matter much, except that it informs a powerful return of its central trope in the midst of "The Master," which is a moving tribute to Freud. Martz shrewdly calls "The Poet" a calm and measured tribute to D.H. Lawrence, and while it is not as distinguished a poem as "The Master," it has its own value and place in H.D.'s achievement.

Tribute to Freud is a rather overpraised book, particularly dear to Freudian literalists from Ernest Jones to the present since it is a kind of hagiography. H.D. herself chats on rapturously, while the old Professor somehow never does get to say anything remotely memorable. Precisely how he clarifies either the poet's bisexuality or her creative inhibitions may escape even the most assiduous and skilled reader. Section 10 of "Writing on the Wall," the first part of the *Tribute*, is both famous and typical:

So much for the Princess, Hanns Sachs, and Walter Schmideberg, the one-time Rittmeister of the 15th Imperial Austro-Hungarian Hussars of His Royal Highness, Archduke Francis Salvator. For myself, I veer round, uncanonically seated stark upright with my feet on the floor. The Professor himself is uncanonical enough; he is beating with his hand, with his fist, on the head-piece of the old-fashioned horsehair sofa that had heard more secrets than the confession box of any popular Roman Catholic father-confessor in his heyday. This was the homely historical instrument of the original scheme of psychotherapy, of psychoanalysis, the science of the unravelling of the tangled skeins of the unconscious mind and the healing implicit in the process. *Consciously*, I was not aware of having said anything that might account for the Professor's outburst. And even as I veered around, facing him, my mind was detached enough to wonder if this was some idea of *his* for speeding up the analytic content or redirecting the flow of associated images. The Professor said, "The trouble is—I am an old man—*you do not think it worth your while to love me*."

("Writing on the Wall")

Presumably such a shock tactic was intended to speed up the transference, but if Freud actually said anything like this, then he was mistaken, as clearly H.D. loved him beyond measure. "But the Professor insisted I myself wanted to be Moses; not only did I want to be a boy but I wanted to be a hero." That certainly sounds like Freud, or by now like a self-parody on his part. There is something quaintly archaic about *Tribute to Freud*, where the Professor's interventions are so accurate, his spiritual efficacy so instantaneous, as to suggest the advent of a new age of faith, the Freud era. A prose memorial provokes our resistances when it seems too pious or too amiably earnest. The pre-Raphaelite aura, hieratic and isolated, with its characteristic effect of a hard-edged phantasmagoria, rescues "The Master" from the cloying literalism of the *Tribute*. "The old man" of the poem is God's prophet, since "the dream is God," and Freud therefore is heard as one who speaks with authority: "his command / was final" and "his tyranny was absolute, / for I had to love him then." The command, at least as H.D. interpreted it, was to accept her own bisexuality as being one with her poethood:

I do not know what to say to God,
for the hills

answer his nod,
and the sea
when he tells his daughter,
white Mother
of green
leaves
and green rills
and silver,
to still
tempest
or send peace
and surcease of peril
when a mountain has spit fire:

I did not know how to differentiate
between volcanic desire,
anemones like embers
and purple fire
of violets
like red heat,
and the cold
silver
of her feet:
I had two loves separate;
God who loves all mountains,
alone knew why
and understood
and told the old man
to explain
the impossible,
which he did.
("The Master")

The phallic or volcanic is evidently preferred by this male God, at least rhetorically, but of the "two loves separate" the "cold / silver / of her feet" triumphs with the re-entry of the dancer in section 5. The force that comes with celebration of the dancer depends upon H.D.'s vision of herself as wrestling Jacob, arguing till daybreak, and of Freud as God or His angel, giving further rhetorical primacy to "the man-strength" rather than to the dancer's leapings:

I was angry with the old man
with his talk of the man-strength,
I was angry with his mystery, his mysteries,
I argued till day-break;

O, it was late,
and God will forgive me, my anger,
but I could not accept it.

I could not accept from wisdom
what love taught,
woman is perfect.
("The Dancer")

That would appear to have meant that a woman's bisexuality or her perfection (in the sense of completeness) was of a different and more acceptable order than a man's bisexuality. The ecstasy of section 5 gently mocks the Freudian "man-strength" even as it salutes the dancer for needing no male, since at least as dancer (or poet) woman is indeed pragmatically perfect. Section 5 has a kind of uncanny force, akin to Yeatsian celebrations of the dancer as image. But the authentic strength of the poem centers elsewhere, in its elegiac identifications of the dead father, Freud, with the earth, and with all the dead fathers. Freud is Saturn, ancient wisdom, and the rock that cannot be broken—a new earth. His temples will be everywhere, yet H.D. cries out: "only I, I will escape," an escape sanctioned by Freud as the freedom of the woman poet. Though D.H. Lawrence is not even alluded to in "The Master," he enters the poem by negation, since it is transformed into a fierce hymn against Lawrence's vision of sexual release:

no man will be present in those mysteries,
yet all men will kneel,
no man will be potent,
important,
yet all men will feel
what it is to be a woman,
will yearn,
burn,
turn from easy pleasure
to hardship
of the spirit,

men will see how long they have been blind,
poor men
poor man-kind
how long
how long
this thought of the man-pulse has tricked them.
has weakened them,
shall see woman,
perfect.
("The Master")

The blindness is precisely Lawrence's in H.D's judgment, and it is hinted at, in muted form, in "The Poet," not so much an elegy for Lawrence as for her failed friendship with him. What seems clear is that her sexual self-acceptance, whether Freudian or not, gave her the creative serenity that made possible the wonderfully controlled, hushed resignation of her wisely limited farewell to Lawrence:

No,
I don't pretend, in a way, to understand,
nor know you,
nor even see you;

I say,
"I don't grasp his philosophy,
and I don't understand,"

but I put out a hand, touch a cold door,
(we have both come from so far);
I touch something imperishable;
I think,
why should he stay there?
why should he guard a shrine so alone,
so apart,
on a path that leads nowhere?

he is keeping a candle burning in a shrine
where nobody comes,
there must be some mystery
in the air
about him,

he couldn't live alone in the desert,
without vision to comfort him,
there must be voices somewhere.
("The Poet")

The wistfulness of that tribute, if it is a tribute, veils the harshness of the critique. A woman can be perfect, but a man cannot, though Lawrence would not learn this. One can imagine his response to H.D.; it would have been violent, but that perhaps would have confirmed her stance, whether sanctioned or unsanctioned by her father and master, Freud.

Marianne Moore

(1887–1972)

For Plato the only reality that mattered is exemplified best for us in the principles of mathematics. The aim of our lives should be to draw ourselves away as much as possible from the unsubstantial, fluctuating facts of the world about us and establish some communion with the objects which are apprehended by thought and not sense. This was the source of Plato's asceticism. To the extent that Miss Moore finds only allusion tolerable she shares that asceticism. While she shares it she does so only as it may be necessary for her to do so in order to establish a particular reality or, better, a reality of her own particulars.

—WALLACE STEVENS

ALLUSION WAS MARIANNE MOORE'S METHOD, A METHOD THAT WAS HER SELF. One of the most American of all poets, she was fecund in her progeny— Elizabeth Bishop, May Swenson, and Richard Wilbur being the most gifted among them. Her own American precursors were not Emily Dickinson and Walt Whitman—still our two greatest poets—but the much slighter Stephen Crane, who is echoed in her earliest poems, and in an oblique way Edgar Poe, whom she parodied. I suspect that her nearest poetic father, in English, was Thomas Hardy, who seems to have taught her lessons in the mastery of incongruity, and whose secularized version of Biblical irony is not far from her own. If we compare her with her major poetic contemporaries—Frost, Stevens, Eliot, Pound, Williams, Aiken, Ransom, Cummings, H.D., Hart Crane—she is clearly the most original American poet of her era, though not quite of the eminence of Frost, Stevens, Crane. A curious kind of devotional poet, with some authentic affinities to George Herbert, she reminds us implicitly but constantly that any distinction between sacred and secular poetry is only a shibboleth of cultural politics.

Some day she will remind us also of what current cultural politics obscure: that any distinction between poetry written by women or poetry by men is a mere polemic, unless it follows upon an initial distinction between good and bad poetry. Moore, like Bishop and Swenson, is an extraordinary poet-as-poet. The issue of how gender enters into her vision should arise only after the aesthetic achievement is judged as such.

Moore, as all her readers know, to their lasting delight, is the visionary of natural creatures: the jerboa, frigate pelican, buffalo, monkeys, fish, snakes, mongooses, the octopus (actually a trope for a mountain), snail, peacock, whale, pangolin, wood-weasel, elephants, race horses, chameleon, jellyfish, arctic ox (or goat), giraffe, blue bug (another trope, this time for a pony), all of La Fontaine's bestiary, not to mention sea and land unicorns, basilisks, and all the weird fabulous roster that perhaps only Borges also, among crucial modern writers, celebrates so consistently. There is something of Blake and of the Christopher Smart of *Jubilate Agno* in Moore, though the affinity does not result from influence, but rather is the consequence of election. Moore's famous eye, like that of Bishop after her, is not so much a visual gift as it is visionary, for the beasts in her poems are charged with a spiritual intensity that doubtless they possess, but which I myself cannot see without the aid of Blake, Smart, and Moore.

I remember always in reading Moore again that her favorite poem was the Book of Job. Just as I cannot read Ecclesiastes without thinking of Dr. Johnson, I cannot read certain passages in Job without recalling Marianne Moore:

> But ask now the beasts, and they shall teach thee; and the fowls
> of the air, and they shall tell thee:
> Or speak to the earth, and it shall teach thee: and the fishes
> of the sea shall declare unto thee.
> Who knoweth not in all these that the hand of the Lord hath
> wrought this?
> In whose hand is the soul of every living thing.

This, from chapter 12, is the prelude to the great chant of Yahweh, the Voice out of the whirlwind that sounds forth in the frightening magnificence of chapters 38 through 41, where the grand procession of beasts comprehends lions, ravens, wild goats, the wild ass, the unicorn, peacocks, the ostrich, the sublime battle-horse who "saith among the trumpets, Ha, ha," the hawk, the eagle, and at last behemoth and leviathan. Gorgeously celebrating his own creation, Yahweh through the poet of job engendered another strong poet in Marianne Moore. Of the Book of job, she remarked that its agony was veracious and its fidelity of a force "that contrives glory for ashes."

"Glory for ashes" might be called Moore's ethical motto, the basis for the drive of her poetic will toward a reality of her own particulars. Her poetry, as befitted the translator of La Fontaine, and the heir of George Herbert, would be in some danger of dwindling into moral essays, an impossible form for our time, were it not for her wild allusiveness, her zest for quotations, and her essentially anarchic stance, the American and Emersonian insistence upon seeing everything in her own way, with "conscientious inconsistency." When her wildness or freedom subsided, she produced an occasional poetic disaster like the patriotic war poems "In Distrust of Merits" and "'Keeping Their World Large.'" But her greatest poems are at just the opposite edge of consciousness: "A Grave," "Novices," "Marriage," "An Octopus," "He 'Digesteth Harde Yron,'" "Elephants," the deceptively light "Tom Fool at Jamaica."

Those seven poems by themselves have an idiosyncratic splendor that restores my faith, as a critic, in what the language of the poets truly is: diction, or choice of words, playing endlessly upon the dialectic of denotation and connotation, a dialectic that simply vanishes in all Structuralist and post-Structuralist ruminations upon the supposed priority of "language" over meaning. "The arbitrariness of the signifier" loses its charm when one asks a Gallic psycholinguistifier whether denotation or connotation belongs to the signifier, as opposed to the signified, and one beholds blank incredulity as one's only answer. Moore's best poems give the adequate reply: the play of the signifier is answered always by the play of the signified, because the play of diction, or the poet's will over language, is itself constituted by the endless interchanges of denotation and connotation. Moore, with her rage to order allusion, echo, and quotation in ghostlier demarcations, keener sounds, helps us to realize that the belated Modernism of the Gallic proclamation of the death of the author was no less premature than it was, always already, belated.

II

Marriage, through which thought does not penetrate, appeared to Miss Moore a legitimate object for art, an art that would not halt from using thought about it, however, as it might want to. Against marriage, "this institution, perhaps one should say enterprise"—Miss Moore launched her thought not to have it appear arsenaled as in a textbook on psychology, but to stay among apples and giraffes in a poem.

—WILLIAM CARLOS WILLIAMS

If I had to cite a single poem by Moore as representing all of her powers working together, it would be "Marriage" (1923), superficially an outrageous collage but profoundly a poignant comic critique of every society's most sacred and tragic institution. As several critics have ventured, this is Moore's *The Waste Land*, a mosaic of fragments from Francis Bacon, the *Scientific American*, Baxter's *The Saint's Everlasting Rest*, Hazlitt on Burke, William Godwin, Trollope, *The Tempest*, a book on *The Syrian Christ*, the Bible, Ezra Pound, and even Daniel Webster (from an inscription on a statue!), and twenty sources more. Yet it is a poem, and perhaps is more ruggedly unified than any other poem of such ambition by Moore.

The poet's own headnote to "Marriage" could not be more diffident: "Statements that took my fancy which I tried to arrange plausibly." The arrangement is more than plausible; it is quite persuasive, though it begins with a parody of the societal *apologia* for marriage:

> This institution,
> perhaps one should say enterprise
> out of respect for which
> one says one need not change one's mind
> about a thing one has believed in,
> requiring public promises
> of one's intention
> to fulfil a private obligation.

No one, I believe, could interpret that opening stance with any exactitude. The substitution of "enterprise" for "institution" qualifies the wryness of "public promises / of one's intention / to fulfil a private obligation," but adds a note both of commerce and of the human virtue of taking an initiative. Who could have anticipated that the next movement of the poem would be this?

> I wonder what Adam and Eve
> think of it by this time,
> this fire-gilt steel
> alive with goldenness;
> how bright it shows—
> "of circular traditions and impostures,
> committing many spoils,"
> requiring all one's criminal ingenuity
> to avoid!

Like nearly every other quotation in this poem, the two lines from Sir Francis Bacon gain nothing for Moore's own text by being restored to their own context. Steel burned by fire does not exactly brighten into a golden bough, so the "gilt" is there partly as anticipation of "criminal ingenuity." Yet "gilt" is in cognitive sequence with "goldenness" and "bright," even if we rightly expect to behold blackened steel. All who have known marriage (as Moore declined to do) will register an unhappy shudder at the force the Baconian phrases take on when Moore appropriates them. Traditions as treasons become circular, and together with impostures can be read here either as performing many despoilments or as investing many gains of previous despoilments. Either way, it might seem as though an ingenuity avoiding this equivocal enterprise could only be taken as criminal by some dogmatist, whether societal or theological.

The poem proceeds to dismiss psychology, since to explain everything is to explain nothing, and then meditates upon the beauty, talents, and contrariness of Eve, a meditation that suddenly achieves Paterian intensity:

> Below the incandescent stars
> below the incandescent fruit,
> the strange experience of beauty;
> its existence is too much;
> it tears one to pieces
> and each fresh wave of consciousness
> is poison.

The detachment of Moore as watcher is not totally lost, but seems (by design) never fully recovered again in the poem. A woman's fine bitterness against the West's endless assault upon Eve is felt in Moore's description of the universal mother as "the central flaw" in the experiment of Eden, itself "an interesting impossibility" ecstatically described by Richard Baxter as "the choicest piece of my life." If Baxter's ecstasy (though not his eloquence) is qualified shrewdly by Moore's contextualizations, Eden is nowhere near so scaled down by her as is Adam, whose male pomp is altogether undermined. He is pretty well identified with Satan, and like Satan is: "alive with words, / vibrating like a cymbal / touched before it has been struck."

Moore's genius at her method allows her the joy of exemplifying her borrowings even as she employs them in a corrective polemic against male slanderings of women:

"Treading chasms
on the uncertain footing of a spear,"
forgetting that there is in woman
a quality of mind
which as an instinctive manifestation
is unsafe,
he goes on speaking
in a formal customary strain.

In the first quotation, Hazlitt is praising his precursor Edmund Burke for a paradoxically certain footing: for power, energy, truth set forth in the Sublime style. Burke is a chasm-treader, sure-footed as he edges near the abyss. But men less given to truth than Burke have very uncertain footing indeed, whether they forget or remember their characteristic brutalities in regard to a woman's "quality of mind." The poem's "he" therefore goes on speaking of marriage in Richard Baxter's ecstatic terms, as though marriage itself somehow could become "the saints' everlasting rest." Fatuously joyous, the male is ready to suffer the most exquisite passage in the poem, and perhaps in all of Moore:

Plagued by the nightingale
in the new leaves,
with its silence—
not its silence but its silences,
he says of it:
"It clothes me with a shirt of fire."
"He dares not clap his hands
to make it go on
lest it should fly off;
if he does nothing, it will sleep;
if he cries out, it will not understand."
Unnerved by the nightingale
and dazzled by the apple,
impelled by "the illusion of a fire
effectual to extinguish fire,"
compared with which
the shining of the earth
is but deformity—a fire
"as high as deep
as bright as broad
as long as life itself,"

> he stumbles over marriage,
> "a very trivial object indeed"
> to have destroyed the attitude
> in which he stood—.

I hardly know of a more unnerving representation of the male fear and distrust of the female, uncannily combined with the male quandary of being obsessed with, fascinated by, not only the female but the enterprise of marriage as well. Moore imperishably catches the masterpiece of male emotive ambivalence towards the female, which is the male identification of woman and the taboo. Here the nightingale, perhaps by way of Keats's erotic allusions, becomes an emblem of the female, while the male speaker, ravished by the silences of the emblem, becomes Hercules suicidally aflame with the shirt of Nessus. The poor male, "unnerved by the nightingale / and dazzled by the apple," stumbles over the enterprise that is Adam's experiment, marriage:

> its fiddlehead ferns,
> lotus flowers, opuntias, white dromedaries,
> its hippopotamus—
> nose and mouth combined
> in one magnificent hopper—
> its snake and the potent apple.

We again receive what might be called Moore's Paradox: marriage, considered from either the male or female perspective, is a dreadful disaster, but as a poetic trope gorgeously shines forth its barbaric splendors. The male, quoting Trollope's *Barchester Towers*, returns us to the image of Hercules, and commends marriage "as a fine art, as an experiment, / a duty or as merely recreation." I myself will never get out of my memory Moore's subsequent deadpan definition of marriage as "the fight to be affectionate." With a fine impartiality, the poet has a vision of the agonists in this eternal dispute:

> The blue panther with black eyes,
> the basalt panther with blue eyes,
> entirely graceful—
> one must give them the path—.

But this mutual splendor abates quickly, and a rancorous humor emerges:

He says, "What monarch would not blush
to have a wife
with hair like a shaving brush?"
The fact of woman
is "not the sound of the flute
but very poison."
She says, "Men are monopolists
of 'stars, garters, buttons
and other shining baubles'—
unfit to be the guardians
of another person's happiness."
He says, "These mummies
must be handled carefully—
'the crumbs from a lion's meal,
a couple of shins and the bit of an ear';
turn to the letter M
and you will find
that 'a wife is a coffin.'

This marvelous exchange of diatribes is weirdly stitched together from outrageously heterogeneous "sources," ranging from a parody of *The Rape of the Lock* (in which Moore herself took a hand) to a women's college president's denunciation of the male love of awards and medals on to a surprising misappropriation of a great moment in the prophet Amos, which is then juxtaposed to a brutal remark of Ezra Pound's. Amos associates the lion with Yahweh:

> The lion hath roared, who will not fear? the Lord GOD hath spoken, who can but prophesy?
>
> Thus saith the LORD; As the shepherd taketh out of the mouth of the lion two legs, or a piece of an ear; so shall the children of Israel be taken out that dwell in Samaria in the corner of a bed, and in Damascus in a couch.

Moore slyly revises the roaring prophet, making the lion every male, and the children of Israel every woman. Pound's dictum, that "a wife is a coffin" is presumably placed under the letter M for "male," and sorts well with Moore's unfair but strong revision of Amos, since the revision suggests that a wife is a corpse. In order to show that her revisionary zeal is savagely if suavely directed against both sexes (or rather their common frailties), Moore proceeds to dissect the narcissism of men

and women alike, until she concludes with the most ironic of her visions
in the poem:

> "I am such a cow,
> if I had a sorrow
> I should feel it a long time;
> I am not one of those
> who have a great sorrow
> in the morning
> and a great joy at noon";

> which says: "I have encountered it
> among those unpretentious
> protégés of wisdom,
> where seeming to parade
> as the debater and the Roman,
> the statesmanship
> of an archaic Daniel Webster
> persists to their simplicity of temper
> as the essence of the matter:

> 'Liberty and union
> now and forever';

> the Book on the writing table;
> the hand in the breast pocket."

Webster, hardly unpretentious, and wise only in his political cunning, is indeed the message inscribed upon his statue: "Liberty and union
/ now and forever." As a judgment upon marriage, it would be a hilarious
irony, if we did not wince so much under Moore's not wholly benign tute-
lage. That Book on the writing table, presumably the Bible, is precisely like
Webster's hand in the breast pocket, an equivocal emblem, in this context,
of the societal benediction upon marriage. Moore's own *The Waste Land*,
"Marriage," may outlast Eliot's poem as a permanent vision of the West in
its long, ironic decline.

Claude McKay

(1889–1948)

THE JAMAICAN CLAUDE MCKAY, WHO WENT FROM MARXISM TO ROMAN Catholicism, was a fierce spirit, whose sonnets have a formalist, baroque intensity that is also now undervalued, as here in "Saint Isaac's Church, Petrograd":

> Bow down my soul in worship very low
> And in the holy silences be lost.
> Bow down before the marble man of woe,
> Bow down before the singing angel host.
>
> What jewelled glory fills my spirit's eye!
> What golden grandeur moves the depths of me!
> The soaring arches lift me up on high
> Taking my breath with their rare symmetry.
>
> Bow down my soul and let the wondrous light
> Of Beauty bathe thee from her lofty throne
> Bow down before the wonder of man's might.
> Bow down in worship, humble and alone;
> Bow lowly down before the sacred sight
> Of man's divinity alive in stone.

This is still the admirer of Leon Trotsky, but the poem's complexity arises out of McKay's repressed awareness that something in his spirit is moving towards conversion. The sestet retreats from the octave's spirituality, and overtly hymns an aesthetic humanism. And yet "The marble man of woe," a representation of the Russian Christ, is not wholly consonant with "man's divinity alive in stone."

The most rugged of McKay's poems is "The Desolate City," a Romantic lament for the lost innocence of the spirit, and another indication of this poet's road to Rome. It may be that McKay, poetically speaking, was born at the wrong time, but too late rather than too early. For all his political anger, which has an authority difficult to withstand, he would have been culturally at home in the Catholicism of Gerard Manley Hopkins and Francis Thompson, a generation earlier than his own.

E.E. cummings

(1894-1962)

THE POET'S FATHER, EDWARD CUMMINGS, WAS BY ALL ACCOUNTS AN impressive person: Unitarian minister, Harvard sociologist, an athlete and outdoorsman, an exuberant personality. He died in a locomotive–automobile collision in the autumn of 1926. "my father moved through dooms of love" was published as number 34 of the *50 Poems* (1934).

Any ambivalence between son and father overtly vanishes in this celebratory poem, though doubtless it remains between the lines, as it were. What renders this elegiac lyric so poignant is its identification with the dead father, and a wonderfully open expression of filial love:

> my father moved through dooms of love
> through sames of am through haves of give,
> singing each morning out of each night
> my father moved through depths of height
>
> this motionless forgetful where
> turned at his glance to shining here;
> that if (so timid air is firm)
> under his eyes would stir and squirm
>
> newly as from unburied which
> floats the first who, his April touch
> drove sleeping selves to swarm their fates
> woke dreamers to their ghostly roots
>
> and should some why completely weep
> my father's fingers brought her sleep:

vainly no smallest voice might cry
for he could feel the mountains grow.

Lifting the valleys of the sea
my father moved through griefs of joy;
praising a forehead called the moon
singing desire into begin

joy was his song and joy so pure
a heart of star by him could steer
and pure so now and now so yes
the wrists of twilight would rejoice

keen as midsummer's keen beyond
conceiving mind of sun will stand,
so strictly (over utmost him
so hugely) stood my father's dream

The characteristic flaw in Cummings is his flagrant sentimentalism, but who would find emotion in excess of the object in this poem? Hyperbolical flaws begin to appear after these first seven stanzas—"his anger was as right as rain" and "his shoulders marched against the dark." Still, the lively metric of the poem partly obscures these banalities. The two final stanzas are pitched so high that they ought not to work, but they do. The father, who preached the social gospel and believed in the potential divinity of all people, returns in the spirit to elevate the son's rhetoric:

though dull were all we taste as bright,
bitter all utterly things sweet,
maggoty minus and dumb death
all we inherit,all bequeath

and nothing quite so least as truth
—I say though that were why men breathe—
because my father lived his soul
love is the whole and more than all

Partly this is effective because Cummings is *not* his father: his own myth did not stress universal love, or potential divinity, but rather isolation, the difficulty of love, the reality of death. That makes more vivid and valuable the transcendence of his filial tribute.

Jean Toomer

(1894–1967)

JEAN TOOMER'S REMARKABLE *CANE* (1923), A SUBTLY INTERWOVEN MEDLEY of prose-poem and verse, was never matched by him again in the more than forty years remaining. *The Blue Meridian* (1929) fades away in contrast with Hart Crane's *The Bridge* (1930), though Toomer and Crane were friends, and some mutual influence was involved. Toomer's immersion in quack spiritualities was fatal both to his work and his sense of identity. And yet, in his brief flowering, he became the authentic poet of what would have to be called black pastoral, as in his marvelous "November Cotton Flower":

> Boll-weevil's coming, and the winter's cold,
> Made cotton-stalks look rusty, seasons old,
> And cotton, scarce as any southern snow,
> Was vanishing; the branch, so pinched and slow,
> Failed in its function as the autumn rake;
> Drouth fighting soil had caused the soil to take
> All water from the streams; dead birds were found
> In wells a hundred feet below the ground—
> Such was the season when the flower bloomed.
> Old folks were startled, and it soon assumed
> Significance. Superstition saw
> Something it had never seen before:
> Brown eyes that loved without a trace of fear,
> Beauty so sudden for that time of year.

This extraordinary lyric is both beautifully wrought and humanly profound. The late blooming of the flower becomes emblematic of a freedom from psychic dearth, the freedom to love.

Robert Graves

(1895–1985)

IN 1948, I WAS ONE OF MANY YOUNG ENTHUSIASTS FOR POETRY WHO FELL in love with *The White Goddess: A Historical Grammar of Poetic Myth* by the lyric poet and popular novelist Robert Graves. Graves died December 8, 1985, at his home in Deya, Majorca, and I began writing this introduction some seven months later, in July 1986, after having reread *The White Goddess* for the first time in many years. Nearly four decades after first reading Graves's remarkable phantasmagoria, I cannot recover the enchantment that the book held for me when I was eighteen. What replaces mystery, and intellectual desire, is the puzzled impression I remember recording back in 1969, the last time I reread *The White Goddess*:

> The shamanism of Empedocles, so strangely reborn in Yeats's *A Vision*, Lawrence's *Fantasia of the Unconscious*, and Graves's *The White Goddess*, proposes a preternatural catharsis to heal a magical spirit in us....
>
> Romantic poetry, in its long history, has been saved ... by its sense of its own tradition, by the liberating burden of poetic influence. Yeats, Lawrence, Graves—despite their varied and real poetic successes—willfully placed their First Romantics too freely and too far away, and.were saved from too crippling a freedom by the relative proximity of their true Romantic ancestors: Blake and Shelley for Yeats, Whitman and Hardy for Lawrence, Keats and Hardy for Graves....
>
> When we turn to the major descendants of Romanticism in modern poetry, we behold a competition to drink of Circe's cup, with only a few notable exceptions. The *daimon* is our destiny, Yeats says, and our destiny is even a kind of justice, but then we

discover that this justice means only the exhaustion of every possible illusion, the completion of every possible emotional relationship. Or, to descend to a lower comedy, Graves tells us that Freud projected a private fantasy upon the world and then Graves offers us the assurance that true poetry worships a barbaric lunar Muse. Both Yeats and Graves show us the nightmare cyclic world of Blake's *The Mental Traveller*, but what Blake tells us is mere unnecessary masochism, Yeats and Graves affirm as imaginative truth, though only Graves insists also on the mutual rendings of poet and Muse as being true love.

Patrick J. Keane, who impresses me as Graves's most persuasive critical defender, argues against this judgment by observing, "it is equally true that Gravesian wildness is tempered by stoicism and a stress on limitation." Yet *ethos* or character does not seem to me the issue. What calls *The White Goddess* and many of the poems founded upon it into question is Graves's curious literalism, which prevents the reader from regarding the White Goddess or Muse as a metaphor for the Gravesian imagination. What cheerfully kept Graves a good minor poet, despite authentic genius, was his distrust of figurative language, and his powerfully reductive tendency to historicize and literalize every manifestation of the Goddess he could discover, whether in life or literature. Just before the end of *The White Goddess*, Graves states his credo, which I am afraid requires both critical correction and experiential skepticism:

> True poetic practice implies a mind so miraculously attuned and illuminated that it can form words, by a chain of more-than-coincidences, into a living entity—a poem that goes about on its own (for centuries after the author's death, perhaps) affecting readers with its stored magic. Since the source of poetry's creative power is not scientific intelligence, but inspiration—however this may be explained by scientists—one may surely attribute inspiration to the Lunar Muse, the oldest and most convenient European term for this source? By ancient tradition, the White Goddess becomes one with her human representative—a priestess, a prophetess, a queen-mother. No Muse-poet grows conscious of the Muse except by experience of a woman in whom the Goddess is to some degree resident; just as no Apollonian poet can perform his proper function unless he lives under a monarchy or a quasi-monarchy. A Muse-poet falls in love, absolutely, and his true love is for him the embodiment of

the Muse. As a rule, the power of absolutely falling in love soon vanishes; and, as a rule, because the woman feels embarrassed by the spell she exercises over her poet-lover and repudiates it; he, in disillusion, turns to Apollo who, at least, can provide him with a livelihood and intelligent entertainment, and reneges before his middle twenties. But the real, perpetually obsessed Muse-poet distinguishes between the Goddess as manifest in the supreme power, glory, wisdom and love of woman, and the individual woman whom the Goddess may make her instrument for a month, a year, seven years, or even more. The Goddess abides; and perhaps he will again have knowledge of her through his experience of another woman.

This is Gravesian autobiography, and as such has a certain limited authority. If the greatest poets in English include Milton, Blake, and Wordsworth, then we can imagine the grim comedy of their reactions to Graves's assurance that they were inspired by the Lunar Muse. Graves had a lifelong contempt for Milton, the butt of his nasty novel *Wife to Mr. Milton*, and had little liking also for Wordsworth, while he managed to so weakly misread Blake's *The Mental Traveller* as not to hear its horror at the dreadful cycle it depicted. "Muse-poets," as Graves describes them, are rather rare. John Keats certainly is the clearest instance of what Graves thinks he means, but that would be the Keats of *Endymion*, not the mature poet of *The Fall of Hyperion* and the great Odes. Graves's favorite lyric, Keats's "La Belle Dame sans Merci," is hardly a celebration of enchantment by the Muse, since the "wretched wight" is starving to death, and cannot be saved. But *The White Goddess*, as Keane admits, loses sight of the reality of human suffering, a loss totally un-Keatsian. Its dedicatory poem, marvelous with bravura, is the purest Graves:

In Dedication

All saints revile her, and all sober men
Ruled by the God Apollo's golden mean—
ln scorn of which I sailed to find her
In distant regions likeliest to hold her
Whom I desired above all things to know,
Sister of the mirage and echo.

It was a virtue not to stay,
To go my headstrong and heroic way

Seeking her out at the volcano's head,
Among pack ice, or where the track had faded
Beyond the cavern of the seven sleepers:
Whose broad high brow was white as any leper's,
Whose eyes were blue, with rowan-berry lips,
With hair curled honey-coloured to white hips.

Green sap of Spring in the young wood a-stir
Will celebrate the Mountain Mother,
And every song-bird shout awhile for her;
But I am gifted, even in November
Rawest of seasons, with so huge a sense
Of her nakedly worn magnificence
I forget cruelty and past betrayal,
Careless of where the next bright bolt may fall.

When Graves reprinted this, under the title of "The White Goddess," as the first poem in *Poems and Satires 1951*, he changed its "I" and "my" to "we" and "our," rather ruining it, at least for me, since its point is the Keatsian assertion of poethood in one's own generation. Behind Graves is Keats's declaration to the scornful Muse, Moneta, in *The Fall of Hyperion*: "I sure should see / Other men here; but I am here alone." Yeats appropriated Keats's assertion for *A Full Moon in March*, and Yeats, as Keane rightly argues, is Graves's true rival as a Muse-poet in our century. To engage Yeats in a poetic agon simply was beyond Graves's powers, and led to some inadequate posturings, and a number of lyrics weaker than perhaps they had to be.

What survives rereading in *The White Goddess* is neither its spurious history nor its tendentious mythmaking, which increasingly seems Graves's romance with Laura Riding writ large (and according to Miss Riding, writ wrong indeed). Nor can many readers tolerate the book's interminable speculations on tree-alphabets, which read like John Ruskin gone even madder than in his weirdest phase:

The thumb of Venus is connected with the palm-tree by its sacredness to the orgiastic goddess Isis, Latona or Lat. Lat was the mother of Nabatean Dusares the vine-god, worshipped in Egypt, and the lowest consonant on the thumb was the vine.

The Jupiter-finger is connected with the furze, or gorse, by the Spring gorse-fires burned in his honour as god of shepherds.

The connexion of the Mercury-finger with the yew is made by Mercury's conducting of souls to the place presided over by the death-goddess Hecate, alias his mother Maia, to whom the yew was sacred.

Fortunately there is a very different Graves who also inhabits the mythographic chapters of *The White Goddess*. Call his an authentic religious sensibility that writes best in negation, and you have him at his strongest:

> What ails Christianity today is that it is not a religion squarely based on a single myth; it is a complex of juridical decisions made under political pressure in an ancient law-suit about religious rights between adherents of the Mother-goddess who was once supreme in the West, and those of the usurping Father-god. Different ecclesiastical courts have given different decisions, and there is no longer a supreme judicature. Now that even the Jews have been seduced into evading the Mosaic Law and whoring after false gods, the Christians have drifted farther away than ever from the ascetic holiness to which Ezekiel, his Essene successors, and Jesus, the last of the Hebrew prophets, hoped to draw the world. Though the West is still nominally Christian, we have come to be governed, in practice, by the unholy triumdivate of Pluto god of wealth, Apollo god of science, and Mercury god of thieves. To make matters worse, dissension and jealousy rage openly between these three, with Mercury and Pluto blackguarding each other, while Apollo wields the atomic bomb as if it were a thunderbolt; for since the Age of Reason was heralded by his eighteenth-century philosophers, he has seated himself on the vacant throne of Zeus (temporarily indisposed) as Triumdival Regent.

Two years before *The White Goddess* appeared, Graves published his most effective novel, *King Jesus* (1946), and eventually risked *The Nazarene Gospel Restored* (with Joshua Podro, 1953). Though the return of matriarchal religion, which is the positive program of Graves's polemic, is now a fashionable notion in certain sects and covens, Graves is not taken as a prophet by current literary feminists. His quest for his kind of historical Jesus may however prove more lasting and disturbing than his celebration of the White Goddess.

II

Graves's curious literalism, which weakens *The White Goddess* and all but a double handful of his poems, constitutes the strength of *King Jesus*. Certain that he tells us the story as it must have been, Graves persuades us at least that he has persuaded himself. Convinced that he had suspended time, Graves insisted that he had recovered the truth about Jesus, and therefore the truth about the origin and meaning of Christianity. Yet *The Nazarene Gospel Restored*, seven years after *King Jesus*, recovers a totally contrary truth, in a clean contradiction that Graves charmingly shrugged off. What *King Jesus* and the *Nazarene Gospel* have in common is a very Jewish, indeed properly Pharisaic Jesus, who takes the Law of Moses to be "sacred and immutable." Graves and Podro divide early Christianity into three factions: the Nazarenes, headed by James and the other surviving disciples of Jesus, who remained loyal to the normative Pharisees; the Alexandrians, essentially Gnostics; Paul and his Gentile churches, who circulated the slander that Jesus condemned the Pharisees rather than some charlatans pretending to be Pharisees. Whether the reader agrees with Graves and Podro that the Nazarenes, rather than the Gnostics or the triumphant Paulines, were the true Christians, is not likely to make much difference. Far more interesting is the authors' contention that Jesus survived the cross, an assertion they share with the ill-assorted literary company of George Moore, Samuel Butler, and D.H. Lawrence.

King Jesus, though hardly one of the neglected masterpieces of narrative in our time, remains far more vital than *The Nazarene Gospel Restored*. Its Jesus is a grandson of Herod the Great, which is at variance with the *Nazarene Gospel*, and indeed only can be called the Gospel according to Graves, since the Nazarenes hardly would have hailed as Messiah an abominable Edomite of the House of Herod. Yet the Herodian Jesus of Graves's novel is the only successful and attractive representation of a personality and moral character to appear anywhere in Graves's prose fiction. Claudius, though newly popular because of a recent television series, is merely a droning voice, scarcely distinguishable from Graves's own. King Jesus speaks a voice of his own, as in the dialogue with the synagogue elders of Capernaum:

> They asked him: "Do you dishonour the memory of the learned Hillel from whom we learned these 'absurd legal fictions', as you call them, these 'falsifications of the Law'?"
>
> "Hillel was a carpenter who never ceased to labour with his hands and remained a poor man to the last. If any man now pleads poverty as an excuse for not studying the Law, it is asked

of him: 'Are you poorer even than Hillel was?' He interpreted
the Law in the spirit of love and laid no burden on the people
that he would not himself undertake with joy. It is written that
when Moses died all the men of Israel mourned for him; but at
the death of Hillel, as at Aaron's death, not only men but women
and children also mourned. Honouring his memory, I say: Sell
your profitable business, merchants, distribute the proceeds to
the poor, return to the boats and nets that you foolishly abandoned, and as you labour on the waters of the Lake remember
again your duty towards your neighbour! For is it not written:
'Six days *shalt* thou labour'? And the learned Shammai, who
received from Simeon son of Shetach, said: 'Love work, and
hate lordship.' And others of the wise have said: 'A man should
hire himself out to a stranger rather than sit idle; let him flay a
carcase in the street to earn his bread rather than say: "I am a
priest", or "I am a great and learned man".'"

"You are called Jesus the carpenter. Where then are your
hammer, saw, chisel and mallet?"

"From a carpenter I have become a shepherd." He displayed
his pastoral staff and mantle. "Let no man envy me my laborious new trade."

"And these idle disciples of yours?"

"Let no man envy them their laborious apprenticeship."

The elders took their leave of him without another word;
and he received no more invitations to preach in any synagogue
of Capernaum.

The vigorous, plain style is Graves at his best, and the portrayal of
his Jesus carries dignity, persuasiveness, and an authentic ethical force.
These are, I think, the virtues of Graves's poetry at its very best. The
Muse-poems, celebrations of the sadistic and vengeful White Goddess, are
less likely to live than what I take to be the best and most bitter love poems
in the language since Hardy:

The Foreboding

Looking by chance in at the open window
   I saw my own self seated in his chair
With gaze abstracted, furrowed forehead,
   Unkempt hair.

I thought that I had suddenly come to die,
    That to a cold corpse this was my farewell,
Until the pen moved slowly upon paper
    And tears fell.

He had written a name, yours, in printed letters:
    One word on which bemusedly to pore
No protest, no desire, your naked name,
    Nothing more.

Would it be to-morrow, would it be next year?
    But the vision was not false, this much I knew;
And I turned angrily from the open window
    Aghast at you.

Why never a warning, either by speech or look,
    That the love you cruelly gave me could not last?
Already it was too late: the bait swallowed,
    The hook fast.

Allen Tate

(1899-1979)

I MET ALLEN TATE ONLY TWICE, AND WAS MOVED BY THE POIGNANCE OF his memories of Hart Crane, his exact contemporary and close friend. Tate's literary criticism was very much in the mode of T.S. Eliot, and I always greatly preferred Tate's own poetry to his work as a critic. Northrop Frye, reviewing Tate's collected essays, found in them what Frye called the Eliotic myth of the Great Western Butterslide, in which a grand slab of classical, Catholic, and royalist butter slides down the centuries and melts, until it congeals again in Eliot's *The Waste Land*.

Though a resolute New Critic, in Eliot's wake, Tate ultimately was as much a late Romantic poet as Eliot proved to be. Though Tate increasingly repudiated Hart Crane's *The Bridge* while hailing Eliot's *The Waste Land*, the idiom of Crane never abandoned the would-be classicist. Crane's pentameter quatrains easily can be mistaken for Tate's while Eliot's fascinating blend of Tennyson and Whitman (his true precursors) yielded a very different mode.

Tate's "Ode to the Confederate Dead" strives to be Eliotic, yet the voice of Hart Crane keeps breaking in:

> The brute curiosity of an angel's stare
> Turns you, like them, to stone,
> Transforms the heaving air
> Till plunged to a heavier world below
> You shift your sea-space blindly
> Heaving, turning like the blind crab.
>
> > Dazed by the wind, only the wind
> > The leaves flying, plunge

This would be at home anywhere in Crane's first volume, *White Buildings*. Even closer to Crane are the majestic quatrains that conclude "The Mediterranean", to me Tate's best poem:

> Let us lie down once more by the breathing side
> Of Ocean, where our live forefathers sleep
> As if the Known Sea still were a month wide—
> Atlantic howls but is no longer steep!
>
> What country shall we conquer, what fair land
> Unman our conquest and locate our blood?
> We've cracked the hemispheres with careless hand!
> Now, from the Gates of Hercules we flood
>
> Westward, westward till the barbarous brine
> Whelms us to the tired land where tasseling corn,
> Fat beans, grapes sweeter than muscadine
> Rot on the vine: in that land were we born.

Tate is a permanent poet, though not of the eminence either of Eliot or of Hart Crane. The savage energy of "Aeneas at Washington" is Tate's own, even if the elegiac splendor of "The Mediterranean" always returns me to the somber and stately quatrains that conclude the canto of *The Bridge* titled "The River".

Sterling A. Brown

(1901-1989)

STERLING BROWN, AT HIS FREQUENT BEST, WAS ABLE TO ASSIMILATE THE strong influences of A.E. Housman, Thomas Hardy, and Robert Frost, and to fuse them in a mode of his own. I should say "modes," for this eclectic poet had several voices, very much his own. The Frostian "Idyll" juxtaposes a sheltered woodland cranny with an intrusive hawk, and sees the deep peace return after the hawk's kill, giving the reader the burden of the final irony: "The stream purred listlessly along, / And all grew quite as peaceful as before."

In another mode developed from Hardy, Brown gives us the poignant "Rain," a remarkable transformation of the sonnet form:

> Outside the cold, cold night; the dripping rain ...
> The water gurgles loosely in the eaves,
> The savage lashes stripe the rattling pane
> And beat a tattoo on November leaves.
> The lamp wick gutters, and the last log steams
> Upon the ash-filled hearth. Chill grows the room.
> The ancient clock ticks creakily and seems
> A fitting portent of the gathering gloom.
>
> This is a night we planned. This place is where
> One day, we would be happy; where the light
> Should tint your shoulders and your wild flung hair.—
> Whence we would—oh, we planned a merry morrow—
> Recklessly part ways with the old hag, Sorrow ...
>
> Outside dripping rain; the cold, cold night.

After that wonderfully gloomy octave, there is the fine poetic shock of "This is a night we planned." The speaker is solitary, erotic loss is overwhelming, and yet everything proceeds by indirection. Thomas Hardy, with his acute sense of life's ironies, might have admired Sterling Brown's "Rain," which precedes Robert Penn Warren in reviving Hardy's spirit.

Langston Hughes

(1902-1967)

Twentieth-century black American literature is so varied that adequate critical generalization is scarcely possible, at least at this time. A literary culture that includes the fiction of Ellison and Hurston, the moral essays of Baldwin, and the extraordinary recent poetry of Jay Wright is clearly of international stature. Langston Hughes may be the most poignant and representative figure of that culture, more so even than Richard Wright. Clearly an authentic poet, Hughes nevertheless seems to lack any definitive volume to which we can turn for rereading. His best book of poems is certainly *Fine Clothes to the Jew* (1927), which retains some freshness and yet has palpable limitations. Ideological defenses of Hughes's poetry are now common and necessarily are represented in this volume. Folk traditions ranging from blues to spirituals to jazz songs to work chants to many other modes do get into Hughes's poetry, but his poems on the whole do not compare adequately to the best instances of those cultural models. Other critics find Hughes Whitmanian, but the subtle, evasive, and hermetic Whitman—still the most weakly misread even as he is the greatest of our poets—had little real effect upon Hughes's poetry. The authentic precursor was Carl Sandburg, and Hughes, alas, rarely surpassed Sandburg.

Social and political considerations, which doubtless will achieve some historical continuity, will provide something of an audience for Hughes's poetry. His first autobiography, *The Big Sea*, may be his most lasting single book, though its aesthetic values are very mixed. Rereading it, plus his second autobiography, *I Wonder as I Wander*, his *Selected Poems*, and *The Langston Hughes Reader*, I come to the sad conclusion that Hughes's principal work was his life, which is to say his literary career. This conclusion is partly founded upon the contrast between Hughes's own writings and the

311

admirable biography by Arnold Rampersad, *The Life of Langston Hughes, Volume 1, 1902–1941* (1986). Reading Rampersad's *Life* is simply a more vivid and valuable aesthetic and human experience than reading the rather faded verse and prose of Hughes himself. Hughes's courage and his persistence made the man more crucial as a representative figure than his intrinsic strength as a writer by itself might have allowed him to have become.

Rampersad, a biographer of uncommon distinction, memorably condenses the essence of Hughes's personal vision in the fifth paragraph of his *Life*:

> As successful as his life seemed to be by its end, with honors and awards inspired by more than forty books, and the adulation of thousands of readers, Hughes's favorite phonograph record over the years, spun in his bachelor suite late into the Harlem night, remained Billie Holiday's chilly moaning of "God Bless the Child That's Got His Own." Eventually he had gotten his own, but at a stiff price. He had paid in years of nomadic loneliness and a furtive sexuality; he would die without ever having married, and without a known lover or a child. If by the end he was also famous and even beloved, Hughes knew that he had been cheated early of a richer emotional life. Parents could be so cruel! "My theory is," he wrote not long before he died, "children should be born without parents—if born they must be."

Most of Hughes's writing, like his overt stances in life, is a reaction-formation away from that origin. Rampersad's skilled devotion uncovers the trace of sorrow that moves remorselessly from a grim family romance (or lack of it) through a refusal to abide or end in alienation. The refusal may be ascribed to Hughes's profound, almost selfless love for his own people, and makes him an authentic and heroic exemplar for many subsequent black American writers. Whatever the inadequacies of Hughes's various styles, his place in literary history is an assured one.

Rampersad, in his essay on Hughes's poetic origins reprinted in this volume, shrewdly notes the mixture of will and passivity that combines in Hughes's art, and relates the passivity to Hughes's apparent asexuality. I wish only that the poetic will in Hughes had been stronger, as it was in Whitman and is now in John Ashbery and Jay Wright, among other contemporaries. What Hughes lacked, perhaps, was a sufficient sense of what Nietzsche called the will's revenge against time, and time's "It was."

Absorbing his own plangencies, Hughes chose not to take revenge upon his familial past. His pride in his family and in his race was too great for that, but what made him a hero of a pioneering black literary life may also have weakened his actual achievement as a poet. Rampersad defends Hughes by comparing him to Whitman, who also had the sense that his life was a larger poem than any he could write. But the poet of "Crossing Brooklyn Ferry" and "As I Ebb'd with the Ocean of Life" could afford that sense better than could the poet of "The Weary Blues" and "Reverie on the Harlem River."

Yet there are moments in Hughes that are unique and testify to a mode of irony almost his own. In *The Big Sea*, Hughes recalls an exchange with his friend of Harlem Renaissance days, the black writer Wallace Thurman. The brief sketch of Thurman, followed by the wise passivity of Hughes's self-revelation, is like a fragment of an art, humorous and wise, that cultural and personal circumstances did not permit Hughes to perfect. Still, it remains a strong testament:

> Wallace Thurman laughed a long bitter laugh. He was a strange kind of fellow, who liked to drink gin, but *didn't* like to drink gin; who liked being a Negro, but felt it a great handicap; who adored bohemianism, but thought it wrong to be a bohemian. He liked to waste a lot of time, but he always felt guilty wasting time. He loathed crowds, yet he hated to be alone. He almost always felt bad, yet he didn't write poetry.
>
> Once I told him if I could feel as bad as he did *all* the time, I would surely produce wonderful books. But he said you had to know how to *write*, as well as how to feel bad. I said I didn't have to know how to feel bad, because, every so often, the blues just naturally overtook me, like a blind beggar with an old guitar:
>
> You don't know,
> You don't know my mind—
> When you see me laughin',
> I'm laughin' to keep from cryin'.

Countee Cullen

(1903–1946)

I HAVE A PARTICULAR FONDNESS FOR COUNTEE CULLEN, AS I DO FOR Edwin Arlington Robinson, who was a benign influence upon Cullen's art, showing him how to be at once Keatsian and oneself. Like Robinson and Keats, Cullen was a highly self-conscious artist who knew that moral concerns could sink a poem without trace. Answering those who would make him only a "protest poet," Cullen eloquently prophesied for the best African American poets after him in his "To Certain Critics":

> No radical option narrows grief,
> Pain is no patriot,
> And sorrow plaits her dismal leaf
> For all as lief as not.

That wry pun upon "leaf" and "lief" is wonderfully typical of Countee Cullen, and is part of his legacy.

Pablo Neruda

(1904–1973)

IN 1930, THE YEAR THAT HART CRANE PUBLISHED *THE BRIDGE*, FEDERICO García Lorca completed the composition of his *Poet in New York*, which includes his "Ode to Walt Whitman." The "Ode to Walt Whitman" of Pablo Neruda was written much later, in 1956, and has very little in common with Lorca's poem, a difference surely deliberate on Neruda's part. Lorca's English, at least in 1930, was nonexistent, and his Walt Whitman was a marvelous phantasmagoria. Neruda translated Whitman, and in some ways knew Whitman, and how Whitman influenced other poets, better than some of Neruda's best exegetes have known. Not that Neruda's "Ode to Walt Whitman" is a good poem, but then paradoxically it is one of his least Whitmanian poems. Insofar as I can judge, Neruda is not only a poet of extraordinarily diverse styles, but of very mixed achievement, ranging from bathos to the high Sublime. Whatever the reader's political sympathies, the last phases of Neruda's life, personal and political, and of his poetry, possess a noble pathos, constantly augmented for us by the hideous survival of the barbaric regime that came into power by murdering Allende, and sacking the home and possessions of the dying national poet. Neruda's directly political poetry, even in much of his *Canto general* (1950), some day may be judged as a generous error, human and humane, but aesthetically inadequate. His later political poetry seems to me scarcely readable, but that is the usual fate of nearly all political poetry of any century. Very little American poetry written in English, and that is overtly political, has survived, or is likely still to join the canon. There is Emerson's fine Channing Ode, written against the Mexican War, and William Vaughn Moody's "An Ode in Time of Hesitation," concerning our land-grab in the Spanish-American War. The poems inspired by our Vietnamese debacle are themselves an aesthetic debacle, as is so much current verse of an ideological kind, reflecting the various passions of our composite School of Resentment. No Victor Hugo has come out of us in North, South, or Central America, or the islands of the Caribbean. American political poetry is perhaps too belated, and Neruda is hardly an exception, nor ought he to have been.

Walt Whitman, despite the ways all too many lame verse writers attempt to see him, was not the ancestor of Allen Ginsberg and other contemporary shamans. Whitman, at his most Sublime, is an immensely difficult and hermetic poet: subtle, evasive, ineluctable, withdrawn, defensive, shy, and endlessly metamorphic. His truest poetic descendants were Wallace Stevens and T.S. Eliot, each of whom repressed him, but the return of the repressed poetic father, partly in the son's own colors, produced their finest poetry. True, deep, poetic influence, a matter I have studied obsessively all my life and attempted to think through as that one thought each of us can hope to think, seems to me to depend upon unconscious or purposive forgetting. As such, it tends to take place in the language in which the poet actually writes his own mature poems. America is not Europe, but American English is also not American Spanish, and Whitman therefore is not the actual precursor of Neruda or Borges, Vallejo or Paz. Whitman is the strongest American poet, and the major figure in American Romanticism, but his language is the language of Shakespeare and of the English Bible. Hispanic poetry, like French, came to Romanticism belatedly, and until our century rather weakly. That must be anyone's impression, but I rely here upon *Children of the Mire* by Octavio Paz, and upon the recent criticism of Roberto González Echevarría, particularly his essay on Nicolás Guillén and the Baroque. The strong Spanish poets before our century were Quevedo, Góngora, and Calderón, a very different grouping from the English line of Chaucer, Spenser, Shakespeare, and Milton, and the descendants of that great fourfold in the High Romantics: Blake, Wordsworth, Shelley and Keats in England, Whitman and Dickinson in America. Neruda's crucial turn, to Blake and Whitman, was clearly an almost desperate effort to find what the Spanish tradition could not give him. Yet Quevedo and not Whitman is clearly his true ancestor, just as his near precursor, who caused him some discomfort, was Vicente Huidobro. T.S. Eliot tried to find ancestors in Dante, Baudelaire, even the rather minor Laforgue, yet remained always the child of Whitman and Tennyson. Neruda's case of poetic influence was not wholly dissimilar.

Neruda, excessive and expressionistic, overtly rhetorical, necessarily delighted in Quevedo, a poet neither Blakean nor Whitmanian. González Echevarría catches the precise dilemma of Neruda's poetic stance, as the critic sets the background for his own investigation into the poetics of Afro-Antilleanism in Nicolás Guillén:

> A central feature of that revision is a return to the Baroque, that is to say, to the work of the major poets of the language, Góngora, Quevedo, and Calderón, and to the Baroque aesthetics formulated by Baltasar Gracián. The inversion of the concept of representation from mimesis to expression envisioned by the Romantics was already implicit in the Spanish Baroque. As the Spanish and Spanish-American Romantics were a mere echo of their European counterparts, the great Hispanic poets of the avant-garde had to search for their poetic foundation not in the Romantics, as their English and German counterparts did, but in the Baroque. While it is a commonplace of Spanish literary history to say that the Generation of '27 in Spain looked to Góngora for inspiration, the fact is that the revision which brought about Góngora's rediscovery began in Spanish America with the *modernistas*—José Martí and Rubén Darío in particular—and continued in the writings of the Mexican Alfonso Reyes during the teens. It also has not been made sufficiently clear that both the Spanish-American and the Spanish writers looked to the Baroque poets because there were no Spanish language romantics worthy of rediscovery or rejection: no Goethe, no Coleridge, no Wordsworth, no Schiller, no Leopardi, only Espronceda, Bécquer, and in Spanish America Heredia, Echeverría, all minor poets, no matter how much we strain to find traces of originality in their works. The great Spanish-language poetic tradition that begins with the *modernistas* and makes yet another start in the twenties with the Generation of '27 has as foundation a rewriting of the Baroques.

Implicit here is a realization that runs counter to the overt assumptions of Formalist, Anglo-American literary Modernism: productively accepted contingency must come out of the poetic traditions of one's own language. We cannot choose those whom we are free to love, and poets cannot choose their own precursors. Overdetermination may be much the same process in the erotic and the literary realms. We demand liberty in both, and yet we must compound with the past in both. And in neither past do we confront the universal, but always what is closest at or to home. In Neruda, the place to discover what was closest is in his *Memoirs* (posthumously published, 1974; translated into English by Hardie St. Martin, 1977).

An aspiring poet by the age of six, if we are to credit his account, Neruda had a memory (or a fantasy) of his first poem that is a very dark version of the Enlightenment myth of the birth of what then was called the Poetic Character:

> I have often been asked when I wrote my first poem, when poetry was born in me.
>
> I'll try to remember. Once, far back in my childhood, when I had barely learned to read, I felt an intense emotion and set down a few words, half rhymed but strange to me, different from everyday language. Overcome by a deep anxiety, something I had not experienced before, a kind of anguish and sadness, I wrote them neatly on a piece of paper. It was a poem to my mother, that is, to the one I knew, the angelic stepmother whose gentle shadow watched over my childhood. I had no way at all of judging my first composition, which I took to my parents.
>
> They were in the dining room, immersed in one of those hushed conversations that, more than a river, separate the world of children and the world of grownups. Still trembling after this first visit from the muse, I held out to them the paper with the lines of verse. My father took it absentmindedly, read it absentmindedly, and returned it to me absentmindedly, saying: "Where did you copy this from?" Then he went on talking to my mother in a lowered voice about his important and remote affairs.
>
> That, I seem to remember, was how my first poem was born, and that was how I had my first sample of irresponsible literary criticism.

Like Whitman before him, Neruda came to associate the genesis of his poetry with the death of the father. Lincoln, particularly in the magnificent elegy, "When Lilacs Last in the Dooryard Bloom'd," became a surrogate father for Whitman, as Neruda understood, and that was Neruda's own placement of Walt Whitman, a knowing substitution of the greatest poet of the Western Hemisphere for José del Carmen Reyes, the trainman, the first and most important of Neruda's irresponsible literary critics. The "deep anxiety ... a kind of anguish and sadness" testifies to what might be called a Primal Scene of Instruction, in which the poem to the mother meets the father's indifference, and a second narcissistic, scar is formed.

Neruda's poem, "The Father," hardly can be termed an elegy, and its fiercely effective conclusion chills the reader:

Mi pobre padre duro
allí estaba, en el eje de la vida,
la viril amistad, la copa llena.
Su vida fue una rápida milicia
y entre su madrugar y sus caminos,
entre llegar para salir corriendo,
un dia con más lluvia que otros dias
el conductor José del Carmen Reyes
subio al tren de la muerte y hasta ahora no ha vuelto.

(My poor, hard father,
there he was at the axis of existence,
virile in friendship, his glass full.
His life was a running campaign,
and between his early risings and his traveling,
between arriving and rushing off,
one day, rainier than other days,
the railwayman, Jose del Carmen Reyes,
climbed aboard the train of death, and so far has not come back.)
(tr. Alastair Reid)

The irony, as Neruda must have known, is that the hard father was the best gift that the poet's genius could have received, just as the substitution of the figure of Whitman as idealized father must be a knowing irony also. Frank Menchaca shrewdly observes that: "Neruda also must have understood that the self which claims to be everywhere freely available in Whitman's poetry is nowhere to be found." The sublime evasions that constitute *Song of Myself* offer Whitman to everyone, and on what do not seem to be Whitman's own terms, though they are. This is the phenomenon that Doris Sommer wittily terms "supplying demand" in her essay on the fatherhood of Whitman in Neruda, Borges, and Paz. She argues that: "Neruda's admiration for the master may have displaced Whitman's narcissism with love for others; but ... ironically, by re-placing self-love with the hierarchy-producing secondary narcissism of hero worship." I think Sommer describes part of the normal process of poetic influence, and I myself would suggest that Borges and Paz, lesser poets than Neruda (though Borges is of similar eminence in his fictions, and Paz as a man-of-letters), actually benefited more from Whitman because they understood him far less well than Neruda did. An idealized father is best misunderstood.

Neruda's misreadings (in what I think I can call the Bloomian sense) of Whitman were creative only when they were deliberate, a process that Sommer again depicts accurately:

> Ironically, an heir such as Pablo Neruda seems indifferent to the problem; he will destroy his teacher by resuscitating older models that never even tempted the reader with a promise of equality and the like of whom Whitman had kissed off in the Preface to his poems. Neruda's colossal *Canto general* (1950) writes in and closes off the spaces for the poet's interlocutor by returning the model of America's new fragmented "epic" to a familiar tradition of apparently seamless romantic narrative. It sets Whitman's rawness right; it tames the earlier and more revolutionary aesthetic until what is left of Whitman is the figure of the father, something Whitman claimed he never wanted to be. Neruda thus reaffirms the political usefulness of representative romance over a poetry of "pure possibility" and reestablishes the hierarchy of poet over people that Whitman had managed (however briefly) to level.

I disagree only with "Whitman's rawness," since that is merely Whitman's deception of his reader; no poetry could be more delicate and finished, while pretending to be tough and raw, and *Canto general* is far rawer than Whitman even pretends to be. Compare to the end of *Song of Myself* the conclusion of *The Heights of Macchu Picchu*, the crown of *Canto general*:

> contadme todo, cadena a cadena,
> eslabón a eslabón, y paso a Paso,
> afilad los cuchillos que guardasteis,
> ponedlos en mi pecho y en mi mano,
> como un río de rayos amarillos,
> como un río de tigres enterrados,
> y dejadme llorar, horas, días, años,
> edades ciegas, siglos estelares.
>
> Dadme el silencio, el agua, la esperanza.
>
> Dadme la lucha, el hierro, los volcanes.
>
> Apegadme los cuerpos como imanes.

Acudid a mis venas y a mi boca.

Hablad por mis palabras y mi sangre.

(tell me everything, chain by chain,
link by link, and step by step,
file the knives you kept by you,
drive them into my chest and my hand
like a river of riving yellow light,
like a river where buried jaguars lie,
and let me weep, hours, days, years,
blind ages, stellar centuries.

Give me silence, water, hope.

Give me struggle, iron, volcanoes.

Fasten your bodies to me like magnets.

Hasten to my veins to my mouth.

Speak through my words and my blood.)
(tr. John Felstiner)

Like Whitman, Neruda addresses the multitudes, multitudes in the
valley of decision. His expressionistic tropes are true to the High Baroque:
river of light, buried jaguars, "struggle, iron, volcanoes," and the dead
workmen magnetizing Neruda's language and the very drives within him.
This is intensely moving, but perhaps rather strenuous when juxtaposed to
the quiet authority of our father, Walt Whitman:

I depart as air.... I shake my white locks at the runaway sun,
I effuse my flesh in eddies and drift it in lacy jags.
I bequeath myself to the dirt to grow from the grass I love,
If you want me again look for me under your bootsoles.

You will hardly know who I am or what I mean,
But I shall be good health to you nevertheless,
And filter and fibre your blood.

Failing to fetch me at first keep encouraged,

> Missing me one place search another,
> I stop some where waiting for you.

Walt is out there, up ahead of us, but patiently waiting, somewhere. The reader is anxious to catch up, but Walt is beyond anxiety, since he is early, while the reader is belated: "Will you speak before I am gone? Will you prove already too late?" At the close of *Heights of Macchu Picchu*, we wonder if the poet is not oppressed by belatedness, even as he urges the dead workers to speak through him. But Neruda, who meditated upon Whitman throughout a lifetime, learned the lesson beautifully, in the superb Whitmanian conclusion of his justly famous poem, "The People":

> Por eso nadie se moleste cuando
> parece que estoy solo y no estoy solo,
> no estoy con nadie y hablo para todos:
>
> Alguien me está escuchando y no to saben,
> pero aquellos que canto y que to saben
> siguen naciendo y llenarán el mundo.
>
> (So let no one be perturbed when
> I seem to be alone and am not alone;
> I am not without company and I speak for all.
>
> Someone is hearing me without knowing it,
> but those I sing of, those who know,
> go on being born and will overflow the world.)
> (tr. Alastair Reid)

The direct model is clearly the two uncanny tercets that end *Song of Myself*. I might not have believed anyone could come so close to Whitman's splendor as Neruda does here, in a poetic act at once bold and generous. Whitman's grand closure is superbly interpreted by Neruda's self-valediction. Neruda and Whitman together seem to be alone and are not alone; they keep each other company and each speaks for all. Someone among us, or within us, is hearing Neruda and Whitman without knowing it, without knowing who they are, but they are good health to us nevertheless. Here, at least, Neruda too stops somewhere waiting for us.

Robert Penn Warren

(1905-1989)

ROBERT PENN WARREN, BORN APRIL 24, 1905, IN GUTHRIE, KENTUCKY, AT the age of eighty is our most eminent man of letters. That truism is vitalized by his extraordinary persistence of development into a great poet. A reader thinks of the handful of poets triumphant in their later or last phases: Browning, Hardy, Yeats, Stevens, Warren. Indeed, "Myth of Mountain Sunrise," the final poem among the new work in the fifth Warren *Selected Poems*, will remind some readers of Browning's marvelous "Prologue" to Asolando, written when the poet was seventy-seven. Thinking back fifty years to the first time he saw Asolo (a village near Venice), Browning burns through every sense of loss into a final transcendence:

> How many a year, my Asolo,
> Since—one step just from sea to land—
> I found you, loved yet feared you so—
> For natural objects seemed to stand
> Palpably fire-clothed! No—

"God is it who transcends," Browning ends by asserting. Warren, older even than Browning, ruggedly remains the poet of immanence, of something indwelling and pervasive, though not necessarily sustaining, that can be sensed in a mountain sunrise:

> The curdling agony of interred dark strives dayward, in stone
> strives though
> No light here enters, has ever entered but
> In ageless age of primal flame. But look! All mountains want
> slow-

ly to bulge outward extremely. The leaf, whetted on light, will cut
Air like butter. Leaf cries: "I feel my deepest filament in dark rejoice.
I know the density of basalt has a voice."

Two primal flames, Browning's and Warren's, but at the close of
"Myth of Mountain Sunrise" we receive not "God is it who transcends,"
but: "The sun blazes over the peak. That will be the old tale told." The
epigraph to the new section of this *Selected Poems* is from Warren's favorite
theologian, St. Augustine: "Will ye not now after that life is descended
down to you, will not you ascend up to it and live?" One remembers another epigraph Warren took from the *Confessions*, for the book of poems *Being
Here* (1980): "I thirst to know the power and nature of time." Warren now
has that knowledge, and his recent poems show him ascending up to living
in the present, in the real presence of time's cumulative power. Perhaps no
single new poem here quite matches the extraordinary group of visions and
meditations by Warren that includes "Red-Tail Hawk and Pyre of Youth,"
"Heart of Autumn," "Evening Hawk," "Birth of Love," "The Leaf,"
"Mortmain," "To a Little Girl, One Year Old, in a Ruined Fortress" and so
many more. But the combined strength of the eighty-five pages of new
poems that Warren aptly calls *Altitudes and Extensions* is remarkable, and
indeed extends the altitudes at which our last poet of the Sublime continues to live, move and have his being.

II

Warren's first book was *John Brown: The Making of a Martyr* (1929).
I have just read it, for the first time, and discovered, without surprise, that
it made me very unhappy. The book purports to be history, but is Southern
fiction of Allen Tate's ideology, and portrays Brown as a murderous
nihilist, fit hero for Ralph Waldo Emerson. Indeed I find it difficult to
decide, after suffering the book, whether the young Warren loathed Brown
or Emerson more. Evidently, both Brown and his intellectual supporter
seemed, to Warren, instances of an emptiness making ruthless and passionate attempts to prove itself a fullness. But *John Brown*, if read as a first
fiction, does presage the Warren of *Night Rider* (1939), his first published
novel, which I have just re-read with great pleasure.

Night Rider is an exciting and remorseless narrative, wholly characteristic of what were to be Warren's prime virtues as a novelist: good story-
telling and intensely dramatic unfolding of the moral character of his
doom-eager men and women. Mr. Munn, upon whom *Night Rider* centers,
is as splendidly unsympathetic as the true Warren heroes continued to be:

Jerry Calhoun and Slim Sarrett in *At Heaven's Gate* (1943), Jack Burden and Willie Stark in *All the King's Men* (1946), Jeremiah Beaumont and Cassius Fort in *World Enough and Time* (1950). When Warren's crucial personages turned more amiable, starting with poor Amanda Starr in *Band of Angels* (1955), the books alas turned much less interesting. This unfortunate phenomenon culminated in Warren's last novel (so far), *A Place to Come To* (1977), which Warren himself ranks with *All the King's Men* and *World Enough and Time*. I wish I could agree, but re-reading *A Place to Come To* confirms an earlier impression that Warren likes his hero, Jed Tewksbury, rather too much. Without some real moral distaste to goad him, Warren tends to lose his narrative drive. I find myself wishing that Tewksbury had in him a touch of what might be called Original John Brown.

Warren's true precursor, as a novelist, was not Faulkner but Conrad, the dominant influence upon so many of the significant American novelists of Warren's generation. In one of his best critical essays, written in 1951 on Conrad's *Nostromo*, Warren gave an unknowing clue as to why all his own best work, as a novelist, already was over:

> There is another discrepancy, or apparent discrepancy, that we must confront in any serious consideration of Conrad—that between his professions of skepticism and his professions of faith ...
>
> Cold unconcern, an "attitude of perfect indifference" is, as he says in the letter to Galsworthy, "the part of creative power." But this is the same Conrad who speaks of Fidelity and the human communion, and who makes Kurtz cry out in the last horror and Heyst come to his vision of meaning in life. And this is the same Conrad who makes Marlow of "Heart of Darkness" say that what redeems is the "idea only" ...
>
> It is not some, but all, men who must serve the "idea." The lowest and the most vile creature must, in some way, idealize his existence in order to exist, and must find sanctions outside himself ...

Warren calls this a reading of Conrad's dual temperament, skepticism struggling with a last-ditch idealism, and remarks, much in T.S. Eliot's spirit:

> We must sometimes force ourselves to remember that the act of creation is not simply a projection of temperament, but a criticism and a purging of temperament.

This New Critical shibboleth becomes wholly Eliotic if we substitute the word "personality" for the word "temperament." As an analysis of Conrad's dramatism in his best novels, and in *Nostromo* in particular, this has distinction, but Warren is not Conrad, and like his poetic and critical precursor, Eliot, Warren creates by projecting temperament, not by purging it. There is no "cold unconcern," no "attitude of perfect indifference," no escape from personality in Eliot, and even more nakedly Warren's novels and poems continually reveal his passions, prejudices, convictions. Conrad is majestically enigmatic, beyond ideology; Warren, like Eliot, is an ideologue, and his temperament is far more ferocious than Eliot's.

What Warren accurately praises in Conrad is not to be found in Warren's own novels, with the single exception of *All the King's Men*, which does balance skepticism against belief just adroitly enough to ward off Warren's moralism. *World Enough and Time*, Warren's last stand as a major novelist, is an exuberant work marred finally by the author's singular fury at his own creatures. As a person who forgives himself nothing, Warren abandons the Conradian skepticism and proceeds to forgive his hero and heroine nothing. Re-reading *World Enough and Time*, I wince repeatedly at what the novelist inflicts upon Jeremiah Beaumont and Rachel Jordan. Warren, rather like the Gnostics' parody of Jehovah, punishes his Adam and Eve by denying them honorable or romantic deaths. Their joint suicide drug turns into an emetic, and every kind of degradation subsequently is heaped upon them. Warren, a superb ironist, nevertheless so loves the world that he will forgive it nothing, a stance more pragmatically available to a poet than to a novelist.

III

Warren's poetry began in the Modernist revival of the Metaphysical mode, as a kind of blend of Eliot's *The Waste Land* with the gentler ironies of Warren's own teacher at Vanderbilt, John Crowe Ransom. This phase of the poetry took Warren up to 1943, and then came to an impasse and, for a decade, an absolute stop. *At Heaven's Gate*, *All the King's Men* and *World Enough and Time* belong to that silent poetic decade, and perhaps the major sequence of his fiction usurped Warren's greater gift. But he was certainly unhappy in the later stages of his first marriage, which ended in divorce in 1950, and it cannot be accidental that his poetry fully resumed in the late summer of 1954, two years after his marriage to the writer Eleanor Clark, and a year after the birth of his daughter, the accomplished poet Rosanna Warren.

The book-length poem, *Brother to Dragons* (1953, revised version

1979), formally began Warren's return to verse, and is undoubtedly a work of considerable dramatic power. I confess to admiring it only reluctantly and dubiously, ever since 1953, because its ideological ferocity is unsurpassed even elsewhere in Warren. Much improved in revision, it remains unnerving, particularly if the reader, like myself, longs to follow Emerson in forgiving himself, if not everything, then at least as much as possible. But Warren—unlike Emerson, Nietzsche, Yeats—does not wish us to cast out remorse. Like his then master Eliot, though in a more secular way, Warren was by no means reluctant to remind us that we *are* Original Sin. *Brother to Dragons* is rendered no weaker by its extraordinary tendentiousness, but is not necessarily persuasive, if you happen not to share its moral convictions.

Warren's shorter poems, his lyrics and meditations, evolved impressively through three subsequent volumes: *Promises* (1957), *You, Emperors and Others* (1960) and a *Selected Poems* (1966), where the new work was grouped as *Tale of Time*. I recall purchasing these volumes, reading them with grudging respect, and concluding that Warren was turning into a poet rather like Melville (whom he was to edit in a *Selected Poems of Herman Melville*, in 1970) or the earlier Hardy. Warren's poems of 1934 through 1966 seemed interestingly ungainly in form, highly individual in genre and rhetoric, and not fundamentally a departure from Eliot's High Modernist mode. A poetry of belief, I would have judged, rather dismissively, and not of overwhelming concern if a reader was devoted to Hart Crane and Wallace Stevens, and to contemporary volumes such as Elizabeth Bishop's *Questions of Travel* (1965) and John Ashbery's *Rivers and Mountains* (1967). I could not foresee the astonishing breakthrough that Warren, already past the age of sixty, was about to accomplish with *Incarnations* (1968) and *Audubon: A Vision* (1969). Other critics of Warren's poetry see more continuity in its development than I do. But in 1968 I was a belated convert, transported against my will by reading *Incarnations*, and able at least to offer the testimony of a very reluctant believer in a poetic greatness now become indisputable and maintained by Warren throughout these nearly two decades since he began to write the poems of *Incarnations* in 1966.

IV

Incarnations opens with a closely connected sequence of fifteen poems called *Island of Summer*, which is the volume's glory. Unfortunately, Warren has included only five of these in his new *Selected Poems*, but they are the best of a strong group, and I will discuss only those five here, since Warren subtly has created a new sequence or a condensed *Island of*

Summer. Like the original work, the sequence is a drama of poetic incarnation, or the death and rebirth of Warren's poethood. In what is now the opening meditation, "Where the Slow Fig's Purple Sloth," Warren associates the fig with fallen human consciousness and so with an awareness of mortality:

> When you
> Split the fig, you will see
> Lifting from the coarse and purple seed, its
> Flesh like flame, purer
> Than blood.
> > It fills
> The darkening room with light.

This hard, substantive riddling style is now pure Warren, and has very little in common with the Eliotic evocations of his earlier verse. "Riddle in the Garden" even more oddly associates fruits, peach and plum, with negative human yearnings, suicidal and painful, and with a horror of inwardness. A violent confrontation, "The Red Mullet," juxtaposes the swimming poet and the great fish, eye to eye, in a scene where "vision is armor, he sees and does not / Forgive." In a subsequent vision of "Masts of Dawn," the optical effect of how "The masts go white slow, as light, like dew, from darkness / Condensed on them" leads to what in some other poet might be an epiphany, but here becomes a rather desperate self-admonition, less ironic than it sounds: "We must try / To love so well the world that we may believe, in the end, in God." This reversed Augustinianism preludes an overwhelming conflagration of Warren's poetic powers in the most ambitious poem he has yet written, "The Leaf."

When he was fifteen, Warren was blinded in one eye by a sharp stone playfully thrown by a younger brother, who did not see that Warren was lying down on the other side of a hedge. Only after graduating from Vanderbilt, did Warren get round to having the ruined eye removed and replaced by a glass eye. Until then, the young poet suffered the constant fear of sympathetic blindness in his good eye. There may be some complex relation between that past fear and Warren's most remarkable and prevalent metaphor of redemption, which is to associate poetic vision both with a hawk's vision and with a sunset hawk's flight. This trope has appeared with increasing frequency in Warren's poetry for more than half a century and even invades the novels. So, in *A Place to Come To*, Jed Tewksbury endures the same vision as he loses consciousness after being stabbed:

I remember thinking how beautiful, how redemptive, all seemed. It was as though I loved him. I thought how beautifully he had moved, like Ephraim, like a hawk in sunset flight. I thought how all the world was justified in that moment.

"The Leaf" centers itself upon the image of a hawk's redemptive flight, with the difference from earlier Warren being in the nature of the redemption. Opening with a renewed vision of the fig as emblem of human mortality and guilt, and of "the flaming mullet" as an encounter in the depths, the poem proceeds to an episode of shamanistic force:

Near the nesting place of the hawk, among
Snag-rock, high on the cliff, I have seen
The clutter of annual bones, of hare, vole, bird, white

As chalk from sun and season, frail
As the dry grass stem. On that

High place of stone I have lain down, the sun
Beat, the small exacerbation
Of dry bones was what my back, shirtless and bare, knew. I saw

The hawk shudder in the high sky, he shudders
To hold position in the blazing wind, in relation to
The firmament, he shudders and the world is a metaphor, his eye
Sees, white, the flicker of hare-scut, the movement of vole.

Distance is nothing, there is no solution, I
Have: opened my mouth to the wind of the world like wine, I wanted
To taste what the world wind dried up

The live saliva of my tongue, my tongue
Was like a dry leaf in my mouth.

Nothing in Warren's earlier poetry matches this in dramatic intensity, or in the accents of inevitability, as the poetic character is reincarnated in him by his sacrificial self-offering "near the nesting place of the hawk." Much of Warren's earlier guilt and sorrow comes together here, with beautiful implicitness: the fear of blindness, the decade of poetic silence, the failure of the first marriage, and most mysteriously, a personal guilt at poetic origins. The mystery is partly clarified in the poem's next movement:

The world is fruitful, In this heat
The plum, black yet bough-bound, bursts, and the gold ooze is,
Of bees, joy, the gold ooze has striven
Outward, it wants again to be of
The goldness of air and—blessedly—innocent. The grape
Weakens at the juncture of the stem. The world

Is fruitful, and I, too,
In that I am the father
Of my father's father's father. I,
Of my father, have set the teeth on edge. But
By what grape? I have cried out in the night.

From a further garden, from the shade of another tree,
My father's voice, in the moment when the cicada ceases, has
        called to me.

Warren's father had died in 1955, at the age of eighty-six. Robert Franklin Warren, who wanted above everything to be a poet, became a banker instead, solely to support not only his own children, but also a family of young children bequeathed to him by his own father, who had married again and then died. Reflecting upon all this, Warren has said: "It's as if I've stolen my father's life," somberly adding: "If he had had the opportunity I did, with his intelligence and energy, he'd have done a lot better than I did."

This is probably part of the sorrow heard in: "I, / Of my father, have set the teeth on edge." Experientially, it would be the larger part, but imaginatively it may yield to the burden of a more strictly poetic inheritance, the Eliotic influence, which Warren almost involuntarily here disavows and surmounts. Eliot's "not the cicada" from *The Waste Land* becomes here the moment when Eliot's presence in Warren's voice ceases, to be replaced by the poetic voice that Robert Franklin Warren had to abandon. The return of the father's voice becomes the blessing of Warren's new style, the gift given by Warren in his father's name. By reversing the Biblical trope from Jeremiah 31:29–30, in which the children's teeth are set on edge, Warren ironically celebrates the harshness of his new style:

The voice blesses me for the only
Gift I have given: *teeth set on edge*.

In the momentary silence of the cicada,

I can hear the appalling speed,
In space beyond stars, of
Light. It is

A sound like wind.

From this poem on, Warren rarely falters, whether in *Audubon: A Vision* or in the half dozen books of shorter poems (or new sections in selected volumes) that have followed. The achievement throughout these books necessarily is mixed, but there are several scores of poems that manifest all the stigmata of permanence.

V

I want to look at. just one of these poems, because it raises again, for me and for others, the ancient problem of poetry and belief. The poem is "A Way to Love God" from *Can I See Arcturus From Where I Stand?*, the sheaf of new poems in the *Selected Poems* before the one under review. I quote only the poem's final vision, which is no grislier than the ones preceding it:

But I had forgotten to mention an upland
Of wind-tortured stone white in darkness, and tall, but when
No wind, mist gathers, and once on the Sarré at midnight,
I watched the sheep huddling. Their eyes

Stared into nothingness. In that mist-diffused light their eyes
Were stupid and round like the eyes of fat fish in muddy water,
Or of a scholar who has lost faith in his calling.

Their jaws did not move. Shreds
Of dry grass, gray in gray mist-light, hung
From the side of a jaw, unmoving.

You would think that nothing would ever again happen.

That may be a way to love God.

By loving God, Warren always appears to mean loving the truth, in all its dreadfulness. This is an ancient polemic in all his work, poetry and prose, and does not beg the questions of truth but rather asserts a necessarily personal conviction as to the truth. Warren, despite the critical efforts of his more pious exegetes, is a skeptic and not a believer, but a Bible-soaked skeptic. His way of loving God is to forgive himself nothing, and to forgive God nothing. The aesthetic consequences of this stance, in a poetry written since 1966, seem to me wholly admirable, while the spiritual grimness involved remains a formidable challenge for many readers, myself among them. Missing from this new *Selected Poems* is a notorious sequence, "Homage to Emerson, On Night Flight to New York," to be found in the *Tale of Time* section of *Selected Poems: 1923–1975*. I don't regret its deletion, but it has a cognitive value in clarifying Warren's life-long distaste for Emerson. Here is its first part, "His Smile":

> Over Peoria we lost the sun:
> The earth, by snow like sputum smeared, slides
> Westward. Those fields in the last light gleam. Emerson—
>
> The essays, on my lap, lie. A finger
> Of light, in our pressurized gloom, strikes down,
> Like God, to poke the page, the page glows. There is
> No sin. Not even error. Night,
>
> On the glass at my right shoulder, hisses
> Like sand from a sand-blast, but
> The hiss is a sound. that only a dog's
> Ear could catch, or the human heart. My heart
>
> Is as abstract as an empty
> Coca-Cola bottle. It whistles with speed.
> It whines in that ammoniac blast caused by
> The passages of stars, for
> At 38,000 feet Emerson
>
> Is dead right. His smile
> Was sweet as he walked in the greenwood.
> He walked lightly, his toes out, his body
> Swaying in the dappled shade, and
> His smile never withered a violet. He
>
> Did not even know the violet's name, not having
> Been introduced, but he bowed, smiling,
> For he had forgiven God everything, even the violet.

When I was a boy I had a wart on the right forefinger.

The final line is perhaps redundant, since the entire poem vigorously thrashes Emerson for his supposedly deficient sense of fact. Accusing Emerson of an abstract heart is not original with Warren, but I wince properly at the effective anti-transcendentalism of: "At 38,000 feet Emerson / Is dead right." At ground level, I believe Emerson to be dead right also. "His Smile" is a good polemic, and should be admired as such. The vexed issue of poetry and belief rises rather when I re-read a poem like "A Way to Love God," which is a sublime nightmare from my perspective, but a truth from Warren's. A secularized conviction of sin, guilt, and error is an obsessive strand in all of Warren's work, and for him it helps constitute a stance which is more than rhetorical. However, the effect is only to increase his *otherness*, the rich strangeness of a kind of poetic strength wholly different from the best living poets of my own generation: Ashbery, Merrill, Ammons and others, and from their precursor, Stevens.

Ideological ferocity never abandons Warren, but he passionately dramatizes it, and he has developed an idiom for it that is now entirely his own. He would appear to be, as I have intimated elsewhere, a sunset hawk at the end of a great tradition. I doubt that we will ever again have a poet who can authenticate so heroic a stance. He has earned, many times over, his series of self-identifications with aspects of the truth. The second new poem in the *Selected Poems*, "Mortal Limit," is a sonnet celebrating again his great image of the hawk:

> I saw the hawk ride updraft in the sunset over Wyoming.
> It rose from coniferous darkness, past gray jags
> Of mercilessness, past whiteness, into the gloaming
> Of dream-spectral light above the last purity of snow-snags.
>
> There—west—were the Tetons. Snow-peaks would soon be
> In dark profile to break constellations. Beyond what height
> Hangs now the black speck? Beyond what range will gold eyes see
> New ranges rise to mark a last scrawl of light?
>
> Or, having tasted that atmosphere's thinness, does it
> Hang motionless in dying vision before
> It knows it will accept the mortal limit.
> And swing into the great circular downwardness that will
>   restore

The breath of earth? Of rock? Of rot? Of other such
Items, and the darkness of whatever dream we clutch?

So long as he abides, there will be someone capable of asking that
grand and unanswerable question: "Beyond what range will gold eyes see /
New ranges rise to mark a last scrawl of light?"

W.H. Auden

(1907-1973)

Attacking bad books is not only a waste of time but also bad for the character.

—AUDEN

While an author is yet living we estimate his powers by his worst performance, and when he is dead we rate them by his best.

—JOHNSON

SECONDARY WORLDS IS A BAD BOOK, AND AUDEN'S WORST PERFORMANCE. These four lectures in memory of T.S. Eliot deal in turn with *Thomas Cranmer*, a pious verse drama by Charles Williams; Icelandic sagas; the three opera libretti by Auden and Chester Kallman; the relation between Christian belief and the writing of poetry. Since the title, *Secondary Worlds*, refers to works of art as against "the primary world of our everyday social experience," the rationale for printing these four talks as a book must be their linked relevance to what has long been Auden's overt polemic against the Romantic view of poetry. Coleridge's ill-chosen terms, Primary and Secondary Imagination, are here subverted by Auden's wit, since by secondary Auden, unlike Coleridge, does mean "inferior."

Of all Auden's writings, *Secondary Worlds* comes most directly out of the neo-Christian matrix of modern Anglo-Catholic letters: Eliot, Williams, C.S. Lewis, Tolkien. I search in vain only for references to Dorothy Sayers. Auden comp ensates with a quotation from *The Future of Belief*, by Leslie Dewart, a book one might not otherwise know:

> The Christian God is not *both* transcendent and immanent. He is a reality other than being Who is present to being, by which presence He makes being to be.

335

"To believe this," Auden modestly says, "is to call into question the art of poetry and all the arts." In *The Dyer's Hand*, an admirable performance, Auden remarked that "the imagination is a natural human faculty and therefore retains the same character whatever a man believes." In his new book, the imagination of a humane man-of-letters and talented comic poet appears to be hardening, which would be a loss.

Johnson definitively stated the difficulties of devotional verse when he observed that the good and evil of Eternity were too ponderous for the wings of wit. The mind sinks under them, and must be content with calm belief and humble adoration, attitudes admirable in themselves but perhaps not conducive to the writing of poems. One of Auden's many virtues is that, unlike Eliot and other literary Christians, he has spared us, and mostly refrained from devotional verse. *For the Time Being*, a work dear to many churchwardenly critics, is a long and unhappy exception, but even it, unlike much Eliot, does not offer us the disciplined humility of the poet as our aesthetic experience.

It is of course one thing to deprecate the possibility of Christian poetry, or of poetry being Christian, and quite another to deprecate poetry itself, all poetry. In Auden's criticism, and particularly *Secondary Worlds*, the two are not always kept apart. When this happens, I find it is bad for my character. On a higher level the experience of reading Auden then becomes rather like reading Kilmer's *Trees*. "Poems are made by fools like me," yes, and by Dante, Milton, Blake, and Homer, but only God makes primary worlds. Or, as Auden says:

> it is possible that artists may become both more modest and more self-assured, that they may develop both a sense of humour about their vocation and a respect for that most admirable of Roman deities, the god *Terminus*. No poet will then produce the kind of work which demands that a reader spend his whole life reading it and nothing else. The claim to be a "genius" will become as strange as it would have seemed to the Middle Ages.

It is possible that other artists may become more like Auden. It is likelier that other critics may become more like him for, with Arnold and Eliot, he is a poet-critic who appeals greatly to critics, little as the splendor of becoming a "poet of professors" appeals to him. Books about Auden all tend to be fairly good, just as books about, say Wallace Stevens, tend to be quite bad. This is probably not because admirers of Stevens love him less well than the lovers of Auden, but because more genuinely difficult poets do not reduce to structures of ideas and images so readily as Auden does.

Auden's poetry now maintains a general esteem among academic critics. If one's judgment of Auden's poetry is more eccentric, one needs to take up the sad burden of literary dissent. Auden has been accepted as not only a great poet but also a Christian humanist sage not because of any conspiracy among moralizing neo-Christian academicians, but because the age requires such a figure. Eliot is gone, and Auden now occupies his place, though with a difference. The difference is refreshing; Auden is wittier, gentler, much less dogmatic, and does not feel compelled to demonstrate the authenticity of his Christian humanism by a judicious anti-Semitism. He has more wisdom and more humor than Eliot, and his talent is nowhere near so sparse, as the enormous range of his lyrics shows. I think it unfortunate that he should find himself in apostolic succession to Eliot, but *Secondary Worlds* seems to indicate that the succession is not unwelcome to him.

Much of *The Dyer's Hand*, despite its generosity as criticism, is darkened by Auden's obsessive doubts about the value of art in the context of Christianity. Similar doubts have maimed many writers, Tolstoi and Hopkins in particular. Insofar as Auden's uneasiness has prevented him from devotional poetry, he has gained by it, but unfortunately the effect upon him has been larger, and has resulted in a trivialization of his art. As a songwriter he remains supreme, being certainly the best in English in the century, but as a reflective poet he suffers from the continual evanescence of his subject matter. As a satirist, he may have been aided, yet the staple of his poetry is neither song nor satire but rumination on the good life, and his notion of the relation between Christianity and art has troubled that rumination. Auden is one of the massive modern sufferers from the malady of Poetic Influence, a variety of melancholy or anxiety-principle that our studies have evaded. Poetic Influence, in this sense, has little to do with the transmission of ideas and images from an earlier poet to a later one. Rather, it concerns the poet's sense of his precursors, and of his own achievement in relation to theirs. Have they left him room enough, or has their priority cost him his art? More crucially, where did they go wrong, so as to make it possible for him to go right? In this revisionary sense, in which the poet creates his own precursors by necessarily misinterpreting them, Poetic Influence forms and malforms new poets, and aids their art at the cost of increasing, finally, their already acute sense of isolation. Auden, like Byron, gives the continual impression of personal sincerity in his poetry, but again like Byron this sincerity is the consequence of a revisionary swerve away from the sincerity of the precursor. In Byron's case of Poetic

Influence the great precursor was Pope, with his highly dialectical sincerity; with Auden the prime precursor is Hardy, and the poetic son's sincerity is considerably more dialectical than the father's.

Auden, in his very fine *New Year Letter* (1 January 1940, at the height of his poetic power), wrote an important poem about Poetic Influence. His precursors are invoked there as a summary tribunal sitting in perpetual session:

> Though
> Considerate and mild and low
> The voices of the questioners,
> Although they delegate to us
> Both prosecution and defence,
> Accept our rules of evidence
> And pass no sentence but our own,
> Yet, as he faces them alone,
> O who can show convincing proof
> That he is worthy of their love?

He names these fathers and judges: Dante, Blake, Rimbaud, Dryden, Catullus, Tennyson, Baudelaire, Hardy, and Rilke, connecting this somewhat miscellaneous ninefold (except for Dryden, there for his mastery of the middle style) by their common sense of isolation, fit companions "to one unsocial English boy." Of all these, Auden's most characteristic poetry is closest to Hardy's, not merely in its beginnings, and like Hardy Auden remains most convincing as a ruminator upon human incongruities, upon everything valuable that somehow will not fit together. Auden's best poems, such as the justly esteemed *In Praise of Limestone*, brood upon incongruities, swerving from Hardy's kind of poem into a more double-natured sense of ruinous circumstance and thwarted love, yet retaining their family resemblance to Hardy. But where Hardy's strenuous unbelief led him to no worse redundancies than an occasional sharp striving after too palpable an irony, Auden's self-conscious belief and attendant doubt of poetry mar even *In Praise of Limestone* with the redundancy of uneasy and misplaced wit:

> But if
> Sins can be forgiven, if bodies rise from the dead,
>   These modifications of matter into
> Innocent athletes and gesticulating fountains,
>   Made solely for pleasure, make a further point;

> The blessed will not care what angle they are regarded from,
>   Having nothing to hide,

The blessed, as Auden says so often in prose, need neither to read nor to write poems, and poems do not describe their sanctity with much success, as Auden also sadly notes, contemplating the verse of Charles Williams. Close thy Auden, open thy Stevens, and read:

> If, then, when we speak of liberation, we mean an exodus; if when we speak of justification, we mean a kind of justice of which we had not known and on which we had not counted; if when we experience a sense of purification, we can think of the establishing of a self, it is certain that the experience of the poet is of no less a degree than the experience of the mystic and we may be certain that in the case of poets, the peers of saints, those experiences are of no less a degree than the experiences of the saints themselves. It is a question of the nature of the experience. It is not a question of identifying or relating dissimilar figures; that is to say, it is not a question of making saints out of poets or poets out of saints.

Theodore Roethke

(1908–1963)

THEODORE ROETHKE SHARES WITH ELIZABETH BISHOP AND ROBERT PENN Warren the distinction of having emerged as the strongest survivors of what could be called the middle generation of modern American poets, which included Robert Lowell, John Berryman, Delmore Schwartz, and Randall Jarrell. This generation came after the succession from E.A. Robinson and Frost through Pound, Eliot, Moore, Stevens, Williams, and Crane, and before the group that includes Ashbery, Merrill, Ammons, James Wright, Snyder, Merwin, Hollander, Kinnell, and others. The fate of a middle generation is hard, particularly when its older contemporaries included half a dozen poets of authentic greatness. The shadows of Stevens and of Eliot still hover in Roethke's last poems in *The Far Field* (1964), which seems to me as derivative a volume as his first, *Open House* (1941).

Dead much too soon, at fifty-five, Roethke did not have time to work through to another achievement as original as his best book, *The Lost Son* (1948), published at the crucial age of forty. My own sense of Roethke's eminence is founded almost entirely on *The Lost Son*. Elizabeth Bishop was unwaveringly strong, from first to last, while Warren became a great poet at the age of sixty, and maintained this eminence for fully two decades after. Roethke is upon his heights, in my judgement, only in *The Lost Son*, but the book is so marvelous that it justifies placing Roethke with Bishop and Warren in his own generation.

The Lost Son is alive in every poem, but the most memorable include "Big Wind," "Frau Bauman, Frau Schmidt, and Frau Schwartze," "The Waking," and four remarkable sequences: "The Lost Son," "The Long Alley," "A Field of Light," and perhaps the most distinguished, "The Shape of the Fire." Since "The Shape of the Fire" is the Roethke I love best, I choose it for an introductory commentary here. Resenting insinuations that the sequence was too much

340

influenced by Dylan Thomas, Roethke rather eagerly took up a suggestion of W.H. Auden's, and asserted that Thomas Traherne was his true source. The source sensibly can be found in Walt Whitman, the most benign of influences upon Roethke, and the hidden influence upon Eliot and Stevens, two of Roethke's masters. Unlike say Yeats, whose effect upon Roethke was overwhelming and destructive, Whitman worked deep within Roethke to help bring to birth what was best in Roethke's own imagination.

The shape of the fire is the shape or form of Roethke's inspiration, and is the dominant if implicit trope of the sequence, until it becomes explicit in the sunlight of section 5. I take it that the title helps guide us to the realization that the poem is not about the first or natural birth, but instead concerns the second birth into poetic vision. The painful birth imagery of section 1 is more a farewell to mothering nature than a celebration of her function.

> What's this? A dish for fat lips.
> Who says? A nameless stranger.
> Is he a bird or a tree? Not everyone can tell.

> Water recedes to the crying of spiders.
> An old scow bumps over black rocks.
> A cracked pod calls.

> Mother me out of here. What more will the bones allow?
> Will the sea give the wind suck? A toad folds into a stone.
> These flowers are all fangs. Comfort me, fury.
> Wake me, witch, we'll do the dance of rotten sticks.

> Shale loosens. Marl reaches into the field. Small birds pass
>   over water.

> Spirit, come near. This is only the edge of whiteness.
> I can't laugh at a procession of dogs.

> In the hour of ripeness the tree is barren.
> The she-bear mopes under the hill.
> Mother, mother, stir from your cave of sorrow.

> A low mouth laps water. Weeds, weeds, how I love you
> The arbor is cooler. Farewell, farewell, fond worm.
> The warm comes without sound.

Roethke was reluctant to associate himself with Rimbaud; there is a Notebook comment of 1944 in which he oddly remarks: "The error of Rimbaud: the world is chaotic, therefore I must be." Hart Crane was the American Rimbaud, as he meant to be; Roethke will not survive a poetic comparison with either. But "The Shape of the Fire" is the most Rimbaldian of Roethke's poems, in its aggressivity and its deep rebellion against nature. The aggressivity subverts the referential aspect of the poem, while the rebellion dissolves any clear sense of a unified subjectivity in Roethke's use of "I." "What's this?" dismisses nature as the "dish for fat lips" that the poem's voice declines to devour. The "nameless stranger," whether bird or tree, is a messenger from beyond nature guiding the poet's Rimbaldian drunken boat over the black rocks of an intransigent nature, to the music of a call from "a cracked pod," also now beyond natural process.

An immense ambivalence in this poet, longing for the maternal even as he is guided out of it, is impelled to fall back on the rejected image of mothering in order to accomplish the new emergence into a vision antithetical to nature's. The prayer to be mothered out of the mother is accompanied by parallel antitheses: a sea nursing the wind, toad folding into a stone, flowers that are fangs, a fury that comforts. Even the contra-natural is viewed dialectically, as the awakening patroness is addressed under the name of witch, and the dance of deliverance from process becomes one of rotten sticks.

If the spirit beckoned near is identified as Whitman's, then the highly Whitmanian affirmation is wholly contextualized: "Weeds, weeds, how I love you." The fat lips of the opening are replaced now by the low mouth lapping water, emblem here of the rebirth into the incarnation of what the eighteenth century called the Poetical Character. Perhaps the most brilliant stroke in section 1 is the final trope, where the soundless warm of the shaping fire replaces the fond warm of what Blake called the state of Generation.

After the relative clarity of this first section, Roethke gives us the most difficult movement, not only of "The Shape of the Fire," but of any poem he ever published. It yields a surreal coherence to repeated rereadings, while defying the heresy of any paraphrase. To me it seems a total success, representing as it does the startled awakening to the poetic condition, a state of origins where every prior expectation has been twisted askew. Eye, ear, nose, foot have relocated themselves, and the nameless stranger of annunciation has been replaced by an hallucinatory listener, Roethke's version of Blake's Idiot Questioner, flat-headed, replete with platitudes and rubber doughnuts, and greeted by the poet with a question one might ask of Satan: "Have you come to unhinge my shadow?"

A poignant tentativeness attends the poet's new state, near allied, as it must have been for Roethke himself, to the disorders of schizophrenia. After a child-like nonsense song of this new innocence, Roethke cries out: "Who waits at the gate?" The answer does not seem to be the abandoned "mother of quartz" with her renewal of the whispers of family romance, but the wasp and other emblems of antithetical redemption of section 3:

> The wasp waits.
> The edge cannot eat the center.
> The grape glistens.
> The path tells little to the serpent.
> An eye comes out of the wave.
> The journey from flesh is longest.
> A rose sways least.
> The redeemer comes a dark way.

The center, being prolific, will hold against the devouring edge or circumference. If the long journey from flesh to poetic incarnation is longest, this is because, as St. John of the Cross suggested, you must go by a dark way, wherein there is no knowing. Roethke indeed does get back to where he does not know, to the childhood world of section 4: "Death was not. I lived in a simple drowse." Dylan Thomas's "Fern Hill" and much of Traherne are doubtless analogues, but Wordsworth is closer, as James Applewhite has indicated. These intimations of immortality guide us to the fifth and final section, the strongest passage in. all of Roethke, an epiphany both Whitmanian and Wordsworthian:

> To have the whole air!—
> The light, the full sun
> Coming down on the flowerheads,
> The tendrils turning slowly,
> A slow snail-lifting, liquescent;
> To be by the rose
> Rising slowly out of its bed,
> Still as a child in its first loneliness;
> To see cyclamen veins become clearer in early sunlight,
> And mist lifting out of the brown cat-tails;
> To stare into the after-light, the glitter left on the lake's surface,
> When the sun has fallen behind a wooded island;
> To follow the drops sliding from a lifted oar,
> Held up, while the rower breathes, and the small boat drifts
>   quietly shoreward;

> To know that light falls and fills, often without our knowing,
> As an opaque vase fills to the brim from a quick pouring,
> Fills and trembles at the edge yet does not flow over,
> Still holding and feeding the stem of the contained flower.

Certainly one of the most American of visions, this splendor is extraordinary for its gentle but taut control of the nearly ineffable. What the sequence gives us is truly the shape of the fire, the shape of the movement: to have, to be, to see, to stare, to follow, and at last to know. To know what? A falling, a filling to the brim, a trembling at the edge that will not flow over: these are the shapes of the creative fire transformed into a sustaining light. Roethke concludes with the image of a light still holding and feeding, a mothering light that contains the flower of restored consciousness as its child. The trope, almost Dantesque, achieves an aesthetic dignity worthy of Wordsworth or Whitman, true founders of the tradition that chose Roethke, at his rare best, as its own.

Elizabeth Bishop

(1911–1979)

THE PRINCIPAL POETS OF ELIZABETH BISHOP'S GENERATION INCLUDED Roethke, Lowell, Berryman, Jarrell, and, in a different mode, Olson. Whether any of these articulated an individual rhetorical stance with a skill as sure as hers may be questioned. Her way of writing was closer to that of Stevens and Marianne Moore, in the generation just beyond, than to any of her exact contemporaries. Despite the differences in scale, her best poems rival the Stevens of the shorter works, rather than the perhaps stronger Stevens of the sequences.

Bishop stands, then, securely in a tradition of American poetry that began with Emerson, Very, and Dickinson, and culminated in aspects of Frost as well as of Stevens and Moore. This tradition is marked by firm rhetorical control, overt moral authority, and sometimes by a fairly strict economy of means. The closing lines in *Geography III* epitomize the tradition's self-recognition:

> He and the bird know everything is answered,
> all taken care of,
> no need to ask again.
> —Yesterday brought to today so lightly!
> (A yesterday I find almost impossible to lift.)

These poignant lines have more overt pathos than the poet ever allowed herself elsewhere. But there is a paradox always in the contrast between a poetry of deep subjectivity, like Wordsworth's or Stevens's or Bishop's, and a confessional poetry, like Coleridge's or that of Bishop's principal contemporaries. When I read, say, "The Poems of Our Climate," by Stevens, or "The End of March," by Bishop, I encounter eventually the overwhelming self-revelation of a profoundly subjective consciousness. When I read, say, "Skunk Hour" by Lowell or one of Berryman's sonnets, I confront finally an opacity, for that is all the confessional mode can yield. It is the strength of Bishop's tradition that its clarity is more than a surface phenomenon. Such strength is cognitive, even analytical, and surpasses philosophy and psychoanalysis in its power to expose human truth.

There are grander poems by Bishop than the relatively early "The Unbeliever," but I center upon it here because I love it best of all her poems. It does not compare in scope and power to "The Monument," "Roosters," "The Fish," "The Bight," "At the Fishhouses," "Brazil, January 1, 1502," "First Death in Nova Scotia," or the extraordinary late triad of "Crusoe in England," "The Moose," and "The End of March." Those ten poems have an authority and a possible wisdom that transcend "The Unbeliever." But I walk around, certain days, chanting "The Unbeliever" to myself, it being one of those rare poems you never evade again, once you know it (and it knows you). Its five stanzas essentially are variations upon its epigraph, from Bunyan: "He sleeps on the top of a mast." Bunyan's trope concerns the condition of unbelief; Bishop's does not. Think of the personae of Bishop's poem as exemplifying three rhetorical stances, and so as being three kinds of poet, or even three poets: cloud, gull, unbeliever. The cloud is Wordsworth or Stevens. The gull is Shelley or Hart Crane. The unbeliever is Dickinson or Bishop. None of them has the advantage; the spangled sea wants to destroy them all. The cloud, powerful in introspection, regards not the sea but his own subjectivity. The gull, more visionary still, beholds neither sea nor air but his own aspiration. The unbeliever observes nothing, but the sea is truly observed in his dream:

> which was, "I must not fall.
> The spangled sea below wants me to fall.
> It is hard as diamonds; it wants to destroy us all."

I think that is the reality of Bishop's famous eye. Like Dickinson's, its truest precursor, it confronts the truth, which is that what is most worth seeing is impossible to see, at least with open eyes. A poetry informed by that mode of observation will station itself at the edge where what is most worth saying is all but impossible to say. I will conclude here by contrasting Bishop's wonderful trope of the lion, in "The End of March," to Stevens's incessant use of the same figure. In Stevens, the lion tends to represent poetry as a destructive force, as the imposition of the poet's will-to-power over reality. This image culminates in "An Ordinary Evening in New Haven":

Say of each lion of the spirit

It is a cat of a sleek transparency
That shines with a nocturnal shine alone.
The great cat must stand potent in the sun.

Against that destructive night in which all cats are black, even the transparent ones, Stevens sets himself as a possible lion, potent in the light of the idea-of-ideas. Here, I take it, Bishop's affectionate riposte:

They could have been teasing the lion sun,
except that now he was behind them
—a sun who'd walked the beach the last low tide,
making those big, majestic paw-prints,
who perhaps had batted a kite out of the sky to play with.

A somewhat Stevensian lion sun, clearly, but with something better to do than standing potent in itself. The path away from poetry as a destructive force can only be through play, the play of trope. Within her tradition so securely, Bishop profoundly plays at trope. Dickinson, Moore, and Bishop resemble Emerson, Frost, and Stevens in that tradition, with a difference due not to mere nature or mere ideology but to superb art.

Robert Hayden

(1913-1980)

I MET ROBERT HAYDEN ONLY ONCE, WHEN SOMETIME IN THE EARLY 1970S I lectured at Ann Arbor, and had the privilege of a personal conversation with him for rather more than an hour or so. We talked about the Baha'i gardens in Haifa, which I had visited in the later 1950s, and also about the poetry of W.B. Yeats, on which I had recently published a long book, and of Hart Crane, who still seems to me an unexamined presence in several of Hayden's strongest poems.

Like Jay Wright, Hayden is a major modern American poet, as well as forming a quartet, together with Ralph Ellison, Toni Morrison, and Jay Wright, one that seems to me the crown of African American literary achievement up to this moment (I write in May 2004). Hayden (1913–1980) is a permanent poet, canonical in a sense that current politicism continues to deride. Cultural fashions fade away, and literary survival always depends upon three criteria: aesthetic splendor, cognitive power, and wisdom. If the United States emerges from the triumphalism of George W. Bush, a time will come when much current rant and cant will dwindle into period pieces, at best. Hayden, a maker and not an image of political correctness, will be read long after louder voices have vanished into the void.

Hayden was at his best in poetic sequences, though some of his lyrical poems are as rewarding. Like Yeats and Hart Crane (and the young Jay Wright of *The Homecoming Singer*), at his most memorable, Hayden is an incantatory poet. His characteristic rhetorical movement is invocation, rather as Yeats invokes his Tower or Hart Carne, Brooklyn Bridge. Most of Hayden's critics regard him as invoking black history, but they oversimplify the basis for his rhetorical art. You can be a very bad poet no matter how incessantly you call upon the West African past, or the horrific sadism of the English, Spanish, and Portuguese slave traders and owners of the Americas. Hayden matters because he is an authentic poet, one of the best of his generation (which included Elizabeth Bishop, Theodore Roethke, May Swenson, and the still overesteemed Robert Lowell). He told me, with a reticence worthy of his best poems, that he was fascinated by the *impacted* quality of Hart Crane's rhetoric, and in some respects he resembles Crane more than he does Yeats, whom his teacher W.H. Auden had commended to him as a model.

Like Crane, who hymned an Unknown God, Hayden was a religious poet, but of the highly eclectic Baha'i persuasion, a heresy from Iranian Islam. Inwardness and aesthetic elitism mark Hayden's highest achievements, as they do the Pindaricism of Jay Wright, for whom Hayden's freedom from spuriously black ideological "criticism" provided a beacon. Hayden's poetic integrity, like Jay Wright's, was absolute, and invariably courageous, in the mode of Ralph Ellison, who insisted that the American and European literary traditions were as much his possession as was the example of Richard Wright.

All this is merely preamble to a rather rapid survey of a few of Hayden's superb sequences, of which *Middle Passage* is the most famous. Both Hart Crane and T.S. Eliot are both drawn upon and evaded in Section III in particular, where an Eliotic allusion, in *The Waste Land*, to Shakespeare's *The Tempest*, fuses with the high rhetoric of Crane's Columbus approaching the New World in the "Ave Maria" canto of *The Bridge*:

> Shuttles in the rocking loom of history,
> the dark ships move, the dark ships move,
> their bright ironical names
> like jests of kindness on a murderer's mouth;
> plough through thrashing glister toward
> fata morgana's lucent melting shore,
> weave toward New World littorals that are
> mirage and myth and actual shore.
>
> Voyage through death,
>   voyage whose chartings are unlove.
>
> A charnel stench, effluvium of living death
> spreads outward from the hold,
> where the living and the dead, the horribly dying,
> lie interlocked, lie foul with blood and excrement.

> *Deep in the festering hold thy father lies,*
> *the corpse of mercy rots with him,*
> *rats eat love's rotten gelid eyes.*

The dispassionate tonalities of this extraordinary passage stem from Hayden's poetic reticence, his characteristic rhetoric of litotes or understatement, in a reaction-formation against Crane's ecstatic hyperboles and Eliot's hyperbolic ironies. For Crane, Columbus is a mystical (if cruel) disciple of the prophet Isaiah, while Eliot's Tiresias is death-in-life desperately waiting for the grace of Anglican conversion. Hayden, a black Baha'i, longs for a more universal salvation. His Cinquez, hero of the *Amistad* Mutiny, is the emblem of all those, of whatever origin, who sought the Blessing that America ought to constitute, however far from that ideal it continues to fall:

> Voyage through death
>   to life upon these shores.

Runagate Runagate is not as intricate and fully written as *Middle Passage*, but it too dares and sustains a high rhetoric:

> Tell me, Ezekiel, oh tell me do you see
> mailed Jehovah coming to deliver me?

My late friend, the great poet-novelist Robert Penn Warren, fiercely hated John Brown, upon whom he had written his first book. One day, at lunch with Warren, I commended John Brown as a prophet, though violent in the extreme, yet in the best of causes. Warren, too urbane to argue, presented me at the next week's lunch with a copy of his *John Brown: The Making of a Martyr*. Loving and honoring Warren's memory, I still follow Emerson and Thoreau and vote for Hayden's sequence, *John Brown*, which honestly admits the prophet's responsibility for "Bleeding Kansas":

> Doing The Lord's work with saber
> sharpened on the grindstone
> of The Word:
>   Bleeding Kansas:
>
> the cries of my people the cries
> of their oppressors harrowed
> hacked—poison meat for Satan's
> maw.

> I slew no man but blessed
> the Chosen, who in the name
> of justice killed at my command.
>
> Bleeding Kansas:
>   a son martyred
> there: I am tested I am trued
> made worthy of my servitude.
>
> Oh the crimes of this guilty
> guilty land:
>   let Kansas bleed.

Of John Brown, Hayden says simply: "he died/for us." Few American poets have understood so well their hopelessly paradoxical country. Hayden, in the concluding stanza of his *American Journal*, joins Walt Whitman in apprehending what may be beyond comprehension:

> confess i am curiously drawn unmentionable to
> the americans doubt i could exist among them for
> long however psychic demands far too severe
> much violence much that repels i am attracted
> none the less their variousness their ingenuity
> their elan vital and that some thing essence
> quiddity i cannot penetrate or name

John Berryman

(1914–1972)

"I BEGAN WORK IN VERSE-MAKING AS A BURNING, TRIVIAL DISCIPLE OF THE great Irish poet William Butler Yeats, and I hope I have moved off from there." That is John Berryman in 1965, and he added: "Then came Yeats, whom I didn't so much wish to resemble as to *be*." Then came Auden, by Berryman's own testimony. "Winter Landscape" was cited by Berryman as his first poem in his own voice, and *Homage to Mistress Bradstreet* as his true break-through. That there are breakthroughs in the development or unfolding of a strong poet cannot be denied; the burden for literary criticism always must be to determine which poets inevitably compel the canon to make place for them. Roethke in his two best volumes achieved strength and then fell away from it. Robert Lowell, concerning whom I seem to be the only dissenter in our nation, did not achieve it, either in the manner of Eliot and Tate, or in that of W.C. Williams. Berryman I find the largest puzzle of his poetic generation, though I believe he will be judged at last only by *The Dream Songs*. To compare them, as some admirers do, to *Song of Myself*, is palpably an error; they are neither of that mode nor anywhere close to that astonishing eminence.

Berryman, like Lowell, continues to be overpraised in Britain, where both are associated with Anne Sexton and Sylvia Plath. This is hardly fair to Berryman, but British critics such as John Bayley and A. Alvarez seem to like their American poets to be suicidal, mentally ill, and a touch unruly, "beyond the Gentility Principle," as Alvarez phrases it. Wallace Stevens, in the judgment of Bayley, is inferior to Berryman and Lowell, which is roughly akin to my proclaiming that Alice Meynell and Charlotte Mew wrote better poems than Thomas Hardy, which I am not about to proclaim. Perhaps Berryman has some permanent poems, but they are hard to locate if you start out with his admirers' hyperbolical guides, which have little actual relation to the terrain of the work itself.

Yeats never left Berryman, who made extraordinary efforts to stop *sounding* like Yeats. That is a perfectly normal procedure in severe cases of poetic influence; Browning's remarkable diction and syntax resulted from his need to stop being Shelley, and the Browning dramatic monologue, with its purported objectivity, was a swerve away from the flamboyant subjectivity of the Shelleyan lyric, or the autobiographical romance of the *Alastor* variety. It would be wonderful if Berryman had become the American Browning, but alas he did not. *The Dream Songs* are not *Men and Women*, and *Love & Fame* is not *Asolando*. In the spirit of having named Lowell as our William Mason, and Plath as our Felicia Hemans, I could call Berryman our "Festus" Bailey or our Alexander Smith, creator of that other masterpiece of the Spasmodic School, *A Life Drama*. Berryman's similarity to Bailey and Smith is quite uncanny, and like Mason and Hemans in their eras, the Spasmodics had critical admirers as profusely enthusiastic as Alvarez, Bayley, Mendelson, and other loyal Berrymanians. Contemporary acclaim is sometimes a very bad indication of a poet's future canonicity.

The poem by Berryman I love best is the proper answer to me, or to anyone else who has the temerity to worry the issue of poetic survival. Here is the last stanza of his superb "A Professor's Song":

> Alive now-no-Blake would have written prose,
> But movement following movement crisply flows,
> So much the better, better the much so,
> As burbleth Mozart. Twelve. The class can go.
> Until I meet you, then, in Upper Hell
> Convulsed, foaming immortal blood: farewell.

Yes, yes indeed, a more than palpable hit, but there precisely is the maddening and necessary question: among the poets, whose blood is immortal? No one likes the question, poets least of all, but it has to be asked, and answered. The cost of belatedness is not a shrinking of literary space, but of the reader's time. I have had the experience of being denounced in this regard, in print and out, by a vociferous bevy of literary journalists, inchoate rhapsodes, and academic impostors, but they too must choose whom they will read in the time they have, and even they must recognize that we cannot reread everyone. Berryman's poetry does not repress this dilemma, no poetry wholly can, however implicitly the sorrow is addressed, and Berryman, even more than most of his contemporaries, was obsessed with this burden. Elizabeth Kaspar Aldrich is particularly shrewd in noting how central this anxiety was to Berryman's imagination. She quotes his splendid remark, from the same 1965 interview that acknowledged the influence of Yeats and Auden: "A poem's force may be pivoted on a missing or misrepresented element in an agreed-upon or imposed design." Someone indeed is always missing, or misrepresented. Aldrich, who loves *Homage to Mistress Bradstreet* more than I do, though I must acknowledge it an ambitious and admirable poem, catches the precise function of crossing over that it fulfilled:

> The "more" that Berryman's poem attempts seems to me, finally, a foredoomed willing-into-being of a burdensome past (the "present" of Anne's world against which she rebels, to which she finally submits) the real burden of which is its quality of absence. Thus, extreme identification with his heroine represents an attempted appropriation of a past from which he is— by the very fact of a literary ancestor like Hawthorne—all the more displaced. But the very hopelessness of the effort is the extraordinary power of *Homage to Mistress Bradstreet*. This is a poem which celebrates impossibilities. The impossibility of living in the faithless void of the present time, the impossibility of being an American poet at all—these are celebrated in this most American of poems in verse Berryman equalled but never surpassed. And it is the nearly impossible intensity of the poet's emotion—need, rage, longing, grief—that this verse contains, and that his Muse/mistress/subject is able to embody. Anne Bradstreet could, paradoxically, embody for Berryman the very weaknesses and absences from which his poetic effort had hitherto suffered—his breakthrough, at what he described as enormous cost; thereafter, *The Dream Songs* and Henry.

I find this persuasive and poignant, though I am uneasy as to all that celebration of impossibilities. "The impossibility of being an American poet at all"—but we have had Whitman, Dickinson, Frost, Stevens, Marianne Moore, Hart Crane, R.P. Warren, Elizabeth Bishop, John Ashbery, James Merrill, A.R. Ammons and, if you will, Eliot, Pound, W.C. Williams and more. Are we to say of *The Dream Songs* also that the very hopelessness of the effort is their extraordinary power? Poetic ambition is vital to poetic strength, and is commendable, and perhaps (*pace* Allen Tate) the poetic will *can* perform the work of the imagination. Like *Homage*, *The Dream Songs* would move even the stoniest of critics, but the question cannot be one of pathos alone. Mad songs are a major lyric genre in our language, and Yeats excelled in them, in and for our century. Late Yeats always hovers nearby in *The Dream Songs*, by which I do not mean the Yeatsian *persona* of Crazy Jane and Tom the Lunatic but the mask of Yeats himself, the wild old wicked man, sometimes appearing as Ribh. What is absent in *The Dream Songs*, inevitably, is the strongest Yeats, the poet who could end almost his last poem by discarding all his own mythologies and personae, and cry aloud in a perfection of agnostic recognition of dying and death:

> O Rocky Voice
> Shall we in that great night rejoice?
> What do we know but that we face
> One another in this place?

Berryman, confronted by that, as all of us are, could only yield, as all of us yield. His own achieved mode, as here in the first stanza of *Dream Song* 88, remained Yeatsian, but without enough perhaps of a swerve into individual difference:

> In slack times visit I the violent dead
> and pick their awful brains. Most seem to feel
> nothing is secret more
> to my disdain I find, when we who fled
> cherish the knowings of both worlds, conceal
> more, beat on the floor,

The violent dead poet here, whose brain is picked, necessarily is Yeats. Berryman, who fled the living world while cherishing the knowings of both the living and the dead, conceals more than Yeats, beats on the floor (a trope taken from Yeats), and finds by rereading Yeats that his own deepest secrets are revealed there, to his own disdain. This has the power of sincerity, but not enough is missing, not enough is misrepresented, and the design is manifestly imposed.

Octavio Paz

(1914–1998)

PAZ RECEIVED THE NOBEL PRIZE FOR LITERATURE IN 1990, ONE OF THE
sounder choices. He possessed, and retains, a unique eminence in Mexican
literature up to this time. Primarily a poet-critic, nevertheless his most
influential books are likely to be *The Labyrinth of Solitude* (1950), which is a
quest for the Mexican identity, and *Sor Juana Or, The Traps of Faith* (1988),
a critical biography of the poet Juana Ramírez, who became Sor Juana Inés
De La Cruz (1651–1695), the major literary figure of the City of Mexico in
seventeenth-century New Spain.

An eclectic and idiosyncratic international poet-critic, and certainly
one of the principal Spanish-language poets of the twentieth century, Paz
paradoxically is most original in his exploration of the very vexed question
of Mexican national identity. Doubtless there are and will be rival attempts
to define what might be called the genius of Mexico, and some Mexican
feminists already denounce *The Labyrinth of Solitude* for implicitly taking
the side of what it exposes and criticizes, the Mexican male myth that their
women first betrayed them to, and with, the invading Spaniards. And yet I
cannot see how Paz could have been clearer:

> In contrast to Guadalupe, who is the Virgin Mother, the
> *Chingada* is the violated Mother. Neither in her nor in the
> Virgin do we find traces of the darker attributes of the great
> goddesses: the lasciviousness of Amaterasu and Aphrodite, the
> cruelty of Artemis and Astarte, the sinister magic of Circe or the
> bloodlust of Kali. Both of them are passive figures. Guadalupe
> is pure receptivity, and the benefits she bestows are of the same
> order: she consoles, quiets, dries tears, calms passions. The
> *Chingada* is even more passive. Her passivity is abject: she does

not resist violence, but is an inert heap of bones, blood and dust. Her taint is constitutional and resides, as we said earlier, in her sex. This passivity, open to the outside world, causes her to lose her identity: she is the *Chingada*. She loses her name; she is no one; she disappears into nothingness; she *is* Nothingness. And yet she is the cruel incarnation of the feminine condition.

If the *Chingada* is a representation of the violated Mother, it is appropriate to associate her with the Conquest, which was also a violation, not only in the historical sense but also in the very flesh of Indian women. The symbol of this violation is Doña Malinche, the mistress of Cortés. It is true that she gave herself voluntarily to the conquistador, but he forgot her as soon as her usefulness was over. Doña Marina [The name given to La Malinche by the Spaniards.] becomes a figure representing the Indian women who were fascinated, violated or seduced by the Spaniards. And as a small boy will not forgive his mother if she abandons him to search for his father, the Mexican people have not forgiven La Malinche for her betrayal. She embodies the open, the *chingado*, to our closed, stoic, impassive Indians. Cuauhtémoc and Doña Marina are thus two antagonistic and complementary figures. There is nothing surprising about our cult of the young emperor—"the only hero at the summit of art," an image of the sacrificed son—and there is also nothing surprising about the curse that weighs against La Malinche. This explains the success of the contemptuous adjective *malinchista* recently put into circulation by the newspapers to denounce all those who have been corrupted by foreign influences. The *malinchistas* are those who want Mexico to open itself to the outside world: the true sons of La Malinche, who is the *Chingada* in person. Once again we see the opposition of the close and the open.

The Mexicans thus see themselves as the sons of La Malinche, and regard her as the *Chingada* personified. Since Paz was writing as a poet, he received all the misunderstandings that he risked: "an elegant insult against Mexican mothers." More accurately, as Paz remarked, *"The Labyrinth of Solitude* was an attempt to describe and understand certain myths; at the same time, insofar as it is a literary work, it has in turn become another myth." Involved here is a disagreement on Paz's part with Claude Lévi-Strauss, set forth in a wise little book (1967):

... Lévi-Strauss affirms that there is a real kinship between myth and music and not between myth and poetry. Myth as distinguished from poetry can be translated without any appreciable loss in the translation ...

Paz adds that translation, for a poem, "implies transmutation or resurrection." A poem by Paz, translated into English by Elizabeth Bishop or Mark Strand is another poem and yet the same poem. This is a version of the Mexicans respecting their President, while behind the respect is the traditional image of the Father. Yet Paz ends his *Labyrinth* on an ominous note:

Every moribund or sterile society attempts to save itself by creating a redemption myth which is also a fertility myth, a creation myth ... The sterility of the bourgeois world will end in suicide or a new form of creative participation.

Paz has been dead for more than two years, and his Mexico currently is becoming both more bourgeois and more Catholic. A superb Surrealist poet, whether in verse or prose, Paz founders in prophecy, as everyone has done in opposing the endlessly driven onward march of bourgeois societies. But that does not lessen the insight nor the visionary power of *The Labyrinth of Solitude*. Himself of mixed Spanish and Indian ancestry, Paz explains Mexican "solitude" by the original trauma of the Spanish Conquest, though as a diplomat and world-traveler he came to know that there are different modes of "solitude" in every national culture.

The starting-points for Paz in defining the difference between the United States and Mexico is that the Native Americans were essentially nomads, while the native Mexicans were settled peoples, farmers rather than hunters. To this was added the differences between Protestant England and the Spain of the Counter-Reformation. So far, that seems obvious enough; Paz manifests his particular genius for locating differences by passing beyond historical origins to spiritual insight:

The Mexicans' vision of death, which is also the hope of resurrection is as profoundly steeped in Catholic eschatology as in Indian naturalism. The Mexican death is of the body, exactly the opposite of the American death, which is abstract and disembodied. For Mexicans, death sees and touches itself; it is the body emptied of the soul, the pile of bones that somehow, as in the Aztec poem, must bloom again. For Americans, death is what is not seen: absence, the disappearance of the person. In the Puritan consciousness, death was always present, but as a moral entity, an idea. Later on, scientism pushed death out of the American consciousness. Death melted away and became unmentionable. Finally, in vast segments of the American population of today, progressive rationalism and idealism have been replaced by neo-hedonism. But the cult of the body and of pleasure implies the recognition and acceptance of death. The body is mortal, and the kingdom of pleasure is that of the moment, as Epicurus saw better than anyone else. American hedonism closes its eyes to death and has been incapable of exorcising the destructive power of the moment with a wisdom like that of the Epicureans of antiquity. Present-day hedonism is the last recourse of the anguished and the desperate, and expression of the nihilism that is eroding the West.

Capitalism exalts the activities and behavior patterns traditionally called virile: aggressiveness, the spirit of competition and emulation, combativeness. American society made these values its own. This perhaps explains why nothing like the Mexicans' devotion to the Virgin of Guadalupe appears in the different versions of Christianity professed by Americans, including the Catholic minority. The Virgin unites the religious sensibilities of the Mediterranean and Mesoamerica, both of them regions that fostered ancient cults of feminine divinities, Guadalupe-Tonantzin is the mother of all Mexicans—Indians, mestizos, whites—but she is also a warrior virgin whose image has often appeared on the banners of peasant uprising. In the Virgin of Guadalupe we encounter a very ancient vision of femininity which, as was true of the pagan goddesses, is not without a heroic tint.

There is much here to acknowledge, and much to argue. Paz had a limited understanding of the American Religion, which he identified with Puritan New England. But the United States, since about 1800, has not been Protestant in the European way, and instead has developed a complex configuration of new faiths that are more than sects: Southern Baptists, Adventists, Mormons, Pentecostalists, and others. Our hedonists are not that different from those of other nations, and our denial of death has something to do with the astonishing national belief (eighty-nine percent, according to Gallup) that God loves each of us on a personal and individual basis. Sane Mexicans do not walk and talk with Jesus; an astonishing number of ordinary citizens of the United States do.

And yet Paz troubles me when he opposes Mexico's vision of femininity to that of the United States, though in this area someone regularly condemned as a "patriarchal critic" had better exercise wariness. The myth of La Malinche or the *Chingada*, unforgettably expounded by Paz, is alien to the United States, yet it is the center of *The Labyrinth of Solitude*, which on rereading flowers into a two hundred page prose-poem, rather than what Paz himself describes as "a book of social, political and psychological criticism."

Halfway through his *Labyrinth*, Paz gives us a remarkable excursus upon Sor Juana, which decades later exfoliated into his superb biography of the first major Hispanic poet in the New World:

> Despite the brilliance of her career, the pathos of her death, and the admirable geometry that shapes her best poetic creations, there is something unrealized and fragmentary in the life and work of Sor Juana. We can sense the melancholy of a spirit who never succeeded in forgiving herself for her boldness and her condition as a woman. Her epoch did not provide her with the intellectual nourishment her appetite required, and she herself could not—and who can?—create a world of ideas in which to live alone. An awareness of her singularity was always very alive in her: "What can women know except the philosophy of the kitchen?" she asked with a smile. But the wound hurt her: "Who would not believe, hearing such general applause, that I have voyaged full-sail on the handclaps of popular acclamation?" Sor Juana was a solitary figure. Indecisive and smiling, she lived an ambiguous life; she was conscious of the duality of her condition and the impossibility of her task. We often hear reproaches against men who have not fulfilled their destinies. Should we not grieve, however, for the ill fortune of a woman who was superior both to her society and her culture?

Eloquently plangent, this still would not have prepared me for Paz's *Sor Juana*, which is a baroque masterwork, and though a critical biography in form, fulfills the project of *The Labyrinth of Solitude*, and perfects Paz's lifelong meditation upon Mexican identity. What emerges most vividly from *Sor Juana*, aside from its depiction of the culture of later seventeenth-century Mexico, is the poetic splendor and final personal tragedy of Sor Juana, destroyed by "the traps of faith," the spiritual tyranny of a Church resisting all enlightenment, and obliterating a woman poet of genius for the sole sake of eliminating an anomaly, an autonomous creative spirit:

It is scarcely necessary to point out the similarities between Sor Juana's personal situation and the obstacles we Mexicans have experienced during the process of modernization. There was an insoluble contradiction between Sor Juana and her world. This contradiction was not merely intellectual; it was fundamental, and can be located in three main areas. The first was the opposition between her literary vocation and the fact that she was a nun. At other moments, although not in New Spain, the Church had been tolerant and had harbored writers and poets who, often in blatant disregard of their religious responsibilities, had devoted themselves exclusively to letters. Their cases, however—the most notable being those of Góngora, Lope de Vega, Tirso de Molina, and Mira de Amescua—differ from that of Sor Juana in an essential point: they were poets and dramatists but not intellectuals. Both vocations, poet and intellectual, converged in Sor Juana. In late seventeenth-century Spain and its domains, a priest or nun with an intellectual vocation was restricted to theology and sacred studies. This incompatibility was aggravated by the fact that Sor Juana's extraordinary intellectual restlessness and her encyclopedic curiosity—Sigüenza's also—coincided with a moment of paralysis in the Church and exhaustion in Hispanic culture.

The second area of discord was Sor Juana's gender. The fact that a woman—what is more, a nun—should devote herself so single-mindedly to letters must have both astounded and scandalized her contemporaries. She was called the "Tenth Muse" and the "Phoenix of America": sincere expressions of admiration that must have set her head spinning at times. She tells us in the *Response* that no lack of criticism and censure accompanied this praise. The censure came from influential prelates and was founded on a point of doctrine. It was not by chance that in his appeal to Sor Juana asking her to forsake secular letters the Bishop of Puebla quoted St. Paul. It was one thing to be tolerant with Lope de Vega and Góngora, both bad priests, and another to be lenient with Sor Juana Inés de la Cruz. Although her conduct was beyond reproach, her attitudes were not. She was guilty of the sin of pride, a sin to which the vain feminine sex is particularly susceptible. Pride was the ruin of Lucifer, because hubris leads to rebelliousness. Sor Juana's critics saw a causal relationship between letters, which lead a woman from her natural state of obedience, and rebelliousness. Sor Juana had disproved the inferiority of women in intellectual and literary matters and made her attainments a source of admiration and public applause; to the prelates this was sin, and her obstinacy was rebellion. That is why they demanded a total abdication.

As Paz shows, Sor Juana's great, Hermetic poem, *First Dream*, differs profoundly from the visions of St. John of the Cross and of St. Teresa. John of the Cross quested to get to a point where there was no knowing, and St. Teresa wished to be possessed by God's light. Both were impatient with reason, but Sor Juana, sublimely reasonable, desired to illuminate all things, in a quest both more Neoplatonic and more encyclopedic than it was specifically Christian. She was the last great poet of Spain's Baroque Age, and that the Church violated her creative integrity was its own sin against the spirit.

Paz, an eclectic religionist, more Hindu and Buddhist than Christian, had an instinctive empathy for Sor Juana's doomed Hermeticism. She stands in his work as the other personification of the scapegoated *Chingada*, at the other end of the historical and spiritual world from the reviled La Malinche. It fascinates me that Octavio Paz, a great erotic poet and universal critic of poetry, composes his two major prose achievements upon two victims of what has to be called the vision of Mexican masculinity, the nature of which remains so resistant to change.

Gwendolyn Brooks

(1917–2000)

GWENDOLYN BROOKS SAYS OF HER PRE-1967 POETRY: "I WASN'T WRITING consciously with the idea that blacks *must address* blacks, *must write* about blacks." Certainly, her work after 1967 is very different from her poems composed before she turned fifty. I prefer the earlier achievement, a judgment (if it is one) that is harmless since every essayist in this volume, except for Langston Hughes, centers upon the later Brooks.

The famous lyric, "The Bean Eaters" ironically and memorably celebrates:

Two who are Mostly Good,
Two who have lived their day,
But keep on putting on their clothes
And putting things away.

This wry turn upon the universal still seems to me Brooks's strength, as does "The Crazy Woman," an eloquent extension of the Mad Song tradition:

I'll wait until November.
That is the time for me.
I'll go out in the frosty dark
And sing most terribly.

If I contrast these with the poem of 1969, "The Riot," I come to see that I am not yet competent to judge the poet who was reborn in 1967. The satiric eye is still there, and the dominant stylistic influence remains T.S. Eliot. Yet the style and the stance seem not to cohere:

Because the Poor were sweaty and unpretty
(not like Two Dainty Negroes in Winnetka)
and they were coming toward him in rough ranks.
In seas. In windsweep. They were black and loud.
And not detainable. And not discreet.

I like that: "In sea. In windsweep," and I grant that the poem's sentiments are admirable, if you believe (as most of us really do) that only violence is the valid answer to violence. The difficulty here, as in the celebrated ballad, the "Anniad," is that Brooks risks becoming a period piece,
at some later time when American society has progressed beyond its long
history of injustice. Ideological verse remains ideological; its paradoxes
flatten out too easily. Gwendolyn Brooks is acclaimed for her self-trans-
formations, as nearly all the essays here demonstrate. Whether she has sacrificed part of her gift in an exemplary cause seems to me a legitimate question.

James Dickey

(1923–1997)

I FIRST READ JAMES DICKEY'S EARLY POEM, "THE OTHER," SOME TWENTY
years ago. Having admired his recently published book, *Drowning With
Others*, I went back to his first book, *Into the Stone*, at the recommendation
of a close friend, the poet Alvin Feinman. Though very moved by several
of the earlier poems, I was affected most strongly by the one called "The
Other." It has taken me twenty years to understand why the poem still will
not let me go, and so I begin with it here. I don't think of Dickey as a poet
primarily of otherness, but rather as a heroic celebrator of what Emerson
called "the great and crescive self," indeed of the American self proper,
which demands victory and disdains even great defeats. Dickey, as I read
him, is like what Vico called the Magic Formalists or Blake named the
Giant Forms. He is a throwback to those mythic hypotheses out of which
strong poetry first broke forth, the bards of divination whose heroic vitalism demanded a literal immortality for themselves as poets. But even a
Magic Formalist learns that he is at best a mortal god.

The pain of that learning is the central story of Dickey's poetry, and
I choose to evade that pain here in order to emphasize Dickey's counter-
song of otherness. Since I will take him scarcely into his middle years, I will
be ignoring all of his most ambitious poetry, "the later motion," as he has
called it. Though his work from 1965 to the present clearly is more problematic than the poems I will discuss, its achievement quite possibly is of a
higher order. But it is too soon to prophesy Dickey's final stature, and criticism must discourse on what it loves before it broods upon the limits of the
canonical. What I know and love best, so far, in Dickey's poetry is "the early
motion," and the counter-song of otherness in that motion moves me most.
I have circled back to that poem, "The Other," and turn to it now to locate
an origin of Dickey's quest as a poet.

That origin is guilt, and guilt ostensibly of being a substitute or replacement for a brother dead before one was born. Freud, I think, would have judged such guilt to be a screen memory, and I am Freudian enough to look or surmise elsewhere for the source of guilt in the poems of *Into the Stone*. From the beginning of his poetic career, Dickey was a poet of Sublime longings, and those who court the Sublime are particularly subject to changeling fantasies. The poem he titled "The Other" is manifestly Yeatsian, whether directly or through the mediation of Roethke, but the argument already is Dickey's own, and in all respects it is the meter-making argument, and not the derived diction and metric, that gives this poem its great distinction. Indeed Dickey, an instinctive Emersonian from the start, despite his Southern heritage, literalizes Emerson's trope of a meter-making argument by the extraordinary device of packing the seventy-seven lines of this lyrical reverie into what has always felt to me like a single sentence. How could there be a second sentence in a poem that identifies itself so completely with the changeling's will to be the other, when the other ultimately is the god Apollo?

Somewhere, Dickey identified his triad of literary heroes as the unlikely combination of Keats, Malcolm Lowry, and James Agee, presumably associated because of their early or relatively early deaths, and because of their shared intensity of belief in what could be called the salvation history of the literary art. But Dickey is very much a poet of Sensibility, in the mode that Frye once defined as *the* Age of Sensibility, the mode of Christopher Smart and of William Collins, among other doomed poets whose threshold stance destroyed them upon the verge of High Romanticism. The Keats who moves Dickey most, the Keats of the letters, is the culmination of the major theme of the poets of Sensibility, the theme that, following Collins, I have called the Incarnation of the Poetical Character. Lowry and Agee, though I don't recall Dickey mentioning this, were curiously allied as verse writers by the overwhelming influence that Hart Crane exerted upon both of them. Dickey seems to prefer Crane's letters to his poems, which oddly parallels his preference of Keats's letters. But Keats and Crane, like Lowry and Agee in their verse, represent fully in their poems the Incarnation of the Poetical Character, where the poet, in the guise of a young man, is reborn as the young god of the sun. That is clearly the genre of Dickey's "The Other," but the clarity is shadowed by Dickey's early guilt concerning what the poem accurately names as "my lust of self."

What self can that be except the magic and occult self, ontological rather than empirical, and in Yeatsian or Whitmanian terms, self rather than soul? The guilt that shadows Dickey's marvelous seventy-seven-line utterance is the guilt induced by what Freud came to call the above-I or the over-I (the superego), a rather more daunting though no less fictive entity than Emerson's Oversoul. Emerson had the shrewdest of eyes for anxiety, but Freud's eye, as Wallace Stevens once wrote, was the microscope of potency. The guilt of family betrayal must ensue from the changeling fantasy of the family romance, and for Freud (as for Kenneth Burke), all romance is family romance. But the family romance of the poet *as* poet tends to depart from the domain of the merely biographical family. Dickey's assertion of self as person was the desire to rise from the "strength-haunted body" of a "rack-ribbed child" to the Herculean figure he has been since, a titanic form among contemporary poets. But since poems can attempt the truth only through fictions or tropes, the poem of "The Other" is compelled to treat the child's aspiration as the drive towards becoming Apollo, poetry itself. The youthful Henry James, reviewing *Drum-Taps*, scorned Whitman as an essentially prosaic temperament trying to lift itself by muscular exertion into poetry. The elderly Henry James, weeping over the great *Lilacs* elegy, scorned his own youthful review; but, properly modified, it can give us a critical trope for reading Dickey: an essentially poetic temperament lifting itself by muscular exertion into poetry.

Dickey's most curious characteristic, from "The Other" through *Puella*, is his involuntary but striking dualism, curious because so heroic a vitalist ought not to exemplify (as he does) so Pauline and Cartesian a mind–body split, or even so prevalent a sense of what Stevens termed the dumbfoundering abyss between ourselves and the object. What the poem surprisingly shows for and to Dickey is that his own body becomes his brother, or Apollo, or "the other." If the body is the divine other, then pathos becomes both sublime and grotesque, because the body must change, and the final form of that change is death. "The Other" is almost the first of Dickey's poems, and in some ways he has never surpassed it, not because he has failed to develop, but because it is unsurpassable. The whole of Dickey is in it already, as the whole of Shelley is in *Alastor*, or the whole of Yeats is in *The Wanderings of Oisin*. I repeat that this does not mean that Dickey simply has unfolded; so restless and reckless an experimentalist is outrageously metamorphic. But all his changes quest hopelessly for a disjunctiveness his temperament refuses to allow him. The "holes" that space out the poems of his major phase never represent discursive gaps or even crossings from one kind of figuration to another. Instead, they impressively mark or punctuate the exquisite desperation of the will to live, the lust of self that is not to be railed at, because it does represent what Keats called "a sickness not ignoble": the sickness unto death of heroic poetry.

"The Other," like so much of Dickey's best work, is very clearly a Southern American poem, and yet its Incarnation of the Poetical Character is necessarily universal in its imagery and argument. This is the universal purchased at the high cost of what was to be a permanent guilt, the guilt of a poet who as poet greatly desired *not* to be egocentric, despite the demands of the mythology that found him from the start. Those demands are felt even in the opening movement of "The Other":

> Holding onto myself by the hand,
> I change places into the spirit
> I had as a rack-ribbed child,
> And walk slowly out through my mind
> To the wood, as into a falling fire
> Where I turned from that strength-haunted body
> Half-way to bronze, as I wished to.

Dickey's natural religion always has been Mithraism, the traditional faith of soldiers, and certainly the most masculine and fierce of all Western beliefs. Despite the Persian origins of Mithra, Rome assimilated him to Apollo, and Dickey's major alteration is to make the Incarnation of the Poetical Character into a Mithraic ritual. The "bronze" of this first stanza will be revealed, later in the poem, as both the statue of Apollo and the body of the sacrificial bull slain by Mithra. As the boy Dickey slings up the too-heavy ax-head, he prays

> To another, unlike me, beside me:
> To a brother or king-sized shadow
> Who looked at me, burned, and believed me:
> Who believed I would rise like Apollo
>
> With armor-cast shoulders upon me:
> Whose voice, whistling back through my teeth,
> Counted strokes with the hiss of a serpent.
> Where the sun through the bright wood drove
> Him, mute, and floating strangely, to the ground,
> He led me into his house, and sat
> Upright, with a face I could never imagine,
>
> With a great harp leant on his shoulder,
> And began in deep handfuls to play it.

"Burned" is the crucial trope here, since the brother, as god of the sun, leads only into the heat and light that is the house of the sun. The oracular hiss is Pythian, though the voice truly becomes Dickey's own. What Dickey, *in the poem*, develops most brilliantly is the figure of downward movement, which is introduced in the second stanza as the combined fall of sweat and leaves, and further invoked in the fall of light. Later in the poem, music falls, followed in the final line by the casting down of foliage. All these fallings substitute for the hidden ritual in which the bull's blood falls upon the Mithraic adept, the warrior in the act of becoming Apollo:

My brother rose beside me from the earth,

With the wing-bone of music on his back
Trembling strongly with heartfelt gold,
And ascended like a bird into the tree,
And music fell in a comb, as I stood
In a bull's heavy, bronze-bodied shape
As it mixed with a god's, on the ground,
And leaned on the helve of the ax.

The "great, dead tree" of the poem's second stanza might be called Dickey's first major fiction of duration, the origin of his quarrel with time. Being Dickey's, it is the liveliest of dead trees, yet it cannot propitiate this poet's poignant longing for a literal immortality:

Now, owing my arms to the dead
Tree, and the leaf-loosing, mortal wood,
Still hearing that music amaze me,
I walk through the time-stricken forest,
And wish another body for my life,
Knowing that none is given
By the giant, unusable tree

And the leaf-shapen lightning of sun,
And rail at my lust of self
With an effort like chopping through root-stocks:
Yet the light, looming brother but more
Brightly above me is blazing,
In that music come down from the branches
In utter, unseasonable glory,

Telling nothing but how I made
By hand, a creature to keep me dying
Years longer, and coming to sing in the wood
Of what love still might give,
Could I turn wholly mortal in my mind,
My body-building angel give me rest,
This tree cast down its foliage with the years.

"This tree" is at last Dickey himself as fiction of duration, the poet become his own poem, indeed "made / By hand," and so a house made by hands, a mortal body. When desire can turn monistic, for Dickey, it can become only a mortal turn, a trope knowing it is only trope. The other is divine, but only as Apollo or Mithra was divine, rather than as Jesus or Jehovah. A poem "about" a body-building child has transformed itself into the Sublime, into the body-building angel who has never since given Dickey any rest.

Retrospectively, I suppose that the poem "The Other" first moved me because so few American poems of twenty years ago had anything like Dickey's remarkable ability to be so humanly direct and yet so trustingly given to the potential of figurative language. The Dickey of the early motion seemed to have found his way back, almost effortlessly, to the secrets of poetry. I remember that the first poem by Dickey that I read was the title poem of *Drowning With Others*, a title that is itself an unforgettable trope, worthy of Emily Dickinson's apprehension that an acute consciousness, even when aware of neighbors and the sun, of other selves and outward nature, still died quite alone, except for its own identity, a totemic single hound. What is Sublime in the self finally is capable only of "drowning with others," but that is only part of what is central in what remains one of Dickey's most singular and enduring poems.

If I remember aright, Dickey himself doesn't much like this poem, and thinks it obscure rather than strong. Indeed, I recall his insistence that he wrote the poem only so as to give status to his book's title. His account of the poem's referential aspect was strangely literal, but I think this is one of his poems that sneaked by him, as it were:

There are moments a man turns from us
Whom we have all known until now.
Upgathered, we watch him grow,
Unshipping his shoulder bones

Like human, everyday wings
That he has not ever used,

Releasing his hair from his brain,
A kingfisher's crest, confused

By the God-tilted light of Heaven.
His deep, window-watching smile
Comes closely upon us in waves,
And spreads, and now we are

At last within it, dancing.
Slowly we turn and shine
Upon what is holding us,
As under our feet he soars,

Struck dumb as the angel of Eden,
In wide, eye-opening rings.
Yet the hand on my shoulder fears
To feel my own wingblades spring,

To feel me sink slowly away
In my hair turned loose like a thought
Of a fisherbird dying in flight.
If I opened my arms, I could hear

Every shell in the sea find the word
It has tried to put into my mouth.
Broad flight would become of my dancing,
And I would obsess the whole sea,

But I keep rising and singing
With my last breath. Upon my back,
With his hand on my unborn wing,
A man rests easy as sunlight

Who has kept himself free of the forms
Of the deaf, down-soaring dead,
And me laid out and alive
For nothing at all, in his arms.

I read this as another lyric of poetic incarnation, a rather less willing assumption of the divine other, perhaps even a defense against the Orphic predicament, but still a revision of the poem "The Other." Indeed, I wonder if one way of characterizing Dickey's obsessive strength as a poet is to say that he cannot stop rewriting that essential early poem. For the man who turns from us in the opening line of "Drowning With Others" is the Orphic Dickey, poet and divine other. Like the rich-haired youth of Collins, or Coleridge's youth with flashing eyes and floating hair, or Stevens's figure of the youth as virile poet in "Mrs. Alfred Uruguay," this other Dickey has hair released into "a kingfisher's crest, confused / By the God-tilted light of Heaven." Apollo is reborn again, but as Orphic drowning man, fit version of the poet of Sensibility in America, be he Hart Crane or Roethke or Agee or Dickey. But if the man turning from us in this poem is Dickey in the act of Sublime apotheosis, then whoever is that "I" rather desperately chanting this hieratic spell? Perhaps that is why Dickey as commentator judged this grand lyric too obscure, despite its palpable strength.

Our poet is weird in the true sense, one of the Fates (as Richard Howard, lexicographer among bards, might remind us), and his natural mode is the uncanny. What he has done here may be obscure to his spectral self, but his magic or occult self gathers his spectral self, until even that "I" keeps "rising and singing / With my last breath." And so truly neither self dies, or can die, in this soaring lyric of divination. Perhaps there is a touch, not indeliberate, of Dylan Thomas in the metric here, and even allusive overtones of Thomas at moments in the diction. That resemblance may even be a hidden cause of Dickey's distaste for his poem, but I remark upon it to note the difference between the poets, rather than their shared qualities. On mortality, the warrior Dickey cannot deceive himself, but a poet whose totem seems to be the albatross does not fear death by water. Few lines are as characteristic of Dickey as "And I would obsess the whole sea."

I take it that "drowning with others" is a trope for "winging with others," and that the dominant image here is flight, and not going under. Flight of course is Freud's true trope for repression, and an Orphic sensibility never ceases to forget, involuntarily but on purpose, that its vocation is mortal godhood, or not dying *as a poet*. Drowning with others, then, as a trope, must mean something like dying only as the immortal precursor dies or writing poems that men will not let die. Though its scale is small, this is Dickey's *Lycidas*, even as *The Zodiac* will be his cosmological elegy for the self. The child building up a Mithra-like body is still here in this poem, but he is here more reluctantly, caught up in the moments of discovering that a too-closely-shared immortality becomes mortality again, the stronger the sharing is known.

Dickey, being one of our authentic avatars of the American Sublime, exemplifies its two grand stigmata: not to feel free unless he is alone, and finally to know that what is oldest in him is no part of the Creation. After two poems wrestling with otherness, I need to restore his sense of solitude, his Emersonian self-reliance, and the great poem for this in his early motion is "In the Mountain Tent," which appropriately concludes the book *Drowning With Others*. I remember that Dickey contrasts this with the more famous "The Heaven of Animals," a lovely poem, but not one with the power of this meditation:

> I am hearing the shape of the rain
> Take the shape of the tent and believe it,
> Laying down all around where I lie
> A profound, unspeakable law.
> I obey, and am free-falling slowly
>
> Through the thought-out leaves of the wood
> Into the minds of animals.
> I am there in the shining of water
> Like dark, like light, out of Heaven.
>
> I am there like the dead, or the beast
> Itself, which thinks of a poem—
> Green, plausible, living, and holy—
> And cannot speak, but hears,
> Called forth from the waiting of things,
>
> A vast, proper, reinforced crying
> With the sifted, harmonious pause,
> The sustained intake of all breath
> Before the first word of the Bible.
>
> At midnight water dawns
> Upon the held skulls of the foxes
> And weasels and touseled hares
> On the eastern side of the mountain.
> Their light is the image I make
>
> As I wait as if recently killed,
> Receptive, fragile, half-smiling,
> My brow watermarked with the mark
> On the wing of a moth

And the tent taking shape on my body
Like ill-fitting, Heavenly clothes.
From holes in the ground comes my voice
In the God-silenced tongue of the beasts.
"I shall rise from the dead," I am saying.

Whether a Christian or not, this speaker appears to entertain a belief in the resurrection of the body. Even in this solitude of spirit, the uncanny in Dickey, his *daimon*, enters with the poem's implicit question: Whose body, mine or that of the other? Is it every man who shall rise in the body, or is it not a more Gnostic persuasion that is at work here? The Gnostic lives already in the resurrected body, which is the body of a Primal Man who preceded the Creation. What a Gnostic called the Pleroma, the Fullness, Dickey calls beautifully "the waiting of things." The dead, the animals, and Dickey as the poem's speaker, all hear together the Gnostic Call, a vast crying out of the waiting of things. Without knowing any esoteric Gnosticism, Dickey by poetic intuition arrives at the trope of the Kabbalistic holding in of the divine breath that precedes the rupture of Creation. What Dickey celebrates therefore is "The sustained intake of all breath / Before the first word of the Bible." That word in Hebrew is *Beresit*, and so the vision of this poem is set before the Beginning. At midnight, not at dawn, and so only in the light of a rain image reflected from the beasts, Dickey speaks forth for the beasts, who have been silenced by the Demiurge called God by Genesis. In Dickey's own interpretation, the man experiences both a kinship with the beasts and a fundamental difference, since he alone will rise from the dead. But I think the poet is stronger than the poet-as-interpreter here. To rise from the dead, in this poem's context, is merely to be one's own magical or pneumatic self, a self that precedes the first word of the Bible.

It isn't very startling to see and say that Dickey, as poet, is not a Christian poet, but rather an Emersonian, an American Orphic and Gnostic. This is only to repeat Richard Howard's fine wordplay upon what could be called the Native Strain in our literature. What startles me, a little, is to see and say just how doctrinal, even programmatic, Dickey's early Orphism now seems. The Orphism has persisted, emerging with tumultuous force in the superbly mad female preacher of Dickey's "May Day Sermon," which I recommend we all read directly after each time we read Jonathan Edwards's rather contrary sermon, "Sinners in the Hands of an Angry God." Rhetorically, though, that is a very different Dickey than the poet of *The Early Motion*, whose Orphism perhaps is the more persuasive for being almost overheard, rather than so emphatically heard.

I turn my charting of the early motion to Dickey's next book, *Helmets*, which so far may be his most distinguished single volume, a judgment in which I would neither want nor expect him to concur. "Helmet," as a word, ultimately goes back to an Indo-European root that means both "to cover and conceal," but also "to save," which explains why "helm" and "helmet" are related to those two antithetical primal names, Hell and Valhalla. Dickey's book, of course, knows all this, Dickey being a preternaturally implicit knower, both as a poet and as a warrior—or, combining both modes, as an archer and hunter. Had I time and space, I would want to comment on every poem in *Helmets*, but I will confine myself to its two most ambitious meditations, "Approaching Prayer" and the final "Drinking from a Helmet." Certain thematic and agonistic strains that I have glanced at already can be said not to culminate but to achieve definitive expression in these major poems. I qualify my statement because what is most problematic about Dickey's poetry is that nothing ever is allowed to culminate, not even in *The Zodiac*, or "Falling," or "May Day Sermon." So obsessive a poet generally would not remain also so tentative, but Dickey's is a cunning imagination, metamorphic enough to evade its exegetes.

As a critic himself obsessed with the issue of belatedness, I am particularly impressed by the originality of "Approaching Prayer," which Dickey rightly called "the most complicated and far-fetched poem I've written." I should add that Dickey said that some fifteen years ago, but it is good enough for me that his observation was true up to then. The far-fetcher was the good, rough English term that the Elizabethan rhetorician Puttenham used to translate the ancient trope called metalepsis or transumption, and "Approaching Prayer" is certainly an instance of the kind of poem that I have learned to call transumptive. Such a poem swallows up an ever-early freshness as its own, and spits out all sense of belatedness, as belonging only to others. "Approaching Prayer" is at moments Yeatsian in its stance and diction, but what overwhelmingly matters most in it can only be called "originality." I know no poem remotely like it. If it shares a magic vitalism with Yeats and D.H. Lawrence, its curious kind of wordless, almost undirected prayer has nothing Yeatsian or Lawrentian in its vision. And it is less like Dickey's true precursor, Roethke, than it is like Robert Penn Warren's masterful "Red-Tailed Hawk and Pyre of Youth," which, however, was written long after it and perhaps may even owe something to it.

Originality in poetry, despite Northrop Frye's eloquent assertions, has little to do with the renewal of an archetype. Instead, it has to do with what I would call a struggle against facticity, where "facticity" means being so incarcerated by an author, a tradition, or a mode that neither author nor reader is aware of the incarceration. Dickey calls his poem "Approaching Prayer," but as his revisionist or critic, I will retitle it "Approaching Poetry" or even "Approaching Otherness." I grant that Dickey has said, "In this poem I tried to imagine how a rather prosaic person would prepare himself for the miraculous event which will be the prayer he's going to try to pray," but surely that "rather prosaic person" is a transparent enough defense for the not exactly prosaic Dickey. No one has ever stood in Dickey's presence and felt that he was encountering prose. The poem's speaker is "inside the hair *helmet*" (my emphasis), and this helmet too both conceals and saves. At the poem's visionary center, the boar's voice, speaking through the helmet, gives us the essential trope as he describes his murder by the archer: "*The sound from his fingers, / Like a plucked word, quickly pierces / Me again.*" The bow, then, is poetic language, and each figuration is a wounding arrow. Who then is slaying whom?

Like any strong poet, Dickey puts on the body of his dead father, for him, let us say, the composite precursor Yeats/Roethke. Shall we say that the strong poet, in Dickey's savage version, reverses the fate of Adonis, and slays the boar of facticity? I hear the accent of another reversal, when Dickey writes:

> My father's sweater
> Swarms over me in the dark.
> I see nothing, but for a second
>
> Something goes through me
> Like an accident, a negligent glance.

Emerson, in his famous epiphany of transmutation into a Transparent Eyeball, chanted: "I am nothing; I see all; the currents of the Universal Being circulate through me; I am part or particle of God." Dickey's surrogate sees nothing, but for a second is all, since that something going through him, glancingly negligent, accidental, also makes him part or particle of God. Addressing beasts and angels, this not so very prosaic personage speaks both as beast and as angel. But to whom? To part or particle of what is oldest, earliest in him, to the beyond that comes straight down at the point of the acceptable time. But acceptable to whom? The God of the hunt is hardly Yahweh Elohim. Dickey's closing chant salutes the God through the trope of "enough": a violent enough stillness, a brain having enough blood, love enough from the dead father, lift enough from the acuity of slaughter—all enough to slay reason in the name of something being, something that need not be heard, if only "it may have been somehow said."

The apocalyptic Lawrence of the last poems and *The Man Who Died*, and the Yeats of the final phase, celebrated and so would have understood that "enough." As an American Orphic, as pilot and as archer, Dickey is less theoretic, more pragmatic, in having known just that "enough."

If I were writing of the later Dickey, the poet of "The Firebombing," "Slave Quarters," "Falling," and *The Zodiac*, then I would invoke Blake's Proverbs of Hell on the dialectics of knowing enough by knowing more than enough. But I am going to conclude where Dickey himself ends *The Early Motion*, with the gracious approach to otherness that characterizes the nineteen fragments that constitute "Drinking from a Helmet." Dickey remarks that the fragments are set between the battlefield and the graveyard, which I suspect is no inaccurate motto for the entire cosmos of what will prove to be the Whole Motion, when we have it all. Though it is a suite of war poems, "Drinking from a Helmet," even in its title, moves toward meaning both of Dickey's major imaginative obsessions: divination through finding the right cover of otherness, and salvation from the body of this death through finding the magic body of the poet.

A survivor climbs out of his foxhole to wait on line at a green water-truck, picking up another's helmet to serve as a drinking vessel. Behind him, the graves registration people are laying out the graveyard for those still fighting. The literal force of this is almost too strong, and conceals the trope of divination, defined by Vico as the process of evasion by which the poet of Magic Formalism achieves godhood—a kind of mortal godhood, but immortality enough. Drinking from a helmet becomes the magic act of substitution, fully introduced in the luminous intensity of fragment VIII:

> At the middle of water
> Bright circles dawned inward and outward
> Like oak rings surviving the tree
> As its soul, or like
> The concentric gold spirit of time.
> I kept trembling forward through something
> Just born of me.

The "something" is prayer, but again in the peculiar sense adumbrated in the poem "Approaching Prayer." Dickey always has been strongest at *invention* (which Dr. Johnson thought the essence of poetry) and his invention is triumphant throughout the subsequent progression of fragments. We apprehend an almost Blakean audacity of pure vision, as the speaker struggles to raise the dead:

I swayed, as if kissed in the brain.
Above the shelled palm-stumps I saw
How the tops of huge trees might be moved
In a place in my own country
I never had seen in my life.
In the closed dazzle of my mouth
I fought with a word in the water
To call on the dead to strain
Their muscles to get up and go there.
I felt the difference between
Sweat and tears when they rise,
Both trying to melt the brow down.

I think one would have to go back to Whitman's *Drum-Taps* to find an American war poem this nobly wrought. Vision moves from Okinawa to rural America, to the place of the slain other whose helmet has served as the vessel of the water of life:

On even the first day of death
The dead cannot rise up,
But their last thought hovers somewhere
For whoever finds it.
My uninjured face floated strangely
In the rings of a bodiless tree.
Among them, also, a final
Idea lived, waiting
As in Ariel's limbed, growing jail.

Ariel, imprisoned by the witch before Prospero's advent, then becomes the spirit of freedom, but not in this poem, where only to "be no more killed" becomes freedom enough. "Not dying wherever you are" is the new mode of otherness, as vision yields to action:

Enough
Shining, I picked up my carbine and said.
I threw my old helmet down
And put the wet one on.
Warmed water ran over my face.
My last thought changed, and I knew
I inherited one of the dead.

Dickey at last, though only through surrogate or trope, is at once self
and other. What was vision becomes domesticated, touchingly American:

> I saw tremendous trees
> That would grow on the sun if they could,
> Towering. I saw a fence
> And two boys facing each other,
> Quietly talking,
> Looking in at the gigantic redwoods,
> The rings in the trunks turning slowly
> To raise up stupendous green.
> They went away, one turning
> The wheels of a blue bicycle,
> The smaller one curled catercornered
> In the handlebar basket.

The dead soldier's last thought is of his older brother, as Dickey's longing
always has been for his own older brother, dead before the poet was born.
Fragment XVIII, following, is the gentlest pathos in all of Dickey:

> I would survive and go there,
> Stepping off the train in a helmet
> That held a man's last thought,
> Which showed him his older brother
> Showing him trees.
> I would ride through all
> California upon two wheels
> Until I came to the white
> Dirt road where they had been,
> Hoping to meet his blond brother,
> And to walk with him into the wood
> Until we were lost,
> Then take off the helmet
> And tell him where I had stood,
> What poured, what spilled, what swallowed:

That "what" is the magic of substitution, and the final fragment is Whitmanian
and unforgettable, being the word of the survivor who suffered and was there:

> And tell him I was the man.

The ritual magic of a soldier's survival has been made one with the Incarnation of the Poetical Character. Of all Dickey's poems, it is the one I am persuaded that Walt Whitman would have admired most. Whitman too would have said with Dickey: "I never have been able to disassociate the poem from the poet, and I hope I never will." What Whitman and Dickey alike show is that "the poet" is both an empirical self, and more problematically a real me or me myself, an ontological self, and yet a divine other. Both poets are hermetic and esoteric while making populist gestures. There the resemblance ends, and to pursue it further would be unfair to Dickey or any contemporary; it would have been unfair even for Stevens or for Hart Crane. The Dickey of the later motion is no Whitmanian; if one wants an American analogue, one would have to imagine Theodore Roethke as an astronaut, which defeats imagination. But I end by citing Whitman because his final gestures are the largest contrast I know to James Dickey's ongoing motions in his life's work. Whitman is up ahead of us somewhere; he is perpetually early, warning us: "Will you speak before I am gone? will you prove already too late?" The burden of belatedness is upon us, but if we hurry, we will catch up to him:

> Failing to fetch me at first keep encouraged,
> Missing me one place search another,
> I stop somewhere waiting for you.

Not Dickey; he cannot stop, yet he has taken up part of the burden for us. Whitman is larger, but then no one is larger, and that largeness is a final comfort, like Stevens's "Large Red Man Reading." Dickey speaks only to and for part of us, but that part is or wants to be the survivor; wants no more dying. Words alone, alas, are not certain good, though the young Yeats, like the young Dickey, wanted them to be. But they can help us to make "a creature to keep me dying / Years longer," as Dickey wrote in the poem of "The Other." I conclude by going full circle, by returning to the poem with the tribute that it could prove to contain the whole motion within it. Dickey cannot "turn wholly mortal in [his] mind," and that touch of "utter, unseasonable glory" will be his legacy.

John Ashbery

(1927-)

IN THE EXQUISITE SQUALORS OF TENNYSON'S *THE HOLY GRAIL*, AS PERCIVAL rides out on his ruinous quest, we can experience the hallucination of believing that the Laureate is overly influenced by *The Waste Land*, for Eliot too became a master at reversing the *apophrades*. Or, in our present moment, the achievement of John Ashbery in his powerful poem *Fragment* (in his volume *The Double Dream of Spring*) is to return us to Stevens, somewhat uneasily to discover that at moments Stevens sounds rather too much like Ashbery, an accomplishment I might not have thought possible.

The strangeness added to beauty by the positive *apophrades* is of that kind whose best expositor was Pater. Perhaps all Romantic style, at its heights, depends upon a successful manifestation of the dead in the garments of the living, as though the dead poets were given a suppler freedom than they had found for themselves. Contrast the Stevens of *Le Monocle de Mon Oncle* with the *Fragment* of John Ashbery, the most legitimate of the sons of Stevens:

> Like a dull scholar, I behold, in love,
> An ancient aspect touching a new mind.
> It comes, it blooms, it bears its fruit and dies.
> This trivial trope reveals a way of truth.
> Our bloom is gone. We are the fruit thereof.
> Two golden gourds distended on our vines,
> Into the autumn weather, splashed with frost,
> Distorted by hale fatness, turned grotesque.
> We hang like warty squashes, streaked and rayed,
> The laughing sky will see the two of us,

Washed into rinds by rotting winter rains.
                  (—*Le Monocle*, VIII)

Like the blood orange we have a single
Vocabulary all heart and all skin and can see
Through the dust of incisions the central perimeter
Our imaginations orbit. Other words,
Old ways are but the trappings and appurtenances
Meant to install change around us like a grotto.
There is nothing laughable
In this. To isolate the kernel of
Our imbalance and at the same time back up carefully
Its tulip head whole, an imagined good.
                  (—*Fragment*, XIII)

An older view of influence would remark that the second of these stanzas "derives" from the first, but an awareness of the revisionary ratio of *apophrades* unveils Ashbery's relative triumph in his involuntary match with the dead. This particular strain, while it matters, is not central to Stevens, but is the greatness of Ashbery whenever, with terrible difficulty, he can win free to it. When I read *Le Monocle de Mon Oncle* now, in isolation from other poems by Stevens, I am compelled to hear Ashbery's voice, for this mode has been captured by him, inescapably and perhaps forever. When I read *Fragment*, I tend not to be aware of Stevens, for his presence has been rendered benign. In early Ashbery, amid the promise and splendors of his first volume, *Some Trees*, the massive dominance of Stevens could not be evaded, though a *clinamen* away from the master had already been evidenced:

The young man places a bird-house
Against the blue sea. He walks away
And it remains. Now other

Men appear, but they live in boxes.
The sea protects them like a wall.
The gods worship a line-drawing

Of a woman, in the shadow of the sea
Which goes on writing. Are there
Collisions, communications on the shore

Or did all secrets vanish when
The woman left? Is the bird mentioned
In the waves' minutes, or did the land advance?
(—*Le Livre est sur la Table*, II)

This is the mode of *The Man with the Blue Guitar*, and urgently attempts to swerve away from a vision whose severity it cannot bear:

Slowly the ivy on the stones
Becomes the stones. Women become

The cities, children become the fields
And men in waves become the sea.

It is the chord that falsifies.
The sea returns upon the men,

The fields entrap the children, brick
Is a weed and all the flies are caught,

Wingless and withered, but living alive.
The discord merely magnifies.

Deepe within the belly's dark,
Of time, time grows upon the rock.
(—*The Man with the Blue Guitar*, XI)

The early Ashbery poem implies that there are "collisions, communications among us, even in confrontation of the sea, a universe of sense that asserts its power over our minds. But the parent-poem, though it will resolve itself in a similar quasi-comfort, harasses the poet and his readers with the intenser realization that "the discord merely magnifies," when our "collisions, communications" sound out against the greater rhythms of the sea. Where the early Ashbery attempted vainly to soften his poetic father, the mature Ashbery of *Fragment* subverts and even captures the precursor even as he appears to accept him more fully. The ephebe may still not be mentioned in the father's minutes, but his own vision has advanced. Stevens hesitated almost always until his last phase, unable firmly to adhere to or reject the High Romantic insistence that the power of the poet's mind could triumph over the universe of death, or the estranged object-world. It is not every day, he says it his *Adagia*, that the world arranges itself in a poem. His nobly desperate disciple, Ashbery, has dared the dialectic of misprision so as to implore the world daily to arrange itself into a poem:

> But what could I make of this? Glaze
> Of many identical foreclosures wrested from
> The operative hand, like a judgment but still
> The atmosphere of seeing? That two people could
> Collide in this dusk means that the time of
> Shapelessly foraging had come undone: the space was
> Magnificent and dry. On flat evenings
> In the months ahead, she would remember that that
> Anomaly had spoken to her, words like disjointed beaches
> Brown under the advancing signs of the air.

This, the last stanza of *Fragment*, returns Ashbery full circle to his early *Le Livre est sur la Table*. There are "collisions, communications on the shore" but these "collide in this dusk." "Did the land advance?" of the early poem is answered partly negatively, by the brown, disjointed beaches, but partly also by "the advancing signs of the air." Elsewhere in *Fragment*, Ashbery writes: "Thus reasoned the ancestor, and everything / Happened as he had foretold, but in a funny kind of way." The strength of the positive *apophrades* gives this quester the hard wisdom of the proverbial poem he rightly calls *Soonest Mended*, which ends by:

> ... learning to accept
> The charity of the hard moments as they are doled out,
> For this is action, this not being sure, this careless
> Preparing, sowing the seeds crooked in the furrow,
> Making ready to forget, and always coming back
> To the mooring of starting out, that day so long ago.

Here Ashbery has achieved one of the mysteries of poetic style, but only through the individuation of misprision.

II

Another misprision is a haunting lyric of belatedness, Ashbery's recent *As You Came from the Holy Land*, where the parodistic first-line/title repeats the opening of a bitter ballad of lost love attributed to Ralegh, one of whose stanzas lingers throughout Ashbery's gentler poem:

I have lovde her all my youth,
  Butt now ould, as you see,
Love lykes not the fallyng frute
  From the wythered tree.

"Her" is the personal past in Ashbery's elegy for the self:

of western New York state
were the graves all right in their bushings
was there a note of panic in the late August air
because the old man had peed in his pants again
was there turning away from the late afternoon glare
as though it too could be wished away
was any of this present
and how could this be
the magic solution to what you are in now
whatever has held you motionless
like this so long through the dark season
until now the women come out in navy blue
and the worms come out of the compost to die
it is the end of any season

you reading there so accurately
sitting not wanting to be disturbed
as you came from that holy land
what other signs of earth's dependency were upon you
what fixed sign at the crossroads
what lethargy in the avenues
where all is said in a whisper
what tone of voice among the hedges
what tone under the apple trees
the numbered land stretches away
and your house is built in tomorrow
but surely not before the examination
of what is right and will befall
not before the census
and the writing down of names

remember you are free to wander away
as from other times other scenes that were taking place
the history of someone who came too late

the time is ripe now and the adage
is hatching as the seasons change and tremble
it is finally as though that thing of monstrous interest
were happening in the sky
but the sun is setting and prevents you from seeing it
out of night the token emerges
its leaves like birds alighting all at once under a tree
taken up and shaken again
put down in weak rage
knowing as the brain does it can never come about
not here not yesterday in the past
only in the gap of today filling itself
as emptiness is distributed
in the idea of what time it is
when that time is already past

Ashbery, probably because of his direct descent from Stevens, tends like Stevens to follow rather precisely the crisis-poem paradigm that I have traced in my map of misreading. This model, Wordsworthian-Whitmanian, never restores as much representational meaning as it continually curtails or withdraws, as I have observed earlier. Ashbery's resource has been to make a music of the poignance of withdrawal. So, in this poem, the "end of any season" that concludes the first stanza is deliberately too partial a synecdoche to compensate for the pervasive absences of the ironies throughout the stanza. Ashbery's turnings-against-the-self are wistful and inconclusive, and he rarely allows a psychic reversal any completeness. His origins, in the holy land of western New York state, are presented here and elsewhere in his work with an incurious rigidity that seems to have no particular design on the poet himself, characteristically addressed as "you." The next stanza emphasizes Ashbery's usual metonymic defense of isolation (as opposed to the Stevensian undoing or the Whitmanian regression), by which signs and impulses become detached from one another, with the catalog or census completing itself in the reductive "writing down of names," in which "down" takes on surprising difference and force. The third stanza, one of Ashbery's most radiant, marks the poem's *daemonization*, the American Counter-Sublime in which Ashbery, like Stevens, is so extraordinarily at home. Ashbery's mingled strength and weakness, indeed his deliberate pathos, is that he knowingly begins where Childe Roland ended, "free to wander away" yet always seeing himself as living "the history of someone who came too late" while sensing that "the time is ripe now." Studying his own habitual expression in his prose *Three*

Poems, he had compared himself explicitly to Childe Roland at the Dark Tower. Here also, his Sublime sense that a Stevensian reality is happening in the war of the sky against the mind is necessarily obscured by a sunset akin to Roland's "last red leer."

Ashbery's finest achievement, to date, is his heroic and perpetual self-defeat, which is of a kind appropriate to conclude this book, since such self-defeat pioneers in undoing the mode of transumption that Stevens helped revive. Ashbery's allusiveness is transumptive rather than conspicuous, but he employs it against itself, as though determined to make of his lateness a desperate cheerfulness. In the final stanza of *As You Came from the Holy Land*, the most characteristic of Shelleyan-Stevensian metaphors, the fiction of the leaves, is duly revealed as a failure ("taken up and shaken again / put down in weak rage"); but the metalepsis substituted for it is almost a hyperbole of failure, as presence and the present fall together "in the gap of today filling itself / as emptiness is distributed." The two lines ending the poem would be an outrageous parody of the transumptive mode if their sad dignity were not so intense. Ashbery, too noble and poetically intelligent to subside into a parodist of time's revenges, flickers on "like a great shadow's last embellishment."

III

Ashbery has been misunderstood because of his association with the "New York School" of Kenneth Koch, Frank O'Hara and other comedians of the spirit, but also because of the dissociative phase of his work as represented by much of a peculiar volume, *The Tennis Court Oath*. But the poet of *The Double Dream of Spring* and the prose *Three Poems* is again the Stevensian meditator of the early *Some Trees*. No other American poet has labored quite so intensely to exorcise all the demons of discursiveness, and no contemporary American poet is so impressively at one with himself in expounding a discursive wisdom. Like his master, Stevens, Ashbery is essentially a ruminative poet, turning a few subjects over and over, knowing always that what counts is the mythology of self, blotched out beyond unblotching.

Ashbery's various styles have suggested affinities to composer-theorists like Cage and Cowell, to painters of the school of Kline and Pollock, and "to an assortment of French bards like Roussel, Reverdy and even Michaux. But the best of Ashbery, from the early *Some Trees* on through "A Last World" and "The Skaters" to the wonderful culminations of his great book, *The Double Dream of Spring* and the recent *Three Poems*, shows a clear descent from the major American tradition that began in Emerson. Even as his poetic father is Stevens, Ashbery's largest ancestor is Whitman, and it is the Whitmanian strain in Stevens that found Ashbery. I would guess that Ashbery, like Stevens, turned to French poetry as a deliberate evasion of continuities, a desperate quest for freedom from the burden of poetic influence. The beautiful group called "French Poems" in *The Double Dream of Spring* were written in French and then translated into English, Ashbery notes, "with the idea of avoiding customary word-patterns and associations." This looks at first like the characteristic quarrel with discursiveness that is endemic in modern verse, but a deeper familiarity with the "French Poems" will evoke powerful associations with Stevens at his most central, the seer of "Credences of Summer":

> *And it does seem that all the force of*
> *The cosmic temperature lives in the form of contacts*
> *That no intervention could resolve,*
> *Even that of a creator returned to the desolate*
> *Scene of this first experiment: this microcosm.*
>
> *... and then it's so natural*
> *That we experience almost no feeling*
> *Except a certain lightness which matches*
> *The recent closed ambiance which is, besides*
> *Full of attentions for us. Thus, lightness and wealth.*
>
> *But the existence of all these things and especially*
> *The amazing fullness of their number must be*
> *For us a source of unforgettable questions:*
> *Such as: whence does all this come? and again:*
> *Shall I some day be a part of all this fullness?*

The poet of these stanzas is necessarily a man who must have absorbed "Credences of Summer" when he was young, perhaps even as a Harvard undergraduate. Every strong poet's development is a typology of evasions, a complex misprision of his precursor. Ashbery's true precursor is the composite father, Whitman-Stevens, and the whole body to date of Ashbery's work manifests nearly every possible revisionary ratio in regard to so formidable an American ancestry. Though the disjunctiveness of so much of Ashbery suggests his usual critical placement with the boisterousness of Koch or the random poignances of O'Hara, he seems most himself when most ruefully and intensely Transcendental, the almost involuntary celebrator "of that *invisible light* which spatters the silence / Of our everyday festivities." Ashbery is a kind of invalid of American Orphism, perpetually convalescing from the strenuous worship of that dread Orphic trinity of draining gods: Eros, Dionysus, Ananke, who preside over the Native Strain of our poetry.

I propose to track Ashbery back to his origins in another essay, but here I have space only to investigate some poems of his major phase, as it seems developing in his two most recent books. To enter at this point a judgment of current American poets now entering their imaginative maturity, Ashbery and A.R. Ammons are to me the indispensable figures, two already fully achieved artists who are likely to develop into worthy rivals of Frost, Stevens, Pound, Williams, Eliot, Crane, and Warren. Merwin, James Wright, Merrill, perhaps Snyder in the school of Williams and Pound, perhaps James Dickey of a somewhat older generation (if he yet returns to the strength of earlier work) are candidates also. Yet all prophecy is dangerous here; there are recent poems by Howard, Hollander, Kinnell, Pack, Feinman, Hecht, Strand, Rich, Snodgrass, among others, which are as powerful as all but the very best of Ammons, Ashbery, Wright. Other critics and readers would nominate quite different groupings, as we evidently enter a time of singular wealth in contemporary verse.

Ashbery's poetry is haunted by the image of transparence, but this comes to him, from the start, as "a puzzling light," or carried by beings who are "as dirty handmaidens / To some transparent witch." Against Transcendental influx, Ashbery knows the wisdom. of what he calls "learning to accept / The charity of the hard moments as they are doled out," and knows also that: "One can never change the core of things, and light burns you the harder for it." Burned by a visionary flame beyond accommodation (one can contrast Kinnell's too-easy invocations of such fire), Ashbery gently plays with Orphic influx ("Light bounced off the ends / Of the small gray waves to tell / Them in the observatory / About the great drama that was being won."). Between Emerson and Whitman, the seers of this tradition, and Ashbery, Ammons and other legatees, there comes mediating the figure of Stevens:

My house has changed a little in the sun.
The fragrance of the magnolias comes close,
False flick, false form, but falseness close to kin.

It must be visible or invisible,
Invisible or visible or both;
A seeing and unseeing in the eye.

These are hardly the accents of transport, yet Stevens does stand precariously, in the renewed light. But even the skepticism is Emerson's own; his greatest single visionary oration is *Experience*, a text upon which Dickinson, Stevens and Ashbery always seem to be writing commentaries:

> Thus inevitably does the universe wear our color, and every object fall successively into the subject itself. The subject exists, the subject enlarges; all things sooner or later fall into place. As I am, so I see; use what language we will, we can never say anything but what we are.... And we cannot say too little of our constitutional necessity of seeing things under private aspects, or saturated with our humors. And yet is the God the native of these bleak rocks.... We must hold hard to this poverty, however scandalous, and by more vigorous self-recoveries, after the sallies of action, possess our axis more firmly....

The Old Transcendentalism in America, like the New, hardly distinguishes itself from a visionary skepticism, and makes no assertions without compensatory qualifications. Still, we tend to remember Emerson for his transparencies, and not the opaquenesses that more frequently haunted him and his immediate disciples. I suspect that this is because of Emerson's *confidence*, no matter where he places his emphases. When Stevens attains to a rare transparence, he generally sees very little more than is customary, but he *feels* a greater peace, and this peace reduces to a confidence in the momentary capability of his own imagination. Transcendentalism, in its American formulation, centers upon Emerson's stance of Self-Reliance, which is primarily a denial of the anxiety of influence. Like Nietzsche, who admired him for it, Emerson refuses to allow us to believe we must be latecomers. In a gnomic quatrain introducing his major essay on self-reliance, Emerson manifested a shamanistic intensity still evident in his descendents:

> *Cast the bantling on the rocks,*
> *Suckle him with the she-wolf's teat,*
> *Wintered with the hawk and fox,*
> *Power and speed be hands and feet.*

This is splendid, but Emerson had no more been such a banding than any of my contemporaries are, unless one wants the delightful absurdity of seeing Wordsworth or Coleridge as a she-wolf. "Do not seek yourself outside yourself" is yet another motto to *Self-Reliance*, and there is one more, from Beaumont and Fletcher, assuring us that the soul of an honest man:

> Commands all light, all influence, all fate
> Nothing to him falls early or coo late.

These are all wonderful idealisms. Whitman, who had been simmering, read *Self-Reliance* and was brought to the boil of the 1855 "Song of Myself." Ashbery, by temperament and choice, always seems to keep simmering, but whether he took impetus from Whitman, Stevens or even the French partisans of poetic Newness, he has worked largely and overtly in this Emersonian spirit. Unfortunately, like Merwin and Merwin's precursor, Pound, Ashbery truly absorbed from the Emerson-Whitman tradition the poet's over-idealizing tendency to lie to himself, against his origins and against experience. American poets since Emerson are all antithetical completions of one another, which means mostly that they develop into grotesque truncations of what they might have been. Where British poets swerve away from their spiritual fathers, ours attempt to rescue their supposedly benighted sires. American bards, like Democritus, deny the swerve, so as to save divination, holding on to the Fate that might make them liberating gods. Epicurus affirmed the swerve, ruining divination, and all poetry since is caught between the two. Emerson, though close to Democritus, wants even divination to be a mode of Self-Reliance. That is, he genuinely shares the Orphic belief that the poet is already divine, and realizes more of this divinity in writing his poems. Lucretian poets like Shelley who find freedom by swerving away from fathers (Wordsworth and Milton, for Shelley) do not believe in divination, and do not worship an Orphic Necessity as the final form of divinity. Orphic poets, particularly American or Emersonian Orphics, worship four gods only: Ananke, Eros, Dionysus and—most of all surely—themselves. They are therefore peculiarly resistant to the idea of poetic influence, for divination—to them—means primarily an apprehension of their own possible sublimity, the gods they are in process of becoming. The gentle Ashbery, despite all his quite genuine and hard-won wisdom, is as much in this tradition as those spheral men, Emerson, Whitman, Thoreau, and that sublime egoist, Stevens, or the American Wordsworth.

The Double Dream of Spring has a limpidly beautiful poem called "Clouds," which begins:

> *All this time he hod only been waiting,*
> *Not even thinking, as many had supposed.*

Now sleep wound down to him as its promise of dazzling peace
And he stood up to assume that imagination.

There were others in the forest as close as he
To caring about the silent outcome, but they had gotten lost
In the shadows of dreams so that the external look
Of the nearby world had become confused with the cobwebs inside.

Sleep here has a Whitmanian-Stevensian cast ("The Sleepers," "The Owl in the Sarcophagus") and the gorgeous solipsism so directly celebrated here has its sources in the same ultimately Emersonian tradition. Though "he," the poet or quest-hero, is distinguished from his fellows as not having yielded to such solipsism, the poem ends in a negative apotheosis:

He shoots forward like a malignant star.
The edges of the journey are ragged.
Only the face of night begins to grow distinct
As the fainter stars call to each other and are lost.

Day re-creates his image like a snapshot:
The family and the guests are there,
The talking over there, only now it will never end.
And so cities are arranged, and oceans traversed,

And farms tilled with especial care.
This year again the corn has grown ripe and tall.
It is a perfect rebuttal of the argument. And Semele
Moves away, puzzled at the brown light above the fields.

The harvest of natural process, too ripe for enigmas, refutes quest, and confirms the natural realism of all solipsists. This poem, urging us away from the Emersonian or Central Self, concludes by yielding to that Self, and to the re-birth of Dionysus, Semele's son. Like his precursor, Stevens, Ashbery fears and evades the Native Strain of American Orphism and again like Stevens he belongs as much to that strain as Hart Crane or John Wheelwright does. In the recent prose *Three Poems*, he ruefully accepts his tradition and his inescapable place in it:

Why, after all, were we not destroyed in the conflagration of the moment our real and imaginary lives coincided, unless it was because we never had a separate existence beyond that of those two static and highly artificial concepts whose fusion was nevertheless the cause of death and destruction not only for ourselves but in the world around us. But perhaps the explanation lies precisely here: what we were witnessing was merely the reverse side of an event of cosmic beatitude for all except us, who were blind to it because it took place inside us. Meanwhile the shape of life has changed definitively for the better for everyone on the outside. They are bathed in the light of this tremendous surprise as in the light of a new sun from which only healing and not corrosive rays emanate; they comment on the miraculous change as people comment on the dazzling beauty of a day in early autumn, forgetting that for the blind man in their midst it is a day like any other, so that its beauty cannot be said to have universal validity but must remain fundamentally in doubt.   (*The Recital*)

The closest (though dialectically opposed) analogue to this passage is the great concluding rhapsody of Emerson's early apocalypse, *Nature*, when the Orphic Poet returns to prophecy:

As when the summer comes from the south the snow-banks melt and the face of the earth becomes green before it, so shall the advancing spirit create its ornaments along its park, and carry with it the beauty it visits and the sons, which enchants it; it shall draw beautiful faces, warm hearts, wise discourse, and heroic acts, around its way, until evil is no more seen. The kingdom of man over nature, which cometh not with observation,—a dominion such as now is beyond his dream of God,—he shall enter without more wonder than the blind man feels who is gradually restored to perfect sight.

Ashbery's apocalyptic transformation of the Self, its elevation to the Over-Soul, is manifest to everyone and everything outside the Self, but not to the blind man of the Self. The Emersonian Self will know the metamorphic redemption of others and things only by knowing first its gradual freedom from blindness as to its own glory. Ashbery's forerunners, the makers of *Song of Myself* and *Notes toward a Supreme Fiction*, were primary Emersonians, involuntary as Stevens was in this identity. Ashbery is that American anomaly, an antithetical Transcendentalist, bearer of an influx of the Newness that he cannot know himself.

IV

I leap ahead, past Frost and Pound, Eliot and Williams, past even Hart Crane, to a contemporary image-of-voice that is another strong tally, however ruefully the strength regards itself. Here is John Ashbery's *The Other Tradition*, the second poem in his 1977 volume, *Houseboat Days*:

> They all came, some wore sentiments
> Emblazoned on T-shirts, proclaiming the lateness
> Of the hour, and indeed the sun slanted its rays
> Through branches of Norfolk Island pine as though
> Politely clearing its throat, and all ideas settled
> In a fuzz of dust under trees when it's drizzling:
> The endless games of Scrabble, the boosters,
> The celebrated omelette au Cantal, and through it
> The roar of time plunging unchecked through the sluices
> Of the days, dragging every sexual moment of it
> Past the lenses: the end of something.
> Only then did you glance up from your book,
> Unable to comprehend what had been taking place, or
> Say what you had been reading. More chairs
> Were brought, and lamps were lit, but it tells
> Nothing of how all this proceeded to materialize
> Before you and the people waiting outside and in the next
> Street, repeating its name over and over, until silence
> Moved halfway up the darkened trunks,
> And the meeting was called to order.
>   I still remember
> How they found you, after a dream, in your thimble bar,
> Studious as a butterfly in a parking for.
> The road home was nicer then. Dispersing, each of the
> Troubadours had something to say about how charity
> Had run its race and won, leaving you the ex-president
> Of the event, and how, though many of these present
> Had wished something to come of it, if only a distant
> Wisp of smoke, yet none was so deceived as to hanker
> After that cool non-being of just a few minutes before,
> Now that the idea of a forest had clamped itself
> Over the minutiae of the scene. You found this
> Charming, but turned your face fully toward night,
> Speaking into it like a megaphone, not hearing

Or caring, although these still live and are generous
And all ways contained, allowed to come and go
Indefinitely in and out of the stockade
They have so much trouble remembering, when your forgetting
Rescues them at last, as a star absorbs the night.

I am aware that this charming poem urbanely confronts, absorbs and in some sense seeks to overthrow a critical theory, almost a critical climate, that has accorded it a canonical status. Stevens's Whitman pro claims that nothing is final and that no man shall see the end. Ashbery, a Whitman somehow more studiously casual even than Whitman, regards the prophets of belatedness and cheerfully insists that his forgetting or repression will rescue us at last, even as the Whitmanian or Stevensian evening star absorbs the night. But the price paid for this metaleptic reversal of American belatedness into a fresh earliness is the yielding up of Ashbery's tally or image of voice to a deliberate grotesquerie. Sexuality is made totally subservient to time, which is indeed "the end of something," and poetic tradition becomes an ill-organized social meeting of troubadours, leaving the canonical Ashbery as "ex-president / Of the event." As for the image of voice proper, the Whitmanian confrontation of the night now declines into: "You found this / Charming, but turned your face fully toward night, / Speaking into it like a megaphone, not hearing / Or caring." Such a megaphone is an apt image for Paul de Man's deconstructionist view of poetic tradition, which undoes tradition by suggesting that every poem is as much a random and gratuitous event as any human death is.

Ashbery's implicit interpretation of what he wants to call *The Other Tradition* mediates between this vision, of poems as being totally cur off from one another and the antithetical darkness in which poems carry over-determined relationships and progress towards a final entropy. Voice in our poetry now tallies what Ashbery in his *Syringa*, a major Orphic elegy in *Houseboat Days*, calls "a record of pebbles along the way." Let us grant that the American Sublime is always also an American irony, and then turn back to Emerson and hear the voice that is great within us somehow breaking through again. This is Emerson in his journal for August 1859, on the eve of being burned out, with all his true achievement well behind him; but he gives us the true tally of his soul:

> *Beatitudes of Intellect.*—Am I not, one of these days, to write consecutively of the beatitude of intellect? It is too great for feeble souls, and they are over-excited. The wineglass shakes, and the wine is spilled. What then? The joy which will not let

me sit in my chair, which brings me bolt upright to my feet, and sends me striding around my room, like a tiger in his care, and I cannot have composure and concentration enough even to set down in English words the thought which thrills me—is not that joy a certificate of the elevation? What if I never write a book or a line? for a moment, the eyes of my eves were opened, the affirmative experience remains, and consoles through all suffering.

V

Of the many contemporary heirs of Whitman and of Stevens, John Ashbery seems likeliest to achieve something near to their eminence. Yet their uncertainty as to their audience is far surpassed in the shifting; stances that Ashbery assumes. His mode can vary from the apparently opaque, so disjunctive as to seem beyond interpretation, to a kind of limpid clairvoyance that again brings the Emersonian contraries together. Contemplating Parmigianino's picture in his major long poem, *Self-Portrait in a Convex Mirror*, Ashbery achieves a vision in which art, rather than nature, becomes the imprisoner of the soul:

> The soul has to stay where it is,
> Even though restless, hearing raindrops at the pane,
> The sighing of autumn leaves thrashed by the wind,
> Longing to be free, outside, lust it must stay
> Posing in this place. It must move as little as possible.
> This is what the portrait says.
> But there is in that gaze a combination
> Of tenderness, amusement and regret, so powerful
> In its restraint that one cannot look for long.
> The secret is too plain. The pity of it smarts,
> Makes hot tears spurt: that the soul is not a soul,
> Has no secret, is small, and it fits
> Its hollow perfectly: its room, our moment of attention.

Whitman's Soul, knowing its true hour in wordlessness, is apparently reduced here and now to a moment only of attention. And yet even this tearful realization, supposedly abandoning the soul to a convex mirror, remains a privileged moment, of an Emersonian rather than Paterian kind. Precisely where he seems most wistful and knowingly bewildered by loss, Ashbery remains most dialectical, like his American ancestors.

The simple diction and vulnerable stance barely conceal the presence of the American Transcendental Self, an ontological self that increases even as the empirical self abandons every spiritual assertion. Hence the "amusement" that takes up its stance between "tenderness" and "regret," Whitmanian affections, and hence also the larger hint of a power held in reserve, "so powerful in its restraint that one cannot look for long." An American Orphic, wandering in the Emersonian legacy, can afford to surrender the soul in much the name temper as the ancient Gnostics did. The soul can be given up to the Demiurge, whether of art or nature, because a spark of *pneuma* is more vital than the *psyche*, and fits no hollow whatsoever. Where Whitman and Stevens are at once hermetic and off-hand, so is Ashbery, but his throwaway gestures pay the price of an ever-increasing American sense of belatedness.

W.S. Merwin

(1927-)

I mean we have yet no man who has leaned entirely on his character,
and eaten angels' fond; who, trusting to his sentiments, found life made
of miracles; who, working for universal aims, found himself fed. He
knew not how; clothed, sheltered, and weaponed, he knew not how,
and yet it was done by his own hands.

EMERSON, *The Transcendentalist* (1842)

MY SUBJECT IS A STILL LITTLE-NOTED PHENOMENON, THE REVIVAL OF THE
Native Strain or Emersonian vision, in the poetry of my own generation of American poets, born in the decade 1925–1935. I cannot survey
all these poets here, and will discuss aspects of the work of only three:
W.S. Merwin, A.R. Ammons, and John Ashbery. My choice is affected
by the limitations of personal taste, and I know it could be argued that
the true continuators of the Emersonian strain are to be located elsewhere, not so much in the School of Stevens and Frost as in that of
Williams and Pound. But I am troubled by the equivocal nature (as it
seems to me) of the achievement of Olson, Duncan and their fellows,
down to Ginsberg, Snyder and younger figures. Emersonian poetry is
a diffuse though recognizable tradition: it includes Jeffers as well as
Hart Crane, the Pound of *The Pisan Cantos* together with the Stevens
of "The Auroras of Autumn," middle Roethke just as much as the later
Aiken. The problem of American poetry after Emerson might be
defined as: "Is it possible to be un-Emersonian, rather than, at best,
anti-Emersonian?" Poe is not an Emersonian poet, but then he is also
not a good poet. Perhaps only our Southern poets, down to Tate and
Warren, could be as un-Emersonian as they were anti-Emersonian; the
best of them now (Dickey and Ammons) are wholly Emersonian. Even

in Emerson's own time, irreconcilable poets emerged from his maelstrom: Dickinson, Thoreau, Whitman, Very, even Tuckerman, whom
Winters judged to be as firm a reaction against Emerson as Hawthorne
and Melville were. American Romanticism is larger than
Emersonianism, but in our time it may no longer be possible to distinguish between the two phenomena. The prophet of a national poetic sensibility in America was the Concord rhapsode, who contains in
the dialectical mysteries of his doctrines and temperament very nearly
everything that has come after.

Let me begin with a representative text, by the indubitably representative poet of my generation, the Protean Merwin. The poem is the wonderful "The Way to the River" from the volume, *The Moving Target*, of
1963. As the poem is about fifty lines, I will summarize rather than quote
it entire. Addressed to the poet's wife, the poem is a kind of middle-of-the-
journey declaration, a creedal hymn reaffirming a covenant of love and a
sense of poetic vocation. Historically (and prophetically) the poem sums
up the dilemma of "the Silent Generation" of young Americans, on the eve
of the astonishing change (or collapse) of sensibility that was to begin at
Berkeley in 1964. After nearly a decade, one sees how brief an episode (or
epicycle) this Time of Troubles was. Merwin, with his curious proleptic
urgency, memorably caught the prelude to that time:

> *The way to the river leads past the names of*
> *Ash the sleeves the wreaths of hinges*
> *Through the song of the bandage vendor*
>
> *I lay your name by my voice*
> *As I go*
> *The way to the river leads past the late*
> *Doors and the games of the children born*
> *looking backwards*
> *They play that they are broken glass*
> *The numbers wait in the halls and the clouds*
> *Call*
> *From windows*
> *They play that they are old they are putting the*
> *horizon*
>
> *Into baskets they are escaping they are*
> *Hiding*

I step over the sleepers the fires the calendars
My voice turns to you

This is the "poverty" of Emerson and Stevens: imaginative need. Merwin joins a tradition that includes the E.A. Robinson of "The Man Against the Sky," the Frost of "Directive," the Stevens of "The Auroras of Autumn" as he too follows Emerson in building an altar to the Beautiful Necessity:

To the city of wines I have brought home a
*   handful*
Of water I walk slowly
In front of me they are building the empty
Ages I see them reflected not for long
Be here I am no longer ashamed of time it is
*   too brief its hands*
Have no names
I have passed it I know

Oh Necessity you with the face you with
All the faces

This is written on the back of everything

But we
Will read it together

The Merwin of this—still his present phase—began with the central poem, "Lemuel's Blessing," which follows the Smart of "Jubilate Agno" for its form (as do so many recent American poets, including Ginsberg, Strand, Donald Finkel) but which is also an Emersonian manifesto. Addressing a Spirit ("You that know the way") Merwin prayed: "Let the memory of tongues not unnerve me so that I stumble or quake." This hymn to Self-Reliance expanded into the most ambitious poem of *The Moving Target*, a majestic celebration of what Emerson called the Newness, "For Now:" "Goodbye what you learned for me I have to learn anyway / You that forgot your rivers they are gone / Myself I would not know you." In *The Lice*, his next volume (and his best), Merwin defined the gods as "what has failed to become of us," a dark postscript to the Emersonian insistence that the poets are as liberating gods. The poems of *The Lice* are afflicted by light, as in this wholly characteristic brief lyric, the poignant

"How We Are Spared":

> *At midsummer before dawn an orange light*
> *   returns to the mountains*
> *Like a great weight and the small birds cry out*
> *And bear it up*

With his largest volume, *The Carrier of Ladders*, Merwin appears to have completed his metamorphosis into an American visionary poet. The book's most astonishing yet most problematic poems are four ode-like "Psalms," subtitled: "Our Fathers," "The Signals," "The September Vision" and "The Cerements." No recent American poet, not even the Roethke of *The Far Field* or Dickey in his latest work, has attempted so exalted a style:

> *I am the son of hazard but does my prayer*
> *   reach you O star of the uncertain*
> *I am the son of blindness but nothing that we*
> *   have made watches us*
> *I am the son of untruth but I have seen the*
> *   children in Paradise walking in lairs each*
> *   hand in hand with himself*
> *I am the son of the warder but he was buried*
> *   with his keys*
> *I am the son of the light but does it call me*
> *   Samuel or Jonah*
> *I am the son of a wish older than water but I*
> *   needed till now*
> *I am the son of ghosts clutching the world like*
> *   roads but tomorrow I will go a new way*

The form is again that of the "Jubilate Agno," but the most important line in this first "Psalm," and in all of Merwin, is very far from Smart's pious spirit:

> *I am the son of the future but my own father*

As a poet, this latest Merwin hardly approaches that impossible self-begetting; the accent of the Pound-Eliot tradition hovers everywhere in even the most self-consciously bare of these verses. Merwin is more impressive for his terrible need, his lust for discontinuity, than for any actual inventiveness. The poignance of his current phase is the constant attempt at self-reliance, in the conviction that only thus will the poet see. Merwin's true precursors are three honorable, civilized representative poets: Longfellow and MacLeish and Wilbur, none of whom attempted to speak a Word that was his own Word only. In another time, Merwin would have gone on with the cultivation of a more continuous idiom, as he did in his early volumes, and as Longfellow did even in the Age of Emerson. The pressures of the quasi-apocalyptic nineteen sixties have made of Merwin an American Orphic bard despite the sorrow that his poetic temperament is not at home in suffering the Native Strain. No poet legitimately speaks a Word whose burden is that his generation will be the very last. Merwin's litanies of denudation will read very oddly when a fresh generation proclaims nearly the same dilemma, and then yet another generation trumpets finality.

Merwin's predicament (and I hope I read it fairly, as I am not unsympathetic to his work) is that he has no Transcendental vision, and yet feels impelled to prophesy. What is fascinating is that after one hundred and thirty years, the situation of American poetry is precisely as it was when Emerson wrote his loving but ironic essay on his younger contemporaries and followers, *The Transcendentalist*, where they are seen as exposing our poverty but also their own. With that genial desperation (or desperate geniality) that is so endearing (and enraging) a quality in his work, Emerson nevertheless urged his followers out into the wilderness:

> But all these of whom I speak are not proficients; they are novices; they only show the road in which man should travel, when the soul has greater health and prowess. Yet let them feel the dignity of their charge, and deserve a larger power. Their heart is the ark in which the fire is concealed which shall burn in a broader and universal flame. Let them obey the Genius then most when his impulse is wildest; then most when he seems to lead to uninhabitable deserts of thought and life; for the path which the hero travels alone is the highway of health and benefit to mankind. What is the privilege and nobility of our nature but its persistency, through its power to attach itself to what is permanent?

Merwin prays to be sustained during his time in the desert, but his poems hardly persuade us that his Genius or Spirit has led him into "uninhabitable deserts of thought and life." Readers distrustful of *The Carrier of Ladders* either emphasize what they feel is a dominance of style over substance or they complain of spiritual pretentiousness. What I find more problematic is something that Emerson foresaw when he said of his Transcendentalist that "He believes in miracle, in the perpetual openness of the human mind to new influx of light and power; he believes in inspiration, and in ecstasy," and yet went on to observe that such a youth was part of an American literature and spiritual history still "in the optative mood." Merwin's optative mood seems only to concern his impersonal identity as poet-prophet; instead of a belief in an influx of light and power, he offers us what we might contrive to know anyway, even if we had not been chilled with him by his artful mutations:

> *To which I make my way eating the silence of*
> *animals*
> *Offering snow to the darkness*
>
> *Today belongs to few and tomorrow to no one*

Emerson's favorite oracular guise was as an Orphic poet. Of the Orphic deities—Eros, Dionysus, and Ananke—Merwin gives us some backward glances at the first, and a constant view of the last, but the Dionysiac has gone out of his poetry. Without the Bacchic turbulence, and haunted by a light that he presents as wholly meaningless, Merwin seems condemned to write a poetry that is as bare of true content as it is so elegantly bare in diction and design. Only the *situation* of the Emersonian Transcendentalist or Orphic Poet survives in Merwin; it is as though for him the native strain were pure strain, to be endured because endurance is value enough, or even because the eloquence of endurance is enough.

Derek Walcott

(1930–)

AFTER READING EACH OF DEREK WALCOTT'S BOOKS AS THEY HAVE APPEARED,
I remain uncertain as to the question of his aesthetic eminence, though few
seem to share my inability to render any verdict, even for myself. Walcott
is an excellent narrator, and is blessed with many verbal gifts. My own bafflement ensues from a concern with poetic voice that centers my own love
for reading and appreciating poetry. Has Derek Walcott developed a voice
altogether his own, the mark of a major poet, or does one hear in him the
composite voice of post-Yeatsian poetry in English?

I want to see if my recent reading of Walcott's long poem, *Tiepolo's
Hound*, will resolve my doubts. The strategy of *Tiepolo's Hound* turns upon
a brilliant doubling of Walcott and the West Indian Impressionist painter
Camille Pissarro, born in 1830, exactly a century before Walcott. In
Pissarro, a Sephardic Jew and so a fellow exile and outsider, Walcott dis-
covers an aesthetic quest he regards as being profoundly akin to his own.

The poem's final section, XXVI, opens with a poignant identity
forged between Pissarro and Walcott:

He enters the window frame. His gaze is yours.

Primed canvas, steaming mirror, this white page
where a drawing emerges. His portrait sighs

from a white fog. Pissarro in old age,
as we stand doubled in each other's eyes.

To endure affliction with no affection gone
seems to have been the settlement in those eyes,

whose lenses catch a glinting winter sun
on mansards and the rigid smoke of chimneys.

This is eloquent and memorable, but do I hear Walcott's voice or an adaptation of the nuanced cadences of Wallace Stevens? Does it matter whose voice it is, when the expression has this much aesthetic dignity? I uneasily recall the poetry of Archibald Macleish, whose eclectic assimilation of Eliot, Pound and others was so wittily satirized by Edmund Wilson in his *The Omelet of A. Macleish*. Here are the closing lines of *Tiepolo's Hound*, which seem to me quite beautiful, but again I hear Wallace Stevens's "hum of thoughts evaded in the mind":

Let this page catch the last light on Becune Point,
lengthen the arched shadows of Charlotte Amalie,

to a prayer's curling smoke, and brass anoint
the branched menorah of a frangipani,

as the lights in the shacks bud orange across the Morne,
and are pillared in the black harbour. Stars fly close

as sparks, and the houses catch with bulb and lampion
to the Virgin, Veronese's and Tiepolo's.

Soon, against the smoky hillsides of Santa Cruz,
dusk will ignite the wicks of the immortelle,

parrots will clatter from the trees with raucous news
of the coming night, and the first star will settle.

Then all the sorrows that lay heavily on us,
the repeated failures, the botched trepidations

will pass like the lights on bridges at village corners
where shadows crouch under pierced constellations

whose name they have never learnt, as the sickle glow
rises over bamboos that repeat the round

of the chartered stars, the Archer, aiming his bow,
the Bear, and the studded collar of Tiepolo's hound.

I cannot deny the distinction of this verse, but the pervasive tonalities of Stevens's kind of impressionism trouble my ear. Walcott, the leading Anglophone poet of the West Indies, is a cultural figure of real importance, and deserves his fame. If I do not find him to be a strong poet, unlike John Ashbery or Seamus Heaney, Geoffrey Hill or James Merrill, Jay Wright or Anne Carson, is that because I set too high a value upon the agonistic element in poetry? My uneasiness may reflect primarily upon myself, and not upon Derek Walcott.

Geoffrey Hill

(1932–)

STRONG POETRY IS ALWAYS DIFFICULT, AND GEOFFREY HILL IS THE STRONGEST British poet now alive, though his reputation in the English-speaking world is somewhat less advanced than that of several of his contemporaries. He should be read and studied for many generations after they have blent together, just as he should survive all but a handful (or fewer) of American poets now active. Such canonic prophecy is founded on the authority of his best work, as I have experienced it in the fifteen years since the publication of *For The Unfallen*, his first book. From his first poem, appropriately "Genesis," on through the *Mercian Hymns*, Hill has been the most Blakean of modern poets. But this is deep or true influence, or Blake's Mental Warfare, rather than the easy transmission of image, idea, diction and metric that superficially is judged to be poetic influence. The merely extrinsic influences on Hill's early verse are mostly American; I can detect the fierce rhetoric of Allen Tate, and the visionary intensities of Richard Eberhart, in some places. Yet the true precursor is always Blake, and the War in Heaven that the strong poet must conduct is fought by Hill against Blake, and against Blake's tradition, and so against Hill himself.

As a war of poetry against poetry, Hill's work testifies to the repressive power of tradition, but also to an immensely individual and deeply moving moral protest against tradition. Like the hero he celebrates in his masterpiece, the *Mercian Hymns*, Hill is a martyrologist. His subject is human pain, the suffering of those who both do and sustain violence, and more exactly the daemonic relationship between cultural tradition and human pain. Confronted by Hill's best poems, a reader is at first tempted to run away, for the intellectual difficulty of the rugged, compressed verse is more than matched by the emotional painfulness and directness of Hill's vision. Hill does not comfort nor console, and offers no dialectic of gain through loss. His subject, like his style, is difficulty; the difficulty of apprehending and accepting moral guilt, and the difficulty of being a poet when the burden of history, including poetic history, makes any prophetic stance inauthentic. In more than twenty years of writing, Hill has given us three very slim volumes, not because his gift is sparse, but because he is too scrupulous to have allowed himself a less organized or less weighted utterance. There are no bad poems in Hill's three books, and so much is demanded of the reader, in concentration and in the dignity of a desperate humanism, that more productive poets are likely to seem too indulgent, by comparison. Hill does not indulge his reader, or himself, and just this remorseless concentration is Hill's assured greatness. The reader who persists will learn to read not only Hill, but other difficult and wholly indispensable poets as well, for only a poet as strong as Hill compels each of us to test his own strength as a reader and so to test and clarify also our own relation to tradition.

Tradition, Freud surmised, was the cultural equivalent of repressed material in the consciousness of the individual. The role of repression in poetry was misunderstood by Freud and has been misunderstood by most of his followers. Freud thought that sublimation was the psychic defense that *worked*, whether in life or in literature, while repression invariably failed, since repression augmented the unconscious. But poetry is figurative language, and in poetry sublimation is accomplished through the self-limiting trope of metaphor, while repression is represented by the expansive trope of hyperbole, with all of its Sublime glories and Grotesque dangers. From the viewpoint of poetry, the "unconscious mind" is an oxymoron, since repressed material in poetry has no place to go but up, onto the heights of what Romanticism called the Imagination. Romantic Imagination, whether in Blake or Coleridge, does not represent a return of the repressed, but is identical with the process of repression itself.

An individual poetic imagination can defend itself against the force of another imagination only by troping, so that a successful defense against poetic tradition always answers repression by an increase in repression. The return of the repressed is only an utopian or apocalyptic dream much indulged in by Marxist speculation, and by assorted contemporary shamans who inspire what is still being termed a counter-culture. Authentic poets show us that Emersonian Compensation is always at work in poetry as in life: nothing is got for nothing. What returns in authentic poetry is never the repressed, but rather the daemonic or uncanny element within repression, which poetic tradition has called by various names, including the Sublime, and the Imagination, both of them hyperbolical figurations for something that has no referential aspect or literal meaning, but that nevertheless guarantees the survival and continuity of poetic tradition. Poets and readers go on questing for one another in order to give a voice to this daemonic impulse that informs and purifies repression. "Purifies" here has no moral or spiritual meaning but refers rather to a process by which the daemonic is reconciled with the writing of poetry.

"Daemonic," in this sense, refers to a realm of power that invades the human world yet seems apart from human origins or human ends. In a very early poem, a visionary lyric in the mode of Eberhart, but like Eberhart reaching back to Blake's "Tyger," Hill laments the inadequacy of poetic language to tell his own experience of daemonic influx:

> I waited for the word that was not given,
>
> Pent up into a region of pure force,
> Made subject to the pressure of the stars;
> I saw the angels lifted like pale straws;
> I could not stand before those winnowing eyes
>
> And fell, until I found the world again.

Hill dislikes his early poems, yet they are not only permanent achievements but also quite essential for understanding all that comes after. "Genesis," for which he has a particular dislike, is superb in itself, a perfect "first" poem, and also a clear intimation of his largest debt to Blake's vision, which is the conviction that the Creation and the Fall were the same event. Another fine early poem, "In Memory of Jane Fraser" (which Hill evidently dislikes most, of all his work), speaks of a single, particular death as uncreating all of nature. For Hill, the natural world is, at best, "a stunned repose," a judgment that allies him to Blake rather than to Wordsworth, Shelley rather than to Keats. Hill's poem on the death of Shelley emphasizes the survival of the animal world, even as Shelley, the Modern Poet proper, or New Perseus, quests aimlessly, "clogged sword, clear, aimless mirror— / With nothing to strike at or blind / in the frothed shallows."

The themes and procedures of both Hill's books of short poems are summed up in what I judge to be his best single poem, the double-sonnet called "Annunciations." Though Hill transcends his own earlier mode in *Mercian Hymns* (as will be seen), "Annunciations" is so important a poem that I will discuss it at some length. A reader who can interpret "Annunciations" can learn to interpret the rest of Hill, and also acquire many insights that will aid in reading any truly difficult poetry of the Post-Romantic tradition. For, in "Annunciations," Hill wrote what later

tradition may judge to have been the central shorter poem of his own generation, a poem that is itself a despairing poetics, and a total vision both of
natural existence, and of the necessary limitations of what we have learned
to call imagination.

An "annunciation" can be any proclamation, but despite Hill's plural
title, the reverberation here depends upon the Annunciation proper, the
announcement of the Incarnation by the Angel Gabriel in Luke 1:26–38.
In some grim sense, Hill's starting-point is the festival (25 March) celebrating Gabriel's announcement. But "the Word" here is not the Logos,
nor simply the words of poetry, all poetry, but the idealization of poetry
that is so pervasive in Western tradition:

> The Word has been abroad; is back, with a tanned look
> From its subsistence in the stiffening-mire.
> Cleansing has become killing, the reward
> More touchable, overt, clean to the touch.

This Word seems more a tourist than an Eliotic explorer; indeed a
hygienic tourist-hunter. Returned, the questers sit together at a literary
feast with their scholarly and critical admirers:

> Now, at a distance from the steam of beasts,
> The loathly neckings and fat shook spawn
> (Each specimen-jar fed with delicate spawn)
> The searchers with the curers sit at meat
> And are satisfied.

I do not know how to interpret this except as an attack upon everyone who has to do with poetry: poets, critics, teachers, students, readers. It
is as though Yeats, after observing in vision his nymphs and satyrs copulat-
ing in the foam, his Innocents re-living their pain and having their wounds
opened again, then attended a banquet in honor of his "News for the
Delphic Oracle." The poem becomes a "specimen-jar," holding an aesthetic reduction of copulation and bleeding wounds. Is such an attack as
Hill's legitimate, since it would apply as much to Homer as to any other
poet? Is Hill attacking a false idealization of poetry or the *Ananke* that governs all poetry? The remainder of the first part of "Annunciations" will not
answer these questions:

> Such precious things put down
> And the flesh eased through turbulence, the soul

Purples itself; each eye squats full and mild
While all who attend to fiddle or to harp
For betterment, flavour their decent mouths
With gobbets of the sweetest sacrifice.

Primarily this is Hill's uncompromising attack upon himself, for more even than Yeats, or even his contemporary Ted Hughes, he writes a poetry whose subject is violence and pain, thus accepting the danger of easing the flesh through a vision of turbulence. Much of the success with readers, particularly British readers, of the later Yeats and of Hughes is surely based upon feeding the reader's eye with imaginary lust and suffering until that eye "squats full and mild." Hill's attack upon "all who attend to fiddle or to harp / For betterment" is therefore an attack upon the most traditional, Aristotelian defense of poetry, an attack upon the supposed function of catharsis. Poems are "gobbets of the sweetest sacrifice," and readers flavor their mouths decently even as decent Christians swallow the bread of communion. It becomes clear that Hill is attacking, ultimately, neither poetry nor religion, but the inescapable element that always darkens tradition, which is that the living, feeding upon the repressions of the dead, repress further and so become the sustenance of the dead. Hill's "sacrifice" is what Nietzsche and Freud would have termed an Antithetical Primal Word, for it is debatable whether the victims commemorated by the poem, or the readers, are the "sacrifice."

The Antithetical Primal Word of the second part of "Annunciations" is of course "love," and here the majestic bitterness of the Sublime triumphs in and over Hill:

O Love, subject of the mere diurnal grind,
Forever being pledged to be redeemed,
Expose yourself for charity; be assured
The body is but husk and excrement.
Enter these deaths according to the law,
O visited women, possessed sons! Foreign lusts
Infringe our restraints; the changeable
Soldiery have their goings-out and comings-in
Dying in abundance. Choicest beasts
Suffuse the gutters with their colourful blood.
Our God scatters corruption. Priests, martyrs,
Parade to this imperious theme: 'O Love,
You know what pains succeed; be vigilant; strive
To recognize the damned among your friends.'

If I could cite only one stanza by Hill as being wholly representative of him, it would be this, for here is his power, his despair and (in spite of himself) his Word, not in the sense of Logos but in the Hebraic sense of *davhar*, a word that is also an act, a bringing-forward of something previously held back in the self. This Word that rejects being a Word is a knowing misprision or mis-taking of tradition, but even the most revisionary of Words remains a Word, as Hill doubtless knows. Being willing to go on writing poems, however sparsely, is to believe that one possesses a Word of one's own to bring forward. When Hill says, "Our God scatters corruption," he means that the God of lovers (and of poets) is antithetical to Himself, that this God is the ambivalent deity of all Gnostics. I take it that "scatters" does not mean "drives away" but rather "increases" corruption by dispersal, which implies that "corruption" takes something of its root-meaning of "broken-to-pieces." Hill's subject then is the Gnostic or Kabbalistic "Breaking of the Vessels," the Fall that is simultaneously a Creation, as in his first, Blakean, chant-poem "Genesis."

Part II of "Annunciations" is thus more of a proclamation against Love than a prayer to Love. Love, addressed under its aspect of repetition, is urged to more honesty, and to a reductive awareness of the body. Corporeal passion lives and dies according to the old dispensation, or law, but Hill comes to proclaim a new Incarnation, which is only a Gnostic dying into yet more sexual abundance. As an incessant martyrologist, Hill grimly announces the imperious as against the imperial or Shakespearean theme. Love, who knows that pains only succeed or follow one another (but are never successful), is urged at least to distinguish its true martyrs among the panoply of its worshippers, and so recognize accurately its valid theme.

Repeated readings of "Annunciations" should clarify and justify Hill's densely impacted style, with its reliance upon figurations of Hyperbole. Hill's mode is a negative or counter-Sublime, and his characteristic defense against the tradition he beautifully sustains and extends is an almost primal repression:

> Not as we are but as we must appear,
> Contractual ghosts of pity; not as we
> Desire life but as they would have us live,
> Set apart in timeless colloquy:
> So it is required; so we bear witness,
> Despite ourselves, to what is beyond us,
> Each distant sphere of harmony forever
> Poised, unanswerable ...

This is again a Gnostic sublimity. Blake could still insist that pity survived only because we kept on rendering others piteous, but Hill comes later, and for him the intoxication of belatedness is to know that our reality and our desire are both negated by our appearance as legatees. It is tradition that makes us into "contractual ghosts of pity." A Beautiful Necessity represses us, and makes us bear witness to a dead but still powerful transcendence. Hill characterizes one of his sequences as "a florid grim music" or an "ornate and heartless music punctuated by mutterings, blasphemies and cries for help." A baroque pathos seems to be Hill's goal, with the ornateness his tribute to tradition, and the punctuation of pathos his outcry against tradition. Hill's is clearly a poetics of pain, in which all the calamities of history become so many poetic salutes, so many baroque meditations, always trapped in a single repetition of realization. Man is trapped "between the stones and the void," without majesty and without justice except for the errors of rhetoric, the illusions of poetic language. Like his own Sebastian Arrurruz, Hill's task is "to find value/In a bleak skill," the poet's craft of establishing true rather than false "sequences of pain."

"It must give pleasure," Stevens rightly insisted, and any critic responding to Hill should be prepared to say how and why Hill's poetry can give pleasure, and in what sense Hill's reader can defend himself from being only another decent mouth opened wide for the poetry-banquet. How is the reader to evade becoming "the (supposed) Patron" so bitterly invoked in the final poem of Hill's first book? The Gnostic answer, which is always a latecomer's answer, is that the reader must become not a patron but one of those unfallen who gave Hill's first book its title:

For the unfallen—the firstborn, or wise
Councillor—prepared vistas extend
As far as harvest; and idyllic death
Where fish at dawn ignite the powdery lake.

The final trope here is perhaps too Yeatsian, but the previous trope that gives back priority to the unfallen has a more High Romantic tenor, looking back to Keats' vision of Autumn. Hill cannot celebrate natural completion, but he always finds himself turning again "to flesh and blood and the blood's pain" despite his Gnostic desire to renounce for good "this fierce and unregenerate clay." Of his incessant ambivalence, Hill has made a strong poetry, one that battles tradition on tradition's own terms, and that attempts to make of its conscious belatedness an earliness. The accomplished reader responds to Hill's work as to any really strong poetry, for the reader too needs to put off his own belatedness, which is surely why we go on searching for strong poetry. We cannot live with tradition, and we cannot live without it, and so we turn to the strong poet to see how he acts out this ambivalence for us, and to see also if he can get beyond such ambivalence.

Hill begins to break through his own dialects of tradition in *Mercian Hymns*, the sequence of prose-poems he published on the threshold of turning forty. His hero is Offa, an eighth century Midlands "king," who merges both into a spirit of place and into the poet celebrating him, particularly the poet-as-schoolboy, for *Mercian Hymns* is a kind of *Prelude*-in-little. Yet here the growth of a poet's mind is not stimulated by nature's teachings, but only by history and by dreams. Transcendence, for Hill, returned or re-entered the sublunary world in old tapestries, sculpture, and metal-work, but mostly in historicizing reverie, which is the substance of these hymns. With *Mercian Hymns*, Hill rather triumphantly "makes it new," and though the obsession with tradition is as strong, much of the ambivalence towards tradition is miraculously diminished. Indeed, certain passages in *Mercian Hymns* would approach sentimentality if the poet did not remain characteristically condensed and gnomic, with the familiar spectre of pain hovering uncannily close:

> We have a kitchen-garden riddled with toy-shards, with splinters of habitation. The children shriek and scavenge, play havoc. They incinerate boxes, rags and old tyres. They haul a sodden log, hung with soft shields of fungus, and launch it upon the flames.

Difficult as Hill was earlier, *Mercian Hymns*, despite the limpidity of its individual sections, is the subtlest and most oblique of his works. It is not only hard to hold together, but there is one question as to what it is "about," though the necessary answer is akin to *The Prelude* again; Hill has at last no subject but his own complex subjectivity, and so the poem is "about" himself, which turns out to be his exchange of gifts with the Muse of History (section X). I suggest that the structure and meaning of *Mercian Hymns* is best approached through its rhetoric, which as before in Hill is largely that of metaleptic reversal or transumption, the dominant trope of Post-Romantic poetry in English. For a full analysis of the trope and its poetic history, I must refer to my book, *A Map of Misreading* and give only a brief account here. Transumption is the trope of a trope, or technically the metonymy of a metonymy. That is, it tends to be a figure that substitutes an aspect of a previous figure for that figure. Imagistically, transumption from Milton through the Romantics to the present tends to present itself in terms of earliness substituting for lateness, and more often than not to be the figure that concludes poems. Translated into psychoanalytic terms, transumption is either the psychic defense of introjection (identification) or of projection (refusal of identity), just as metaphor translates into the defense of sublimation, or hyperbole into that of repression. The advantage of transumption as a concluding trope for belated poems is that it achieves a kind of fresh priority or earliness, but always at the expense of the presentness of the present or living moment. Hill is as transumptive a poet, rhetorically, as Milton or Wordsworth or Wallace Stevens, and so he too is unable to celebrate a present joy.

There is no present time, indeed there is no self-presence in *Mercian Hymns*. Though Hill's own note on the sequence betrays some anxiety about what he calls anachronisms, the genius of his work excludes such anxiety. Nothing can be anachronistic when there is no present:

> King of the perennial holly-groves, the riven sandstone; over-
> lord of the M5: architect of the historic rampart and
> ditch, the citadel at Tamworth, the summer hermitage in
> Holy Cross: guardian of the Welsh Bridge and the Iron
> Bridge: contractor to the desirable new estates: saltmas-
> ter: money changer: commissioner for oaths: martyrolo-
> gist: the friend of Charlemagne.
> 'I liked that,' said Offa, 'sing it again,'

It is not that Offa has returned to merge with the poet, or that Hill has gone back to Offa. Hill and Offa stand together in a figuration that has introjected the past and the future, while projecting the present. Hill's epigraph, from the neglected poet and essayist, C.H. Sisson, analogizes his own conduct as private person and Offa's conduct of government, in all aspects of conduct having to do with "object and justification." Hill's struggle, as person and as poet, is with the repressive power of tradition, with the anxieties of history. Offa is seen by Hill as "the starting-cry of a race," as the master of a Primal Scene of Instruction, an imposition of order that fixates subsequent repression in others, which means to start an inescapable tradition. By reconciling himself with Offa, Hill comes close to accepting the necessary violence of tradition that earlier had induced enormous ambivalences in his poetry.

This acceptance, still somber but no longer grim, produces the dominant tone of *Mercian Hymns*, which is a kind of Wordsworthian "sober coloring" or "still sad music of humanity." But the sequence's vision remains

Blakean rather than Wordsworthian, for the world it pictures is still one in which Creation and Fall cannot be distinguished, and at the end Offa is fallen Adam or every man: "he left behind coins, for his lodging, and traces of red mud." The reader sees that each hymn is like the inscription on one of Offa's hammered coins, and that these coins are literally and figuratively the price of a living tradition, its perpetual balance of Creation and Fall. Hill has succeeded, obliquely, in solving his aesthetic-moral problem as a poet, but the success is as equivocal and momentary as the pun on "succeed" in "Annunciations." Hill now knows better "what pains succeed," and his moving sequence helps his readers to the same knowledge.

No critical introduction to a poet only just past forty in age can hope to prophesy his future development. I have seen no poems written by Hill since *Mercian Hymns*, but would be surprised if he did not return to the tighter mode of For The Unfallen and King Log, though in a finer tone. His achievement to date, as gathered in his volume, seems to me to transcend the more copious work of his contemporary rivals: Hughes, Gunn, Kinsella, Tomlinson, Silkin. Good as they are, they lack poetic strength when compared with Hill. He has the persistence to go on wrestling with the mighty dead—Blake, Wordsworth, Shelley, Yeats—and to make of this ghostly struggle a fresh sublimity. He is indeed a poet of the Sublime, a mode wholly archaic yet always available to us again, provided a survivor of the old line come to us:

> Against the burly air I strode,
> Where the tight ocean heaves its load,
> Crying the miracles of God.

Mark Strand

(1934–)

I HAVE KNOWN MARK STRAND, AS PERSON AND AS POET, FOR MORE THAN half a century. His gift is harbored rather than sparse: that is my interpretation of his major work to date, *Dark Harbor: A Poem* (1993). The poem constitutes a "Proem" and forty-five cantos or sections.

Dark Harbor, like some earlier poems by Strand, is an overt homage to Wallace Stevens. It is as though casting aside anxieties of influences Strand wishes reconcilement with his crucial precursor. The "Proem" sets forth vigorously: "The burning/Will of weather, blowing overhead, would be his muse." But, by Canto IV, we are in the world of Stevens:

> There is a certain triviality in living here,
> A lightness, a comic monotony that one tries
> To undermine with shows of energy, a devotion
>
> To the vagaries of desire, whereas over there
> Is a seriousness, a stiff, inflexible gloom
> That shrouds the disappearing soul, a weight
>
> That shames our lightness. Just look
> Across the river and you will discover
> How unworthy you are as you describe what you see,
>
> Which is bound by what is available.
> On the other side, no one is looking this way.
> They are committed to obstacles,
>
> To the textures and levels of darkness,

417

To the tedious enactment of duration.
And they labor not for bread or love

But to perpetuate the balance between the past
And the future. They are the future as it
Extends itself, just as we are the past

Coming to terms with itself. Which is why
The napkins are pressed, and the cookies have come
On time, and why the glass of milk, looking so chic

In its whiteness, begs us to sip. None of this happens
Over there. Relief from anything is seen
As timid, a sign of shallowness or worse.

This is the voice of the master, particularly in *An Ordinary Evening in New Haven*. Strand shrewdly outdoes Stevens to the glass of milk, setting aside any more metaphysical concerns. An effort is made, for fifteen cantos, to domesticate Stevens, but the great voice, of Stevens and Strand fused together, returns in Canto XVI:

It is true, as someone has said, that in
A world without heaven all is farewell.
Whether you wave your hand or not,

It is farewell, and if no tears come to your eyes
It is still farewell, and if you pretend not to notice,
Hating what passes, it is still farewell.

Farewell no matter what. And the palms as they lean
Over the green, bright lagoon, and the pelicans
Diving, and the listening bodies of bathers resting,

Are stages in an ultimate stillness, and the movement
Of sand, and of wind, and the secret moves of the body
Are part of the same, a simplicity that turns being

Into an occasion for mourning, or into an occasion
Worth celebrating, for what else does one do,
Feeling the weight of the pelicans' wings,

The density of the palms' shadows, the cells that darken
The backs of bathers? These are beyond the distortions
Of chance, beyond the evasions of music. The end

Is enacted again and again. And we feel it
In the temptations of sleep, in the moon's ripening,
In the wine as it waits in the glass.

It is Stevens who tells us that, without heaven, all farewells are final.
What enchants me here are the Strandian variations on farewell. Waves
and tears yield to very Stevensian palms, and to the pelicans of Florida,
venereal soil. A greater meditation, suitable to Strand and Stevens as seers
of the weather, arrives in Canto XXIV:

Now think of the weather and how it is rarely the same
For any two people, how when it is small, precision is needed
To say when it is really an aura or odor or even an air

Of certainty, or how, as the hours go by, it could be thought of
As large because of the number of people it touches.
Its strength is something else: tornados are small

But strong and cloudless summer days seem infinite
But tend to be weak since we don't mind being out in them.
Excuse me, is this the story of another exciting day,

The sort of thing that accompanies preparations for dinner?
Then what say we talk about the inaudible—the shape it assumes,
And what social implications it holds,

Or the somber flourishes of autumn—the bright
Or blighted leaves falling, the clicking of cold branches,
The new color of the sky, its random blue.

Is that final tercet Strand or Stevens? As the sequence strengthens,
deliberate echoes of Josh Ashbery, Octavio Paz and Wordsworth are
evoked by Strand, until he achieves a grand apotheosis in his final canto:

I am sure you would find it misty here,
With lots of stone cottages badly needing repair.
Groups of souls, wrapped in cloaks, sit in the fields

Or stroll the winding unpaved roads. They are polite,
And oblivious to their bodies, which the wind passes through,
Making a shushing sound. Not long ago,

I stopped to rest in a place where an especially
Thick mist swirled up from the river. Someone,
Who claimed to have known me years before,

Approached, saying there were many poets
Wandering around who wished to be alive again.
They were ready to say the words they had been unable to say—

Words whose absence had been the silence of love,
Of pain, and even of pleasure. Then he joined a small group,
Gathered beside a fire. I believe I recognized

Some of the faces, but as I approached they tucked
Their heads under their wings. I looked away to the hills
Above the river, where the golden lights of sunset

And sunrise are one and the same, and saw something flying
Back and forth, fluttering its wings. Then it stopped in mid-air.
It was an angel, one of the good ones, about to sing.

The aura is Dante's, and we are in a spooky place, paradise of poets
or purgatory of poets. If one line above all others in *Dark Harbor* rever-
berates within me, it is: "They were ready to say the words they had been
unable to say—." The accent remains late Stevens, but with a difference is
altogether Mark Strand's.

Jay Wright

(1935-)

ONE CENTRAL IMAGE IN JAY WRIGHT'S POETRY IS CREATION-BY-TWINNING, in which a poem becomes a limbo dance, a gateway out of the Middle Passage of the slave trade, a gateway that is also a logbook, and so a poem for passage. The limbo is a West Indian dance performed under a gradual-ly lowered bar, until the dancer is a spider-man, spread-eagling his arms and legs. Interpreters refer the limbo to the terrible Middle Passage, the route of slave ships from Africa to America, during which the slaves were crowded into so little space that they contorted themselves into human spi-ders. In Jay Wright's art, the limbo is a metaphor for this poet's aesthetic project, a quest for a gateway out of the Middle Passage by making "a log for passage." This logbook offers initiation by twinning, a mode of divine creation in the Dogon mythology of West Africa. There Amma or Yahweh twins himself hermetically as Nommo or Adam, a forerunner for the Black Son of God, who will be the gateway for everyone out of a universal Middle Passage. In his poem, "The Albuquerque Graveyard," Wright had returned to the burial place of early friends and associates:

> I am going back
> to the Black limbo,
> an unwritten history
> of our own tensions.
> The dead lie here
> in a hierarchy of small defeats.
>
> *Selected Poems* 62]

A somewhat later poem, "The Abstract of Knowledge / The First Test," has an intricate passage adumbrating this image of the limbo, at once

Dante's place outside of Hell, Purgatory, and Heaven, and a dance ironically commemorating bondage:

> If you go from the certainty of oneness
> into solitude and return,
> I must divest you of your double
> and twin you in love's seclusion.
> My instruments toll you into limbo;
>
> [*Selected Poems* 180]

Dogon mythology teaches that every being, indeed every object, has
its own language, which is its twin or double, its Nommo or Adam.
Western Hermetism has roughly the same teaching, which influenced
Symbolist poetry, both in Rimbaud and in Hart Crane. Jakob Boehme's
grand phrase for this doubling was "the signature of all things." In many
respects, Jay Wright's poetry attempts to read the signatures of all things,
a daunting project for any poet, but one peculiarly fraught with hazards for
an African-American writer in our America drifting towards Millennium.
The extra-literary pressures placed upon the late Ralph Ellison were
excruciating, and doubtless had their effect in seeing to it that *Invisible Man*
remained a solitary achievement. Ellison once wryly remarked to me that
only internal pressures could be fecund; the evidence for his proud
truthtelling can be found all about us, in all the clamors of Resentment,
emanating as they do from every possible ideology. What Ellison is to the
African-American novel, Jay Wright is to black poetry in the United
States. It is not accidental that Wright has become the Invisible Man:
reclusive, isolated, and ceaselessly meditating in a remote part of Vermont,
alone with his wife. What other context does our self-betrayed culture
afford him? But I have cried out upon these matters too often, and I am so
wearied by Resenters who urge historicizing and politicizing upon me, that
for now I will just forget them, and will analyze and appreciate Jay
Wright's poetry as it sets him in company of his peers: Rilke, Hölderlin,
Hart Crane, Robert Hayden, Paul Celan, and Luis Cernuda, the marvelous Spanish poet of the Sublime who fled Franco and died by his own
hand in Mexico. My love for Wright's poetry goes back a quarter-century
to *The Homecoming Singer* (1971), and has been heightened with each subsequent volume, culminating with *Boleros* (1991). There has been no book
by Wright these last five years, but I will quote and discuss one of his most
recent poems. At sixty-one, Wright is one of the handful of major
American poets that we have alive among us, but alas he is the least read
and studied of them all. Partly this is caused by the authentic cognitive and

imaginative difficulties that his work presents, but partly the neglect of his poetry comes from nearly everyone's wrong-headed expectations of an African-American poet. Wright is a protest poet only as Dante was. A visionary poet, whether William Blake or Hart Crane or Jay Wright, has an agenda that an age of politicized criticism cannot apprehend. Wright is a great religious poet, whose spirituality is a syncretic weave of African, American, and European strands. The American component in this weaving is New Mexican and Mexican, the European is Dantesque, the African most often Dogon. We have little capacity for apprehending so complex and original a spiritual vision, which enhances Jay Wright's poetic difficulty for us. Yet I am speaking of a central American poet, one fully comparable to John Ashbery, A.R. Ammons, and only a handful of others now living among us. That so remarkable and capacious a poet is neglected is another, terrible symptom of our current cultural decay.

The American Sublime, however we mock it, remains the crucial mode of our poetry, from Emerson, Whitman and Dickinson through Wallace Stevens and Hart Crane on to James Merrill, Ammons, and Jay Wright. By the Sublime I intend the Longinian sense of being upon the heights, a transcendental and agonistic mode of aesthetic experience, and one that is highly consonant with extraordinary learning. Learned poets are not infrequent, in all the great poetic traditions. Jay Wright legitimately participates in so many strong traditions that inevitably he is an immensely learned poet. The difficulties presented to the reader are different neither in degree nor in kind from those we have to confront in John Milton or in William Blake. I have expressed my critical conviction that only Wright is of Ralph Ellison's eminence among all African-American creators of imaginative literature, up to this present time. But *Invisible Man* is a post-Faulknerian novel, and has much the same relation to *Light in August* or *Absalom, Absalom!* as these books have to Joseph Conrad's principal fictions. Modern poetry, however, is bewilderingly multiform in its relation to anterior poetry, and Wright is syncretic and diverse to an extraordinary degree. If you compare him to an exact contemporary like the admirable Mark Strand, one of your first conclusions will be that Strand has an intense relation to only a few precursors, Wallace Stevens and Elizabeth Bishop in particular. Strand's *Dark Harbor*, a book-length sequence of marvelous eloquence and poignancy, relies upon its intricate evasions of Stevens's influence, at once embraced without ambivalence, yet also warded-off, lest Strand drown in Stevens. Wright seems to me closest to Hart Crane among American poets, but neither Crane nor the Crane-influenced Robert Hayden are as central to Wright's art as Stevens is to Strand's. Sometimes, particularly in *The Double Invention of Komo*, Wright seems as haunted by T.S. Eliot's *Four Quartets* as Crane was by *The Waste Land*. It can be a touch disconcerting to hear Eliot's voice in Wright's St. Augustine:

> This is the dance of the changeless
> and the changing,
> the spirit's intensity
> for the world's endurance.
> Knowledge is motion in twilight,
> a state of falling into sight;
> one by one,
> the spirit's eyes touch and grow.
> *Peregrinus*, the tense spirit
> tenses and returns to its
> own understanding.
> There is always the going forth
> and the returning;
> there is always the act,
> the slow fusion of being.
> All things,
> by the strength of being joined,
> will continue;
> the sin is to turn away;
> ignorance is inattention ...
>
> [*Double Invention* 51]

In his "Afterword" to *The Double Invention of Komo*, Wright comments upon poetic voicing and its relation to ritual:

> In ritual, one does not step back from vision; one follows it. My poem risks ritual's arrogance. It presents a dominant voice, that of the initiate undergoing Komo's rigorous formalities ...
>
> [*Double Invention* 114]

The "dominant voice" of the poem is certainly Wright's own, though it fascinates me as to just why the later Eliot continues to break in, usurping the celebrant of Bambara ritual. I take the Eliotic intrusions, here and elsewhere in Wright, to be a sign that anthropology and poetry do not necessarily dwell together so comfortably as Wright insists they do. It is well worth remarking that Wright is a poet of the Sublime; he is not an anthropologist, a cultural historian, or a revivalist of archaic African religions.

Yes, he is a soothsayer and reads omens, but primarily as a path to writing his own poems. So fiercely fused are his gifts, at their best, that he transforms ritual into poetry, but never poetry into ritual, the prime flaw of Eliot in the *Quartets*. I learn something about African spirituality by reading Wright, and by following up his references to crucial scholarship upon this matter, but after all one can read his sources without reading him. In a review of Wright's *Selected Poems*, a not unsympathetic poet-critic, Robert B. Shaw, called the author of *The Double Invention of Komo* and *Dimensions of History* "a belated High Modernist," and lamented that readers uneducated in the relevant anthropological sources would require commentaries before they could judge the question of value in Wright's work. Yet, like T.S. Eliot and Hart Crane, Jay Wright at his most appealing is an incantatory writer whose initial impact transcends the necessity of commentary. Pindar is an immensely difficult poet, dense with mythological allusiveness, but his passionate pride in his own agonistic poetic prowess eloquently goes beyond his intricate ecstasies of mythic counterpoint. The high song more than sustains its difficulties, and Pindar always asks and answers the triple-question of the Sublime: more than? less than? or equal to? Excellence in the range and reach of the spirit is always the burden of the Sublime—in Pindar, Hölderlin, Shelley, Hart Crane, and very much in the major phase of Jay Wright.

It is one of the central ironies of our poetry that the major African-American poet, one of whose prime tropes being what he calls "the black limbo," should be our crucial composer of the American sublime ode as we approach Millennium. There are a few living poets of Jay Wright's eminence among us—John Ashbery and A.R. Ammons in particular—but their recent work has turned in other directions. If you define the modern Sublime mode with historical precision, then its central characteristic has to be an ambition of transcendence. The American Sublime, though Wallace Stevens nervously mocked it, is nevertheless well defined by the marvelous conclusion of his "The Idea of Order at Key West":

> The maker's rage to order words of the sea,
> Words of the fragrant portals, dimly-starred,
> And of ourselves and of our origins,
> In ghostlier demarcations, keener sounds.

Wright, neither a poet of the sea nor of those Keatsian portals, labors incessantly to order words of ourselves and of our origins in ways that will render the demarcations ghostlier, the sounds keener. Yet his sense of our origins, and his own, is so multiform and complex, that he gives a new and fuller meaning to the descriptive term "African-American." I scarcely can think of another American poet who has so astonishingly adumbrated that particular hyphen.

Wright's poetry is so large and varied, in scope and design, that I will center now, in some detail, upon my personal favorites among all his published work to date, the sequence of five grand odes that conclude his superb volume, *Elaine's Book* (1988; Elaine being the sister of his wife, Lois). These five poems—"The Anatomy of Resonance," "Journey to the Place of Ghosts," "Saltos," "The Power of Reeds," "Desire's Persistence"—are exalted in tone and stance, and attempt to mount the high places of the spirit. They remind us that Wright, like Hölderlin and Hart Crane, is a secular religious poet. Crane rather wistfully called himself a "Pindar of the Machine Age," while Wright should be termed a "Pindar of the Chaotic Age," for that is where we are now, drifting as we do towards a new Theocratic Age. Perhaps most of our current poets who matter—from A.R. Ammons to Jorie Graham—quest for their authentic spiritual ancestors, a search that is essential to the high, Pindaric mode of invocation and celebration. But no other major poet now writing among us carries out this mission with the urgency and intensity of Jay Wright.

The literary context of Wright's sequence of odes is provided by a startlingly effective blend of Hölderlin and Paul Celan, on the one side, and Aztec poetry, on the other. What allies the two visionary modes, in Wright's implicit interpretation, is a kind of despairing transcendence, a triumph of the Negative over the pseudo-spiritualities of much received religious tradition. In a sense, Wright returns to the argument of his long poem, *Dimensions of History*, where Aztec mythology was employed as an intricate instance of mingled creation and destruction in the world-cycles commemorated by the huge pyramid-temples that still survive. But a mythic history of the contending forces of the Aztec versions of Venus and Mars, for all its brazen power, had to be tempered if Wright was to achieve a subtler and more articulated vision than that of *Dimensions of History*. Hölderlin and Celan are played off by Wright against the Aztec splendor, which he knows was in its way as barbaric as the cruel Catholicism of the Spanish invaders who destroyed the Aztec culture. The suicidal intensity of Hölderlin and of Celan retains a personalism that is alien to the Aztec clash of gods and historical cycles, and Jay Wright's heroic insistence upon the individuality of the poet draws much of its authority from the examples of Hölderlin and Celan.

"The Anatomy of Resistance," the first of Wright's cycle of five odes, takes its epigraph from Hölderlin:

And the bird of the night whirs
    Down, so close that you shield your eyes.

Baudelaire wrote of the wing of madness coming so close that it brushed his ear; Hölderlin records a similar immediacy, so that both poets express the terrible cost of imaginative vision. Wright is concerned, not with the cost, but rather with "the anatomy of resonance," the analysis of that close whirring down that makes the poet apotropaically shield his eyes against his own vision. Seven stages mark this resonance, each headed by a crucial word in Hölderlin's sublime, composite metaphor: *The Bird, Night, Whirs, Down, Close, Shield, Eyes*. I rather should say Wright's revision of Hölderlin's trope, since here is the German original, "Die Kürze," written by Hölderlin in 1798:

«Warum bist du so kurz? liebst du, wie vormals, denn
  «Nun nicht mehr den Gesang? fandst du, als Jüngling, doch,
    «In den Tagen der Hoffnung,
      «Wenn du sangest, das Ende nie!»
Wie mein Glück, ist mein Lied.—Willst du im Abenrot
  Froh dich baden? hinweg ists! und die Erd ist kalt,
    Und der Vogel der Nacht schwirrt
      Unbequem vor das Auge dir.
                  [*Selected Verse*, 15–16]

The title is generally translated as "Brevity," and here is the most literal translation that I can give:

"Why are you so brief? Do you love singing less than you did formerly? since, as a young man, in the days of hope, when you sang, there was no end to your singing!"
  As is my fortune, so is my song. Would you bathe happily in the evening redness? It has vanished! And the earth is cold, and the bird of night whirs uncomfortably down towards your eyes.

Unbequem, "uncomfortably," is taken by Wright as "so close that you shield," the eyes being more than uncomfortable with the whirring that threatens to brush them. Hölderlin laments the end of an early poetic joyousness, a primal exuberance that has yielded to a supposedly more limited, or at least less celebratory art. Adroitly, Wright's first movement, *Bird*, has nothing in it of Hölderlin's "theology of existence":

BIRD

There must be an atmosphere,
or an evergreen,
or the green shading into the red-yellow
                        brown of earth, for the eye,
surely,
some choir in which the ornamented arms
might tune themselves
               to the absolute A of air.
Creatures given to this air
shape their own suspension,
               a process of weight,
thrust away from the body's substance,
and the depths of a woman's body,
               of maple and ash,
hold the arc of another substance,
a memory of unrealized absence.
There is a river here,
where the white heron fastens its claws
to the flat blue surface,
as though it stood in a flowing altar
               to call into the dense grove
of arrested light around the water.
Look and you will see the plume of communion,
a possible intention that arises only here.
It seems that the river has been clay
               for feather and bone,
for the elastic tissue of the bird's voice.
And the ...
words that begin a theology of existence,
a political history of flight,
an interrupted dream of being definite.
               [*Elaine's Book* 68–9]

"The absolute A of air" recalls the last of the "Logbook of Judgments" section in *Dimensions of History*, "Meta-A and the A of Absolutes" available now in *Selected Poems of Jay Wright*):

I am good when I know the darkness of all light,
and accept the darkness, not as a sign, but as my body.
This is the A of absolutes,

the logbook of judgments,
the good sign.

                    [*Selected Poems* 176]

This has been Wright's mature poetics, the Dogon insistence that each being (even an object) has its own language which is its own Adam, its Nommo, the Adamic twin or double, frequently antithetical to the being or object. So "the darkness of all light," an emergence from Plato's cave, is also a log for passage, an emergence from the Middle Passage, the black limbo of bondage. *That* is where we are in the first movement of "The Anatomy of Resonance," in the A of absolutes, the absolute A of air, a purged epiphany or moment of vision, an atmosphere tuned for the poetic eye, which then would require no shielding. And so Wright replaces the bird of the night with the Yeatsian (or even Sarah Orne Jewettian) white heron, for whose voice "the river has been clay / for feather and bone," the clay intimating the red clay out of which Adam or Nommo, antithetical double and twin, has been formed. Therefore Wright characterizes his epigraph, *And the bird of the night whirs / Down, so close that you shield your eyes*, as a theology of existence, and even as "a political history of flight," where "political" takes on the shade of "politic," meaning "prudential" and even "artful," as befits a dweller in the city of poetry. And that is why this epiphany is "an interrupted dream of being definite," since the interruption is the whirring of Hölderlin's bird of night, which now distracts Wright from his absolute A of air, his authentic poetic dream of definite being.

Night, the second movement, rewrites the history of darkness, invoking Cuzco, the ancient Incan capital, rebuilt by the conquering Spaniards upon the ruins of the old, streets of the dead. Cuzco here, in "The Anatomy of Resonance," recalls the destroyed cities of *Dimensions of History*, the Mayan capital Labna, and the Aztec capital Tenochtitlán, upon whose remnants Mexico City is built. Wright's "pecked cross" is not Catholic but Aztec, described in a note to *Dimensions of History* as representing the "four points of the compass," and so as an emblem of the wind and the rain, "pecked" because beaked in Aztec bird symbolism. Out of the absence of light, in a poetically reclaimed lost city of the Americas, a radiant voice rises, in an antiphony with the despairing voice of the Old World Hölderlin, visionary of unredeemed loss. Wright, humbly cognizant that he cannot be Pindar or Hölderlin, nevertheless enters the agon that is the Sublime mode by affirming his African and New Mexican heritages, by again asserting his spiritual ancestry in the splendors that the invading Europeans only could ruin. Beautifully modulated, *Night* is a negative epiphany twinning the serenity of *The Bird*.

Taken together, these first two movements define Wright's swerve away from the tradition of the Sublime, in an intricate irony or allegory reliant upon the Dogon mythology of Anima (Yahweh) and the Seventh Nommo (the Christ or Redeemer) that is always central to Wright's mature poetry. *Whirs*, the third movement, attempts instead an antithetical completion of Hölderlin's whirring resonance, by way of the "devastating hum of the jackal's song":

WHIRS
The jackal has learned to sing in the ash,
a severe chanty in praise of the cock and the fish,
of the aureole balm of evening.
When the moment arrives for singing,
palm leaves that are heavy with windlessness
                    vibrate to a star's breath,
and the ear, attuned to all the harmonies of neglect,
lifts the soteriological wisdom of loss
                    from its parish bed.
There is a moment when the boy comes out of the wood,
his feet slippered with a bee sound, his face
turned to the bull roar following his flight.
The boy carries an apple sound in his head,
something to enhance the dissonant eruption
                    of his new morning.
Now, mother night has dressed herself
to dance to the dulcimer of his spring.
Father now to the boy,
she will lock his arms, and twirl him,
and fill his body with the deep
and devastating hum of the jackal's song.
                    [*Elaine's Book* 70]

A mothering night that transforms to fatherhood centers this stately lyric in which sound prevails, from the jackal's singing its severe chanty of what sustains it through the stellar vibration of palms, sounds of bee, bull, and apple, and the dissonance of the boy's own advent. His spring is a dulcimer, and his dance twirls his body into the resonance of the jackal's chanty. Wright gives us here one of the staples of the Sublime ode, the incarnation of the Poetic Character in the poet's younger self, akin to the sensibility of song's abundance that Hölderlin elegizes as his own first phase. Yet brevity is not Wright's burden; his complex ancestry has its saving strand neither in the Old

World nor in the New, but in the indigenous spiritualities of Africa, which is why the *Whirs* movement celebrates "the soteriological wisdom of loss," in opposition to Hölderlin's Sublime grandeur of loss. Soteriology, in Christianity, is the theological doctrine of deliverance by Jesus, a salvation dependent upon a unique biography, both in and out of time. Wright intimates again, here as elsewhere, a different wisdom of loss, the sacrifice of the Nommo figured in the African jackal, a forager who has learned to sing in the ash of his foraging, and whose song is a cyclic repetition. Amma made love to the earth, which first brought forth a jackal, who in turn violated the earth his mother, all evil subsequently proceeding out of that mismatch. Wisdom is in the cycle, and not in the single manifestation of a savior as much out of time as in it, and so not even in the Seventh Nommo.

Down, the fourth movement, returns to another of Wright's geographies, Scotland, where he lived for a year that has been deeply impressed upon all his subsequent poetry, a North Sea vision playing off against Africa, Old and New Mexico, and upper New England. In *Down*, Wright experiences an emptying-out of the poetic self, a defensive movement of the spirit resting from the Sublime:

DOWN

Under the rock, in the hollow,
there are stones the color of cats' eyes.
Old women who have seen these eyes
know that the body should be eiderdown
and bathed with the water of holy wells
and mineral springs, a blue water
with just the hint of hardness
        a slight taste of sulfur.
So the sinistra side of that other body
would drift to the North Sea,
and come down in its emerald armor,
to be welcomed in a Latin wood,
where a crescent moon peeks over
          the empty seawall.
My dunum and dum boots quiver
on the qui vive,
      anxious
to enlist water again
    to unruffle and fix
the mystery of buried stone.

[*Elaine's Book* 70–1]

The supposed Scottish legend here is a variant upon the Celtic myth of Arthur, and "the other body ... in its emerald armor" becomes, in Wright's vision, not the return of a warrior-king but of a poetic vision reconfirmed by the marvelous lyric, *Close*, the next in "The Anatomy of Resonance":

> CLOSE
>
> Time and the deductive season
> teach an intimacy, reason
> enough to set sail under seal,
> a tenaciously secret keel
> of abbeys and cathedrals, found
> in the strictest boroughs, the round
> plot of land dense with unicorns;
> as in a soul's tapestry, horns
> flagellate the air. Now confined
> near an emerald sun, defined
> by my spirit's strictest account,
> I cling to my dole, and dismount.
> I have filled my bowl with the rose
> smoke of ecstasy in a close.

This intricate little Eliotic poem, with its internal and slant rhymes, is itself a miniature of the daemonic Sublime, fusing the Celtic "emerald sun," the warrior-king returned, with the famous unicorn tapestry, Hermetic record of an emblazoned reality unexpectedly regained. Ecstasy, a close only in the sense of an enclosure, leads downwards to the undoing movement, *Shield*:

> SHIELD
>
> Skewed, perhaps,
> the heart's road bends sinister,
> not out of skin and hide,
>   owing nothing
> to the combustible partition
>   crowning
> those trees
>   a doe's leap away.
> Maude had it right—
> John would be closer to love's blossom.
> She had been given nothing,

> and had only a desire to see
> down the dextrous avenue of self.
> Clearly, Maude knew
>   who would be impaled,
> who would sit on an order's collar,
> what weight the father would bear
>   against his own kind.
> Kindness,
>   or call it the valor of salvation,
>   roots in a shell,
> scaled to catch the rattle of friendship
>   and war heat alliance.
> We are stretched over the heart's house,
> to defend such kindness as remains,
> when the sun, strawberry red,
> dips itself into the lime green water
>   that flows endlessly home.
>   [*Elaine's Book* 72]

Maude is Mary Magdalene, John is the Beloved Disciple, and the account of the "impaling" of Christ has a Gnostic flavoring, as Wright again subtly rejects a Western image of salvation not in accord with the Akan doctrine of God, of Amma who would not bear a weight against his own kind, as the Christian God certainly does in the sacrifice of Jesus. Before he turns to *Eyes*, the final movement, Wright gives us a remarkable epigraph from Paul Celan's *Schneebett* (Snowbed): "Augen, weltblind, in Sterbegeklüft ...," rendered here as "Eyes, worldblind, in the lode-break of dying." *Sterbegeklüft* is a tough word, presumably one of Celan's coinages, and perhaps should be translated as "the fissure (or cleft) of dying." Wright wants the fissure to be a break in a vein of ore, as though dying is itself a wealth:

> EYES
> Old light, at this depth, knows
> the veil of deception, the water valley
> through which it leaps and divides.
> So here, as the south wind alerts the body
> to the season's change, the scarlet poplar
> leaf runs, from point through point,
> a topsy-turvy body to be fixed
>   in a different mirror.

An eye, such as this, may be worldblind
in the lode-break of dying. An eye, such as this,
may be no more than a peacock's tail,
the infant bud in a cutting, or the different
curve of a voice in the earth.
There is a market town in Suffolk,
where the bones and Roman urns and coins
mark a sacred ground with the sound of vision.
Time must tell us everything about sensation
and the way we have come to terms
                                        with our failure
to see anything but the blue point of desire
                                        that leads us home.
                            [*Elaine's Book* 73]

This is the Return of the Dead, of Hölderlin and of Celan, in Wright's own great ode, and confronts the challenge of answering Hölderlin's despairing vision: "And the bird of the night whirs / Down, so close that you shield your eyes." Wright employs his interpretation of Celan to exalt a rekindled poetic eye, one that transcends: "Old light" and the "veil of deception." To be "worldblind, in the lode-break of dying," whatever it meant to Celan, becomes in Jay Wright a marvelously hopeful image for a fresh poetic beginning. It is a loving critique of the Western Sublime of Hölderlin (and of Celan) that Wright presents, yet a critique nevertheless. The American Sublime, in Wright, becomes identical with the black limbo, the dance that takes slaves out of the Middle Passage.

Remembering a market town in Suffolk, where the sound of vision rose for him from a different curve, or dimension of history in the earth, Wright reaffirms the possibility of his own "The Eye of God, The Soul's First Vision," the opening poem of his epic of poetic incarnation, *Dimensions of History*. There Wright combined Dogon and Aztec symbolism in a riddle of initiation that is very different from the poetic election of Hölderlin's Greco-German Sublime. Implicit in the final movement of "The Anatomy of Resonance" is Wright's African mode of twinning, of election-by-substitution, as here at the start of *Dimensions of History*:

Where did I learn to present myself
to the cut of some other voice,
substitute in a mime
my body breaks to contain?

There is Wright's own intricate balance, poised between "the signs of understanding / that I assert, but cannot reach alone," and the solitary eye of Hölderlin and Celan, agonistic and isolate. Time, which for the African-American Wright, is purely a dimension of history, has to tell us everything about the sensation of confronting the whirring bird of the night, a sensation that for Hölderlin is inviolate and single. The Western Sublime mode, which includes the American Sublime before Ralph Ellison and Jay Wright, is indeed a strenuous way of coming to terms with our tendency to see only "the blue point of desire / that leads us home." With reverence for Hölderlin, Wright dialectically terms that kind of transcendence a failure, one that he has come to seal by bringing us an African-Aztec poetic vision as a saving balance. Such an assertion is audacious, yet "The Anatomy of Resonance" goes a good distance towards sustaining it.

"Desire's Persistence," the last of Wright's five odes, will take us back to that home-seeking, High Romantic "blue point of desire," in another poem as elaborate as "The Anatomy of Resonance." Between come three odes, simpler but no less magnificent, all addressing the poetic vocation. "Journey to the Place of Ghosts" takes another epigraph from Celan, yet is almost entirely African in its setting and emphasis. I pass over it here, except to note that its ritual descent to the dead yields a rekindling of the poetic self, but at the expense of a psychic cost more harrowing than any other I recall in Wright's work. "Saltos," with its title hinting at the need to become a spiritual acrobat, follows and again I must neglect its splendors, though the poignance of being "awakened by a sun I will never see" testifies to Wright's awareness that his Africa is purely a vision, and not an empirical experience. "The Power of Reeds," the fourth ode, retrieves lost connections, in a characteristic Wrightian uncovering of the weave that analogizes ancient Greek, African and Mexican Indian visionary songs and singing. This too, though it is the most powerful of these three middle odes, I set aside while noting that again the African strand is the strongest in the weave. Wright, who is sublimely above the vulgar cultural politics of our academies and our journalists, is far more devoted to African culture and scholarship than are the entire camp of Resenters and cultural nationalists.

"The Anatomy of Resonance," by any rational standards of aesthetic eminence is a great poem, but "Desire's Persistence" seems to me even stronger, and is one of the double handful of Sublime achievements by poets of Jay Wright's own American generation. I return therefore to a rather close reading because Wright, as I reiterate, is a legitimately difficult poet who requires exegesis. I am sufficiently unregenerate so that I regard this as a merit, rather than a flaw, of his poetry. The ultimate archetype of the poet for Wright is Dante. Hart Crane, a difficult poet and a strong rhetorical influence upon the young Jay Wright, was drawn to Dante precisely as Wright is, seeking a paradigm for the poet's relation to his own poetry. In some sense, all of Wright's poetry to date constitutes his *Vita Nuova* and his *canzoni*. Though *Dimensions of History* and *The Double Invention of Komo* are epics in the Pound–Eliot mode, both were composed a little early in Wright's career. His work-in-progress, *Transformations*, consists of extended, meditative lyrics, wisdom literature, rather than the celebratory and lamenting odes of *Elaine's Book* and *Boleros*. Unlike Crane, who suffered a death by water at thirty-two, Wright is at the start of his sixties, and I am moved to prophesy that an African-American Dante may yet be revealed to us.

"Desire's Persistence" is indeed as beautiful as it is difficult. Its title comes from the Aztec, as does the line that Wright quarries for the name of the individual movements: "I lift the red flower of winter into the wind." But before we go to the sequence of *I*, *Lift*, *Red*, *Flower*, *Winter*, *Wind*, Wright allows the narrator, Desire, to speak:

> In the region of rain and cloud,
> I live in shade,
> under the moss mat of days bruised
> > purple with desire.
> My dominion is a song in the wide ring of water.
> There, I run to and fro,
> braiding the logical act
> > in the birth of an Ear of Corn,
> polychromatic story I will now tell
> in the weaving, power's form in motion,
> a devotion to the unstressed.
> Once, I wreathed around a king,
> became a fishing-net, a maze,
> > "a deadly wealth of robe."
> Mothers who have heard me sing take heart;
> I always prick them into power.
> > > [*Elaine's Book* 82]

The chanter, Desire, takes on the ambivalent guise of "a fishing-net, a maze / 'a deadly wealth of robe,'" that last presumably an allusion to the shirt of the centaur Nessus that became a fire to consume Heracles. Whether the dangerous desire, "power's form in motion," can be transfigured wholly from a destructive force to a transcending charisma is unclear, even when the chanter, the *I* section, becomes the astral body of resurrection and so an augmented Hamlet, "Dane of Degrees." Yet even the first section ends on the image of fresh life, and this gives a particular aura to "I lift the red flower of winter into the wind." Whatever that meant in its ancient Mexican context, here it carries the burden of vitalization, the blessing of more life, even though the *I* section rocks back and forth between images of rising and descents to the sepulchre:

> Out of the ninth circle,
> a Phoenician boat rocks upward into light
> and the warmth of a name—given to heaven—
> that arises in the ninth realm.
> Earth's realm discloses the Egyptian
> on the point of invention,
>   deprived of life and death,
> heart deep in the soul's hawk,
> a thymos shadow knapping the tombed body.
> Some one or thing is always heaven bound.
> Some flowered log doubles my bones.
> The spirit of Toltec turtledoves escapes.
> A sharp, metaphorical cry sends me
>   into the adorned sepulchre,
> and the thing that decays learns
>   how to speak its name.
>   [*Elaine's Book* 83]

John Hollander has compared Wright to Geoffrey Hill, since they share "a secularized religious power that keeps them questing among the chapels of ruined tropes," though Hollander rightly adds that Hill contends mostly with English poetic history, while Wright's agon gives "a unique relational profundity to the hyphenation itself in 'African-American.'" The dimensions of Wright's personal history, those of an African-American born in Albuquerque and educated in California, have helped him to so uncover the weave of our country's cultural heritages as to make him our only authentic multi-cultural poet of aesthetic eminence, though there are younger poets who follow already on the new roads he has broken. Generally I wince at the term "multi-cultural," because it is a cant term of those who would destroy literary study in the name of what purports to be social justice, but in fact is merely a networking cabal of resentful academic commissars who feel guilty because their teachers (my exhausted self included) once taught them to love poetry for its own sake.

Now I protect myself, because when someone says "multiculturalism" to me, I immediately say: "Ah, yes, you mean the poetry of Jay Wright, at once Hispanic, African, German, Italian, and above all Indic-American and African-American." By then the rabblement have retreated because while they have read Foucault and Lacan, they have read no poems by Jay Wright, fully the peer of John Ashbery and A. R. Ammons and Geoffrey Hill, and so one of the most exalted poets still alive.

My excursus over, I return to "Desire's Persistence," where "the thing that decays learns / how to speak its name." That thing *can* be the resurrected body, returning to an awareness, whether in the ninth Hell or the ninth Heaven of Dante. All of culture, Wright shrewdly implies, shares in a common shamanism, together uttering "a sharp, metaphorical cry," since Wright, like so many heterodox religious poets, locates us in the imaginal world, midway between empiricist reduction and transcendental intensities likely to seem ghostly to many among us. *Lift* concludes with the arcane or astral body and Hamlet's strangely transcendent death, both of which are removed from Wright, yet he himself is curiously removed throughout this movement. His estrangement, more imagined than personal, is enhanced in the brief, reverberating movement called *Red*.

> RED
> The heart, catalectic though it be, does glow,
> responds to every midnight bell within you.
> This is a discourse on reading heat,
> the flushed char of burned moments one sees
> after the sexton's lamp flows
> over the body's dark book.
> There is suspicion
> here that violet
> traces of
> sacrifice
> stand
> bare.
>
> [*Elaine's Book* 84–5]

What syllables does the poet's heart lack? Presumably those that toll the midnight bells of the psyche, intimations of mortality. In the variations of redness—the glowing of the heart, the reading of heat, flushed char, burned moments, flowering lamplight, the violet traces of sacrifice—this masterly, brief lyric reads the body's dark book by the illumination of the majestic Aztec trope: *I lift the red flower of winter into the wind*. We come to see that winter's red flower is an image of resurrection-through-sacrifice, another evidence of the persistence of desire, a persistence at the center of the next movement *Flower*:

FLOWER

This marble dust recalls that sunset
with the best burgundy, and the way,
after the charm of it, the peacocks
escaped their cages on the green.
I would now embellish the flame
that ornaments you,
even as it once in that moment
                                 did.

I carry you blossomed,
cream and salt of a high crown.
You *must* flare,
        stream forth,
blister and scale me,
even as you structure the enveloping kiss,
              sporophore of our highest loss.
                   [*Elaine's Book* 85]

The flame, now of sexual passion, flaming forth, is an extension of the Aztec flower's redness of resurrection. But between comes the *Winter* movement of our decline, an intimation of mortality that prompts one of Jay Wright's triumph in the Sublime mode:

WINTER

Under the evergreens,
the grouse have gone under the snow.
Women who follow their fall flight
tell us that, if you listen, you can hear
their dove's voices ridge the air,
a singing that follows us to a bourne
               released from its heat sleep.
We have come to an imagined line,
                 celestial,
that binds us to the burr of a sheltered thing
and rings us with a fire that will not dance,
        in a horn that will not sound.
We have learned, like these birds,

to publish our decline,
when over knotted apples and straw-crisp leaves,
the slanted sun welcomes us once again
to the arrested music in the earth's divided embrace.

[*Elaine's Book* 85–6]

This intricate music, eloquently arrested and divided, conveys a northern New England ambiance, the poet's most persistent context in these mature years of his solitude. What matters most about this Winter chant is its astonishingly achieved high style, its hushed yet piercingly pitched voice altogether Wright's own. The birds' singing yields to the now soundless, stationary image of desire's flame, a desire paradoxically kept constant by its temporal awareness both of cyclic renewal and of cyclic decline. Since the organizing Aztec metaphor relates to sacrifice and its transformations, we ought not to be startled that the concluding *Wind* movement shifts shamanistically to a woman's identity, desire speaking with a radically altered voice:

WIND
Through winter,
harmattan blacks the air.
My body fat with oil,
I become another star at noon,
when the vatic insistence
of the dog star's breath clings to me.
Though I am a woman,
I turn south,
toward the fire,
and hear the spirits in the bush.
But this is my conceit:
water will come from the west,
and I will have my trance,

be reborn,

perhaps in a Mediterranean air,
the Rhone delta's contention
with the eastern side of rain.
In all these disguises,
I follow the aroma of power.
So I am charged in my own field,
to give birth to the solar wind,
particles spiraling around the line

of my body,
moving toward the disruption,
the moment when the oil of my star at noon
                                    is a new dawn.
                                [*Elaine's Book* 86–7]

Giving birth to the solar wind renews the Aztec sense of desire's persistence, but this shamaness is an African woman, since the harmattan is a dust-laden wind on the Atlantic coast of Africa. Turned towards the flames, she enters her spirit-trance and is reborn, perhaps where the Rhone comes down to the Mediterranean, in a Latin culture. With his reincarnation assigned to her, the poet accepts immolation, joining the finished Tolteca singers, whose work was subsumed by the Aztecs:

        3
I shall go away, I shall disappear,
I shall be stretched on a bed of yellow roses
and the old women will cry for me.
So the Toltecas wrote: their books are finished,
but your heart has become perfect.
                                [*Elaine's Book* 87]

The Toltec bed of yellow roses goes back to the powerful dramatic monologue, "Zapata and the Egúngún Mask," which comes earlier in *Elaine's Book*. There Zapata cries out:

When there is no more flesh for the thorn,
how can I nurture this yellow rose of love between us?
                                [*Elaine's Book* 23]

The yellow rose yields to the Aztec red flower of winter, and Wright's book is finished even as those of the Toltecas are concluded. Yet, addressing himself, he can assert a Sublime consultation: "But your heart has become perfect." Perfect returns to its origin in *perfectus*, complete or finished, fashioned as a carpenter of the spirit might have fashioned it "in the region of rain and cloud."

The step beyond the namings of the Sublime odes in *Elaine's Book* was taken by Wright in his next volume, *Boleros* (1988). Boleros are, in the first place, stately Spanish dances marked by sharp turns, punctuated by foot-stamping, and most dramatically by sudden gestured pauses, when the dancer holds one arm arched over the head. Jay Wright's *Boleros* are intricately interlaced odes, lyrics, and meditations, most of them paced with a deliberate slowness, and many with their own sharp punctuations, positioned and poised archings. Some of the poems are among Wright's finest, and almost all contain astonishing touches of grace and grandeur. Of the forty separate pieces, the central work is the fifth, a three-part ode celebrating and lamenting names and naming, in an American tradition strongest in its founders—Emerson, Whitman, Dickinson—and in their great inheritor, Wallace Stevens. Jay Wright, both more Spanish (by way of New Mexico), and more African in his culture, handles naming and unnaming very differently than did Stevens and his precursors. Take as representative Emersonian unnaming the penultimate section of "The Man With the Blue Guitar":

> Throw away the lights, the definitions,
> And say of what you see in the dark
>
> That it is this or that it is that,
> But do not use the rotted names.

The fifth *Bolero* opens with the rather categorical line: "all names are invocations, or curses," and proceeds to the namelessness of a particular child who never came forth. It is not clear whether the poet laments his own unborn child, or a generic one of

> those who were impeached for unspeakable desire,
> even as they lay in mothers' cave hollow wombs,
> speechless, eyeless, days away from the lyrics of light
> and a naming.
> [*Boleros* 9]

A lyrical second movement of the poem returns to the images of loss and of the child:

> These are memory's accoutrements, reason to have searched
> a flowered place with a name that fits,
> where love's every echo is a child's loss.
> [*Boleros* 10]

Presumably the name that fits invokes the flowered place, and the child's loss is part of the curse of namelessness. Yet the poem's wonderful concluding movement refuses names, whether as invocations or as curses:

All names are false.
The soothsaying leaves call winter a paradox—
a northern traveler on a southern wind.
The ice on a weather-broken barn recalls May poppies.
I would have you recall the exhilaration
of reading broken sonnets, on cinnamon—
scented nights, in a tiled room,
while the charity doctors disputed their loves
                        on the cobblestones below.
I enter again the bells and traces of desire,
call and recall, the pacing of love stalking us.
What is love's form when the body fails,
or fails to appear? What is love's habitation
but a fable of boundaries, lovers passing
athwart all limits toward a crux ansata?
I have carried your name on velvet,
knowing you are free, having never suffered the
heartache of patience that love and naming
that this our divided world requires.
                        [*Boleros* 10–11]

This returns to the Sublime arena of the great ode, "Desire's Persistence,"
for the "bells and traces" surely include that poem. A superb meditation that is
part of the work-in-progress, *Transformations*, resumes the quest for desire's persistence, under the highly appropriate title, "The Cradle Logic of Autumn":

En mi país el otoño nace de una flor seca, de algunos pájaros ...
o del vaho penetrante de ciertos ríos de la llanura.
                        Molinari, "Oda a una larga tristeza"
Each instant comes with a price, the blue-edged bill
on the draft of a bird almost incarnadine,
the shanked ochre of an inn that sits as still
as the beavertail cactus it guards (the fine
rose of that flower gone as bronze as sand),
the river's chalky white insistence as it
moves past the gray afternoon toward sunset.
Autumn feels the chill of a late summer lit
only by goldenrod and a misplaced strand
of blackberries; deplores all such sleight-of-hand;
turns sullen, selfish, envious, full of regret.

Someone more adept would mute its voice. The spill
of its truncated experience would shine
less bravely and, out of the dust and dunghill
of this existence (call it hope, in decline),
as here the blue light of autumn falls, command
what is left of exhilaration and fit
this season's unfolding to the alphabet
of turn and counterturn, all that implicit
arc of a heart searching for a place to stand.
Yet even that diminished voice can withstand
the currying of its spirit. Here lies——not yet.

If, and only if, the leafless rose he sees,
or thinks he sees, flowered a moment ago,
this endangered heart flows with the river that flees
the plain, and listens with eye raised to the slow
revelation of cloud, hoping to approve
himself, or to admonish the rose for slight
transgressions of the past, this the ecstatic
ethos, a logic that seems set to reprove
his facility with unsettling delight.
Autumn might be only desire, a Twelfth-night
gone awry, a gift almost too emphatic.

At sixty, the poet rehearses the season's cradle logic, this sense that what begins anew each autumn, in a blue light, is the prospect of a "diminished voice." What to make of a diminished thing, the Frostian project, suits only Wright's Vermont landscape, but not the persistence of the Sublime in his spirit. He counts the price, instant by instant, tallying what Emerson would have called his cost of confirmation. It is high enough to make him cast out his mythologies; this meditation is remarkably direct and poignant. Or perhaps the mythologies—Dogon, Bambara, Aztec, Romantic Sublime—are held just barely in abeyance in this latest Jay Wright, who beholds no celestial birds, such as Toltec turtledoves, but rather "a bird almost incarnadine." As Wright well knows, you hardly can use the word "incarnadine" without evoking Macbeth's "this my hand will rather / The multitudinous seas incarnadine." Deftly allusive as this is, we are cautioned by it to see that the poet struggles to keep desire's persistence from becoming mere ambition's survival, lest he follow Shakespeare's most imaginative villain and fall "into the sear, the yellow leaf." Autumn's cradle logic finally (and very subtly) is repudiated, since what persists in it is not the desire that will lift the red flower of winter into the wind. *That* desire, more truly Jay Wright's, retains an element of sacrifice, rather than the emphatic persistence of "a Twelfth-night / gone awry."

When Ralph Ellison's *Invisible Man*, nameless and yet at last all-knowing, concluded by going down and living underground, he asserted that he spoke for us, whoever we were. I can trace Ellison's spirit in Jay Wright's poetry, partly because, on a higher frequency, I find that Wright speaks for me. West African religion seems to me the likeliest point-of-origin of our American gnosis, our sense that there is a little man or woman inside the big man or woman. That little being is the true self, the Gnostic spark or *pneuma* that has access to the Seventh Nommo, the black Christ. Twinning or doubling, as we have seen (by glimpses only) is Wright's preferred mode of troping, his downward path to wisdom. Without the power of Wright's metaphors, he could not aid us in our struggle against the jackal who mates with the earth, and who brings forth from the earth the bad verse and worst prose of the counter-culture. Multiculturalism, in our literary journalism and in our ruined literary education, is the ideology that says: our bad writers are no worse than your bad writers. [...] Without standards—aesthetic, cognitive, and imaginative—we will all perish, indeed are perishing already. In one of his better moments, T.S. Eliot spoke of the spirit as "unappeasable and peregrine." I can locate few such spirits among us now: I have to wait for them to locate me. Jay Wright's poetry first found me a quarter century ago, and has not abandoned me since.

Seamus Heaney

(1939-)

AT THIRTY-NINE, WALLACE STEVENS WROTE "LE MONOCLE DE MON Oncle"; at about the same age Yeats wrote "Adam's Curse." Texts of the fortieth year form a remarkable grouping; I can think immediately of Browning's "Childe Roland" and Poe's "Eureka," and I invite every reader to add more (Whitman's "Out of the Cradle" and "As I Ebb'd" suddenly come to mind, but there are many others). I would not say that the Northern Irish poet Seamus Heaney, at forty, has printed any single poem necessarily as fine as "Adam's Curse," but the lyric called "The Harvest Bow" in *Field Work* may yet seem that strong, against all of time's revenges. There are other poems in *Field Work* worthy of comparison to the Yeats of *In the Seven Woods* (1904), and it begins to seem not farfetched to wonder how remarkable a poet Heaney may yet become, if he can continue the steady growth of an art as deliberate, as restrained, and yet as authoritative and universal as the poems of *Field Work*—his fifth and much his best volume in the thirteen years since his first book, *Death of a Naturalist* (1966).

That book, praised for its countryman's veracity and vividness of soil-sense, reads in retrospect as a kind of dark hymn of poetic incarnation, a sombre record of the transgression of having been a Clare-like changeling. Heaney's first poems hold implicit his central trope, *the vowel of earth*, and move in a cycle between the guilt of having forsaken spade for pen, and the redemption of poetic work: "I rhyme. To see myself, to set the darkness echoing." *Door into the Dark* (1969) seems now, as it did to me a decade ago, mostly a repetition, albeit in a finer tone, and I remember putting the book aside with the sad reflection that Heaney was fixated in a rugged but minimalist lyrical art. I was mistaken and should have read more carefully the book's last poem, "Bogland," where Heaney began to open both to the Irish, and to his own abyss. Reading backwards from *Field Work* (and the two other, intervening books) I am taught now by the poet how he passed from description to a visionary negation:

> Our pioneers keep striking
> Inwards and downwards,
>
> Every layer they strip
> Seems camped on before.
> The bogholes might be Atlantic seepage.
> The wet centre is bottomless.

Such a center indeed could not hold, and Heaney was poised upon the verge of becoming a poet of the Northern Irish Troubles, a role he now wisely seeks to evade, but in a morally rich sense of "evade," as I will try to show later. *Wintering Out* (1972) seems stronger than it did seven years ago, when it began to change my mind about Heaney's importance. It is a book about nearing the journey's center, and takes as its concern the poet's severe questioning of his own language, the English at once his own and not his own, since Heaney is of the Catholic Irish of Derry. Few books of poems brood so hard upon names, or touch so overtly upon particular words as words. No single poem stands out, even upon rereading, for this is the last volume of Heaney's careful apprenticeship as he works towards his deferred glory. *North* (1975) begins that glory, a vital achievement by any standards, perhaps a touch dimmed for American critics by the accident of its appearance so close to Geoffrey Hill's *Somewhere Is Such a Kingdom*, which gathered together in America Hill's first three volumes. But the power of *North* is that four years of reading have enhanced it, while *Field Work* seems to me the only recent British book of poems worthy of sustained comparison to the magnificence of Hill's *Tenebrae*, published in 1978.

Heaney's first three books sparred gently with local and contemporary precursors; the alert reader could find the colors and flavors of Kavanagh and Montague, of Ted Hughes and R.S. Thomas. Like the deliberate touches of the late Robert Lowell in *Field Work*, these are all "screen-memories," of interest only as tactical blinds. What emerges in *North*, and stands clear in *Field Work*, is the precursor proper, the middle Yeats, with whom the agon of the strong Irish poet must be fought, as much by Heaney in his maturity as it is by Kinsella, with the agon itself guaranteeing why Heaney and Kinsella are likely to become more memorable than Kavanagh and Clarke, among the Irish poets following Yeats.

I hear behind the poems of *North* the middle Yeats of *The Green Helmet* and of *Responsibilities*, a hearing reinforced by *Field Work*. This is the

Yeats of a vision counting still its human cost, and so not yet abandoned to daemonic presences and intensities:

> I passed through the eye of the quern,
>
> Grist to an ancient mill,
> And in my mind's eye saw
> A world-tree of balanced stones,
> Querns piled like vertebrae,
> The marrow crushed to grounds.

That is Heaney's "Belderg" from *North*, but I do not think Yeats would have disowned it. The enduring poems in *North* include the majestic title-piece, as well as "Funeral Rites," "Kinship," "Whatever You Say Say Nothing," and, best of all, the sequence of poetic incarnation with the Yeatsian title, "Singing School." The poem "North" gave and still gives Heaney his poetics, as a mythic voice proclaims what must be this new poet's relation to the Irish past:

> It said, 'Lie down
> in the word-hoard, burrow
> the coil and gleam
> of your furrowed brain.
>
> Compose in darkness.
> Expect aurora borealis
> in the long foray
> but no cascade of light.
>
> Keep your eye clear
> as the bleb of the icicle,
> trust the feel of what nubbed treasure
> your hands have known.'

The reader of *Field Work* comes to realize that Heaney's eye is as clear, through discipline, as the air bubble in an icicle, as clear, say, as the American eye of the late Elizabeth Bishop. "Funeral Rites" inaugurates what seems doomed to be Heaney's central mode, whether he finally chooses Dublin or Belfast. "Kinship," a more difficult sequence, salutes the bog country as the "outback of my mind" and then flows into a grander trope:

This is the vowel of earth
dreaming its root
in flowers and snow,

mutation of weathers
and seasons,
a windfall composing the floor it rots into.
I grew out of all this

like a weeping willow
inclined to
the appetites of gravity.

Such inevitability of utterance would be more than enough if it were merely personal; it would suffice. Its grandeur is augmented in the last section of "Kinship" when Heaney acquires the authentic authority of becoming the voice of his people:

Come back to this
'island of the ocean'
where nothing will suffice.
Read the inhumed faces

of casualty and victim;
report us fairly,
how we slaughter
for the common good

and shave the heads
of the notorious,
how the goddess swallows
our love and terror.

The problem for Heaney as a poet henceforward is how not to drown in this blood-dimmed tide. His great precedent is the Yeats of "Meditations in Time of Civil War" and "Nineteen Hundred and Nineteen," and it cannot be said in *North* that this precedent is met, even in "Whatever You Say Say Nothing," where the exuberance of the language achieves a genuine phantasmagoria. But "Singing School," with its queerly appropriate mix of Wordsworth and Yeats, does even better, ending poem and book with a finely rueful self-accepting portrait of the poet, still waiting for the word that is his alone:

I am neither internee nor informer;
An inner émigré, grown long-haired
And thoughtful; a wood-kerne

Escaped from the massacre,
Taking protective colouring
From bole and bark, feeling
Every wind that blows;

Who, blowing up these sparks
For their meagre heat, have missed
The once-in-a-lifetime portent,
The comet's pulsing rose.

That is true eloquence, but fortunately not the whole truth, as *Field Work* richly shows. Heaney is the poet of the vowel of earth and not of any portentous comet. In *Field Work*, he has gone south, away from the Belfast violence, heeding the admonition that Emerson addressed to himself in the bad year 1846, when the American slaveholders made war against Mexico:

Though loath to grieve
The evil time's sole patriot,
I cannot leave
My honied thought
For the priest's cant,
Or statesman's rant.

If I refuse
My study for their politique,
Which at the best is trick,
The angry Muse
Puts confusion in my brain.

Like Emerson, Heaney has learned that he has imprisoned thoughts of his own which only he can set free. No poem in *Field Work* is without its clear distinction, but I exercise here the critic's privilege of discussing those poems that move me most: "Casualty," "The Badgers," "The Singer's House," the lovely sequence of ten "Glanmore Sonnets," "The Harvest Bow" (Heaney's masterpiece so far), and the beautiful elegy "In Memoriam Francis Ledwidge," for the Irish poet killed on the Western Front in 1917. All of these lyrics and meditations practice a rich negation, an art of excluded meanings, vowels of earth almost lost between guttural consonants of history. Heaney's Irish sibyl warns him that "The ground we kept our ear to for so long / Is flayed or calloused." The muted elegy "Casualty," which cunningly blends the modes of Yeats's "The Fisherman" and "Easter 1916," concludes in a funeral march giving us the sea's version of Heaney's vowel of earth:

> They move in equal pace
> With the habitual
> Slow consolation
> of a dawdling engine,
> The line lifted, hand
> Over fist, cold sunshine
> On the water, the land
> Banked under fog: that morning
> I was taken in his boat,
> The screw purling, turning
> Indolent fathoms white,
> I tasted freedom with him.
> To get out early, haul
> Steadily off the bottom,
> Dispraise the catch, and smile
> As you find a rhythm
> Working you, slow mile by mile,
> Into your proper haunt
> Somewhere, well out, beyond ...

Even as the slain fisherman's transcendence fuses with Heaney's catch of a poem to send the poet also "beyond," so Heaney has revised Yeats's ambition by having written an elegy as passionate as the perpetual night of the Troubles. Even stronger is "The Badgers," an oblique poem of deepest self-questioning, in which the elegiac strain is evaded and all simple meanings are thwarted. Sensing "some soft returning," whether of the murdered dead or of the badgers, Heaney places upon his reader the burden of difficult interpretation:

> Visitations are taken for signs.
> At a second house I listened
> for duntings under the laurels
> and heard intimations whispered
> about being vaguely honoured.

The first line of this passage does not reach back to Lancelot Andrewes through Eliot's "Gerontion" but rather itself boldly revises John 4:48, "Except ye see signs and wonders, ye will not believe" and perhaps even Matthew 12:38–39. "An evil and adulterous generation seeketh after a sign." The duntings are at once the dull sounds of badgers and, more crucially, the Wordsworthian "low breathings" of *The Prelude* 1,323. Though an external haunting, testifying to the laurels of poetic election "vaguely honoured," they are also Heaney's hard-drawn breaths, in this text and out of it, in a murderous Northern Ireland. Heaney, once so ruggedly simplistic in his only apparent stance, has entered upon the agonistic way of a stronger poetry, necessarily denser, more allusive, and persuasively difficult.

I read this entrance as the triumph of "The Singer's House," a poem I will forebear quoting entire, though I badly want to, and give only the superb three stanzas of the conclusion, where Heaney laments the loss of every thing in his land that should be "crystal," and discovers an inevitable image for his audacious and determined art that would reverse lament and loss:

> People here used to believe
> that drowned souls lived in the seals.
> At spring tides they might change shape.
> They loved music and swam in for a singer
>
> who might stand at the end of summer
> in the mouth of a whitewashed turf-shed,
> his shoulder to the jamb, his song
> a rowboat far out in evening.
>
> When I came here first you were always singing,
> a hint of the clip of the pick
> in your winnowing climb and attack.
> Raise it again, man. We still believe what we hear.

The verve of that final line is a tonic even for an American reader like myself, cut off from everything local that inspires and appalls Heaney. Closer to ordinary evenings in New Haven are the universal concerns that rise out of the local in the distinguished "Glanmore Sonnets" that open, again, with Heaney's central trope: "Vowels ploughed into other: opened ground." Confronting an image of the good life as field work, with art redeemed from violence and so "a paradigm" of new-ploughed earth,

Heaney finds even in the first sonnet that his ghosts come striding back. Against the ghosts he seeks to set his own story as a poet who could heed Moneta's admonition to Keats, or Nietzsche's to all of us: "Think of the earth."

> Then I landed in the hedge-school of Glanmore
> And from the backs of ditches hoped to raise
> A voice caught back off slug-horn and slow chanter
> That might continue, hold, dispel, appease:
> Vowels ploughed into other, opened ground,
> Each verse returning like the plough turned round.

Yet the ninth sonnet is driven to ask with true desperation: "What is my apology for poetry?" and the superb tenth sonnet ends the sequence overtly echoing Wyatt's most passionate moment, while more darkly and repressively alluding to the Yeatsian insight of the perpetual virginity of the soul: "the lovely and painful / Covenants of flesh; our separateness." More hopeful, but with a qualified hope, is the perfect lyric "The Harvest Bow," which I quote in its entirety:

> As you plaited the harvest bow
> You implicated the mellowed silence in you
> In wheat that does not rust
> But brightens as it tightens twist by twist
> Into a knowable corona,
> A throwaway love-knot of straw.
>
> Hands that aged round ashplants and cane sticks
> And lapped the spurs on a lifetime of game cocks
> Harked to their gift and worked with fine intent
> Until your fingers moved somnambulant:
> I tell and finger it like braille,
> Gleaning the unsaid off the palpable,
>
> And if I spy into its golden loops
> I see us walk between the railway slopes
> Into an evening of long grass and midges,
> Blue smoke straight up, old beds and ploughs in hedges,
> An auction notice on an outhouse wall—
> You with a harvest bow in your lapel,

Me with the fishing rod, already homesick
For the big lift of these evenings, as your stick
Whacking the tips off weeds and bushes
Beats out of time, and beats, but flushes
Nothing: that original townland
Still tongue-tied in the straw tied by your hand.

The end of art is peace
Could be the motto of this frail device
That I have pinned up on our deal dresser
Like a drawn snare
Slipped lately by the spirit of the corn
Yet burnished by its passage, and still warm.

Heaney could not have found a more wistful, Clare-like emblem than the love knot of straw for this precariously beautiful poem, or a sadder, gentler motto than: "*The end of art is peace*." Certainly the oversong of the poem, its stance as love-lyric, seems to sing against Yeats's Paterian ringers in the tower, who have appointed for the hymeneal of the soul a passing bell. But the end of married love may be peace; the end of art is agonistic, against time's "it was," and so against anterior art.

The hands which plait the harvest bow are masculine and hardened, but delicate in the office of marriage, which brings in harvest. Implicated in the making is the knowable corona of mellowed silence, not the unreliable knowledge of poetry; and Heaney as poet must both love and stand back and away from this wisdom, paternal and maternal. The fingers which follow a human tradition can move as if moving in sleep—"asleep in its own life," as Stevens said of the child. But Heaney must "tell and finger it like braille," for that is the poet's field of work: "Gleaning the unsaid off the palpable," the slender pickings after the granary is full.

Though his vision, *through her emblem*, in the third stanza approximates a true peace, it breaks into something both richer and more forlorn in what comes after. The young Yeats sang of "The Happy Townland," where "Boughs have their fruit and blossom / At all times of the year" and "all that are killed in battle / Awaken to life again." Heaney, leaving youth, hears in recollections of innocent venery a music that "Beats out of time, and beats, but flushes / Nothing." There is nothing for it to start up since the happy or original townland belongs only to those "still tongue-tied" in the frail device of the harvest bow. Heaney's genius is never surer than in his all-but-undoing of this emblem in his final trope, where the love knot becomes a drawn snare recently evaded by the corn-king, an evasion that

itself both burnishes and animates the knowable corona of achieved marriage. Obliquely but firmly, the struggle of poetry displaces the lover's
stance, and the undersong finds a triumph in the poem's closure.

I verge upon saying that Heaney approaches the cunning stance of
the strong poet, evasion for which I cite not its American theorists and
bards, from Emerson through Whitman and Dickinson to Frost and
Stevens but the central British master of the mode:

> Know ye not then the Riddling of the Bards?
> Confusion, and illusion, and relation,
> Elusion, and occasion, and evasion?

That is Tennyson's Seer, not Emerson's Merlin, and must become
Heaney's poetic, if like Yeats he is to transcend the vowel of earth. It will
be a painful transition for a poet whose heart is with the visionary naturalism of Wordsworth and Keats and Clare (and Kavanagh, Montague, R. S.
Thomas) rather than with a vision fighting free of earth. But there are
signs in *Field Work* that the transition is under way. Heaney ends the book
with a grim rendition of Dante's Ugolino, too relevant to the Irish
moment, and with his not altogether successful title poem which invokes
the Gnostic doubloon of Melville's Ahab. I end here by reading in the
noble quatrains of Heaney's "In Memoriam Francis Ledwidge" a powerful
evasion of a fate that this poet will never accept as his own:

> In you, our dead enigma, all the strains
> Criss-cross in useless equilibrium
> And as the wind tunes through this vigilant bronze
> I hear again the sure confusing drum
>
> You followed from Boyne water to the Balkans
> But miss the twilit note your flute should sound.
> You were not keyed or pitched like these true-blue ones
> Though all of you consort now underground.

Not my way to go, as Heaney tells us, for he is keyed and pitched unlike
any other significant poet now at work in the language, anywhere. The strains
cross-cross in him in so useful an equilibrium that all critics and lovers of poetry must wish him every cunning for survival. To this critic, on the other side
of the Atlantic, Heaney is joined now with Geoffrey Hill as a poet so severe
and urgent that he compels the same attention as his strongest American contemporaries, and indeed as only the very strongest among them.

Anne Carson

(1950-)

THE CANADIAN POET ANNE CARSON IS SO ORIGINAL AND AUTHENTIC IN
her works that I can think of only two other poets of her eminence now
alive and writing in English: John Ashbery and Geoffrey Hill, and they are
a full generation older.

A classical scholar by profession, Carson is a learned poet, but always
with a difference. She is like no one else alive. Emily Brontë and Emily
Dickinson are her authentic precursors. Carson is a poet of the Sublime, in
the sense that she revives in her "Essay with Rhapsody," *FOAM*. Longinus,
the true origin of literary criticism, is her quarry, because his Sublime consists of quotations, "lustres," as Plutarch and Emerson called them. These
come at us like volcanic eruptions, and clearly Carson is fond of active volcanoes, as Longinus must have been:

> Look this is the real Homer who storms like a wind alongside
> the fighting
> men, none other than Homer who "rages as when spearshaking
> Ares or
> ruinous fire in the mountains rages, in folds of deep forest, and
> foam is
> around his mouth."
> —Longinus, *On the Sublime* 9.11; Homer, *Iliad* 15.605-7

Carson's genius is to spot that foam and elucidate it:

> Foam is the sign of an artist who has sunk his hands into his
> own story,
> and also of a critic storming and raging in folds of his own deep theory.

Carson's first book was *Eros the Bittersweet: An Essay* (1986), a meditation upon a trope of Sappho (all of whose fragments Carson has now translated). In the dance of Sappho's mind: "Desire moves. Eros is a verb." Invoking Plato's *Phaedrus*, *Eros the Bittersweet* breaks off (it cannot end, or come to rest) with a luminously resigned paragraph:

> From the testimony of lovers like Sokrates or Sappho we can construct what it would be like to live in a city of no desire. Both the philosopher and the poet find themselves describing Eros in images of wings and metaphors of flying, for desire is a movement that carries yearning hearts from over here to over there, launching the mind on a story. In the city without desire such flights are unimaginable. Wings are kept clipped. The known and the unknown learn to align themselves one behind the other so that, provided you are positioned at the proper angle, they seem to be one and the same. If there *were* a visible difference, you might find it hard to say so, for the useful verb *mnaomai* will have come to mean "a fact is a fact." To reach for something else than the facts will carry you beyond this city and perhaps, as for Sokrates, beyond this world. It is a high-risk proposition, as Sokrates saw quite clearly, to reach for the difference between known and unknown. He thought the risk worthwhile, because he was in love with wooing itself. And who is not?

The wisdom of Socrates was not to think that he knew what he did not know. I suppose that the use of literature for life is reaching wisdom, not to reach wisdom, which cannot be done. Carson is a wisdom writer of genius, rather than a Socratic wise woman. She is an artist who has sunk her hands into her own story, and she has a Homeric effect upon a critic (at least this one), causing me to storm and rage in my own deep theory of influence. Her strong reading of Emily Brontë and of Emily Dickinson is implicit in much of her poetry, and sometimes emerges with fierce explicitness.

Carson's first book after *Eros the Bittersweet* was *Short Talks* (1992), available now as Part II of *Plainwater* (1995). The scariest of these thirty-two prose poems is "On Walking Backwards":

> My mother forbad us to walk backwards. That is how the dead walk,
>   she would say. Where did she get this idea? Perhaps from
>   a bad

translation. The dead, after all, do not walk backwards but they do

walk behind us. They have no lungs and cannot call out but would

love for us to turn around. They are victims of love, many of them.

With my own number of beloved recently dead, I have taken to turning around as I walk. Carson, more even than Geoffrey Hill, makes me uneasy. Her "Introduction" to *Short Talks* serves as prelude to everything she has written since:

> Early one morning words were missing. Before that, words were not. Facts were, faces were. In a good story, Aristotle tells us, ever thing that happens is pushed by something else. Three old women were bending in the fields. What use is it to question us? they said. Well it shortly became clear that they knew everything there is to know about the snowy fields and the blue-green shoots and the plant called "audacity," which poets mistake for violets. I began to copy out everything that was said. The marks construct an instant of nature gradually, without the boredom of a story. I emphasize this. I will do anything to avoid boredom. It is the task of a lifetime. You can never know enough, never work enough, never use the infinitives and participles oddly enough, never impede the movement harshly enough, never leave the mind quickly enough.

This is the task of her lifetime, and since I am two decades older than Carson, one of my likely regrets when I depart is that I will not have absorbed her lifetime's work. I pass on here to what seem her first published verse poems, *The Life of Towns*, a sequence of thirty-six brief meditations, with overtones of Emily Dickinson, who receives the elliptical tribute of "Emily Town":

> Riches in a little room.
> Is a phrase that haunts.
> Her since the mineral of you.
> Left.
> Snow or a library.
> Or a band of angels.
> With a message is.

Not what.
It meant to.
Her.

Dickinson favored no punctuation except dashes—Carson gives us ten periods for ten very short lines. Christopher Marlowe's "infinite riches in a little room" (*The Jew of Malta*) is echoed ironically by Touchstone's allusion to the murder of Marlowe in *As You Like It*: "it strikes a man more dead than a great reckoning in a little room." This becomes the room in her father's house in Amherst where Dickinson wrote her poems and letters. Where is Carson in this poem, or is this not her town, but then, none of the towns in the sequence is hers.

Carson's own story of the self is first told (more or less) in the long narrative essay, *The Anthropology of Water*, that concludes *Plainwater*, where she identifies herself as the only one of the fifty Danaides who did not slay her bridegroom, and thus drowned instead in the deep water:

Water is something you cannot hold. Like men. I have tried.
Father,
brother, lover, true friends, hungry ghosts and God, one by one
all took
themselves out of my hands.

The Anthropology of Water is eloquently memorable, but I prefer *The Glass Essay*, the narrative poem that leads off *Glass, Irony, and God* (1995), where Carson's greatness as a poet first fully emerges. Emily Brontë is Carson's daemon, as Heathcliff was Catherine Earnshaw's. Visiting her mother, who lives alone on a Brontë-like moor in the north of Canada, Carson confronts her main fear: "I feel I am turning into Emily Brontë,/ my lonely life around me like a moor."

The story of loss—of a man called Law—is perhaps the same as in *The Beauty of the Husband* (2001), but there the recital is harsh and direct, while here we are in an atmosphere of glass, where context would be shattered were the poet to express fury. Instead she meditates upon morning visions she calls Nudes: "naked glimpses of my soul." The central vision is the final night with Law, "a night that centred Heaven and Hell,/ As Emily would say." Law is no Heathcliff, only another cad, to the reader, but Carson effectively presents herself as a living wound of love, her own "pain devil," as Heathcliff was Emily Brontë's. The poet-novelist of *Wuthering Heights* and a handful of magnificent lyrics addressed a transcendental Thou in a few poems that seem to me Gnostic hymns to the

Alien God, who is a stranger in this cosmos. All but identified with Emily
Brontë, Anne Carson disengages from this relation to a Thou:

> Very hard to read, the messages that pass
> between Thou and Emily.
> In this poem she reverses their roles,
> speaking not *as* the victim but *to* the victim.
> It is chilling to watch Thou move upon thou,
> who lies alone in the dark waiting to be mastered.
>
> It is a shock to realize that this low, slow collusion
> of master and victim within one voice
> is a rationale
>
> for the most awful loneliness of the poet's hour.
> She has reversed the roles of thou and Thou
> not as a display of power
>
> but to force out of herself some pity
> for this soul trapped in glass,
> which is her true creation.
>
> Those nights lying alone
> are not discontinuous with this cold hectic dawn.
> It is who I am.

Mutually trapped in glass, the two poets again fuse. After a series of
harrowing Nudes, *The Glass Essay* attains its majestic closure:

> I saw a high hill and on it a form shaped against hard air.
>
> It could have been just a pole with some old cloth attached,
> but as I came closer
> I saw it was a human body
>
> trying to stand against winds so terrible that the flesh was
> blowing off
>   the bones.
> And there was no pain.
> The wind

was cleansing the bones.
They stood forth silver and necessary.
It was not my body, not a woman's body, it was the body of us
all.
It walked out of the light.

Overwhelming in context, this remains extraordinary even on its own. There is no consolation in this cleansing, yet there is also no pain. Since this is a vision, and not a privileged moment, we cannot speak of a secular epiphany. Nor can one find the spirit of Emily Brontë in this: it is Anne Carson transcending—momentarily—her own suffering, because erotic loss is universal, male and female. For this visionary moment, melancholia recedes, and we are given an exemplary figure for what Sigmund Freud brilliantly termed "the work of mourning."

The epilogue to *The Glass Essay* is a sequence of eighteen poems called *The Truth About God*. Two of them are astonishing: "Deflect" and "God's Name," both founded upon the early Kabbalah of Isaac the Blind. What is deflected is the light that emanated from the Adam Kadmon, the God-Man:

From the lights of his forehead were formed all the names of
the world.
From the lights of his ears, nose and throat
came a function no one has ever defined.

From the lights of his eyes—but wait—
Isaac waits.
In theory

the lights of the eye should have issued from Adam's navel.
But within the lights themselves occurred
an intake of breath

and they changed their path.
And they were separated.
And they were caught in the head.

And from these separated lights came
that which pains you
on its errands (here my friend began to weep) through the
world.

For be assured it is not only you who mourn.
Isaac lashed his tail.
Every rank of world

was caused to descend
(at least one rank)
by the terrible pressure of the light.

Nothing remained in place.
Nothing was not captured except
among the shards and roots and matter

some lights
from Adam's eyes
nourished there somehow.

The intake of breath is the *zimzum*, God's withdrawal to permit creation, but the lights separate, and the *kelim* or vessels shatter into "shards and roots and matter." Carson adds her own lively touches; Isaac the Blind becomes a dragon of the Deep, lashing his tail and roaring, witnessing the catastrophe creation. "God's Name" also shows Carson as her own Kabbalist:

The name is not a noun.
It is an adverb.
Like the little black notebooks that Beethoven carried

in his coatpocket
for the use of those who wished to converse with him,
the God adverb

is a one-way street that goes everywhere you are.
No use telling you what it is.
Just chew it and rub it on.

Carson will not tell us that adverb but I suspect it is "endlessly," while the verb that goes with it is "suffers." "Book of Isaiah," which follows later in *Glass, Irony, and God* may be Carson's most disjunctive narrative, and the strongest so far. Guy Davenport accurately notes that Carson captures prophetic narrative with a peculiar felicity:

It was a blue winter evening, the cold bit like a wire.

Isaiah laid his forehead on the ground.

God arrived.

Why do the righteous suffer? said Isaiah.

Bellings of cold washed down the Branch.

Notice whenever God addresses Isaiah in a feminine singular verb
   something dazzling is
about to happen.

Isaiah what do you know about women? asked God.

Down Isaiah's nostrils bounced woman words:

Blush. Stink. Wife. Fig. Sorceress—

God nodded.

Isaiah go home and get some sleep, said God.

Isaiah went home, slept, woke again.

Isaiah felt sensation below the neck, it was a silk and bitter sensation.

Isaiah looked down.

It was milk forcing the nipples open.

Isaiah was more than whole.

I am not with you I am *in* you, said the muffled white voice of God.

Isaiah sank to a kneeling position.

New pain! said Isaiah.

New contract! said God.

Carson's comic Sublime evades bitterness, whether in Hebraic context or in the classical convolutions of her extraordinary "novel in verse," *Autobiography of Red* (1998), too long and intricate for me to describe here. A remarkable outburst of Carsonian fecundity gave us *Men in the Off Hours* (2000) and *The Beauty of the Husband* (2001), from which I will draw a few texts for consideration, only to suggest the expanding contours of her achievement. But I cite, as her *intended* aesthetic, the opening paragraph of her "Note on Method" that preludes *Economy of the Unlost* (1999), her study of verbal economy in Simonides and Paul Celan:

> There is too much self in my writing. Do you know the term Lukács uses to describe aesthetic structure? *Eine fensterlose Monade.* I do not want to be a windowless monad—my training and trainers opposed subjectivitystrongly, I have struggled since the beginning to drive my thought out intothe landscape of science and fact where other people converse logicallyand exchange judgments—but I go blind out there. So writing involves some dashing back and forth between that darkening landscape wherefacticity is strewn and a windowless room cleared of everything I do not know. It is the clearing that takes time. It is the clearing that is a mystery.

I do not know what to do with this. Could one imagine Emily Brontë or Emily Dickinson or Gertrude Stein saying: There is too much self in my writing? Lukács, a Marxist, deplored too much self, since the single person is a myth, according to Marx. Why read Carson rather than a thousand other poets now writing, except that she sensibly goes blind in the absurd realm of "objectivity"? That mode or landscape is easy, vulgar, and therefore disgusting: authentic subjectivity is difficult, sublime, and inspiring. In any case, Carson's genius is to write on the self, not fashionably off it.

There is so much superb poetry available by reading *Men In the Off Hours*, that all I can do here is discuss the poem that most moves me, "Father's Old Blue Cardigan," the elegy for the loss of love to Alzheimer's disease:

Now it hangs on the back of the kitchen chair
where I always sit, as it did
on the back of the kitchen chair where he always sat.

I put it on whenever I come in,
as he did, stamping
the snow from his boots.

I put it on and sit in the dark.
He would not have done this.
Coldness comes paring down from the moonbone in the sky.

His laws were a secret.
But I remember the moment at which I knew
he was going mad inside his laws.

He was standing at the turn of the driveway when I arrived.
He had on the blue cardigan with the buttons done up all the
way to the top.
Not only because it was a hot July afternoon

but the look on his face—
as a small child who has been dressed by some aunt early in the
morning
for a long trip

on cold trains and windy platforms
will sit very straight at the edge of his seat
while the shadows like long fingers

over the haystacks that sweep past
keep shocking him
because he is riding backwards.

If that *is* pathos, the control is so firm that I cannot locate the point
where logos takes over. I reread Carson's poem and suddenly remember
the day I encountered an old friend and Yale colleague sitting on the pavement in front of the Graduate School, shoe in one hand and the other hand
counting his toes, over and over. A month before, we had encountered
each other at the same spot, and enjoyed an intense discussion of American
religion, about which he knew everything. The look on his face, as he

counted over his toes, was the small child's expression so precisely caught by Carson's train-ride metaphor.

The Beauty of the Husband, dancing its twenty-nine death-tangos, has the remorseless drive of Freud taking us beyond the pleasure-principle. It would be grisly to select a favorite tango, but I cannot get no. XXII "Homo Ludens," out of my head, though I would like to. The nameless husband, after a three-year separation, takes his wife to Athens, supposedly for reconciliation. At night, in the hotel room, they dispute as ever concerning his serial infidelities, and suddenly his nose begins to bleed:

> Then blood runs down over his upper lip, lower lip, chin.
> To his throat.
> Appears on the whiteness of his shirt.
>
> Dyes a mother-of-pearl button for good.
> Blacker than a mulberry.
> Don't think his heart had burst. He was no Tristan
> (though he would love to point out that in the common version
> Tristan is not false, it is the sail that kills)
> yet neither of them had a handkerchief
> and that is how she ends up staining her robe with his blood,
> his head in her lap and his virtue coursing through her
>
> as if they were one flesh.
> Husband and wife may erase a boundary.
> Creating a white page.
>
> But now the blood seems to be the only thing in the room.
>
> If only one's whole life could consist in certain moments.
> There is no possibility of coming back from such a moment
> to simple hatred,
> black ink.

Cold-heartedly, I might observe that I know no other moment like this, in literature, but that praise seems pointless in confronting Carson's eloquent immediacy. Our lives, even in retrospect, do not consist in certain moments, secular epiphanies that come back to us, glories or humiliations. That is part of the dark wisdom of a long poem that beings: "A wound gives off its own light" and ends with the former husband fictively saying: "Watch me fold this page now so you think it is you."

Yet I don't want to end this brief appreciation of Anne Carson with that voice, but with her own. She is a highly active volcano, and fascinates a critic who has been a Longinian all his long life. Somewhere in *Plainwater* she writes: "Language is what eases the pain of living with other people, language is what makes the wounds come open again." Not language, not at all language, I want to murmur, but only language's rare masters—like Emily Brontë, Emily Dickinson, Anne Carson.

Further Reading

Abrams, M.H. *The Mirror and the Lamp: Romantic Theory and the Critical Tradition*. New York: Oxford University Press, 1953.

Attridge, Derek. *Poetic Rhythm: An Introduction*. New York: Cambridge University Press, 1995.

Bloom, Harold. *the Best Poems of the English Language: From Chaucer Through Frost*. New York: HarperCollins, 2004.

———. *Figures of Capable Imagination*. New York: Seabury Press, 1976.

———. *Poetry and Repression*. New Haven: Yale University Press, 1976.

———. *A Map of Misreading*. New York: Oxford University Press, 1975.

———. *Kabbalah and Criticism*. New York: Continuum, 1975.

———. *The Anxiety of Influence*. New York: Oxford University Press, 1973.

Brooks, Cleanth. *The Well Wrought Urn: Studies in the Structure of Poetry*. New York: Harcourt Brace, 1956.

Brooks, Cleanth, and Robert Penn Warren. *Understanding Poetry* 3rd ed. New York: Holt, Rinehart and Winston, 1960.

Courthope, W.J. *History of English Poetry*. London: Macmillan, 1895–1910.

Eliot, T.S. *The Use of Poetry and the Use of Criticism: Studies in the Relation of Criticism to Poetry in England*. London: Faber and Faber, 1970.

Frye, Northrop. *The Anatomy of Criticism: Four Essays*. Princeton: Princeton University Press, 1957.

Fussell, Paul. *Poetic Meter & Poetic Form* (rev. ed.). New York: Random House, 1979.

Harmon, William, ed. *Classic Writings on Poetry*. New York: Columbia University Press, 2003.

Heaney, Seamus. *The Redress of Poetry: Oxford Lectures*. London: Faber and Faber, 1995.

Hirsch, Edward. *How to Read a Poem: And Fall in Love with Poetry*. New York: Harcourt Brace & Co., 1999.

Hollander, John. *Rhyme's Reason: A Guide to English Verse*, 3rd ed. New Haven: Yale University Press, 2001.

Johnson, Samuel. *Lives of the Poets: A Selection*, J.P. Hardy, ed. Oxford: Clarendon Press, 1971.

Knight, George Wilson. *The Starlit Dome: Studies in the Poetry of Vision.* New York: Oxford University Press, 1971.

Magill, Frank N., ed. *Critical Survey of Poetry: English Language Series.* Pasadena: Salem Press, 1992.

Paglia, Camille. *Break, Blow, Burn: Camille Paglia Reads Forty-three of the World's Best Poems.* New York: Pantheon, 2005.

Parini, Jay, ed. *The Columbia History of American Poetry.* New York: Columbia University Press, 1993.

Parisi, Joseph and Stephen Young, ed. *Dear Editor: A History of Poetry in Letters.* New York: W.W. Norton, 2002.

Paschen, Elise, and Rebekah Presson Mosby, ed. *Poetry Speaks: Hear Great Poets Read Their Work from Tennyson to Plath.* Naperville: Sourcebooks MediaFusion, 2001

Paz, Octavio. *The Bow and the Lyre: The Poem, Poetic Revelation, Poetry and History.* Austin: University of Texas Press, 1987.

Pearce, Roy Harvey. *The Continuity of American Poetry.* Princeton: Princeton University Press, 1961.

Perkins, David. *A History of Modern Poetry: Modernism and After.* Cambridge, Mass.: Belknap Press of Harvard University Press, 1976–1987.

Preminger, Alex, Terry V.F. Brogan, and Frank J. Warnke, ed. *The New Princeton Encyclopedia of Poetry and Poetics.* Princeton: Princeton University Press, 3rd edition, 1993.

Raffel, Burton. *How to Read a Poem.* New York: Plume Books, 1994.

Schmidt, Michael. *The First Poets: Lives of the Ancient Greek Poets.* New York: Knopf, 2005.

———. *Lives of the Poets.* New York: Vintage, 2000.

Spiller, Michael R.G. *The Development of the Sonnet: An Introduction.* New York: Routledge, 1992.

Turco, Lewis. *The Book of Forms: A Handbook of Poetics* 3rd ed. Hanover, NH: University Press of New England, 2000.

Turner, Mark, and George Lakoff. *More than Cool Reason: A Field Guide to Poetic Metaphor.* Chicago: University of Chicago Press, 1989.

Vendler, Helen. *Poems, Poets, Poetry: An Introduction and Anthology* 2nd ed. New York: Bedford/St. Martin's, 2002.

———. *The Given and the Made: Strategies of Poetic Redefinition.* Cambridge, Mass.: Harvard University Press, 1996.

———. *Soul Says: On Recent Poetry.* Cambridge, Mass.: Belknap Press of Harvard University Press, 1996.

————. *The Music of What Happens: Poems, Poets, Critics.* Cambridge, Mass.: Harvard University Press, 1989.

Welsh, Andrew. *Roots of Lyric: Primitive Poetry and Modern Poetics.* Princeton: Princeton University Press, 1978.

Index

About the Author

HAROLD BLOOM is Sterling Professor of the Humanities at Yale University. He is the author of over 20 books, including *Shelley's Mythmaking* (1959), *The Visionary Company* (1961), *Blake's Apocalypse* (1963), *Yeats* (1970), *A Map of Misreading* (1975), *Kabbalah and Criticism* (1975), *Agon: Toward a Theory of Revisionism* (1982), *The American Religion* (1992), *The Western Canon* (1994), and *Omens of Millennium: The Gnosis of Angels, Dreams, and Resurrection* (1996). *The Anxiety of Influence* (1973) sets forth Professor Bloom's provocative theory of the literary relationships between the great writers and their predecessors. His most recent books include *Shakespeare: The Invention of the Human* (1998), a 1998 National Book Award finalist, *How to Read and Why* (2000), *Genius: A Mosaic of One Hundred Exemplary Creative Minds* (2002), *Hamlet: Poem Unlimited* (2003), and *Where Shall Wisdom be Found* (2004). In 1999, Professor Bloom received the prestigious American Academy of Arts and Letters Gold Medal for Criticism, and in 2002 he received the Catalonia International Prize.